Writing
by *Choice*

Third Edition

Writing
by *Choice*

Eric Henderson

With Contributions from David Leach,
Scott Johnston, and Danielle Forster

OXFORD

UNIVERSITY PRESS

OXFORD
UNIVERSITY PRESS

Oxford University Press is a department of the University of Oxford.
It furthers the University's objective of excellence in research, scholarship,
and education by publishing worldwide. Oxford is a registered trade mark of
Oxford University Press in the UK and in certain other countries.

Published in Canada by
Oxford University Press
8 Sampson Mews, Suite 204,
Don Mills, Ontario M3C 0H5 Canada

www.oupcanada.com

First Edition published in 2006
Second Edition published in 2011

Library and Archives Canada Cataloguing in Publication

Henderson, Eric, author
Writing by choice / Eric Henderson. — Third edition.

Includes index.
ISBN 978–0–19–900861–2 (pbk.)

1. Academic writing—Textbooks.   2. Report writing—
Textbooks.   3. English language—Rhetoric—Textbooks.   I. Title.

PE1408.H39 2015   808'.042   C2014-907931-1

Cover image: yang wenshuang/Getty Images

Oxford University Press is committed to our environment.
Wherever possible, our books are printed on paper which comes from
responsible sources.

Printed and bound in Canada

1 2 3 4 — 18 17 16 15

Contents

Readings

SAMPLE PROFESSIONAL ESSAYS

SAMPLE STUDENT ESSAYS

From the Publisher

Oxford University Press is proud to bring you *Writing by Choice*, the definitive text on writing and composition for today's students. Developed not just to teach the basics of writing but to empower students to write well, *Writing by Choice* encourages students to make appropriate choices in their writing by giving them the tools and the knowledge to do so.

This third edition is clearly divided into three parts: a rhetoric with an integrated reader, a research guide, and a grammar and style handbook. The new chapter structure includes learning objectives, marginal definitions and cross-references, current examples, and chapter summaries. The text continues to give detailed treatment to expository, argumentative, and literary essays, illustrating key principles through sample professional and student essays as well as individual and group exercises.

Writing by Choice remains the first choice for engaging students in a comprehensive, widely applicable approach to developing their writing skills and thinking critically about how—and why—they write.

HIGHLIGHTS OF THE THIRD EDITION

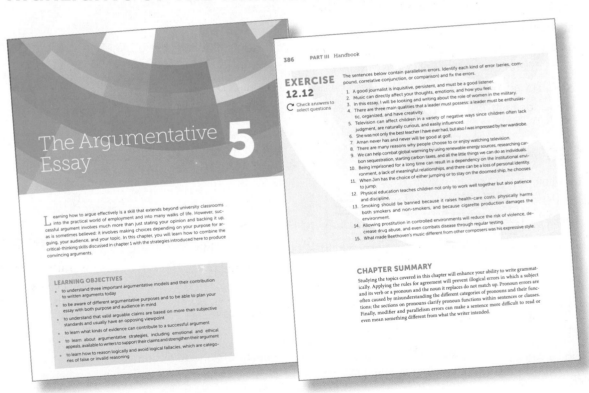

The **new chapter structure** includes learning objectives,
current examples, and end-of-chapter summaries.

Helpful **margin notes** include definitions of key terms and writing tips. Definitions also appear in the **glossary** at the end of the book.

The new **signpost margin notes** contain cross-references for easier navigation.

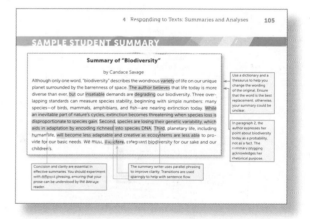

Examples of **student writing** provide readers with a peer-focused approach to honing their skills and developing technique.

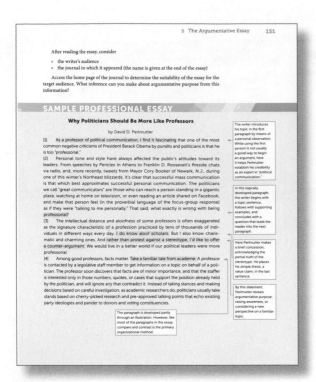

5 The Argumentative Essay   151

Professional essays—almost all of them new—have been selected for currency and readability.

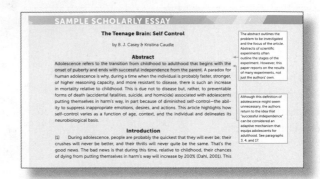

The readings include **paragraph numbers**, encouraging students to refer to specific text in their analyses.

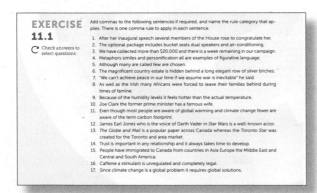

Exercises, including both individual and collaborative activities, provide students with opportunities to practise their skills.

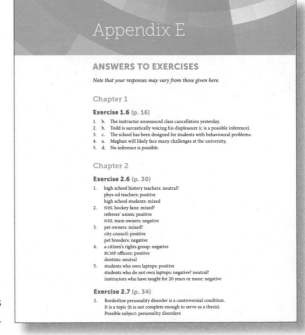

An **icon** ↻ indicates which exercises have an answer key in the appendix.

The **"Fast Track" feature** in the grammar chapters presents a succinct recap of complex rules.

Fast Track

Finding Fragments

Does the word group contain a subject (tells who or what), and is there an action performed by the subject?	If NO . . .	⟶	it's a fragment
Does the word group consist of only nouns/pronouns preceded by prepositions?	If YES . . .	⟶	it's a fragment
Is the only identifiable verb form in the word group an infinitive (e.g., *to be, to know, to learn*)?	If YES . . .	⟶	it's a fragment
Does the only identifiable verb form in the word group end in *-ing, -ed,* or *-en* and is not preceded by a helping verb (e.g., *is, were, has been*)?	If YES . . .	⟶	it's a fragment
Does the word group begin with a subordinating conjunction (one of the words on p. 321), and express a incomplete thought?	If YES . . .	⟶	it's a fragment

A Closer Look

Using Citations Efficiently

Parenthetical references are intended to give the reader as *much* information as possible about the source while interfering as *little* as possible with the essay's content and readability. This is an especially important principle in the Modern Language Association (MLA); however, in both MLA and American Psychological Association (APA) documentation styles, you should not include unneeded citations.

You can avoid citing the same source repetitively in one paragraph *if it is clear you are referring to that one source throughout*. Thus, you can combine references from the same source in one citation. For example, let's say you used three pages from your source, Jackson; when you were finished drawing from that source, you could indicate your use of Jackson this way:

(Jackson 87–89)

This citation would tell the reader that you used that one source continuously for three of her pages—perhaps one

idea from page 87, two facts from page 88, and a paraphrased passage from page 89.

Another strategy for direct and economical documentation is to use a signal phrase to indicate a forthcoming reference. After naming the source and following with the material from the source, for example, a direct quotation or paraphrase, provide the page number. The reader can then clearly see the beginning and end of the source material. Since you have named the author(s) in your own sentence, you do not repeat the name in the citation (see Signal Phrases in chapter 7 on p. 219).

A third strategy is combining in one citation sources that contain the same point. This method is useful when you are summarizing the findings of several studies in the same paragraph and want to avoid excessive citations:

(Drinkwater, 2010, p. 118; Hovey, 2009, p. 75).

The **"A Closer Look" feature** expands on topics of interest, including achieving objectivity in academic writing; reading for style and tone; identifying irony; conducting research in the humanities, the social sciences, and the sciences; and writing indirect thesis statements.

Glossary

absolute phrase A group of words that consists of a noun/pronoun and a partial verb form, modifying the entire sentence.
abstract A condensed summary used in many scholarly essays; it is placed before the study begins, is written by the study's author, and includes its purpose, methods, and results.
adjectivally Acting as an adjective in a sentence.
adjectival modifier A word or phrase that describes or particularizes a noun and usually precedes it.
adjective A word that modifies and precedes a noun or follows a linking verb; it answers the question *Which?, What kind?,* or *How many?*
adverbially Acting as an adverb in a sentence.
adverbial modifier A word or phrase that describes or particularizes a verb; may also modify an adjective or another adverb; a **sentence adverb** may modify the entire sentence.
adverb A word that modifies a verb, an adjective, an adverb, or even an entire sentence; it often ends in *-ly* and answers the question *When?, Where?, Why?, How?, To what degree!,* or *How much?*
alliteration Identical sounds at the beginning of closely placed words.
allusion A historical, religious, mythic, literary, or other kind of outside reference used illustratively or to reveal another aspect of the work.
analogy A logical comparison between two objects in order to help the reader understand the first object. *See also* **metaphor**.
analysis The act of taking something apart or breaking it down in order to look at it closely.
analytical Refers to the activity of breaking something down to see how it is put together and the relationship between the parts.
anapest A foot of poetic metre consisting of two unstressed syllables and one stressed syllable.

anaphora The repetition of words or phrases at the beginning of lines or clauses.
annotated bibliography An expanded bibliography that includes not only the information of standard bibliographies but also brief summaries of related works and, sometimes, appraisals of each work.
antecedent The noun that the pronoun replaces in the sentence.
apostrophe In poetry, an address to an absent or dead person or to a non-human object.
appositive A word or phrase that is grammatically parallel to the previous noun or noun phrase and gives non essential information.
argument A rhetorical mode concerned with persuading a reader to adopt a specific point of view or course of action.
aside In drama, a brief speech intended for the audience, not for other onstage characters.
assonance The repetition of vowel sounds in the middle of closely placed words.
audience Readers with common knowledge, interests, attitudes, reading habits, and/or expectations.
audience orientation The attitudes and emotional/ethical positions that define a typical reader; it could be positive (agreeing with your position), neutral (having no opinion), negative (disagreeing with your position), or mixed (including those who agree and those who disagree).
bibliography A list at the end of the essay of all the sources used in the essay. The title of this list varies by citation style.
blank verse Poetry written in unrhymed iambic pentameter.
block method A method of comparing and contrasting in which a writer considers all points related to one subject of comparison before moving on to the second subject.
Boolean operators Small words used to combine, include, or exclude specific search terms.

The **new glossary** contains an alphabetical listing of the key-term definitions, providing a handy reference for students.

Appendix C

A CHECKLIST FOR EAL WRITERS

The following are some English idiomatic expressions and rules for usage, organized alphabetically by the parts of speech. Although they are not a major part of speech, articles can be confusing for EAL writers, so they have been allotted a separate section, beginning on page 396.

For more complete information, many useful references, including OUP's general ESL dictionaries, can be consulted.

Adjectives

One-word adjectives usually precede the words they modify, except predicate adjectives that follow linking verbs (see p. 313). However, relative (adjectival) clauses follow the nouns they modify and present special challenges for writers (see p. 396).

The following adjectives often give students trouble.

Ago: When you want to refer to a time in the past and relate this time to today, you can use the adjective *ago*; it follows the noun. To refer to a *specific* point in the past, you can give the date (month, day, year) preceded by *on*. See "Times and dates," below.

The first truly successful cloning of an animal occurred more than *ten years ago.* The first truly successful cloning of an animal occurred *on July 5, 1996.*

Few versus a few: Both can precede nouns that can be counted, but *few* means "not many," and *a few* means "some." So, *few* usually refers to fewer of something than *a few!* (Since *a few* has more letters than *few,* you can associate it with more of something than *few.*)

Few Canadians know how to play cricket. However, a few people on my listserv said they would be interested in learning how to play it.

Much versus many: Use *much* before nouns that cannot be counted and *many* before countable nouns. Similarly, use *amount* before uncountable nouns and *number* before countable nouns (see p. 302); use *less* before uncountable nouns and *fewer* before countable nouns (see p. 402).

The Canadian television channel *MuchMusic* features *many* different kinds of music.

Appendices include proofreading methods and guidelines, peer edit forms, and a checklist for EAL writers.

ONLINE RESOURCES

For Instructors

- An **instructor's manual** offers chapter overviews, review questions, discussion starters, collaborative exercises and activities, and answer keys to selected exercises in the book.
- A **test bank** provides multiple-choice and true-or-false questions to assess students' understanding of the chapters.

For Students

- A **student study guide** includes chapter summaries, interactive quiz questions, and links to additional online resources.

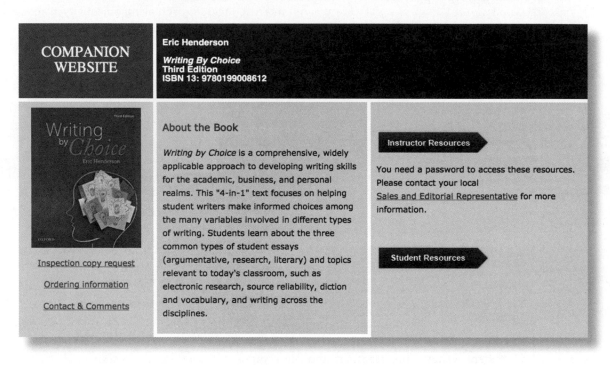

COMPANION WEBSITE

Eric Henderson

Writing By Choice
Third Edition
ISBN 13: 9780199008612

Inspection copy request

Ordering information

Contact & Comments

About the Book

Writing by Choice is a comprehensive, widely applicable approach to developing writing skills for the academic, business, and personal realms. This "4-in-1" text focuses on helping student writers make informed choices among the many variables involved in different types of writing. Students learn about the three common types of student essays (argumentative, research, literary) and topics relevant to today's classroom, such as electronic research, source reliability, diction and vocabulary, and writing across the disciplines.

Instructor Resources

You need a password to access these resources. Please contact your local Sales and Editorial Representative for more information.

Student Resources

www.oupcanada.com/Writing3e

Preface

By the time students begin post-secondary study, most are familiar with the do's and don'ts of writing essays, having usually been taught rigid guidelines for the writing of essays. While guidelines are essential, they should not hamper thought or expression. They should not deprive writers of choices, but enhance their ability to make *informed* choices given the wide range of variables affecting different kinds of writing tasks.

At the university level, student writers are capable of, and should assume responsibility for, making informed choices. Only by doing so can they take up the challenges offered by their studies and by the wide variety of workplace writing tasks that may lie ahead. In a world that increasingly values solutions to its problems, the knowledgeable, adaptable writer will always be in demand, since written forms of communication are likely to reach the widest possible readership—to be heard, considered, and acted on. This is true not only of formal academic essays written for professors but also of other communications designed for a specific purpose, such as applying for a student exchange or training opportunity.

As the Contents pages reveal, the composition sections of *Writing by Choice* are not organized around the teaching of the traditional rhetorical modes. Detailed treatment is given to three kinds of essays: expository, argumentative, and literary—the kinds typically assigned in first-year composition and literature courses. Specialized writing contexts are also considered: the appendices include proofreading guidelines and hints; strategies for writing in-class or examination essays; and help for overcoming the challenges of EAL student writers. The grammar and the composition sections stress the step-by-step approach of identifying, applying, and integrating.

Almost all of the examples in the text, including the many exercises, are taken from students' writing, which reinforce rules and concepts as they apply to realistic, everyday writing contexts—ones that have occurred and will occur to students as they write. The writing by students represents a wide variety of disciplines, reflecting the diverse interests of today's students. Several selections from the academic and professional worlds of the kind that students encounter in their research also are included as teaching/learning devices.

Exercises are designed to engage students on their own as well as in group or collaborative environments. Many instructors consider editing by peers an indispensable part of collaborative learning; peer edit forms are included in an appendix. An important feature of this text, full-length student essays illustrate expository, argumentative, and literary essays, as well as critical analyses and responses. The importance of summarizing is reflected in the text as well. MLA and APA documentation styles are outlined in a separate chapter, along with the rudiments of the notes' style.

The third edition of *Writing by Choice* retains the core features of the first and second editions, as described above. However, much of the material has been rewritten and redesigned to meet the needs of today's students (and instructors) to access relevant information quickly and efficiently.

ACKNOWLEDGEMENTS

Preparing the third edition of *Writing by Choice* has given me an opportunity to reflect on the privilege of working with many knowledgeable and enthusiastic experts at Oxford University Press Canada in editorial, management, marketing, and sales over the last decade; I particularly want to thank developmental editor Leah-Ann Lymer, copyeditor Leslie Saffrey, and production manager Steven Hall for their proficiency and professionalism.

I would like to express my gratitude to Chris Higgins, formerly of the University of British Columbia, for her pioneering work on Chapter 7 in the first edition. Several named and anonymous reviewers offered detailed comments, which proved invaluable in planning the many changes and additions for this third edition. I would like to thank the following reviewers, as well as those who elected to remain anonymous, for their thoughtful feedback:

Rhonda Anderson, University of Saskatchewan
Jay Timothy Dolmage, University of Waterloo
Adam Lawrence, Cape Breton University
Craig Melhoff, University of Regina
James Christian Parsons, University of Ottawa
Jennifer Payson, University of British Columbia
Matte Robinson, St Thomas University
Thea Todd, Camosun College

I also thank the students in my composition and literature classes at the University of Victoria who agreed to have their work published here; I can show no greater appreciation than by noting their willingness to respond to my emails long after classes had ended!

Some ten years ago, amid self-doubts occasioned partly, perhaps, by too many years teaching continuing education, I at last took up the suggestion of Madeline Sonik that a 40-page writing text called "The Gremlins of Grammar" could aspire to something more; for that challenge, I will always be grateful.

Eric Henderson

Writing
by *Choice*

PART I
Rhetoric with Integrated Reader

When you enter a college or university, you can expect to do a lot of writing. Thus, the skills you have acquired from your previous schooling will be important. For most students, however, these skills represent a beginning, not an end: they need to be expanded and refined in order to meet the variety of challenges—in writing, reading, and thinking—you will encounter.

Educator Daniel J. Boorstin once defined education as "learning what you didn't even know you didn't know." In addition to the review presented in Part I, you will be introduced to unfamiliar terms, concepts, and methods—"what you didn't even know you didn't know." Learning to master them, with the aid of examples and exercises to practise your new skills, will be vital to success in all your courses.

Although writing and organizational skills are fundamental to this success, many students are surprised by the amount of reading they have to do in their post-secondary courses. Many assignments will require you to read and comprehend challenging texts for various purposes, including discussing them with other students, responding to them in writing, summarizing them, or analyzing them. This is where critical thinking often comes in: most of these activities require you to break down an idea, topic, argument, or passage of text to evaluate its validity or the author's style, techniques, or use of rhetoric. Thus, we begin Part I by looking at the interconnections among reading, thinking, and writing.

When you know the kinds of questions to ask about texts and the ways to approach them, you will be ready for chapters 2 and 3, which focus on developing basic skills in writing successful essays and paragraphs. Becoming familiar with these skills will enable you to build on them to write with a specific purpose in mind. Chapter 4 focuses on summarization and critical analyses. Chapters 5 and 6 highlight the development of more complex writing and critical-thinking skills to master the argumentative essay and the literary analysis, respectively.

1 Foundations: Reading and Thinking

Many of the tasks ahead will require you to read challenging texts efficiently and thoughtfully. By using the strategies discussed in this chapter, you will be on your way to becoming a more confident reader and thinker. You will learn to use the reading strategy that best matches your reading purpose and to ask questions to facilitate the reading process. Specific techniques are given to help you understand what you are reading.

What does it really mean to be a critical thinker? This chapter will help you develop your critical thinking skills so you can apply them successfully to a wide variety of texts.

LEARNING OBJECTIVES

- to learn how a proactive approach to reading, thinking, and writing will help you acquire the skills for success

- to be able to identify selective reading strategies and use them effectively when reading challenging works

- to be able to ask appropriate questions at different stages of the reading process

- to use strategies to help determine the meanings of unfamiliar words and expand your vocabulary

- to understand the importance of critical thinking and use it to analyze essays

A PROACTIVE APPROACH

New challenges await us at every stage of our lives. When a student enters university or college, many of these challenges are connected to reading and thinking and, of course, writing. The various subjects you study will approach the acquisition of knowledge and skills differently, but responding to these challenges will be central to your progress. However, acquiring knowledge and skills is never a passive process. Crucial to your success is your ability to take a proactive approach to your learning. When you are proactive, you act with an awareness of a future problem or need, taking a first step toward a positive outcome. Once this outcome has been achieved, you are ready to tackle the next challenge, whether in reading, thinking, or writing—or all three—building the skills necessary for success.

> When you are proactive, you act with an awareness of a future problem or need. In this sense, you help to ensure a positive or problem-free outcome to something—for example, to the writing assignments in your university/college courses.

The proactive reader

- Responds critically and analytically to challenging texts (see p. 8)
- Employs selective reading practices, fitting reading strategy to reading purpose (see p. 7)
- Reads carefully for meaning, using techniques to understand important words by context (see p. 12)
- Understands that texts are designed for specific readers and purposes (see chapter 2, p. 18)

The proactive thinker

- Uses critical thinking in reading/writing tasks: questions, compares, (re)considers, analyzes, responds (see p. 13)
- Makes inferences (conclusions based on evidence) about what is being read (see p. 14)

The proactive writer

- Writes for a specific audience and purpose, for example, by using appropriate essay/paragraph organization and development (see chapters 2–7)
- Understands the value of clear, grammatical writing and an effective style in communicating to an audience (see chapters 9–12)

Chapters 1–3 stress the interconnections among reading, thinking, and writing, and, in this way, encourage a proactive approach to these three challenges. In this chapter, we discuss proactive strategies for reading and thinking.

THREE-WAY READING

Most of us read for pleasure, at least sometimes. We choose what, when, and where we want to read. This kind of reading is primarily a one-way activity; reading to grasp content is essentially "passive reading." But this one-way activity becomes two-way when you begin responding to the text. In a literary text, you may make personal associations—recollections, emotions, desires—or experience the simple pleasure of escaping into another world that is, in some way, like your own. Consider, for example, the beginning of the short story "Friend of My Youth," by Alice Munro:

> I used to dream about my mother, and though the details in the dream varied, the surprise in it was always the same. . . . In the dream I would be the age I really was, living the life I was really living, and then I would discover that my mother was still alive. . . . Sometimes I would find myself in our old kitchen, where my mother would be rolling out piecrust on the table, or washing the dishes in the battered cream-colored dishpan with the red rim. But other times I would run into her on the street, in places where I would never have expected to see her.
>
> —Munro, Alice. *Friend of My Youth*. Toronto: Penguin, 1991. Print.

In theory, someone could read this passage merely by focusing on the meanings of the words and trying to grasp the literal meaning of the passage. But most readers will find themselves connected in some deeper way, forming associations that depend on their own experiences and outlook. Engaging with a text this way can be considered two-way reading. Your engagement could be just as deep or meaningful as three-way reading, discussed below, but the nature of the engagement is different.

Consider the beginning of another text, also about dreams, roughly the same length as the first:

> Religion was the original field of dream study. The earliest writings we have on dreams are primarily texts on their religious and spiritual significance. Long before psychoanalysts, sleep laboratory researchers, and content analysts arrived on the scene, religious specialists were exploring dreams in a variety of ways: using dreams in initiation rituals, developing techniques to incubate revelatory dreams and ward off evil nightmares, expressing numerous dream images in different artistic forms, and elaborating sophisticated interpretive systems that related dreams to beliefs about the soul, death, morality, and fate.
>
> —Doniger, W., & Bulkley, K. (1993). Why study dreams?
> A religious studies perspective. *Dreaming: Journal
> of the Association of Dreams*, 3(1), 69–73.

Did you read this paragraph differently from the fictional one? There may have been specific words or phrases, such as *content analysts* or *incubate revelatory dreams*, that caused you to reach for a dictionary; in the first paragraph, the language was probably more familiar.

Importantly, in reading the second paragraph, you likely went beyond one- or two-way reading. Though you may have formed some personal associations, you probably reacted more critically: the writers were making general statements about the use of dreams in religious societies and cultures. If you had continued to read the article, you would have drawn conclusions based on the writers' statements and the way they were presented. You would have begun, perhaps, to ask, Is the claim valid? Is it truthful?

Reliable? Is it consistent with previous claims? When you engage in this process and ask these kinds of questions, you are responding *critically* to a work.

A writer may say something directly or may present evidence from which the reader can draw a conclusion. For example, Doniger and Bulkley provide factual evidence that ancient societies developed highly sophisticated methods for studying dreams—perhaps just as complex as the methods of today's psychoanalysts and dream researchers. The writers don't directly *say* that the ancient methods were as complex, but readers could make that **inference**. (See p. 14.)

The main point is that while both passages above require you to react at some level beyond simple comprehension, the second passage calls forth a more critical response. In critical thinking, you read actively to test the validity of an author's statements, by considering the logic and consistency behind them, and to determine whether the evidence supports the author's claims.

Three-Way Reading and Academic Writing

In *three-way reading* you respond **critically** or **analytically** (or both) to the text. Three-way reading applies to fiction as well as nonfiction. In fact, when you study literature in university or college, analyzing and critical thinking are often stressed more than personal responses.

For example, in an analysis of a literary work for your English class, you employ the vocabulary of literary criticism to analyze the writer's theme and devices used to convey it. As part of an analysis of Munro's story "Friend of My Youth," you might consider her use of the first person (*I*) point of view and its relation to the work's theme. Similarly, if you were interested in creative writing, you could read the Munro text by focusing more on her writing techniques, generalizing on her use of first person and its specific value for fiction writers. In both cases, your analysis reflects skill acquisition relevant to the area you are studying (i.e., literature or creative writing).

As a homework assignment, you may be asked to write an analysis based on a three-way reading of an essay you've studied (see chapter 4). As you write, you are completing a cycle: you read a text; you think about it critically and analytically; you write down your thoughts, making them conscious, thereby closing the cycle of learning that started with reading. You can then go back and begin the cycle again by rereading the piece, rethinking it, and, perhaps, using your more developed perceptions by writing about it again. Analyzing essays and other texts and thinking about the conscious choices that writers make will lead you to reflect on your own writing processes and enable you to make sound and conscious choices in *your* own writing.

Three-way reading is essential to your success in responding to the kinds of challenging texts you encounter in university. At times, your reading could focus on, for example, understanding if you need to summarize the main finding of a source to use it in a research essay. At other times, your instructor might ask you to respond to a text, using your personal experience or observations about a topic. More often than not, you will be asked to use the "high-level" critical and analytical skills that are the hallmark of academic writing.

→ See chapter 6 for information about writing responses and literary analyses.

When a reader makes an **INFERENCE**, or infers, he or she draws a conclusion based on the evidence presented (i.e., the reader is not directly told what to conclude *from* the evidence). See Applying Critical Thinking, page 14.

CRITICAL describes the activity of weighing or evaluating something, such as the validity of a statement.

ANALYTICAL refers to the activity of breaking something down to see how it is put together and the relationship between the parts.

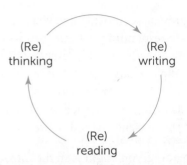

One-way reading = reading to understand meaning (content)
Two-way reading = reading to respond (associative/personal)
Three-way reading = reading to analyze techniques (critical/analytical)

FIGURE 1.1 Three-Way Reading

A Closer Look

Objectivity and Academic Writing

As you develop reading and critical-thinking skills, as discussed above, the level and nature of your engagement with a text will become increasingly complex, and you will need to take a more impersonal approach to what you are analyzing, to "stand back" and use the tools and resources that abound for careful study of texts. It is natural, then, to express yourself differently than if you were responding to a text in a more personal way; thus, it will no longer reflect your deeper purpose to say *I feel* or *I believe* or emphasize your feelings or opinions about a work.

The use of more objective forms of expression, or a more impersonal tone, goes hand-in-hand with this new engagement. For example, it is usually unnecessary to address your reader as *you* or to refer to yourself in the first person (*I*, *me*, *my*, etc.); doing so may even suggest a bias. Observing other forms of expression is important, too, in academic writing: you should avoid conversational-style writing and writing with a gender or other kind of bias.

EXERCISE 1.1

Collaborative Exercise: Writing Objectively

In the following short passage, identify specific words and phrases that may not be suitable for academic writing—because of subjective language, an overly conversational style, or gender bias.

> Some people have criticized full body scanners used at airports as an invasion of your privacy. However, I disagree, as the image generated blurs the face of a passenger, and you would have no possible idea who a person is just from the image. However, these machines cannot detect items hidden inside a passenger's body, which, I admit, might be a downside to their use. But, overall, I believe the machine is a far cry from the invasiveness of a physical search, a.k.a., the infamous "pat down."

TYPES OF SELECTIVE READING

University-level reading is not all detailed, close reading but is governed by choices; it is selective. In other words, *how* you read depends on both *what* you read and *your purpose* for reading. **Scanning** and **focused reading** are different types of **selective reading** suited to different purposes.

When you scan, you read for the gist of an essay or its main points, or to identify specific features. To scan effectively, you often need to know *where* to look. For example, if you want to get the gist of a reading, you might scan the introduction to find the thesis; although not *all* introductions include a thesis, the introduction is the first place to look. For main ideas, you might look at the first sentences of paragraphs (they are often topic sentences). You could also scan a table of contents or list of references for key words. Note that scanning as defined here is not the same thing as idle browsing where you casually glance through a webpage or magazine to see what interests you. Like focused reading, scanning is reading with a purpose.

When you practise focused reading, you concentrate on smaller blocks of text. You read for detail and sometimes for tone or style. In this sense, focused reading is specialized reading—it asks you to become a specialist (historian, literary critic, sociologist, mathematician) in your reading of the text.

Matching Reading Type and Purpose

In university-level reading, scanning is often combined with focused reading, for example, in research. Following three stages will help you research effectively:

1. When you begin research, you need to *scan* catalogue entries, journal indexes, book content pages and indexes, reference books, databases, and other types of sources in order to find materials to develop your topic.
2. Once you have located most of your sources, *scan* the most valuable articles, books, and websites to identify the main ideas or concepts relevant to your topic.
3. After identifying these ideas/concepts, practise *focused reading* to understand them and see how they fit with your thesis or with the ideas of other writers.

Scanning and focused reading are most effective when you employ them as deliberate strategies, asking specific questions in order to get as much from the reading as possible without wasting your time. Guidelines and strategies for selective reading are discussed in Responding Critically and Analytically through Questions, page 8. Some basic strategies for scanning and focused reading are outlined in table 1.1.

SCANNING is a reading strategy in which you look for key words or sections of a text.

FOCUSED READING is a close and detailed (i.e., word-by-word) reading of a specific, relevant passage.

SELECTIVE READING is a reading strategy designed to meet a specific objective, such as scanning for main points or reading for details.

Find a one-sentence definition of a topic of interest in one of your textbooks. Begin by scanning the index (an alphabetical listing of content found at or near the end of a book) for the topic; for example, in a sociology text, you could look for *sexuality* or *deviance*; in a psychology text, you could look for *depression* or *motivation*. Scan the entries under the topic; finally, scan the referenced pages themselves to locate the definition.

EXERCISE 1.2

TABLE 1.1 Basic Strategies for Scanning and Focused Reading

SCANNING	FOCUSED READING
Scanning begins when you know your purpose for reading and what you are looking for.	Focused reading begins when you have identified important or relevant passages.
Knowing where to look will help you scan efficiently.	Breaking down the passage will help you access complex material—for example, separating main points from sub-points and claims from supporting details and examples.
In scanning, skip irrelevant parts of the text.	In focused reading, read the passage first for comprehension; then, apply active reading skills.
With practice, scanning can be done quickly.	Focused reading is a methodical process, but practice will enable you to read faster and more deeply.
Activities associated with scanning include note-taking and cross-referencing (see chapter 7, Research Note-Taking, p. 201).	Activities associated with focused reading include summarizing, paraphrasing, and direct quotation (see chapter 7, Using Sources in the Composing Stage, p. 211).

RESPONDING CRITICALLY AND ANALYTICALLY THROUGH QUESTIONS

Focused reading can be triggered by asking questions about a written work. These can be asked before you read, while you read, after you have completed the first reading for content, or during later readings. Some questions relate to content, such as one asking for the specific date of a historical event; others require you to read critically or analytically, such as one asking about the causes of a historical event. Active reading typically involves responding to different kinds of questions at different times.

Before Reading

If you wanted to go on a trip somewhere far away, you probably wouldn't just head for the nearest terminal and purchase a ticket; you would learn about that place before you risked your money. Pre-reading questions can give you an agenda, just as planning a trip enables you to prepare an itinerary.

Whether your topic involves the analysis of a literary work, the investigation of changes to municipal policies, or researching an aspect of Aboriginal culture, various pre-reading questions can help you determine the text's usefulness. Questions about the writer could alert you to his or her qualifications, the audience for whom the book or essay was written, and possible biases of the writer.

However, the starting place for most readers is a work's title, which can convey information about content, organization, and other important features. For example, consider the assumptions you would make about works with the following titles, both of which refer to the settlement of Canada's Prairies:

> Buckley, Helen. *From Wooden Ploughs to Welfare: Why Indian Policy Failed in the Prairie Provinces.*

> Owram, Doug. *Promise of Eden: The Canadian Expansionist Movement and the Idea of the West, 1856–1900.*

Both titles contain words that inform their readers about purpose and content, as well as time and place. The first title suggests its author analyzes the causes of the failure of Indian policy. In the second title, the words *Promise of Eden* and *idea* suggest Owram focuses on perception and ideology behind the movement during the years indicated. As opposed to non-academic works, the titles of academic studies need to inform readers about content. Sometimes, as with the two titles above, the main title summarizes the work through an appealing image or stylistic device (Buckley uses the alliteration of "*Wooden*" and "*Welfare*"), while the subtitle (following the colon) gives specific information about content.

EXERCISE 1.3

Many of your textbooks include references to journal articles, books, and other media. These could be found in the content, or under Notes, Bibliography, or Suggestions for Further Reading. Using a textbook in your favourite subject, choose the titles of two journal articles or books referred to and analyze them word for word. In at least one sentence for each title, describe what you think the work is about.

After you consider a work's title, other pre-reading questions include the following:

- *How long is the text?* Knowing the length of a text will help you form a realistic reading plan.
- Is there *an abstract* that summarizes the entire essay? Usually, the abstract precedes the essay, giving an overview of the writer's hypothesis, method, and results (see A Closer Look: Other Types of Summaries—The Abstract in chapter 7, p. 213). In a book, the Preface, Introduction, or Foreword might give you a summary, thus saving you from unneeded reading. The editor of an essay collection may summarize each essay in an introduction or foreword.
- Is the work *divided into parts*? Are there headings throughout the essay?
- *Who is the author?* Do/should you know anything about him or her? (e.g., his or her *profession*? Nationality?)
- Is the author a member of a specific organization, group, or community?
- Does he or she seem to be *an expert*?
- When was the work written?

- *To whom is the work addressed?* The general public? Experts? A refereed journal contains many articles that have been evaluated by knowledgeable peers; it will be seen as more reliable by your instructors if you are writing a research essay. Similarly, a scholarly book publisher might be more reliable than a trade publisher.
- What is the *level of language*? Does it seem difficult, specialized? If the answer is "yes," you may have to do a little background reading or exploratory research—and ensure you have your dictionary handy.

EXERCISE 1.4

Using the same material as in exercise 1.3, choose three of the above questions and further analyze the book or journal article. Write a short response to each question.

First Reading

It's a good idea to first read the essay or chapter for content and general impressions. You may prefer to leave highlighting until your second reading, when you have a better idea of the relative importance of the various passages.

Some people prefer to make annotations—comments, thoughts, questions, or additions—in the margin of the text (assuming they own the text!). Still other people prefer to keep their own responses and the source text apart. Responding in some way is the most natural way to make it relevant to you, even if that means you just write abbreviations or symbols, such as ?, ??, !, N.B., or *, **, or ***, in the margin to denote levels of importance. Also see Research Note-Taking in chapter 7, page 201.

Questions to ask yourself during and after the first reading might include

- What are your impressions of the first few paragraphs?
- Is there a distinct introductory section?
- What kinds of words are used? More specifically, what is the vocabulary level (simple, sophisticated, general, specialized)? Is **jargon** used?
- What is the purpose of the text (e.g., to persuade, explain, describe, analyze, combination of these)?
- What is the work's main point or thesis?
- Are the work's main points identifiable (in paragraph topic sentences, for example)?
- Do the points seem well supported? Is enough detail provided?
- Are secondary sources used? Does the writer use footnotes, endnotes, or parenthetical references?
- Is the text easy to follow? Are the points clearly expressed or is the meaning sometimes unclear? Note areas where the meaning is unclear.
- Does the author seem to shift his or her focus or change his or her position at any point? Does he or she qualify points or contradict him- or herself?

> **JARGON** consists of words and expressions used within a designated group or in a particular discipline that its members would understand but that people outside the group would not necessarily understand. Jargon is a kind of specialized diction.

- Does the work seem to build? Does it get stronger or weaker?
- Is there a distinct concluding section? Is it satisfying?

Second Reading

In your second (and later) readings of a work, your ability to apply critical and analytical skills is crucial. With practice, these skills will become active in all your reading.

- Is the introduction effective? Why or why not?
- What specific strategies does the writer use to draw you into the work (e.g., question, quotation, anecdote, narration, description, analogy)?
- Is the author's purpose in writing clear from the start?
- What is the work's tone (i.e., the writer's attitude to the subject matter—for example, familiar, objective, detached, casual, humorous, ironic, formal, informal)?
- Can you put the thesis in your own words?
- How are the points backed up? What kinds of evidence are used (e.g., examples, illustrations, facts, statistics, authorities, personal experience, analogies)?
- How does the writer organize the work? Is one method used more than any other (compare/contrast, definition, cause and effect, narration, description, division, other)?
- Does the author appear reliable? Fair?
- How are the main points arranged? Is the strongest point placed near the beginning, middle, or end? Are the points arranged in the most effective order?
- Does the work appeal more to logic or to emotion?
- Does the writer appeal to a set of values or standards?
- What inferences should readers make? Is reason used effectively?
- Do specialized language, insufficient background, long or poorly constructed paragraphs, ineffective writing style, inconsistencies, or contradictions in the argument affect clarity at any time?
- Is the conclusion effective? Why or why not?

The questions above cover many different aspects of the writing process discussed in this textbook.

For specific strategies for reading scholarly essays, see page 228.

FOCUSED READING AND COMPREHENSION

As mentioned, focused reading requires attention to specific words.

In your readings, you will sometimes encounter unfamiliar words. At other times, although the word looks familiar, *the way it is being used* seems unfamiliar. This is a natural by-product of language and its evolution; in the process of reading, you will not only increase your vocabulary by learning new words and new uses for old words but come to appreciate the nuances of words and the way they contribute to the subtlety of a writer's thought.

Learning strategies that help you understand a word in the context of the sentence is a first step in becoming a proactive reader. Studying other writers' language can improve your own writing as well as sharpen your critical-thinking skills, as discussed below, on page 14.

Word Meanings

Comprehension is vital as a starting point in just about everything you read. This section focuses on strategies to increase comprehension. Dictionaries are indispensable tools for writing, whether you are a professional writer or a student writer. They are also an essential part of reading. But while a good dictionary is part of the key to understanding challenging texts, it is certainly not the only one.

Because the texts you read in university may be more challenging than those you are used to, looking up every unfamiliar word would be time-consuming and distracting. Thankfully, you don't need to know the precise meaning of every word you read; you need to know the exact meanings of the most important words but only approximate meanings for others.

Since relying *only* on a dictionary is inefficient, you should cultivate reading practices that minimize the constant use of a dictionary. Refer to a dictionary when needed, for example, to confirm a word's meaning; otherwise, try to determine meanings by

- looking at surrounding words, which often give a clue to meaning
- looking at the idea the writer is trying to express
- noting similarities with words you *do* know

Important words are often revealed through context—the words around them. If a writer does not define difficult words, he or she may use synonyms or rephrasing to make their meanings easy to grasp. Writers may also use an unfamiliar word in such a way that the surrounding words clarify its meaning.

Using Context or Similarities to Determine Word Meanings

In the following sentences from the essay at the end of this chapter, "Embrace the Mediocrity Principle" (p. 19), words before or after the italicized words can be used to determine their meanings:

> [The principle's] acceptance as a guiding 21st century *paradigm* . . . just might save humankind from its own bloated sense of superiority and greed.

A paradigm is something that *guides*, such as a pattern; *21st century* could further suggest that a paradigm is an enduring pattern.

> [Homer-Dixon] describes how the current convergence of global crises can no longer be dismissed by the "Don't Worry, Be Happy" voices of *hucksters* promoting status, wealth, and consumption.

With the words that follow *hucksters*, the writer appears to be criticizing people who sell consumer goods. You might conclude that the word refers to people who take advantage of others' naivety to make a sale.

Particularly important concepts may be defined. Early in the essay, two important principles are defined (p. 19):

> Welcome to The Mediocrity Principle . . . . *Unlike the famous Peter Principle that says people rise to fulfill their incompetence,* the new and very real *Mediocrity*

Principle says that wherever astronomers look, the universe . . . sinks into trans-galactic commonness.

When a writer does not define a word, you may be able to infer its meaning by examining the idea the writer is trying to express. In the following example, it is apparent that Gould has challenged a major finding of Charles Darwin.

. . . the late Harvard University paleontologist Stephen Gould pilloried Darwin's theory, saying evolution comes about, in part, through fluke and global catastrophe, not just through a species' inherent superiority.

In fact, the verb *to pillory* means something stronger than simply "challenge": "to hold up to public ridicule." Since Darwin's theories are publicly accepted, the choice of *pilloried* seemed a suitable one.

The meanings of words can often be determined because they look like other, familiar words. One could guess that *ghettoization*, part of the phrase *regional economic ghettoization* in paragraph 13 of the essay on page 19, is related to *ghetto*, a place in which a minority group lives, cut off from the more privileged.

Reading carefully to determine both the immediate context and the encompassing idea of the sentence can help you determine a word's meaning. Remember that the object is not necessarily to make the word part of your writing vocabulary but to enable you to know how the author is using it—to recognize its **connotation**. However, the discovery of a word's connotation can be an opportunity to learn more about the word's meanings and make it part of your writing vocabulary. Thus, learning a word's connotations can help expand your vocabulary and make you a stronger reader *and* writer.

CRITICAL THINKING

What Is Critical Thinking?

Responding actively to a text develops your **critical-thinking** abilities. One meaning of the adjective *critical* is "making a negative comment, criticizing." However, the root of *critical* comes from a Greek word that means "to judge or discern, to weigh and evaluate evidence." When you apply critical thinking, you weigh the evidence and come to a conclusion. Critical thinking can be defined as *a series of logical mental processes that lead to a conclusion*. Critical thinking may involve

- analyzing
- comparing
- evaluating
- questioning
- rethinking
- synthesizing (putting together)

Much of what we do today is done quickly. This is true not only of video games, texting, tweeting, and other forms of social messaging, but also in business, where "instant" decisions are often valued (especially if they turn out to be good decisions!).

> A word's **CONNOTATION** is its associations or implications, whereas a word's denotation is its basic, or dictionary, meaning. Connotation may depend on context.
>
> **CRITICAL THINKING** can be defined as a series of logical mental processes that lead to a conclusion.

However, because critical thinking involves many related activities, speed is not an asset. In fact, since critical thinking is a process, the best way to succeed is to slow down, *to be more deliberate in your thinking* so you can complete each stage of the process.

This section is not designed to *make* you think critically, since you probably would not be at university or college if you did not use critical thinking daily. Rather, it is meant to *make you more conscious of the process*, especially when you read and analyze an essay or when you write one. Critical-thinking skills are triggered whenever you read a work in order to comment on it, such as during a classroom discussion or debate, or to use it for support in your essay. The previous section, Responding Critically and Analytically through Questions, provided guidelines to help you become a careful reader who asks important, relevant questions.

Applying Critical Thinking

Critical-thinking skills also apply to many everyday situations—from deciding what courses to take to what clothes to wear. Although choosing clothes might seem trivial, consider the importance of comparing, questioning, weighing, and rethinking if you were deciding on an outfit for an important job interview. What factors might affect your choice? These could range from the type of job you are applying for, the dress code of the company, the clothes you feel most confident in, or the weather on the day of the interview.

Critical thinking, then, involves making choices, but the most highly developed critical thinking is more than simple choice-making: it involves making the *best* choice from a range of possibilities. When you read an essay or a book, or evaluate a real-life situation, you are often not directly told what to think. You might be given evidence and left to infer the meaning. When you infer, you arrive at a probable conclusion based on what you read (or see). The *best* inference (or choice) is the *most probable* one after all the evidence is weighed.

Much research relies on inferences: astronomers, for example, study the phenomenon of black holes by observing the behaviour of matter that surrounds the black hole. They know that before gas is swallowed up by a black hole, it is heated to extreme temperatures and accelerates. In the process, X-rays are created, which escape the black hole and reveal its presence. Scientists cannot actually see black holes, but they can *infer* their existence through the emission of X-rays.

EXERCISE 1.5

Consider the following situation:

You invite a new friend for a coffee, but she does not show up. The next day, you meet her unexpectedly and ask her what happened. She pauses for a few seconds and then says matter-of-factly, "Well, actually, I was abducted by aliens, and they just released me." What do you make of her statement? What inferences are possible? Which are more likely? What could you say or do to ensure that your conclusion was the most probable one?

Possible inferences:

Probable inferences:

How to ensure that your inference is correct:

A Closer Look

Critical Thinking in Literature Classes

Learning how to analyze literary works means applying specific reading strategies to interpret literature, arriving at the best inferences to make your reading more complex and/or subtle. When you read a poem, short story, or novel, the writer doesn't tell you the work's theme, explain how a symbol is being used, or list the traits of the main character. Instead, he or she embeds theme, symbol, and character within the work, enabling you, the reader, to draw conclusions about their significance.

Training and practice in critical thinking will help you read literature more deeply. Interpreting literary works often requires a sensitivity to irony, indirection, subtext, and style—one reason why reading good literature can be challenging yet rewarding. See A Closer Look: Reading for Style and Tone, below (p. 18), and the sample student essay by Kiyuri Naicker on page 181.

You use critical thinking as you read whenever you evaluate and draw conclusions about claims and about the evidence or sources of these claims. It is important to remember that critical thinking is a *process of engagement* with a text (or a situation) that may change as you read (or learn more about the situation).

The critical thinker questions assumptions, tests the evidence, and accepts (or rejects) conclusions after careful analysis. When questions arise, the critical thinker seeks answers within the text itself but may also seek relevant outside sources. For example, in the case of the coffee invitation described in the box above, you might ask the woman's friends about her belief in aliens—or about her sense of humour.

In analyzing arguments, the critical thinker should carefully evaluate the writer's claims and look for failures in logic or misuse of emotion (see Logical, Emotional, and Ethical Fallacies in chapter 5, p. 137). He or she should also consider points that the writer *does not* raise. Is the writer avoiding certain issues by not mentioning them? Expository (fact-based) writing can also produce disagreement and contradictory findings. For example, researchers determining the effectiveness of a new drug or investigating the connection between television viewing and violence may arrive at different conclusions. What can account for the differing results? Attempting to answer this question involves critical thinking, too.

> Using critical thinking in arguments involves breaking down the arguer's use of reason and questioning what is both said and not said. Using critical thinking in exposition could involve analyzing why researchers' findings are different from one another.

Breaking Down Critical Thinking

Controversial topics often evoke a strong, emotional response. However, for the critical thinker, they are an opportunity to exercise one's reasoning skills. Take, for example, the claim that cats are smarter than dogs. Here are some areas to evaluate when you analyze a writer's argument:

- *Consider the writer's credibility.* Is the writer regarded as an expert? For example, is he or she a researcher into animal behaviour? A veterinarian? An animal trainer? Someone who has owned both dogs and cats? Owned cats only? Could the writer have a bias against dogs? Are there any errors in logic, such as "My neighbour's dog jumps up on me all the time; therefore, dogs are not smart"? Has fact been carefully distinguished from opinion?

- *Consider the nature of the thesis/main points.* Specific claims are more convincing than general ones. Since there are many different dog breeds, it would be difficult to generalize about the intelligence of *all* dogs.

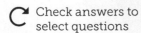
In argument, a warrant provides the basis for a claim. This term is discussed in chapter 5, page 115.

- *Consider the basis of the statement.* You can look beyond the statement to ask what it is based on—for example, a definition. There are various ways to define and measure intelligence: physiologically (e.g., the weight of the brain in proportion to the weight of the body) and behaviourally (e.g., trainability, adaptability, independence). Those who think dogs are more intelligent may point to trainability as the intelligence factor, while cat fanciers may point to adaptability or independence.

- *Consider the method.* How does the writer attempt to prove his or her claim? Since intelligence can be measured, a method that measured it scientifically would be more credible than one that relied on personal experience—especially since many pet-lovers may be opinionated about their pets' intelligence.

- *Consider the support.* In critical thinking, you must evaluate the nature of the evidence and the way the writer uses it. Typical questions might include, What kind of evidence does the writer use? Does the writer rely too much on one kind of evidence or one source? How many sources are used? Are they current sources (recent studies may be more credible than older ones)? Does the writer ignore some sources (e.g., those that found dogs more intelligent than cats)?

- *Draw your conclusion.* While analyzing and questioning are important during your reading of the work, synthesizing (putting together) is the final-stage activity that leads to your conclusion(s). *Your goal is to determine whether the weight of evidence supports the writer's claim.* You might consider how weaker points affect the validity of the findings. Are there any gaps or inconsistencies in the chain of reasoning?

EXERCISE 1.6

↻ Check answers to select questions

As discussed in this section, we use critical thinking and inferences every day. The following scenarios call for critical-thinking skills by asking us to make inferences.

A. What inferences could be made in each case?

B. Is there a best (i.e., most probable) inference? Justify your choice of the most probable inference. If you believe no inference can be made, explain what kind of information you would need to make an inference.

1. You arrive at your 8:30 a.m. class after missing yesterday's class because you overslept. You are surprised to see an empty classroom. As well, there is no one you recognize from class hanging around outside, and there is nothing posted on the wall or door to show that the instructor is ill.
    Inferences:
    a. You have mistaken either the time or the room.
    b. The instructor announced class cancellation yesterday.
    c. The instructor is ill, but no one put up a notice.
    d. No inference is possible. (What further information is needed?)

2. It was Todd's roommate's turn to cook dinner, but when Todd got home, his roommate was glued to the TV and the kitchen looked untouched. "Wow! Something smells great," enthused Todd.
   Inferences:
   a. Todd has a poor sense of smell.
   b. Todd is sarcastically voicing his displeasure.
   c. Todd is trying to give his roommate a hint that he should start dinner.
   d. No inference is possible. (What further information is needed?)

3. The students at the school work in isolated workstations; their desks face the walls. Social interaction is structured and supervised. Time-out rooms are small, windowless areas without furniture or carpeted floors; the doors have keyed locks. The cells are painted bright colours: pink, yellow, and blue; the light switch for each cubicle is on the outside.
   Inferences:
   a. The students at the school are thoroughly dedicated to their studies.
   b. School designers have provided the optimal conditions for study.
   c. The school has been designed for students with behavioural problems.
   d. No inference is possible. (What further information is needed?)

4. All was not eager anticipation for Meghan. She chose to attend the largest university in the province, and she found herself frequently feeling lost, both geographically and socially. She had to take a campus bus to get to some of her classes on time. Most of her classes were large with well over 100 students; one class had 250 students. She was used to smaller class sizes in high school with support from her resource teacher. Although she arranged for support through the university's Office of Disability Services, Meghan realized that she would have to approach the professors to describe her learning problems and request accommodations. Meghan also felt disorganized. Although her roommates had purchased their texts, yearly organizational calendars, and other materials, Meghan had no idea where to begin; her fear of failure was increasing by the moment.
   Inferences:
   a. Meghan will likely face many challenges at the university.
   b. Meghan will likely give up and go home.
   c. Meghan's fears are likely unfounded, as the many resources available at the university will help her adjust to her new life.
   d. No inference is possible. (What further information is needed?)

5. Binkley paid for all the travel and expenses, and what was only 12 months ago a very new and controversial transaction has today left Binkley a healthy man—and the first of 16 people who have successfully received organs through MatchingDonors.com.
   Inferences:
   a. The author believes that this method of soliciting donors is wrong.
   b. The author believes that this method of soliciting donors is, at the very least, ethically questionable.
   c. The author sees nothing wrong with this method of soliciting donors.
   d. No inference is possible. (What further information is needed?)

A Closer Look

Reading for Style and Tone

Straightforward, direct writing is rightly praised (especially by writing instructors!). However, a writer may employ a more complex or indirect style than that needed for simple communication. Why would a writer choose to use *indirect* means to get his or her points across?

TONE is the writer's attitude toward the subject matter or audience and can be determined by the writer's language and style. In **SATIRE**, a writer uses humour and an ironic tone to poke fun at an individual, a group, or society itself—the target of the satire.

Such a style can make writing more interesting or the thesis more convincing. Alert readers will understand that the writer's indirectness is serving a purpose and read the essay in light of that purpose. Readers who do not notice this may be confused by the essay or misinterpret it.

A writer's style consists of features that (1) make the writing distinctive—for example, a descriptive style might use many adjectives—and (2) reflect the audience or purpose in writing. For example, an informal style could indicate familiarity with average readers or their values; if a writer's purpose was to parody (make fun of) someone, the style might reflect this through exaggeration. Features of style, then, can include diction (word choice), sentence structure and length, and the use of literary devices, such as imagery or metaphors. (Note that *style* also has other meanings in writing—see chapters 8 and 12).

Sometimes readers need to use their critical-thinking skills to "read between the lines" and understand the author's **tone**—his or her attitude toward the subject matter or audience. Tone is usually revealed through language and style, including features like diction or specific stylistic choices, like the use of metaphors or humour. For example, in **satire**, a writer uses humour and an ironic tone to poke fun at an individual, a group, or society itself—the target of the satire.

EXERCISE 1.7

Collaborative Exercise: Determining Tone

What is the author's tone in the following passage? Is it one more of amusement or of contempt? What, specifically, shows you the writer's attitude? As you practise focused reading on this passage, pay particular attention to the author's word choices.

> They're the impulse buys piled up next to the cash register. They're the books stocked by Urban Outfitters and hipster gift stores. They're the books you pick up, laugh at, and figure would be just about right for that co-worker who's into sci-fi *(The Space Tourist's Handbook)* [or] the friend who watches too much TV *(Hey! It's That Guy!: The Fametracker.com Guide to Character Actors)*. . . .
>
> Pop-culture-inspired handbooks for situations you're never going to face featuring information you're never going to need, these gimmicky, kooky, sometimes just plain stupid books have at least one thing in common: There are more and more of them out there, because they sell.
>
> —Hal Niedzviecki, *The Globe and Mail*, 2005

Think of a recent episode of a TV comedy, an article in a magazine, or a website in which satire was used. Can you identify the target of the satire (i.e., whom it was directed against)? Was the target announced or did a reader/viewer have to infer it? Consider specific features that contributed to the satire and write a short response in which you identify the target of the satire, along with passages, images, dialogue, and so on, that pointed to the target.

SAMPLE PROFESSIONAL ESSAY

Before reading the essay below, consider any relevant questions on pages 9–10 that might apply to this essay. After reading "Embrace the Mediocrity Principle," answer the questions that follow, focusing on making inferences based on content and credibility, along with tone and style, where applicable.

SAMPLE PROFESSIONAL ESSAY

Embrace the Mediocrity Principle

by Daniel Wood

[1]   The shoe has dropped. But few are inclined to embrace the implications of the discoveries in the last few years that there are, almost certainly, *millions* of Earths out there and that the big rock you inhabit is as ordinary as phlegm.

[2]   Welcome to The Mediocrity Principle—astrophysicists' scary gift to the third millennium. Unlike the famous Peter Principle that says people rise to fulfill their incompetence, the new and very real Mediocrity Principle says that wherever astronomers look, the universe—and, by extension, all its constituents—sinks into trans-galactic commonness.

[3]   The Earth isn't the least unique. *Ipso facto*: neither are you. You're unalterably average.

[4]   It's an idea that, cosmologically speaking, has been a long time coming. But, its acceptance as a guiding 21st century paradigm, say pundits of impending environmental and economic apocalypse, just might save humankind from its own bloated sense of superiority and greed.

[5]   Welcome to 2012: Year of the Hairshirt. The year the 99 per cent got mad. The year that sardines trump swordfish and mediocrity begins to replace excess. Frugalism is the new black.

[6]   In a Very Brief History of Time (169 words), this is how the Earth and its occupants have fallen into disgrace. A few centuries ago, people in the West thought this planet was the centre of the universe, that it began in 4004 BC (on Saturday, Oct. 22, to be exact), and that humans were made in the image of God. Copernicus, Galileo, and Darwin put large holes in these beliefs.

[7]   In the early 20th century, astronomer Edwin Hubble said a lot of those stars out there aren't stars at all. They're distant galaxies—billions of them, each containing billions of stars.

[8]   To make matters worse for humankind's sense of uniqueness, it soon became clear that time didn't start with The Big Guy in 4004 BC, but with The Big Bang in 15 billion BC.

[9]   Now, using information from the Hubble and Kepler telescopes, 707 of what's-predicted-to-be millions of distant exoplanets have been identified—including newly found Kepler-22b that sits in the so-called Goldilocks Zone, neither too far nor too near to its Sun to make it a good candidate for warmth-loving, carbon-based life. In fact, there are almost certainly tens of millions of life-sustaining, Earth-like rocks out there. We live, it appears, on a commonplace hunk of granite, Coca-Cola, and chop suey surrounded by 10,000,000,000,000,000,000,000 stars and innumerable solar systems.

[10]   "Why should we assume there is anything special about us? Mediocrity is the universal rule," says Alexander Vilenkin, the Boston cosmologist who in 1995 coined the phrase The Mediocrity Principle.

[11]   As this was happening, the late Harvard University paleontologist Stephen Gould pilloried Darwin's theory, saying evolution comes about, in part, through fluke and global catastrophe, not just through a species' inherent superiority. Now, humans can no longer claim to be Heavenly or even evolutionarily blessed; we're the result—in part—of renegade luck.

Headed for newt status?

[12]   Goodbye creationism. Goodbye self-importance. Goodbye security. That might have been the appropriate reaction were it not for one thing. The Earth today is facing one of those planetary catastrophes that Gould and his doom-saying associates have often spoken about. And the catastrophe is *us*.

[13]   The planet's systems are breaking down: global warming, economic disintegration, energy and food crises, the accelerating extinction of species, rampant pollution, AIDS, regional economic ghettoization, and the threat of worldwide terror. The list is long and familiar.

[14]   Sixty-five million years ago, the dinosaurs failed to adapt to change and became, in time, newts. Mediocrity was *forced* on them. Today, there are creepy species waiting in the wings—rats, blackberries, cockroaches, lawyers—ready to claim humanity's position atop the Pig Pile. (Remember, the planet's dominant life-form throughout history is slime.)

[15]   It's beginning to look as if the wackos carrying the placards reading "The End Is Nigh," are right. Unless . . . UNLESS: This planet's brainiest inhabitants accept that The Mediocrity Principle applies to them. With apologies to Marshall McLuhan, *medium* is the message.

[16]   Tad Homer-Dixon is no wacko. He's a University of Waterloo professor of international affairs and author of the 2001 Governor-General award-winning book *The Ingenuity Gap*.

[17]   In it he describes how the current convergence of global crises can no longer be dismissed by the "Don't Worry, Be Happy" voices of hucksters promoting status, wealth, and consumption.

[18]   "The conceit of sustainable development," says Homer-Dixon, "is you can have your cake and eat it, too. You can't. There's only *so much*. The cliff-edge *is* out there."

[19]   As Homer-Dixon sees it, there are two human options for the future: 1) capitulation to drastic worldwide regulations and limits . . . or 2) chaos.

[20]   To achieve the former, there'd have to be restrictions on consumption and on freedoms that—to use Homer-Dixon's phrase, "would be Holland—*times 10*." It would be a world of unimaginable technocratic order, enforced mediocrity, and eco-police. Flagrant extravagance would be a crime.

[21]   That is the *good* option. To achieve the latter—chaos—Earthlings just have to keep doing what we're doing now. This route leads to fortified enclaves of wealth scattered amid widespread political and environmental collapse, plus the quarantine of entire sections of the planet. It would be—again using Homer-Dixon's analogy, "a patchwork of global anarchy—like many, many Haitis."

[22]   Which option would you choose?

Selling mediocrity

[23]   The point man for global mediocrity is Vancouver's Kalle Lasn, the founder of award-winning *Adbusters* magazine, and creator of the unlikely "Buy Nothing Day." His is not an easy task. In a world of exceptionalism, glitz, and vacuous spectacle, the satisfactions of the ordinary are, he knows, made to appear third-rate.

[24]   For example, recent ad copy hyping the Nissan Altima read: "May Promote Feelings of Superiority." There are no ads anywhere promoting the virtues of mediocrity. Lasn knows this because he has produced 25 anti-commercials and sought to air them on the three big American TV networks. His success rate? Zero for 25.

[25]   "Consumption is the mother of all evils," he says as he studies the foyer of a big-box Toys 'R' Us near his office. Colourful, inflated swimming pool animals float overhead. "People think business and technology will save us. But that's science fiction. Calamities lie ahead. Ordinariness will be resisted. In time, there'll be hell to pay. This over-consumptive culture of ours is going to die very hard."

[26]   As he leaves the store, he admits that he doesn't have much hope for the future. But he does, he says, have faith . . . in the *potato*. He'd dug one that morning in his backyard garden and fried it up for breakfast. At the memory, he smacks his lips.

Embrace our boringness

[27]   There are, cynics acknowledge, a few hopeful signs that mediocrity might take root amid a society that has, since the corporate scandals and economic turmoil of recent years, grown disenchanted with excess.

[28]   But it's a long descent from taking million-dollar golden handshakes from Fannie Mae to finding happiness in wearing bunny slippers and watching reruns of *Celebrity Pets*. That is a fall too far. Mediocrity is not about tastelessness. It's not about bad. It's not the Lada or carpet bowling or people who say, "Yo!" Mediocrity eschews the snobbishness of Calvin Klein for the practicality of Sears. Mediocrity does not go ga-ga over miniature summer squashes, when there are plenty of zucchinis—grown locally, of course.

[29]   Mediocrity embraces home haircuts, tap water, elbow patches, Scrabble nights, and naps. Mediocrity celebrates the winners of the annual Darwin Awards for their fatal stupidity. They are the true heroes!

[30]   Mediocrity looks for guidance to Despair, Inc.—a real business whose motto is: "Increasing Success by Lowering Expectations" and whose logo features the Leaning Tower of Pisa.

[31]   Mediocrity has as its most respected voice the man who gave the commencement address at his Yale University alma mater in 2001 and said there was nothing wrong with getting Cs. He'd done it himself. The usual venue for his speeches has been The White House.

[32]   There are some who'd argue that the Truth is out there and that extraterrestrials lurk at the periphery of our vision. The Mediocrity Principle provides a simpler explanation.

[33]   Mediocrity says there are no aliens nearby in their flying saucers because—despite humankind's efforts to simultaneously Disneyfy and destroy the planet—the Earth is a boring destination for intergalactic travellers.

[34]   This planet, it now seems, is likely just one of millions of ordinary way stations in the universe—a dull place like Kapuskasing where you'd only stop if your car broke down.

Source: *The Tyee*, 24 December 2008. © Daniel Wood. Reprinted with permission.

EXERCISE 1.9

1. Sum up the Mediocrity Principle in one to two sentences by using your own words.
2. How effectively does Wood support his thesis concerning the Mediocrity Principle? What would you consider his strongest point?
3. What is the only way, according to Wood, that global catastrophe could be prevented? Do you think he is generally hopeful about humanity's future?
4. What do you think *anti-commercials* are (see paragraph 24)? How could you find out if your inference is correct?
5. Analyze paragraphs 1–3 for their style. You could consider word choice/level of language, sentence structure, use of the second-person pronoun (*you*), or other strategies that reveal the author's style.
6. Identify the author's tone (i.e., apparent attitude toward his subject) in paragraph 14. Does it seem the same in paragraph 27? Identify the author's tone in one other paragraph in which it seems different from that in paragraphs 14 and 27.
7. What are the Darwin Awards?
8. Why does Wood not give the name of the man who, he says in paragraph 31, is the voice of mediocrity?
9. Why do you think Wood chooses the particular examples he does in the last section, "Embrace our boringness"? Do you believe they help support his thesis?
10. Do you agree with Wood's thesis? Write a 500-word response in which you explain your agreement or disagreement, using your critical-thinking skills and referring specifically to the essay itself.

EXERCISE 1.10

From the following list, choose five words you're unfamiliar with and try to determine their meaning by their context or similarity in "Embrace the Mediocrity Principle." (See p. 12—13 for strategies.) When you've written a short definition of the word, look it up in a reliable dictionary to confirm its meaning. Then, use the word in a sentence of your own that would enable another writer to guess its meaning. Finally, give the sentence to a classmate and have him or her determine the meaning by context.

Note: If you read five essays per week and learned the meanings of just five new words per essay, you could increase your vocabulary by 100 words per month!

bloated (paragraph 4)	convergence (paragraph 17)
capitulation (paragraph 19)	cosmologist (paragraph 10)

disenchanted (paragraph 27)   pundits (paragraph 4)
enclaves (paragraph 21)   renegade (paragraph 11)
flagrant (paragraph 20)   vacuous (paragraph 23)
inherent (paragraph 11)

CHAPTER SUMMARY

Chapter 1 introduces you to effective reading and thinking strategies, providing a foundation for the kinds of challenging tasks, including writing ones, common at the university level. Many tasks involve three-way reading, that is, reading critically and analytically. Reading a text usually begins by scanning for general or specific content, followed by focused reading of one or more passages. Because you will undoubtedly encounter many unfamiliar words in your reading, develop the habit of determining word meanings by context. Developing critical-thinking skills is also crucial to three-way reading and involves analyzing, questioning, weighing evidence, and reaching the best, or most probable, conclusion.

2 The Writing Situation

This chapter begins by identifying the two main factors that influence the writing situation: why you are writing (writing purpose) and who you are writing to (audience). A step-by-step overview of the writing process follows with guidelines on what to expect and how to succeed at each stage: pre-writing, researching, organizing, composing, and revising. The chapter concludes with a review of the four rhetorical modes with examples of each.

LEARNING OBJECTIVES

- to understand the importance of your purpose for writing
- to know who you are writing to and learn strategies for addressing specific readers so they will respond in the way you wish
- to be able to break the essay-writing process into stages and become familiar with the goals and objectives applicable to each stage
- to learn to utilize pre-writing strategies and outlines
- to be aware of the benefits and potential pitfalls of composing on the computer
- to understand the specific tasks involved in revision
- to learn the differences between the four rhetorical modes: exposition, argument, narration, and description

WRITING PURPOSE

Before you begin writing, you need to consider the factors that influence your writing task, including your purpose for writing and your audience. Purpose refers to more than your reason for writing, as the questions below make clear: Will you be choosing your own topic or have you been given a specific topic? If the latter, will you have to narrow the topic? What kind of writing will you be doing? What form will it take (e.g., response, formal essay, research proposal, lab report)?

- What main activities are involved (e.g., informing, explaining, arguing, narrating, describing, summarizing)?
- Does the assignment stress new tasks or does it ask you to apply familiar concepts and practices?
- What specific skills will you need to demonstrate? For example, will you have to define, synthesize, analyze, compare and contrast, or classify? If the assignment includes a specifically worded question or statement, pay attention to verbs, such as *evaluate* or *assess, summarize, explore, explain, argue for or against, discuss, describe*. Each indicates a different purpose.
- Will you be using your own ideas? Where will they come from (opinions/personal experience, readings, class or group discussions)?
- Will the assignment test originality—new approaches to an old problem (inventiveness, imagination, creativity)?
- Should your language be formal, like that of most academic disciplines? Is the occasional use of contractions and/or informal diction acceptable?
- Will you be using ideas from books and articles or other secondary sources (e.g., interviews, surveys)?
- What kind of preparation will be needed?
- Will you be submitting work in progress, such as pre-writing, self-survey, proposal, outline, plan, or rough draft?
- How long does it need to be?
- How much time do you have for the assignment? For example, an in-class exam would require a different assessment of purpose than that of an essay assigned weeks in advance.

WRITING TO AN AUDIENCE

Almost everything is written for an **audience**—readers with common interests, attitudes, reading habits, and expectations. Like book publishers and web designers, student writers need to "design" their essay for an audience or a typical reader. When physicist Stephen Hawking set out to write his famous book on cosmology, *A Brief History of Time*, he took his audience into account, as is evident in his first paragraph. Italics show where readers are specifically addressed:

> Where did the universe come from? How and why did it begin? Will it come to an end, and if so, how? These are questions that are of interest to *us all*. But modern science has become so technical that only a very small number of specialists are

> A writer's **AUDIENCE** is composed of readers with common knowledge, interests, attitudes, reading habits, and/ or expectations. In order to write to a specific audience, you should be aware of relevant characteristics of your readers.

able to master the mathematics used to describe them. Yet the basic ideas about the origin and fate of the universe can be stated without mathematics in a form that *people without a scientific education* can understand.

Hawking begins with straightforward questions that he says interest us all, meaning curious people with no scientific training. He chooses direct language and simple sentence structure. If he were addressing his book to specialists, he probably would not have used the phrase *a very small number of specialists*. Perhaps he would have said *cosmologists, astrophysicists, and mathematical physicists*, specifically addressing these readers.

The tone of the passage also shows his concern with audience. It is inviting and implies that a non-specialist reader can understand difficult concepts. Clearly, Hawking wrote the way he did because he wanted to meet the expectations of his target audience.

EXERCISE 2.1

You could consider the writer–reader relationship a kind of contract with responsibilities on both sides. What responsibilities to the reader would a writer have in this relationship? What responsibilities would a reader have? Add to the list in table 2.1, assigning additional responsibilities in this contractual arrangement.

TABLE 2.1 Responsibilities of Reader/Responsibilities of Writer

RESPONSIBILITIES OF THE READER	RESPONSIBILITIES OF THE WRITER
1. to read attentively and closely	1. to use appropriate language and a clear, readable style
2. to test the writer's claims for logic and consistency	2. to reason fairly, logically, and with consistency
3.	3.
4.	4.
5.	5.

EXERCISE 2.2

Collaborative Exercise: Using Reader-Based Prose

Identify places in the following paragraph where the writer has failed to use reader-based prose in writing to an audience of non-specialists (i.e., who are unfamiliar with the pollination process). This could be due to unfamiliar words, missing information, or unclear relationships among points.

Pollination is a well-known process that involves the transport of pollen grains from the male reproductive organ. This process allows cross-fertilization and genetic diversity in the sessile plant world and enables the plant to produce seeds, resulting in a new generation. Organisms called pollinators carry out this necessary process. The honeybee has proven an effective pollinator, but native bee populations are declining. Some examples of uncommon pollinators include *leptonycteris curasoae*, which has a mutualistic relationship with the columnar cactus.

—Buchmann, S. L., & Nabhan, G. P. (1997). *The forgotten pollinators.*
Island Press: Washington, D.C.

A Closer Look

Reader-Based Prose: Writing *to* an Audience

Reader-based prose is focused on the reader. Specifically, it is geared toward the particular audience the essay is designed for and uses words and concepts this reader will understand. It can be a good idea to visualize an audience made up of typical readers before you begin composing; in this way, your reader will be not just an abstraction but a specific group. Rather than just writing *for* your instructor, focus on writing *to* a specific group—for example, your peers, people who share an interest in your topic, or people knowledgeable about your topic—using language they would understand. For example, although you may write a research essay *for* your instructor to mark, you are actually writing it *to* other researchers with expertise in the topic, your audience.

However, remember that in formal writing you should not address your audience directly using the second-person pronoun, *you*. Using *you* implies you know your reader well or that he or she is a member of a specific group whose characteristics you know well. For example, the second-person pronoun is often used in this book because it is written to a specific group: university students in writing and composition classes.

In contrast with reader-based prose, **writer-based prose** is much less directed to its audience: private journal writing is one example of a writing activity where there is no need to acknowledge a reader. Another example is freewriting (see Freewriting and Clustering, p. 36); after you have used freewriting to uncover your thoughts and feelings about a topic, you then need to begin shaping that topic to a specific reader.

Because reader-based prose is directed to an audience, you must ensure it is error-free and clear in its meaning. Ideas need direct and concise expression. In addition, there should be no obvious gaps in logic, nor should you assume a reader knows something just because you know it. In some cases, you may have to define terms or clarify specific points. Even if the intended audience has specialized knowledge about a subject, it is best to assume that *the reader knows less about the subject than you do.*

READER-BASED PROSE is focused on the reader by making clear communication a priority and acknowledging the role of the reader in the communication process.

WRITER-BASED PROSE is focused on the writer and the expression of his or her feelings or thoughts.

Although it's useful to visualize an audience that consists of more than just your instructor, of course it's also important to acknowledge your instructor as a reader by following directions given for the assignment. For example, if you are required to include a title page with the instructor's name beneath the name or number of the course, not including this information would be failing to meet the needs of your audience (your instructor). The presentation of your essay demands your careful attention since instructors vary in their requirements; for instance, one instructor may require you to use 12-point size type while another may say that a point size between 10 and 12 is acceptable.

An audience can be profiled by the knowledge and interest levels of typical readers.

Audience Factors

Audience refers to the person or people you are writing to—for example, fellow students, members of another peer group, your instructor, or a knowledgeable expert. An audience can be profiled in a variety of ways, which can affect your decision on what to include or not to include, what level of language to use, how to develop your ideas, how much background to provide, what kind of support to use, and other concerns.

You can use two main criteria to profile your audience:

- *Knowledge*: the background, expertise, or familiarity with the subject
- *Interest level*: the extent of audience interest or potential interest

Awareness of an audience's level of knowledge and interest can be determined through various questions such as those listed below.

Knowledge and Interest Levels

The knowledge and interest levels of an audience can be measured on a scale ranging from low to high. Thus, an audience that has little knowledge about your topic but is very interested can be represented as *low knowledge–high interest*. A reader with a great deal of knowledge about and interest in your topic can be represented as *high knowledge–high interest*. Such a reader could be an expert as most experts in a field possess both knowledge and interest. Scholarly writers seldom have to adopt strategies to entice their readers to keep reading, as they are usually interested in the topic to begin with; however, if your audience could be classified as "low or medium interest," you should find ways to stimulate interest, beginning with your introduction (see p. 71 for strategies).

The following questions can help determine the knowledge and interest levels of your audience.

Knowledge and Interest Questions

1. How much do you know about your potential readers? How much do you need to know? What might they value? What ambitions and goals might they possess? How could your writing appeal to their values and goals?
2. In what ways might the members differ from you? From one another? Consider such factors as their location, age, gender, occupation, education, ethnic and/or cultural background, social status, politics, religion, hobbies, and entertainment.
3. Is there a specific group of individuals you want to reach (other students, scientists, people your age, people of different ages)?
4. If your readers' knowledge about a subject is less than your own (for example, if you are writing on a specialized topic), what would help them better understand the topic (background information, facts and figures, examples, analogies or comparisons, references to experts)?
5. If your readers' interest in a subject is less than your own, what could help them better relate to the topic (examples, questions, anecdotes or short narratives, personal experience)?

Finally, the following questions could be also relevant to the way you address your audience:

- What kind of writing does your audience expect or appreciate (simple and direct, complex, subtle, original)?
- Would humour or irony be appropriate?
- How could your audience affect your writing style or your tone?

Collaborative Exercise: Audience Knowledge and Interest Level

What assumptions could you make about the knowledge and interest levels of readers of the following?

1. a blog
2. a trendy e-zine
3. an academic English journal
4. a book about recent discoveries in paleontology
5. a bestselling book on a topical subject

EXERCISE 2.3

Explore the databases your university subscribes to. The journals found on these databases are usually written for high knowledge–high interest audiences. For example, the *International Journal of Clinical Practice* is written for people in the medical field, and most of the articles use terminology that these professionals are familiar with.

1. Find an article that was written for a knowledgeable audience.
2. Use a database to find an article about the same topic but that was written for a more general audience (you might try searching magazines or newspapers).
3. Compare the prose and writing styles of the two articles. For example, find examples of language written for the different audiences. Which article would you cite if you were writing for your instructor? Which article would you cite more if you were writing for your peers in the classroom?

EXERCISE 2.4

Audience Orientation

When your writing purpose is to convince someone, you need to consider an additional audience factor in order to present a strong, effective argument: your audience's orientation to the topic. **Audience orientation** refers to the attitudes and emotional/ethical positions that define a typical reader. Once you have determined audience orientation, you can then use argumentative strategies that would be convincing to your reader.

> In argument, an audience can be profiled by its orientation to the topic, that is, the attitudes and emotional/ethical positions that define a typical reader. An **AUDIENCE'S ORIENTATION** to the topic could be positive (agree with your position), neutral (have no opinion), negative (disagree with your position), or mixed (include those who agree and those who disagree).

An audience can have *positive*, *neutral*, *negative*, or *mixed* orientations toward the subject, the writer, or the writer's thesis.

- *Positive*: holds the same view as the writer, or is more likely to agree than disagree
- *Neutral*: does not feel strongly one way or the other
- *Negative*: differs from the writer's view or is more likely to disagree than agree
- *Mixed*: is divided between those who agree and those who disagree

→ For more information on approaches and audience strategies, see chapter 5, Strategies for Argument and Rebuttal.

Assessing audience orientation to your thesis is especially vital in argument. Will most of your readers agree or disagree with your viewpoint, or will they have no opinion? Many people form attitudes about matters of common interest, though they may be open to other views. Stem-cell research, for example, has many supporters and opponents. If you write an essay on a controversial topic like stem-cell research, knowing the views of your readers could help you decide on your approach

EXERCISE 2.5

Collaborative Exercise: Audience Orientation

Consider the subject of stem-cell research. How might the opinions of members of a scientific community differ from those of a religious community? Would all scientific or religious communities have identical attitudes? What could affect differences? What about an audience of first-year biology students? Come up with two statements that could represent the beliefs and opinions of members of the scientific community and two statements that could represent members of a religious community. (Of course, individuals within both communities could hold very different views from one another.)

Orientation Questions

The following questions can be used to help determine the orientation of your audience.

1. What is your audience's attitude toward your topic or viewpoint? If you are unsure, how could you find out? What preconceived opinions might its members hold? What has informed these opinions (for example, education, culture, or environment)? Do you need to be sensitive to the audience's background? For example, are you a vegan writing to an audience of cattle farmers?
2. If you expect your readers to disagree with you, how could you make them more open-minded?

EXERCISE 2.6

Five topics are given in table 2.2 with a group of potential readers for each. From what you know or can assume about the topic and audience, complete the third column indicating the audience's probable orientation (positive, neutral, negative, or mixed) to the topic.

↻ Check answers to select questions

TABLE 2.2 Topic/Audience Table

TOPIC TO ARGUE	AUDIENCE	ORIENTATION
mandatory physical education in school	high school history teachers	
	phys-ed teachers	
	high school students	
abolishing NHL hockey fights	NHL hockey fans	
	referees' union	
	NHL team owners	
compulsory pet neutering	pet owners	
	city council	
	pet breeders	
use of taser guns by the RCMP	a citizens' rights group	
	RCMP officers	
	dentists	
laptops in the classroom	students who own laptops	
	students who do not own laptops	
	instructors who have taught for 20 years or more	

WRITING: THE COMPOSING PROCESS

Having considered the two important pre-writing factors, purpose and audience, we can turn to an overview of the writing process.

The Traditional Linear Model

One of the most common models used in teaching writing is the linear one that asks you for a written "product," usually an essay or a report. The traditional linear model recognizes that in virtually all writing, the writer has a purpose or goal toward which he or she steadily progresses. This model can be divided into stages:

1. *Pre-writing:* thinking about, coming up with, and narrowing a topic
2. *Research:* finding background information and supporting evidence (This stage could involve intensive library resources or simply consist of examining your knowledge about a topic.)
3. *Organization:* determining the order of points; outlining

4.   *Composing (first draft):* getting down your ideas in paragraph form
5.   *Revising (final draft):* revising and editing to achieve the finished version

Pre-writing (sometimes called inventing) is an explorative stage in which you may start with a subject or a topic but no thesis. This is the point where pre-writing strategies come in—systematic methods to generate ideas (see Subjects versus Topics, p. 33, and Pre-writing Strategies, p. 34). When you have enough ideas and have made connections among some of them, you are ready to write a thesis statement.

As you continue expanding and exploring the topic through research, you will construct an outline, clarifying the relationships among your points. Then, you will begin

A Closer Look

Process-Reflective Writing

Although the focus on writing in this book is the linear one in which you use a planned, stage-by-stage approach, many professional writers use an approach that is more process-oriented than goal-oriented. Of course, they have a goal in mind, but their progress toward that goal depends less on pre-determined choices and more on reflection; thus, it is sometimes referred to as a process-reflective method or, more informally, as "revision on the fly" as the process-reflective writer may "rethink" a point before moving to the next one.

Typically, composing involves periods of intense writing balanced by periods of reflection, which may lead you to further develop an idea, to qualify it, or perhaps to abandon it in favour of another line of thought. You may stop to recall, analyze, or reconsider.

Underlying this method is an appreciation of the connection between writing and thinking. As you write, your thinking is affected in two related ways: a choice, once made, excludes options that may have existed before, but it also creates new options. In this way, what you *have written* directs what you *will* write. By writing down your thoughts, you become conscious of them, and they become subject to your control. As a result, your thinking becomes clearer. It is said that clear thinking produces clear writing—likewise, writing (especially clear writing) produces clearer and more directed thinking. In process-reflective writing, you *reflect on* your process in order to make both your writing and thinking clearer.

Process-reflective writing is especially useful for exam essays where you do not have time to prepare a detailed outline (see The In-Class Essay or Examination Essay in Appendix B, p. 390). However, you can also use this method throughout the composing process, for example, if you find your thoughts headed in a different direction from what is indicated in your outline. Indeed, you may prefer one composing method to the other or combine them. The object is the same: to produce a rough draft with organized, well-developed points.

Here are some tips for process-reflective writing:

- If you are uncertain whether your words reflect your intended meaning, try rephrasing the point and choose the version that best captures your meaning.
- Consider transitions (see chapter 3, Transitions between Sentences, p. 66) to help develop a point; then, ask if the transition reflects the relationship between ideas that you want to convey.
- If you are unsure where a point is going, consider leaving some blank space and use a previous sentence or point as a new starting place.
- Keep your thesis in mind throughout, but don't be afraid to depart from it if necessary; it can be changed or reworded later.
- Don't worry about grammatical or mechanical errors; focus on clarity and the complete expression of your ideas.
- Don't worry about length; unneeded details or less important points can be deleted during the next draft.

your rough draft, working toward unified, coherent, and developed paragraphs. After you have completed the draft, you will revise it, paying particular attention to grammar, punctuation, sentence structure, and mechanics.

Practical benefits of learning and using this traditional model are that it applies directly to many university and workplace tasks in which objectives are clearly defined and form is important—such as scientific experiments, formal research essays, and business reports—and that it can be adapted to a variety of specialized functions.

STAGES IN ESSAY WRITING

Pre-writing

External factors could determine how much time you devote to the pre-writing stage. If you are assigned a specific topic, you won't have to spend as much time at this stage as someone who is simply told to "write on a topic of your choosing."

Subjects versus Topics

A **subject** contains many potential topics. Consider your school subjects: history is a subject, but it can be broken into many different topics—for example, different civilizations, social/political movements, and time periods (e.g., History of the Labour Movement in Canada, The Origins of Modern Japan), which might correspond to different history courses you can enroll in. Other subjects, like psychology or English literature, can be similarly broken down.

Modern technology, *global warming*, and *energy sources* are examples of essay subjects. A subject could also be more specific than these examples (*iPhones*, *species extinction*, and *alternative energy sources* could also be considered subjects). A **topic** differs from a subject in being narrower or more focused. Similarly, a **thesis** is more focused than a topic because it makes a specific comment on the topic or tells the reader how you will approach the topic. A statement that contains a thesis will need support; a statement that consists of only a subject or topic will usually not need support.

Below we will consider using pre-writing strategies to come up with a topic. These strategies sometimes result in a thesis and even in some main points for your essay, but at other times, your thesis is not clear to you until after you've begun your research. However, your topic *should always* be clear before you begin your research.

> A **SUBJECT** contains many potential **TOPICS**; a thesis is narrower and more focused than a topic.
>
> A **THESIS** is a formal statement that includes both your topic and your approach to, or a comment on, the topic. A more developed thesis would include your main points. See chapter 3, The Thesis Statement, page 78.

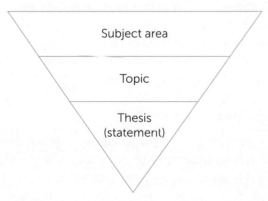

FIGURE 2.1 Subjects versus Topics

EXERCISE 2.7

C̶ Check answers to select questions

Read through the following list. Decide whether each statement is a subject, a topic, or a thesis. If it is a topic, identify the subject; if it is a thesis, identify the topic and the subject. There may be more than one possible topic or subject, as in the example below:

The discrepancy between men's and women's golf coverage is due to sexism.

It is a *thesis* (the statement makes a comment about a topic).

Topic: men's and women's golf coverage

Possible subjects: golf, sports coverage, sexism in society

1. Video games are bad for youth.
2. Borderline personality disorder is a controversial condition.
3. The federal government should change the drinking age across Canada to 18.
4. More hybrid cars are on the market than ever before.
5. Whales are one of many threatened species today.
6. "Managed trade" involves government intervention, such as the imposition of tariffs.
7. Cruelty to animals often goes unpunished.
8. Studying the classical languages in school is unnecessary today.
9. Many varieties of dance and dance styles exist today.
10. Enrolling in a dance class can help people with disabilities.

Topic Hunting

Your instructor may tell you to find your own topic or to narrow a given subject to a manageable topic. In the first case, you would start from scratch. Here are some questions you can consider if you need to come up with a topic from scratch:

- Where do your interests lie (hobbies, leisure pursuits, reading interests, extra-curricular activities)?
- What would you like to find out more about? Curiosity is a good motivator. What topic do you think readers might like to learn about? Thinking of *other* people's interests can guide you to a worthwhile topic. What topic could benefit society or a specific group in society (for example, students at your university)?
- Can you think of a new angle on an old topic? Neglected areas of older topics can present new opportunities for exploration. For example, modern technology and lifestyle have created many new addictions.

Pre-writing Strategies

Pre-writing strategies clarify your thoughts about the subject and enable you to generate ideas, some of which you will use in your essay; others can be discarded as you further clarify your topic. Pre-writing can lead to a tentative thesis statement and, in many cases, your main points.

Pre-writing strategies include

- *asking questions* about the subject or topic
- *brainstorming*
- *freewriting*
- *clustering* or *mapping*

Although pre-writing techniques work by association, each has unique strengths, and one may be more useful than another for a particular kind of writing. Table 2.3 (p. 37) lists some uses of pre-writing techniques. The most important thing is that you learn to work with whatever methods serve you well.

Questions and Brainstorming

Asking questions and brainstorming are tried-and-true approaches for finding out more about a subject. Although you can pose any questions, asking the traditional journalistic questions—*Who?*, *What?*, *Why?*, *When?*, *Where?*, and *How?*—can be helpful for almost any subject, such as *roommates*:

Who? Who make the best roommates? (worst?)

What? What are the qualities of an ideal roommate?

Why? Why are roommates necessary? (or not?)

When? When is the best time to start looking for a roommate?

Where? Where can you find a roommate? Where can you go for privacy when you have a roommate?

How? How do you go about finding a good roommate? How do you get along with a roommate?

In brainstorming, you write down words, phrases, or sentences that you associate with a subject and then look for what they have in common. How can they be connected and categorized? You can often combine brainstorming with one or more pre-writing methods. For example, if you began by asking the journalistic questions about the subject *roommates*, you could brainstorm the qualities of an ideal roommate, using the question *What?* to generate a list. You could continue to use these two methods by then asking why these important qualities contribute to a good roommate.

In addition to listing random associations on one subject, you could set up the brainstorming session by applying different criteria to a topic. For example, using a topic like *private versus public health care*, you could list your associations under *pro* and *con*; you could also list similarities and differences between two related items, such as two addictive substances, two movie directors, or two racquet sports; or you could divide a general category, such as contemporary music, into sub-categories and list your associations with each. These specific kinds of lists are useful when you know that your essay will employ a primary method of organization

By using pre-writing techniques, you can narrow down a subject to a usable topic. However, not all topics can be turned into effective thesis statements. Some are too broad while others are too narrow. If the topic is too broad, it will be hard to do more than provide a general overview. Your essay may also be difficult to plan and write because there will be so much you could say about the topic. On the other hand, if your topic is too specific, you could feel yourself limited by the topic's scope; you may also have problems researching it if there's not much available.

Pre-writing techniques help generate potential topics and main points for an essay. Asking questions, brainstorming, freewriting, and clustering are pre-writing techniques.

such as cost–benefit, compare and contrast, or classification/division. See chapter 3, page 85.

Freewriting and Clustering

In freewriting, you write for several minutes without stopping. You can freewrite without a topic in mind and see where your subconscious leads you, or you could begin with a specific subject or topic, though you may end up writing about something else. That is fine. You do not need to censor or edit yourself, or concern yourself with spelling or grammar. You are concerned with flow and process and should not worry about mechanics or content. You do not need to punctuate or use capital letters: you just write without lifting your pencil from the page, or just continue typing without editing. The important principle is that you do not stop writing. If you can't think of anything to say, you write something anyway, such as "I can't think of anything to say" until another idea or association comes to you.

If you enjoy freewriting, you can follow it with a looping exercise. In looping, you underline potentially useful words, phrases, or sentences; then, you choose the best one to focus on as the beginning point for more freewriting. You can also take the most useful phrase, sum it up in a sentence, and begin freewriting using this sentence as a starting point. Although freewriting is a popular pre-writing strategy, you can use it at any point in the composing process—if you get stuck on a particular point or experience "writer's block" when drafting your essay.

Freewriting has several functions:

- It can free you from writer's block. A typical problem in beginning to write is feeling you have nothing to say.
- It gives you access to ideas or feelings you might not have known about.
- Combining freewriting with looping can help you narrow down a topic and, sometimes, come up with a thesis and main points.

Clustering, or mapping, represents your thoughts graphically rather than linearly. Near the centre of a blank piece of paper, write down and circle your subject and then think of related words or phrases, which you record and circle, connecting each with the word or phrase that gave rise to it. Clustering produces distinct groups of related words and phrases, which may be developed into main points. You can often see other relationships between circles in one cluster and those in another. In the example in figure 2.2, dotted lines represent other possible connections.

Figure 2.2 is the result of a group clustering exercise that began with the subject *vitamins*, and produced this thesis statement: "Because of media hype and the promise of good health, more people than ever are taking vitamins before they really know the risks involved."

Research

Although research is associated with reliable secondary sources accessed through your library, sources may include interviews and other field research. Also, research may involve determining what you already know about a topic and consolidating

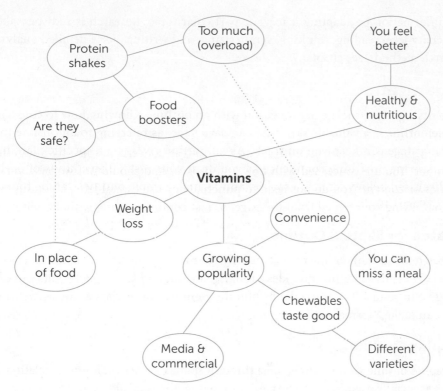

FIGURE 2.2 Group Clustering

TABLE 2.3 Pre-writing Strategies

PRE-WRITING STRATEGY	DESCRIPTION	USES
questioning	asking questions about subject/topic	expository (informational) essays in the sciences or social sciences where a thesis can be framed as a specific question or series of questions you will try to answer
freewriting	timed writing in which you write without stopping or editing yourself	personal essays or responses in which you try to make subjective connections with the topic
brainstorming	writing down in point form associations with a subject/topic	• collaborative work in which all group members can give input • exam questions in which you need to generate main points quickly
clustering	representing ideas by series of circles and connecting lines, showing their relationships	argumentative essays, which rely heavily on logical connections; good for those who prefer spatial to linear representations

this information or adapting it to your particular topic. Research is indispensable to university-level reading, thinking, synthesizing, and writing. For a detailed analysis of research methods, see chapter 7.

Organization

Students rightly associate organization with an outline. Knowing how to construct a usable outline is a valuable skill that can save time, as referring to an outline in the drafting stage can keep you on track. As an outline gives you a specific plan, it can be reassuring, instilling confidence as you draft your essay. Three kinds of outlines are discussed below: scratch, graphic, and formal. Sample outlines can be found on pages 39 and 40.

Scratch (or Sketch) Outline

> Three types of outlines, designed for different purposes, are the scratch, graphic, and formal outline.

A scratch (or sketch) outline represents only your main points, usually just by a word or phrase. The scratch outline provides a rough guideline and gives you flexibility in developing your points. It is especially helpful for planning an in-class essay, where limited time can make a formal outline impractical.

Graphic Outline

A graphic outline shows connections through spatial, rather than linear, relationships and is especially useful for writers who work best with visual aids. One way to construct a graphic outline is to put your main points in rectangular boxes and use vertical arrows to show the order of the points. Horizontal or diagonal arrows can show sub-points or supporting points.

A graphic outline typically looks more like a working outline than a formal outline does. As needs are redefined, changes can be shown through arrows, parentheses, crossings-out, or additional boxes (or other shapes). You can think of a graphic outline as a set of temporary road signs, aiding and guiding the traffic of your thoughts during construction.

Figure 2.3 shows a graphic outline applied to the five stages of essay writing. Vertical arrows represent the sequence of stages (the main points), while diagonal arrows indicate sub-points—composing choices for writers. The two-pointed arrow shows the interrelationship between questioning and brainstorming discussed previously. The parentheses around *research* indicate that research may or may not be part of the composing process. Finally, the vertical arrows under *final draft* show that each activity in the oval is performed in the order indicated. The arrows, then, show sequence, while the use of ovals, rather than rectangles, calls attention to the fact that *re-seeing*, *editing*, and *proofreading* should not be treated as major stages like *pre-writing*, *outlining*, *first draft*, and *final draft*. Graphic outlines must be logical but, as mentioned, can be customized to reflect the writer's needs.

Formal Outline

> **FORMAL OUTLINE**
> A kind of outline that shows the relationships between the different levels of points.

The **formal outline** includes sub-points as well as main points, so you are able to represent more of your essay's structure. In a formal outline, you can see at a glance how the

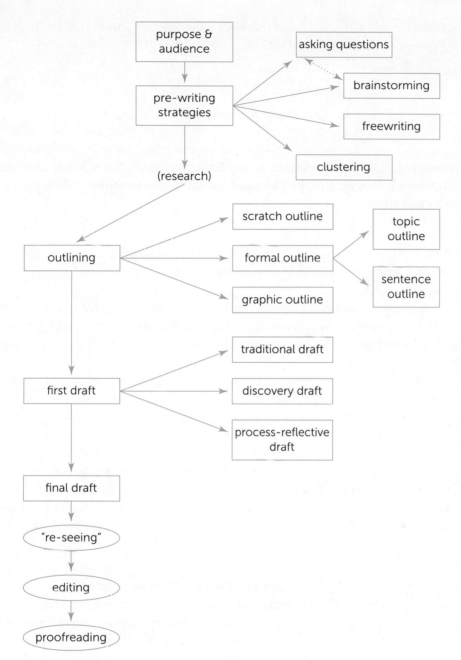

FIGURE 2.3 Graphic Outline

parts interrelate—which is especially useful in a longer essay and in one employing a complex structure, such as a compare-and-contrast or research essay. A formal outline can give a writer a sense of security: the writer's points and sub-points can be consulted often during the composing stage.

A formal outline shows the relationships between the different levels of points (main point, sub-point, sub-sub-point, etc.), using coordination and subordination.

Coordinate (equal) and subordinate (not equal) elements are shown through the numbering system common to formal outlines:

I.
    A.
    B.
           1.
           2.
                a.
                b.

II.
    A., etc.

Points I, II, etc. are coordinate or equal, as are sub-points A, B; 1, 2; etc. However, sub-points A and B are subordinate (not equal) to main points I and II, just as 1 and 2 are subordinate to A and B.

The first level (main) points are not indented, but each successive level is indented one or more spaces from the previous level. An outline made up of main and sub-points is a two-level outline; one with main points and two levels of sub-points is a three-level outline.

Formal outlines can differ in their format and detail. A **topic outline** shows paragraph topics and their development, usually through just a word or phrase. A **sentence outline** shows more detail and uses complete sentences in parallel format. You may be asked to submit a formal outline either before or when you submit the final version of your essay. A formal outline can be compared to an engineer's blueprint, revealing how a structure will be put together. For an example of a formal sentence outline, see the outline by Iain Lawrence on page 223. An example of a two-level topic outline follows. This outline was used as the basis for a student essay. Inevitably, the writer made a few changes when she drafted the essay; for example, she changed paragraph order, switching II and III.

A **TOPIC OUTLINE** shows paragraph topics and their development, usually through just a word or phrase. A **SENTENCE OUTLINE** shows more detail and uses complete sentences in parallel format.

Topic Outline for "Arts and the BC Government: The Deepest Cut"
  I. Introduction
      A. Public appreciation of the arts
      B. Thesis: budget cuts to the Arts in BC are a bad decision
  II. History
      A. History of arts cuts in BC
      B. History of Canadian artists' earnings
  III. Facts and Figures: 2010/2011 Budget Cuts
      A. Current status of arts funding
      B. Government's response to budget cut disputes
  IV. Economic Factors
      A. Global arts budgets
          1. Comparisons to other provinces
          2. Comparisons to other countries

    B. Studies that support investment in the arts
     1. Revenue
     2. Employment
   V. Community
    A. Public response to the cuts
    B. Why Canadians should care
  VI. Conclusion
    A. Summary of main points
    B. Future consequences
    C. Emotional appeal

General Guidelines for Outlining

1. Divide outlines into introduction, paragraphs for development, and conclusion.
2. Plan for a *minimum* of five paragraphs unless told otherwise. For longer essays, five will probably not be enough.
3. Ensure you have one main idea per paragraph.
4. Divide your main ideas (points) into sub-points (at least two per paragraph) that develop the main idea.
5. Represent the relationship between main ideas and their points of development (or sub-points) graphically by indenting sub-points or, more formally, use a combination of letters and numbers.
6. Ensure that the main points and sub-points are ordered logically.

Composing: First Draft

Getting words on paper in sentence and paragraph form is the most challenging stage for many writers. Whichever composing method you feel most comfortable with (see p. 31 and 32), in the first draft, your focus should be on setting your ideas down.

Composing on the Computer

Over the past 20 years, networked computers have transformed research and writing for students and professionals alike. Most campuses offer access to Internet-equipped workstations in labs and libraries, and many universities supply free wireless Internet (WiFi) in classrooms and other study spaces. At home, students use desktop computers, laptops, tablets, and even powerful smartphones to search for information, compose drafts, and share their writing via the Internet with teachers, fellow students, and the rest of the world—all with the push of a button.

  Some students still prefer to use pen and paper to complete the early stages of the writing process, such as brainstorming, outlining, and first drafts. For revisions, many students will print a rough draft and make changes or marginal notes with a pen or pencil. That said, composing on a computer or even a tablet can be fast and efficient. Sentences, paragraphs, or entire sections can be moved to improve coherence or to experiment with a new order of ideas and examples. Experienced writers learn to save text they're unsure about and copy it to the end of the document or into a separate file, where they can access it later.

There are now a variety of software applications (some freely available on the Internet) that allow writers to gather information and visually organize ideas into digital outlines, flow-charts, and concept maps. Most university instructors require a final draft formatted on a word processor, either printed out or submitted digitally (as an email attachment or via an online course management system). Instructors may also specify word-processing requirements, such as margins, line spacing, paragraph indentation, font size and font preference, and a computer-generated word count.

Composing with Care

Word processors and networked computers offer many advantages but also a few drawbacks, most of which can be surmounted by using composing common sense. Two areas are discussed below: proofreading and plagiarism.

Even if most of your work is done on the computer, it's strongly recommended that you print a final version of your essay and carefully check your hard copy for typos and spelling and grammar errors. Spell-checkers do a good job of identifying obvious spelling errors but will not catch mistakes that depend on context or usage—for example, they may fail to flag misspellings of *their/there*, *to/too*, or *woman/women*. Spell-checking software will fail to spot missing words in sentences.

→ See Appendix A for more about proofreading.

In addition, as unwary authors type, Auto-Correct and Auto-Complete functions in some programs can insert unintended words. A digital thesaurus can expand students' vocabularies but can also lead to the inappropriate usage of unfamiliar new words. For these reasons, professional writers and editors will often proofread a paper copy of their final drafts backward, reading from the end to the beginning, so they don't gloss over typos.

Digital documents stored and accessed in "the cloud" using online tools such as GoogleDocs or Dropbox allow students to access their projects from multiple devices and different locations. Cloud-based storage can also be used to collaborate on writing projects but can blur the line of authorship and run afoul of an assignment's requirement for individual originality. In addition, documents stored online can be accidentally deleted by other users who have shared access to the folder.

When researching a topic using the Internet, students can easily locate information and ideas from online journals or other websites and then transfer this material into document files with a simple copy and paste. However, a failure to keep track of and then properly cite the origins of such research can lead to accidental plagiarism. Some universities employ plagiarism-detection software to scan digital copies of student submissions for evidence of borrowed text. The unacknowledged use of someone else's words or ideas, even unintentionally, can be a serious academic infraction. For that reason, it's important to manage each stage of the writing process carefully, so you can keep track of your research borrowings and not get confused by the different versions on your computer or by the many edits on any one page. Many word processors include a footnote function that allows writers to add links to quoted or paraphrased material as they write and then generate a Works Cited page or a list of attributions.

→ For more about what constitutes plagiarism, see chapter 7, page 213.

Organizing Computer Files

The keys to successful composing on the computer are careful planning and organization. After completing a stage in the process, create a folder and save the latest version (file) of your notes, outline, drafts, etc. to this folder, labelling it for later use. You will appreciate being able to identify the most recent file, especially if your work on a paper is interrupted. The following file, for example, which includes the course code, project name, version, and date, will be easy to retrieve: *ENGL135_ResearchDraft1_15March*. When you open the file, use the Save As function after you make your first change to the document (for example, a deletion or addition) and rename the document—for example, *ENGL135_ResearchDraft2_19March*; then proceed with the draft.

When you create successive versions of a document, you create a digital "trail." If, for example, in your second draft, you want to refer back to your outline to locate a source that you didn't use in your first draft, or a paragraph that you deleted from the first draft, you can do so. Although most word-processing programs have the auto-save feature, you should save your document every few minutes in case your computer crashes or power is lost. Also, consider backing up files to a mass-storage device, such as a USB flash drive, an external hard drive, or a cloud-based Internet storage service. This will ensure that, even if your computer's hard drive crashes, the document is saved to a secondary location.

Another way to create a trail is to use the Track Changes function (found under the Review tab in Microsoft Word). This enables you to make multiple edits and keep track of them by having all text—the original and the new text—in one place. If you delete or change material, you will see this material with strike-through marks, along with any replacement text. Using Track Changes through many different versions of the same document can be distracting, however. Consider saving different versions if one tracked version becomes hard to follow.

Many word-processing programs also include a Comment function. By highlighting a portion of text and clicking Insert Comment, you can use pop-up boxes to make notes to yourself, such as areas to follow up on or the source from which you took this information. This feature is especially useful in collaborative work where comments by individual group members appear in different colours, with each user identified. Your instructor may use the Comment function to give typed feedback on digital submissions.

Most universities today have temporary network storage space available for students' university-related work, which you can access from the institution's workstations as well as your personal laptop or home computer. Instructions for accessing and using this space are usually available through your institution's computing help centre or similar site. Avoid frustration by making sure you know the proper channels and procedures for saving and retrieving your documents, as well as your university's policies on the maximum total file size for data storage and deadlines after which your documents might be deleted.

Revising: Final Draft

The final draft probably is the most undervalued stage of the writing process. Many student writers think the final draft is the place to apply a few necessary touch-ups. They may have assumed they were supposed to "get it right the first time." However, professional writers almost never do, so why should this be expected of student writers?

> **REVISION**, which means "to see again," involves various activities and could involve taking a thorough second look at purpose and audience, organization, paragraph development, clarity, grammar, and the like; it is a very important stage in the composing process.

Remember that early drafts are essentially rough efforts to put your thinking into words. To change the rough into final requires a new focus: *the written document*. When you revise, you want to build on its strengths as well as repair any weaknesses. This process could involve any or all of the following:

- Fine-tuning
- Overview of purpose and audience
- Clarifying meaning
- Underscoring ideas
- Solidifying structure

The acronym FOCUS can serve as an aid to memory. It is important to remember that while there is no "right" order in revision, proofreading should always be the final stage.

Overview of Purpose and Audience

Ask yourself whether the essay fulfills its purpose and whether it speaks to your intended audience. You may decide you need to adjust your introduction to clarify your purpose. You might find that some of your words were too informal for your audience and that you need to find words to replace them.

Clarifying Meaning

Try reading the essay aloud. Will your audience understand your meaning? Have you always expressed what you meant? Wherever a sentence seems awkward or just overly long, consider rephrasing for clarity.

It is hard to be objective when you look back at what you have written, especially if you have just written it. Allotting at least a few hours between completing the first draft and revising will help you see your essay more objectively. Also, getting someone else to read over your paper can give you valuable input, especially if he or she can point to unclear passages. Seeing the places where other people have difficulty will highlight those places for close attention.

Underscoring Ideas

In your body paragraphs, your main ideas are introduced and developed. These paragraphs should reinforce your thesis and support your points. Reviewing your body paragraphs might mean going back to your notes, outline, or early drafts to see if you can further support an idea that now strikes you as undeveloped. Or you might include an example, illustration, or analogy to make an abstract or general point more concrete and understandable. Do not settle for *almost*. Ask yourself if all your points are as strong as they *could* be.

What if you now see that a point is underdeveloped but you do not know how to go about developing it further at this stage? Remember that pre-writing strategies can be used at any point in the process; their main purpose is to generate ideas. Try a brief freewriting session (or whichever method works best for you) to help you expand on the undeveloped point.

Another important principle of paragraph writing is **emphasis**. Stressing specific words, sentences, and ideas will direct your reader to what is most important. This does not usually mean using italics but rather making sure that the most important ideas are easy to find. Some of the strategies mentioned under paragraph coherence (for example, see Repetition and Synonyms on p. 66) will help create emphasis.

Solidifying Structure

In order to solidify your structure, return to your outline. Does your essay's structure reflect your original plans for it? Do you see any weaknesses in the outline you didn't see before? Can the structure of the essay be made more logical or effective? If the essay's structure seems strong, look at each paragraph as a mini-essay with a topic sentence, full and logical development of the main idea, and a concluding thought. All paragraphs need to follow a logical sequence. Is the paragraph unified and coherent as well as adequately developed? Are paragraphs roughly the same length, or are some conspicuously short or long?

When you revise, you want to make your essay strong*er*, clear*er*, and *more* readable. When writers make changes to their drafts, it is often because they discover better ways to say what they wanted to say. After all, you know much more about your topic now than you did at any other stage in the composing process—so this is the best (and last!) chance to develop your essay to its full potential.

Fine-Tuning

Working on the final draft will almost certainly involve some small-scale changes and corrections. Fine-tuning can be divided into editing and mechanics.

Editing

In the crucial revision stage of editing, the focus shifts to sentences and words. This means ensuring that each sentence is grammatical, that your expression is clear and concise, and that you have used appropriate transitions between sentences. You can also refine your style, for example, by checking if there is enough sentence variation. Can you combine sentences to produce more complex units, or can you use different sentence types to make your prose more interesting?

Proofreading

Mechanics involves ensuring that your essay conforms to your instructor's requirements, for example, in its format and presentation, such as the presence of a title page, spacing, and the like. The final review should involve proofreading for mechanical errors, such as spelling and typos. For a full treatment of efficient writing and editing strategies, as well as proofreading guidelines, see Appendix A.

RHETORICAL MODES OF DISCOURSE

Essays can be classified according to the traditional ways of organizing information. These are known as the **rhetorical modes** of discourse: exposition, argument, narration, and description. Because argumentative and expository essays are discussed

---

EMPHASIS is drawing the reader's attention to important words, sentences, or ideas to make them easy to find.

When you revise, you want to make your essay strong*er*, clear*er*, and *more* readable. When writers make changes to their drafts, it is often because they discover better ways to say what they wanted to say. After all, you know much more about your topic now than you did at any other stage in the composing process—so the revision stage is the best (and last!) chance to develop your essay to its full potential.

The four **RHETORICAL MODES** are argument, exposition, narration, and description.

in detail in later chapters, they will be introduced here only briefly. Narration and description are discussed more fully beginning on page 47 of this chapter as well as briefly below.

EXPOSITORY VERSUS ARGUMENTATIVE ESSAYS

EXPOSITION is a rhetorical mode concerned with explaining and informing a reader.

ARGUMENT is a rhetorical mode concerned with persuading a reader to adopt a specific point of view or course of action.

Expository writing can be contrasted with persuasive or argumentative writing. **Exposition** explains and informs; **argument** attempts to persuade your audience to see your viewpoint. An expository research essay in the sciences doesn't usually state the writer's opinions (if it does, it is considered argumentative); its conclusions result from the use of fact-based sources, such as scientific studies. The writer of an expository essay may consider different or contrary views on a controversial issue without taking sides; in argument, the writer takes sides and defends his or her position.

Although these seem like fundamental differences, the dividing line between exposition and argument is not always a solid one, and many of the same skills and strategies are applicable to both.

Here are some elements that exposition and argument *share*:

- Both can use factual information and reliable sources to support main points.
- Critical thinking is essential to successful expository and argumentative writing.
- In both, your voice should remain objective and your language neutral.

Table 2.4 lists some ways that exposition *differs* from argument.

TABLE 2.4 Expository versus Argumentative Writing

IN EXPOSITORY WRITING	IN ARGUMENTATIVE WRITING
You use a fact-based thesis (see p. 52).	You use a value- or policy-based thesis (see p. 52).
You begin with an open mind and see where your exploration takes you.	You begin by considering where you stand on an issue and how you can support your position.
In your body paragraphs, you look at the available evidence and rely on critical thinking for your conclusion.	In your body paragraphs, you draw the reader's attention to supporting evidence but do not ignore or distort contradictory evidence.
Research is usually an integral part of expository writing.	Research is not always necessary in argumentative writing (although your instructor may ask you to include research to strengthen your argument).
If you are writing on a controversial topic, you do not take sides, though you may explain the position of both sides using objective language.	You take a side and try to win your argument fairly by using logic and using emotion where appropriate.

Sample thesis for an expository essay:

The skeletal evolution of the penguin enabled it to adapt to an ocean environment.

In this case, the writer will inform and explain.

Sample thesis for an expository essay that might use some argument:

We can take several steps to alleviate the impact of global warming on the emperor penguin habitat on Roosevelt Island.

How do you think argument might be involved—either directly or indirectly? What assumption is the writer making about the topic that the reader would be expected to agree with?

Sample thesis for an argumentative essay:

Nations must act quickly and collectively to put an end to global warming, which is destroying penguin habitats in the Antarctic sub-continent.

Verbs like *must* and *should* usually signal an argumentative thesis.

NARRATION AND DESCRIPTION

Recall the excerpt by Alice Munro in chapter 1 (p. 4) in which the writer is telling a story. That is what **narration** does: it tells about something that has happened, relating incidents (usually, but not always, chronologically) and revealing character. The narrative pattern is commonly used in fiction and in personal essays; it can be used occasionally in fact-based essays as well.

The Munro excerpt is also descriptive as it gives the reader concrete, sensual information. **Description** mainly evokes the sense of sight, but it can also make use of the other senses. If you use description in an expository essay, it is important to be as concrete as possible and avoid general, abstract words or phrases. The phrase *the ordinary guy in the gravy-stained tee shirt*, used in the second excerpt below, helps readers see details clearly in their mind.

Narration and description are often used to convey immediacy. The selective use of either in factual writing can lend drama, directness, and impact to your essay. Consider the following sample openings of fact-based expository essays.

In the narrative paragraph below, the student writer uses the story of a young Pakistani hero to introduce an essay on education of females in Pakistan.

Narration:

In July 2013, a 14-year-old Pakistani girl, Malala Yousafzai, was shot in the head by a Taliban gunman for promoting the education of women.

NARRATION tells about something that has happened, relating incidents and revealing character.

DESCRIPTION gives the reader concrete, sensual information.

Malala lived in the Taliban-controlled Swat District of northern Pakistan where skirmishes often took place between the Taliban and the Pakistan military. The actions of Malala and other girls in the area had come to the attention of the BBC, who in 2009 asked Malala to write a blog on life under Taliban rule. As she became increasingly active politically, she attracted the attention of the international community, which saw her as a hero. Once an ordinary schoolgirl, she and her family were catapulted into a dangerous world of death threats. After the shooting, she lay in a coma and was airlifted to England where she gradually recovered. On July 13, 2013, she spoke to the UN, calling for worldwide access to education for girls.

—Shannon Clark

The academic writer in the excerpt below uses description to introduce her topic. In fact, the author interweaves description with important detail about her topic and writing purpose to create an interesting, yet informative, introduction:

Description:

This article looks at Michael Moore's persona—the aggrieved, aggressive maverick, the know-it-all who knows nothing—to explore the idea of authorial voice and persona in nonfiction filmmaking. Michael Moore, the everyman, the ordinary guy in the gravy-stained tee shirt whose job it is to look after our interests, seems to be the authority that is no better than we are, but who has more guts. Smart, but appearing to be unschooled, his belligerent air of thwarted entitlement and his anti-intellectualism point to a contradictory set of values and viewpoints, paternalistic authority on the one hand and rugged delinquency on the other, that are sometimes hard to splice together.

—Spence, Louise. Working-Class Hero: Michael Moore's Authorial Voice and Persona. *The Journal of Popular Culture* 43.2 (2010): 368–80. Print. (368)

EXERCISE 2.8

Collaborative Exercise: Narration and Description

1. In the excerpt about Malala Yousafzai, identify words and phrases that use narration, telling us what happened (nouns and verbs are especially important).
2. In the excerpt about Michael Moore, identify words and phrases that use description, giving us a clear picture of the subject (adjectives are especially important).

CHAPTER SUMMARY

Asking questions about your writing purpose and intended audience before beginning a writing assignment will help you anticipate challenges and plan effectively. By taking into consideration audience knowledge and interest levels, you can use strategies suited to typical readers, making them receptive to your thesis. After considering pre-writing factors like purpose and audience, the chapter focuses on stages in the writing process: specific choices for generating and narrowing ideas; options for outlining; useful composing strategies; and, the underrated stage, revising. The chapter concludes by introducing the four modes of discourse, emphasizing exposition and argument.

3 Essay and Paragraph Essentials

In this chapter, you will be introduced to choices for organizing both the essay itself and its paragraphs. In this way, the chapter highlights essay structure and the interconnections between the parts of the essay, as well as paragraph structure and its key features. Essay introductions are analyzed with extensive sections on attracting reader interest and crafting strong thesis statements. The rhetorical patterns are then introduced, with examples, to help you choose the best methods for developing your main points.

LEARNING OBJECTIVES

- to understand how an essay can be divided and the relationships among the parts
- to learn the types of claims and their uses in different kinds of essays
- to learn the importance of using evidence for support and the kinds of evidence, including primary and secondary sources, facts/statistics, experts, examples, case studies, and precedents
- to break the paragraph into topic sentence, support, and paragraph wrap
- to be able to write body paragraphs that are unified, coherent, and well developed
- to use precise word choice, logical sentence order, repetition and synonyms, and transitions to help create effective paragraphs
- to be able to write successful introductions that announce the topic, thesis, and main organizational method, as well as establish the writer's credibility

- to be able to make effective choices in developing thesis statements that are interesting, specific, manageable, clearly phrased, and focused on one topic
- to be able to write successful conclusions that reinforce and/or extend the thesis
- to understand the rhetorical patterns and use them effectively in your essay

THE ESSAY: AN ANALYTICAL MODEL

An essay can be analyzed, or "broken down," in different ways. For example, you can divide an essay's structure into introduction, body paragraphs, and conclusion. When you are asked to write a critical analysis, you may analyze the writer's use of logic and reason, the reliability of sources, the tone or style of writing, the writer's background or bias, and the like.

The elements discussed below are common to most essays—from scholarly studies for specialized readers to the kinds of essays you will write. But whether you are reading an essay or writing one, you will often begin by identifying the claim, a general assertion about the essay's topic.

Kinds of Claims

An essay makes a **claim**, usually expressed in the thesis (see p. 33), and then provides support. Thus, we can divide the essay into two main parts, whether it is argumentative or expository: the *claim* and the *support*. Claims can be subdivided into different types: fact, value, extended value, and interpretation.

Claims of Fact

A **claim of fact** is usually an **empirical** claim that is developed by inductive reasoning, which uses valid evidence-gathering methods such as observation and measurement. Claims of fact are common to most expository essays and are supported by academic studies, facts, and statistics.

Claims of Value

A **claim of value** is an ethical claim and appeals to one's values or morals; such values could be related to a religious, philosophical, social, cultural, or other system. A claim of value can be developed by deductive reasoning where standards of good or bad, right or wrong, are accepted as **premises**.

Claims of Extended Value

A **claim of extended value** goes beyond a value claim to call for some kind of action to fix a problem or improve a situation. For example, a proposed change to a law that gives people more control over something in their lives may be based on a value: it will produce a more democratic society. It can be developed by inductive and deductive reasoning.

An argumentative essay usually seeks to convince its audience to adopt a position or make a change; an expository essay explains or informs its audience.

A **CLAIM** is a statement that a writer will attempt to prove in an essay. A **CLAIM OF FACT** is an assertion supported by empirical methods such as measurement and observation. A **CLAIM OF VALUE** asserts a value or moral quality. A **CLAIM OF EXTENDED VALUE** asserts the need for an action.

EMPIRICAL denotes a scientific method based on observation and measurement.

A **PREMISE** is a statement assumed to be true.

For more on inductive and deductive reasoning, see chapter 5, page 125.

Most topics can be explored through any of these three claims, depending on *the way the claim is presented*; from this, you can see how important it is to phrase your thesis precisely. In an expository essay, the claim will be presented as factual. In an argumentative essay, the claim will usually be presented as one of value or extended value. If you were asked to write an essay on the topic of *homelessness*, for example, your claim could take a form similar to one of the following:

> *Factual claim:* Because of the unsettled economic climate, homelessness is increasing in most Canadian provinces.

For support, the writer might use inductive reasoning, perhaps by presenting economic data to help prove a relationship between economic instability and incidence of homelessness.

> *Value claim:* In a society of excess, our indifference to the problem of the homeless on our doorsteps is an indictment of our way of life.

For support, the writer might use deductive reasoning and make emotional and ethical appeals to the reader.

> *Extended value claim:* To solve the problem of homelessness in our city, council needs to increase the number of permanent shelters, erect temporary shelters in downtown parks, and educate the public about this escalating social problem.

For support, the writer could appeal to the reader's values but would focus more on practical, "real-world" solutions. Both inductive and deductive reasoning could be used.

Claims of Interpretation

A **claim of interpretation** is a specialized type of value claim. In a literary analysis, a writer may use an interpretive claim and support it by references to the primary (literary) text as well as, perhaps, to secondary sources. A writer in a discipline such as history, philosophy, or cultural studies also may use a claim of interpretation if the main purpose is to weigh and interpret the evidence found in either primary or secondary sources. For example, a writer could claim that the defeat of Athens in the Peloponnesian War was inevitable because of the internal conflicts within Athens itself, using the interpretations of scholars for support. Because a claim of interpretation can often be challenged, it can be considered a kind of argumentative claim.

Interpretive claims can be used outside the humanities, for example, to analyze a trend or predict an outcome. Since the future is always, to a degree, unknown, an essay with such a claim will be essentially argumentative.

Support: Evidence and Credibility

Informed readers will not accept a claim without **support**—in other words, without **evidence** to back it up. But evidence alone is not enough. To convince your reader that your claim is justified, you need to show **credibility**. Evidence may be wasted if you do not present yourself as believable.

A **CLAIM OF INTERPRETATION** analyzes a text or trend or argues for an outcome.

SUPPORT for a claim is provided by evidence and reinforced by a writer's credibility.

EVIDENCE, such as studies and examples, helps back up a claim.

A writer's **CREDIBILITY** is established by his or her knowledge, reliability, and fairness.

Later in this chapter (p. 60), you will find more information about claims and thesis statements.

A Closer Look

Hypotheses and Question Claims

A specialized type of claim used in the introductions of academic essays involving experimentation is a **hypothesis**, a prediction about the experiment's outcome. However, although a hypothesis sounds inconclusive, when the researchers write up the experiment, they know its outcome, that is, whether the hypothesis was verified or not.

A **question claim** might be appropriate if the writer is exploring an area that has not been well researched or if the results are controversial. For example, student writer Iain Lawrence phrases as a question his claim concerning the effect of sports on childhood aggression in his essay found in chapter 7 (p. 225); he answers the question in his conclusion after analyzing the research on the topic. (You should ask your instructor before using a question claim in your introduction.)

> A **HYPOTHESIS** is a prediction about an experiment's outcome.
>
> A **QUESTION CLAIM** is a claim (thesis) in the form of a question.

Organization of Evidence

You support your claim through your main points and sub-points. These points function effectively when appropriate organizational methods are used and when the points are ordered logically (climax, inverted climax, or mixed order of points). Organizational methods include definition, chronology, classification/division, cause–effect, problem–solution, and compare and contrast (see p. 85).

> → See chapter 5, Organizing an Outline for Argument (p. 142), for more on ordering points.
>
> → See Rhetorical Patterns (p. 85), for more on organizational methods.

Kinds of Evidence

A writer provides support through specific *kinds* of evidence. Depending on your topic, the instructions for the assignment, and your discipline, you may use some kinds of evidence more than others.

Writing in the humanities often relies on primary, or original, sources. If you write an English essay, for instance, you will probably use many quotations from literary works. The primary sources commonly used in historical research are contemporary documents, such as newspapers, letters, and other records from the time period.

Social sciences writing often focuses on facts and figures, statistics and other numerical data, case studies, interviews, questionnaires, and observation. Scientific studies may use similar kinds of evidence but rely on direct methods that involve experimentation. Examples are important in just about every discipline.

Using a variety of evidence, rather than relying solely on one kind, will likely produce a stronger essay. However, it's important, especially if you are using research, to find **hard evidence** to support your key points. Hard evidence includes facts, statistics, and statements from authorities (experts). Soft evidence alone, such as examples and illustrations, might make your essay readable and understandable, but hard evidence will make it more convincing.

> **HARD EVIDENCE** is authoritative evidence that includes facts, statistics, and expert opinions.

A Closer Look

Reliability of Statistics

You probably have heard people say that statistics lie or that numbers can be twisted to mean whatever you want them to mean. It's important that you take statistics from reliable sources and pay attention to the wording of the passage to assess bias or distortion. Use caution with statistics cited by people or organizations promoting a particular cause or viewpoint. For example, surveys conducted by special interest groups can be subtly deceptive (see chapter 7, Reliability of Sources, p. 193).

Consider the case of a union that wants to put pressure on the government by making its case public. The group's executive pays for a full-page ad in major newspapers, claiming 93.7 per cent support among the public. The questions to ask are, "Who were the survey's respondents?" "How many were surveyed?" "How was the survey conducted?" Perhaps in this situation a small number of people who happened to be walking by the picket lines were stopped and surveyed. Perhaps the survey was conducted on the union's website. Reliable sources disclose their information-gathering methods, which you can evaluate.

Remember that statistics and factual data are often used for a specific purpose; evaluate them individually and keep this purpose in mind. Also bear in mind that well-known sources like People for the Ethical Treatment of Animals (PETA), or groups with a clear political leaning, such as the Fraser Institute, may give more importance to documented studies that agree with the organization's mission but pay less attention to other reliable findings.

Facts and Statistics

It is hard to argue with facts. For this reason, factual information, like the findings from research, is the strongest kind of evidence in research essays, whether expository or argumentative.

All the essays in chapter 7 make effective use of facts and statistics.

Authorities and Experts

When you apply for a job, you may be asked for letters of reference. Unless your would-be employer asks specifically for a character reference, you would normally submit letters from knowledgeable experts—perhaps from your former bosses or those you have worked with. They would be considered authorities who could support your claim of competence and testify that you are a good candidate for the job.

Authorities can be used to support your claim if they have direct knowledge of your subject. Authorities who are not experts have less credibility. For example, in an essay that argues a scientific or mathematical point, citing Albert Einstein would provide hard evidence. In an essay about vegetarianism, citing Einstein would provide soft evidence as he is not considered an expert on the topic. You will usually locate experts as you research your topic. However, it's also possible to conduct an interview with an expert, asking questions relevant to your claim. See A Closer Look in chapter 7, Field Research: Interviewing, page 210.

Examples, Illustrations, Case Studies, Precedents

While hard evidence provides direct support, **soft evidence** might make your points more understandable or convincing, and includes examples, illustrations, case studies,

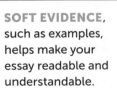

SOFT EVIDENCE, such as examples, helps make your essay readable and understandable.

and precedents. We use examples in both speech and writing. To support his argument, a teenager arguing for his independence might give several examples of friends who live on their own. Examples should always be relevant and representative. The teenager's parents might refute the examples by pointing out that they are not representative—for example, that one friend, Shawn, has a full-time job and that another, Giovanna, spent the summer travelling before moving out of her parents' house.

In most writing, examples bring a point home to the reader by making it specific and concrete. Examples are especially useful if you are writing for a non-specialist, as they make it easier to grasp a complex or an abstract point.

Illustrations are detailed examples that often take the form of anecdotes or other brief narratives. Student writer Luke Neville-Rutherford uses the example of a recent racial incident to help support his value claim that racism in soccer undermines the sport. After the example, the writer briefly analyzes its significance:

> In October 2011, Luis Suarez, a professional soccer player with Liverpool FC, and his opponent from Manchester United, Patrice Evra, took part in many heated verbal exchanges during their match. Later, it was revealed that cameras had recorded Suarez addressing racial expletives to Evra at least 10 times. After the English Football Association (FA) investigated the incident, they fined Suarez £40,000 and handed out an eight-match ban, determining that the controversial player's actions "damaged the image of English football around the world" (FA Report). However, in a rematch, Suarez ignored Evra during the traditional pre-match handshake, further aggravating a sensitive situation. Although unfortunate in the short run, publicity surrounding the incidents served to raise racism awareness, while the forceful actions of the FA deserve commendation.

Case studies are often used as support, particularly in the social sciences, education, and business; they can also be the focus of research studies. A case study is a carefully selected example that is closely analyzed in order to provide a testing ground for the writer's claim. Because case studies are real-life examples, they can be used to support a hypothesis (a prediction). For example, to find out if involving youth in decision making could produce a safer school environment, a Vancouver school planned a series of student-led initiatives and activities. The results showed that that the students felt safer and had improved their pro-social and conflict resolution skills. The outcome supported the hypothesis concerning the effectiveness of youth self-governance.

Precedents are examples of how particular situations were dealt with in the past. Judgments in courts of law establish precedents that influence future decisions. Once you have established some course of action as a precedent, you then apply it to your argument. Successfully using precedents as evidence depends on your ability to convince the reader that both

1. similar conditions apply to your topic today
2. following the precedent will produce a desirable result

For example, if you were arguing that Canada should offer free post-secondary studies to all academically qualified individuals, you could refer to the precedent

ILLUSTRATIONS are detailed examples that help make your essay readable and understandable.

CASE STUDIES are carefully selected examples that are closely analyzed to support a claim.

PRECEDENTS are examples of how particular situations were dealt with in the past and may be used in arguments to convince a reader that similar situations exist today and would benefit from similar action.

of Denmark, one of the first countries to provide universal access to post-secondary schooling. Then you must make it clear that both

1. the situation in Denmark is comparable to that in Canada
2. Denmark has profited by this system, so Canada will also likely benefit from a similar course of action

Other Kinds of Evidence

Analogy, description, and personal experience as evidence are suggestive and indirect; they cannot by themselves prove a claim.

Analogy, a kind of comparison (see p. 90), and description (see p. 47), can be used to make a point easier for the reader to understand and relate to. Like narration, description may also play a limited role in argument, perhaps to attract interest in the essay's introduction or to set up a main point.

Personal experience could take the form of direct experiences or observation. Recounting an experience can help the reader relate to your topic. You should keep your voice objective when using personal experience; any bias will undermine your credibility. Personal experience can effectively support a value claim. For example, if you had witnessed a dog fight, your observations on dog fighting could support the claim that dog fighting is cruel. Similarly, if you have had personal experience with homeless people by working in a food bank, you could use your experience to help support an extended value claim.

Credibility

Demonstrating credibility as a writer strengthens your claim. Three factors contribute to credibility:

- knowledge of the topic
- reliability/trustworthiness
- fairness

> You demonstrate your **KNOWLEDGE** of a subject when you present strong, well-supported points.
>
> You demonstrate your **RELIABILITY** when your writing is well-structured, clear, and grammatical.

Your knowledge by itself doesn't make you credible. Consider again the analogy of job-hunting: when you send out your résumé, you want to impress prospective employers with your experience and knowledge; however, during the interview, the employer will likely ask questions that pertain more to your reliability as an employee than to your knowledge—for example, "Why do you want to work for us?" "Where do you see yourself in five years?" "Why did you quit your last job?" Furthermore, when employers check your references, questions of your reliability are bound to arise. Similarly with essay writing, along with conveying knowledge, you must convince the reader that you are reliable.

You demonstrate **knowledge** through your points and their support. But you can present yourself as knowledgeable without being thought reliable. You instill confidence in your **reliability** or trustworthiness when you can answer "yes" to questions like the following:

- Is your essay well structured?
- Are your paragraphs unified, coherent, and well developed?

- Is your writing clear? Is your grammar correct? Is your style effective?
- Have you used the conventions of your discipline?
- Have you used critical-thinking skills effectively? Are your conclusions logical and well founded?

You must demonstrate **fairness** in an argumentative essay, where it is often important to consider opposing views. A writer who is fair comes across as objective in addressing the other side, avoiding slanted language that reveals bias. While you can demonstrate reliability by avoiding misuse of reason, you can demonstrate fairness by using emotional appeals moderately and selectively (discussed in more detail in chapter 5). The question of fairness can also arise in an expository essay if you are not objective in your use of the evidence.

> You demonstrate **FAIRNESS** when your arguments are objective and when you do not misuse reason or emotion.

The Unity of the Essay

An effective essay is really one entity with many interdependent parts. In figure 3.1 below, each part coexists with the other parts; none is an isolated entity that you can simply inject into an essay mechanically or without considering where it fits in. This interrelatedness is evident in many places in a successful essay. In writing essays, you can ask questions like:

- "Am I using the kinds of evidence favoured by my discipline?"
- "Am I organizing this evidence logically?"
- "Have I used enough sources?"
- "Is my essay well structured and is my writing clear and grammatical?"
- "Have I used evidence fairly?"

When reading an essay in order to analyze it, you can ask similar questions about the writer and the essay. When you analyze, you break something down into parts so you can look closely at each part. The interdependence of the parts of the essay can then

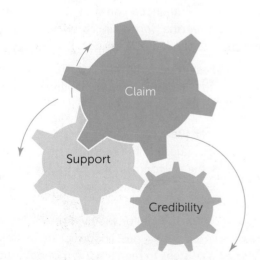

FIGURE 3.1 Interrelatedness of Credibility, Support, and Claim

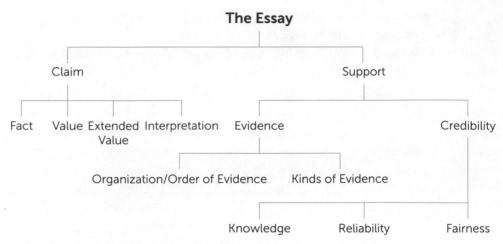

FIGURE 3.2 The Essay: An Analytical Model

be clearly seen. For example, grammatical errors affect the writer's reliability, thus reducing credibility and weakening support for the claim. Understanding the relatedness of the different parts should enable you to approach your own writing critically and give you the tools to analyze other writing.

EXERCISE 3.1

C Check answers to select questions

It is important that you be able to distinguish between factual claims and value claims. Although there may not always be a firm line between exposition and argument, you may be asked to write an essay that is clearly either one or the other; and, of course, your reader should recognize what kind of essay he or she is reading.

Determine whether the statements below are most suited to argument, exposition, or literary analysis by putting an *A*, *E* , or *L* beside them. In addition, identify any tentative claims.

1. British Columbia's environmental policy is superior to Alberta's policy.
2. Legislators should impose an outright ban on smoking on public open-air patios.
3. Diplomacy and militarism are the two main approaches to foreign policy which, though sometimes used independently, are much more effective when used in combination.
4. How does bullying inflicted through technology differ from traditional bullying, and how can this form of bullying be prevented?
5. 3M's tradition, strategy, and corporate image have helped it maintain its top-ten ranking in *Fortune* magazine year after year.
6. In spite of a few studies that question the health benefits of organic products, they remain the best choice for the environmentally conscious consumer.
7. Our fascination with celebrity doings and misdoings is undermining the fabric of North American society.
8. Hip hop today acts as a cultural bridge for widely diverse groups of young people to communicate across racial, class, religious, linguistic, and national divisions.
9. The government should take steps to regulate the monopolistic practices of airlines today.

10. Probably nobody in the history of psychology has been as controversial—sometimes revered, sometimes despised—as Sigmund Freud.

11. What are the physical effects of artificial and natural tanning? What are the risks involved, and what can be done to educate the public about both?

12. Despite the recent upsurge in the purchase of ebooks, traditional books will remain the mainstay for people who genuinely enjoy reading.

13. An increasing number of people today object to a legal system that relegates animals to the status of property with no rights to protect their interests in court.

14. Seamus Heaney uses sensory imagery, alliteration, and onomatopoeia to invoke the power of a natural setting and the intensity of the child's awakening.

15. We hypothesize that eating meat will lead people to constrict their moral concerns for animals. —Loughnan, S., Haslam, N., & Bastian, B. (2010). The role of meat consumption in the denial of moral status and mind to meat animals. *Appetite, 55,* 156–159. doi:10.1016/j.appet.2010.05.043

Each of the 15 simple thesis statements below contains a claim of fact, value, or extended value. Identify the kind of claim, and then turn the original claim into the two other kinds of claims (one sentence for each new claim). You may make any changes in wording you wish as long as the topic remains the same.

EXERCISE 3.2

↻ Check answers to select questions

Example:

Thesis Statement: The human race cannot afford to ignore the tremendous potential benefit of embryonic stem-cell research to find cures for many diseases.

Kind of Claim: Claim of value: the writer asserts that stem-cell research is beneficial.

A. Supporters of stem-cell research believe in the promise of embryonic stem cells to help repair damaged cells in the body, but its opponents believe that their use would encourage the destruction of human embryos.

Kind of Claim: Claim of fact: the writer asserts that both sides of the stem-cell controversy will be analyzed.

B. Recent developments in stem cell research have created new opportunities for researchers in biomedical technology, which should be backed by laws that do not restrict its use on religious or ethical grounds.

Kind of Claim: Claim of extended value: the statement advocates an action on the basis of what the writer believes is a "greater good."

1. The smartphone's dominance of the mobile phone market is due mostly to its increasingly sophisticated operating system.

2. The lyrics of rap music are inherently anti-social and encourage violence.

3. Women should not be allowed to serve in the military in anything but administrative roles.

4. The international community must take strong and decisive action against countries with anti-gay laws.

5. After completing high school, a student should travel for at least a year before proceeding to college or university.
6. It is necessary to provide more funding for technology in today's classrooms and to spend less on teachers' salaries.
7. Senate reform is one of the most pressing political issues today and should be addressed by the current government.
8. With many sports teams, clubs, and cultural groups on campus, students who do not participate in extracurricular activities are not getting good value for their education.
9. School uniforms provide many benefits to students and their parents.
10. The government should subsidize organically grown food.
11. Recreational use of steroids can cause physical and psychological damage to the user.
12. Before committing more resources to space exploration, we should work to solve global problems, such as poverty, that affect people every day.
13. Although factory farming provides a constant supply of meat, it has many drawbacks for the consumer, the environment, and the animals themselves.
14. Parents should have the right, within reason, to discipline their child as they see fit.
15. While advocates of a shorter work week believe that this measure will help our troubled economy, opponents say it will only weaken it and create social problems.

ESSAY AND PARAGRAPH STRUCTURE

A paragraph must be organized to serve specific functions:

- to introduce and develop a point
- to provide a smooth and logical connection to what precedes and follows the paragraph (introductory and concluding paragraphs are discussed as special cases, p. 71 and 83)

Like an essay, a paragraph has a beginning, a middle, and an end. The beginning announces what is to follow, usually in the **topic sentence** (in a paragraph) or the *thesis statement/claim* (in an essay). Without a clear topic sentence, the paragraph will lack force and unity. The middle of the paragraph develops the main point, while the ending provides a satisfying conclusion. The concluding sentence may act as a *wrap* by summarizing the main idea in the paragraph, in this way functioning much like the conclusion of an essay.

The difference between an essay and a paragraph is, of course, that the essay ends with the conclusion. A successfully constructed body paragraph not only provides a satisfying ending but also leads the reader into the following paragraph. This is often done through a transition—a word or phrase that provides a logical connection.

| The **TOPIC SENTENCE** contains the paragraph's main idea. |

Topic Sentence

A topic sentence introduces the main idea in the paragraph, while the other sentences in the paragraph develop it. The topic sentence is usually the first sentence in the paragraph for the same reason that the thesis statement usually occurs in the introduction (first paragraph) of the essay: it provides a logical starting point and makes the paragraph easy to follow.

A Closer Look

Theses and Topic Sentences

If we compare the structure of a paragraph and an essay, the topic sentence is like the thesis statement, in that both are generalizations that apply to the paragraph and the essay, respectively. In comparing a paragraph to a sentence, the topic sentence functions similarly to an independent clause: the topic sentence expresses the main idea in the paragraph just as the independent clause contains the main idea in the sentence. Typically, the other sentences in the paragraph illustrate or expand on the main idea by giving more detail, just as dependent clauses and phrases give more detail within the sentence. The interconnectedness of essay, paragraph, and sentence is thus underscored through these kinds of coordinate (equal) and subordinate (unequal or dependent) relationships.

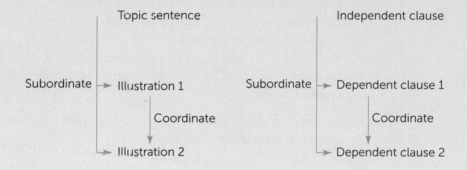

In each set of sentences, choose which one would make the best topic sentence for the paragraph. Remember that the topic sentence states the main (most general) point.

1. Essay Topic: The 100-Mile Diet
   a. In small communities, stores often use local products to produce their own wares.
   b. Eating locally is one way to sustain the local economy and farming community.
   c. For example, on Vancouver Island, most grocery stores sell dairy products from Island Farms and other regional dairies.

2. Essay Topic: Cellphones
   a. Recent studies have found that the brain cannot handle all the multi-tasking we try to do.
   b. We interrupt our meals, leave conversations, and forget to concentrate on our driving in order to answer our cellphones.
   c. Cellphones dominate the lives of many Canadians today.

3. Essay Topic: Physical Education Classes
   a. Physical education classes teach skills and knowledge not usually stressed in other classes.
   b. Skills like physical coordination and teamwork are developed in PE classes.
   c. PE classes allow more opportunities for social interaction, which is an essential skill in building future relationships and careers.

EXERCISE 3.3

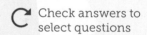 Check answers to select questions

The **PARAGRAPH WRAP** reinforces the main idea.

Paragraph Wrap as Conclusion

The **paragraph wrap** reminds the reader what the paragraph was about. However, the wrap doesn't just repeat the topic sentence; it reinforces its importance using different words. In the following paragraph, student writer Jordan Van Horne successfully wraps the main idea, which is introduced in the first (topic) sentence:

> If speed limits were abolished on highways, the necessity for law enforcement officers to patrol the highway for speeders would be curtailed. As a result, police chiefs might have more officers to assign to special community projects, such as MADD or drug awareness projects in elementary schools. These officers could spend their time on a variety of social and community projects that would benefit a large number of youths precisely at the time when they need this guidance. In addition, more officers could be allotted to other important areas that are typically understaffed today, such as surveillance and patrol duty to prevent drug smuggling. Surely the presence of police in the community or their dedication to large-scale projects such as drug smuggling would be more beneficial to public safety than having them patrol the highways.

Do not end a paragraph by introducing the topic of the following paragraph, which would disrupt the unity of the paragraph.

A wrap is especially effective in a longer paragraph (more than five sentences) where the reader might lose track of the main idea.

Connecting Paragraphs by Using a Transition

Whether or not the paragraph contains a wrap, it's important that the reader can connect it to what follows. A well-constructed paragraph not only states the main point, develops it, and reinforces it but also leads the reader smoothly to the next point (paragraph), like a well-oiled hinge connecting two solid objects. This can be done through a transition: a word, phrase, or clause that links ideas. The question to ask yourself is whether the reader can follow your train of thought easily from one paragraph to the next.

In the following excerpt from a student essay, Marissa Miles began her new paragraph with a dependent clause transition (underlined) before introducing the topic for the paragraph (no underlining). From the transition, you can see that the previous paragraph focused on the fostering of independence through home schooling.

> <u>Although the qualities of independence and self-motivation are important in a home-schooled education</u>, its flexibility enables the child to learn at his or her own pace, matching progress to the child's natural learning processes.

The writer of the following paragraph has combined an indirect reference to the preceding paragraph with the topic sentence of the current one:

> Another crucial function of genetic engineering is its application to the pharmaceutical industry.

> —Student writer Neil Weatherall

In formal writing, avoid the kinds of transitions used to connect sentences *within* paragraphs, such as *consequently*, *for example*, *moreover*, and similar words and phrases (see Transitions between Sentences, p. 66 below). They are not usually strong enough to connect main ideas from one paragraph to the next. Using transitions to connect ideas within a paragraph is discussed below under Coherence (p. 64).

PARAGRAPH FUNDAMENTALS

Good paragraphs are unified, coherent, and well developed. Unity, coherence, and development are discussed below.

Unity

Each paragraph should focus on *one* central idea announced in the *topic sentence*. Although it's usually best to place your topic sentence at the beginning, *the topic sentence anchors thought in the paragraph,* so this anchoring *could* occur in the beginning, middle, or end. In a unified paragraph, all sentences in the paragraph relate to the main idea, wherever that idea occurs.

Paragraphing, however, is not a mechanical process. Although the principle of one idea per paragraph is sound and logical, it may sometimes be difficult to tell where one idea ends and the next one begins. This is especially true in a rough draft where you are trying to get your ideas down and may not always be attentive to paragraph structure. Therefore, when you revise your essay, an important question to ask is whether each paragraph contains one main idea.

Also, in revising, you may see that one paragraph is much longer than the others. In such cases, you can determine a logical place to divide the paragraph into two smaller paragraphs. In the case of short paragraphs, you should consider combining them, as short paragraphs may come across as simplistic. When combining short paragraphs ensure that logical transitions are used to connect sentences.

> A unified paragraph focuses on one central idea announced in the topic sentence.

Collaborative Exercise: Paragraph Unity

The lengthy paragraph below could be divided into shorter paragraphs. Determine the natural paragraph breaks and mark where the new paragraphs should start. Remember to avoid a succession of very short paragraphs; occasionally, short paragraphs may be acceptable, but too many of them make for choppy and disconnected writing. Be prepared to justify your choices.

EXERCISE 3.4

↻ Check answers to select questions

According to Davis and Tarasuk (1994), the working definition of food poverty, or hunger, as it is known in Canada is "the inability to obtain sufficient, nutritious and personally acceptable food through normal food channels or the uncertainty one will be able to do so" (p. 1). In Canada, hunger is very rarely seen to the extent that it occurs in impoverished nations, but that does not mean it is not happening or that it is not a very real and imminent concern. In fact, chronic hunger affects millions of Canadians, especially those who are unemployed, have low incomes, or are inadequately supported by welfare and social assistance (Riches, 1999). The most well-known and widespread concern about Canadian hunger was in the 1930s, during the height of the Great Depression. Since then, there have been small-scale attempts across Canada to deal with hunger, but it was not until the early 1980s when hunger once again became a growing concern. The first official food bank opened in Edmonton, Alberta, in 1981 due to growing need (Davis & Tarasuk, 1994). Since 1981, the number of hungry Canadians has grown every year. Unlike in the United States, Canada has never had any type of official record of exact numbers of Canadians who are unable to obtain enough to eat; these numbers can only be estimated using data from the use of food assistance programs. They can never be an entirely accurate measure, as not every chronically hungry person will utilize a food assistance program. Nonetheless, every year many Canadians are forced by necessity to turn to the support of many different food assistance programs, such as food banks.

—Student writer Adele Horbulyk

In the following paragraphs, one sentence is off-topic, affecting the paragraph's unity. Identify the sentence that doesn't belong and explain why it is off-topic.

1. The requirement to display the N (new driver) sign on your vehicle is a reasonable one. It allows other drivers to recognize that the driver may be inexperienced. These drivers may drive more cautiously around the novice driver. It also alerts law enforcement officials to the fact that the driver is learning how to cope in traffic. However, officers have been known to pull over an N driver even if they have no legitimate reason to do so. Since alcohol consumption is often high in teenagers, the N sign in the rear window enables police to monitor for drunk driving more effectively. The requirement is therefore beneficial for both other drivers and the police.

2. The ability to concentrate during classes can easily be affected by a student's lack of activity. Most students find it difficult to sit around for six hours each day with only a lunch break, during which they might also do nothing but sit and eat. Exercise gives students relief from simply passively taking in information hour after hour. It especially helps children with high energy levels who find it hard to sit still. In addition, exercise is a solution to the ever-growing problem of obesity. By breaking up the day by at least one compulsory period of activity, students will be able to retain more information and perform better academically.

Coherence

The word *cohere* means "stick together." Someone who is *in*coherent doesn't make sense; the words or ideas don't stick together. By contrast, someone who is coherent is easy to follow. It is the same with a paragraph: one that lacks coherence is hard to follow. As a result, the words and the ideas do not stick in the reader's mind.

Here is the opening of an essay about the need for a nutritional diet. Although the ideas are quite simple, the paragraph isn't easy to follow. Try to determine why this is the case.

Original: Most children throughout Canada depend on their parents to provide them with the proper nutrients each day. There are many contributing factors that make this ideal unachievable, and this lack can cause children to cultivate a serious disease known as obesity.

Now consider a rewritten version of this paragraph. Do you find it easier to follow? Why?

Revised: Most Canadian children depend on their parents for adequate daily nutrition. However, many factors can prevent them from achieving their nutritional ideal, which may result in obesity, a serious medical disorder.

Part of the problem with the original paragraph lies in the words themselves: *cultivate* and *disease* are not the best words in this context. However, what also helps the words and ideas stick together is the careful use of repetition and transitions. In the rewritten version, the writer has replaced *this ideal* with *their nutritional ideal*, linking *ideal* to *nutrition* in the first sentence. By adding the transition *however* and replacing *and* by *which*, the relationship between the ideas becomes clearer.

Most Canadian children depend on their parents for adequate daily *nutrition*. *However*, many factors can prevent them from achieving *their nutritional ideal*, *which* may result in obesity, a serious medical disorder.

You can use specific methods, discussed below, to ensure your paragraphs are **coherent**, or easy to follow.

Word Choice

A major cause of incoherence is the fundamental problem of choosing the word that best conveys your meaning. In a rough draft, you may write the first word that comes to mind without considering whether it is the most precise word. Reader-based prose focuses on using the words that best convey your thoughts. Consider the following paragraph in which the writer is discussing the complex phenomenon of change. What word should the writer have used instead of the italicized word?

Change is a natural process resulting from interconnected systems in the biosphere, hydrosphere, lithosphere, and atmosphere. However, there is evidence today that human activity, including consumption and urbanization, is *exasperating* such changes.

When you consider what words to use, remember that it is not always a case of the right word versus the wrong word. Often, more than one word can convey your intended meaning, so it may be a question of choosing the *best word for the given context*. Whenever you use a word that is not part of your everyday vocabulary, you should confirm its meaning by looking it up in a dictionary. For written assignments, it's helpful to exchange your writing with someone else and pay attention to any passages that strike your reader as unclear.

A **COHERENT** paragraph is easy to follow.

→ Strategies for learning word meanings are discussed in Word Meanings in chapter 1, page 12; see also chapter 9, Working toward Precision: Wise Word Choices, page 289. Common usage errors are listed in Common Words That Confuse, in chapter 9, page 301.

→ Rhetorical patterns are discussed beginning on page 85.

Understanding the meaning of words is important for both reading and writing. If you do not understand a word when you are reading, this can affect *your understanding* of the essay. As mentioned, if you do not understand the meaning of a word when writing, this can affect *your reader's understanding* of your essay.

Rhetorical Patterns

Coherent paragraphs often follow a distinct pattern. Paragraphs can be given a chronological, cause–effect, classification/division, compare and contrast, or other pattern.

Logical Sentence Order

Recall that your writing is closely connected to your thinking and that you need to make your thought process clear to your reader. If one idea does not logically proceed from the previous one, then the paragraph will not be coherent. Similarly, there may be one or more gaps in a paragraph that need to be filled in, perhaps by inserting a sentence. Many writers number their main points in order to make the sequence of ideas easy to follow.

Repetition and Synonyms

Repeating key phrases can help the reader follow the main idea in the paragraph. Using synonyms (words that mean the same thing as, and can therefore replace, other words) can also help you reinforce key words without sounding repetitive. Experienced writers often consider the rhythm of the sentence, placing key words at strategic points in the paragraph.

Parallel Structures

Writers can also use parallel and/or balanced structures to achieve coherence. One of the reasons why so many readers can remember the beginnings and endings of Charles Dickens's novels is that Dickens often employed balanced structures: "It was the best of times; it was the worst of times" (*A Tale of Two Cities*).

→ See The Parallelism Principle, chapter 12, page 381, for more information about grammatical parallelism.

Transitions between Sentences

Transitional words and phrases guide the reader from one sentence to the next, signalling the exact relationship between them. Often, just adding the right transitional words gives the paragraph the coherence that is needed. However, if you fail to use a transition to connect two ideas, the reader may find it hard to follow the paragraph's development. Some of the most useful transitions are listed below.

Note how the word *However* in the paragraph above tells the reader that the idea in the second sentence contrasts with the idea in the first one. *However* is a transition of contrast.

Types of Transitions

- *Limit or concession:* admittedly, although, it is true that, naturally, of course, though

- *Cause and effect:* accordingly, as a result, because, consequently, for this reason, if, otherwise, since, so, then, therefore, thus
- *Illustration:* after all, even, for example, for instance, indeed, in fact, in other words, of course, specifically, such as
- *Emphasis:* above all, assuredly, certainly, especially, indeed, in effect, in fact, particularly, that is, then, undoubtedly
- *Sequence and addition:* additionally, after, again, also, and, and then, as well, besides, eventually, finally, first . . . second . . . third, furthermore, in addition, likewise, meanwhile, next, moreover, similarly, subsequently, too, while
- *Contrast or qualification:* after all, although, but, by contrast, conversely, despite, even so, however, in spite of, instead, nevertheless, nonetheless, on the contrary, on the one hand . . . on the other hand, otherwise, rather (than), regardless, still, though, whereas, while, yet
- *Summary or conclusion:* in conclusion, in effect, in short, in sum, in summary, so, that is, thus, to summarize

In the following paragraphs, student writer Grace Chau uses transitional words and phrases, repetition, and balanced constructions—all of which serve to make the paragraphs more coherent. If these words and phrases were taken away, much of the paragraphs would be unclear. Transitions are in boldface type, repetitions are in italic, and balanced constructions are underlined.

> **In contrast to** allopathy, in Traditional Chinese Medicine (TCM), organs are viewed as "networks"—**that is**, functional physiological and psychological domains—**rather than** discrete anatomical structures. All our organs are related; **in fact**, our body, our behaviour, and the environment we are in are also interconnected. **In other words**, TCM focuses more on the *context* where the disease exists than on the disease itself. **Such emphasis** on *context* implies that the way people get sick and can be treated are highly personalized.
>
> People with different *symptoms* may have the same underlying problem, requiring similar treatments; yet people with the same *symptom* may need completely different remedies. While we are equally endowed with our basic parts, our lungs, heart, kidneys, liver, and so on, our way of coordinating these parts is individualized. **For example**, if arthritis is due to an invasion of "heat" (inflammation), it is different from the same condition with a different cause—**for example**, "cold" (reduced circulation) or "dampness" (accumulation of fluids). **In the first case**, practitioners would administer cooling herbs; **in the others**, warming or diuretic herbs would be used.

A unified paragraph refers to one central idea; in a coherent paragraph, one sentence leads logically to the next sentence. Figure 3.3 shows two diagrammatic representations of unity and coherence in which the sentences are represented by arrows.

→ When you use transitional words or phrases to connect one idea to the next, be careful to punctuate correctly. See chapter 11, Semicolon (p. 345) for punctuation rules governing transitional words and phrases.

In formal writing, do not begin a sentence with the transitions *and, but, or, so,* or *yet.* They should be used to connect two main ideas *within* a sentence.

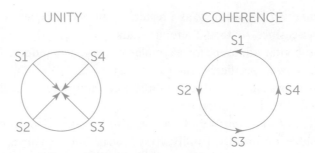

FIGURE 3.3 Unity and Coherence Diagrams

EXERCISE 3.5

↻ Check answers to select questions

Paragraph Coherence

I. Coherence through Word Choice

In the sentences below, replace the italicized words with words that better convey the intended meaning, using a dictionary as required.

1. Today's prospective car buyers should consider buying a hybrid electric vehicle as the benefits clearly outweigh the *detriments*.
2. The *volume* of competition and training that goes into golf requires a high level of physical fitness.
3. The recent *expansiveness* of the Internet frees shy adolescents from the constraints of a face-to-face relationship.
4. The narrow *physique* of glacial fjords protects them from the effects of high waves and storm damage.
5. The safest way to protect the principles of democracy is to keep the division between church and state *tangible*.
6. Sports today have become more competitive, and parents may *enlist* their children in competitive sports at too young an age.
7. Our capabilities in combating infections have begun to *regress* as many strains of bacteria have become *resilient to* antibiotics.
8. Adopting a vegetarian lifestyle would no doubt have a major *impact toward* ending world hunger.
9. The fashion industry today *distributes* the idea that young women should conform to one *implausible* ideal.
10. To *assure* that teenagers do not drive drunk, the drinking age should be raised to 19, when teens are mature enough to deal *respectably* with alcohol.

II. Coherence through Paragraph Development

You can organize paragraphs in different ways: by chronology (time order), by comparing and contrasting, by division (dividing a general category into specific ones), and other methods (see p. 85).

1. How are the ideas organized in these paragraphs?
2. Besides the main organizational method(s), find other ways that the writer has achieved coherence.

3. What do you think the writer might have written about in the third paragraph?

> They came over the land bridge connecting Asia with Alaska, those first men of the Western Hemisphere. The date was between 20,000 and 30,000 years ago. They were hunters, dressed in the skins of the animals they hunted. Their weapons were stone-tipped spears. All this was long before Homer, before the dynasties of Egypt, before Sumer and the Land of the Two Rivers, and, of course, long before the Christian Bible was written. At that time, the glaciers that covered Canada and parts of the northeastern United States during the last ice age were melting. They melted first along river valleys, which turned into great misty, fog-haunted corridors between receding walls of ice.
>
> The hunters roamed south along those corridors, pursuing animals for food and clothing. They died eventually, as all people do, and their children came after them in the long stammering repetition of humanity everywhere. The animals they hunted were principally caribou, bear, and mammoth—the latter long since extinct in North America. Camps of those early men have been discovered recently. They are the ghostly forbears of modern Indians and Eskimos.
>
> —Al Purdy, "Aklavik on the Mackenzie River"

III. Coherence through Sentence Order

The 10 sentences below are taken from a paragraph by student writer Stina Grant. Combine them in the most logical order to form a coherent paragraph. Supply any necessary links between one sentence and the next, and be prepared to justify the order you used to achieve coherence. (Note: citations have been omitted for clarity's sake.)

1. The effects of bullying can be devastating.
2. Many adults can recall incidences of bullying while growing up—either as participants or observers.
3. To address bullying as a society, we need to understand its root causes and motivations.
4. Norwegian researcher Dan Olweus was a pioneer in this unacknowledged field.
5. Olweus defined bullying as an aggressive act committed repeatedly by an individual or a group that intimidates, harasses, mistreats, or excludes others either directly or indirectly.
6. Bullying started to receive research attention in the early 1970s.
7. Bullying can be physical or psychological, verbal or non-verbal.
8. Victims go to school every day fearing harassment and humiliation.
9. Many experts believe that the psychological scars left from bullying can last well into adulthood.
10. The concept of bullying is not new.

IV. Coherence through Transitions

Using transitions can help sentences cohere, or stick together. The following paragraph lacks transitions. Provide logical connections between the sentences by choosing the appropriate transitions from the list below, filling in the blanks. In part 2, one transition has been given to you.

1. _____ many educators and parents have praised the Harry Potter series, some Christian parents have called for a ban on the books in their schools and libraries.

Some churches have even gone as far as burning the books, citing biblical injunctions against witchcraft, _____ those in Exodus and Leviticus. _____ some Christians believe the books are compatible with Christianity, _____, that they embody basic Christian beliefs.

although

however

indeed

such as

2. Massive energy consumption is having a negative impact on the planet. _____, in the summer of 2006, western Europe experienced some of the hottest weather on record. <u>Moreover</u>, this temperature increase is not an isolated occurrence. _____, almost every credible scientist today believes that the earth is experiencing climate change due to the emissions of greenhouse gases from cars and coal-burning power plants. Ninety per cent of the energy used in the US comes from fossil fuels such as oil, coal, and natural gas (Borowitz 43), _____ problems arise from other sources, too. _____, nuclear power plants leave radioactive by-products, making storage difficult. _____, dams are not much better, as nearby populations must be relocated, and the surrounding habitat is destroyed.

~~moreover~~

but

for example

in fact

unfortunately

for example

V. Coherence through Use of Repetition, Parallel Structures, and Transitions

1. Read the paragraph below to determine how the writer has used transitions and repetition to achieve coherence. Underline transitions and repetitive devices. Identify the topic sentence. One of the ways to achieve coherence is to number your points, though unnecessary numbering can add to clutter. Do you think that it was a good choice for the writer to number his points? If so, why?

> Critics of the World Trade Organization argue that its approach to globalization causes more harm than good because it undermines democracy. The WTO is undemocratic in several respects. First, ambassadors from member nations are appointed, not elected. Second, the coalition known as the "Quad," comprising the European Union, the United States, Japan, and Canada, holds almost all the real power. In theory, at least, such decisions as new membership, rule changes, and rule interpretations of WTO rules should be voted for with a three-quarters majority. In practice, however, the "Quad" determines the WTO agenda. Third, WTO trade talks are held in secret to avoid public criticism and scrutiny. Furthermore, an organization that is not elected controls trade so effectively that it possesses the power to supersede the power of elected communities, states, and even nations on any issue, however ambiguous, related to trade.
>
> —Student writer Tao Eastham

2. Read the paragraph below to determine how the writer has used transitions and repetition to achieve coherence. Underline transitions and repetitive devices. Identify the topic sentence. This paragraph is an introductory paragraph to a chapter of a book. What topic do you think will be developed in the next paragraph? Why?

> The news media's power to trivialize anything that comes to their attention is almost magical. News service advertisements talk about providing a "window on the world" or a report on "history in the making." But the nightly television newscast and the daily newspaper fall far short of these ideals. Instead, we get a fast-paced smorgasbord of unconnected and disembodied news stories where meaning and context are lost in the rapid-fire delivery of colourful prose and dramatic pictures. As a result, much of what passes for news is instead isolated, unconnected, and almost meaningless bits of information—in effect, the news is trivialized. This trivialization operates at both the structural level of news gathering and dissemination, and at the level of individual news stories. We have termed this style "the trivialization effect."
>
> —adapted from R.A. Rutland, *The Newsmongers*.

SPECIALIZED PARAGRAPHS: INTRODUCTION AND CONCLUSION

The Introduction

Almost everything you read begins with an introduction. Even if it is not labelled "introduction," it acts as one by previewing what follows. It presents the main idea and, probably, the organization pattern of the document—whether it is a book, an article in a scholarly journal, a class essay, or a sales proposal. The introductions students are asked to write usually consist of one paragraph that fulfills specific functions, and that should, like all paragraphs, be unified, coherent, and well developed.

You can compare the preparations for writing the essay's introduction to the care you would take when meeting someone for the first time. Just as there are people you don't notice because they don't present themselves well, or whom you notice for the wrong reasons, so there are introductory paragraphs that aren't noticed or are noticed for the wrong reasons. As the introduction is one of the most important parts of your essay, it is worth spending time crafting it to meet the requirements discussed below. It will draw the reader into the essay and provide necessary information, satisfying the expectations of your audience.

Catching the Reader's Interest: Logical, Dramatic, and Mixed Approaches

The introduction should create reader interest while informing the reader of the essay's topic. Although most of your essay's "substance"—your main points and sub-points, the supporting details—will be placed in the middle (body) paragraphs, an ineffective

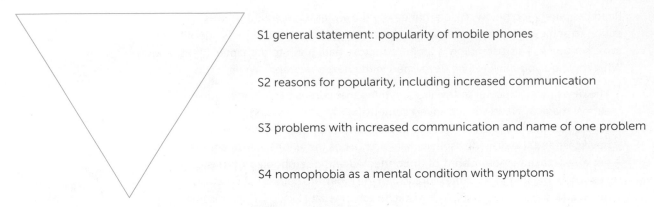

S1 general statement: popularity of mobile phones

S2 reasons for popularity, including increased communication

S3 problems with increased communication and name of one problem

S4 nomophobia as a mental condition with symptoms

FIGURE 3.4 Inverted Pyramid Structure

introduction could mean that these details are wasted as the rest of the essay may not be read. Keeping the reader's interest while introducing the topic can be achieved through two main methods.

Logical Introduction

The *logical* approach is the traditional way to create interest. You begin with the general and proceed to the specific; the most specific is your thesis statement. This is also called the *inverted pyramid* structure.

Writers of expository, argumentative, and literary essays often use this method. A logical opening enables you to situate your own approach to a topic within a larger context. In this way, you establish the topic's significance as you progressively become more specific. Your thesis statement is usually the last sentence of the introduction while the preceding sentences build your emphasis.

Student writer Celeste Barnes-Crouse uses the pyramidal structure to move logically from the general to the specific in the introduction below. She briefly discusses the recent popularity of mobile phones, comments on their many uses, then introduces some disadvantages before revealing her thesis in the last sentence. (See Figure 3.4).

> Although mobile telephones have been used for decades, their popularity with the average person began to surge less than a decade ago. Since then, people have seen the advantages of near-constant access to their phones, such as increased communication at the workplace or with family, along with better response to emergencies. However, the hazards of constant communication affect daily life as well, like talking and texting while driving, text addiction, classroom and workplace disruptions, and, increasingly, nomophobia: the fear of being without one's cellphone. Social and economic pressures of the 21st century have caused restricted cellphone use to become a valid medical condition in society with a range of symptoms, and its global prevalence is rising.

Other kinds of logical approaches can also be used, For example, the writer below begins by mentioning something *familiar* and proceeds to the *unfamiliar*:

While intelligence quotient (IQ) has long been a useful tool to determine one's intelligence, a new development in the study of human intellectual experience has expanded to include one's emotional state. It is called Emotional Intelligence, or EQ.

—Student writer Chin-Ju Chiang

Dramatic Introduction

The *dramatic* approach can be used in various ways: you could begin with an interesting quotation, a thought-provoking question, a personal experience, an illuminating statistic, a description of a scene, or a brief narrative with the objective of surprising or intriguing your reader. Although it is used more often in argument than in exposition, it can prove effective in some expository essays as well, as the example below illustrates. In the following paragraph, the student writer creates a scenario that enables the reader to experience an unfamiliar martial art first-hand, just as she experienced it:

Imagine a circle of adults and children dressed in white pants with different coloured cords around their waists. Everybody is clapping and singing in an unfamiliar language—entranced by what is unfolding within the circle. Musicians are playing drums, tambourines, and an instrument that looks like a stringed bow with a gourd attached. There is an inescapable feeling of communal energy within the circle. Uncontrollable curiosity lures the unknowing spectator; peering into the circle exposes two people engaged in an intense physical dialogue. Kicks and movements are exchanged with precision and fluidity, which create a dance-like choreography. What is being witnessed is called a *roda* (pronounced ho-da, it means "circle" in Portuguese). A person's first encounter with this intriguing display of physicality and grace is an experience not easily forgotten. I did not forget my first *roda*, and, consequently, I later began training in this Brazilian form of martial arts—*Capoeira* (pronounced cap-where-a).

—Student writer Kerry Hinds

The main function of the dramatic introduction above is to evoke a scene, but a writer might want to evoke an emotional response. Although some of the same strategies as those mentioned apply, the stress here is not on surprise but on an emotional connection between writer and reader. However, if you use this approach, you need to ensure that the typical reader will respond in the way you wish. An emotional opening needs to be sufficiently broad so that most people will share your feelings about the issue. An emotion-based introduction is sometimes used by a writer who wants to alert the public to an important concern—for example, a serious health risk or the incidence of missing children.

Rewrite the two complete student paragraphs above using other approaches—i.e., use the dramatic approach for the first paragraph and the logical approach for the second one. (In order to do so, you might have to do some research.)

EXERCISE 3.6

Mixed Approaches

A writer using the *mixed approach* combines different methods to attract interest.

- *Dramatic–logical*: The writer could begin with a question or challenging statement and then proceed to develop the rest of the paragraph through the logical approach.
- *Logical–dramatic*: The writer could use a "reversal" strategy, beginning with a general statement before dramatically turning the tables and arguing the opposite.

The writer of the paragraph below employs the *logical–dramatic* strategy to introduce her topic, the use of fur in today's society. After explaining the practical function of fur in humanity's past, in the second half of the paragraph she turns the tables and begins her argument that using fur today is wasteful and unnecessary:

> Since the beginning of time, people have depended on fur. Cavemen wore animal skins as clothing; furthermore, after an animal, such as a buffalo, was killed, the flesh would be eaten and the bones would be used in tool-making. They used as much of the animal as possible due to their spiritual beliefs and because with few other resources, it made sense to waste as little as possible. Wearing fur in that age was a necessity: it was warm, practical, and readily available. Today, it is a far different story. Fur is part of the upscale fashion industry, but killing wild animals for their skin extends beyond fur fanciers; it is a luxury product for many different consumers today, such as owners of cars with leather upholstery. There are more than 40 different animal species that are killed for their skin, and not a single one needs to be.
>
> —Student writer Grace Beal

Whatever approach you use, the way you choose to create interest should be relevant to your topic, your purpose in writing, and your audience. For example, if you were trying to argue in favour of euthanasia, or another issue with a built-in emotional aspect, and you knew your audience opposed it, a strongly emotional opening might not be a good approach because you would risk alienating your readers.

> When choosing the type of opening to use, consider your topic, purpose, and audience.

Other Features of the Introduction

The introduction serves other important functions:

- It announces your topic and the main point. The thesis statement, occurring near or at the end of the introduction, gives the main point of the essay and should have two parts: the topic itself plus a comment on the topic (see The Thesis Statement on p. 78, below).
- It introduces the writer. The introduction is the place where the reader comes to know that he or she is in competent hands. The introduction is the writer's first chance to establish *credibility* by showing knowledge, reliability, and

A Closer Look

The Introduction in Scholarly Writing

Writers in the academic disciplines often use a slightly different approach in their introductions as their essays, typically, are much longer and more complex than the introductions you will write. For example, their research might consist of dozens of sources. They might begin by giving background, such as an overview of the major works in the field or the various positions relevant to the topic. The writer will then link these studies, particularly the last ones mentioned (usually the most recent ones), to his or her own approach, directly showing what he or she expects to add to the knowledge about the topic.

As in a student essay, the introduction concludes with a thesis statement, but this may take a different form from the kind of thesis you write (see The Thesis Statement, below). For example, it might be a question or hypothesis (prediction) about the results of the study, particularly if the study is an experiment. The authors of a study on the effects of bullying on the victims made the following prediction:

> We hypothesized that individuals become perfectionistic in an attempt to escape or minimize further abuse.
>
> —Miller, J. L., & Vaillancourt, T. (2007). Relation between childhood peer victimization and adult perfectionism: Are victims of indirect aggression more perfectionistic? *Aggressive Behavior*, 33, 233.

An **essay plan** is also common in scholarly introductions: the author outlines the parts of the essay often using the first-person voice, as this example illustrates:

> In the first half of this paper, we explore the essence of this debate, with a particular focus on women entrepreneurs in Canada. In the second half of the paper, we tell the stories of these two Canadian entrepreneurs who have started technology-based businesses.
>
> —Lynes, J., Wismer, S., & Andrachuk, M. (2011). The role of education in entrepreneurship: Two Canadian stories. *Advancing Women in Leadership*, 31, 14–22.

For an example of an academic introduction, see "The Teenage Brain: Self-Control" (p. 229).

As a student, you will likely be asked to *read* scholarly studies that begin with a direct and concise statement of the problem or purpose and may even include the study's findings in the introduction. This is often the case with scientific articles designed for those with specialized knowledge. However, unless you are writing a report for a science or business course, the essays you are asked to *write* will likely have introductions similar to those discussed in this chapter.

> An **ESSAY PLAN** is the form the thesis can take when the author outlines the parts of the essay, often using the first-person voice.

trustworthiness. These qualities should come across through good writing and by appearing rational, fair, and in control.

- It indicates *how* the writer will develop the main points. What organizing method will be used? Organizational patterns are discussed below (p. 85).

Introduction Length

Some successful introductions are quite brief; others are longer. The length may depend partly on the length of the essay itself; it may also depend on your decision whether to list the main points of your essay in an expanded thesis (but you should not *develop* your main points here) or give background information. As a guideline, an introduction

> In addition to stimulating reader interest, an introduction should announce the topic and main point, reveal the main organizational method, and establish the writer's credibility.

should not be more than 10–15 per cent of the length of the essay, but you should check with your instructor for specific guidelines.

Starting at the Beginning

You could think of the introduction as gradually building up to its last sentence, your thesis statement. However, you should not focus all your energy on the last sentence at the expense of the first sentence. Your opening sentences need to be carefully crafted too. An ineffective opening may be too general, too abrupt, obvious, irrelevant, or exaggerated. Using the analogy of meeting someone for the first time, you could say that a general, obvious, or irrelevant opening is the equivalent of a weak handshake and an averted glance rather than a firm handshake and direct eye contact. An abrupt or exaggerated opening could be compared to an overly aggressive greeting and vice-like, rapid hand pumping.

Weak Openings

A weak opening may fail to engage a reader's interest by being too broad; it should be directly related to your topic (see "Exaggerated claim" below, where generalizations lack validity). Similarly, obvious and irrelevant claims may bore a reader.

Too general or obvious:

> This is the technology age.

> Many people consider hockey Canada's sport.

Irrelevant, or "so what?":

> Few people know that sea otters can live to the age of 15 years.

This could be an effective opening if the statement really fell into the category of "believe it or not"—but it doesn't.

The reader of this statement might wonder how the writer's experience is relevant to the reader:

> When I attended high school, I took every opportunity to be actively involved in all the physical education classes and sports organizations available.

One variant of a dramatic opening is asking the reader to imagine a specific scenario. If you use the "imagine" opening, ensure what you are asking the reader to imagine is realistic and interesting to a general audience.

> Imagine you are behind the wheel of a formula racing car, about to complete the final lap for your first NASCAR victory.

Such an opening would likely interest a reader only if he or she were interested in stock-car racing.

Too abrupt:

> First Nations' self-determination and self-government must come from within.

Do not begin your essay with a statement that could serve as your thesis as it could alienate readers who disagree with you. Bear audience in mind, then, when you craft your essay opening.

The statement above could serve as an effective thesis statement once the reader has been prepared for it.

Exaggerated claim:

> Nowadays everyone has a cellphone in their pocket or backpack.

Many people in your city do not own a cellphone; there are few claims that justify the use of *everyone*.

> The largest health epidemic in today's society is obesity, especially among children.

Many health "epidemics" exist today, and obesity among children is certainly one of them. However, the statement would appear more credible if it were qualified, perhaps by the addition of ". . . some experts believe" Or "One of the largest. . . ."

Collaborative Exercise: Evaluating Openings

EXERCISE 3.7

↻ Check answers to select questions

In groups, consider the following opening statements and what makes each effective or ineffective. Rate each on a scale of 1 to 5, where 1 represents a very weak opening and 5 represents an abrupt or exaggerated one. Give a 3 rating if the opening seems good, neither too weak nor too strong. Then, discuss how those not rated 3 could be revised to make them more effective and interesting.

1. Franz Anton Mesmer discovered hypnosis in the 1770s.
2. Although email began as a modern communications miracle, it has become the greatest nuisance ever invented.
3. I guess we would all like to look like Rihanna if we could.
4. There are many issues surrounding end-of-life treatment of terminally ill individuals.
5. Why not buy the best-made sports car the world has to offer?
6. The movement of people away from the Catholic Church today is mostly due to its teachings on issues like abortion, women's equality, and homosexuality.
7. A few years ago, the Fédération Internationale d'Escrime (FIE) passed several unpopular rule changes in the sport of fencing.
8. In all American literature, no character ever gave more thought to moral decisions than Huckleberry Finn does.
9. Fighting is a part of hockey—no ifs, ands, or buts.
10. Health and academic success have long been considered interrelated.
11. Mixed martial arts is the best entertainment value available today.
12. Imagine that you are a woman standing before a mirror.
13. What is a bylaw?
14. Western society today increasingly accepts different lifestyles and personal choices, giving many marginalized individuals greater freedom to live as they choose.
15. High school students should have the chance to participate in a wide variety of non-competitive activities in their physical education classes.

Writing an introduction requires time and patience. You should not feel discouraged if, after having produced an outline, you cannot quickly come up with a strong introduction. It may be best to return to your introduction *after* you've written the rest of the essay. In fact, some instructors believe that the introduction should be the last part of the essay you write.

For the difference between a subject, a topic, and a thesis, see page 33.

A **SIMPLE THESIS STATEMENT** announces the topic and main point; an **EXPANDED THESIS STATEMENT** includes your main points in the order in which they will appear in your essay.

The Thesis Statement

Nearly all essays need a thesis statement—the main point of your essay, or what you will be attempting to prove. A thesis statement has two parts: the *topic* and the *comment*. It does not just state a topic. Consider this example:

> My essay will be about life in residence at the University of the South Pole.

The sentence above states a topic and does not comment on it. But a thesis might be as follows:

> Life in residence at the University of the South Pole helps prepare you for life after university.

This sentence makes a comment about the topic. "Life in residence at the University of the South Pole" is the topic; "helps prepare you for life after university" is the comment. It tells the reader how you will be addressing the topic, what your focus will be.

Kinds of Thesis Statements

Simple thesis statements have the two required parts, like the example above.

Expanded thesis statements give more detail by including your main points:

> Life in residence at the University of the South Pole helps prepare you for life after university by making you independent, by reinforcing basic life skills, and by teaching you how to get along with other penguins.

Just as a simple thesis statement goes further than a topic, so an expanded thesis statement goes further than a simple thesis statement by answering questions like *How?* or *Why?*, by accounting for or justifying the main idea: *How* does life in residence prepare one for life after university?

Here's an example of a topic, followed by a simple thesis statement and an expanded one that answers the question *Why?*:

> *Topic:* School uniforms

> *Simple thesis statement:* Making school uniforms mandatory has many advantages for students.

> *Expanded thesis statement:* Making school uniforms mandatory has many advantages for students because they eliminate distractions, encourage a focus on academics, and reduce competition based on appearances.

Should you use a simple or expanded thesis statement in your essay? Simple thesis statements may be sufficient for shorter essays and are sometimes used in fact-based (expository) essays in which you attempt to answer a question or solve a problem. In argumentative essays, you try to convince your reader of something. An expanded thesis statement that announces all your points in the introduction gets you off to a forceful start. Check with your instructor for specific guidelines about simple versus expanded thesis statements.

A Closer Look

Indirect Thesis

In an indirect thesis statement, the main point or thrust of your argument is not explicitly stated but is implied in your introduction. Writers of expository essays do not often use indirect thesis statements, though experienced writers may sometimes use them in informal-style essays. One of the best-known examples of an indirect thesis statement is in Jonathan Swift's satiric essay "A Modest Proposal," published in 1729. Swift advocates the sale of one-year-old children to the wealthy, who will buy them to eat! The "modest proposal" is designed to call attention, in an absurdly callous way, to the problem of poverty in Ireland, which Swift felt was being ignored by the wealthy.

Effective Thesis Statements

An effective thesis statement should be interesting, specific, and manageable.

- *Interesting*: The thesis is likely to attract the reader, especially the general reader, to the topic and the essay.
- *Specific*: The thesis isn't so general, broad, or obvious that it lacks relevance; it informs the reader about what follows.
- *Manageable*: The thesis sounds as if it can be reasonably explored in the space of the essay; the writer can successfully carry out what is promised in the thesis.

Ineffective Thesis Statements

Although a thesis statement may be ineffective because it is not interesting, specific, or manageable, other problems may also make it ineffective. An unclear thesis statement may confuse a reader because of the phrasing or because the writer wasn't clear about the topic itself. Unclear phrasing:

> Pets are important in that they can unify, can heal, and are an inevitable part of human nature.

Do we know what the writer means by these items? The writer needs to be more detailed and precise:

> *Revised:* Pets are important in bringing people together, helping them recover from an illness or depression, and enabling them to express important human values, such as love.

A thesis statement may be unclear because it seems to straddle two topics rather than centring on one. This could be the result of the writer's early uncertainty: he or she may not yet know the essay's major focus. In revising your essay, you should always ensure that your thesis accurately reflects the essay's main point. In this example, we don't know whether this essay will be about excessive dieting or body image:

> Many youths are obsessed by dieting today because of the prominence our society places on body image.

Fast Track

Thesis Statement Checklist

✔ Have you written a complete thesis statement, not just a topic?

✔ Does it have two parts (simple thesis statement)?

✔ Is it interesting, specific, and manageable?

✔ Have you included your main points in the order they will appear in your essay (expanded thesis statement)?

✔ Is there enough detail to enable the reader to understand your main points (i.e., it is clearly phrased)?

✔ Is it clear what one topic the thesis will focus on (i.e., it does not appear vague or appear to straddle two topics)?

✔ Is it worded objectively and not self-consciously?

✔ In arranging your main points, have you applied parallel structure?

To successfully revise this thesis, the writer needs to narrow the topic to one specific area, such as one of the following:

> unhealthy diets and the problems they create
>
> the effects of body image on youths
>
> the relationship between body image and dieting

→ When you use an expanded thesis statement, you need to express your main points in parallel structure; otherwise, the thesis could be hard to follow (see The Parallelism Principle in chapter 12, p. 381).

In addition, many instructors will want you to avoid a stiff and self-conscious thesis statement that refers directly to the writer or to the essay's purpose:

Ineffective: I (or, This essay) will examine the phenomenon of online gambling and argue in favour of strict government regulation of this growing industry.

Revised: Online gambling is an increasing concern to governments today and should be subject to strict regulations.

A clear thesis begins with the writer's clear thoughts. As in all writing, clear thinking produces clear expression. On the other hand, the thesis you start with shouldn't be considered fixed. As you write your outline or rough draft and uncover areas about your topic you weren't aware of before, you may want to go back and revise your thesis.

EXERCISE 3.8

↻ Check answers to select questions

A. If you were asked to write an essay on computer games, which of the simple thesis statements below would be suitable? Rate each according to whether it is interesting, specific, and manageable. Be prepared to explain your decisions.

1. Computer games provide one of the most entertaining pastimes we have today.
2. Violence in computer games is affecting children these days by increasing the number of shootings in schools.
3. Computer gaming companies will do anything to sell their product.

4. Computer games take away our free time by creating a dependency that is very hard to escape once we are hooked.
5. Computer games are a great babysitter for children.

B. Write an effective thesis statement on the topic of computer games, using any pre-writing technique you feel comfortable with and making sure that you include the requirements of a good thesis statement.

C. The following thesis statements are either simple or expanded. Identify the type. If they are simple thesis statements, add detail, turning them into expanded thesis statements.

1. Regular, moderate doses of stress not only are inevitable in today's world but also can be good for you.
2. As consumers, we must keep ourselves informed about the activities of the industries we support.
3. Although poor waste management has already had a significant impact on the planet, through recycling, waste reduction programs, and public education, future damage can be minimized.
4. Education is viewed as a benefit to individuals, but too much education can have negative results.
5. Many people today misunderstand the meaning of success.

Collaborative Exercise: Writing Strong Thesis Statements

In groups, use a pre-writing technique to formulate a simple thesis statement that has the five criteria discussed above. Begin with a choice of broad subject areas, such as the ones suggested below. When each group has come up with a thesis statement and written it on a piece of paper, exchange it with another group's and have that group evaluate it according to the criteria below. Give one mark for each item if the thesis statement is

- interesting
- specific
- manageable
- well phrased
- clearly on one topic

When each group has completed the evaluation process, discuss the ratings and the rationale behind them.

After each group has received feedback on its thesis statement and revised it accordingly, use another pre-writing technique to come up with three main points. Then reword the simple thesis statement so that it is an expanded thesis statement. It can again be marked as above.

Possible topics: aliens, backpacking, clothes, diet, exercise, Facebook, geeks, humour, identity theft, justice, karma, leadership, malls, nature, open relationships, pets, Quebec, reality TV, smartphones, taboos, university, vegans, Wikipedia, Xbox, youth, Zen Buddhism

EXERCISE 3.10

↻ Check answers to select questions

Evaluate the following introductory paragraphs according to the criteria discussed in the previous pages. Does each function as an effective introduction? Specifically consider the following:

- Which method(s) did the writer use to create reader interest (logical, dramatic, mixed)?
- Is the opening effective? What makes it effective (or not)?
- Identify the thesis statement. Is it interesting, specific, and manageable? Simple or expanded? Clearly written and well focused?
- Has the writer established credibility (shows knowledge, seems reliable/trustworthy)?
- Is the essay's main organizational pattern (e.g., chronology, compare and contrast, cause–effect, problem–solution, cost–benefit) apparent?

1. Clothing has always reflected the times, and a prime example is the bathing suit. From their most cumbersome and unattractive beginnings to the array of styles we see to-day, bathing suits have always reflected the lives of the women who wore them and the society in which they lived. In the last hundred years, roles of the sexes, improvements in women's rights, changes in the economy, and perceptions of body image have all played a part in bathing suit design.

   —Student writer Stephanie Keenlyside

2. The sport of bodybuilding has evolved considerably through the ages. Starting with muscle man competitions, it has now turned into what some would call a "freak show." Bodybuilding is a sport that requires its athletes to display their best aesthetically pleasing physiques on stage; they are judged according to specific criteria. Many factors leading up to the judging itself contribute to the outcome of the competition; for example, nutrition from whole foods and supplements, and low body fat percentage from proper diet and cardiovascular training all contribute to the success of the competitors. Steroids, too, are a major factor in professional events like the International Federation of Bodybuilding and Fitness (IFBB) competitions, where athletes are not tested for drug use. Anabolic steroid abuse plays a large role in bodybuilding, often resulting in adverse health effects.

   —Student writer Mike Allison

3. Newport High School, a large school in the city of Bellevue, Washington, was recently selected as a Blue Ribbon National School of Excellence by the U.S. Department of Education. Earning this prestigious award was the result of years of steady increase in SAT scores, ITED scores, and the number of AP tests taken by its students. Newport also offers the widest range of AP classes available to students in the Bellevue School District. How were they able to do this? It is simple: administrators worked hard to cut most of the fine arts programs to make room for a large number of academic classes. Many schools in the US and Canada today are pushing aside creative learning classes to make room for honours and advanced placement classes in an effort to boost their school's reputation. However, what is the cost to the students attending these schools? Fine arts are crucial to the development of the child's self-image, intellectual capacity, and mental health, and time must be allotted for such classes in high school.

   —Student writer Tyler Nicol

Evaluate the following introductions according to the criteria discussed above. For example, you could consider whether the openings are successful, whether the writer creates interest and appears credible, and whether the thesis statement is clear and focused. Then, rewrite them, correcting any weaknesses you find. You can use your own material or ideas, but try not to increase the length of the paragraphs (approximately 130 words).

EXERCISE 3.11

1. Something drastic needs to be done about obesity among teenagers today! Over the last decade, there has been a disturbing trend toward teenage obesity. Teenagers today would rather lodge themselves in front of the TV or play video games for hours on end than get some form of physical exercise. This problem becomes pronounced in high school because physical education is not compulsory in most schools. However, PE classes have a lot to offer. Participation can reduce the risk of heart failure, improve overall fitness, promote good health habits, improve self-discipline and skill development, boost self-confidence, increase academic performance, and enhance communication and co-operative skills. Obesity is an alarming trend among high school students today and should be a concern to both students and their parents.

2. Recently, there has been much concern over the increasing mortality in adult male worker honeybees. This phenomenon is referred to as "colony collapse disorder" and results in the death of colonies of honeybees over the winter. The disorder in managed honeybee colonies has been seen in the United States, Canada, and throughout Europe. Combined with the equally disturbing decline in the unmanaged bee population in several countries, this points to a large-scale problem. Humans rely on bee-pollinated crops for their food consumption; perhaps 30% of our foods are derived this way (Kearns & Inouye, 1997). In addition, the decline in the bee population could have a devastating effect on the natural ecosystem. Investigating the factors surrounding this decline is, therefore, of great concern to humans, and a way to fix this global problem needs to be found.

The Conclusion

Unlike the surprise ending of some fiction, the conclusion of an essay should be prepared for every step of the way—both by the introduction and by the points that are developed within the essay itself. So, a surprise ending to an essay indicates serious structural problems in the body. On the other hand, a conclusion that simply repeats the thesis statement is predictable and redundant, leaving the reader with the impression of a static, undeveloped argument.

In your conclusion, you should bring the reader back to reconsider the thesis statement in light of its development in the body paragraphs. The conclusion *recalls both* the thesis statement and the essay's supporting points.

Two Kinds of Conclusions

The conclusion can underscore the importance of the thesis in two ways: (1) it can reiterate the thesis using different words, perhaps by a call to action if you are arguing for a

A Closer Look

The Conclusion in Scholarly Writing

As in student essays, conclusions in scholarly essays

- Summarize the main points and findings
- Generalize about the topic or suggest applications/further study

Unlike conclusions in most student essays, they may

- Be longer than the introduction and well developed
- Mention other relevant studies and compare findings
- Make specific recommendations

In an essay describing an experiment, the conclusion will often be titled "Discussion" and begin by stating whether the hypothesis was proved; the researchers may also mention their study's limitations.

Recognizing the key features of scholarly introductions (p. 71) and conclusions will help you access information quickly and enable you to meet the challenges of reading at the university level.

> The conclusion reinforces the thesis statement in light of what has been discussed in the body paragraphs. A **CIRCULAR CONCLUSION** is mainly concerned with stressing the main point; a **SPIRAL CONCLUSION** looks beyond the thesis, applying it or suggesting further research.

Introduction

Conclusion

FIGURE 3.5
Introduction and Conclusion

practical change of some kind; (2) it can suggest a specific way that the thesis could be applied, ask further questions, or propose other ways of looking at the problem. These two strategies suggest two patterns:

- **circular conclusion**: recalls and reinforces the thesis
- **spiral conclusion**: recalls the thesis but also leads beyond it

A circular conclusion "closes the circle" by bringing the reader back to the starting point. It is particularly important that a circular conclusion does not simply repeat the thesis statement word for word but shows how it has been supported. A circular conclusion might reinforce the importance of the thesis by making an ethical or emotional appeal, for example, by reminding the reader that the action argued for in the thesis is morally the best choice. A spiral conclusion might point to implications of the thesis or suggest follow-up research.

Whereas the introduction often starts with the general and works toward the specific (the thesis statement)—the "inverted pyramid" structure—the conclusion often works from the specific to the general, as shown in figure 3.5.

Specific things to avoid in the conclusion are

- restating the thesis statement word for word
- mentioning a new point; conclusions should reword the old in an interesting way, not introduce something new
- giving an example or illustration to support your thesis; examples belong in your body paragraphs
- writing a conclusion that is longer than your introduction

Set your conclusion beside your introduction to check that it fulfills all the functions of a conclusion discussed above and relates to your introduction in a satisfactory way.

DEVELOPING YOUR ESSAY THROUGH SUBSTANTIAL PARAGRAPHS

Like introductions and conclusions, middle, or body, paragraphs benefit from being well planned in order to make your points accessible to your reader. Information can be broken down and presented through organizational or developmental methods, called **rhetorical patterns**. Well-developed paragraphs contain supporting information organized by consistent patterns. They not only expand on the main idea but also increase the essay's coherence.

The writer may choose to use one main pattern for the essay itself and other patterns in supporting roles. For example, an essay may set out to examine a cause–effect relationship but may use different methods from paragraph to paragraph to introduce, clarify, illustrate, or expand the main points.

Choosing the appropriate organizational patterns is one of the keys to writing a complete and interesting essay. Which patterns should you use for your essay?

Ultimately, your choice will depend on factors like your purpose in writing, topic, audience, kind of essay, and primary pattern. First, we will consider the many ways that writers can develop their key points through paragraphs that use different rhetorical patterns. However, because definition is an excellent starting point for many essays, using definition is discussed separately on page 93. Also, because organizing an essay by the compare and contrast patterns can be more complex than by other patterns, compare and contrast essays are discussed beginning on page 94.

> **RHETORICAL PATTERNS** are methods of breaking down information and presenting it to the reader.

Rhetorical Patterns

A topic may lend itself to a particular rhetorical pattern. In fact, in some cases, this pattern follows logically from the topic itself. For example, for the topic *Which is more important at college or university: acquiring skills or getting good grades?*, you might guess that the essay should use the compare and contrast pattern. For the topic *Solutions to the problem of homeless people*, you would know that the essay should be organized as problem–solution where you briefly describe the problem and then suggest ways to solve it. On the other hand, if the topic question were *Do you believe that homeless people today are a problem?* you might develop your essay in a similar way, but the *problem* of homelessness would be much more important than the solutions. Even if the topic determines the *main* way that the essay should be developed, there will likely be opportunities to consider different rhetorical patterns in individual paragraphs. These patterns are discussed below.

Analysis, meaning "separating" or "breaking down," is sometimes considered a distinct pattern. When you analyze, you take something apart in order to look at it closely. You analyze when you divide and classify, compare and contrast, consider problems and solutions, identify costs and benefits, and the like. Analysis is one of the keys to critical thinking.

One way to generate patterns of organization is to ask questions about the topic. Each question in table 3.1 leads to a particular method for developing a paragraph. If,

> **ANALYSIS** involves taking something apart in order to look at it closely.

TABLE 3.1 Rhetorical Patterns

QUESTION	RHETORICAL PATTERN
What is it?	definition
When did it occur?	chronology
How do you do it? *or* How does it work?	process analysis/"how to"
What kinds/categories are there?	classification/division
What causes/accounts for it? What is the result/effect?	cause–effect
How can it be shown?	example/illustration
How can it be (re)solved?	problem–solution
What are the advantages/disadvantages?	cost–benefit
How is it like something else?	analogy
How is it like and/or unlike something else?	compare and contrast

for example, your topic is *fast foods*, you could use any of the patterns below to help develop an essay on this topic, depending on the question you choose to focus on in each paragraph.

Definition: What Is It?

Define something in an essay in order to tell the reader precisely what you will be talking about. Defining a term, such as an abstract concept, can also help you understand your topic better and, perhaps, help you organize your main points. By *fast foods*, do you mean something like a Big Mac? Do you mean food that you can buy at a store that is quickly heated and eaten? Both could be considered fast foods, but they are not the same.

Chronology: When Did It Occur?

In the **chronological** pattern, you trace the topic's *development over time*. For example, when did fast foods begin, and when did they begin to affect people and society? Tracing the evolution of fast foods in the last 25 years might reveal that many fast-food restaurants have expanded their choices and reduced their portion sizes to counter the perception that these foods are unhealthy. Applying this rhetorical pattern, then, could also involve a cause–effect or problem–solution approach.

> Bacteria have plagued humanity since the beginning of the species. When an infection took hold of our distant ancestors, there was little

When you **DEFINE** something, you tell the reader what you will be talking about.

A **CHRONOLOGICAL** pattern traces the topic's development over time.

→ For more about definition in essays, see Using Definition in an Essay, page 93.

to do but wait and hope the body could fight off the microscopic enemy. It was in 1928 that Alexander Fleming made the discovery that revolutionized medicine, the antibiotic that became known as penicillin. Although it wasn't until 1942 that it could be used medically, it ushered in an era in which humans were no longer helpless victims of unseen bacteria. Over time, procedures from simple vaccinations to major surgeries became safe due to the ability to eliminate the risk of infection. Unfortunately, many of these advancements are threatened today as more bacteria are becoming resistant to traditional antibiotic treatment.

—Student writer Robert Flemmer

Process Analysis: How Does It Work?

Although **process analysis** usually appears in a fact-based essay that relates the chronological, step-by-step stages of a *process*, you can also use this rhetorical pattern in an argumentative essay—for example, if you wanted to convince a reader that one games system was easier to operate than another. This pattern can also be used for non-technical subjects—for example, "How to Impress Your Boss, or Professor, in Ten Easy Steps." Since the production of fast-food burgers is often a regimented process, you could describe this process from the time a customer places an order to the time it is handed to him or her.

> When you use **PROCESS ANALYSIS**, you give the step-by-step stages of a process.

Successful conflict resolution requires a willingness to listen, respect the other's point of view, and engage in a constructive dialogue. The first, crucial step is to define the problem in terms both parties will agree with. This is often the most challenging stage, which is why it is important to speak neutrally and to use "I messages" to communicate. In the next stage, consider solutions without judging their merit. When both participants have given input, objectively discuss the most feasible options, arriving at one acceptable to both (it will probably not be one heavily favoured by one or the other). In implementing the solution, stress the positives and encourage actions in which members have equal responsibilities. Finally, be prepared to reevaluate and readjust goals and responsibilities in the interests of a long-term solution.

—Student writer Drew Dawson

Classification/Division: What Kinds Are There?

In **classification**, you begin with a large number of items—for example, commonly known members of the animal kingdom—which you organize into more manageable groups: mammals, birds, fish, reptiles, and amphibians. Each category, such as mammals, could in turn be organized into still smaller units, such as rodents, primates, and carnivores. Fast-food burgers can easily be classified as well: hamburgers, chicken burgers, fish burgers, veggie burgers.

> When you use **CLASSIFICATION**, you organize items into manageable groups.

When you use **DIVISION**, you break a topic down into parts.

In **division**, you are more concerned with how the individual parts relate to the whole. You break a topic down into parts in order to better understand or explain the whole (the topic). For example, to illustrate how essay structure works, you can divide the essay into introduction, body paragraphs, and conclusion. In her essay on the detection of habitable planets outside the solar system, student writer Carly Morgan discusses three main detection methods:

> The first is direct imaging, which is ideal as we are able to see the planet itself, but this method is rarely successful. In the radical velocity method, the Doppler shift of light from the star can be used to detect an orbiting planet; it can be analyzed to identify a red or blue shift, which would indicate a planet of substantial mass causing gravitational effects on the star. The transit method utilizes NASA's spacecraft Kepler, which continuously monitors the brightness of 157,000 stars to see if the star's light dims; if it does, it could indicate a planet passing in front of the star (Marcy, 2010, p. 435).

Cause–Effect: What Is the Cause? Or, What Is the Effect?

When you use **CAUSE–EFFECT**, you consider the reasons for or consequences of something.

You can use the **cause–effect** pattern to organize an entire essay or in one or more paragraphs to analyze a main point. When you deal with causes, you consider the reasons for or antecedents of an occurrence; effects are essentially results or consequences. For example, since fast food has often been blamed for obesity, you could look at studies that link obesity (effect) to unhealthy diets (cause). Cause–effect studies are particularly common in the sciences and social sciences. The following excerpt from an introduction shows that the essay will focus on a controversial psychological hypothesis; a reader could infer that causes and effects will be discussed:

> The cathartic model of anger postulates that when people do not express their anger, feelings of frustration build up until they are released in some way. If the release fails to occur, the individual could explode, much like a balloon that fills until it bursts. The theory of catharsis has been debated for decades, and researchers are split in their findings. Does the act of expressing our anger reduce our feelings of aggression, or does venting make us more susceptible to further aggression when frustrating situations arise?
>
> —Student writer Karen Lacoursiere

Example/Illustration: How Can It Be Shown?

When you use **EXAMPLES**, you give specific instances or occurrences to help a reader understand or relate to a point.

Using a concrete **example** is an excellent way to support a point and clarify an abstract idea. This rhetorical pattern can be combined with other methods, such as cause–effect, cost–benefit, or compare and contrast. For example, if you were using the cause–effect method to develop the point that fast foods save valuable time (an effect), you might discuss the convenience of drive-through lanes at fast-food restaurants as one example; another example might be the use of an assembly line to prepare the food. Examples are indispensable in most writing and may consist of brief expansions of a point or more developed explanations. Student writer Lindsay Banh gives examples of social media before expanding on a key example supporting her claim about a rapidly developing Internet phenomenon:

> Social media websites like YouTube, Facebook, Twitter, Instagram, and Tumblr have enabled users to participate in national and international events, such as the 2008 and 2012 US presidential elections. More recently, users of social media have found a way to target audiences to bring awareness to issues of importance and achieve justice. In 2012, a documentary about the atrocities of Joseph Kony and his Lord's Resistance Army went viral. The International Criminal Court had been unsuccessfully trying to prosecute Kony but was hampered by the fact that his operations took place in remote and impoverished regions of Africa, not in major cities. However, within four days of its release, the 30-minute video *The Invisible Children* had generated more than 38 million views on YouTube and became a trending sensation over Twitter (CBC News World).

Problem–Solution: How Can It Be (Re)Solved?

The **problem–solution** pattern could focus on a problem, a solution to a problem, or both a problem and its solution. For example, a problem with fast foods is their dubious nutritional value. After stating this problem, you could propose ways that fast foods could be made healthier, offering solutions. In his critique of the global food system and its polarizing effect on the "have-nots," A. Haroon Akram-Lodhi discusses both problems and solutions; however, in the following passage, he stresses the need for a solution:

> When you use **PROBLEM– SOLUTION**, you analyze a problem, solutions to the problem, or both.

> Together we must end a global food regime in which one person's inexhaustible cornucopia requires the creation of a community of hunger. . . . Together we must build a food system where everyone can get the food they need. The world's small-scale peasant farmers and landless waged workers want . . . to be able to feed themselves, securely, without having to submit themselves, like vassals, to the multifariously macabre agreements and arrangements of the market. They are hungry for change. We, who are the world's wealthy, have to imaginatively transform and inventively revolutionize what we expect of our food. We have to be hungry for change.
>
> —Akram-Lodhi, A. Haroon. *Hungry for Change: Farmers, Food Justice and the Agrarian Question*. Halifax: Fernwood Publishing, 2013. Print. (6–7)

Cost–Benefit: What Are the Advantages and Disadvantages?

Analyzing something often involves weighing the advantages and disadvantages, the pros and cons. **Cost–benefit analysis** can be applied to many topics as few things in life come without some costs. You could apply cost–benefit analysis to fast foods, for example, by focusing on the individual, community, or perhaps even global costs or benefits. In an expository essay, cost–benefit analysis involves the objective weighing of pluses and minuses.

> When you use **COST–BENEFIT ANALYSIS,** you weigh the advantages and disadvantages of something.

However, if you were *arguing* that the benefits were more important than the costs, you might well consider the costs first and *then* the benefits, leaving the strongest argument for the last. In the passage below, student writer Kristen Carlton takes the opposite stance, first mentioning the benefits before discussing the costs. She uses cost–benefit analysis to introduce her topic, positive psychology:

> Since the founding of psychology by Wilhelm Wendt in 1879, the field has accomplished major achievements. Several disorders listed in the most recent edition of the *DSM*, the manual of the American Psychological Association, are either treatable or curable. A science of mental illness was created, in layperson's terms, to make people less miserable. However, with the good came the bad. Psychologists and psychiatrists began focusing mainly on the negative in human nature that needed treatment; psychology had forgotten about improving normal lives. Treating mental illness was not all to be done: surpassing everyday potential was possible. A new branch of psychology, positive psychology, has begun to emerge over the past decade. This new scientific method investigates positive human development, breaking away from the traditional focus on human failure (Gable & Heidt, 2005).

Analogy: How Is It Like Something Else?

An **analogy** or **metaphor** is a comparison between one object and a second object that, except for the point of comparison, is unlike the first one. Analogies and metaphors help the reader better understand the original object. For example, you could compare fast foods to the fast pace of society itself.

Analogies are *logical* comparisons and should not strain the reader's credulity. However, a writer might deliberately use an analogy to surprise the reader and enable him or her to visualize a situation. The author below uses a colourful analogy to appeal to his audience, many of whom will have seen or know about the movie he refers to:

> Watching a fight in the National Hockey League is reminiscent of the 2002 movie *Gladiator* in which two people fight to the death while the crowd yells from above for blood. Although fighters in the NHL are obviously not trying to maim or kill their opponents, the reaction of the crowd as they stand, raise their arms, and scream in unison is similar. Fights in the NHL serve primarily as a crowd pleaser and an outlet for spectators' frustrations.
>
> —Student writer Erik Lehman

Compare and Contrast: How Is It Like and/or Unlike Something Else?

To **compare and contrast** is to systematically identify similarities and differences between two things. When you compare and contrast, you begin by finding logical bases of comparison and then analyze similarities and/or differences. In arguing that one hamburger restaurant is better than another, for example, you could use as bases of comparison their prices, their food quality, their hygienic values, and the friendliness of their staff.

When you use **ANALOGY**, you logically compare one object to another one in order to help the reader understand the first object.

When you use a **METAPHOR**, you compare one object to another one not usually associated with the first one.

When you **COMPARE AND CONTRAST**, you consider similarities and/or differences between two things.

→ For more about the compare and contrast pattern and an example of a compare and contrast essay, see page 94.

In the following paragraph, the writer announces the rhetorical pattern in the topic sentence; however, she uses other patterns as well. Along with the main rhetorical pattern, identify two other patterns in the paragraph.

> Vegetarianism, derived from a Latin word meaning "to enliven," was practised in ancient Greece as early as the sixth century BCE by the Pythagoreans, and its reputation has spread to many other countries since then. It is a way of life in China, India, Japan, Pakistan, and even in North America with more than 14 million vegetarians. Since its beginnings, many well-known people have been non-meat-eaters, including Socrates, Plato, Leonardo da Vinci, Charles Darwin, Thomas Edison, Albert Einstein, and Isaac Newton. The term "vegetarian" refers to someone who does not eat any flesh; however, there are many varieties of vegetarianism. If one eats no flesh (red meat, poultry, fish), but consumes dairy and egg products, one is said to be a lacto-ovo vegetarian (the most popular type in North America). Pesco-vegetarians eat seafood but avoid red meat and poultry. Vegans are "strict vegetarians," who not only avoid consuming any type of animal but also avoid anything manufactured from animals (soap, leather, wool, honey, gelatine). Any form of vegetarianism is a healthy way of living, which not only benefits humans but also benefits animals and the planet itself.
>
> —Student writer Jessica Charbonneau

EXERCISE 3.12

↻ Check answers to select questions

→ Development through narration and description, less commonly used in academic essays, is discussed in chapter 2 on page 47.

Find two body paragraphs from one student or professional/academic essay in this textbook. (Do not use an introduction or conclusion.) Identify the rhetorical pattern used in each paragraph and analyze the effectiveness of the paragraph's development. Try to come up with at least three relevant points for each paragraph.

EXERCISE 3.13

Below are 10 general topics. Using two different organizational methods per topic, come up with two topic sentences for each topic. Here are some examples using the topic *rap music*:

EXERCISE 3.14

1. *Cause–Effect*: Rap music, with its reliance on ever-changing slang, has expanded people's vocabulary; for instance, one's boyfriend is called one's "boo."
2. *Chronology*: The style of rap music has evolved considerably since it first gained popularity with North American youth in the early 1990s.
3. *Problem–Solution*: It may seem somewhat ironic, but it is possible that many of the problems addressed in rap lyrics could be solved through this very same medium.
4. *Compare and Contrast*: Rap and hip hop music of the late 1980s and early 1990s, with its offensive lyrics and radical counter-cultural appeal, can be compared in terms of its sociological implications to the rock'n'roll revolution of the late 1960s and early 1970s.
5. *Cause–Effect*: Rap music has been used as a vehicle for an oppressed minority to get its voice heard.

6. *Process*: To create rap music you need a DJ to provide the beats by mixing records, and an MC who takes the beats and contributes the vocals to make the finished product.
7. *Classification*: There are many different forms of rap; these include hip hop, hard core, and R&B.
8. *Definition and Division*: Rap is a unique form of music that is built around heavy bass beats mixed with sharp, quick lyrics. There is a whole spectrum of rap music, ranging from slow love ballads to fast-paced dance songs.
9. *Cost–Benefit*: Though rap may lead young people to openly and healthily question authority and the status quo, it can lead some adolescents to commit acts of violence against society.
10. *Analogy*: Rap can be compared to the insistent and repetitive chants of an evangelistic preacher.

Topics:

alternative schooling	privacy
animal rights	public speaking
eating disorders	same-sex marriage
evolution	sports violence
organ transplants	stress

EXERCISE 3.15

Collaborative Exercise: Providing Support

Taking one of the claims for each statement in exercise 3.2 earlier in the chapter, determine how you would most effectively support it in the body of an essay. This exercise could take the form of a group discussion, or your group could write out a strategic approach, referring as specifically as possible to those parts under Support in figure 3.2.

Strategies to Consider

Organization of Evidence: Which patterns of organization/development would you likely use? Which could be used?

Kinds of Evidence: Which kinds of evidence would most effectively back up your claim?

Credibility: Which of the three categories of credibility—knowledge, reliability, fairness—seem the most important? Why? What general or specific strategies could you use to ensure your support is credible?

→ See Kinds of Evidence (p. 53) and Credibility (p. 56).

ESSAYS USING A PRIMARY PATTERN

Primary versus Secondary Patterns

If you use one of the patterns above as the primary method to support your thesis statement, you will likely use other rhetorical patterns in supporting roles. Some are almost always used to organize paragraphs and rarely as a controlling pattern for the entire essay. It is difficult to write an essay using *only*, or even primarily, example/illustration or analogy.

Using Definition in an Essay

In an argumentative essay, defining something is often the first stage of an argument in which you go on to develop your thesis statement through means other than definition. On the other hand, a definition essay can expand and elaborate on a subject, using a variety of rhetorical patterns to do so.

When you use definition as a starting point, your success in getting a reader to agree with your definition will help establish your credibility and, in this way, strengthen your argument. Defining something also enables you to set the terms on which you want your argument to rest: successful definition enables you to take control of a controversial or abstract topic.

Although definition in an argumentative essay can be effective, it is often an essential part of an expository essay. Essays in the natural sciences and social sciences often begin by defining terms that the writer will employ throughout the essay. It may be crucial for the writer to establish the sense or connotation of terms that have been used in a variety of ways in the writer's discipline (see the cloning example below). An academic text—above all, an introductory textbook—often includes a glossary or index of common terms that is designed to make it easier to apply terms correctly.

A reader often needs to know exactly how you are going to use a term, as definitions can change over time and may depend on cultural, social, or other factors. For example, the way you would define *privacy* today would likely be different from the way it would have been defined 25 years ago, partly because of technologies that have made it easier for others to access personal information.

In the examples below, the writer defines a concept, consumerism, in order to use it in a specific way in his or her essay. Each definition is affected by the writer's purpose. In the first example, the writer will argue that consumerism plays a negative role in society. In the second example, taken from the introduction to an expository essay, the writer defines consumerism as a basic economic principle. She then connects the definition to one aspect of consumerism—consumer protection, her topic.

> Our lives today are defined by consumerism and revolve around it. We seem to constantly be purchasing or planning to purchase an item that will somehow make our lives easier or more enjoyable. Indeed, consumerism is the culture that promotes excessive shopping and buying without considering the use or importance of the products we buy.
>
> —Student writer Rob McDannold

> Most people use money as an exchange between goods and services, and it is essential to understand one's rights as a customer. Nowadays, most products require labelling because they inform the customers about the contents and specifications of the product, giving customers the right to choose between different products and not be affected by misleading advertising. Consumerism is a modern movement to help protect the consumer against useless, inferior, or dangerous products, misleading advertisement, unfair pricing, and other important concerns.
>
> —Student writer Kelly Kao

In argument, a definition can set the terms on which your argument will rest. In exposition, a reader often needs to know how you are going to use a term, as definitions can change over time and may depend on cultural, social, or other factors.

A writer may sometimes give a broad or common definition to lead up to the definition most pertinent to the essay. It would have been misleading if the writer of the paragraph below had cited only the broad definition and not defined the specific way he is using the term *cloning*.

> In the past decade, cloning has been scrutinized by the media, yet cloning has been going on in nature since the origins of life. By definition, clones are "a group of two or more individuals with an identical genetic makeup derived, by asexual reproduction, from a single common parent or ancestor" (Haran, 2008, p. 13); cutting a worm in half, in fact, creates a clone. However, for the purpose of this essay, "cloning" will refer to the artificial production of a genetically identical cell or tissue. Cloning is broken into two main categories: reproductive cloning, the production of a whole duplicate being, and therapeutic cloning, creating cloned tissue from stem cells harvested from a cloned embryo.
>
> —Student writer Chris Batt

Definition is a fundamental part of many of the academic essays you will read, and grasping a definition can help you know how to read the essay itself. In the following paragraph from the introduction of an academic essay, the writers use detailed criteria established by a creditable organization to help explain the methodology of their own essay.

> According to the Association for Experiential Education (AEE), experiential education is an educational process whereby a learner "constructs knowledge, develops skill, and clarifies values from direct experiences and reflection on that experience" (AEE, 2007). Principles associated with this definition include involving a learner on multiple levels (e.g., intellectually, socially, and emotionally); having a learner contemplate and examine her or his personal values; encouraging a learner to become aware of her or his own biases, judgements, and preconceptions, and to reflect critically on these; and promoting a personal learning process that has implications for future learning (AEE, 2007). The educator's role is to provide experiences that facilitate learning and are congruent with these principles.
>
> —Rye, B. J., Elmslie, P., & Chalmers, A. (2007). Meeting a transsexual person: Experience within a classroom setting. *Canadian On-Line Journal of Queer Studies in Education*, *3*(1).

The Compare and Contrast Essay

Compare and contrast can be used as the main rhetorical pattern in either an argumentative or an expository essay. As compare and contrast essays can be challenging to organize, consider using the three-step approach:

1. Ensure that the topics you want to compare are, indeed, comparable. For example, it is not possible to compare the health-care system in the United States to the educational system in Canada. While it might be possible to compare the health-care systems of the two countries, such a topic might be too broad to be manageable.

However, it might be manageable to compare the health-care systems of two Canadian provinces.

2. After you have determined that the topics are comparable and that the essay is manageable, choose two or three bases of comparison for the main points of your essay, ensuring that each basis is logical and can be applied to both subjects being compared.

3. To ensure that the essay is clearly laid out with the points easy to follow, you can choose between two organizational methods, the block or point-by-point method.

Block and Point-by-Point Methods

In the *block method*, you consider all the points that relate to your first subject of comparison, which becomes your first block of material. Next, consider all the points as they apply to the second subject of comparison, your second block. When you compare the second subject, you use the same order as you did with the first.

In the *point-by-point method*, you consider one basis of comparison as it applies to each subject and continue until you have considered all the bases of comparison. In the following outline, *A* and *B* represent your subjects, or what you are comparing, and the numbers represent your points, or bases of comparison:

Block Method

A: Subject of comparison
       1. basis of comparison
       2. basis of comparison
       3. basis of comparison
B: Subject of comparison
       1. basis of comparison
       2. basis of comparison
       3. basis of comparison

Point-by-Point Method

1. Basis of comparison
       A: subject of comparison
       B: subject of comparison
2. Basis of comparison
       A: subject of comparison
       B: subject of comparison
3. Basis of comparison
       A: subject of comparison
       B: subject of comparison

Below, the two methods are applied to the identical topic and bases of comparison.

Topic: Compare and contrast benefits of walking to benefits of cycling.

Block Method

A: Cycling
       1. transportation
       2. exercise

        3. health

        4. cost

  B: Walking

        1. transportation

        2. exercise

        3. health

        4. cost

Point-by-Point Method

1. Transportation

      A: cycling

      B: walking

2. Exercise

      A: cycling

      B: walking

3. Health

      A: cycling

      B: walking

4. Cost

      A: cycling

      B: walking

Sample Essay: Compare and Contrast

After reading this essay, answer the questions that follow, which focus on audience, paragraph development, and essay organization.

For another example of a compare and contrast essay, see "Why Politicians Should Be More Like Professors" in chapter 5 (p. 151).

SAMPLE PROFESSIONAL ESSAY

House Plants Are Better Than Dogs

by Jeff Halperin

[1]   Some people believe that a home isn't a home without a dog. To hear these people talk, you'd think that shedded hair, sharp fangs, and crap on carpets are trivial matters. They're barking money pits, these dogs, and for too long we've been under the false impression that they're better than houseplants. Let's investigate.

[2]   Unlike dogs, plants will forever maintain their poise no matter how many times you ring the doorbell. Calm, cool, and collected, the houseplant is a model of patience and even temperament. They bow down to nobody, see no race or class. Perfectly reflecting the modern zeitgeist, plants represent the highest ideal of egalitarian tolerance. Dogs, on the other hand, are famous for attacking mailmen—an obvious gesture of class warfare.

[3] You can be sure plants won't harass company at your next dinner party, but don't be fooled into thinking they're entirely dormant. They grow in response to Bach fugues, which would be a compliment to their ear, too, if they had one.

[4] In light of nuclear disaster and the rising cost of gas, there's a big hubbub about how best to harness the sun's energy. But plants already settled this millions of years ago. Living off the sun's rays, plants are their own solar panels. Scientifically way ahead of us and financially more responsible, plants don't need government handouts for their energy exchange program. Shame dogs don't eat rain and sunshine, eh?

[5] It's not all economics. Plants give back oxygen without even being asked. That is a real kindness because you can hardly overstate the importance of oxygen. Plants can't help but be givers. In comparison, dogs only give you something with the understanding that you'll throw it back to them over and over in an endlessly futile cycle. Also, dogs need to go to school just to figure out how to sit down or play dead. Plants don't need to be taught to play dead. They're autodidacts.

[6] Admittedly, there's something to be said for a dog that quietly nestles on your lap after a hard day's work. But ask yourself: has your dog signed a contract indicating he won't revert to pissy pre-housebroken days? What if some horrible canine violence on TV suddenly provokes him and he becomes a biter? Plants offer unrivalled peace of mind. You can take plants at their word. Nothing can make them bite you or crap under your bed.

[7] Finally, after years of attachment, your plant will grow and so will your pleasure with it. With casual care, your plant can actually outlive you. No matter how much you care for your dog, it will end up dead in a crumpled heap on the floor. If you have kids, they'll cry. All's well that ends well, but it never ends well with dogs.

[8] Yes, dogs can be sweet, cuddly, and affectionate—they aren't wholly without commendable traits, even though it's much, much better to get a houseplant. But in all fairness, at least dogs are a cheaper, lower maintenance, and cuter alternative to getting a baby.

Source: *The Walrus*, 21 July 2011. Reprinted by permission of the author.

EXERCISE 3.16

1. Briefly analyze the essay's introduction. Consider the effectiveness of the opening and the thesis statement. Is Halperin successful in establishing his approach to the topic of dogs versus houseplants?
2. How could you characterize the writer's tone? Give specific examples. How could awareness of tone affect your reading of the essay?
3. Analyze one of the body paragraphs, using criteria discussed in this and/or previous chapters.
4. Identify the compare and contrast method Halperin uses and the bases for comparison. You can use the appropriate diagrammatic model on page 95, above, to show method and bases for comparison.
5. Write an essay of 500 words (roughly the length of the essay above) in which you compare two subjects not usually compared. You can write argumentatively, claiming that one side is better than the other (see chapter 5), or explain both sides without arguing for one or the other.

CHAPTER SUMMARY

Chapter 3 provided you with helpful guidelines for planning your essay, as well as ensuring that your paragraphs are unified, coherent, and well developed. The analytical model enables you to look at the essay as a complete entity with interrelated parts. To successfully support a claim, you need to consider what kinds of evidence to use and how to organize the evidence. Your credibility as a writer depends on more than just your knowledge about your topic: your reliability and fairness should come across to a reader. Introductions and conclusions should also be planned to satisfy readers' expectations and convey relevant information in an appealing way. In planning well-developed paragraphs, you can use a variety of rhetorical patterns; definitions and examples of common patterns are given.

Responding to Texts: Summaries and Analyses

4

Your assignments will sometimes require you to study an essay by using critical thinking, organizational, and writing skills. Two common forms this can take are the summary and the critical analysis, each of which requires a unique approach: while a summary represents another writer's ideas, a critical analysis examines how the essay was put together and the author's use of reason. In this chapter, you will learn how to write effective summaries and critical analyses, practical skills that will enhance your general thinking, reading, and writing abilities throughout your academic career.

LEARNING OBJECTIVES

- to understand the value of summarizing in developing your comprehension, prioritizing, and concision skills

- to learn how to summarize by identifying the main points of the source text and putting them in your own words

- to apply strategies for writing effective précis summaries

- to understand the purpose of a critical analysis and the ways it differs from a rhetorical analysis and a critical response

- to study the ways a text can be broken down and the strategies to use when writing your critical analysis

- to appreciate the importance of referring specifically to the source text to support your claims about its strengths, weaknesses, and significance

SUMMARIES, ANALYSIS, AND RESEARCH PAPERS

In a **SYNTHESIS** you "put together," such as combining the findings of sources in a research essay.

Three common assignments in university courses are summaries, critical analyses, and research papers. As summaries and critical analyses are focused on source texts, they differ from research papers (discussed in chapter 7), whose main purpose is to investigate how issues or problems have been dealt with by experts. Although a research paper uses analysis, it also uses **synthesis**; that is, you "put together" your essay by combining your own words and critical-thinking skills with the findings of reliable sources to help guide you to a conclusion about the issue or problem.

Summaries, critical analyses, and research papers vary in their purpose, audience/ style, structure, and typical activities, as shown in table 4.1; each also highlights

TABLE 4.1 Three Common Reading/Writing Assignments

TYPE OF ASSIGNMENT	PURPOSE	AUDIENCE/STYLE	TYPICAL ACTIVITIES AND STRUCTURE
précis summary	• to demonstrate comprehension, concision, and ability to identify main points	• writer must use own words and write clearly so a reader unfamiliar with the original text could understand its essence	• scanning and focused reading • comprehension • rephrasing and using synonyms • inferring main points • follows order of points in source text
critical analysis	• to examine how a text is constructed and whether the argument is effective • to assess text's importance/ influence • to better understand types of texts, their uses, and their effectiveness	• written in formal style/objective voice for audience knowledgeable about rhetorical practices and strategies	• focused reading • comprehension and critical thinking • analyzing and evaluating used throughout • stating main features of source text in thesis • breaks down text to provide support for thesis • focuses on source text
research paper	• to answer a question, solve a problem, test a hypothesis, or interpret a text • to better understand the research process and evaluate sources	• written in formal style/objective voice for audience of varying interest in and knowledge of the topic • may include jargon (specialized terms and concepts)	• scanning potential sources • focused reading for main ideas/ findings • synthesizing used throughout • using logical order of points to arrive at conclusion • uses fact-based thesis • evaluates sources • examines issue/problem/ hypothesis

specific writing skills. However, selective reading is crucial in each. The summary and critical analysis are discussed below. A full treatment of the research essay is given in chapter 7.

SUMMARY: THE PRÉCIS

The Value of a Summary

In contrast to many other writing tasks, in a **summary** you do not interpret or comment on the source text. When you summarize, you include the main points and discard less important information. A précis is a specific kind of summary. It contains the main ideas of a complete work, or a major section of a work, and can be thought of as a miniaturized version of its longer, more detailed original.

Writing full-length summaries sharpens both your reading and writing skills. As you read a work for summarization, your first concern is with its meaning. A summary may be unclear because the writer began summarizing without clearly understanding the source. As always, clear thinking helps produce clear writing. The best way to test the effectiveness of a summary you've written is to have others read it and ask them if they can grasp the essence of the original from your summary. If they cannot do this, you need to work on clarity and precision.

However, a précis summary does more than test comprehension skills. To summarize successfully, you must distinguish the more important ideas from the less important ones. To help you see the relationship between main points and sub-points, it can be useful to make a two-level outline before you begin writing your summary.

Finally, a précis must be written concisely, using simple constructions and plain language. Stress basic sentence elements, like nouns and verbs. If you waste words, your summary will be inefficient, but if you write concisely, you can include more points from the original, making your summary better than one that includes fewer points.

Pointers for Précis Writing

A précis

- is accurate and retains the essence of the original
- includes the main ideas
- includes the most important developments of these ideas if there is room
- omits examples and illustrations, unless very important
- follows the same order of ideas as the original
- does not add anything to the original
- uses concise prose
- is in your own words but may retain significant words from the original; *place quotation marks* around significant words, phrases, or sentences that you cite directly
- uses brief transitions where necessary to connect ideas, but avoids wordy phrases—e.g., "the writer goes on to say that . . . "
- is approximately 20–25 per cent as long as the original

> When you **SUMMARIZE**, you include the main points and discard less important information.

> See Organization, chapter 2, page 38.

> As important as it is to develop summarizing skills, in most writing, summarizing should supplement, not replace, analysis. For example, a succinct summary of the source text in a critical analysis will set the stage for your own analysis. In a literary analysis, plot summary should also be kept to a minimum.

A Closer Look

Specialized Kinds of Summaries

The précis summary is only one kind of summary. In your reading you may encounter other kinds; you may even be asked to write one or more of them as part of your coursework:

An **ABSTRACT** is a condensed summary used in many scholarly essays and placed before the study begins.

A **LITERATURE REVIEW** is a condensed survey of articles that appears in scholarly introductions.

An **ANNOTATED BIBLIOGRAPHY** is an expanded bibliography that includes summaries and appraisals of key works on the topic.

- An **abstract** is a condensed summary used in many scholarly essays; it is placed before the study begins, is written by the study's author, and includes the study's purpose, methods, and results.
- A **literature review** is a condensed survey of articles on one topic that appears in the introduction of many scholarly essays and informs the reader about previous research.
- An **annotated bibliography** is an expanded bibliography that includes not only the information of standard bibliographies but also brief summaries of related works and, sometimes, appraisals of each work.

Rhetorical Stance

If the essay you are summarizing aims to persuade its reader rather than to present factual information, you may need to acknowledge its rhetorical purpose by separating fact from opinion. For example, one professional writer begins an essay in this way:

> In the course of two years' research for a book on how we think about pain, I've spoken to neurologists, doctors, artists, therapists of every stripe, as well as psychologists—the frontline workers. And frankly, I preferred the people selling healing magnets to most of the psychologists. They were bad communicators. They couldn't make eye contact. They seemed more interested in certain folds in the brain than in helping human beings cope with pain.
>
> —Marni Jackson, "Every Breath You Take: A Former Hospital Pain Specialist Puts His Faith in the Powers of Meditation," *Maclean's* (16 August 1999).

If you did not acknowledge the writer's words as opinion, you could seriously misrepresent her:

Misleading: Psychologists generally communicate badly and are shifty-eyed.

However, you could acknowledge the author's rhetorical purpose this way:

Marni Jackson preferred "the people selling healing magnets" to the majority of psychologists she spoke to.

In expressing rhetorical purpose through verbs like *believes* or *argues*, you show the writer's attitude toward the subject. But do not characterize the writer's stance as negative or infer a bias. Summaries should *represent*, not judge. Therefore, choose your words carefully.

Précis Planning

You can summarize using three steps:

1. Read the work for the first time to learn its purpose, thesis, intended audience, rhetorical stance, etc.
2. When you reread it, note its major points, along with the most important sub-points and/or key examples, and from these points write an outline. Look up any words you're unsure about; remember that accuracy is essential. Make notes that might help you clarify the writer's ideas, rephrasing important content.
3. Following your outline, write a summary that includes all the main points. If you have room for more than the main points, include the most important sub-points to reach the required word range. When you've completed the first draft, refer to the checklist on page 101 before revising. Importantly, ensure that the summary is essentially in your own words and that you have put quotation marks around any words or phrases taken directly from the source.

Where to Find Main Ideas

Scan the essay, looking for important ideas in the most likely places: the thesis statement at the end of the introduction and the main ideas in topic sentences of major paragraphs, often the first sentence of a paragraph. However, not all topic sentences are the first sentences of paragraphs—indeed, not all paragraphs have topic sentences. Furthermore, not every paragraph will contain a major idea, so there will not necessarily be a predictable relation between the original's number of paragraphs and the number of points in your outline.

In scanning *paragraphs*, remember that main points can usually be connected to the thesis. In scanning *sentences*, look for main ideas in independent clauses.

Sample Précis

In the example below, the summary writer made notes in the margin, which focus on identifying main points. From these notes and the outline, the final summary was created; it appears on page 105 and is 20 per cent of the original (132 words). If you were writing a critical analysis of this essay, the notes would look different, focused more on rhetorical strategies, such as style, tone, language, and argument.

> *Rhetorical purpose* refers to the reason for writing. In argument, the rhetorical purpose is usually to convince the reader to change his or her mind.
>
> When summarizing, be especially careful *not* to
> - become too general or vague; be *specific* but *not detailed*
> - distort the writer's meaning in any way; use *your words* but *the writer's ideas*

SAMPLE PROFESSIONAL ESSAY

Biodiversity

by Candace Savage

[1]   "Biodiversity" is an attempt to invoke the splendour of the living world with a single word. Just six syllables but they flood the mind with images: fish, bright as petals, dart

The images are designed to grab our attention, but the word "biodiversity" is obviously important, stressed throughout the essay and mentioned in the conclusion.

The main idea in this paragraph elaborates on the first paragraph. The writer stresses the wonders of life-forms.

She introduces the problem, humanity's threat to biodiversity. She begins analyzing the problem in the next paragraph.

She divides biodiversity into three different measures, each of which is developed in the rest of the essay. Each measure could be considered an important point and should be included in the summary. The statistics in this paragraph are detail and should not be included.

This sentence contains the most important idea, not the rhetorical question in the first sentence.

Although the first sentence introduces the topic, the main idea in this paragraph is in the last sentence, which makes a specific statement about the loss of genetic variability. The detail in the paragraph builds toward this statement, which is directly connected to the essay's thesis.

From the phrasing and placement at the end of the essay, it is obvious that this is a main point: the important idea that humans and their future are at stake whenever species survival is threatened.

Here the writer makes a plea for biodiversity.

through a coral reef; herds of caribou stream across frozen lakes; bees thrum, wings beat, buds burst with greenery. This miracle planet teems with living things.

[2]   The United Nations-declared International Year of Biodiversity extends an invitation to celebrate this panoply of protoplasmic inventions, the only life, so far as we know, in the cosmos. Think of it: an infinity of rock and dust, and in the midst of nothingness, one mid-sized blue planet, with more than 1,400,000 different species squiggling around on it. Although it is difficult to be certain, life is probably richer and more diverse at present than at any other time in the long history of Earth. Lucky us, to be alive at just the right moment.

[3]   If only our luck could hold a little longer. If only we didn't know that the runaway demands of a single species, Homo sapiens, are increasingly being met at the expense of the intricate life going on around us.

[4]   Biodiversity is usually assessed at three conceptually separate but intersecting layers, using different measures. At present, all of the measures suggest we are headed for trouble. Take the number of species. According to the International Union for Conservation of Nature's Red List of Threatened Species, 12 percent of all the birds in the world, 21 percent of mammals and 30 percent of amphibians are in imminent danger of going extinct. A majority of predatory marine fish are also on the brink. What does it do to our hearts to know that our burgeoning population and gotta-have-it entitlements have already pushed more than 17,291 species to the limits?

[5]   Will life go on without the Pacific population of the basking shark or the spiky blossoms of the pink milkwort, both endangered in Canada? Without a doubt, it will. Extinction is as inevitable as death and just as natural. You could even see it as a good thing, since it opens up space for new species to evolve. But when extinction outpaces innovation, the losses quickly mount. Food webs are weakened and genetic resources are lost, with consequences that reverberate long into the future.

[6]   This brings us to the second layer of biodiversity assessment: genetic variability. With rare exceptions, every organism is genetically unique so the more individuals a species can muster, the more genetic resources it has. Similarly, local populations often become adapted to local conditions (wild roses that grow on the prairies are subtly different than those on the forest fringe) and each variation adds to the species' genetic vocabulary. The more genetically diverse a species is—the more possibilities are encoded in its DNA—the more likely it is to respond successfully to future change. Tragically, the World Wildlife Fund's Living Planet Index indicates that, globally, vertebrate species are diminishing in both population and range, an indirect indication that their genetic inheritance is eroding.

[7]   The cumulative effect of these losses, whether of species or genes, is to reduce the adaptive capacity—the creativity—of the living world. It is at this third level of complexity, where we take in the whole, wild rumpus of life at a single glance, that the importance of biodiversity to humankind becomes most vivid. Ecosystems, such as forests, rangelands and rivers, all provide life-sustaining goods and services to humanity, including pollination, fertile soil, clean water, pure food and a breathable atmosphere, to say nothing of inspiration and spiritual renewal. The more species that can fulfill each of these functions, the more secure our future will be. We don't even want to think about the corollary.

[8]   Protecting biodiversity will bring solace not only to us but to our children and theirs for generations to come. Let the beauty slip away? Leave a legacy of ruin and loss? Just six syllables: It's not an option.

Source: "Biodiversity: What is Biodiversity" by Candace Savage appeared in *Canadian Geographic*, June 2010. Reprinted by permission of the Author.

SAMPLE STUDENT SUMMARY

Summary of "Biodiversity"

by Candace Savage

Although only one word, "biodiversity" describes the wondrous variety of life on our unique planet surrounded by the barrenness of space. The author believes that life today is more diverse than ever, but our insatiable demands are degrading our biodiversity. Three over-lapping standards can measure species stability, beginning with simple numbers: many species—of birds, mammals, amphibians, and fish—are nearing extinction today. While an inevitable part of nature's cycles, extinction becomes threatening when species loss is disproportionate to species gain. Second, species are losing their genetic variability, which aids in adaptation by encoding richness into species DNA. Third, planetary life, including human life, will become less adaptable and creative as ecosystems are less able to pro-vide for our basic needs. We must, therefore, safeguard biodiversity for our sake and our children's.

> Use a dictionary and a thesaurus to help you change the wording of the original. Ensure that the word is the best replacement; otherwise, your summary could be unclear.

> In paragraph 2, the author expresses her point about biodiversity today as a probabllity, not as a fact. The summary phrasing acknowledges her rhetorical purpose.

> Concision and clarity are essential in effective summaries. You should experiment with different phrasing, ensuring that your prose can be understood by the average reader.

> The summary writer uses parallel phrasing to improve clarity. Transitions are used sparingly to help with sentence flow.

Take a section from one of the readings in this textbook, such as "Headed for newt sta-tus?" from "Embrace the Mediocrity Principle," (p. 19) or "Overgeneralization 2: Adoles-cents have no prefrontal cortex" from "The Teenage Brain: Self-Control" (p. 221) and write a summary of it approximately 20 per cent of the length of the original.

EXERCISE 4.1

THE CRITICAL ANALYSIS

A **critical analysis** is something like a literary analysis in which you break down a text in order to discuss its theme and techniques. Both rely on your knowledge of the kind of text you are analyzing. For example, you need to be familiar with a literary form you are analyzing just as you need to be familiar with critical thinking in order to break down an argument. On the other hand, in a literary analysis you usually do not evaluate the work itself (i.e., say whether it is good or bad), but much of a critical analysis could focus on strengths and weaknesses. Above all, a critical analysis should demonstrate your ability to analyze such elements as the writer's purpose, audience, use of reason, and argumentative strategies.

> A **CRITICAL ANALYSIS** should demonstrate your ability to analyze such elements as the writer's purpose, audience, use of reason, and argumentative strategies.

A Closer Look

Critical Analyses and Rhetorical Analyses

According to common usage, a *critical analysis* stresses an author's reason and thinking processes, while a *rhetorical analysis* stresses a writer's style and technique, his or her use of language designed to persuade an audience. Both analyses involve breaking down a text in order to show how it was put together for a particular purpose and audience. There is often considerable overlap in the use of these two terms. In this book, the term *critical analysis* is used to encompass a writer's use of linguistic resources as well as critical-thinking skills. However, a more specific discussion of language and style as they apply to rhetorical analyses is presented in chapter 9 (pp. 300–301).

A *critical response* may require some of the same skills as a critical analysis, but most responses are balanced between analysis of one or more of the essay's main points and your own opinion or observations about an issue raised in the text you have read.

> → For general guidelines for reading challenging essays, see Responding Critically and Analytically through Questions in chapter 1, page 8.

Below are some questions you can use to help you read texts as well as plan and write critical analyses. (Of course, guidelines for critical/rhetorical analyses can vary greatly from instructor to instructor and from assignment to assignment.)

Reading and Other Planning Strategies

- What do you know about the author? Does he or she appear qualified to write on the topic?
- What is the essay's thesis? Its main points?
- Are points supported by specific and relevant detail? Do the sources seem reliable?
- What inferences should readers make? Are they reasonable and valid?
- Does the author create interest in the topic? How? Would other strategies have helped?
- How does the author make the issue relevant to the reader? Does he or she appeal to the reader's concerns and values? How?
- How is the essay organized? What kinds of strategies and techniques facilitate understanding? Could organization or content been made clearer?
- Who is the intended audience? The level of language? Is the voice or tone appropriate? How could you describe it?
- Does the author include distinctive stylistic features (analogies, metaphors, imagery, anecdotes, non-standard sentence structure)?
- Is reason used effectively? Are there flaws in logic?
- Does the essay appear free of bias? Is the voice objective?
- Has the author acknowledged the other side? How has he or she responded to the opposing viewpoint?
- Does the author make emotional appeals? Are any extreme or deceptive?

Writing Strategies

- In your introduction, name the text and author, and give information concerning the author's background and/or publication information, if relevant.
- Briefly summarize the author's approach and main points.
- Conclude your introduction with your thesis, commenting on the essay's effectiveness and/or significance; be specific; simply saying that the essay is effective/ineffective is not enough.
- If the essay is argumentative, your thesis should evaluate the author's use of reason and argumentative strategies
- Use your body paragraphs to support your thesis with clear and detailed points; ensure that each paragraph focuses on one main point and that points are connected logically so your analysis is easy to follow.
- Refer directly to the text often; use direct quotation for major points and summarize or paraphrase less important points (see Methods of Integrating Sources, chapter 7, p. 217).
- Keep your tone (attitude) neutral and your voice and language objective.

See Tina Lalonde's student analysis that follows the professional essay below.

Sample Essay for Critical Analysis

The essay below is the source text for the sample student critical analysis that follows it.

SAMPLE PROFESSIONAL ESSAY

Tarmageddon: Dirty Oil Is Turning Canada into a Corrupt Petro-state

by Andrew Nikiforuk

[1]   Europeans once regarded Canada as a decent "dogooder" democracy, celebrated for its vast forests, pristine waters, and pleasant cities. But the rapid development of the tar sands, the world's largest energy project, has not only blackened the country's environmental reputation, but also dramatically undermined its political and economic character.

[2]   Oil, a politically corrosive resource, has unsettled the nation. Ever since Canada supplanted Mexico and Saudi Arabia nearly a decade ago as the No. 1 oil supplier to the United States, the federal government has become an increasingly aggressive defender of hydrocarbons and little else.

[3]   The nation's dismal record on climate change, and minimal investments in green energy, simply reflect a growing dependence on oil revenue, oil volatility, and petroleum lobbyists. As a consequence, Canada now shares the same sort of unaccountability and lack of transparency that marks fellow petrostates such as Saudi Arabia. Nowadays, Canada is, as one *Toronto Star* columnist pointedly put it, "a nation that doesn't say much, doesn't do much, and doesn't seem to stand for much."

[4]   Canada's dramatic transformation began with the rapid exploitation of the tar sands in the mid-1990s. This resource, a true symbol of peak oil, is neither cheap nor light. Bitumen, an inferior and ultra-heavy hydrocarbon that resembles asphalt, is so thick that it can't move through a pipeline unless diluted with a solvent.

[5]   Bitumen also contains so much carbon (and so little hydrogen) that it must be upgraded into "synthetic crude," a product with a higher sulphur, acid, and heavy metal content than West Texas crude or North Sea oil. As a consequence, bitumen remains the world's most capital-intensive oil at $6080 a barrel; in contrast, U.S. domestic crude can be produced at $10 a barrel.

[6]   Although industry studies claim that bitumen production is only 15% dirtier than light oil, the facts speak otherwise. The U.S. National Energy Technology Laboratory, for instance, recently calculated that jet fuel made from bitumen has a carbon footprint 244% greater than fuel made from U.S. domestic crude. While Statoli, Norway's state-owned company, reports greenhouse gas emissions of 8 to 19 kilograms per barrel in the North Sea, production emissions in the tar sands range from 22 to 417 kilograms or higher. In addition, scientists report a disturbing lack of public transparency on tar sands emissions reporting.

[7]   Nevertheless, every major global oil company has joined the bitumen boom. To date, the $200 billion scramble has directly industrialized 1.4 million hectares of forest—the equivalent of 40 Denvers or 17 Berlins.

[8]   The spectacle has not been pretty. Open pit mines the size of cities excavate shallow bitumen deposits in the forest, while steam plants inject deeper formations with as many as 12 barrels of steam to melt just one barrel of bitumen. Both recovery methods create enormous environmental messes.

[9]   The mines generate extraordinary volumes of toxic waste, which companies store in massive unlined dykes. These geologically unstable "tailing ponds" occupy 140 square kilometres of forest along the Athabasca River and contain a variety of fish-killers and cancer-makers, including arsenic, cyanide, naphthenic acids, and polycyclic aromatic hydrocarbons. Any breach of these impoundments would be catastrophic for the world's third-largest watershed, the Mackenzie River Basin.

[10]   Federal and provincial standards for reporting the volume of pollutants in these waste sites, and for reducing mining waste, didn't materialize until 2009. Even Boston-based Cambridge Energy Research Associates has decried the total lack of transparency on the reporting of tar ponds seepage into ground water or surface water.

[11]   The steam plants have equally impressive footprints. These heavily subsidized enterprises are fragmenting a forest the size of England with wells and pipelines. A fifth of Canada's natural gas demand goes into boiling the water to melt out the bitumen. This makes the energy intensity of steam plants so high that, at one joule of energy to make 1.4 joules of bitumen, there is little net gain in energy from the process.

[12]   The amount of groundwater pumped through these steam plants keeps growing, and threatens the hydrology of the entire region. Opti-Nexen, a large steam plant operator, initially calculated that it would take two barrels of steam to make one barrel of bitumen. Now the company boils up to six.

[13]   Due to its energy and water intensity, the tar sands has become its own carbon-making nation within Canada. It now accounts for 5% of the nation's emissions and pollutes the global atmosphere with 40 mégatonnes of greenhouse gases a year. That's nearly double the annual emissions of Estonia or Latvia. By 2020, the project will likely exceed the emissions of Belgium, a nation of 10 million people. (These industry calculations do not

include the burning of the oil in cars or the destruction of peat-lands, forests, and grasslands by the mines and natural gas drillers.)

[14]   The most poisonous legacy of the tar sands project has been its impact on public policy. Canada, once a global leader on tackling ozone pollution and acid rain, now has no effective climate change policy. Canada is the only signatory to the Kyoto Protocol that has completely abandoned its targets. It now ranks 59th out of 60 countries on responsible climate action: only Saudi Arabia boasts a worse record.

[15]   At the failed Copenhagen talks last year, an almost invisible Canada, one of the world's top ten emitters, gave a mere three-and-a-half-minute presentation. Even Saudi Arabia managed a six-minute talk.

[16]   Canada's Prime Minister, Stephen Harper, the son of an Imperial Oil executive, hails from the tar sands-producing province of Alberta, where a third of the population conveniently does not believe in climate change. Like many of Saudi Arabia's élites, Harper remains a bona-fide climate change skeptic—if not an outright denier. He has also appointed climate change deniers to important scientific posts. One of his close associates, Ken Boessenkool, even works as an oil industry lobbyist. Many of his fishing buddies support the country's pro-oil, anti-climate-action lobby group, Friends of Science.

[17]   Given that corporate taxes on tar sands production yield the federal government nearly $5 billion a year, steady oil revenue has trumped the public interest. The country has opposed low carbon fuel standards in the U.S., while Canada's Foreign Affairs branch says it "will resist efforts to label one form of energy as appropriate, such as renewables." Canada's Environment Minister, Jim Prentice, openly criticizes provinces such as Quebec for implementing green policies that reduce fossil fuel consumption.

[18]   Like Saudi Arabia, Canada has increasingly relied on foreign temporary workers, whose numbers (250,000) now exceed permanent immigrants, to develop its oil fields. In 2008, Alberta actually had 20 times as many temporary foreign workers (from places as diverse as China, South Africa, and the Philippines) as the U.S. in proportion to its population.

[19]   Abuses by brokers and employers abound. A 2009 report by the University of Sussex concluded that Canadian authorities, much like Saudi politicians, view temporary workers as "stocks that can be brought in or out as required." The Canadian and Alberta governments have also failed to consult local workers, unions, and the general public about their temporary foreign worker programs.

[20]   Although industry and government describe the tar sands as "Canada's new economic engine," the project has in reality given Canada a bad case of the Dutch Disease. This economic malaise, a form of deindustrialization, takes its name from a 1977 Economist article that detailed how a natural gas boom hollowed out the manufacturing base of the Netherlands. Gas exports inflated the value of the Dutch guilder, which in turn undermined the ability of its manufacturers to export their goods.

[21]   Thanks to rapidly growing tar sands exports (from 600,000 barrels a day in 2000 to 1.3 million barrels today), the loonie, as the Canadian dollar is known, has now reached parity with—and may soon surpass—the U.S. dollar in value. But the high-priced loonie has made it particularly difficult for Canadian manufacturers to sell their goods. A 2009 study by Luxembourg's Centre for Research in Economic Analysis confirmed that Canada's oil-priced currency has indeed hammered industries as varied as textile mills, electronics, fabricated metal, and paper. It concluded that 54% of the nation's manufacturing employment losses (nearly 5% of the workforce) were due to the rapid tar sands development from 2002 to 2007.

[22]   Unlike Norway, the world's most transparent petro-state, Canada has also failed to exercise any fiscal accountability over its non-renewable oil wealth. The country has no sovereign fund and has saved no wealth to date, much to the consternation of the Organization for Economic Cooperation and Development (OECD), which concluded in a damning 2008 report that "other nations have shown much more restraint and foresight in managing their resource revenues to mitigate boom-and-bust cycles."

[23]   In addition, neither Canada nor Alberta charges much for the bitumen. Alberta has even described its royalty regime as a "give-it-away" scheme. Alberta's share from a $60 barrel of oil is a mere 30 cents, one of the lowest royalties in the world. The province also permits corporations to deduct royalties for federal corporate tax purposes.

[24]   Nevertheless, Alberta still garners nearly a third of its revenue from hydrocarbons. To date, much of it has been used to lower taxes, manipulate public sentiment, and recklessly build infrastructure to fuel more tar sands development. Ruled by one political party for an astounding 38 years, Alberta's government has been increasingly described as incompetent, authoritarian, and corrupt.

[25]   Canada has yet to have a national debate about the pace and scale of the tar sands development. Until it acknowledges the project's cancerous hold on national life, Canada will increasingly become an unstable petro-state marginalized by oil price volatility and global carbon politics.

Source: *CCPA Monitor* 17.1 (2010), 10–11.

SAMPLE STUDENT CRITICAL ANALYSIS

Critical Analysis of "Tarmageddon: Dirty Oil Is Turning Canada into a Corrupt Petro-state" by Andrew Nikiforuk

by Tina Lalonde

[1]   "Tarmageddon: Dirty Oil is Turning Canada into a Corrupt Petro-state," by Andrew Nikiforuk, is an unrelenting condemnation of Canada's government and its rapidly expanding tar sands. Drawing on nationalistic pride and alarm over Canada's international reputation, Nikiforuk's article successfully educates and informs its readers about the dangers of the tar sands. The environmental and financial ramifications are illustrated, and he alludes to government misinformation and lack of transparency. Although he is writing for the general public, the article appeared in a 2010 issue of *The Canadian Centre for Policy Alternatives Monitor*, a progressive publication geared toward social and economic justice that presumably has subscribers more informed on social issues than the average reader. Nikiforuk systematically lays out the basics of the tar sands and bitumen. The reader is shown the implications of the unrestrained expansion of what is arguably one of the world's largest contributors to climate change and global warming. The author's thesis is clear from the title, but it should be added that he feels Canada's civic character is being undermined as well. As if to convey his urgency and his determination to raise the alarm, the author delivers his points with all the subtly of a sledgehammer. He leaves room for little doubt on his own position, and indeed, leaves the reader little opportunity to come to a conclusion other than the one presented.

Lalonde's introduction is thorough and informative. She provides a context for the essay and mentions its appearance in a "progressive publication." She briefly summarizes the author's approach and thesis and discusses the writer's success in reaching his intended audience. The last two sentences suggest possible limitations or weaknesses in the argument.

[2]   Nikiforuk uses many effective techniques to dramatic effect; even the title demands attention. Furthermore, as the title suggests, he does not mince words. The reader is kept engaged with wordplay and vivid imagery. Wordplay is also used very effectively to create the tone the author is trying to convey. In the introduction, imagery of an abundant, beautiful, and natural Canada is almost immediately "blackened" to metaphorically create an image of Canada's fallen status. Although one could call such language slanted, it nevertheless conveys the author's view perfectly. Oil's depiction as politically "corrosive" as it eats away at governmental integrity, the tar sand's depiction as having a "cancerous hold," and the prediction that it will leave a "poisonous legacy" are all undeniably effective. Imagery also evokes strong feeling. "Fragmented forests the size of England" (p. 108) and "open pit mines the size of cities" (p. 108) are compelling images that contribute to understanding the colossal impact on the environment. Similarly, the forty mega-tonnes of yearly emissions from the tar sands are equated with the emissions of small European countries in a successful comparison that imparts the sheer scale of pollution generated. Factual, credible comparisons and contrasts are used, via academic studies, government reports, and industry observations, to show differences between governmental policies and transparency, levels of pollution, study results, and global environmental responsibility. Contrast is also used to illustrate unfavourable similarities in human rights abuses, environmental irresponsibility, and political self-induced blind-spots.

[3]   Although Nikifork's style is compelling, no alternative viewpoints are presented: no common ground is established upon which a hostile, or even an undecided, reader might agree. Additionally, no concessions are made to the other side of the tar sands debate. The author apparently lacks sympathy for people who view the tar sands as a necessary evil in order to feed their families. Perhaps he regards the short term benefits as inconsequential when compared to the long term, and possibly irrevocable, damages the tar sands could bring. . . . The lack of a feasible solution or compromise offered could be regarded as a major omission, but as Nikiforuk points out in his conclusion, "Canada has yet to have a national debate about the pace and scale of the tar sands development" (p. 110). Perhaps he felt no solutions could present themselves until Canadians were given enough information to examine the issue.

[4]   In a mere two years since the publication of "Tarmageddeon," the debate about the Canadian tar sands has exploded onto the national, and even the international, stage. Although this essay was written before the tar sands were such a hot button topic, it foreshadows the divisiveness and political upheaval in the nation today. Written with clarity by someone who appears extremely knowledgeable on the subject, "Tarmageddon" assumes a great importance today. Although it may be biased, uncompromising, and possibly even hostile, it successfully gives a resolute nudge to the nation's collective conscience.

Lalonde analyzes three specific stylistic features of "Tarmageddon." Here she refers to wordplay and imagery, which are then analyzed; comparisons and contrasts are discussed near the end of the paragraph. Structurally, it might have been better to include the third feature in the same sentence in which she mentions wordplay and imagery.

While Lalonde summarizes Nikiforuk's points, she is also analyzing their effectiveness. Another way to structure a critical analysis is to briefly summarize its main points first; the rest of the essay can then focus on analysis.

Note the many specific references to the text in this paragraph. Lalonde effectively uses a combination of direct quotation and summary. Note that she uses direct quotations to stress significant phrasing, reserving summary for points where phrasing is less important.

This paragraph addresses the essay's weaknesses; however, Lalonde uses critical thinking to account for them and does not simply dismiss them as flaws. She has made it clear in her introduction that she believes the essay has more strengths than weaknesses; therefore, it is logical that she devotes more space to the former (par. 2) than the latter (par. 3).

In her conclusion, Lalonde notes the essay's relevance today. Her final sentence reinforces her balanced appraisal of the text. Note that her criticisms are expressed in a dependent clause while the important point about the essay's possible effect on its audience occurs in an independent clause.

EXERCISE 4.2

Write a critical analysis of the essay "Embrace the Mediocrity Principle" on page 19.

CHAPTER SUMMARY

Many of your class assignments will require you to use texts in various ways. Summaries and critical analyses, discussed in this chapter, require focused reading for contrastive purposes: when summarizing, you include only the most relevant points and discard detail. When writing a critical analysis, you use your knowledge of texts and critical thinking to evaluate the writer's structure and similar features, along with his or her use of reason. Pointers are provided to enable you to master the valuable skills of writing summaries and critical analyses.

The Argumentative Essay 5

Learning how to argue effectively is a skill that extends beyond university classrooms into the practical world of employment and into many walks of life. However, successful argument involves much more than just stating your opinion and backing it up, as is sometimes believed: it involves making choices depending on your purpose for arguing, your audience, and your topic. In this chapter, you will learn how to combine the critical-thinking skills discussed in chapter 1 with the strategies introduced here to produce convincing arguments.

LEARNING OBJECTIVES

- to understand three important argumentative models and their contribution to written arguments today

- to be aware of different argumentative purposes and to be able to plan your essay with both purpose and audience in mind

- to understand that valid arguable claims are based on more than subjective standards and usually have an opposing viewpoint

- to learn what kinds of evidence can contribute to a successful argument

- to learn about argumentative strategies, including emotional and ethical appeals, available to writers to support their claims and strengthen their argument

- to learn how to reason logically and avoid logical fallacies, which are categories of false or invalid reasoning

- to decide whether to use a rebuttal strategy in your essay and which would be the best strategy considering your purpose, audience, and topic
- to be aware of choices in the way you structure your argumentative essay

EVERYDAY ARGUMENTS

Argument is so ingrained in our lives that it might seem strange to devote space to what people do naturally. A teenager argues with his parents that he is old enough to live on his own; a lawyer argues a complex point of law before a Supreme Court judge. What is the difference between these arguments? Complexity might be one difference, but another lies in the likelihood that both the teenager and the parents will present the argument at least partly in emotional terms.

This is not the case with the lawyer who knows that her credibility is built more on logic, precedent, and reason than on emotion. It could be a good strategy for a defence lawyer to create sympathy for a defendant, but the lawyer would have to do this indirectly, perhaps through the emotional testimony of character witnesses—not by displaying emotion herself. Whereas the teenager and his parents probably do not plan their strategies in advance, the lawyer's case will be built on careful planning. The kind of arguing you will do at the university level has more in common with that of the prudent lawyer than that of the passionate parent.

Although the roots of argument are embedded in the public discourse of Greek and Roman orators, it has been adapted to many contemporary functions: for example, editorials and letters to the editor, proposals, and the process of mediation all rely on argument. Advertising tries to influence us through persuasive means—often either self-serving logic or emotions. When you design your résumé, you try to persuade an employer to hire you over someone else. Thus, the argumentative essay exercises the logical and critical-thinking skills you use every day.

Rhetoric and Argument

Rhetoric has taken on a range of meanings today but can be defined broadly as the use of effective modes of communication. In this chapter, we will work within the narrower meaning of **rhetoric** as the structure and strategies of argumentation used to persuade the members of a specific audience.

Aristotle and Argument

Greek philosopher Aristotle (384–322 BCE) used the word *rhetoric* to stress a speaker's awareness of the choices available in any given situation to affect an audience. He believed that a general audience would often need to be persuaded—that showing knowledge alone was not enough.

Laying much of the groundwork for classical argument in his book *Rhetoric*, Aristotle divided arguments into three kinds: those founded on

- reason (**logos**)
- morality (**ethos**)
- emotion (**pathos**)

As it is applied to argument, **RHETORIC** refers to the structure and strategies of argumentation used to persuade the members of a specific audience.

Arguments founded on **LOGOS** rely on appeals to reason and logic. Arguments founded on **ETHOS** rely on appeals to ethics and morality. Arguments founded on **PATHOS** rely on appeals to emotions.

Of the three, the most important appeal is to a reader's reason. Ethical appeals play a major role, too, mostly in establishing your credibility as an arguer. Aristotle reasoned that an audience will be more convinced by an argument if the arguer is seen as "understand[ing] human character and goodness in their various forms" (*Rhetoric* Book I, chapter 2). Aristotle also stressed the connection between emotional appeals and knowledge of one's audience, knowing the audience's "hearts."

> Aristotle believed that the effective arguer had to understand the "hearts" of his audience, their feelings and beliefs.

A Closer Look

Two Modern Models of Argument: Rogers and Toulmin

Both models discussed in this section stress the use of planning and the awareness of an audience; each makes a unique contribution to the art of argument.

Argument based on the ideas of Aristotle is often called traditional argument and stresses an adversarial approach. In contrast to traditional argument, the approach of Carl Rogers (1902–1987) emerges out of communication theory and involves "see[ing] the expressed idea and attitude from the other person's point of view." Rogerian strategies include framing your argument in terms the other person will accept. For example, the teenager arguing to live on his own could use Rogerian argument to express his parents' concerns and his appreciation for them.

The main strength of the Rogerian system is its focus on the audience. In traditional arguments, arguers may be encouraged to "imagine" a community of critics, and thus to anticipate counterpoints and sharpen one's *own* points, but not to genuinely engage in a dialogue with one's critics. The Rogerian approach encourages establishing common ground—points of agreement—with your audience. The arguer may concede a point in order to appear fair.

While the Rogers model broadened the concept of argumentation to include both sides in a respectful dialogue, the system of Stephen Toulmin (1922–2009) deepened the concept of argument. Toulmin based his ideas on the way lawyers present their cases before courts, realizing that claims need to be based *on* something. In other words, claims must be justified. One of Toulmin's important contributions is the concept of the warrant, the foundation of an argumentative claim, linking the claim to the evidence.

Another aspect of Toulminian argument is the need to qualify claims, to avoid unqualified statements. A qualified claim will be more acceptable to a reader, who may reject an overly broad claim as unrealistic. For example, the parents of the independent-minded teenager may argue that 18 isn't old enough to live on one's own, but a qualified claim, such as "many 18-year-olds aren't ready to live on their own," is more realistic.

See table 5.1 for a summary of the major features of the argumentative models of Aristotle, Rogers, and Toulmin.

Appeals to reason, emotion, and ethics all can be used in argument, as can finding common ground with your audience. The following "real-life" scenario demonstrates the various facets of arguments as outlined above:

→ For an explanation of the common ground strategy, see page 128.

→ For an explanation of the concession strategy, see page 128.

You are disappointed by an essay grade and arrange to meet your instructor in her office. By your effective use of reason, you try to convince her that your mark does not reflect your true abilities, while conceding the validity of some of her criticisms; *concessions* are used in many arguments. Going through the paper systematically, you focus on points that seem arguable, asking for clarification or elaboration and presenting your counterclaims. As you do, you appear a responsible, conscientious student: you make an *ethical appeal*.

You appeal to her fair-mindedness, reiterating her helpfulness, your interest in the course, and your desire to do well. In this way, you

Continued

TABLE 5.1 Three Argumentative Models

ARGUMENTATIVE MODEL/THEORY	ORIGINAL USES	KEY CONCEPTS/ TERMS	USES IN AN ARGUMENTATIVE ESSAY
Aristotle	oratory/public speaking	logical, ethical, and emotional appeals	• understanding inductive and deductive kinds of reasoning • using reason effectively • establishing authority and trustworthiness • appealing appropriately to audience emotions
Rogers	psychology/ interpersonal communication	common ground, consensus	• acknowledging opposing views • laying grounds for trust and openness • reaching consensus and mutual understanding • making concessions
Toulmin	law	claim, warrant, data (evidence)	• providing foundation for/developing a claim to make it convincing • tying claim to evidence • qualifying claim to avoid generalizations

→ To see how the warrant provides a foundation for your claim, see Solidifying the Claim through the Warrant, page 127.

establish *common ground*, as you would try to do with the reader of your essay. As well, you do not come across merely as one who wants a better mark, but as one who is interested in learning how to write a better essay. In doing so, you are giving a valid *foundation to your claim* much more than you would be if you said something like "I need a B− in this course so I can get into my program."

If you argue with integrity, you will leave a good impression. Emotional appeals, such as tearfully bemoaning your stressful life, are apt to be less successful, but subtle appeals may have influence.

EXERCISE 5.1

Recall a recent argument.

1. Begin by briefly describing the circumstances that led to it.
2. Divide a page in half vertically and summarize each point raised by "your side" and "the other side."
3. Simply report what was said (do not embellish with interpretations of the meaning of what was said)—each side's point of view and the counter-argument, if there was one. When a new point begins, draw a horizontal line to separate it from the previous point.
4. In a couple of paragraphs, analyze the strengths and weaknesses of each point.
   • Did the point make an appeal to reason? An emotional appeal? An ethical one?
   • Was an opinion supported? Were facts used to support an opinion?
   • Were the points logically related to one another?
   • Was the argument resolved? If so, how?

In your analysis, identify any flaws, such as simplifications and generalizations. Try to be as objective as possible to *both* sides.

ARGUMENTATIVE PURPOSE

Approaching argument as a "one size fits all" is limiting. An argument can have many purposes, large or small, as was suggested above in the examples of the Supreme Court lawyer and the teenager. These include

1. defending your point of view
2. seeking to change a situation
3. promoting consensus
4. drawing attention to a problem/raising awareness
5. reaching a common understanding
6. interpreting a text

These purposes are explained below.

1. Defending Your Point of View

The most common reason for everyday arguments is probably to defend a viewpoint or express an opinion. Such an argument often uses a value claim, asserting that the arguer's point of view is good, fair, or right in order to convince the reader or listener to adopt a new position. Arguments that use a value claim are sometimes called position arguments. In her comparison essay, student writer Kristen Carlton supports her value claim that ebooks are superior to hardcovers (see appendix B, p. 392).

2. Seeking a Change

When you seek to change a situation, you argue for or against a specific action or change using an extended value claim. These kinds of claims go further than simple value claims and are often written to governments and other authorities. Arguments that use extended value claims are sometimes called proposal arguments. For example, the designers of the health services campaign on page 134 argue against a government proposal.

3. Promoting a Consensus

On the surface, it might seem unnecessary to use argument if an audience already agrees with you, but many written arguments appear in publications whose readers share core values or opinions about a controversial issue. Argument implies agreement, as well as disagreement; thus, argument can be used to affirm consensus. In the case of the teenager and his parents, consider how the teenager might have argued if his audience were his friends rather than his parents. An arguer may also seek to solidify common bonds with a reader in order to change a situation.

4. Drawing Attention to a Problem/ Raising Awareness

An arguer may seek to draw attention to a subject that has been ignored or overlooked. Instead of attempting to effect change, the writer is more concerned with "raising consciousness," perhaps as a first step toward change. If the issue is a serious one for your audience, you need to convince the reader that the problem is urgent and that attention is crucial. On the other hand, you may just want to get your reader to see a situation from a new perspective. In either case, to write successfully with this argumentative purpose, you need to be familiar with the knowledge level of your audience. In "Embrace the Mediocrity Principle," in chapter 1, page 19, Daniel Wood attempts to change his readers' perceptions concerning our "mediocrity" as a species. See also Dalton Anderson's essay in this chapter, page 144.

5. Reaching a Common Understanding

Arguing for a common understanding, such as a "middle ground," is often more practical than just asserting a one-sided claim. Such an argumentative purpose could involve arriving at a compromise or weighing both sides to determine the stronger one. In either case, the successful arguer may shift the attitude of *both* sides from firm opposition to flexibility. To argue effectively with this purpose in mind, you need be familiar with both positions; hence, the Rogerian approach is often useful (see above, p. 116). These arguments are often called conciliation arguments. For an example of a conciliation argument, see "Should Veiling Be Banned in the Courtroom?", by Brydon Kramer, page 147.

6. Interpreting a Text

When you interpret a text, for example, a poem in a literature class, you make a claim about the work and defend it by citing specific passages within the work and, sometimes, by citing what other people have said (secondary sources). See chapter 6.

Combining Argumentative Purposes

Of course, an argumentative essay can combine two or more purposes. For example, in his essay on allowing face veils in court (later in this chapter on p. 147), Brydon Kramer lays two opposing arguments before the reader to get both sides to see each other's point of view (purpose 5); however, in his conclusion, he argues that the court should change its practice (purpose 2).

As suggested above, intended audience goes hand-in-hand with argumentative purpose. Just as you would not begin planning an argument without a topic, you should not begin planning without a purpose and an audience in mind. If a bargaining committee were planning a strategy for improving the conditions for its workers, an article that appeared in the union newsletter would probably be designed to *promote consensus*, to solidify union members. If it took out advertising space in a local newspaper, the purpose might be to *raise awareness* of issues they considered important. However, when the members of the committee sat down with management, they would have to adopt a new objective: knowing that neither side is likely to get its way on all issues, they might plan a strategy that would give them several key points without giving up too much (*reaching a common understanding*).

For more about audience, see chapter 2, page 25.

TABLE 5.2 Purpose and Audience

PURPOSE	CLAIM	AUDIENCE
defending your point of view (position argument)	value	neutral or opposed
seeking to change a situation (proposal argument)	extended value	neutral or opposed
promoting affiliation	value or extended value	agree
raising awareness	value	neutral (unaware of issue)
reaching a common understanding (conciliation argument)	extended value	mixed: opposed relative to each other's position

Determine the argumentative purpose for the claims below. Assume that the audience is a general one, composed of readers with low to medium knowledge of the topic—except topics directly relevant to university students.

EXERCISE 5.2

1. Despite the popularity of reality TV, many are unaware of the adverse effects these shows have on viewers.
2. Employers should have the legal right to monitor their employees' email and Internet use with or without the employee's consent.
3. Municipal casino bans are necessary to preserve other local businesses and help curb the rising crime rate.
4. When you consider the difficulty in becoming a professional athlete today, the short length of their careers, and the physical and mental demands of constantly being in the spotlight, it is easy to justify their salaries.
5. After registration is completed, students should receive vouchers to purchase their textbooks and not be required to pay for them in addition to their tuition.
6. While it is often stated that Canada's immigration and multiculturalism policies are the main reasons for immigration, it is economic opportunity, political stability, and the positive Canadian image that are largely responsible.
7. Wireless laptops and tablets should be permitted in classrooms across campus, but they should be subject to guidelines to ensure their legitimate use, along with a student probationary system in the event of misuse.
8. Factory farming should be eliminated due to its inhumane practices, the health of consumers, and its effect on the planet.
9. Despite the controversy, stem cells are the key in unlocking the secrets of curing illnesses, diseases, and injuries that were long believed to be incurable.
10. Embryonic stem-cell research has a healthy future in Canada as long as we approach new regulations with caution and acknowledge the legitimate ethical issues at stake.

A Closer Look

Argument or Exposition

In most cases, a reader needs to know whether he or she will be reading an argumentative or expository essay. Thus, when you argue to raise awareness in order to get the reader to see a new perspective (purpose 4), you need to word your thesis as an argument. A fact-based claim that informs the reader about a new direction of research should also be worded so that the reader knows he or she will be reading an expository essay. In the thesis statements below, the wording helps clarify what kind of essay will follow:

> → For comparisons of expository and argumentative writing, see chapter 2, page 46.

Expository essay claim (to inform): New research into violent video games suggests that playing some violent games could increase vision and higher level brain functions. [The writer will be investigating current research on the topic.]

Argumentative essay claim (to raise awareness): The perception that violent video games are bad for you is being challenged by new research. [The writer will be arguing that new research into video games is worthy of the reader's attention.]

Another kind of expository essay that may seem to straddle the line between fact and argument is common in scholarly research: here the claim is framed as a question or problem that needs investigation. In the conclusion, the researcher answers the question and/or makes recommendations to improve the situation. In her comparison essay, student writer Sarah Matheson phrases the factual claim as a question. Her conclusion shows her use of critical thinking: at the end, she makes a recommendation resulting from her findings:

Expository claim: The bottom line concerning therapy is that it needs to succeed. In the treatment of mentally ill individuals, which therapeutic method is more effective: psychotherapy or pharmacotherapy?

Conclusion based on research: Research is divided with some studies indicating that psychotherapy is more effective, while other research indicates that pharmacotherapy is better. In fact, it depends on factors like the type of mental illness, individual preferences, the severity of the illness, and even the age of the individual. After a treatment is given, successful results can range from a reduction of symptoms to an improvement in the quality of life and social functioning of the patient. Generally, the combined effects of psychotherapy and pharmacotherapy have proven more effective in the treatment of a mental illness compared to either therapy alone. In the future, further research can be conducted to examine the use of combined therapies and their effectiveness on patients with mental illnesses.

ARGUABLE CLAIMS

Opinion, Facts, and Argument

In contrast to facts, which can be verified by observation or research, opinions can be challenged. As you will see, for a position on a topic to be argued, there is usually an opposing view that can be challenged. Although facts can be used to support the thesis of an argumentative essay, effective arguers are always clear about when they are using facts and when they are using opinion. In reading, use your critical-thinking skills to ask if the writer always clearly separates facts from opinion. If not, he or she might be guilty of faulty reasoning (see p. 136).

The following statement cannot be challenged:

Fact: The distance between the earth's equator and the moon averages 384,400 kilometres.

Now consider the following two pairs of sentences, each consisting of a fact and a related opinion:

Fact: According to moon-landing conspiracy theories, the 1969 *Apollo* moon landing was faked.

Opinion: The *Apollo* moon landing didn't actually take place; it was all a hoax.

Fact: On 13 November 2009, NASA announced that water had been found on the moon.

Opinion: Now that water has been found on the moon, humans should set up colonies at the moon's poles by 2050.

Collaborative Exercise: Fact and Opinion

EXERCISE 5.3

Consider the two pairs of statements above on the topic of humans on the moon.

1. Discuss the ways that fact differs from opinion in each case.
2. Come up with two other topics and write two statements for each, a fact and an opinion. Make sure they are phrased so that either fact *or* opinion is obvious.

Let's say you see two friends emerging from a showing of a popular movie. With raised voice and exaggerated gestures, friend A states categorically that *The Hunger Games* is the best movie of the year. Matching friend A gesture for gesture, friend B insists that *The Hobbit: An Unexpected Journey* was a much better movie. To support her claim, friend A cites *The Hunger Games*'s "awesome visual effects." Friend B's counter-claim is that the action in *The Hobbit* was "out of this world." Who is right?

Neither is "right" because you cannot base a rational argument on purely subjective standards. On the other hand, you might be able to base an argument on the superiority of one movie over another if you compared the elements of suspense in both, or the quality of the acting or directing—if you could apply measurable standards to both.

Other kinds of claims are also not arguable. You could not easily write an argumentative essay on the virtues of good health, as there is no opposing view. Similarly unarguable are obvious claims, such as "social media is very influential on many youth today."

Arguable claims must (1) be based on more than subjective standards; and (2) have an opposing viewpoint. In addition, successful claims should be specific, interesting, and manageable.

→ To review claims and thesis statements, see The Thesis Statement, chapter 3, page 78.

Specific, Interesting, and Manageable Claims

You also need to ensure that your claim is *specific*, *interesting*, and *manageable*. Below, we focus on a sample argumentative claim, showing the kinds of questions you can ask to help you develop a strong and effective thesis for an argumentative essay.

Specific Claim

A specific claim identifies a topic that has been narrowed down and your specific approach to it. In addition, a specific claim is worded precisely.

> *Vague claim:* Parents of children who play hockey would like to see fighting eliminated from the game at all levels.

This claim is not specific enough to suggest what kind of argument will follow or even if the essay will focus on argument rather than exposition: *parents*, *would like to see*, and *at all levels* are vague. Also, the phrase *eliminated from the game at all levels* is non-specific and illogical: what has this got to do with the parents who don't like seeing their children fight? To make your claim specific, consider using an expanded thesis statement that includes your main points, as the reader will see at a glance that you have supported your claim. In the following revised thesis statement, the claim is expressed more clearly through specific words and includes the main points. *Should* clearly reveals an extended value claim:

> *More specific argumentative claim:* Fighting should be prohibited in hockey since violence gives young hockey players a negative model and reinforces a "win at all costs" mentality.

Although a claim may be specific if it is precisely worded, it is often a good idea to define concepts central to your argument. In the claim above, the writer might define what is meant by *fighting*. Does the dropping of hockey gloves or excessive physical contact constitute the beginning of a fight? Does a fight begin when there is a third player involved? Definition enables the writer to make a topic more specific.

An "all or none" claim is also non-specific. Where your claim is too broad, you should either use qualifiers to restrict its scope or reword it to make it more realistic. Examples of qualifiers include *a few*, *in part*, *many*, *often*, *several*, *some*, *sometimes*, and *usually*. In addition, you can use verbs and verb phrases that qualify and limit, such as *contribute to*, *may*, *play a role in*, and *seems*.

Interesting Claim

To help make your claim interesting, draft it with a specific audience in mind. In the claim about fighting in hockey, the intended audience is hockey parents as well as coaches, managers, and other hockey executives—people who can make changes. Those who never watch hockey or don't have children playing hockey might not be interested.

Along with audience interest, an important consideration is the viewpoint of your audience.

- Are most people to whom the argument is addressed likely to agree with you? Disagree? Be neutral?
- Will they possess general knowledge of the topic?
- Is the topic a current one that most will have heard of?

These kinds of questions will be even more relevant when you structure your essay and support your claim. For example, if your audience includes many opponents, it may be important to establish common ground and to convince them that you have similar values and goals. See below, Strategies for Rebuttal, page 131, for specific audience strategies.

Manageable Claim

Although the manageability of a claim will be determined partly by whether it is specific and interesting, it will also depend on essay length, availability of support, and the complexity of the issues that need to be addressed. A claim that promises more than the writer could achieve in a medium-length essay would not be manageable.

Extended value claims, which try to persuade people to take action, go beyond simply proving something is bad or unfair. Often needed are realistic solutions or at least suggestions that these kinds of solutions exist. Is the proposal realistic? To say that a government should increase funding to post-secondary education by 25 per cent is probably not realistic given the current economy. If your proposal isn't realistic, it may be best to change your claim to one of value or else reword it.

The claim about hockey violence was found to be arguable, specific, and interesting (to its intended audience), but is it *manageable*?

Fighting should be prohibited in hockey since violence gives young hockey players a negative model and reinforces a "win at all costs" mentality.

The issue of banning fighting throughout hockey, especially at the professional level, seems too complex to be manageable if the issues relating to young hockey players are also addressed. Realistically, would the fact that many hockey players act as role models for younger players motivate those who manage the game to ban fighting? To make the statement manageable, the writer could focus *either* on the way that fights in professional hockey undermine hockey players as role models *or* on the consequences of fighting in minor hockey:

Value claim: Fighting in professional hockey gives young hockey players a negative model since violence reinforces a "win at all costs" mentality.

Extended value claim: Fighting should be prohibited in minor hockey at and below the midget level since violence reinforces a "win at all costs" mentality.

Remember that all claims need to focus on one main topic, not to straddle two related topics. In addition to being specific, interesting, and manageable, they must also be clearly written.

EXERCISE 5.4

C Check answers to select questions

Collaborative Exercise: Evaluating Claims

In discussion groups, evaluate the 10 claims below, determining whether they would make good thesis statements for an argumentative essay. Are the claims arguable, specific, interesting, and manageable?

1. Cloning should be prohibited as it will mean the end of natural selection.
2. Since underage drinking is a major problem today, it wouldn't make sense to lower the drinking age any further.
3. *The Simpsons* is a much funnier sitcom than *Family Guy*.
4. Email is a very useful form of communication today as it is accessible, fast, and far-reaching.
5. Sex education needs to play a greater role in schools so that the number of pregnancies can be reduced and teenagers will practise safer sex.
6. No-fault insurance has made it easier for insurance companies to stay in business.
7. Internet dating services are innovative, convenient, and affordable alternatives to the singles scene.
8. It is better to have a summer job in retail than in customer service; though the pay is less, you meet nicer people.
9. Legal guidelines are needed for genetic testing as it may threaten our privacy, lead to harmful gene therapy, and have dangerous social costs.
10. Because of the dangerousness of the sport utility vehicle, people should have to prove they really need an SUV before being permitted to purchase it.

Kinds of Evidence

Value and extended value claims, like factual claims, need support. In chapter 3, evidence was divided into two main categories: hard evidence and soft evidence. Fact-based essays, not surprisingly, depend mostly on facts, statistics, and scientific studies. In argument, factual sources may be important as support, along with soft evidence, such as examples, analogies, anecdotes, narration, or even personal experience. However, what will always be crucial regardless of your purpose for arguing is the careful use of reason and logic.

Working Your Claim: The Rational Basis of Argument

Two kinds of reasoning methods are used in logical arguments: through *inductive* or *deductive* reasoning, assumptions and **premises** can be validated and a conclusion can be made.

Because it is often more important in arguments, where the arguer asks the reader to accept general statements, most of the following section focuses on deductive reasoning. However, both inductive and deductive reasoning work differently to form conclusions; therefore, readers should understand the basis of both.

> A **PREMISE** is a statement, assumed to be true, that leads to a conclusion.

Inductive Reasoning

Induction, or **scientific reasoning**, arrives at a conclusion based on specific occurrences, which are observed and recorded. The conclusion, then, is the result of the accumulation of evidence through controlled and objective methods of evidence gathering. Inductive reasoning is called scientific reasoning because scientific research frequently relies on the collection and analyzing of specific data to arrive at a conclusion.

People like to make jokes about the weather by using faulty inductive reasoning. How often have you heard someone say, "Whenever I wash my car, it rains," or "Every time I bring my umbrella, it's a sunny day, but the first day I forget it, it rains"?

Two questions to ask yourself when using inductive reasoning are

1. Have you provided enough support for each statement you make?
2. Have you been logical and consistent in applying your reasoning method?

Several examples of faulty inductive reasoning are given in table 5.3 that begins on page 138—for example, doubtful causes and hasty generalization.

Deductive Reasoning

Deductive reasoning can be broken down into three parts, represented by three statements:

- a general statement: the *major premise*
- a specific statement: the *minor premise*
- the conclusion

Below is an example of this three-part structure, known as a *syllogism*, that illustrates the deductive method:

Major premise: All property owners in the municipality must pay taxes.

Minor premise: I am a property owner in the municipality.

Conclusion: I must pay taxes.

However, consider the following syllogism:

Major premise: All people who live on the west coast of North America are in danger from earthquakes.

Minor premise: Nancy lives in California.

Conclusion: Nancy is in danger from earthquakes.

If one of the premises is wrong, as is the major premise above, the conclusion will be invalid. Part of the problem with the statement is that it is too general. Try to avoid overly general claims:

More specific major premise: All people who live on the southern part of the San Andreas Fault are in danger from earthquakes.

Minor premise: Nancy lives on the southern part of the San Andreas Fault.

Conclusion: Nancy is in danger from earthquakes.

INDUCTION (SCIENTIFIC REASONING) arrives at a conclusion based on specific occurrences, which are observed and recorded.

Logical fallacies in inductive reasoning can develop (1) where there is not enough evidence to make a generalization; or (2) where the means for gathering the evidence are faulty or biased.

DEDUCTIVE REASONING arrives at a conclusion based on a general statement applied to a specific statement.

Here are two questions to ask yourself when using deductive reasoning:

1. Does the major premise (general statement) apply to the people or situation described in the minor premise (specific statement)?
2. Is it a valid generalization?

Like inductive reasoning, deductive reasoning can be faulty, such as when it is used to exclude or persecute minorities; many forms of stereotyping are based on faulty deductive reasoning—by drawing a conclusion about a person based solely on his or her membership in a racial or religious group.

Now consider the following set of premises, which can be presented in syllogistic form:

Major premise: It is wrong not to treat the environment with respect.

Minor premise: In building the pipeline, the company is not treating the environment with respect.

Conclusion: The company is wrong to build the pipeline.

Major premise: It is right to treat business interests as primary.

Minor premise: In building the pipeline, the company is treating business interests as primary.

Conclusion: The company is right to build the pipeline.

Even though the conclusions are contradictory, in each syllogism the conclusion is logical if the major premise is accepted as true. As an arguer, you need to ensure that any general claims you make will be ones your audience will accept. Similarly, when you analyze an argument, consider the validity of any general statements, especially as they apply to the intended audience.

> Sound use of inductive and deductive reasoning will help produce a logical argument and increase your credibility as an arguer. However, making logical fallacies (see p. 137), which involve faulty use of reason, such as drawing a conclusion despite a lack of evidence or making a generalization that isn't true, will reduce your credibility.

EXERCISE 5.5

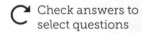 Check answers to select questions

Collaborative Exercise: Detective Work

Read the following short scenarios and analyze how the police reached their decision (i.e., analyze their reasoning methods) or why the investigation failed.

A.   Were *inductive* methods involved? If they were flawed, was the problem due to a lack of evidence or faulty methods of evidence gathering?

B.   Were *deductive* methods involved? If so, what generalization was made?

1.   *Scenario:* After a robbery at an expensive and seemingly burglar-proof home, the police investigation settled on two possible suspects. One suspect had been seen near the house near the time of the robbery, but had never previously been arrested. The second suspect had not been seen near the home but was not able to account for his movements that night; furthermore, he had two prior robbery convictions. *Result:* Police brought the second man in for further questioning.

2.   *Scenario:* Police believed they would easily be able to identify the suspect of an assault when they discovered blood samples on the floor and wall of the crime scene. But the crime scene officer, who was working on his first case, neglected to prepare the samples correctly, and they deteriorated. *Result:* Police were unable to come up with a suspect.

Solidifying the Claim through the Warrant

One way to test the logical connection between your claim (or any important point) and its support is through the basis for the claim, the **warrant**. A warrant solidifies the connection between claim and evidence. If the warrant is obvious to the reader, it does not have to be announced. The following warrant is clear without being stated:

Claim: I have to buy a new watch.

Evidence: It says the same time as it did 30 minutes ago.

Warrant: My watch is broken.

A warrant can arise from various sources, including physical laws, human laws, assumptions, premises, common knowledge, aesthetic values, or ethical principles. For an argument to be successful, the reader must agree with the warrant, whether stated or implied.

See figure 5.2, "Please Sign Our Petition": A Case Study, on page 134, which illustrates how claims, warrants, and support work together to produce an effective argument in the workplace about the need for a company's health services.

STRATEGIES FOR ARGUMENT AND REBUTTAL

Strategies for Arguments

As discussed above, most successful arguments depend on the careful use of reason, what Aristotle termed *logos*. However, other strategies can be considered in the planning stage or inserted to strengthen a point in the composing or revision stages. These strategies include the following:

- *Definition:* explaining what something is, especially in order to use the definition as a basis for support
- *Comparison:* noting similarities and/or differences
- *Common ground:* getting your readers to see that you share some of their values or concerns
- *Concession:* acknowledging the validity of an opposing point in order to appear fair
- *Appeal to reader interests:* showing how opponents might benefit by adopting your claim
- *Emotional (pathos) or ethical (ethos) appeal:* appealing subtly to the feelings or morality of your reader
- *Attention-grabbing techniques:* finding ways to keep the reader interested in your topic

Your decision to use these strategies could depend on factors like your

- topic
- argumentative purpose
- audience

These strategies are discussed below.

The two student argumentative essays at the end of this chapter, page 144 and page 147, make use of inductive and deductive reasoning respectively.

A **WARRANT** is a statement that tests the logical connection between a claim and its support.

Aristotle's three appeals are discussed on page 114–115.

Definition

➜ For more about definition, see chapter 3, Using Definition in an Essay," page 93.

It can be important to define a concept in order to prepare for its use in your essay. For example, if you want to argue that dance should be considered a sport, you can define precisely what is meant by *sport*. A definition most readers would agree with could be a springboard into your thesis, showing how dance skills reflect your definition of sport. Student writer Brydon Kramer defines *culture* in order to rebut an opposing claim about immigrants (p. 147).

Comparison

➜ For more on comparison, see Compare and Contrast in chapter 3 (p. 94).

Comparisons can be an effective argumentative strategy to make a claim more concrete and convincing. For example, if you establish criteria for judging the excellence of a film (perhaps by using definition), you could argue that *Harry Potter and the Deathly Hallows—Part 2* satisfies those criteria. However, you might be able to strengthen your points by comparing this film with another in the series, say, *Harry Potter and the Order of the Phoenix*, which does not satisfy your criteria. Similarly, you could compare *Deathly Hallows* favourably with a classic fantasy film, such as the original *Star Wars* film, noting similarities between them. Comparisons are used in "Should Veiling Be Banned in the Courtroom?" and "Why Politicians Should Be More Like Professors."

Common Ground

Values are involved in most arguments. Especially for audiences that are neutral or opposed, appealing to common ground is an effective strategy. This can be done by demonstrating that you share basic values with your reader, such as the need for a healthy and safe environment, though you may disagree on specifics. However, reinforcing common goals or reminding readers of shared values can also work when your writing purpose is to strengthen a consensus. In the conclusion of her essay on banning performance-enhancing drugs, student writer Shelby Gurney stresses the benefits of drug-free athletics to future generations; she ends by reinforcing her main points by appealing to common ground:

> When professional athletes are good role models, they will benefit children in the future, who learn that an athlete can excel without harmful drugs. Ridding sport of these drugs will not be easy, but the effort is worthwhile as long as people care about fairness, integrity, health, and the meaning and value of sport.

Concession

Agreeing in part with an opponent's argument is applicable to audiences that are neutral or opposed to your view. It shows your reasonableness and fairness, inviting the reader to approach your view with a similar respect. After making the concession, you will usually follow with a strong point of your own. In the excerpt below, student writer Spencer Cleave addresses an opposing point concerning the US embargo against Cuba. After a concession (italicized below), he introduces a counter-claim that he will develop in his next paragraph:

Many supporters of the maintenance of the trade embargo against Cuba contend that the Cuban government fails to uphold the human rights of its population. *It is true that Cuba has had a number of human rights violations in its past.* However, many reforms have recently been made by the government in an attempt to remedy its human rights problems. These efforts show that the government has a desire to improve the conditions within its own nation.

Making concessions is also common when the argumentative purpose is to reach a compromise.

Appeal to Reader Interests

Important in almost all arguments is getting the reader to see benefits—either personally or as a member of a community—in adopting your view. In her essay on safe-injection sites, student writer Kerry Hinds first addresses mild opponents by pointing out the disadvantages drug users must overcome; when she argues that these sites would reduce health-care costs, she addresses other opponents, those motivated more by practical than by humanitarian concerns:

> If we wish to control the spread of AIDS, we cannot look at AIDS as strictly a drug-user's disease; many non-users get infected also. If money is not put into [safe-injection] programs such as these, our health-care system will be further burdened with the care of chronically ill patients, costing the taxpayers even more money than the cost of opening a clinic. Without foresight and action, the health of non-users will be further compromised and our health-care system will be further debilitated.

Emotional and Ethical Appeals (Pathos and Ethos)

Although most effective arguments are driven more by reason than by emotion, appeals to emotion or ethics help a reader personalize a topic (pathos) or universalize it (ethos) and can be especially useful in extended value claims where an action is required. In the following brief examples, the student writers use appeals in their conclusions to motivate a reader:

> We all have the power through our dietary choices to end the inhumane practices of factory farming and the suffering of our fellow creatures. Sometimes forgotten is that its victims are living, breathing beings that deserve to be respected and treated well.
>
> –Kaitlin Pitre

> It is a person's moral responsibility to protect those who are being victimized and to prevent bullying from taking and ruining more lives than it already has.
>
> —Layne Robinson

A Closer Look

Arguments in Advertising

A common form for argument to take is advertising. Of course, we are surrounded by ads in a variety of media every day. However, advertising works best if the advertiser knows its audience. Take, for example, a skin-care product targeted to young women. An advertiser might use comparisons and appeals to reader (viewer) interests while ignoring common ground and concession strategies. To support its extended value claim to get you to buy the product, the advertiser might use a split screen to compare a smooth leg to a stubbly one and end with an image of the young woman in her workplace competently giving orders to her subordinates (appeal to reader/viewer interests).

By contrast, a non-profit group might make emotional appeals through graphic images of impoverished children, suggesting, too, that both the organization and the reader/viewer share basic concerns, such as the need to end poverty, the need for educational access, and the like (common ground). Concessions wouldn't serve the need of most advertisers, though a famous exception is Avis Rent-a-Car, whose tagline for 50 years (until 2012) was "When you're only number two, you try harder."

→ For examples of specific techniques to attract interest, such as questions, anecdotes, and description, see Dramatic Introduction, chapter 3, page 73.

When deciding whether or not to use these kinds of appeals, consider your audience and argumentative purpose. It may not be a good idea to use a strong emotional appeal if you are writing on factory farming and most of your readers are dedicated meat-eaters, as it could alienate them. However, comparisons, common ground, and appeals to reader interests could be apt strategies in this instance.

Attention-Grabbing Techniques

Using a hook can draw a reader into your essay, especially if your topic might be perceived as dry; it can also be used if your argumentative purpose is to raise awareness.

EXERCISE 5.6

Discuss in groups or individually analyze in writing the effectiveness of the "Help save the lipstick" advertisement by the World Wide Fund for Nature (Singapore) in figure 5.1, considering the strategies mentioned in A Closer Look: Arguments in Advertising, along with any other points relevant to argument. Remember that when you analyze an argument, you should consider purpose, audience, use of reason, and argumentative strategies. While an analysis of a written source could consider language and linguistic resources, at least part of your analysis of this ad should consider its visual effects and the way(s) they are created.

Before analyzing the ad, use at least two reliable sites to determine the origins, aims, and reputation of the WWF.

- Consider the following questions before discussing specific strategies:
- Who is the ad designed for? How, specifically, does it appeal to this viewer/reader?
- Might other viewers/readers respond favourably to the ad's message? Why or why not?

- What was your immediate response to the image and its headline? Did you read all of the text below the headline? How did this text affect your response?

FIGURE 5.1 This advertisement, produced for the World Wide Fund for Nature (Singapore), encourages the use of certified sustainable palm oil.

Source: Photo Credit: Alain Compost/WWF-Canon; Poster credit: Courtesy World Wide Fund for Nature.

Strategies for Rebuttal

For most arguments, you need to consider how to respond to the other side. In the **rebuttal** (also called the refutation), you raise the opposing points to reveal their weaknesses, which strengthens your own argument. As with other argumentative strategies, whether and how you choose to make a rebuttal will depend on your topic, your argumentative purpose, and your audience. Two main approaches are discussed below.

Strategy A: Acknowledgement

Acknowledging the other side is important in most arguments; however, if your writing purpose is to promote consensus, it may not be important. If your audience is likely composed of those who mildly disagree, a good strategy is to acknowledge the other side and oppose it by a strong argument. You might also choose to use strategy A if your readers were unfamiliar with the points on the other side; spending too much time on the opposing view could work against you.

In the following example, student writer Laura Benard represents the opposing viewpoint by a prepositional phrase (*Despite the aesthetic value*) ahead of her thesis

> **REBUTTAL** means raising an opponent's points in an argument in order to reveal their weaknesses, thereby strengthening your own argument.

statement. She treats the opposing argument, that people use pesticides to make their lawn look attractive, as obvious:

> Despite the aesthetic value of weed-free, green lawns, the negative impacts of maintaining lawns by means of pesticide, lawn mower, and water use are so great that lawn owners should adopt less intensive maintenance practices or consider lawn alternatives.

If you use the acknowledgement strategy, you can phrase the acknowledgement as a dependent clause that contains the less important (opposing) information and follow with your own claim in an independent clause:

> Although some may argue [major point of opposition argument], the fact is [your thesis].

However, it is sometimes a good idea to provide background or a brief summary of the opposing view. Deciding how much space to spend on the other side requires striking a balance between the desires to demonstrate your fairness and to present a strong argument of your own. When you summarize the other side, ensure you

- use an objective tone and neutral language
- are concise and clear
- state the other side's points fairly

Strategy B: Point-by-Point Rebuttal

Consider the following rebuttal strategies for different audiences:

- For a neutral reader familiar with the topic and the major points of debate (such as arguments about legalizing marijuana, abolishing capital punishment, and other often-debated topics), it is a good strategy to raise all opposing points and rebut each one. If a topic is less familiar, acknowledge only the major counter-arguments, ensuring that your points are stronger (or use strategy A, above).
- For neutral or strong opponents of your claim who may not be knowledgeable about the topic, consider acknowledging their side and conceding minor points. An important aspect of rebuttal is anticipating your opponents' objections so that you can rebut such points in advance. Acknowledging your opponents' views should show that, having analyzed them, you find them inadequate. Consider using strategy B: point-by-point rebuttal, then, if your audience strongly disagrees.
- When writing for opponents who are knowledgeable about the topic, consider responding thoroughly to the other side: since your reader will likely be familiar with many of the arguments in its favour, by ignoring them, you could lose credibility. If your overall purpose is to reach a compromise, your objective here will be to find common ground. In either case, you would raise individual points, usually beginning with an opposing point, and respond to its weaknesses. Usually, you will stress the opposing point's inadequacies or inconsistencies and

Summary of Argumentative Strategies: Among the argumentative strategies you can consider are definition (p. 128), comparison (p. 128), common ground (p. 128), concession (p. 128), appeal to reader interests (p. 129), emotional and ethical appeals (p. 129), attention-grabbing techniques (p. 130), acknowledgement rebuttal (p. 131), point-by-point rebuttal (p. 132).

draw attention to faulty reasoning. However, if your goal is to find common ground, you will assume the role of a constructive critic rather than that of a strong opponent. In either case, though, your voice should be unbiased and objective. See Brydon Kramer's essay in this chapter, page 147.

For three of the topics listed below:

1. Choose one of the two purpose options (to keep it simple, the audience can always be considered neutral).
2. Keeping in mind topic, purpose, and audience, select the most appropriate strategies discussed on pages 128–132 and summarized in the margin on page 132.
3. Write one paragraph per topic justifying the strategies you chose.

EXERCISE 5.7

TOPIC	ARGUMENTATIVE PURPOSE (P. 117)	AUDIENCE (NEUTRAL)*	STRATEGIES
negative effects of music videos on adolescent girls	1. defend view 2. raise awareness		
permitting exotic pets to be sold in Canada	1. change situation 2. raise awareness		
The Occupy movements were a failure	1. defend view 2. reach understanding		
energy drinks	1. change situation 2. raise awareness		
cigarettes should be declared illegal	1. change situation 2. promote consensus		
Mac computers vs. PCs	1. defend view 2. reach understanding		
body piercing	1. promote consensus 2. raise awareness		
body checking in minor hockey	1. defend view 2. raise awareness		
banning fast-food outlets near schools	1. change situation 2. reach understanding		
citizen justice	1. promote consensus 2. reach understanding		

*As discussed in chapter 2, audiences can vary according to their knowledge and interest levels, as well as their orientation to the topic. Audiences could also be classified in other ways—for example, by age range, education, vocation, and so on.

This chapter began by noting the importance of argument in all aspects of our lives. Figure 5.2 is adapted from an information campaign of a medical service company in response to a government decision to restructure the company's services. Although the form of the argument is obviously different from that of an essay, notice that in its essentials it follows the argumentative model discussed above. The writers also used argumentative strategies, such as concessions and common ground. Numbers and letters have been added in order to make it comparable to body paragraphs in an outline.

As with most arguments, the claim is announced early. It is an extended value claim, asking the reader to take an action—signing a petition—however, it is grounded in a value claim, that government plans could "compromise one of the best lab systems." To support this claim, the company cites various facts and statistics in a list; these purport to show that the labs provide essential services. Underlying the claim and connecting it to the evidence is the warrant: the premise that people are happy with and care about the services the lab provides. If the warrant is not accepted by the reader, the claim will be ineffective.

The argument begins by summarizing three points of the opposing position. Systematically, the points are refuted in the next two sections. For example, point A under "What the Government Is Planning" is countered by two points under "What this means to patient care" (A.1 and A.2.). The argument is developed through cause–effect: a 20 per cent cut (cause) will affect patients and patient care.

WE NEED YOUR SUPPORT! PLEASE SIGN OUR PETITION

The government plans to fundamentally change how laboratory services are delivered. These plans jeopardize the lab services you depend on.

These plans could also compromise one of the best lab systems there is—one that has been serving patients in communities across our province for more than 45 years.

I. WHAT THE GOVERNMENT IS PLANNING

A. It has already announced a 20 per cent cut in the fees it pays to community labs for the testing services we provide.

B. It is planning to dismantle the existing province-wide system and create six independent lab delivery systems—one within each of the health authorities.

C. It is planning to establish a bidding process that would see each health authority going to tender for all outpatient lab services.

II. WHAT THIS MEANS TO PATIENT CARE

A. 1. Alone, the magnitude of the fee cuts will affect patients and patient care.
A. 2. The government's other plans will bring a period of complete instability, turning today's system upside down.

B. The government's plans will result in six fragmented systems—potentially providing six levels of service and access—and six new bureaucracies to manage them.

C. Applying a competitive bidding process to laboratory medicine comes at a very high risk. Price is always a major factor in a competitive bidding process, and lowest bids come with reduced access service levels.

III. OUR CONCERNS

A. The government based its plans on flawed, faulty, and unsubstantiated data.

B. We don't understand why the government chose to dismantle a system that works well, instead of building on its strengths.

C. We fully support the government's goals. However, we don't agree with the way it is trying to achieve these goals.

FIGURE 5.2 "Please sign our petition": A Case Study

IV. WHAT WE'VE DONE

A. 1. We've told the government repeatedly that we support its goals and can help them achieve them. We've told the government to put its plans on hold so that we can talk to them about less disruptive alternatives.

A. 2. We've told patients and physicians about the government's plans and how they could affect lab services and service levels.

WHAT WE'RE DOING NOW

B. 1. We're asking people who value the services we provide to show their support by signing our petition.

B. 2. If you want to know more about the government's plans and our concerns, please visit our website.

C. *If you care about protecting the lab services you rely on—please sign our petition.*

Community Lab Facts:

- For more than 45 years, physicians and their patients have relied on the quality cost-effective diagnostic testing and information services community labs provide.
- The testing and information services we provide help doctors diagnose, treat, and monitor their patients.
- **Every day**, the 1,600 people working in community labs
  - provide a selection of several hundred different tests, from routine to specialty diagnostics.
  - support early discharge hospital programs by providing access to lab testing at home and in the community.
  - perform more than 55,000 tests on the 16,000 patients who visit one of our labs.
  - visit more than 700 patients in their homes and in long-term care facilities, at no charge to the patient or health-care system.
  - deliver more than 5,000 specimens to public testing agencies at no cost to the patient, agency, or health-care system.
  - transmit lab results electronically via PathNET to more than 3,000 physicians.
  - support our services through an extensive collection and transportation network, information technology, and analytical expertise that's taken years to develop.

FIGURE 5.2 (*Continued*)

In addition to countering the major points of the government's argument, the company is concerned with establishing its credibility. Topic II addresses patient care, focusing concern directly on the reader. Topic III Point C attempts to find common ground in an effort to show fairness to the government side: "We fully support the government's goals."

IV serves as a conclusion to the argument. The information in Points A, B, and C in effect summarizes the claim by rewording it: in the claim/thesis in the first paragraph of the piece, the phrase "jeopardize the lab services you depend on" is used; compare—"affect lab services and service levels, "value the services we provide," and "protecting the lab services you rely on." Point C makes an emotional appeal with its deliberate choice of the words *care* and *protecting*.

EXERCISE 5.8

In groups or individually, analyze the argument presented in figure 5.2 and evaluate its effectiveness, using the questions below as guidelines.

1. Consider your own position toward the issues. Do you have any knowledge about this issue or similar issues relating to government decisions about health care (or education)? How do government decisions affect you and/or other people who use these kinds of services? What are the sides of the debate? Which side do you support? How might your prior knowledge and opinions affect your response to this argument or others like it?

2. Is there anything that would have made the argument more effective? Be as specific as possible.

3. Are there any questionable appeals to emotion or ethics? Are there any logical fallacies? Why do you think the company does not give specific information in main point III, sub-point A: "The government based its plans on flawed, faulty, and unsubstantiated data"?

4. Analyze the refutation, bearing in mind topic, audience, and purpose. Why do the authors employ Strategy B to refute the three points mentioned in main point I, which gives background about the government's position?

5. What specific changes would you make if you were writing this argument as a formal essay? In what ways does it differ from a formal essay? (See chapter 9 for some of the characteristics of informal writing.)

6. Imagine that one year has passed. The government is proceeding with its plans; some lab employees have lost their jobs, and there are dire predictions in newspaper editorials that our health care will be directly affected. How do you think the company's argument might change in response? Write a revised claim that reflects the new current conditions. Choose one specific form: informal brochure for distribution, letter to the editor/editorial, or argumentative essay.

CATEGORIES OF FAULTY REASONING

Many arguments are based on opinion, but in order to be convincing, the arguer should not come across as *opinionated*. Argument at the university level isn't writing with an "attitude": in effective arguments, writers express themselves objectively, using neutral language.

Consider the following passage in which the writer makes it clear to the reader that he is opinionated; however, if the reader is overwhelmed by opinion, he or she may well miss the points:

> Institutions of higher learning are meant for people hoping to broaden their interests and knowledge in order to contribute to society. I, myself, agree with this principle, and I also agree that a degree can help me acquire a job and be good at it. Along with this, I do not doubt that these institutions facilitate higher cognitive functioning. What I do not agree

with is the approach that these institutions have toward the sciences. In fact, I oppose the favouritism that is always shown to the sciences whenever financial matters are considered.

Rewrite the paragraph above, eliminating the references to opinion and first-person pronouns (*I*, *me*, etc.). Does the revised paragraph sound more forceful? How is credibility improved?

EXERCISE 5.9

Logical, Emotional, and Ethical Fallacies

Ineffective arguments with logical, emotional, or ethical fallacies detract from the writer's credibility. Misuse of reason affects reliability: we don't trust someone who misuses reason. Misuse of emotional appeals shows unfairness to the other side: emotional fallacies *exploit* emotions, so are very different from legitimate appeals to emotion.

Some fallacies are founded on faulty inductive reasoning, for example, cause–effect fallacies; others are grounded in the faulty use of deductive reasoning, in which invalid generalizations are made. Table 5.3 lists 20 common argumentative fallacies. Avoid these in your own writing and look for them in the arguments of your opponents. Identifying them and analyzing their faults will enhance your credibility.

These fallacies were categorized many years ago, and you may hear them referred to by their old Latin names. In table 5.3, their Latin names have been replaced by more modern descriptive labels.

Use critical thinking to decide whether the writer has used faulty reasoning or has manipulated emotion. There may be times when, for example, only two valid alternatives exist (vs. either–or fallacy). Analogies can be used in argument, but a false analogy makes an extreme or illogical comparison. Similarly, a precedent can be used for support in argument (see p. 55) but is different from the tradition fallacy in being based in logic.

You can consider most fallacies oversimplifications that, as such, fail to do justice to the complexities of an issue. The writer using them weakens his or her argument, as a reader using critical thinking could say, "Wait a minute; that doesn't make sense." When you argue, you want your statements to be forceful and effective—not to provoke suspicion. Otherwise, the reader might commit the fallacy of rejecting your entire argument (hasty generalization) because in one instance you misused reason.

A writer needs to look closely and objectively at *how* he or she argues and ensure that (1) arguments are always founded on logic and (2) that appeals to emotion and ethics are moderate—avoiding excessive praise or condemnation. Watching out for the first will make the writer appear reliable and trustworthy; watching out for the second will make the writer appear fair.

When you oversimplify or misuse emotion, you weaken your argument and give the critical thinker an opportunity to reject your claims.

TABLE 5.3 Common Logical, Emotional, and Ethical Fallacies

TERM	DESCRIPTION	EXAMPLE
Inductive		
certain consequences ("slippery slope")	a common fallacy that insists that a result is inevitable based on an oversimplified cause–effect relationship	If we legalize marijuana, other, more dangerous drugs are going to end up being legalized as well, and we will end up with a drug culture.
doubtful causes	a cause–effect fallacy that insists that a result is inevitable and cites too few causes to support that result; it bases an argument on a relationship that may not exist	He looked unhappy after the exam; he must have failed miserably. (This argument assumes there could be only one cause for his unhappiness—if, indeed, he was unhappy.)
either–or (false dilemma)	suggests that there are only two available options, one of which will be unacceptable to the audience	Either I borrow the car tonight or my life is over. (Consider that cry "you're either with me or against me," which takes the logical either–or fallacy and gives it an emotional thrust.)
false cause	another cause–effect fallacy; asserts that simply because one event preceded another one there must be a cause–effect relationship between them	Neesha wore her favourite socks to class the day she failed a test; consequently, she threw the socks away.
hasty generalization	forms a conclusion based on insufficient evidence	I talked to two people, both of whom said the text was useless, so I will not buy it. (Two people may not be an adequate sample.)
Deductive		
authority worship	accepts unquestioningly the argument of an authority solely on the basis of who says it	He spent 17 years on the Atomic Energy Board. He must know everything there is to know about his subject.
circular reasoning	draws a conclusion on the basis of an unproven premise as if it didn't need proving.	I'm an "A" student. How can the teacher give me a B–?
false authority	argues on the basis of a presumed or unspecified authority	Studies show that people would support a law for raising the drinking age. (What specific studies show this?)
false analogy	compares two things that are, in fact, not alike	How can people complain about circuses that use wild animals in their acts? We keep animals that were once wild in small spaces, such as cats, in our homes.
fuzzy categories	insists that there is no fundamental separation between two ideas or objects, or no point where one clearly becomes the other. This fallacy appears when terms are imprecisely defined	A student argues with Professor Fuddle that there is no reason why his English essay received a C. After the professor agrees to a C+ grade, the student repeats the argument that there is no clear distinction between

Continued

TERM	DESCRIPTION	EXAMPLE
		a C+ and a B- and, using this flawed logic, eventually works his mark up to an A!
"it does not follow"	suggests that there is a logical connection (such as cause–effect) between two unrelated areas	I worked hard on this essay; I deserve at least a B+ for my effort. (Marks are usually awarded for results, not for effort.)
longevity	argues the validity of something solely because it has existed for a long time	How can war be wrong when people have been fighting each other since the dawn of civilization?
red herring	attempts to distract the reader, often by using an ethical fallacy	*Heart of Darkness* is not racist because Conrad's target was the greed of Europeans. (The writer does not address racism but draws attention to another issue.)
straw man	misrepresents an opponent's main argument by substituting a false or minor argument. If the audience agrees with the minor argument, they may dismiss the overall argument	Thaddeus Tuttle points out that while women have not achieved wage parity with men, they often take maternity leaves, which means they don't work as much as men.
tradition ("that is the way we have always done it")	argues for a course of action because it has been followed before, even if the same conditions no longer apply	You shouldn't ask if you can go to Toronto for the Thanksgiving weekend. This is a time you always spend with your family.
Emotional/ethical		
bandwagon	argues in favour of something because it has become popular	Everyone has seen the movie. We have to see it tonight.
desk-thumping (dogmatism)	asserts a claim without supporting evidence on the basis of what the arguer passionately believes	It is everyone's moral obligation to oppose the new tax.
guilt by association	takes a view contrary to that of a supposedly disreputable person or group, based only on the arguer's opinion of that person or group	How bad can whale hunting be when an extremist group like Greenpeace opposes it?
name-calling	assigns base motives to or insults an individual or group (see "slanted language")	Pharmaceutical companies' long hold on patents denies needed medicines to the poor and is just plain greedy.
name-dropping	uses the fact that some popular person or group supports something as an argument in its favour	Tiger Woods has endorsed Nike, Inc., products since 1996. On the other hand, when celebrity endorsements backfire, the celebrity's name becomes negatively associated with a product and the corporate-celebrity relationship quickly ends. (See guilt by association fallacy.)

EXERCISE 5.10

↻ Check answers to select questions

Find the Fallacies

The following story by student writer Alison James contains at least five errors in reasoning. Try to classify them according to the logical and emotional fallacies referred to above:

> Last week, Tina and her boyfriend, Steve, were running late for a reservation at their favourite restaurant. They were trying to figure out the quickest route so they would not lose their table. Tina suggested taking the side streets in order to avoid the traffic lights. Steve suggested that, while there are traffic lights on the main street, there was a chance they would hit all the green lights; but if they took the side streets, they would have to stop at all the stop signs. He added that the speed limits were faster on the main street than on the side streets where the speed limit was 30 km/h.
>
> Tina rebutted, "But nobody actually drives 30 on those streets!"
>
> Steve replied, "But we could get stuck behind a little old lady, and everybody knows how slowly they drive. Besides, we can speed on the main street; there are never any cops on that street, so we won't get a ticket."
>
> Tina said, "No, let's take the side streets: we always go that way. And there have been two accidents recently on the main street, so the side streets are safer."
>
> Neither of them was convinced by the other's argument (perhaps because they were so faulty), and they missed their reservation after all!

Slanted Language

In addition to misusing logic and emotion, a writer can show a lack of objectivity by using *slanted* or *loaded language*. Such language can take many forms, ranging from extreme direct statements to qualifiers (adjectives or adverbs) that more subtly convey a bias. When slanted language is direct and offensive, it is easy to spot. For example, if you dismissed the other side as *evil* or their argument as *horrible* or *disgusting*, you would reveal your bias. When you use strongly slanted language, even a reader who agrees with your stance could take offence and question your fairness.

However, slanted language can be less obvious, for example, when words play unfairly on the connotations, rather than the denotations, of language—in other words, on the negative *implications* of particular words, rather than on their literal meanings. A writer's careful and conscious use of a word's connotations can be effective in an argument, but if the purpose is to distort the truth, then the writer's credibility is at stake. For example, in the passage below, *removed from office*, rather than the more neutral *voted out of office*, plays unfairly on the connotations of the first phrase. The italicized words in the following reveal slanted language:

> In the recent election, the *reigning* political *regime was removed from office* as a result of the *atrocities they had committed* against the people of the

province. The voters believed the new government would improve things, but when you achieve such easy victory there is a tendency to overlook the reason for your victory: the people who elected you. Today, the government is ignoring the middle class, *betraying* the very people who *naively* voted them into office.

Collaborative Exercise: Making a Stronger Argument

The following paragraphs suffer from faulty logic, unfair emotional appeals, and slanted language. In groups, analyze each argument, determine what fallacies and inconsistencies make it ineffective, and suggest improvements to make the argument stronger.

EXERCISE 5.11

↻ Check answers to select questions

1. Genetically engineered foods are being sold in most supermarkets without anyone knowing that we are being used as guinea pigs for the corporations developing this technology. The general public is being kept in the dark entirely, and the way that this food is being sold is through one-sided advertising. The public is being told that genetically engineered foods are a safe and effective way to grow a lot of food faster by inserting genetic material of one species into another. Though the proponents of genetically engineered foods attempt to convince the public that this technology will save lives, the reality is that major biotechnology companies are developing genetically engineered food crops to maximize their profits. Corporations would have us believe that the reason why 19,000 children starve to death daily is because of inefficient agricultural practices, but the world currently produces enough food today to provide a decent diet for every person on this planet. In spite of this fact, genetically engineered foods are being sold as the cure for Third World starvation. This, however, is simply not true. The motives of the companies selling genetically engineered foods are not to save the lives of starving people, but to line their own pockets by profiting from the biotechnological industry. As a society, we should move to force governments to ban the development of genetically engineered foods before it is too late.

2. The legalization of marijuana would destroy society as we know it today. The typical Canadian would be exposed to many harsh drugs, such as coke, crack, and heroin, because of the increased acceptance of drugs within the community. Rehabilitation clinics for chronic drug users would be a huge drain on the economy. There would have to be new laws and screenings implemented to prevent people from working with heavy machinery or operating a motor vehicle while impaired by marijuana. Canadian business owners would be dissatisfied with many of their employees, and then discrimination would rear its ugly head. Firing someone for smoking marijuana and not being productive at work is not discrimination; however, the point would be made that it is. Clearly, our society would sink to a despicable level if this drug were legalized.

ORGANIZING AN OUTLINE FOR ARGUMENT

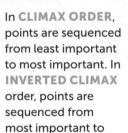

In **CLIMAX ORDER**, points are sequenced from least important to most important. In **INVERTED CLIMAX** order, points are sequenced from most important to least important.

When outlining and drafting an argumentative essay, you should pay attention to the order of your main points. Ensure that they are ordered logically—i.e., from least to most important point—**climax order**—or from most important point to least important—**inverted climax**—whichever is most relevant for your argument; other orders are possible. You do not have to include all the elements listed below nor follow the same order of parts. For example, it may not be necessary to include background if the issue is well known to most readers. The rebuttal may not require a lot of space and, depending on the topic and other factors, you might choose to place it before, rather than after, your main points.

Rhetorical Function of Parts

A **DELAYED CLAIM** is not announced until the evidence has been provided.

The most common pattern in formal writing is the classical model (or its variants) described here. Other patterns are possible, including **delayed claim**, which can be useful if you expect strong opposition or if your opening is dramatic or memorable in another way. In this pattern, you do not announce your claim until you have provided the evidence, so your claim, in effect, acts as the conclusion. (Although professional writers sometimes use a delayed claim, you should check with your instructor before doing so.)

Your argumentative purpose could also affect your organization. If you are arguing to reach a common understanding, as student writer Brydon Kramer does in the essay on page 147 of this chapter, you might give equal space to both sides and conclude by explaining how this common understanding can be met.

I. Introduction

- gains reader's attention and interest
- includes your claim that includes argumentative purpose
- establishes your credibility (knowledge, reliability, and fairness)

Body Paragraphs: II, III, and IV

II. Background

- presents background information, if relevant

III. Lines of Argument

- presents good reasons (logical, emotional, and ethical appeals) to support thesis; draws on assumptions, premises, and warrants
- uses all relevant evidence—facts, statistics, examples, views of experts/authorities
- presents reasons in specific order related to argument

IV. Refutation

- considers opposing points of view
- notes both advantages and disadvantages of opposing views
- argues that your thesis is stronger than opposing view and more beneficial to the reader

V. Conclusion

- summarizes argument
- expands or elaborates on the implication of your thesis
- makes clear what you want reader to think or do
- may make final strong ethical or emotional appeal

Argumentative Plan

EXERCISE 5.12

Part 1: Creating an Audience Profile

1. After you have chosen an arguable topic for an argumentative essay (see p. 120), create an audience profile by considering the three criteria characterizing an audience discussed in chapter 2.
2. In a group of three, take turns interviewing the other two members of your group, asking them questions that will enable you to assess your audience according to its
    - knowledge
    - interest level
    - orientation (agree, disagree, neutral, or mixed)
3. Write a one-paragraph description of what you have found, allotting at least a couple of sentences to each criterion.

Part 2: Creating an Argumentative Plan from Your Profile

Use the information about audience in Part 1 to create an audience plan based on your audience, topic, and argumentative purpose. The focus of the plan should be on specific strategies that would convince your audience given the topic and purpose. Include as many strategies as possible among those discussed on pages 128–132, explaining what each would contribute to the essay.

SAMPLE ARGUMENTATIVE ESSAYS

The most common argumentative purposes are to defend a viewpoint using a value claim and to recommend an action or a change a situation using an extended value claim. Essay 1 uses a value claim in the introduction. However, the two essays that follow illustrate other argumentative purposes: to reach a common understanding (Essay 2), and to raise awareness (Essay 3).

The essays illustrate many of the strategies discussed in this chapter.

For examples of argumentative essays that do not use research, see "Embrace the Mediocrity Principle" in chapter 1 (p. 19), "House Plants Are Better Than Dogs" in chapter 3 (p. 96), and the sample in-class student essay in Appendix B (p. 392).

To conserve space, the essays here are single-spaced and References and Works Cited sections are not on separate pages. The essays do not follow essay format requirements for title pages or identification information. For the correct ways of dealing with essay presentation, see Appendix A, page 388.

1. Sample Student Argumentative Essay—MLA Style

SAMPLE STUDENT ESSAY

The Gluten-Free Epidemic

by Dalton Anderson

[1]   Gluten-free dieting has been one of the most popular health trends in the last decade. This diet has received plenty of attention from health enthusiasts who claim eating gluten-free is one of the easiest ways to lose weight. Even professional athletes, such as the NBA's Steve Nash and tennis star Novak Djokavic, have jumped on the gluten-free bandwagon (Gulli 58). Studies have confirmed that eating gluten-free benefits the small percentage of the population afflicted with Celiac Disease, but there is no indication that gluten-free is beneficial to the average, healthy consumer. In fact, evidence suggests that eating gluten-free can be detrimental to a consumer's wallet and well-being.

> Anderson's thesis expresses a value claim. However, in his conclusion, he goes beyond this to make a recommendation to his readers.

[2]   There is only one rule to the gluten-free diet: consumers can eat whatever they wish, but their food cannot contain gluten. This problematic protein is constructed from gliadin and glutenin (Boissonneault et al. 13). Gluten is essential to many baking techniques because it supports the structure for pastries and other wheat products. Interestingly, gluten is also found in products that the average consumer wouldn't imagine having a connection to gluten, such as soy sauce, hot dogs, beer, and toothpaste (Gulli 55). Therefore, the common availability of gluten-containing foods makes a gluten-free diet very difficult to follow, especially considering that bread is the most consumed product in every country (Troncone, Auricchio, and Granata 330).

> Although this paragraph gives mostly background information, Anderson efficiently makes an argumentative point in the last sentence.

[3]   Dr. William Davis was the first pioneer for the gluten-free revolution. Davis's book, *Wheat Belly,* promises that by removing wheat (and, therefore, gluten) from the reader's diet, the reader will "lose 20, 30, or 50 pounds just within the first few weeks" (10). The solution is simple: "eliminate the wheat, eliminate the problem" (12). Since the release of *Wheat Belly,* the popularity of gluten-free dieting has skyrocketed. Twenty-five percent of consumers now look for gluten-free options when shopping (Boissonneault et al. 13). Gluten-free has grown into a $6.2 billion worldwide market that continues to expand every day with large companies like Kellogg's, Campbell, and Domino's all converting to get a share of the market. Gluten-free options make up a $90 million market in Canada alone (Gulli 55). In addition, the market is expected to grow 20% annually for the foreseeable future (Mitchell 9).

[4]   Most of the consumers who make up this emerging market are people who don't have a medical requirement to eat gluten-free. Currently, the only portion of the population restricted to eating gluten-free for life is the small percentage suffering from Celiac Disease. Celiac Disease is a rare autoimmune disease that affects 1% of the population (Zannini et al. 13) and occurs in individuals who are genetically sensitive to gluten (Troncone & Jabri 582). The disease is caused by an irregular reaction of specialized white blood cell to the gliadin portion of gluten. Celiacs usually suffer from wheat allergy and gluten sensitivity as well, which are conditions that are more common in the general public (Boissonneault et al. 13). Celiacs who consume gluten may experience anemia, skin lesions, chronic diarrhea, osteopenia, and

> Anderson uses four sources in this relatively short paragraph, carefully placing his citations so the reader is clear on where the information comes from. See chapter 7, page 213, and chapter 8 for more about citations.

infertility (Troncone et al. 329). These severe effects of Celiac Disease are why a gluten-free diet is needed for a Celiac's entire life.

[5]   Celiac Disease is commonly misdiagnosed for gluten sensitivity or wheat allergy. Proper diagnosis between these conditions is almost impossible because suitable testing requires patients to be exposed to gluten for several months (Boissonneault et al. 17). Even then, a definitive result may not be found. All of these conditions are similar in symptoms and differ primarily in hormone and blood cell levels associated with each disease. For example, an elevated amount of the antibody "IgE" indicates that the patient is suffering from a wheat allergy. Gluten sensitivity and wheat allergies are more common in the general population than is Celiac Disease, however. Seven percent of the population suffers from gluten sensitivity while 5 percent of the population suffers from wheat allergy (Boissonneault et al. 13). A gluten-free diet is the only medical nutrition therapy for Celiac Disease, gluten sensitivity, and wheat allergy that can ease the symptoms of these conditions (Troncone et al. 329).

[6]   While a gluten-free diet may be the only treatment for those with Celiac Disease, there is no scientific proof that eating gluten-free aids consumers with other conditions or those who are looking to lose weight. Although many consumers are convinced that they have experienced great results since they converted to eating gluten-free, in fact, these results generally occur from an overall improvement in their diet (Cadenhead and Sweeny 161). Switching to gluten-free diets requires consumers to be aware of everything they are eating. This means that many processed foods that contain gluten are eliminated from a consumer's diet in exchange for "basic, nutrient-dense, whole foods" (161). For example, consumers may be so concentrated on avoiding gluten that they stop buying potato chips, not because the chips are unhealthy but because the chips contain gluten. Thus, they may not realize that they feel healthier because they've stopped eating junk food. Average consumers may also experience a placebo effect, where they have a perceived improvement in health, despite no medical improvements. Furthermore, many unsubstantiated claims exist saying that gluten-free dieting helps patients with irritable bowel syndrome, autism, and autoimmune disorders, but these claims are surrounded by controversy in the scientific community and are, at the very least, unproven (Boissonneault et al. 13).

[7]   While positive evidence supporting gluten-free dieting remains unsubstantiated by science, many reports have investigated the negative effects of gluten-free dieting. Currently, many gluten-free food options lack the necessary nutrients that make up a healthy diet. By avoiding whole grains and cereals, dieters are missing integral parts of balanced eating habits such as fibre, vitamin B (Cadenhead & Sweeny 161) and minerals like calcium and iron (Zannini et al. 229). These whole grains also provide plenty of energy to engage metabolic processes (Cadenhead & Sweeny 161). Even the original pioneer of the gluten-free diet admits that the current gluten-free options are not very beneficial. In a recent interview, William Davis admitted that current gluten-free options are "nonsense" because they are "made with 'junk carbohydrates,' which raise blood sugar and are contributing factors to hypertension, cataracts, heart disease, and cancer" (CBC). Gluten-free options are often lower in quality and have worse "mouth-feel" and "off-flavors" (Zannini et al. 229).

[8]   Moreover, gluten-free options may not even be entirely gluten-free. Processing problems at large food preparation plants may lead to harmful gluten contamination and compromise the gluten-free nature of the product (Zannini et al. 229). Cross-contamination can occur practically at any time during the preparation of meals, but it is especially common when gluten-free substances are prepared on the same surfaces as other gluten-containing

Anderson uses inductive reasoning to support the claim that gluten-free diets don't help most people and, in fact, can be detrimental to one's health. He relies on research studies. This contrasts with Kramer who uses mostly deductive reasoning in his argument (p. 147).

Continued

items. Restaurant foods may contain undeclared gluten in their dishes as well (Lomangino 7). Sheila Crowe (qtd. in Lomangino) discovered a New York City chef who admitted to serving high-gluten-containing pasta entrees to customers who specifically asked for gluten-free meals because he believed that gluten-free items were identical to regular food items (7).

Note the use of facts and statistics in this paragraph: they are used to support the claim here that gluten-free options can be costly. They also give Anderson credibility by showing his knowledge.

[9]   Gluten-free options are also hurting consumers' wallets as much as their health. In Canada, gluten-free products are 242% more expensive than the counterpart regular product on average (Stevens & Rashid 147). For example, churches in Canada can buy gluten-free wafers for $23 for a 1000-piece box instead of boxes of 1000 regular wafers for $10 (Gulli 55). For most consumers following this health trend, finding gluten-free items is a large challenge as well. Of their entire stock of items, grocery stores, on average, carry only 36% gluten-free products. The price of many gluten-free items may also vary between different shopping venues. The lack of available gluten-free options at reasonable prices may affect an individual's compliance and dedication to the diet, which may lead to nutritional consequences and complications (Lee et al. 423).

Rather than simply repeat his value claim, Anderson ends by making recommendations. Verbs like *should* and *needs* suggest that action is required—an extended value claim.

[10]   Consumers should recognize that gluten-free dieting is not a reliable method for controlling eating habits. While many people see gluten-free as a healthy option, this is certainly not the case. Gluten-free products should be left for the small minority of the population afflicted with Celiac Disease and other gluten-related medical issues. More scientific analysis needs to be dedicated to investigating the nutritional benefits of gluten-free options for the average consumer. Consumers should wait until gluten-free products are proven to provide the same nutritional value to consumers as regular products do, as many of the common substitutes for gluten like oats and cornstarch are not viable replacements. Consumers need to be patient for the development of gluten-free products in order to keep themselves from hurting their health and their wallets; it is much too early to jump on the gluten-free bandwagon.

Works Cited

Boissonneault, Gilbert, et al. "Disorders Triggered by Gluten." *Journal of the American Academy of Physicians Assistants* 26.3 (2013): 13–17. *Academic Search Complete*. Web. 8 May 2014.

Cadenhead, Kathleen, and Margo Sweeny. "Gluten Elimination Diets: Facts for Patients on This Food Fad. *BC Medical Journal* 55.3 (2013): 161–65. *Academic Search Complete*. Web. 10 May 2014.

CBC. "Gluten-Free Is 'Nonsense' Says *Wheat Belly* Author." *CBCNews: British Columbia*. Canadian Broadcasting Company, 24 Oct. 2013. Web. 7 May 2014.

Gulli, Cathy. "Gone Gluten-Free." *Maclean's* 16 Sept. 2013: 55–59. Print.

Lee, Anne, et al. "Economic Burden of a Gluten-Free Diet." *Journal of Human Nutrition & Dietetics* 20.5 (2007): 423–30. *Academic Search Complete*. Web. 14 May 2014.

Lomangino, Kevin. "Are 'Gluten-Free' Foods Really Gluten-Free?" *Clinical Nutrition Insight* 39.3 (2013): 7–8. *Ovid*. Web. 16 May 2014.

Mitchell, Richard. "Going Gluten-Free." *Refrigerated & Frozen Foods Retailer* Oct. 2010: 9–12. *LexisNexis Academic*. Web. 16 May 2014.

Stevens, Laci, and Mohsin Rashid. "Gluten-Free and Regular Foods: A Cost Comparison. *Canadian Journal of Dietetic Practice and Research* 69.3 (2008): 147–50. *Academic Search Complete*. Web. 10 May 2014.

Troncone, Riccardo, Renata Auricchio, and V. Granata. (2008) "Issues Related to Gluten-Free Diet in Coeliac Disease." *Current Opinion in Clinical Nutrition and Metabolic Care* 11.3 (2008): 329–33. *Ovid*. Web. 10 May 2014.

Troncone, Riccardo, and Bana Jabri. "Coeliac Disease and Gluten Sensitivity." *Journal of Internal Medicine* 269.6 (2011): 582–90. *Ovid*. Web. 10 May 2014.

Zannini, Emanuele, Julie Miller Jones, Stefano Renzetti, and Elke K. Arendt. "Functional Replacements for Gluten." *Annual Review of Food Science and Technology* 3 (2012): 227–45. *Academic Search Complete*. Web. 10 May 2014.

EXERCISE 5.13

1. Whom do you believe Anderson is writing to in his essay? Do you think his argument is well suited to this audience? Why (not)?

2. a. Why do you think he uses so few direct quotations, preferring summary overall? (You could look ahead to chapter 7, which discusses the use of sources.)

   b. Comment on his use of Davis as a source in paragraphs 3 and 7.

3. Has Anderson included an adequate number of sources to support his claims? Is there a good sampling of sources—for example, from a variety of media —or do you think he has relied too much on one source or type of source? Explain your answer with examples.

4. Analyze paragraph 6 for unity, coherence, and development, considering the use of methods discussed in chapter 3 (p. 63, p. 64, p. 85).

5. a. Consider the effectiveness of the structure of Anderson's essay (see Rhetorical Function of Parts, p. 142).

   b. Referring specifically to his introduction and conclusion, analyze their contribution to the essay as a whole.

2. Sample Student Argumentative Essay—APA Style

For another example of an essay using APA style, see the essay by Iain Lawrence on page 200.

SAMPLE STUDENT ESSAY

Should Veiling Be Banned in the Courtroom?

by Brydon Kramer

[1]　　In 2007, Canadian courts were confronted with the task of balancing religious freedom with the right to a fair trial when a Muslim complainant (known as N.S.), who had alleged that her uncle and cousin had sexually assaulted her as a child, requested to remain veiled while testifying (Makin, 2012). This case highlights the tensions that sometimes arise out of multiculturalism. To start with, multicultural policies attempting to accommodate cultural practices often result in contending liberties, especially when the practices at stake challenge dominant norms. In the case of N.S., many worried that allowing the complainant to veil

Continued

In his introduction, Kramer provides background, beginning with the specific case that gave rise to conflicting principles. He impartially represents both sides before announcing his thesis in the last sentence. Although Kramer announces his preferred outcome, by fairly representing arguments on both sides, he encourages an open and reasoned approach to an emotionally charged topic. See Two Modern Models of Argument: Rogers and Toulmin, page 115.

In this paragraph, Kramer summarizes the court's decision, using direct quotation in block format to stress the importance of the court's exact wording. In paragraph 8, he again uses direct quotation in citing the view of the dissenting judge in the case of N.S.

Kramer uses definition to support his opposition to the claim of multiculturalism critics that immigrants should not be given "special rights."

while testifying would hinder the defendants' right to a fair trial. These worries have led to a violent clash between religious freedom and the "judicial norms that address the probative functions of . . . courts" (Schwartzbaum, 2011, p. 1536). Furthermore, as Okin suggests (as cited in Song, 2005, p. 474), multicultural policies often promote cultural accommodation at the expense of gender equality. By accommodating religious head scarves, which she claims place unfair constraints on women, the patriarchal hierarchies within minority cultures are entrenched. Despite these tensions, many argue that forcing Muslim women to unveil in courtrooms may further alienate an already marginalized group of individuals, forcing them to make an impossible choice between their culture and the justice system (Howard, 2012, p. 159). Importantly, banning the *niqab* in courtrooms could discourage victims of abuse from coming forward. Therefore, the costs of banning the *niqab* outweigh its benefits.

[2]   In response to N.S.'s case, on December, 20, 2012, the Supreme Court of Canada decided that there are occasions when "religious beliefs must bow to social and legal norms" (Makin, 2012); thus, the court established a set of criteria to evaluate cases where cultural and/or religious practices contend with an individual's access to justice. *Niqab*-wearing women possessing sincere religious beliefs may be required to unveil while testifying if

> (a) this is necessary to prevent a serious risk to the fairness of the trial, because reasonably available alternative measures will not prevent the risk; and (b) the salutary effects of requiring her to remove the *niqab* outweigh the deleterious effects of doing so (Chief Justice Beverly McLachlin, as cited in Makin, 2012).

[3]   This decision reflects the court's recognition that an extreme approach towards the issue of the *niqab* would fail to "accommodate and balance sincerely held religious beliefs against other interests, [which] is deeply entrenched in Canadian law" (Chief Justice Beverly McLachlin, as cited in Makin, 2012).

[4]   Some opponents of multiculturalism argue that granting groups special rights is unjust, especially in the case of immigrants who voluntarily immigrate; however, such an assumption underestimates a culture's importance. Culture is any "well-integrated, well-bounded, and largely self generated entit[y] defined by a set of key attributes, including a shared language, history, and values" (Song, 2005, p. 474). When the attributes of a culture become embedded in institutions, they form a "societal culture" (Kymlicka, 1995, p. 76). According to Kymlicka, access to this culture "provides its members with meaningful ways of life across the full range of human activities, including social, religious, recreational, and economic life, encompassing both public and private spheres" (p. 76). This context of choice grants individuals meaningful options that allow them to live their lives according to what they conceive as "good." Consequently, Margalit and Raz assert (as cited in Kymlicka, 1995, p. 89) that an individual's access to a "societal culture" is crucial.

[5]   Unfortunately, not all cultures possess the institutions required to provide their members with meaningful options; for example, immigrant cultures that have been relocated to new territories and have left behind their institutions no longer possess "societal cultures" (Kymlicka, 1995, p. 78). Instead, immigrants must gain access to the institutions of the dominant group by adopting national languages, public holidays, and state symbols; however, integration into a foreign culture requires acculturation and is extremely difficult. Thus, some accommodations are necessary to allow minority groups access to the majority's "societal culture" (p. 89).

This is often achieved through group-differentiated rights, which emerge in multicultural policies. In the case of N.S., allowing her and other Muslim women to veil in courts would assist them in integrating into the dominant "societal culture." However, as noted above, allowing Muslim women to veil in courts leads to two major challenges.

[6]   First, many assert that multicultural policies, which seek to accommodate cultural practices, hinder gender equality. Feminists argue that multicultural policies often sacrifice women at "the altar of protection for group rights" by accommodating cultural practices that are inherently sexist (Beaman, 2011, p. 460). Many view the *niqab* as a symbol of female oppression that places unequal restrictions on Muslim women. Such a belief is reflected by the French Conseil d'Etat's statement in 2010 (as cited in Howard, 2012, p. 149), claiming that the veil "testifies to a profoundly in-egalitarian conception of the relationship between men and women." Such views are supported by the claim that women and young girls may be coerced to veil against their will by men in their families and communities; for example, in *Begum v. Head Teacher and Governors of Denbigh High School*, 2006, several girls feared that if the school allowed students to veil, they would face pressures from their fathers and older brothers to veil as well (Howard, 2012, p. 151). Thus, according to this argument, allowing women to veil in courts entrenches systems of patriarchy within Muslim culture and generates a disturbing paradox: by accommodating a group's cultural practices, multicultural policies enable some groups to preserve practices that oppress their most vulnerable members, which are often women.

[7]   The second argument in favour of banning the *niqab* from court is the belief that allowing a witness to veil compromises the fairness of a trial. This argument reflects the tensions that arise when cultural practices challenge the norms of the majority culture. In the case of the Canadian justice system, "there is a deeply rooted presumption . . . that seeing a witness's face is important to a fair trial, enabling an effective cross-examination and credibility assessment . . ." (Chief Justice McLachlin, as cited in Makin, 2012). Allowing a woman to hide her face behind the *niqab* while testifying directly contradicts this presumption. Furthermore, if Muslim women are able to veil in courts, judges may be forced to allow others to cover their face as well. Future cases may use N.S. as precedents in order to allow a plaintiff or defendant to cover the face for insincere reasons, such as to hide his or her demeanor. Song (2005) calls this "the boomerang effect," which occurs when "the legal accommodations of cultural practices within minority cultures . . . boomerangs back" to threaten the justice of future trials (p. 482).

[8]   Although these are powerful arguments, the consequences for banning the *niqab* from the courtroom are potentially very serious. First, viewing the veil as a symbol of oppression, say its opponents, risks creating a harmful stereotype. In fact, the meaning attributed to the *niqab* and other religious head scarves by those who veil is often very different from that assumed by those in a non-Islamic culture. For the former individuals, veiling does not necessarily represent their subordination to men, but may serve as an ethical and religious signal; affirmation of one's identity, or a means for negotiating it; and/or a political act (Howard, 2012, p. 153). As Judge Tulkens suggests (as cited in Howard, 2012, p. 153) in *Sahin v. Turkey*, 2007, "wearing a head scarf has no single meaning. . . . [I]t does not necessarily symbolize the submission of women to men, and there are those who maintain that, in certain cases, it can be a means of emancipating women."

[9]   Furthermore, banning the *niqab* from the courtroom may result in a counteractive backlash by marginalizing all those who veil, whether or not by choice. Madam Justice

Continued

The last sentence in this paragraph provides a transition. The first sentence of paragraph 6 serves as a topic sentence, announcing the first of the two challenges to the argument for veiling.

As he does in the previous paragraph, Kramer thoroughly explains the arguments for banning the *niqab*, providing support from reliable sources, including feminists, a politician, a judge, and an academic.

A precedent is a kind of evidence, derived from its legal use, often useful in arguments unrelated to law cases.

In the topic sentence, Kramer makes the transition between summarizing the "powerful" points on one side to the "serious" ones on the other, keeping his voice objective. He devotes roughly the same amount of space for each side.

<table>
<tr><td>

Kramer strategically presents his strongest point in his last body paragraph. By citing the dissenting opinion in the N.S. case, Kramer draws attention to his own reason-based argument. Like a good lawyer, he weights the relative strengths of each point, concluding on the basis of what he believes is the stronger argument.

</td><td>

Rosalie Abella, representing the dissenting voice for the ruling in N.S., argues that the effects of forcing women to unveil greatly outweigh the advantages: "In particular, . . . sexual assault complainants may be unwilling to come forward and lodge complaints" (Makin, 2012). Women may be forced to make an impossible decision: to step forth as a complainant, which would potentially force them to remove their veil, or to let the crime in which they were a victim go unnoticed. As Schiek notes (as cited in Howard, 2012, p. 159), "[a] headscarf ban would in fact hinder steps towards emancipation by Muslim women, who are not (yet) prepared to adapt to Western ideals of equality, and thus not allow them to integrate [into the justice system]"; thus, a ban on veiling in courtrooms could lead to deleterious and far-reaching effects that would not serve the needs of justice. Justice Abella also argues that courts regularly hear from witnesses whose demeanors may be altered because of surgery or stroke, yet do not disqualify the witness's testimony (Makin, 2012). She argues that women who choose to veil should be able to receive similar accommodation.

</td></tr>
</table>

Beginning with an acknowledgement of the strong pro-banning argument, Kramer focuses on the strongest argument against the ban, explaining why he believes this is the most compelling point.

[10]   Multicultural polices that accommodate cultural practices that challenge dominant norms often result in serious tension between principles held up as sacrosanct. In the case of N.S., the rights to religious freedom and a fair trial, along with principles of gender equality, all violently clash. Although accommodating multicultural practices that are embedded in patriarchal systems may fail to address gender inequality within these cultural groups, the risk of cultural backlash presents a more prominent threat. In the context of N.S., this backlash may result in an unwillingness on the part of sexual assault complainants to come forward and lodge complaints at the cost of preserving a judicial norm; thus, in order to prevent heinous crimes like sexual assault from going unpunished, Muslim women should be allowed to veil in courts.

References

Beaman, L. G. (2011). "It was all slightly unreal": What's wrong with tolerance and accommodation in the adjudication of religious freedom? *Canadian Journal of Women and the Law, 23*(2), 442–463.

Howard, E. (2012). Banning Islamic veils: Is gender equality a valid argument? *International Journal of Discrimination and the Law, 12*(3), 147–165. doi: 10.1177/1358229112464450

Makin, K. (2012, December 20). Witness may be required to remove *niqab* while testifying. *Globe and Mail*. Retrieved from http://www.theglobeandmail.com/news/national/witness-may-be-required-to-remove-niqab-while-testifying-top-court/article6588243/?page=all

Kymlicka, W. (1995). *Multicultural citizenship.* New York, NY: Oxford University Press.

Schwartzbaum, A. (2011). The *niqab* in the courtroom: Protecting free exercise of religion in a post-Smith world. *University of Pennsylvania Law Review, 159*(5), 1533–1576.

Song, S. (2005). Majority norms, multiculturalism, and gender equality. *American Political Science Review, 99*(4), 473–489. doi:10.1017/S0003055405051828

3. Sample Professional Essay

Before reading this essay, you can review the questions discussed in chapter 1, Responding Critically and Analytically through Questions, page 8. As the essay is journalistic rather than scholarly, the writer does not cite his sources.

After reading the essay, consider

- the writer's audience
- the journal in which it appeared (the name is given at the end of the essay)

Access the home page of the journal to determine the suitability of the essay for the target audience. What inference can you make about argumentative purpose from this information?

SAMPLE PROFESSIONAL ESSAY

Why Politicians Should Be More Like Professors

by David D. Perlmutter

[1]   As a professor of political communication, I find it fascinating that one of the most common negative criticisms of President Barack Obama by pundits and politicians is that he is too "professorial."

[2]   Personal tone and style have always affected the public's attitudes toward its leaders. From speeches by Pericles in Athens to Franklin D. Roosevelt's fireside chats via radio, and, more recently, tweets from Mayor Cory Booker of Newark, N.J., during one of this winter's Northeast blizzards, it's clear that successful mass communication is that which best approximates successful personal communication. The politicians we call "great communicators" are those who can reach a person standing in a gigantic plaza, watching at home on television, or even reading an article shared on Facebook, and make that person feel (in the proverbial language of the focus-group response) as if they were "talking to me personally." That said, what exactly is wrong with being professorial?

[3]   The intellectual distance and aloofness of some professors is often exaggerated as the signature characteristic of a profession practiced by tens of thousands of individuals in different ways every day. I do know aloof scholars. But I also know charismatic and charming ones. And rather than protest against a stereotype, I'd like to offer a counter-argument: We would live in a better world if our political leaders were more professorial.

[4]   Among good professors, facts matter. Take a familiar tale from academe: A professor is contacted by a legislative staff member to get information on a topic on behalf of a politician. The professor soon discovers that facts are of minor importance, and that the staffer is interested only in those numbers, quotes, or cases that support the position already held by the politician, and will ignore any that contradict it. Instead of taking stances and making decisions based on careful investigation, as academic researchers do, politicians usually take stands based on cherry-picked research and pre-approved talking points that echo existing party ideologies and pander to donors and voting constituencies.

The writer introduces his topic in the first paragraph by means of a personal observation. While using the first person is not usually a good way to begin an argument, here it helps Perlmutter establish his credibility as an expert in "political communication."

In this logically developed paragraph, the writer begins with a topic sentence, follows with supporting examples, and concludes with a question that leads the reader into the next paragraph.

Here Perlmutter makes a brief concession, acknowledging the partial truth of the stereotype. He places his simple thesis, a value claim, in the last sentence.

By this statement, Perlmutter reveals argumentative purpose: raising awareness, or considering a new perspective on a familiar topic.

The paragraph is developed partly through an illustration. However, like most of the paragraphs in the essay, compare and contrast is the primary organizational method.

Short sentences are rhetorically effective here: each unambiguous statement suggests a stage completed in the steady progress toward the goal of a factual consensus.

[5]   The best scholarly research allows for being wrong. Hypotheses are proposed. Evidence accumulates. Scientific consensus evolves. Young scholars, and not a few senior ones, raise new ideas. Heresies become orthodoxies, and in time they, too, are often modified or overturned. Scholars can admit the limitations of their knowledge when answers are elusive. Politicians, on the other hand, seem incapable of saying "I don't know" in response to any question.

[6]   Arguments involve facts, not spin. Good scholars don't spin. A professor may certainly make the case to her colleagues or students that one theory best explains known facts. But unlike politicos, faculty members spend their time worrying about methodologies, not persuasive strategies. Professors don't conduct focus groups and audience testing, or devise sound bites and slick videos to cloak their most ridiculous policy positions and campaign promises with clever slogans, buzzwords, optics, or metaphors. Professors don't think, "My research is pleasant to the ear and appealing to the emotions, so facts be damned." We adhere to an ancient wisdom: The Book of Job castigates those who would "darkeneth counsel by words without knowledge."

[7]   Playing "gotcha" is rare and frowned upon. When a colleague—or a student, for that matter—misspeaks and accidentally makes some preposterous claim, only the most churlish pedagogue will mock, pounce on the mistake, and cite the error as proof that his "opponent" should be dismissed completely. But politics, as practiced these days by politicians and polemical commentators, is one long trivial game of gotcha. Anything—even the slightest infelicitous word choice—that can be twisted negatively by an opponent is used for the next attack ad or ranting op-ed.

In his second-last body paragraph, Perlmutter does not rely on comparison and contrast but on one specific virtue of good professors: their recognition of the importance of collaboration. However, a contrast can be inferred by the writer's diction. What words apply to politicians in this paragraph?

[8]   It's fine to be partisan about ideas, but governing must be collaborative. Professors can be passionate and sometimes argumentative. They can believe with fervor in a theory of society, or even on whether to install blackboards or whiteboards in a new classroom. But every day, on thousands of campuses, millions of students are educated without any disruption by academic partisanship. There is no filibustering. More than in any other trade, professors will sit down, work together with people with whom they hold deep ideological differences, and get the job done.

Perlmutter puts an important point in the words of an expert; however, he doesn't identify this person, which might have made his point stronger.

[9]   Call it aloofness if you must, but the truth is that contemplative, thoughtful, evidence-seeking research, conducted for the purpose of finding answers rather than scoring political points, would better serve our country than puffery, posturing, and cant. As a political consultant I know observed, "People want black and white, but we have so many problems that are gray." We need to stop feeding the general dysfunctional tendency toward oversimplifying complex problems and admit that difficult issues must be handled by smart and reflective people.

The writer concludes his essay with a concession and an ethical appeal.

[10]   I realize that in this essay I have employed the conceit of contrasting the best professors with the worst politicians. In truth, I have met and known many people in the political class who are brilliant, honest, and dedicated to the commonweal. I have met and heard of faculty members who are unprincipled and self-serving. My point, however, is that the best characteristics of the best professors can be of great service to the country, and we should encourage and reward them in our leaders, not mock them.

Source: From "Why Politicians Should Be More Like Professors" by David D. Perlmutter in *The Chronicle of Higher Education* 57.25, 2011. Reprinted by permission of the author.

CHAPTER SUMMARY

Chapter 5 discusses the mode of argumentation beginning with three argumentative models, those of Aristotle, Carl Rogers, and Stephen Toulmin. Each model is identified by its dominant features; however, they share a planned strategic approach to argument that distinguishes effective argumentation at the university level from everyday spontaneous arguments where opinions dominate. Planning begins with choosing an argumentative purpose and ensuring that the topic is arguable. The remainder of chapter 5 focuses on the careful use of reason and effective argumentative strategies. Categories of poor reason and misused emotion are also discussed.

6 The Literary Essay

By the time you get to university, you probably have considerable experience reading and discussing literary works. This chapter is designed to refine these skills, making you a more thoughtful reader of poetry, fiction, and drama. Three kinds of writing assignments are discussed, but the chapter's focus is on literary analyses, including the use of research in analyses. A step-by-step approach is taken to developing your points, and key terms and techniques are highlighted for the four genres of literature.

LEARNING OBJECTIVES

- to understand what a literary analysis is and how it differs from a response or evaluation

- to learn the different ways literary works can be analyzed, including the text-centred, or close reading, approach and the context-centred approach, which views the work within an established context or theory

- to understand the value of an effective planning strategy and the steps you can use to help you write a literary analysis

- to learn how to identify specific features, such as sound devices, imagery, and figurative language, and apply them to literary works, especially poetry

- to learn how to identify specific features of fiction, such as narration, point of view, and conflict, and apply them to short stories and novels

- to learn how to identify the sub-genres of drama, such as comedy, satire, and tragedy, and their specific features
- to enable you to identify the kinds of secondary sources used in research and integrate them effectively into your literary research essay

GENERAL FEATURES OF LITERARY ESSAYS

Although the literary essay has unique characteristics, it has features in common with other kinds of essays you have written or will write. In its structure, the literary essay is like an argumentative or expository essay.

- It begins with an introduction that contains a thesis statement directly related to the works you are analyzing.
- It includes several well-developed body paragraphs.
- It ends by summarizing your main points and reiterating your thesis.

Attention to grammar, punctuation, and mechanics is important. You will also need to pay close attention to diction (word choice), syntax (word order), and sentence structure. In sum, you will need to give as much thought to clarity, coherence, and concision as you do with other essays.

Writing literary essays also develops your inference-making abilities. To analyze a work deeply, you need to "read between the lines" to explore character, theme, setting, tone, and the like, examining their significance and interrelations. Thus, studying literature helps develop critical-thinking skills.

The claim you make in a literary essay is one of interpretation: in effect, you are arguing that the approach you take to the work, or theme, is valid and worth exploring. In the body paragraphs, much of your support should come from primary sources, the texts you are analyzing. You may also use research (secondary sources) to help support your interpretation.

As with other disciplines, a literary vocabulary and methodology have developed over the years, enabling those who analyze literary texts to express their ideas about a work. Many students of literature are already acquainted with much of this vocabulary and with the essential practices of literary interpretation through English courses in high school or, perhaps, through discussing stories, poems, or novels with family or friends.

Many students are also familiar with current movies, which, of course, have plots, settings, characters, and themes similar to those of written texts: thus, most students are well prepared to read and analyze literary texts. It is, therefore, not so much a question of learning a new category of discourse than of expanding and refining what you already know to adapt to the more sophisticated analyses expected at the post-secondary level.

In analyzing literature, we make inferences about character, situation, theme, and the like. The author doesn't directly state what the themes are; rather, we use critical thinking to draw conclusions concerning character, situation, and theme. Thus, studying literature helps develop critical-thinking skills (see chapter 1, p. 13).

A theme can be defined as the over-arching meaning or universal qualities in a work. Many of the work's elements, such as character, setting, language, imagery, and poetic techniques, contribute to its theme(s). You should refer to a work's theme, rather than its *message*. Literary works seldom are written just to communicate a message.

Because an analysis is objective, you should not use quantitative words like *great* and *amazing*; in most analyses, you avoid first-person references such as *I believe . . . , I will show . . . , it seems to me . . . .*

Kinds of Literary Essays

You can analyze a literary work in several ways:

- A "response," such as a journal entry, is concerned with your personal or "gut" reaction to a work: the ways it affects you or makes you feel, or the ways it leads you to reflect on your own attitudes, values, or experiences.
- An evaluation uses objective criteria to judge a work's quality; *informed* opinion supports your claims about the work's worth or relevance. Evaluations refer directly to the work and use accepted standards for assessing a work, such as plausibility, quality of writing, originality, or universal appeal.
- A literary analysis focuses on the author's techniques, connecting them to the work's theme. For example, it might show how
  - figurative language contributes to the work's theme
  - imagery helps set a work's mood
  - the first-person voice enables us to identify with the narrator

→ For more information about integrating research sources, see chapter 7, pages 217–222.

Research

A literary research essay includes secondary sources, for example reviews, commentaries, articles, or books. As in any essay involving research, you integrate your own ideas and language with the ideas and language of others (see p. 178–179).

Text-Centred and Context-Centred Approaches

Two of the most common approaches to a literary analysis are text-centred and context-centred ones.

- A *text-centred approach* is focused on the text itself and involves focused reading.
- A *context-centred approach* views the work within an established context, such as a historical or cultural one.

The text-centred and the context-centred approaches are discussed in more detail below. The two essays in this section illustrate these different approaches:

- The student essay on "Stopping by Woods on a Snowy Evening" (p. 162) illustrates the text-centred approach.
- The student essay on "The Yellow Wallpaper" and "My Papa's Waltz" (p. 181) is a research paper that combines text- and context-centred approaches.

Reading can refer to the cognitive act of processing words (the familiar sense of reading a book) or to the intellectual process of understanding a literary work's meaning through *analysis* (which means a "breaking up" or "loosening"). *Reading*, then, is an activity. *A reading* is an *interpretation* of a work as a result of reading and analyzing it.

ON THE ROAD TO THE ROUGH DRAFT

Although there are many ways to explore a literary work, having some guiding principles in mind can be useful. A step-by-step approach to developing a literary research essay follows, but you can go about the steps in any order you wish or omit certain steps if they are not relevant to your topic or requirements.

A Closer Look

Evaluating a Student Essay

Take a moment to consider the following statements:

There aren't really any objective criteria for grading a literary essay!

❑ True
❑ False

I can say whatever I want as long as I back it up!

❑ True
❑ False

There seems to be one reading of a work—and it's the prof's!

❑ True
❑ False

For the most part, instructors grade by objective standards, even if these standards aren't always comparable to those in disciplines where there are clearly right or wrong answers: some essays are more complete, coherent, or consistent than others. Three standards that pertain to your use of primary texts are discussed at the end of this feature, The 3 C's of Criticism; or, How *Not* to Get a C on Your Essay.

It is essential that you support your points by referring directly to the literary work itself, but that doesn't mean that simply referring to a passage provides that support. You need to ensure that you have used the text logically and effectively: in particular, you must show the reader that your reference is *representative* and *relevant*.

Representative and relevant references clearly illustrate the point you are trying to make. In the first example below, the writer has not provided a strong enough context for the quotation; it is not representative. In the second, the quotation does not bear out the claim the writer makes for it; it is not relevant.

In Dickinson's "Because I could not stop for Death," adulthood is depicted in the line *The Dews drew quivering and chill*.

The statement needs elaboration. When you use a direct quotation to support a point, ask *How?*, *Why?*, or *What?* For example, you could ask "*How* does the line depict adulthood?" or "*Why* is this important to the theme of the poem?"

Revised: In Dickinson's "Because I could not stop for Death," the poet's metaphor for life is a carriage ride that passes through childhood and middle age before arriving, after the sunset of life, at an age in adulthood where the falling of the dew is experienced: "The Dews drew quivering and chill."

The writer could then consider Dickinson's unusual choice of words *drew quivering*, asking, perhaps, why these words are important, what effect they have on the reader, or how they relate to the work's theme.

The second quotation below, intended to illustrate the narrator's obsession, reveals only her weariness:

The longer that the narrator is confined to the room, the more obsessed with the yellow wallpaper she becomes: "It makes me tired to follow [the pattern]."

How does the quotation relate to the narrator's obsession? *What* does it show about the narrator or her situation in the isolated room? This version is more revealing:

Revised: The longer that the narrator is confined to the room, the more obsessed with the yellow wallpaper she becomes: "It dwells in my mind so."

A work's meaning is a function of the complex interplay of many factors. Unlike didactic works (ones with clear messages), literary works do not often have a fixed meaning; instead, they may offer numerous, but certainly *not limitless*, possible readings.

The 3 C's of Criticism; or, How *Not* to Get a C on Your Essay

The best readings of a work demonstrate coherence, consistency, and complexity, using the tools you are given to analyze works of literature.

- *Coherence*: the reading makes sense; the points are clearly made, are well expressed, and can be easily followed by a reader.

- *Consistency*: the reading contains no apparent contradictions nor is one aspect of the whole given much greater prominence at the expense of other equally important elements; it takes into account the entire work. Even a close analysis of a specific passage should be related to the work as a whole.
- *Complexity*: the reading is not superficial or simplistic but is detailed and multi-dimensional, given word length and other requirements.

Obviously, other factors could have a bearing on your grade, such as whether you wrote on topic or strayed from it or whether you gave equal space to all the texts you used; originality may also be important. Furthermore, paragraphing, grammar, punctuation, sentence structure, appropriate level of language, and mechanics of form and presentation are significant factors, as they are in most essays. If you used research in your essay, your effective use of secondary sources and correct documentation also are crucial.

Method for Developing an Outline or a Draft

1. *Read and reread* the work. You will be surprised by what you *didn't* see on your first reading.
2. *Commit your thoughts and feelings to writing.* If you have been keeping a response journal, review it and supplement it with new perceptions or expand on what you wrote earlier.
3. *Ask questions*, such as the kinds referred to under How to Approach a Poem (p. 163); most questions are relevant to literary works in general. If you don't think you have firmly grasped the content of the work, try paraphrasing or summarizing it. In novels, plays, long poems, and even short stories, you might construct a section-by-section, chapter-by-chapter, or scene-by-scene breakdown, clarifying what happens to whom when and where. This can also help you locate key textual references later on.
4. *Briefly consider information about the author*: the age he or she lived in; his or her nationality, philosophy, beliefs; and other works he or she has written. Review your class notes about the writer and the works or browse secondary sources, such as reliable websites, to see how others have approached the work.
5. Try to narrow your focus to *one or two important areas*—for example, structure, point of view, imagery, tone, mood, symbolism—whichever seem important.
6. *Make connections and find patterns to come up with a thesis statement.* Connections and patterns in a work of poetry, drama, or literary prose can guide you toward a reading that is coherent, consistent, and complex. Literary conventions, such as structure and organization, imagery, poetic devices, setting, and point of view, as well as historical, cultural, or social connections, to mention a few, suggest many patterns through which a work can be explored. For example, if you find a striking image in a work, see if you can find similar images; once you find a *pattern* of such images, describe the connections that can be made to larger features of the work, such as character, structure, or point of view. Write a tentative sentence or two that includes the main point or theme of the work and connect it to your topic.
7. Although your personal response might have been important in your early reading and thinking about a work, it is now time to step back, *to make the transition from personal feelings and associations to objective, critical analysis.*
8. *Do your research.*
    a. Decide on a method of organized note-taking.

→ See chapter 7, Research Note-Taking, page 201.

b. Don't concentrate on precise expression or correct grammar right now. It is important, though, that you record examples and page references as you write.

c. Move from the general to the specific to develop your points, from concept to detail, from the large-scale to the small-scale, and from general claims to textual references. As well, consider transitions to help link ideas (see p. 62).

9. Continually test your points and the examples from the literary work against your thesis. Work toward expanding points that support your thesis, but don't necessarily discard valid and important points that don't directly support your thesis.

Technique is the means by which the poet, dramatist, or fiction writer expresses his or her artistic vision. Therefore, in your analysis you might consider the kinds of devices the writer has used. The technical aspects of the text you are analyzing will vary according to

- genre—for example, a poem *may* rely more on stylistic and figurative devices than other genres do; fiction writers rely on specific structural and narrative techniques.
- the formal elements of a tradition to which the work belongs (sonnet, elegy, ode, or initiation story, for example). Texts within a tradition can be explored in part through the conventions of that tradition, which the author may follow closely, disrupt, or adapt to suit his or her purposes.
- your topic; you may be required to write on imagery, setting, point of view, or dramatic structure.

See Organization in chapter 2, page 38.

10. You may now have enough information to begin constructing an essay outline, the basis for your first draft. In the outline, focus on the relationship between your points.

Two Tips for Analyzing Literature

1. Avoid telling what happens in the work; assume your reader knows the work and has read it recently. Summarize information about plot, character, and setting to set up your point, but a summary is not an analysis; summarizing too much wastes space.

2. When you refer to the text, *use the present tense* to describe action and character; this is known as the literary present. In the following passage, from a student essay on Ted Hughes's poem "Hawk Roosting," the verbs have been italicized to illustrate how the literary present is used to represent the actions in the poem and their textual significance. In the last two sentences, Darcy Smith uses the past tense to depict actions in the past outside of the poem.

> The hawk's flight "direct/Through the bones of the living" *is* a particularly sinister image, reinforcing the hawk's vision that he *controls* all life. All these images *project* a sense of divine, or more likely demonic, power. The imagery in the last stanza *suggests* how the hawk's egotism *represents* human nature. In the first line of this stanza, the hawk *observes*, "The sun is behind me." The sun *was considered* a god by many ancient civilizations. Ancient Egyptian pharaohs, for instance, *claimed* their divine right to rule *originated* in being descended from the sun.

Also use the present tense to refer to the words of critics: "Levin *claims* . . . ."

→ You may want to look at "How to Approach a Poem" on page 163 before reading the analysis below.

Theory into Practice: A Sample Poetry Analysis

Robert Frost's poem "Stopping by Woods on a Snowy Evening" is often included in poetry anthologies.

Assignment

The assignment was to write a 500- to 700-word textual analysis of "Stopping by Woods on a Snowy Evening." A textual analysis focuses largely on the text itself, paying attention to the poet's technique and the relations between techniques and theme.

Stopping by Woods on a Snowy Evening
by Robert Frost

	Metre	Rhyme Scheme
Whose woods these are I think I know.	˘ ˊ ˘ ˊ ˘ ˊ ˘ ˊ	a
His house is in the village though;	˘ ˊ ˘ ˊ ˘ ˊ ˘ ˊ	a
He will not see me stopping here	˘ ˊ ˘ ˊ ˘ ˊ ˘ ˊ	b
To watch his woods fill up with snow.	˘ ˊ ˘ ˊ ˘ ˊ ˘ ˊ	a

My little horse must think it queer
To stop without a farmhouse near
Between the woods and frozen lake
The darkest evening of the year.

He gives his harness bells a shake
To ask if there is some mistake.
The only other sound's the sweep
Of easy wind and downy flake.

The woods are lovely, dark and deep.
But I have promises to keep,
And miles to go before I sleep,
And miles to go before I sleep.

Preliminary Considerations

"Stopping by Woods on a Snowy Evening" presents particular challenges to the student writer: its simplicity is deceptive. When you first read it, you might find its simplicity appealing. To help you get beyond "first impressions," ask questions about the poem; try to find patterns that lead to a tentative thesis.

- *What first strikes you about the poem?* Perhaps its regularity. It consists of three four-line stanzas with an identical rhyme scheme and a fourth stanza with identical end-rhymes. In creating the poem, the poet has employed a strict formal pattern: stanza length, rhyme, and metre are regular.
- *What actually is happening in the poem?* Remarkably little. The poet himself seems lost in his thoughts, fallen into a kind of trance as he looks into the woods. Most readers at one time or another will have experienced a similar feeling to the poet's: being caught by a strong, indefinable feeling while performing some ordinary task. This might be a good place to begin exploring the poem, perhaps by writing down your associations or freewriting on the topic.

- *What one main area should you focus on?* In the poem, the speaker is thoughtful, so one area to explore might be the mood that his thoughtfulness evokes. Mood can be defined as the predominant tone of the poem created by the poet's language or approach to character and/or setting. To develop this theme, you might want to focus on how language and setting combine to evoke a solemn mood.

Consider this tentative thesis statement: "The speaker draws the reader into the poem by creating, through simple rhythms, diction, and the device of repetition, a familiar mood of solemnity while contemplating something mysterious." Although not fully developed yet, it identifies important elements that you can expand on. It specifies mood, setting, and three devices: rhythm, diction, and repetition.

Here are some rough notes about the poem. In the final version that follows, you can see that the writer hasn't used all the points, but has applied the principle of selection, using those points that seem to best support the thesis.

Stanza 1:

- Metre is regular: there are four iambs (metrical unit with an unstressed and a stressed syllable) in each line, making it iambic tetrameter. The rhyming scheme is, likewise, quite regular: aaba bbcb ccdc dddd. Diction: simple words: mostly one-syllable words and a few two-syllable ones.
- *His house, his woods*: repetition suggests importance of ownership; *He will not see me stopping here*: would not approve?
- Sets up opposition between woods and the house in the village: do the woods really "belong" to the man in the village? Nature vs. civilization? Narrator vs. owner?

Stanza 2:

- Horse seems to think speaker's behaviour is unusual, not his habit to stop like this; he is a man of routine or business, perhaps—horses, too, are creatures of habit, under control of humans: a *work* horse? Action vs. thought?
- Setting is particularized: "*between* the woods and the frozen lake": alternatives?
- Time is specific: significance of *darkest evening of the year*: winter solstice; the word *dark* recurs in final stanza; but in contrast to the *dark* is the snow: whiteness.

Stanza 3:

- *Harness* suggests captivity, containment: *bells* suggest celebration: Christmas?
- Speaker attributes human qualities to the horse: *thinking* (l. 5), *asking* (l. 10): personification.
- The sound of the shaking bells contrasts with the *only other* sound, that of the wind.
- *Easy* suggests the easy way, the simplest choice? It is easy to give way to what you desire, not so easy to commit to what you *must* do.
- *Downy* conveys softness, comfort, like a pillow: you don't usually think of wind as *easy*, and snowflakes are in reality cold, ice crystals.

Stanza 4:

- Line 13 contains two repeated words: *woods* and *dark*; besides being *dark*, the woods are *lovely* (appealing? tempting?) and *deep*; these words suggest seduction, being drawn toward something potentially dangerous and deceptive; or is he in fact being drawn toward something beautiful, profound, and truthful? Alternatives again! the speaker abruptly reminds himself that he has *promises to keep*: what kind of promises and to whom or what?
- He has distance to travel before he can sleep; sleep can refer to literal sleep (when the journey is done) or perhaps to death—the end of life's journey?
- Why does the speaker repeat the last line? Is he confidently repeating what must be done (reinforcing his choice) or does repetition further the idea of a kind of spell that he can't break away from?

These notes suggest that the poem is built not just on regularity but also on contrasts, on *oppositions between two worlds*. In the essay itself, the writer stressed both these elements but decided that one is more important than the other. This analysis, of course, is far from the only one possible; nevertheless, it is well supported by the text and is coherent, consistent, and complex, within the 500- to 700-word requirement.

SAMPLE STUDENT ESSAY

Mystery or Mastery? Robert Frost's "Stopping by Woods on a Snowy Evening"

by Kaja Vessey

[1]   Though most of us prefer a planned and orderly life, we may at times surrender to a spontaneous impulse. The first-person narrator of Robert Frost's "Stopping by Woods on a Snowy Evening" yields to such an impulse, stopping by woods to "watch [them] fill up with snow" and falling deeper into their mystery—or, some would say, their mastery. Similarly, the poet draws the reader into the poem by creating a familiar mood of solemn contemplation, using simple diction and basic rhythms.

[2]   By constructing a seemingly straightforward poem that employs a regular iambic tetrameter metre with a relatively predictable rhyming scheme of aaba bbcb ccdc dddd, the poet stresses the ordinariness of his experience. Despite this ordinariness, the poem relies on tensions or oppositions to suggest how our perception can at times transcend the ordinary. However, in the end, the poem's regularity affirms a commitment to worldly routine: although the woods hold a mysterious temptation, "lovely, dark and deep," they do not hold mastery: "But I have promises to keep . . . ."

[3]   One of the tensions configured by the poem is between the village, representing civilization, and nature. In the first stanza, the poet tentatively identifies the owner of the woods, but since the man lives at some distance, he will not see the poet "stopping here / To watch his woods fill up with snow." Already, a tension is established between the private world of the poet, who has access to nature, and the public world of ownership or business,

which separates even the owner from his legacy in nature. Even the horse seems part of the world the poet has left behind. The horse "thinks" his stopping is "queer" and "ask[s] if there is some mistake." The poet hears the harness bells shaking, but the impatient call to routine is opposed by the subtler sound, "the sweep / Of easy wind and downy flake." The adjectives "easy" and "downy" could convey comfort, relaxation, sleep—the "easy" succumbing to his tranquil feeling; or the lure of the woods could suggest a treachery in nature, the temptation to drop his responsibilities and simply give himself up to sleep, and inevitable death through exposure to cold, in the winter woods at night.

[4]   End rhyme also supports the idea of being drawn to the woods: in stanzas one to three, the rhyme in the third line is picked up in the stanza that immediately follows, creating a hypnotic effect. But as the poet falls deeper under the spell of the woods, he abruptly recalls he has "promises to keep." What are these promises? The "darkest evening" might refer to the winter solstice, and the image of the shaking bells suggests it is near Christmas. Are his "promises" connected to religious or familial duties? Perhaps he is facing some other darkness, a disappointing relationship, awareness of advancing age, sorrow, or pain associated with a loved one.

[5]   The repetition of lines 15 and 16 could suggest the progressive intensifying of the spell; more likely, though, they consciously reassert his need to complete the journey and fulfill his obligations. The poem's regular structure, rhyme, and metre, along with simple diction, suggest that he remains committed to his routines even while he is lured by the woods. Like most people, worldly responsibilities restrain him from falling under the power of an undefined impulse; his deeper commitment, like ours, is to duty to the world he knows. As he continues his physical journey and reaches his goal, he may well recall his "stopping by woods" much more than the journey. Our breaks from routine are usually more memorable than the routine itself.

THE LITERARY GENRES: POETRY, THE SHORT STORY, THE NOVEL, AND DRAMA

The **genres** of literature include poetry, drama, the novel, the short story, and nonfiction prose (essays). Smaller divisions, or sub-genres, are sometimes made—a short story might be classified as myth, fairy tale, fantasy, mystery, western, horror, or science fiction, each of which might be further subdivided.

Much of what has been discussed above relates to what the genres of literary writing have in common. The sections on poetry, fiction (the short story and the novel), and drama below focus on their unique characteristics and challenges. Various ways to approach your reading and study of each genre are discussed.

How to Approach a Poem

Two approaches, the text-centred approach and the context-centred approach, apply to all the literary genres, so much of the information below applies to more than poetry.

Text-Centred Approach: The "Inside-Out" Approach

The text-centred approach uses the wide range of writing strategies and poetic devices available to the poet. Because it explores the connections between the formal

> The **GENRES** of literature include poetry, drama, the novel, the short story, and nonfiction prose (essays). They may be further divided into sub-genres.

elements of a work and its meaning, it is called the **formalist** method. Here are some strategies that you as a reader and writer can apply to analyze the poem "from the inside out."

- *Look at the poem's structure*, the arrangement of parts. Are there distinct divisions? What are their functions? What does each contribute to the whole? Do they suggest a movement or progression of some kind? Do they parallel/contrast with one another?

  Many poems are divided into *stanzas*, units of two or more lines that often share metre, rhyme scheme, etc. Within these units structural devices include **parallelism** (simple repetition or "echoing") and *juxtaposition* (words or images placed beside others for effect). *Anaphora* (repetition of words or phrases at the beginning of lines or clauses) and *chiasmus* (in the second of two parallel phrases, the inversion of the order followed in the first) are specific kinds of parallelism. Examples of smaller structural elements include *caesura*, a pause in the middle of a line, and *enjambment*, one line running into another rather than being *end-stopped,* having a logical and syntactic stop at the end of a line.

- *Listen to the poem*. Read the lines aloud. What kind of rhythm do they have? Is it regular, with repeated units recurring at predictable intervals? If so, can you characterize the poem's metre? *Scansion* is the reading of a line of poetry to determine the pattern of stressed and unstressed syllables. Are there exceptions to the regular metre? If so, what is their significance?

  If the poet uses *rhymes*, where are they? At the end of each line? Are they ever in the middle of a line (*internal rhyme*)? Do the words rhyme exactly, or do they just sound similar with identical vowel or consonant sounds on the last stressed syllable (*near rhyme*)? If there is a distinctive pattern of rhyme, what is it?

  Are there other aural features in the poem, such as closely placed words with repeated sounds at their beginnings: *alliteration*? Or with repeated vowel sounds in their middles—*assonance*? Are there examples of *onomatopoeia*, words that sound like their meanings (e.g., *buzz, splash*)? Is there **euphony** (words that have a pleasing or melodic sound) or *cacophony* (words that sound harsh or disagreeable)?

> Remember that the "voice" in the work is not necessarily that of the poet; a literary work is not usually a reliable form of autobiography. Writers may use facts or apparent truths about themselves, but these facts will not necessarily play a role in your analysis of the work.

A Closer Look

Metre

Metre refers to repeated patterns of stressed and unstressed syllables in lines of poetry. The name of the metre is determined by the basic unit of measurement (the foot) and the number of feet in a line. The four most common feet are

the *iamb* (one unstressed + one stressed syllable) ˘ ´

"Ŏn éither síde the ríver líe" (Alfred, Lord Tennyson)

the *trochee* (one stressed + one unstressed syllable) ´ ˘

"Týger, Týger, búrning bríght" (William Blake)

the *anapest* (two unstressed syllables + one stressed syllable) ˘ ˘ ´

´ ˘ ˘ ´ ˘ ˘ ´ ˘ ˘ ´
"When the voices of children are heard on the green" (Blake)

the *dactyl* (one stressed syllable + two unstressed syllables) ´ ˘ ˘

´ ˘ ˘ ´ ˘ ˘ ´ ˘ ˘ ´ ˘ ˘
"lurching through forests of white spruce and cedar" (Alden Nowlan)

A line that contains three feet is called a *trimeter*, one that contains four feet is a *tetrameter*, and one made up of five feet is a *pentameter*. Thus, a poem with lines composed of five iambs is written in *iambic pentameter*. *Blank verse*, the closest to the rhythms of everyday English speech, is written in unrhymed iambic pentameter. Blank verse is used in much narrative and dramatic poetry, including parts of Shakespeare's plays.

- *Identify the poem's speaker* (the main *voice* in the poem) *or narrator* (if the poem is narrated—told as a story).

   Can you determine the speaker? Not just *who* it is, but also his or her perspective? How is the poem told? Does the poet seem to be addressing anyone or anything? Is the person or object absent, as in an *apostrophe*?

   What is the *mood* of the poem, and how does it make you feel? Is a predominant emotion expressed? Is it constant, or is there a shift at some point?

   What is the poem's *tone*, or attitude to the subject/audience? Does the poet use **irony**? See A Closer Look: Irony, below.

   Is *hyperbole* (extreme exaggeration) used? *Understatement* (drawing attention to something by minimizing it)? Hyperbole is common in comic works; either hyperbole or understatement can be used to convey irony.

A Closer Look

Irony

Irony may exist where there are two levels of meaning: the apparent (literal or surface) meaning and another intended (non-literal or deeper) meaning. Irony may differ in degree according to its purpose and, traditionally, is divided into three types.

- In *verbal irony*, the literal and intended meanings of language are at odds. Verbal irony resembles sarcasm, but irony is usually more indirect and subtle than sarcasm, which simply states something as its opposite.
  - *Sarcasm*: Mr. Bennet in Jane Austen's novel *Pride and Prejudice* refers to his worthless son-in-law: "I am prodigiously proud of him."
  - *Verbal irony*: "Yet graceful Ease, and Sweetness void of Pride, / Might hide her Faults, if *Belles* had

Faults to hide" (Alexander Pope). The last clause is ironic since the "belle," Belinda, is mortal and, of course, *does* have faults.
  - In his anti-war poem "Dulce et Decorum Est," the irony of Wilfred Owen is much harsher. His graphic images of a youth dying from a gas attack render ironic the patriot's claim that "dulce et decorum est"—it is "sweet and right to die for your country." While the title affords an example of verbal irony, the poem, as an indictment of war and the "lie" of those who promote its glory, exemplifies situational irony (see below).
- In *dramatic irony*, the reader/audience possesses an awareness about the character or situation that the character doesn't have. For example, in many of

Shakespeare's comedies, people are disguised, and while the audience is aware of these disguises, most of the characters are not. **Tragic irony** exists if the reader/audience is aware of a situation that the hero is oblivious to and which will lead to disaster; for example, the audience in Shakespeare's *Othello* learns of Iago's treachery long before Othello does.

- In *situational irony*, a situation appears to point to a particular outcome but results in the reverse of the expected one. For example, it is ironic that Pip, the protagonist of Charles Dickens's novel *Great Expectations*, discovers that his benefactor is not the wealthy Miss Havisham but the convict Magwitch.

> **DICTION** refers to the writer's word choice. **SYNTAX** is word order.

- *Pay close attention to stylistic devices and figures of speech*. Some of the more important devices are **diction**, **syntax**, and allusion. Figures of speech include metaphor, metonymy, synecdoche, simile, and personification. Other rhetorical elements are logic-centred; they include paradox and oxymoron (the verbal juxtaposition of contraries, as in *darkness visible* or *terrible beauty*). Another device is an ellipsis (words left out).

A Closer Look

Common Devices

A *metaphor* is an indirect comparison between two things not usually considered similar:

> Love . . . is the star to every wandering bark (Shakespeare).

Love is compared to a star and the lover is compared to a *bark* or ship; *star* and *bark* are metaphors for love and the lover, respectively. Metaphors can be divided into the *tenor* (the object being compared—*love*, the lover) and the *vehicle* (the image to which the tenor is linked—*star*, *bark*).

A *simile* is a comparison using *like* or *as* or a similar word/phrase:

> The holy time is *quiet as a Nun* (William Wordsworth).

Metonymy is the substitution of an object or idea for a related one:

> A *goose's quill* has put an end to murder (Dylan Thomas).

The poet refers to a document signed by a king with a quill pen; it is actually the person, not the quill, who "put an end to murder."

An *allusion* is a historical, religious, mythic, literary, or other kind of outside reference used thematically or to reveal another aspect of the work:

> This man had kept a school / And rode our *wingèd horse* (W.B. Yeats's allusion to the mythological horse Pegasus, associated with poetry).

- *Look at the poem's imagery*. Try to discover patterns of images: words conveying sense impressions, particularly sight. What kind are they? Can you characterize them? Which senses do they refer to? How do the images connect with other elements to lead you to a reading of the poem?

  Does the writer use the image as a *symbol*? A traditional symbol, such as the sea, a star, or the heart, has specific cultural or cross-cultural associations; a *contextual symbol* resides in the way the author uses it, its context.

Context-Centred Approach: The "Outside-In" Approach

The context-centred analysis employs all of the technical terminology of textual criticism, but relates it to an encompassing context. Literary works can be explored through different perspectives:

- biographical
- historical
- cultural/racial
- gender-based
- theoretical and others

The context-centred critic employs connections between literary art and the "real" world, and considers many of the oppositions between life and art stressed by the text-centred critic as limiting. Some of the most common poetic contexts are discussed briefly below (most of them also apply to other genres).

- *Convention and form in poetry.* You may be concerned with viewing a poem in a larger context, such as a poetic tradition or form with its requirements or expectations. You could look at the ways that the poem conforms to conventions, the ways that it departs from them, or the ways that the writer adapts the conventions for his or her own purposes.

  Broadly speaking, poetry can be classified as lyric, narrative, or dramatic: *lyric* ("song") poetry expresses strong emotions or thoughts in relatively brief form. *Narrative poetry* tells a story and tends to be longer. **Dramatic poetry** has drama-like qualities, such as a speaker who addresses an imaginary listener (dramatic monologue). Both narrative and dramatic poetry can be lyrical; as well, a lyric could have narrative or dramatic elements.

  Other traditional poetic forms include
  - lyric poetry: ode, elegy, sonnet, villanelle, haiku
  - narrative poetry: ballad, epic
  - dramatic poetry: dramatic monologue

  Each form employs specific conventions. For example, the *sonnet* always has 14 lines and has two possible stanzaic arrangements: the *Italian* or *Petrarchan* form with an eight-line *octave* and a six-line *sestet*, and the *English* or *Shakespearean* form with three *quatrains* (four lines each) and a *couplet* (two lines). *Fixed forms* allow for little flexibility, while *open forms*, like free verse, do not conform to any set conventions of stanza, rhyme, or metre.

- *The biographical context.* Who/what were major influences in the poet's life? Does the poem appear addressed to someone the poet knew, or are names or places in the poem connected with the writer's life?

  Although the poet is viewed critically as the creator of the work, and not the autobiographical equivalent of the voice, speaker, or narrator, in **confessional poetry** autobiography is used to express emotional intensity. The tone can range from despair to anger. Nonetheless, you should not assume that the voice of the poem is *identical* with the biographical poet. Sylvia Plath, an

American confessional poet (1932–1963), said this about the relationship between art and personal experience:

> I think my poems come immediately out of the sensuous and emotional experiences I have, [but] I think one should be able to control and manipulate experiences, even the most terrifying . . . with an informed and intelligent mind.

- *The historical/social context.* Can the poem be studied as a historical or social document? In the following excerpt, student writer Rory Wizbicki explores Al Purdy's poem "The Country North of Belleville" in a historical context. The poem details the hardships of poor, immigrant, nineteenth-century farmers who travelled to Canada in the hope of finding prosperity and freedom in a new country:

> Although, geographically, the plots north of Belleville are every farmer's nightmare, within this shallow soil lies their blood, sweat, and tears produced from endless days of work and toil. A farmer becomes so connected to his land, "plowing and plowing [his] ten acre field" that the "convulsions [begin to] run parallel with his own brain" (57). The land is both his greatest enemy and his most respected companion. Despite his plot's stubborn resistance to human cultivation, a man of this area "might have some/opinion of what beauty/is and none deny him/for miles" (5–8). The timeless beauty and respect for the land are paralleled by the lasting cultural values engraved into the farmer's stony fields.

- *The cultural, racial, or gender-based context.* Awareness of a writer's culture has been instrumental in broadening the canon of literature in the last few decades. For example, the fact that Dionne Brand is of black heritage, that Eden Robinson is of Aboriginal heritage, or that Margaret Atwood strongly identifies with the feminist movement can be important in analyzing the ways in which their works give voice to the marginalized.

  Did the poet contribute to a social, political, or aesthetic movement? Was the poem written in response to a "cause"? Cultural, racial, gender, socio-economic, and class issues can serve political ends in poems of protest or resistance; they may express collective or personal empowerment.

  The traditional (Western) canon was based on the opinion of critics and readers—chiefly white, middle-class, and male—that particular works met high artistic standards and were most worthy of study. With the increasing interest in previously marginalized writers, creative works today encompass a wide range of human experiences. The literary canon now includes a wide variety of cultural, racial, ethnic, economic, and gendered perspectives.

- *The theoretical perspective.* Literary criticism may seek to incorporate theory and practice from other disciplines—for example, linguistics, visual art, history, education, philosophy, psychology, anthropology, economics, and mythology. Modern literary theory often stresses the ways that literary art depends on and engages with aspects of language and culture. The interdisciplinary approach to literature enables us to study it from many different perspectives.

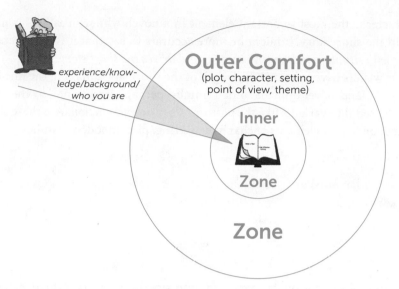

FIGURE 6.1 A Model for Reading and Interpreting Fiction

Fictional Forms

One way of classifying fiction is by its length. In general, a **short story** is a fictional narrative of fewer than 15,000 words; a **novella** is 15,000–40,000 words; a **novel** is more than 40,000 words.

Analyzing a work involves exploring its themes, or controlling ideas, along with the other elements mentioned above. A novel's or short story's characters may seem unusual, its plot unlikely, and its setting unfamiliar, but there will usually be something familiar about its themes: they might focus on love, death, suffering, renewal, or human relationships. Through the work's themes, the reader can make connections with his or her own experience—themes universalize the writer's work.

Fiction is often analyzed according to what you can call the *comfort categories* (these can be applied to any other literary works as well). In fiction, the comfort categories include the traditional areas of plot, character, setting, point of view, and theme. Essentially, the comfort categories relate to basic questions you often ask of a work of fiction or narrative poem in order to begin analyzing it: *What?*, *Who?*, *Where and when?*, *How?*, and *Why?*

As figure 6.1 shows, a reader's response to a work of fiction will depend partly on his or her experience, knowledge, and background. Because each reader brings a different set of experiences and expectations to a work, no two analyses will be identical. Even though we share the critical tools for analyzing fiction (that "outer zone" containing the comfort categories of plot, character, setting, point of view, and theme), in the "inner zone" one can apply the more complex tools for analyzing fiction discussed below. Being familiar with the many resources for analyzing fiction will enable you to respond more fully to the work, producing an in-depth reading.

The Short Story

The difference between a short story and a novella or novel cannot be judged simply by length. Edith Wharton (1862–1937), an American short story and novel writer, stated

> Fiction can be classified by its length: a **SHORT STORY** is fewer than 15,000 words, a **NOVELLA** is 15,000–40,000 words, and a **NOVEL** is more than 40,000 words.

that character is the most important element in a novel, while "situation" is more important in the short story. It might be more accurate to say that it is the *interaction of character with situation that creates conflict and drives the short story.*

Just as writers have extended the length of the short story, making the line between story, novella, and novel difficult to determine—perhaps irrelevant—so the story has been condensed into variants like the *postcard story* or *microfiction*. Are these short stories? Can you identify elements of character, setting, plot, mood, or conflict?

> For sale: baby shoes, never worn. —Ernest Hemingway

> The last man on Earth sat alone in a room. There was a knock at the door. —Anonymous

---

EXERCISE 6.1

Collaborative Exercise: What Is a Short Story?

Most students have had experience reading short stories. Below, two students have given their own definition of what a short story means to them.

A. Discuss the merits and/or limitations of the definitions.
B. Come up with your own one- to two-sentence definition of the short story, focusing on what makes it successful for you. (The same activity could be used with the poem, play, or novel.)

Students' Definitions

1. It should provide some kind of continuous dream which the reader can enter, commune with, and leave having felt something.
2. It is a fully realized world. After passing through this world, the reader sees his or her own world differently.

The Single Effect

One of the earliest developers of the short story, American Edgar Allan Poe (1809–1849), claimed that, unlike the novel, the successful short story should be of a length to be read at one sitting and should focus on one effect that serves to unify its elements. According to Poe, writers of short fiction should decide on this single effect and select incidents that help bring it about. Thus, Poe stressed the *economy* of the story—the use of atmosphere, dialogue, mood, imagery, and so on, that results in a unified effect. In many short stories, the single effect relates to a discovery a character makes about nature, society, other people, or him- or herself.

The Novel

A **novel** is an extended fictional prose narrative involving one or more characters undergoing significant experiences over a span of time. The term is from the Italian *novella*, a short, realistic prose form popular in the late medieval period. The word *novel* means "new," and early fictional narratives brought to English a new prose form, very different from the popular romances of the Middle Ages that depicted the imaginary exploits

> A **NOVEL** is an extended fictional prose narrative involving one or more characters undergoing significant experiences over a span of time.

of heroes. English novels were notable at first for their realism, though the novel is not always a realistic form (see p. 173).

How to Approach Fiction

Some tools for analyzing stories, novels, and novellas are discussed below. Many of the terms also are useful in analyzing drama and narrative or dramatic poetry.

Plot

The plot is the arrangement or sequence of actions in a story, novel, or drama.

The plot structure usually has identifiable elements. You may be familiar with the pyramidal division of plot into *rising action*, *climax* (the high point of the conflict or the turning point), and *falling action* (*resolution* or *denouement*). In many dramas, novels, and stories, the rising action is preceded by the *exposition*, which introduces background information. The *initiating incident* begins the rising action. *In medias res* describes the strategy of beginning a story in the midst of an important action.

Fiction involves one or more kinds of **conflict**, which usually take the form of obstacles the character must overcome to achieve a goal. Conflict—the driving force behind the occurrences of a short story, novel, or drama—may arise from the character's motivation or through forces lying outside the character. The conflict is usually introduced early and instigates the rising action.

Many other structural devices lend coherence to a story; for example, authors may use a *framing* technique in which the beginning and the end mirror one another in setting or situation. In some novels, a character narrates the beginning and the end, and the story of the main character evolves within this narrative frame. Other forms of *parallelism* can be used to suggest similarities or differences between characters, or to show the development in a character at different points in a novel.

Plots may be closed or open-ended. A traditional way to provide *closure*, especially in novels of social interaction, such as the *novels of manners* of Jane Austen, is through a marriage. The actions or events of the plot may be closely related or only loosely related, as in the episodic plot of a picaresque novel, in which case, the structure may take the form of a journey. A *quest* is a journey with a specific goal, usually a valuable object. The quest is completed when the hero/heroine overcomes all the obstacles and has brought the object back to his or her society. However, the *quester* may fail in the quest; invariably, the failed quester undergoes a learning experience while trying to satisfy the terms of the quest.

The incidents that make up a plot can be ordered in various ways: most simply, they may be arranged chronologically (time order); even in the chronological order, however, other devices or effects can be used—for example, the writer may use *foreshadowing*, creating suspense through the anticipation of a future action or result, or *flashbacks*, moving back in time to narrate important events, perhaps as a character recollects them.

Character

One reason why novels became so popular from their early evolution was the way that character was highlighted. Novels allowed for a diversity of approaches to character type and development.

> Fictional and dramatic plots can be divided into exposition, rising action, climax, and falling action (resolution or denouement). In terms of **CONFLICT**, the rising action represents increasing tension; the climax represents the high point of the conflict, while the falling action represents the relaxation of the conflict.

Novels usually have at least one round character, or protagonist, and several flat (minor) characters. Minor characters can act as antagonists, foils, or in other ways to highlight traits of the protagonist or advance the plot.

According to writer James Joyce, an *epiphany* represents a character's (or reader's) sudden recognition of something personally illuminating in an ordinary event or object.

SETTING is the place and time of the work.

Character type. Novels usually have at least one *round* (fully developed and complex) character and several *flat* (one-dimensional, undeveloped) ones. The main character in a work of fiction or drama is called the *protagonist*, usually the round character. The novel may also have an *antagonist*, who opposes the protagonist. An antagonist often reveals hidden or submerged aspects of the protagonist. A *foil* is a character who *contrasts with* another character, though the two characters aren't necessarily opponents.

Character development. Character may be disclosed through narration, description, dialogue, or action. Character development usually occurs through a learning experience: in an *initiation story*, a young protagonist makes the transition to adulthood, from innocence to experience. The learning could result from suffering and culminate in an intense moment of recognition or insight. In short fiction, James Joyce introduced the concept of the *epiphany*, a character's sudden recognition of something personally illuminating in an ordinary event or object.

Setting

Setting is the place and time of the work. In contrast to short stories, novels usually have more than one main setting, and the time may be brief, such as days, or lengthy, such as years. Setting can be shown through concrete detail conveyed through diction and imagery. Use of imagery can also create a specific atmosphere, which may help set a mood. *Regionalism* is the realistic portrayal of the beliefs and behaviours of characters from a distinct area, such as Stephen Leacock's Orillia, Ontario, and Alice Munro's southwestern Ontario.

Narration

Narrative point of view is the perspective or angle of vision from which the narrative is told.

Narrator field of vision. An *omniscient* ("all-knowing") *narrator* sees and tells the whole story in the third person, moving to different scenes and in and out of characters' minds; a *limited omniscient narrator* can move in and out of the minds of one or more characters, but often is limited to the consciousness of the main character; a *first-person narrator* reports from his or her own experiences using the first-person (*I*) voice.

Narrator involvement. A first-person narrator may be detached from the action, narrating events from the *observer* or uninvolved perspective. This narrator can also, of course, be involved in the action. First-person *involved* narrators may narrate events in which they play a significant role. A writer may use special techniques to represent internal consciousness, such as *inner monologue* or *stream of consciousness* to show the mind in flux or the transient emotions, thoughts, and sensations of a character.

Narrator reliability. Narrators may be reliable or unreliable. A reliable narrator can be trusted to give a truthful picture of events and character. Most third-person narrators are reliable.

An *unreliable narrator* may be naive: he or she may not be in possession of all the facts or may be too inexperienced to see things as they are or to make sound judgments.

The *naive narrator*, then, may be limited in his or her capacity to understand and explain, such as Mark Twain's young narrator, Huck, in *Adventures of Huckleberry Finn* (1885).

On the other hand, a narrator may consciously or unconsciously deceive the reader, in order to avoid confronting unpleasant facts about him- or herself or because of a bias. A writer's use of an unreliable narrator produces irony, as there is a discrepancy between the narrator's perceptions and the reality of a situation. Through unreliable narration, writers convey the complexity of perception and the human capacity for (self-)deception.

Orientation to Reality

Realism in the novel has produced many sub-genres, including social realism, psychological realism, and historical realism. Because the term *realism* is so broad, it is difficult to define. In the general sense, it refers to the need of the fictional writer to portray things as they really are. Realism also can be considered a distinct literary tradition that began in Europe as a response to *romance* and to contemporary scientific discoveries about the place of humans in the universe—for example, the theory of evolution that gained prominence after Charles Darwin published *On the Origin of Species* in 1859. Since it seemed less truthful for artists to dwell on idealized human traits, writers turned increasingly to the everyday interactions of ordinary people, using realistic detail to portray middle-class characters in a recognizable environment.

Naturalism is an outgrowth of realistic writing in the late nineteenth and early twentieth centuries that stressed humanity's helplessness before external forces, such as those of one's society or natural environment, or before internal ones, such as heredity. Frequently, naturalistic writers portray their protagonists as victims of fate.

Reality, however, is not an absolute term. A work may be essentially realistic while utilizing a symbolic framework, although on the surface, symbols and realistic detail might seem incompatible. Similarly, *science fiction* and *fantasy* may invert or subvert standards of objective reality and still be considered realistic; in this case, the relevant question would not be "Could it happen in our world?" but "Could it happen *in the world created by the writer*?" **Magic realism** combines the objectively real and the surprise of the unreal or unexpected; in magic realism, the created world is magical and real at the same time. **Metafiction** defines its own boundaries of the real by focusing on the story itself as the testing ground of the "real"; one of the themes in a work of metafiction is the status of fiction and fiction-making: metafiction uses the work itself to explore this status and, more broadly, to question the ways we construct our own reality.

Much critical writing today attempts to examine the many faces of **postmodernism**. Postmodernism is certainly not restricted to fiction; indeed, it incorporates diverse aspects of contemporary culture. Although difficult to define, postmodernism in literature tends to reject such assumptions as the authority of the author, univocal (one-voice) perspectives, unifying narratives, and other "absolutes"; in their place, it stresses plurality, possibility, and "play."

How to Approach Drama

When you think about drama, you may recall plays you studied in high school, including those by William Shakespeare. Most of Shakespeare's plays are classified as

Narrators can be classified according to their field of vision (omniscient, limited, first-person), involvement (observer, involved), and reliability (reliable or unreliable because of their naivety or deceptiveness).

REALISM is a literary method or tradition in which the writer seeks to show things as they are.

NATURALISM stresses the role of external forces, such as nature, or internal forces, such as heredity, in characters' lives.

MAGIC REALISM combines the objectively real and the surprise of the unreal or unexpected.

METAFICTION uses the work to explore the nature of fiction and the role it plays in our lives.

POSTMODERNISM rejects "absolutes" in literature, such as the authority of the author, stressing possibility and "play."

tragedies or comedies, but the general term *drama* (from the Greek *dran*, "to do" or "to perform") refers to a story acted out on a stage or in front of a camera. Thus, when you read a play, it is essential to imagine it as performance and spectacle—not just as dialogue on a page.

Aristotle (384–322 BCE) called drama an "imitated human action." He declared that a drama should observe the three *unities* of time, place, and action. By **unity of time** he limits the play's action to approximately one day; by **unity of place** he limits it to one setting; and by **unity of action** he limits it to a single set of incidents "having a beginning, a middle, and an end." Although the unities are not strictly observed by many playwrights, their observance helps create dramatic focus and intensity, necessary elements in theatre where the audience must remain attentive for at least two hours to absorb the full experience of the spectacle.

Comedy

In viewing human limits as weaknesses, comedy mocks, but sometimes celebrates, the lesser—such as the physical—self. Comedy uses laughter as a form of displacement, enabling its audience to identify the "other" as silly, pretentious, or unimportant. Countless examples exist in the contemporary media—from television and YouTube skits to improvisations and stand-up routines. From a literary perspective, however, certain types of comedy had a "serious" function.

The humour of high comedy (characterized as **wit**) appeals more to the intellect, having such targets as social pretensions and character inconsistencies. It typically has a complex function, dealing with serious issues like human relationships—even dealing with the subjects of tragedy from a perspective of lightness and humour.

Satire can be considered a separate genre from comedy, although it often evokes laughter from informed audiences. Satire uses ridicule and irony to undercut or critique human institutions. Satire may be mild, intended to make society's members more aware (Horatian satire) or harsh, intent on attacking these institutions (Juvenalian satire). There is sometimes a fine line between comedy and satire. In **parody**, the writer imitates another literary work, poking fun at it and/or revealing its weaknesses.

Comic plot. Fortune, chance, and coincidence are the major external forces that drive the plot of literary comedy; inner forces that determine comic action include motivations like physical desire, greed, envy, ambition, and concern with appearances. In the end, base human desires usually are punished, while continuity is suggested by a marriage between the most worthy characters.

Comic theme. One of the most important themes in drama is that of identity, perhaps because in drama the onstage character is isolated in a way that he or she usually is not in a novel. **Asides**, **monologues**, and **soliloquies**—speeches in which a character reveals his or her own thoughts for the ears of the audience alone—can be used to underscore this sense of isolation, as well as to suggest self-reflection and inner conflict. Comedy may revolve around exchange and multiplicity of identity. In most of Shakespeare's comedies, for example, there are frequent changes of identity and/or mistaken identities.

Drama is an imitated human action in which the **UNITIES OF TIME, PLACE, AND ACTION** help create dramatic focus and intensity.

WIT is humour that appeals to the intellect.

SATIRE uses ridicule and irony to undercut or critique human institutions.

PARODY pokes fun at a literary work or reveals its weaknesses.

An **ASIDE** is a brief speech intended for the audience, not for other onstage characters. A **MONOLOGUE** is a continuous speech by one character. A **SOLILOQUY** is a continuous speech by one character alone on the stage. It usually reveals the character's thoughts and feelings to the audience.

Tragedy

Tragedy celebrates the "greater" self by juxtaposing human strengths and endurance with powerful outer forces; tragedy involves disastrous change from happiness to suffering and, usually, the death of the protagonist (the **denouement** or **catastrophe**). This suffering arouses a complex mix of emotions in its audience, especially fear and pity. Traditionally, the characters of tragedy are high-status individuals, such as rulers; this, however, is not the case with most tragedies written in the last 200 years. It is still essential, though, that we see the tragic protagonist as admirable.

Tragic plot. The exterior forces of fate or destiny are associated with tragedy; the inner force that drives the protagonist in classical tragedy is pride (**hubris**) or some such trait that exists in an extreme or distorted form (**tragic flaw**, or **hamartia**).

Tragic theme. Tragedy involves the tearing away and negation of identity. In both ancient Greek and Shakespearean tragedy, the protagonist is a king or high-status figure, making the fall from the greatest height as devastating as possible for both the individual and society, for the loss of the monarch would affect the whole social fabric. Shakespeare's King Lear falls from king to an old man divested of kingly power to a madman in a storm in a wilderness prior to his death.

The **DENOUEMENT** is the outcome or resolution of the play's conflicts. **CATASTROPHE** is the resolution (denouement) in tragedy; it usually results in the tragic hero's death.

HUBRIS means tragic pride.

A **TRAGIC FLAW** or **HAMARTIA** is a character's weakness that leads to his or her downfall.

THE LITERARY RESEARCH ESSAY

Since full information about conducting research and using secondary sources and documenting them appear in chapters 7 and 8, this section focuses on specific strategies for dealing with literary sources.

For more about the distinction between primary and secondary sources, see chapter 7, page 203.

Primary and Secondary Sources

Primary sources are the literary works (original sources) that you are analyzing; primary sources could also include letters, interviews, or diary entries of the writer. **Secondary sources** are studies (books, articles, and other media) that comment on or analyze one or more aspects of the primary work. Secondary sources include criticism relating to the work itself or to the writer's life (biographical criticism), as well as historical, cultural, linguistic, and other kinds of discourse that incorporate literary works. Using secondary sources in your analysis will strengthen your paper by showing how your observations about a work relate to what others have said.

How to Use Secondary Sources

1. Use a source to provide general information or to introduce something you will be discussing:

   Provide general information: Gerald Vizenor, a contemporary critic and Native American spokesperson, writes that "movies have never been the representations of tribal cultures; at best, movies are the deliverance of an unsure civilisation" (179).

   Introduce: Author Miriam Bird once said, "travel is more than the seeing of sights; it is a change that goes on deep and permanent, in the ideas of the living" (11).

PRIMARY SOURCES comprise original material, such as poems, stories, novels and plays.

SECONDARY SOURCES comprise material that comments on, explains, or interprets primary sources.

Similarly, the journeys the two characters undergo leave an indelible effect on them, changing the way they see the world and respond to others.

2.   Use a source to support, explain, or expand your point:

Support: It is not vanity that drives the protagonist, an unproven knight, in Browning's narrative poem "Childe Roland to the Dark Tower Came," and he is far from idealistic as well. As James Stonewall states, "it is a simple desire to finish his quest, to finally put an end to his journey, that motivates Roland" (76).

Explain/Expand: The wreck itself is a dense image, and through its complexity, Rich is able to illustrate the complexity of myths. The wreck represents "the history of all women submerged in a patriarchal culture; it is that source of myths about male and female sexuality which shape our lives and roles today" (Mcdaniel, par. 7).

3.   Use a source to disagree or to qualify:

Disagree: Donohue's fixation on the "elfin child" Pearl places undue emphasis on the ways we redeem our (innocent) children, rather than on the novel's more important concern with the ways society judges sin.

Qualify: Herb Wyile asserts that Chance "displays . . . insidious racism. His vision for his epic is grounded in a self-exculpatory, racist triumphalism characteristic of the western" (3). This may be the case, but since it is Chance's perspective, he likely considers it the truth.

➤ For reliability of Internet sources, see chapter 7, page 193.

Reliability of Secondary Sources

As with secondary sources for other research essays, you must be careful with the kinds of sources you use, especially if you use the Internet for research; university-related websites are the most reliable.

Reliable sources include critical studies of the work (books, articles in journals or from essay collections, etc.); other media and online resources affiliated with universities; and officially designated agencies or organizations.

Unreliable sources include Internet sites that feature essays on specific literary works by unnamed authors, or writers who give their name but not their credentials; discussion groups; and other unofficial postings, such as the home pages of enthusiasts or unofficial postings of student essays.

The expansion of the Internet has made commercial "study guides" readily accessible, but these are of questionable value. Remember that these quick-fix guides invariably present mechanical and superficial treatments of generic topics; they are seldom insightful or offer a reading that you wouldn't be more than capable of yourself. You should ask your instructor before using such a source, and, of course, if you do use one, you must cite it correctly.

Recent Sources

Unless you are specifically commenting on the reception of the work in the time it was written or the cultural/historical conditions that affected the work, prefer current sources to older ones as you would in other disciplines where older sources often become outdated. Another advantage of beginning with recent criticism is that such sources often refer to useful older criticism.

Most post-secondary institutions offer access through their library systems to online versions of scholarly journals. For example, the databases *Academic Search Complete*, *Project Muse*, or *Literature Online* (LION) enable students to access full-text articles in a wide variety of literary journals, from general ones to those specializing in the literature of a specific time period; literature of a particular country or region; literature categorized by genre; literature associated with movements; literature and culture; literature on an individual author; and interdisciplinary studies.

For online searches, see chapter 7, Online Searches, page 205.

Drafting and Revising the Literary Essay

The works you use as primary and secondary sources may be stylistically dense with some unfamiliar words and challenging concepts. However, you need to write in a direct and straightforward fashion to communicate their themes and ideas. Dealing with the complexities of literary and critical texts can present challenges to you as a writer and thinker: remember that convoluted language or sentence structure impedes understanding of complex thought; it also wastes words.

See chapter 9 for writing and style tips for literary research essays.

Introduction and thesis statement. Like any essay, the literary analysis should include an introduction with an identifiable thesis, which should name the topic and primary works. Your thesis should clearly indicate your approach to the topic.

Two sample introductions follow: in the first, student writer Loni Getty develops her introduction logically, beginning with a generalization and narrowing it down to a specific thesis:

See chapter 3, page 78, for information about thesis statements.

> The New World's struggle to forge a distinct identity outside the shadow of Old World Europe is reflected in much of the fiction of nineteenth-century American writers. Two such fiction writers, Herman Melville and Nathaniel Hawthorne, explore and question this evolving American identity by constructing characters who are outsiders forsaking the dominant values of their time. In Hawthorne's *The Scarlett Letter* Hester Prynne rejects the repressive intolerance and rigidity of America's Puritan values, while Melville's Bartleby, in "Bartleby, the Scrivener," withdraws from the materialistic, self-centred individualism of Wall Street, New York, and American business ideals. Each character struggles to function in a world that lacks empathy and basic kindness.

In the second introduction, from an exam essay, Richard Sexton uses the dramatic method by applying a brief quotation to the topic of freedom before narrowing it to a specific thesis:

> In George Orwell's novel *1984*, one of Big Brother's infamous slogans is "Freedom Is Slavery." American writers such as Mark Twain and Herman Melville also explored this paradox in the previous century. Twain's *Adventures of Huckleberry Finn* and Melville's "Bartleby, The Scrivener" have

main characters in situations where they are least free when they have gained physical freedom. Both works embody this central paradox of freedom and enslavement.

Body paragraphs—integration of sources. Take care to integrate direct quotations effectively. The challenge in writing literary essays, because you will probably refer often to the text to support your points, is to weave quotations logically and gracefully into your sentences. The following is not well integrated:

> The moose is seen as a strong, noble figure: "like a scaffolded king, straightened and lifted his horns" (30).

To be grammatical and clear, something must be added:

> *Revised:* The moose is seen as a strong, noble figure: "[L]ike a scaffolded king, [he] straightened and lifted his horns" (30).

→ See chapter 7, page 221, for more information on making changes to a direct quotation.

Remember that much of the support in a literary analysis will come from primary sources: you make a point and follow with a quotation. As a general rule, do not provide a direct quotation and follow it by a comment about it. Doing so will produce a choppy and mechanical analysis:

> "His fin, / Like a piece of sheet-iron, / Three-cornered, / And with a knife-edge" (3–6). In these lines, E.J. Pratt uses imagery to reveal the shark's machine-like power.

> *Revised:* In these lines, E.J. Pratt uses imagery to reveal the shark's machine-like power: "His fin, / Like a piece of sheet-iron, / Three-cornered, / And with a knife-edge" (3–6).

Similarly, do not insert a long direct quotation into the middle of your sentence if it results in an awkward structure. The quotation below is not very long, but the revised version is better integrated:

> In the third line, Stafford uses imagery, "This is the field where grass joined hands," to stress the unity of the scene.

> *Revised:* In the third line, Stafford uses the image of a "field where grass joined hands" to stress the unity of the scene.

→ See chapter 7, page 217, for how to use block format. For information on integrating sources, see page 217.

When citing from primary texts, check all your references carefully. Poetry citations should refer to line numbers rather than page numbers. Use the solidus (slash) to indicate line divisions in poetry with a space on both sides (/). For three or more lines of poetry, indent and use block format. For prose, use block format when you quote more than four lines of text.

If the poem is divided into sections, precede the line number by the section number, separating the two by a period. Thus, a parenthetical citation for the last four lines of Samuel Taylor Coleridge's "The Rime of the Ancient Mariner" would look like this: (VII.622–25). For short poems, such as Robert Frost's "Stopping by Woods on a Snowy Evening," line numbers usually are optional, but you should check with your instructor.

For works of fiction in various editions, you should cite the page numbers in your edition; then follow with a semicolon, a space, and chapter (ch.) or section (sec.) number. Plays should be referenced by act number, scene number, and line numbers, separated with periods with no spaces in between.

Examples:

In the end, Tess acknowledges her punishment: "'I am ready,' she said quietly" (417; ch. 58).

"The rarer action is / In virtue than in vengeance" (*The Tempest* 5.3.27–28).

The following body paragraph from student Stefan Virtue's essay on Edgar Allan Poe's "The Cask of Amontillado" illustrates the successful integration of a primary and a secondary source. Because Virtue alternates between his sources, he needs to include a complete parenthetical citation each time. He also integrates his quotations grammatically and smoothly, adding information he considers necessary:

> Montresor and Fortunato wend their way through the catacombs replete with the implied juxtaposition of wine, skulls, and skeletons. At this stage in the story, Fortunato has forgotten about Montresor's great and numerous family. He asks about the Montresors' coat of arms and motto. Montresor describes the shield as "[a] foot crush[ing] a serpent rampant whose fangs are embedded in the heel. . . . *Nemo me impune lacessit* [no one insults me without punishment]" (Poe 18). Montresor's mockery of Fortunato, with its ironic foreshadowing, fails to deter Fortunato from his quest for the Amontillado. Symbolically, Fortunato is already bound and helpless by the vice of the grape (Platizky 207). Finally, after arriving at the end of the vaults, Montresor chains Fortunato to the granite wall, and mockingly and sarcastically "implore[s]" (Poe 19) his victim to return, teasing him sadistically until the last brick is in place (Platizky 207).

Conclusion. Like the conclusion of any essay, the conclusion of a literary analysis should remind the reader of the thesis, perhaps by rephrasing it or by summing up one or two of the essay's most important points. Below, student writer Jessica Boyle concisely summarizes the differences between the stories' protagonists while suggesting their universality:

> Women may have various responses in their struggles for power and control in a male-dominated society. Some accept their fate; some fight for their freedom. Some ultimately accept the benefits and comforts in letting another person govern their life, as the sisters in Mansfield's "Daughters of the Late Colonel"; others, like the narrator in Gilman's "The Yellow Wallpaper," are willing to accept the risks of the struggle—even at the cost of their sanity.

Titles. When coming up with a title for a literary essay, be especially careful it isn't too broad; it should refer directly to the works you analyze:

Too broad: "Humanity's Quest"; "The Desire for Freedom"; "Distortion of Reality in Modern Literature"; "The Theme of Race."

→ For the use of ellipsis points to omit words in direct quotations, see chapter 7, Omitting Material: Ellipses, page 220.

→ For more about using brackets and ellipses in direct quotations, see chapter 7, page 219.

By specifying the titles of the individual work(s), the writers could have made their essay titles more meaningful and useful. On the other hand, a title may be specific but uninformative:

> *Uninformative:* "An Essay on Stephen Crane's 'The Monster'"; "Ted Hughes's 'Hawk Roosting'"

> ***Informative and Interesting:***

> "A Frankenstein of Society's Making: Stephen Crane's 'The Monster'"

> "A Hawk's Guide to Megalomania"

→ See chapter 8, pages 241–252, for specifics of MLA documentation.

Sample Student Literary Research Essay—MLA Style

The following essay explores a theme common to a short story and a poem, using the texts and secondary sources for support. The short story, "The Yellow Wallpaper," is summarized, and the poem, "My Papa's Waltz," is reproduced below.

SAMPLE STUDENT ESSAY

Summary of "The Yellow Wallpaper," by Charlotte Perkins Gilman, first published in 1892

[1]   "The Yellow Wallpaper" comprises journal entries of an unnamed woman narrator over a period of three months, during which her husband, John, has leased "a colonial mansion." The couple has a new baby, looked after by a nanny, and the narrator is forbidden any activity, including writing, while she recovers from "nervous depression." Although she believes that work and change would do her good, she complies with her husband's wishes, except for writing in her journal, which she hides from her husband and sister-in-law. Confined to an upper room she believes was once a nursery, she is repelled by its yellow wallpaper, but for lack of anything to do studies it intently, becoming more and more obsessed by it.

[2]   Over time, she discovers a pattern beneath the surface, and what begins as "a formless sort of figure" later becomes a woman or several women "creeping behind the pattern." The woman shakes the bars of the outer pattern, which are revealed by moonlight; during the day, the trapped woman, like the narrator, is "subdued." The narrator's physical health improves as her obsession deepens; she suspects John and his sister also take an interest in the wallpaper. In the week before the expiry of the lease, the narrator thinks she sees the woman creeping about the grounds. On the last day, the narrator is determined to free the woman forever and, to do so undisturbed, locks the door and throws the key out a window. Armed with rope to tie up the woman if she tries to get away, the narrator completes the job by ripping off the wallpaper. In the final scene, the narrator is creeping around the room's perimeter as John enters, then faints. Stepping over him, the narrator says, "I've got out at last. . . . And I've pulled off most of the paper, so you can't put me back!"

"My Papa's Waltz"

by Theodore Roethke

The whiskey on your breath
Could make a small boy dizzy;
But I hung on like death:
Such waltzing was not easy.

We romped until the pans
Slid from the kitchen shelf;
My mother's countenance
Could not unfrown itself.

The hand that held my wrist
Was battered on one knuckle;
At every step you missed
My right ear scraped a buckle.

You beat time on my head
With a palm caked hard by dirt,
Then waltzed me off to bed
Still clinging to your shirt.

Gilman's "The Yellow Wallpaper" and Roethke's "My Papa's Waltz": An Exploration of Ambivalence

by Kiyuri Naicker

[1]   We often look at our world in terms of opposites or dualities. Only the bravest writers attempt to explore the grey areas of life where binaries converge and borders are not clearly defined. Some have persevered and created scenarios in which our traditional methods of perception fail us, forcing us to peer into this undefined area. Much can be uncovered about human nature in these instances. Two authors, in particular, have excelled in examining these interstices as they occur in domestic relationships: Charlotte Perkins Gilman and Theodore Roethke. The works analyzed here investigate what lies between the poles of sanity and insanity, abuse and affection. The ambiguous situations they have created draw our attention to societal concerns and ultimately urge us to question how we interpret the world around us.

[2]   At the turn of the century, relatively little was understood about the progression of mental disorders. In her story "The Yellow Wallpaper," Gilman takes us on one woman's journey into madness through a first-person perspective. The story describes the transitional period between sanity and insanity, during which reality slips away and disorder slowly takes over. This fictitious account is based on Gilman's own experiences with neurasthenia and depression, which she underwent early in her marriage. A widespread belief during this period was that mental illness in women stemmed from moral deviance, and it was treated accordingly. In Gilman's case, her physician concluded that she needed to live as domestic a life as possible and limit herself to two hours of "intelligent" life a day. "The Yellow Wallpaper" was written to challenge the prevalent "domestic ideology" of the time; it is largely regarded as a feminist work. In this blurry region of conflicting realities, issues concerning the role of women in a patriarchal society, especially in relation to the medical world, began to surface. The narrative Gilman created "chronicles how women have been socially, historically, and medically constructed as not only weak, but sick beings" (Suess 61). The character never overtly accuses her oppressors for the state she finds herself in, but the story places the blame for the narrator's insanity on her situation rather than on herself. Jeannette King and Pam Morris explain that early feminist readings such as this were important because they

Continued

Naicker uses several near-synonyms for the *in-between* area her essay explores, including *the grey areas*, the *interstices* and the *transitional period*, avoiding repetition.

It is a good idea to name the works in your introduction, even if they are named in your title.

Naicker uses a logical introduction, contrasting common, everyday perceptions with those of "the bravest writers." She concludes her introduction by naming the authors and the specific dualities they attempt to bridge. In her last sentence, she considers the effect of the works on readers, which she follows up on in her conclusion.

Naicker uses two different citation formats here. In the first one, she includes the author's last name and page number; in the second she includes only the page in parenthesis as she names the authors in a signal phrase (*Jeannette King and Pam Morris explain*).

"rectified the tendency to enclose the heroine's problems within her own abnormal psycho-logical state" (37). This story forces one to look at what has actually transpired in the mind of the narrator, something that was generally avoided at the time in the treatment of mental disorders. As is evident in the narrator's interactions with her physician husband, the capac-ity of women to assess their own mental health was not taken seriously, and their concerns regarding their conditions were often marginalized. The outcome of this story points to the dangers of inadequate communication between physician and patient. Paula A. Treichler, for instance, reads the story as "an indictment of the complex and unhealthy relationship between women and medical language" (72).

[3]   It is also an indictment of the view towards women and creativity at the time. The narrator's writing was seen to be the cause of many of her problems, and any attempts she made to continue with her craft were done in a furtive and guilty manner. Conrad Schumaker believes that it demonstrates "what happens to the imagination when it is defined as fem-inine (and thus weak) in a patriarchal Victorian society that values only the practical" (591). The original purpose of this piece was therefore to change the view of the prescribed "rest cure" for women with neurasthenia; however, the cure itself had roots in a patriarchal med-ical realm that came under the magnifying glass as a result. The imposed confinement that Gilman underwent and the negative effects she consequently suffered are apparent in the story; the physician husband acts lovingly but succeeds in imprisoning his wife and driving her over the brink of sanity. Apart from providing an early feminist perspective, this story also illustrates how easily we can hurt those we love, and how trusting we can be of our aggressors.

[4]   Roethke explores this balance between affection and abuse more thoroughly in "My Papa's Waltz." Through his carefully ambivalent description, he has created a piece in which the two coexist in the same energetic scene. Roethke went to considerable lengths in his word choice to create ambiguity. Original poetic manuscripts reveal many revisions, the most drastic occurring in the fourth stanza. The first two lines originally read, "The hand wrapped round my head / Was harsh from weeds and dirt," but were changed to "You beat time on my head / With a palm caked hard by dirt" in the printed version (McKenna 38). The diction in the revision is much more strongly ominous.

[5]   In contrast, one of the earlier titles was "Dance with Father," but the title was later changed to "My Papa's Waltz" (39). The final title has more affectionate, lighthearted over-tones. This has the effect of "plung[ing us] into the comic and tragic tension" of the poem (Janssen 44). Speculation on the tone of this poem has divided many readers. This effec-tively illustrates the extent to which interpretation depends on an individual's perspective. According to H.R. Swardson,

> The words of a poem create a series of filters that eliminate possible mean-ings. In the universe of possible readings, comparatively few precipitate through all the filters. But in a poem like "My Papa's Waltz," several differ-ent readings do succeed in making their way through. At that point, the "preferred reading" is not found in the text, but in the interaction of reader and text. (4)

[6]   Those who see the joy in the poem place much emphasis on the rhythm and simple rhyme of the piece, and take the image of the waltz literally. The drunken fa-ther is seen as playfully tipsy, lavishing affection on the boy, which readers may have

Side annotations:

Naicker uses repetition to connect an important idea in the previous paragraph to the topic of this paragraph.

In her context-centred approach to "The Yellow Wallpaper," Naicker refers to several feminist critics. She does not include direct quotations from the primary source, though doing so might have strengthened her support.

Naicker's focus in paragraph 3 is on the medical model and creativity; however, in her last sentence, she refers to another theme in "The Yellow Wallpaper," providing a transition to her discussion of "My Papa's Waltz." Although her focus is different in the two works, such a link helps unify her essay.

To support her claim about word choice, Naicker contrasts early with later versions of the poem. She uses a direct quotation from a critic, Janssen, to comment on the significance of these contrasts. Seamless integration of primary and secondary sources increases her credibility.

By using block format, Naicker stresses the quotation's importance. Indeed, during the following lengthy paragraph, Naicker analyzes different "interactions" between reader and text.

experienced with their own usually reserved fathers after they have had a few drinks. However, those who see the darker side of the poem view the waltz and rhythm ironically. These elements set a dizzying pace for the succession of fearful images remembered by the boy. The whiskey on his father's breath, the shaking room, his frowning mother, and the marred hand of his father (possibly from previous beatings) all flash past him on this terrifying journey around the kitchen. Words like "battered," "scraped," "death," and "beat" are implicated in recounting fear rather than joy. The element of alcohol also enhances the potential for violence and loss of control, according to many. As Bobby Fong observes, "The poem is like a seesaw, where the elements of joy . . . are balanced against the elements of fear . . . . A seesaw tips easily, and 'My Papa's Waltz' is susceptible to the pressure of personal experience" (80).

[7]   Given that both elements are present, it is more pertinent to question why they are there rather than argue for one perspective over the other. The ambivalence of the poem illustrates the extent to which the poles of affection and abuse converge, especially for those in dependent relationships. For example, it is possible that the child knows on some level that a terrifying incident has transpired, but in recalling the incident has "regressed into areas of the psyche where powerful thoughts and feelings—the raw materials and driving power of our later lives—remain under the layers of rationale and of civilized purpose" (Snodgrass 81). According to Snodgrass, he is therefore, out of civility and self-preservation, refraining from mentioning the abuse that has occurred. However, it is more likely that the boy himself does not know where the rapture ends and the terror begins. He has difficulty in separating the abusive monster from the loving father, and perhaps does not view them as distinct, opposing forces, as we tend to do. When the "waltz" ends, he still clings to his father who carries him up to bed. Roethke seems to be suggesting that the two extremes are perhaps not as distant as we would like to imagine. Blurring the lines in such a volatile situation makes it easy to understand how domestic violence is perpetuated through generations. The boy in this case has not attached solely negative connotations to the event and may find himself interacting with his own future son in this manner. The whole scene lends itself well to the idea of perpetuity, as stated by Ronald Janssen:

> As an image of still larger patterns, the idea of the waltz raises the image of the dance of death, the dance of life, and we are led to think not only of the succession of daily experiences but also the succession of generations as a kind of pattern as the younger generation moves into the older. (45)

[8]   Despite the indefinite tone and imagery of the poem, it still succeeds in conveying the nuances of a very complex scene. The tone manages to avoid being deliberately condemning in addressing a highly sensitive subject, and as a result invites honest interpretation and introspection.

[9]   Both the works discussed above provide complex and subtle social commentaries. Gilman and Roethke have explored everyday domestic life that exists between the dualities around which we tend to cluster. Their force lies in what they have left unsaid, leaving room for interpretation and, through it, self-examination. By leading us into areas we would normally never venture, they raise issues in feminism and domestic violence that are still pertinent today. As these authors' works suggest, relationships are seldom simple or polar.

Continued

A clear topic sentence sets up this important paragraph, which addresses the subtle relationships in the poem.

Naicker refers to Snodgrass in order to disagree with him. See How to Use Secondary Sources, page 175.

Naicker makes a generalization about the poem's social relevance. Note the way that she weaves general and specific commentary to create a multi-layered reading of the poem.

Though brief, Naicker's conclusion reiterates her introduction, for example, by rephrasing her statement about the authors' purpose to "urge us to question how we interpret the world around us." In her last sentence, she emphasizes the works' relevance to today's reader.

Works Cited

Fong, Bobby. "Roethke's 'My Papa's Waltz.'" *College Literature* 17 (1990): 79–82. Print.

Janssen, Ronald. "Roethke's 'My Papa's Waltz.'" *Explicator* 44.2 (1986): 43–44. Print

King, Jeannette, and Pam Morris. "On Not Reading Between the Lines: Models of Reading in 'The Yellow Wallpaper.'" *Studies in Short Fiction* 26.1 (1989): 23–32. Print.

McKenna, John J. "Roethke's Revisions and the Tone of 'My Papa's Waltz.'" *ANQ* 11.2 (1998): 34–39. Print.

Schumaker, Conrad. "'Too Terribly Good To Be Printed': Charlotte Gilman's 'The Yellow Wallpaper.'" *American Literature* 57.4 (1985): 588–99. Print.

Snodgrass, W.D. "That Anguish of Concreteness—Theodore Roethke's Career." *Theodore Roethke: Essays on the Poetry*. Ed. Arnold Stein. Seattle: U of Washington P, 1965. 81. Print.

Suess, B.A. "The Writing's on the Wall: Symbolic Orders in 'The Yellow Wallpaper.'" *Women's Studies* 32.1 (2003): 79–97. Print.

Swardson, H.R. "The Use of the Word 'Mistake' in the Teaching of Poetry." *ADE Bulletin* 91 (1988): 4–13. Print.

Treichler, Paula. A. "Escaping the Sentence: Diagnosis and Discourse in 'The Yellow Wallpaper.'" *Tulsa Studies in Women's Literature* 3.1–2 (1984): 61–77. Print.

→ For information about MLA citation style, see chapter 8, pages 241–252.

CHAPTER SUMMARY

Chapter 6 discusses strategies for reading literary works and writing about them, focusing on the literary analysis. After comparing two main approaches to literary works, the text-centred and context-centred approaches, the features of the four major literary genres—poetry, short fiction, the novel, and the drama—are discussed with many examples provided. The chapter gives specific strategies for structuring and developing literary analyses and ends by outlining the challenges of the literary research essay.

PART II
Research Guide

American writer Zora Neale Hurston described research as "formalized curiosity. It is poking and prying with a purpose," which, over the course of centuries, has enabled us to better understand ourselves and our world.

Learning about research is learning a method. Like scholarly researchers, student researchers build on the work of others. Although undergraduate student researchers do not typically further knowledge in the sense that established scholars do, the research essay (often called a research paper or research project) provides a useful and enduring model. It might be more accurate to say that student researchers are like artisans learning a craft, building future skills by following in the footsteps of others in pursuit of a goal:

> Artisans pursue the creative blending of materials, tools, techniques, design, form, and function, often to enable them to realise the vision which inspired them. . . . Likewise, the academic researcher starts with a question, which can only be satisfactorily answered by blending appropriate data, concepts, research design, research methods, analytical techniques, and so forth. . . .
>
> Whether it is a completely original outcome or a new representation of something familiar, the finished work of both the artisan and the researcher should resonate with their intended audience, as capturing and explaining some aspect of their subject. Although the finished research product must be rigorously informed, the unique fusion of method, data, and the researcher means that it is, in many ways, as much art as science.
>
> —Guthrie, Cathy. "On Learning the Research Craft: Memoirs of a Journeyman Researcher." *Journal of Research Practice* 3 1 (2007): 1–2.

From a more practical perspective, when you are assigned a research essay, you will be exercising a number of valuable and interrelated skills, including planning, selective reading, critical thinking, evaluating and summarizing sources, analyzing, synthesizing, organizing, integrating, and documenting your sources. Because of the scope of activities involved, research essays provide a vital learning experience. Chapters 7 and 8 focus on all these—and other related—skills in a chronological sequence, beginning with an answer to the questions What is research and what does it involve?, and ending with the important final stage of source documentation.

7 Writing a Research Essay

As you advance in your post-secondary career, research will assume a greater importance. This research may involve direct experimentation, for example in your science labs. However, it will almost certainly involve greater exposure to the research of others, which you will then use to help answer a research question or solve a problem; becoming familiar with the research process is therefore critical. The purpose of this chapter is to introduce effective research methods—from coming up with a research topic, to finding useful sources, to the final stages of integrating and documenting these sources—to help you master the research skills essential to success in your chosen discipline.

LEARNING OBJECTIVES

- to understand the differences between exposition, writing concerned with explaining, and argument, writing that attempts to persuade the reader to adopt a point of view

- to understand what research is and the activities typically associated with it; to understand that successful research is a process that can be broken down into several stages

- to learn how to evaluate sources according to specific criteria so you can use credible sources in your essay

- to understand what a research proposal is and how it can help you in the early stages of research

- to understand the differences between primary and secondary sources
- to appreciate the value of using peer-reviewed journal articles in your research
- to learn different methods for integrating sources—summary, paraphrase, direct quotation—and when they should be used
- to be clear on what plagiarism is and the steps you can take to avoid it
- to learn how to show the reader that you have omitted material or made changes to a direct quotation

EXPOSITION, SYNTHESIS, AND RESEARCH

Research is associated with **expository writing**, which *informs* or *explains*, rather than argues. However, arguments can often be strengthened by research: using secondary sources, such as facts and statistics from government websites, the results of academic studies, or the opinions of experts, can make your claim more convincing (see chapter 5). Similarly, if you are asked to use research in a literary analysis, in addition to analyzing primary sources—the works themselves—you will analyze the views of experts to give more credibility to your thesis (see chapter 6).

Research comes from the French *rechercher*, "to seek again": exploring, checking, and re-checking are integral to research. In an expository research essay, claims of fact are generally used, and you don't set out to argue for one side or the other; instead, after determining your research question, you analyze the validity of the conclusions of various researchers on the topic and, from these findings, answer your question about your topic.

Research, then, is concerned with much more than just *finding out*. In research projects, you use critical thinking to *apply* your knowledge and synthesize what you learned to draw a conclusion about your topic. Thus, while exposition implies research, research implies synthesis—putting together what you have learned.

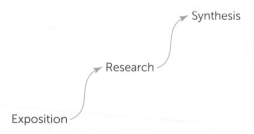

Synthesis

Research

Exposition

As a philosophical term, synthesis is the third, higher stage of truth that results from the combination of thesis and antithesis. In chemistry, synthesis refers to the formation of a more complex compound from two or more chemical elements. These definitions suggest what you do when you use the findings of others to help explain your topic: you create a synthesis, or "a higher stage of truth."

EXPOSITION is a term for writing concerned with informing or explaining, as distinct from arguing or persuading.

In expository research essays, you synthesize by bringing together the findings of researchers to draw a conclusion about your topic.

STAGES IN THE RESEARCH PROCESS

Although the research process is not always linear, it can be broken down into distinct stages. As you work toward your goal of investigating a problem, you can monitor your progress by using the questions below as a checklist. At the end of each stage, you should sense that you are building toward your goal and have completed the tasks before proceeding to the next stage in what Cathy Guthrie above calls a "journey."

The stages are briefly described below with reference to the essay of student writer Iain Lawrence whose outline and draft appear on pages 223–228.

Research: Finding and Exploring

This step involves determining your topic and sources (see Subjects versus Topics in chapter 2, p. 33). Once you have selected your topic, you may have to narrow it down so that your essay is not too general, perhaps by thinking about your own interests in relation to the topic.

Student writer Iain Lawrence wanted to research some aspect of sports. As he had a four-year-old son, he began thinking about the value of children's sports and sports leagues. Preliminary research in textbooks and other general sources guided him to the topic he eventually settled on: the relationship between participation in sports and childhood aggression. See his proposal (p. 200), outline (p. 223), and essay (p. 225).

After you have a topic and have begun your research, it is helpful to write a *research proposal* (p. 199), which includes your purpose, topic, thesis, and main points, as well as a tentative list of source material.

Questions to Ask

- Where do your interests lie?
- Do you have a knowledge base you can use to begin exploring the topic?
- If the topic is unfamiliar, how can you obtain background information?
- What do you hope to discover about this subject?
- How can you narrow down your topic?
- To whom are you writing? Who is your audience?
- What kinds of sources are appropriate given your topic and audience? Where can you find them?
- Have you given yourself sufficient time to research, synthesize, organize, compose, document, and revise?

Synthesis (I): Assimilation

After you have found your sources, you assimilate them: by taking notes and summarizing where appropriate, you demonstrate that you can accurately represent another person's ideas and use them with your own ideas. This vital stage of the research essay is discussed on pages 201–203; summarizing is discussed in Summary: The Précis in chapter 4, page 101 and below, Summary, page 211. When you have done these tasks, you are ready to begin to organize your points and structure your essay.

As Iain Lawrence recorded information, he was already beginning to evaluate its usefulness and connect information from different sources. In reading peer-reviewed journals on child development, Lawrence came across several definitions of aggression and had to decide on the relative importance of each. He then sorted them into categories and focused on the most relevant ones.

During this stage, as you decide how the material is going to be used and where it belongs in your essay, your goal should be much clearer than in the finding and exploring stage. You should begin to see your essay "coming together" as you work toward building your essay's structure, the next stage.

Questions to Ask

- Is your research geared toward supporting your research question?
- How do the sources help you explore the topic?
- Have you understood the results of the studies you've looked at and/or the positions of the experts whose works you have read?
- Are all your sources credible? Recent? Relevant?
- Have you summarized adequately and/or quoted accurately all sources you might use?
- Have you recorded the authors' names, titles, page numbers, and other bibliographic information accurately?
- How do the different experts' views or conclusions fit together?
- Are there opposing positions? Do some findings challenge others, for example?
- Has your research changed your approach to the topic? Do you need to change your thesis?

Organization: Arranging

Every essay needs a structure; often this will be shown through an outline, a kind of blueprint for the writing stage. Strategies for outlining are discussed in chapter 2; an example of a topic outline is given on page 40. An example of a detailed sentence outline is on page 223.

For Lawrence, a comprehensive outline was essential, and the composing stage was directly linked to his detailed outline. Although he relied on the outline, he continued to develop some of his points as he worked on his rough draft. A formal outline can be useful, but it shouldn't be considered unchangeable.

Questions to Ask

- What kind of outline should you use?
- Is there a natural organizational method you should use (chronological, cause–effect, problem–solution)?
- Do your points thoroughly explore the topic?
- Are any points inadequately developed? How can they be further developed?
- Do all your points include sub-points?
- What points are most essential and what sources are most relevant?
- Are you off topic anywhere?

- How should the points be ordered (e.g., from least important to most important)?
- Does your chosen structure reflect your purpose? Will it be easy for your reader to follow?

Synthesis (II): Composing

During the first-draft stage, synthesis takes place at the linguistic or the textual level, as you integrate your sources into your essay. Thus, how you use direct quotations, summary, and paraphrase will be crucial (see Using Sources in the Composing Stage, pp. 211 and 212).

Lawrence makes minimal use of direct quotation, preferring to summarize findings in his own words and reserve direct quotations for emphasis. His choice was determined partly by essay length: summary enabled him to convey information efficiently, and he could therefore include more sources in his essay, enhancing his credibility. By contrast, Brydon Kramer uses direct quotations often as precise wording is important (see p. 147). When you write an English or a history essay, direct quotations are usually crucial.

Questions to Ask

- Have you used sources consistently to support your points? Have you depended too much on one or a few sources?
- If you are working directly from an outline, can you see any points that need further development? Do any overly long paragraphs need to be subdivided?
- Which sources should be summarized, which paraphrased, and which quoted directly? (This will depend on various factors including length, importance, and phrasing of the source.)
- Could you have unintentionally plagiarized by failing to cite a source or by citing it incorrectly? (If in doubt, check with your instructor.)
- Can you use ellipses to omit less important parts of a direct quotation?
- Have you provided smooth transitions between quotations and your own writing?
- Is the language level consistent throughout? Is it appropriate for your audience?
- Are direct quotations grammatically integrated and easy to read?
- Have you double-checked quotations for accuracy?
- Is your own writing clear, grammatical, and effective?

→ See Omitting Material: Ellipses (p. 220).

Documenting: Following Procedures

In this final stage of the research essay, you follow the documentation guidelines as laid down by the authority of your discipline. The two main scholarly methods for parenthetical referencing are those of the Modern Language Association (MLA) and the American Psychological Association (APA). Some journal and book publishers use notes as a referencing system, following, for example, the Chicago Manual of Style (CMS) or the Council of Science Editors (CSE); still others use variants of one of these systems. The major documentation methods are outlined in chapter 8. Lawrence, whose disciplines were biology and psychology, used APA style (see pp. 252–263).

Questions to Ask

- What documentation style is expected for the essay?
- Where can you find reliable information on documenting? (Sources of information on documentation must be both accurate and current.)
- If you have used electronic sources, are you clear on acceptable methods for documenting them?
- Do you know exactly what needs to be documented and what does not? For example, is it possible that the reader could confuse your ideas or observations with those of a secondary source?
- Have you carefully documented other people's words and ideas without cluttering the essay with unnecessary citations?
- Have you included *all* the sources in your essay in your alphabetical list at the end of your essay?

Table 7.1 summarizes the five stages discussed above. Remember to pay close attention to grammar, style, and clarity. Demonstrating your knowledge of previous research on your topic will help convey your reliability as a researcher; paying strict attention to the formal writing standards of the academic disciplines will help convey your reliability as a writer.

TABLE 7.1 Stages in Writing a Research Essay

STAGE	ACTIVITIES	WRITING TASKS	TEXTBOOK READINGS
Research	finding, exploring, scanning	• pre-writing, narrowing topic • research proposal	The Research Proposal (p. 199); Researching Your Topic (p. 197)
Synthesis (I): Assimilation	focused reading, assimilating ideas from sources	• note-taking • summarizing	What Is Research? (p. 192) Summary: The Précis (p. 101)
Organization	arranging, determining structure	• formal outline	Formal Outline (p. 40)
Synthesis (II): Composing	integrating at textual level	• summary • paraphrase • direct quotation • mixed format	Source Citation and Plagiarism (p. 213) Methods of Integrating Sources (p. 217)
Documentation	following guidelines	• in-text citations • bibliography section	Why Document Your Sources? (p. 239); Source Citation and Plagiarism (p. 213)

A Closer Look

Coming Up With a Title

Your research essay's title, like all essay titles, should be informative, reflecting content and your approach to the topic. Clearly, a title like "Major Research Paper" conveys neither. The title "Attention Deficit Disorder" announces only the topic; it says nothing about content or approach. "The Mozart Effect and Cognitive Processing" is also broad. "Treating Attention Deficit Disorder without Drug Interventions" and "Does Listening to Classical Music Enhance Intelligence?" are both informative and clear.

Although the title of an argumentative essay is often designed to arouse interest, the title of an expository essay should focus on conveying information efficiently. Do not wait until you have finished your essay before choosing a title. As possible titles occur to you as you research, outline, or compose, write them down for further consideration. A blank title page and a looming deadline can make a last-minute decision difficult; remember that your title will be the first part of your essay that is read. Here are some suggestions to make title selection easier:

- Nouns are usually the keywords in titles. If you are stuck for a title, choose three or four important nouns in your essay or ones that sum up your main points; then, look for the best way to connect them (e.g., *video games + children + aggression* becomes "The Effects of Video Games on Childhood Aggression").

- If your title seems too long, consider dividing it into two parts with a colon (e.g., "The Negative Impacts of the International Monetary Fund's Policies on Argentina's Social Disparities" could become "The Impacts of the International Monetary Fund's Policies on Argentina: Fanning the Flames of Social Disparity").

- A two-part title could pose a central question that the essay will answer (e.g., "Tablets in Today's Classroom: Distractions or Educational Tools?").

- Although an expository essay title may not need to attract a reader's interest, a catchy title may convey information more efficiently than one that is more straightforward (e.g., "Airbrushed to Perfection: Media and Teenagers' Self-Esteem" conveys essentially the same information as, and is more interesting than, "Unrealistic Images in the Media and Their Effects on Teenagers' Self-Esteem").

WHAT IS RESEARCH?

Although you may not realize it, research is probably familiar to you. It is unlikely you will have made many important life decisions without researching them beforehand, whether deciding which model of smartphone to buy or which post-secondary schools to apply to. In the case of schools, you may have browsed websites, talked to other people—perhaps current students, graduates, or school counsellors—and considered various academic and non-academic criteria. However, you probably placed the highest value on *factual evidence*: programs, prerequisites, tuition fees, housing, and campus size.

Decision making based on research is a life skill, and analysis, judgment, and evaluation are involved in the decision-making process. Research assignments in university ask you to analyze, compare, assess, and synthesize the scholarship of experts in your subject area, generally by discussing multiple positions on a problem. Simply rephrasing these sources is not necessarily research, nor is summarizing your own opinions or experiences.

One common approach to organizing a research paper is to compare and contrast the similarities and differences between two or more ideas. Another method is to evaluate the strengths and/or weaknesses of an idea based on criteria that you create or borrow from experts. The following step-by-step example involves both compare-and-contrast and evaluation to draw a conclusion about each source.

1. Identify a problem:

    the effect of playing video games on aggressive or violent behaviour

2. State a claim or hypothesis about this problem (what the writer will explore or prove):

    Violent video games can cause aggression in teenagers.

3. Describe the points made by one or more "experts" concerning the claim:

    Researcher A's research shows a significant increase in emotional arousal and a decrease in brain activity in areas responsible for self-control after teenagers played a violent video game for 20 minutes. Researcher A used brain scans to detect changes in activity in different areas of the brain.

    Researcher B's research shows a small but significant relationship between playing violent video games and thoughts and behaviour after the period of game playing. She studied young teenagers who completed questionnaires about their video playing habits and their aggressive thoughts and behaviour.

4. Decide on the merits of these experts' approaches to the thesis:

    Researcher A's finding is more convincing than that of Researcher B because his method provides direct evidence that playing video games altered parts of the brain associated with aggressive behaviour. However, it did not investigate aggressive acts; therefore, his study did not attempt to link video game playing and aggressive behaviour.

    Researcher B's study found a positive correlation (association) between game playing and aggression, but it was small and was based on self-reports, which may not always be reliable.

5. Conclude with your judgment on the thesis, either by rating the experts' approaches or by suggesting a new way of thinking about the problem:

    Researcher A has convinced me that there is physical evidence linking violent video games and aggressive impulses. Even though Researcher B's finding suggests a link between game playing and aggressive thoughts and behaviour, the evidence is less compelling due to the study's method. Clearly, though, both studies could be valid sources in an essay that explores the effects of violent video games.

Reliability of Sources

Experts are highly experienced or educated people who have produced significant work on a subject. Partly because of the expansion of the Internet, you need standards for screening the quality of the information that you can access today.

When assessing the credibility of a secondary source, consider the words of the porcine dictator in George Orwell's *Animal Farm*: "[S]ome animals are more equal than others." The ease with which anyone with basic computer skills can publish online has created both new opportunities and new challenges for researchers.

Searching the Internet for smartphone prices and using it for academic research require different criteria; research is focused on the trustworthiness of the author. Many thoughtful and well-respected authors use the Internet to reach others who share their interests; however, it is important to judge a website author's motivation carefully.

The Internet has increasingly become an arena for personal opinion, some of it informed, much of it uninformed. Moreover, "digital advocacy" has rapidly become a form of mass protest. Individuals or groups garner support for a cause in order to argue for their position (for example, by having visitors "sign" petitions) against government and other policy makers. Visual appeal and a sophisticated design may help make such sites *appear* credible and reliable.

Today's student researcher must be able to distinguish between reliable and unreliable sources, as well as objective ones and those with a viewpoint to promote. In general, assess a website or any non-library source by ensuring that it satisfies the four "Re's" of research (the first two apply particularly to websites):

1. *Reputable*
2. *Reliable*
3. *Recent*
4. *Relevant*

➜ See Opinion, Facts, and Argument in chapter 5, page 120.

1. *Reputable*: Reputable websites make their purpose known to readers (many have an easily accessible mission statement or an "About Us" page). They also support their statements with verifiable facts and figures, and make known their evidence-gathering methods. Most reputable websites are associated with a well-established organization. Reputable websites clearly distinguish between fact and opinion.
2. *Reliable*: You can trust the information posted on reliable sites. To determine the reliability of a website not associated with familiar organizations, verify the information in another source that you know is reliable. Checking and double-checking are signs of good research.
3. *Recent*: Since attitudes and analyses change over time, recent information allows you to consider the latest developments in your field. Internet information is often current (in some cases, currency refers to hours or days rather than weeks or months!), and content several months old may be outdated. This can be true even of reputable and reliable sites, like some government websites. Always check the date of the website's creation or its most recent update.
4. *Relevant*: Using sources that are not directly relevant to the point you wish to make disrupts your essay's unity; a "padded" References or Works Cited page also reduces your credibility. Ask if there is a *direct* connection between your point and its support, and whether it is the *best* support you can find.

These criteria apply particularly to open-access resources, from Google Scholar to the enormously vast array of commercial, governmental, and personal websites that anyone can view. These contrast with the authoritative resources accessed through your institution's library home page.

The way you use open-access resources, or whether you use them at all, depends on what kind of information you are looking for. You should first consider your purpose for seeking out a source. Is it for reliable information from an objective source with evidence-gathering methods beyond reproach (Statistics Canada, for example), or is it to learn about a particular viewpoint? In the latter case, it might be acceptable to use a website that advocates a position or supports a cause as long as you make that position clear in your essay.

Finding a Research Question

Research often begins with the statement of a problem or with a research question. It could also take the form of a hypothesis, as it does in many scientific experiments where the researcher states the expected or probable result of the experiment; the experiment is set up to test the hypothesis. Student researchers, too, could then conduct research to determine whether their prediction is valid. For example, you could hypothesize that there is a causal relationship between children playing violent video games and aggression. However, if no such relationship is discovered, your original hypothesis is still valuable. Whether hypotheses are proven or not, you have discovered something new about your topic.

Choose five topics from the list below and formulate a research question or hypothesis for each. Make sure it is specific enough to serve as a thesis statement in an essay.

EXERCISE 7.1

Example:

Topic: organic foods

Question: Do organic foods hold measurable health benefits for humans?

Hypothesis: Although organic foods have environmental benefits, they do not hold measurable health benefits for humans.

alternative energy sources	genetic engineering
bullying	globalization
campus housing	hybrid vehicles
cosmetic surgery	over-the-counter medications
deforestation	pet overpopulation
early development of humans	private health care
educational spending	religious education
endangered species	social networking
fashion industry	traditional media
file-sharing	weight-loss methods

A Closer Look

Knowledge and Research across the Disciplines

Although many principles of research apply to all disciplines, research goals and methods can vary across the disciplines. Here we define humanities, the social sciences, and the sciences, and consider the kinds of research associated with each.

Humanities: A branch of human knowledge concerned with examining the tools that humans use to express and represent themselves. Humanities writing focuses on how ideas and values are used to interpret human experience, analyzing primary sources to draw conclusions about their literary themes, historical/cultural significance, theoretical basis, or universality.

When you write an essay in the humanities, you will probably use direct quotations from primary sources; in English literature, these are the poems, plays, novels, and short stories you are studying. In history, these are documents such as old newspapers, letters, treaties, and the like. However, incorporating such references in your essay does not constitute research; you will need to analyze and synthesize secondary sources—what other critics have said about the primary works and the ways they have interpreted them. Studies in the humanities often try to situate primary works within an overarching context—for example, in relation to a literary or philosophical theory.

> Reports and scientific studies often use the IMRAD structure with the following standardized sections and headings: **I**ntroduction, **M**ethods, **R**esults, **A**nd **D**iscussion.

The claim in a humanities essay is often interpretive: the writer justifies his or her decision to interpret a poem or historical event in a specific way, arguing that this perspective is a worthwhile way to consider the poem or event. Evidence from primary and secondary sources is used to support this kind of claim.

Sciences: A branch of human knowledge concerned with the study of natural phenomena using empirical methods to determine or validate its laws.

The empirical method is the basis of most scientific study: researchers begin with a hypothesis and design an experiment to test its validity. The closeness of empiricism and science is apparent in the fact that the empirical method is often known as the *scientific method*. Empiricism has a long and complex history in Western thought dating back before Aristotle. At the root of most empirical systems (scientific and philosophical) is the belief that knowledge is derived from the senses. Sixteenth-century philosopher Francis Bacon stressed the need for careful and controlled observation to produce a generalization about the subject investigated— the foundation of the scientific method as it developed throughout the centuries.

Written experiments in the sciences typically share a common structure, beginning with an Introduction, followed by sections titled "Methods," "Results," and "Discussion" (or "Conclusion"), known by the acronym IMRAD. The "Methods" section explains in precise detail how the experiment is set up, enabling future researchers to duplicate or build on it. The "Discussion" section interprets the raw data generated through the experiment and suggests ways that the findings can be applied.

Social sciences: A branch of human knowledge concerned with collective human behaviour and the systems we create to study this behaviour (e.g., social, psychological, or political ones).

Research in the social sciences (sometimes called social and behavioural sciences to differentiate them from natural sciences) deals with the ways that humans are affected by social, political, or economic systems. Information can be classified according to its purpose; for example, economics is a system concerned with how society deals with money and the creation and consumption of goods and services, whereas political science is concerned with how governments and other political bodies affect society.

The social science researcher identifies an aspect of human behaviour to investigate and designs an experiment with a hypothesis or main question in mind. The subject (usually human) is observed, and the results are measured and interpreted; the hypothesis is either proved or disproved. Such experiments, like those in the natural sciences, use a *quantitative* methodology, i.e., the results of the experiment can be quantified and conclusions can be drawn from the numerical data. The researcher can then determine whether there is a valid relationship between the data and the hypothesis.

Another common method in the social sciences is quantifying the results of questionnaires or surveys. Interviews and observation may generate data, which is then interpreted by the knowledgeable specialist.

Observing groups or individuals is common social science research.

Rather than seeing studies in the humanities, social sciences, and sciences in isolation, however, some writers today focus on their similarities or on how thought in the humanities can inform thought in the sciences and vice versa. As well, much research today is cross-disciplinary, concerned with issues that transcend the traditional divisions. Other disciplines, such as law, business, and education are intrinsically interdisciplinary in their nature or scope.

Researching Your Topic

Beginning to Explore

In most cases, especially if you are free to choose your own topic, beginning and narrowing the search for material related to your topic will be something you do yourself. Looking for a general work, such as a textbook, in your subject area is a useful first step. A general work likely includes a bibliography (alphabetical listing of sources), which you can scan for relevant titles and authors. Consult works on your subject in the library's reference section, such as indexes, encyclopedias, dictionaries, and comprehensive guides; many such library resources are available online. Internet search engines and subject directories can also provide excellent starting points, suggesting general topics that you can narrow down.

When you find potentially useful sources, you can add them to your **working bibliography**, a list of books, articles, and other texts you plan to look at. For a book, scan the index and the table of contents to determine how helpful the source will be. If it looks promising, read the writer's "Introduction," "Preface," or "Foreword." The author often summarizes his or her approach and provides chapter-by-chapter summaries there. For an article, read the abstract (short summary that precedes a science or social science journal article).

Your working bibliography will likely not exactly match the final list of works you actually use; the purpose of a working bibliography is to lead you to relevant sources. Remember to note the date of a book's publication from the copyright page (the back of the title page). Prefer more recent works, not only because they will be up to date but also because they may draw on relevant previously published works and provide you with other useful sources. Sometimes just scanning the "Works Cited" or "References" section at the end of a recent work will suggest potential sources.

Most university libraries have user-friendly interfaces that enable you to begin with a subject area that provides fast links to more specific information. In the sample shown in figure 7.1, clicking the link in a subject category takes you to a list of resources for that subject, for example, journal collections and useful databases.

> Your **WORKING BIBLIOGRAPHY** is the list of books, articles, and other texts you plan to look at.

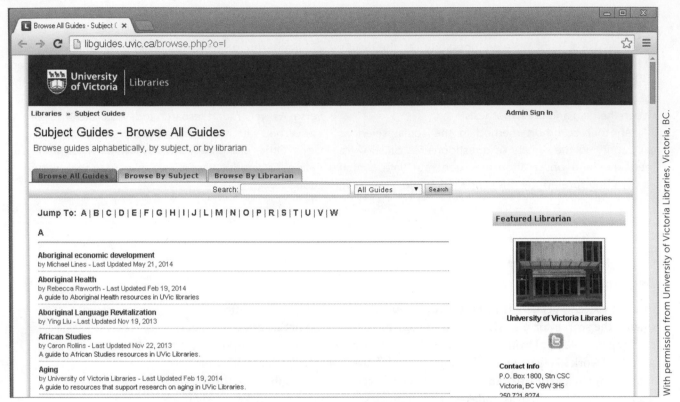

With permission from University of Victoria Libraries, Victoria, BC.

FIGURE 7.1 Searching a Database by Subject Guide Category

EXERCISE 7.2

Choose one question/hypothesis that interests you from the list you made in exercise 7.1. Using a textbook, encyclopedia, or subject guide available from your library, generate three specific questions related to the main question/hypothesis you came up with. You could use one of the four pre-writing methods discussed in chapter 2, Pre-Writing Strategies, page 34, to help generate the questions.

EXERCISE 7.3

Using a general reference work, such as an encyclopedia or subject dictionary, locate the entries for the topic you used in exercise 7.2. One source common to most university libraries is *Oxford Reference Online*, which includes many guides in 20 subject areas, such as biology, computing, economics and business, and environmental sciences. For example, if your topic is organic foods, *The Oxford Encyclopedia of Food and Drink in America* is a possible source. When you have located an entry:

- summarize it in about 100 words

or

- use some of the information to help answer one of the three questions you created in exercise 7.2. Your instructor may specify a length for this answer.

The Research Proposal

Proposals are common in student research projects and in workplace writing, especially in engineering, business, and education. Non-profit organizations and individuals also use them to apply for grants. The ability to make the proposal sound worthwhile may convince the granting agency that the writer is the best person for the project. Similarly, as an essay writer, you want your subject to appear worth investigating, and you want to be perceived as credible.

In the professional world, a proposal can be detailed and complex. It can be divided into introduction/overview, background information and/or statement of the problem, goals and objectives, methods, available resources, needed resources, and conclusion. Sometimes writers include dates for the completion of specific parts of the process—for example, the date to finish preliminary research. As a student, writing even a short proposal can help clarify your thinking and provide a rough plan.

A proposal may mark the initial stage of the project, consisting of just an "expression of interest," perhaps a paragraph or two explaining your topic and why you are interested in exploring it. Or, it may be submitted later in the process and include a formal outline.

A Simple Proposal: Purpose and Methodology

A research proposal should include, at a minimum

1. *Purpose*: a statement about your topic, along with your research question, hypothesis, or problem to be investigated
2. *Research methodology*: a brief description of how you plan to locate the major sources

1. Purpose

a. Announce the area you want to explore. You can also briefly state why you want to explore this area and/or why it might interest other people or be of concern to them.
b. Include a tentative thesis statement; of course, you can amend it later.
c. Outline at least three to four main points (or questions) in addition to your thesis.

2. Research Methodology

a. Relevant background could include anything you need to find out about before you begin writing.
b. Mention the *kinds of sources* you will likely use; what resources are suggested by the topic or your discipline? Which will likely be most useful: books, journals, magazines, Internet sources? What kind of preliminary research are you planning? In addition to primary and secondary sources, consider whether alternative sources, such as interviews or surveys, might be useful; give book/journal and article titles, if possible.
c. You should anticipate what organizational methods you will be using (e.g., cause–effect, compare and contrast, classification/division, problem–solution).

Sample Research Proposal

Here is the research proposal for the student essay that appears in this chapter (p. 225). It satisfies the requirements of research proposals as discussed above. By giving details and specific references to research sources, Lawrence demonstrates his credibility as a researcher.

SAMPLE STUDENT PROPOSAL

The Impact of Sport on Levels of Inappropriate Childhood Aggression

by Iain Lawrence

Purpose

[1]   Parents are often told that involvement in aggressive sports such as martial arts will help shy or passive children develop a sense of self-esteem and confidence; at the same time, they are told that such sports will promote respect for others and function as a channel for inappropriate aggression in anti-social or aggressive children. Are such claims warranted, and do other "aggressive" sports, such as lacrosse, hockey, or perhaps even soccer, provide a healthy outlet for aggression, or do they simply encourage further inappropriate behaviour? The central question for this research project is "Does involvement in 'aggressive' sport mitigate inappropriate childhood aggression?"

Methodology

[2]   Key terms, such as "inappropriate aggressive behaviour" and "aggressive sport," will be defined and distinguished where necessary from their counterparts, such as "acceptable aggressive behaviour" and "high-energy sport." Since this research paper is only about 1,500 words, it will be important to remain focused on the task of answering the general question described above, rather than narrowing the focus too much, for example on one particular sport. Further research could examine whether specific sports reduce or control inappropriate aggression in children. In addition to defining key terms, this research project will provide a literature review to try to determine the current knowledge about the relationship between children and aggressive sports.

[3]   Key sources will be found primarily in peer-reviewed journals devoted to childhood development. Those with a focus on child psychology will likely be relied on heavily. An example of such a source is "A Qualitative Study of Moral Reasoning of Young Elite Athletes," by Long, Pantaléon, Bruant, and d'Arripe-Longueville, published in the journal *The Sport Psychologist*. Textbooks discussing the proven emotional and social benefits of different sports will also be useful for this project, especially as starting places. An example of a book containing such information is Gatz, Messner, and Ball-Rokeach's *Paradoxes of Youth and Sport* (2002), an authoritative collection of essays on youth and sports.

RESEARCH NOTE-TAKING

Keeping clear records during the research phase of the essay-writing process allows you to read material efficiently as well as save time (and your sanity) when you write your paper. You should make notes as you research your sources, ensuring that you record the following information:

- the complete names of the authors, editors, and translators
- the name of the book, journal, magazine, newspaper, or website affiliation or sponsor
- the name of the specific article, chapter, section, or website with the full publication details, including date, edition, or translation; for a journal article, include volume and issue number; for Internet sites, include the date the site was created or updated
- for books, the name of the publisher and the company's location (including province/state or country)
- for Internet sites, the day you viewed the page and either the URL or the **digital object identifier (DOI)**
- a direct quotation, a summary, or a paraphrase of the writer's idea; *if it is a direct quotation, make sure you put quotation marks around it*
- the page numbers you consulted, both those from which specific ideas came and the full page range you looked at (for unnumbered online documents, use some other marker, such as paragraph numbers or section headings)

> Record page numbers for *all* specific references, not just for words that you plan on quoting directly in your essay.

Organizing Research Notes

One time-honoured method of organizing your notes is to write them on index cards (remember to number them). You can also record notes in a journal and use tabs to section the book into particular headings. If using a computer, you can create a record-keeping system by creating multiple document files in a folder (see chapter 2, p. 43). In addition, there are various software programs that can help you organize your research, such as EndNote (http://www.endnote.com), Bibliographix (http://www.bibliographix.com), and Nota Bene (http://www.notabene.com), which are databases.

> The **DIGITAL OBJECT IDENTIFIER (DOI)** is a number–alphabet sequence that begins with the number 10 and is often found on documents obtained electronically through databases. In APA documentation style, it is the last element in the citation.

RefWorks is another program you can use to keep track of source material (http://www.refworks.com). If you enter the bibliographic information into the system, it will create a "Reference" or "Works Cited" page (depending on whether you specify APA or MLA style, which are discussed in chapter 8). Furthermore, you can electronically send catalogue or database search results directly to RefWorks; it's not necessary to manually enter records.

Alternative citation managers include Zotero (https://www.zotero.org), which works seamlessly with the Web, making it easy to capture records from internet searches as well as database search results. Mendeley (http://www.mendeley.com), a reference manager and "academic social network," is especially useful for collaborative projects and sharing information. Both systems are popular with scholars and students as they offer cutting-edge features, along with flexibility and ease of use.

Before submitting a final paper, review all the entries to ensure you have eliminated any sources you have decided not to use in your essay.

Cross-Referencing

Cross-referencing your notes can make it easier to retrieve your information when you are writing your essay. In addition to listing keywords on index cards or visual aids like mind maps (graphic organizers), you can use a commenting feature within computer files. Some word-processing programs let you make cross-references within single documents (in Word, for example, this is found under Insert, then Cross-reference in the drop-down menu). Computer databases often have built-in, keyword-based cross-referencing systems.

Some systems, like RefWorks and Zotero, offer tagging features. Tagging is an easy way to categorize items by attaching descriptive words to them. You can tag your information with whatever relevant keyword or term you would like associated with that item. These tags allow you to sift through your information by using the categories that you deem relevant.

Some Useful Research Strategies

Assimilating

Begin the research by gathering definitions of the keywords and phrases in your thesis statement.

- Read or view potential sources with the thesis statement in mind. Resist getting sidetracked by unconnected material.
- Judge whether or not a book will be worth your time by looking up your keywords and phrases in the index at the back of the book. Similarly, read the abstracts of articles.
- Consider how your information can be strung together using transitional words and phrases like *as a result of, because, on the other hand*, or *in contrast*.
- Try to find at least one example to support every major statement you wish to make.

Arranging

- After your research, construct a rough outline showing the structure of your paper by creating primary and secondary headings corresponding to the major elements of your thesis statement. Under the headings, list the lines of reasoning and/or examples that support these points.
- Decide how many pages you will allot for each section of the paper, bearing in mind the relative importance of each point and the paper length.
- Look over your outline. Do you have sufficient examples to support your major statements?
- Review the assigned word count. Do you have enough material in your study notes to fill the pages? If not, is more research needed? Consider laying out your

A Closer Look

Using Contradictory Evidence

In the initial research stage, you will need to find sources relevant to your topic; however, not all studies on a given topic come to the same conclusion. You will have to assess their differences, perhaps by analyzing their respective strengths and weaknesses. This process of weighing the conclusions involves critical thinking and is a fundamental part of research.

In the humanities, your thesis is often based on the interpretation of a text, so you must carefully show how the interpretations of critics differ from each other and, perhaps, from your own interpretation. Above all,

contradictory interpretations should not simply be dismissed without explanation or analysis.

If you do not address contradictory studies, the reader may wonder why. For example, many recent studies have attempted to show the health benefits of vitamins. If you are investigating the benefits of vitamin E in preventing heart disease and have found that credible evidence exists, you still need to acknowledge contradictory studies, especially recent ones, and explain how these findings fit into your claim about the value of vitamin E.

---

paper in a word-processing program according to the suggested page number count. Use manual page breaks (under Insert in most programs) to create document sections that follow your outline, so that you can judge whether you're writing too much or too little for any section.

- Design a timeline for each of the steps in your paper, if you haven't already done so, to ensure all sections will be included in your final version.

THE SEARCH IS ON: LOCATING AND USING SOURCES

Almost all research can be electronically mediated in some way, as libraries have become interactive and virtual clearing houses for information storage and distribution. There are more kinds of source materials available than ever before; most of the important ones are discussed below.

Primary and Secondary Sources

A major goal of university-level research is to read or view original material, known as primary sources. The ability to analyze and integrate secondary sources, the literature that has grown up in response to the original work, is also a principal goal of post-secondary learning. You need to be able to distinguish between *original* authors and the *commentary on* their work. Literary analyses often include or quote primary source material but are considered secondary sources. Essay assignments frequently include a requirement that both primary and secondary sources be identified and referenced.

A primary source could be the later edition of a work. For example, a recent edition of *The Merchant of Venice* is acceptable as a primary source in an undergraduate's work because first editions are rare. Personal documents, such as letters and journals, and raw scientific data are also considered primary sources. A secondary source for *The Merchant of Venice* would be another writer's analysis of and commentary on the play, material about Shakespeare's theatre or Elizabethan English, and so on. An encyclopedia entry is also considered a secondary source.

Kinds of Secondary Sources

Reference sources such as indexes, almanacs, encyclopedias, dictionaries, and yearbooks can provide you with concise summaries of statistics, definitions, and biographies, and may also provide a reading list of the principal primary and secondary sources. This type of broad-spectrum information is widely available on the Internet. For instance, a Google search of "black hole" and "encyclopedia" returns results that include the *Encyclopaedia Britannica*, the *Columbia Encyclopedia*, *Encarta Encyclopedia*, and numerous library-based sites offering further links to information on the subject. The *Britannica* entry includes a listing of relevant books, articles, websites, magazine articles, and videos on black holes.

Books and Articles

Once you've developed a basic understanding of your topic, you can look for books and journal articles that specifically address your research question/thesis statement. Continue your research by locating the books and periodicals mentioned in your preliminary search of reference materials.

A book can be a unified work written on a single theme; a compilation of articles, essays, or chapters by a number of authors around a topic; or a collection of pieces by a particular author that have already been published individually. Books can be located online through an author or title search or through a database.

Today's libraries increasingly have e-book collections that can often be accessed from your library's home page. As with print resources, you can scan the table of contents and index in order to find references to your key words and phrases; you can usually search for these within the full text of the book.

Periodicals are published regularly—for instance, monthly, yearly, or daily. Examples include magazines, journals, yearbooks, and newspapers. Unless you are writing about an extremely current aspect of contemporary culture, you will probably be concentrating on journals, which publish articles written by academics, scientists, and researchers. The most respected journals are peer-reviewed: experts in that field have assessed the work prior to its publication.

There are thousands of scholarly journals publishing a wealth of current and authoritative research on just about any topic you can imagine. The best way to access them is through your institution's library, which purchases subscriptions to the journals they consider most important to faculty and students.

Locating a hard copy (paper copy) of a journal article generally begins with a library's electronic catalogue, either in the library or via the Internet. Let's say you want to find an article listed in the bibliography of a well-known textbook on your topic. You'll need the

Journals contain scholarly articles and reviews written by experts for other experts. The most reliable journals are peer-reviewed: articles have been evaluated by specialists before publication.

detailed information that makes up what is called a citation, which includes much more than the author's name and the name of the journal:

Author(s) Name(s): Zigler, E. F., & Gilman, E.

Publication Year: 1993

Article Title: Day care in America: What is needed?

Journal Name: Pediatrics

Volume and Issue Number: 91, 2 (an issue number is not always required in your citation, but you should record it in case it is needed)

Page Numbers: 175–178

The complete citation written in APA style (see chapter 8, p. 252) looks like this:

Zigler, E. F., & Gilman, E. (1993). Day care in America: What is needed? *Pediatrics, 91*(2), 175–178.

Most library catalogues let you select "journals only" in the search options and then search for the journal name (as opposed to the article title or author name). You'll be given a call number that will direct you to a location in the library where you'll find issues of the journal (either unbound or bound into a book). Look up the volume month or issue, and then follow the page numbers to the article.

Online Searches

A full-text journal article accessed through a database is almost always the same as in the print version of the journal. Databases also may house a blend of scholarly and non-scholarly information, including popular magazines, newspapers, and non-peer-reviewed journals, along with government-produced documents. In addition, databases supply links to the growing number of journals that don't publish a paper version at all and are available only online: electronic journals, or e-journals.

Although database interfaces can vary, most function on the principle of keywords (including authors' names). For instance, EBSCO*host* contains a number of databases, including *Academic Search Complete*, providing links to several thousand journals and millions of articles by using a combination of keywords, search limiters, and search expanders.

By entering your keywords in the **find** or **search** box, you can retrieve any article that contains your keywords in either the title or the body of all of the thousands of periodicals available through EBSCO*host*. (If you want to use a phrase such as "homeless teens," you must use quotation marks unless the field provides the option to search two or more words as a phrase.)

The number of hits can be overwhelming. For this reason, EBSCO*host* allows you to select limiters on your search, including a time period of publication and the option to search only peer-reviewed journals (see figure 7.2). There is also an advanced search

The **FIND** or **SEARCH** function in a database lets you search quickly through many articles by using keywords.

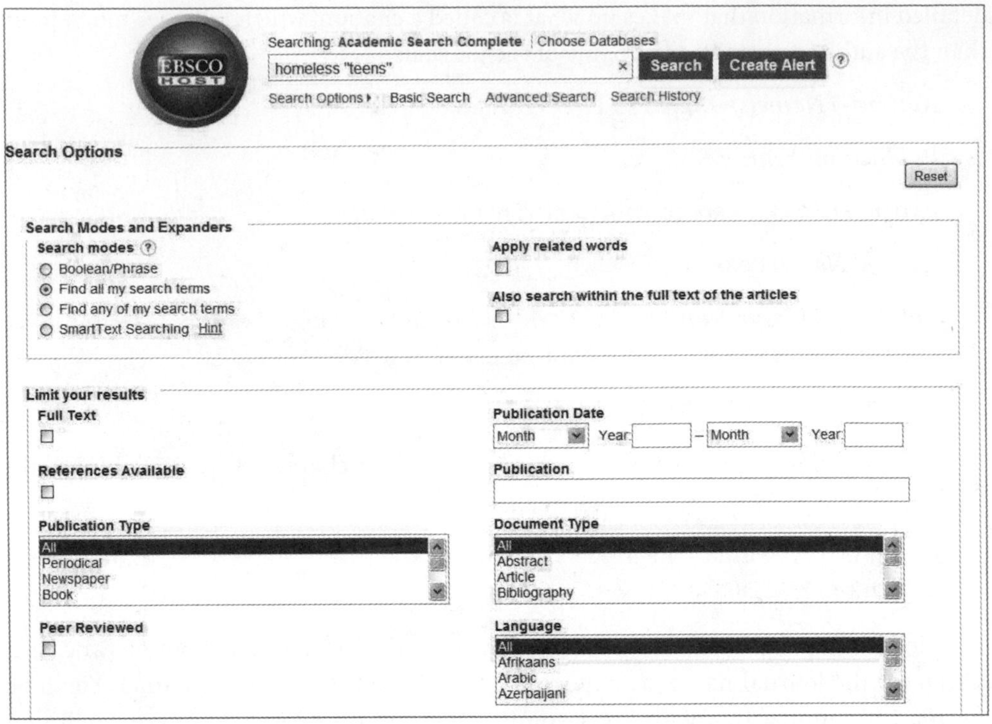

FIGURE 7.2 An EBSCO*host* page showing basic search options, including limiters like peer-reviewed journals, publication date ranges, and publication type.

window, which permits you to define various combinations of keywords and search limiters or expanders. Each academic discipline has specialized databases and indexes that concentrate on publications that are particularly relevant to that field; database descriptions will help you find the right ones; as well, databases have a link to online help.

Boolean operators are used to customize your search. Search limiters include the words AND and NOT. If you type AND between two or more search terms, your results will combine search terms; if you type NOT between search terms, your results will omit what follows NOT. If you use OR as a search expander, your results will include *at least one* of the terms.

Let's say you were undecided about the topic you wanted to explore but were seriously considering researching either caffeine or alcohol. A database search on "caffeine OR alcohol" using EBSCO*host* turns up approximately 200,000 entries. Thinking that you might want to compare caffeine and alcohol, you use the limiter AND, which produces 800 results. In order to exclude entries about tobacco from your search, you add a second limiter, "NOT tobacco" and hit Search. Using the two limiters ("caffeine AND alcohol NOT tobacco") produces 600 results. Using more descriptive keywords is often advisable. For example, "caffeine addiction AND alcohol addiction" produces fewer than 100 results.

Finally, many databases allow you to combine your keywords without using Boolean operators: you simply enter your terms and choose the correct search mode. For

> **BOOLEAN OPERATORS** are small words used to combine, include, or exclude specific search terms.

A Closer Look

Ten Popular Databases

The following comprehensive and subject-specific academic databases offer authoritative articles, reports, and abstracts, along with links to other relevant sources for students of many disciplines and interests.

Academic Search Complete, on the EBSCO*host* platform, is the leading comprehensive multi-disciplinary database for academic research. In addition to more than 7,000 full-text periodicals, including 6,300 peer-reviewed journals, it provides indexing and abstracting for over 12,000 publications including journals, monographs, reports, and conference proceedings.

Business Source Complete provides indexing and abstracting for more than 1,300 scholarly journals and business periodicals. It includes full-text journal articles for all business disciplines, including marketing, management, accounting, and economics. Additional non-journal full-text content includes financial data, books, monographs, major reference works, conference proceedings, case studies, investment research reports, industry reports, and market research reports.

ERIC (Education Resource Information Center) is the bibliographic database for scholarly education journals and other education-related information. In addition to journal articles, ERIC includes records for books, research syntheses, conference papers, technical reports, policy papers, grey literature, and other education-related materials. It is best known for its sizable series of short synopses on pertinent topics (ERIC Digest Records) written by educational experts.

Google Scholar is a website for scholarly research in all disciplines. It enables basic and advanced searching across the web for scholarly content like books, articles, abstracts, theses, and other sources from academic publishers, universities, scholarly websites, and more. Many sources link to abstracts and previews or to full text available freely online or through your library.

Historical Abstracts and **America: History and Life:** Historical Abstracts is the most comprehensive, scholarly database for researching the history of the world, excluding North America, from 1450 to the present. America: History and Life is a key database for the history of North

America. It indexes literature back to 1964 on the history and culture of the United States and Canada from prehistory to the present.

JSTOR is a full-text scholarly journal archive of more than 1,000 leading academic journal titles in the humanities, social sciences, and sciences. It also includes selected books and other materials for scholarly research. Journals are full-text from the first volume and issue, but recent issues (the last three to five years) are generally not available.

MLA International Bibliography is the leading bibliographic database for research on modern languages, literatures, folklore, and linguistics. In addition to print and electronic journal articles in these disciplines, MLA provides citations for books and e-books, book articles, dissertation abstracts, and websites, and links to full-text items available online or through your library.

PsycINFO contains more than one million citations and summaries of journal articles, book chapters, books, dissertations, and technical reports in the field of psychology. It also includes information about the psychological aspects of related disciplines such as medicine, psychiatry, nursing, sociology, education, pharmacology, physiology, linguistics, anthropology, business, and law.

Sociological Abstracts provides abstracts and indexing for over 1,800 journals in sociology and related disciplines in the social and behavioural sciences. It also provides abstracts for books, book chapters, dissertations, and conference papers with coverage back to 1952. Cited reference linking is provided for articles added to the database since 2002, showing how many times an article has been cited in other papers.

Web of Science consists of six comprehensive citation databases in the sciences, social sciences, arts, and humanities, including Science Citation Index Expanded, Social Sciences Citation Index, and Arts & Humanities Citation Index. It provides coverage back to 1900 of thousands of scholarly journals, books, book series, reports, and conference proceedings. Web of Science is also the leading database for cited reference searching.

example, in Basic Search in EBSCO*host*'s Academic Search Complete, the search mode *Find all of my search terms* is equivalent to AND, and the search mode *Find any of my search terms* is equivalent to OR. Many other databases and catalogues now work similarly, including Google Scholar.

Truncation and Wildcards

Boolean searches often allow truncation and wildcard symbols. Truncation symbols enable you to include all variants of a search term. For example, using the asterisk as the truncation symbol in "teen*" will ensure that your search results include the terms *teen*, *teens*, and *teenager*. Wildcards are used within a word, for instance in "colo#r" to include alternative spellings (*colour* and *color*), or in "wom?n" to include variable characters (*woman* and *women*). Most databases and catalogues use the asterisk (*) or question mark (?) as the truncation or wildcard symbol. Some databases may also use the pound sign (#) or another symbol. If you are not sure what symbol to use, check the help menu, usually located in the upper right-hand corner of your screen. The help menu will also provide information on other advanced search strategies that can be used in that particular catalogue or database.

Saving Search Results

Most databases and online catalogues let you save your search results. You can mark a result to be saved by checking a box or adding it to a folder, and then choose from several options—usually print, email, save, or export. Export often includes an option to download or export to the bibliographic management software of your choice, such as RefWorks or EndNote. Some databases also allow you to create a personal account so that you can customize your preferences, save and retrieve your search history, organize your research in folders, or set up email alerts and RSS feeds.

EXERCISE 7.4

Using the same topic you began to explore in exercise 7.2, come up with some keywords based on the summary and/or question you came up with in exercise 7.3. Using the information discussed above, locate at least three potential sources for a research essay on your topic.

The Value of Library Research

Libraries continue to be valuable resources for researchers at all levels of expertise; they have materials not available online and are staffed by professionals who understand how information is organized and interrelated. Most libraries have reference librarians who can save you time and direct you to sources you might never come across on your own. Furthermore, libraries hold many important records, including

- indexes for many periodicals, images, films, microfiche files, and videos
- theses and dissertations (book-length documents written by university students as part of their advanced degree requirements)

A Closer Look

Using "One-Stop" Search Tools

In most university libraries, you can search from the library's home page using a single search box. "Unified discovery systems," such as Summon and EBSCO Discovery Service, are the library's equivalent to search engines like Google, quickly returning copious results on just about any topic. However, more content does not always mean better content; for best results, discovery tools should be used alongside subject-specific databases. The following highlights some of the pros and cons of using Summon, a common discovery tool, versus research databases.

Strengths

- Summon is easy to use, as almost any term you enter will yield results. It is important, however, to take advantage of the refine/limit features—for example, to separate peer-reviewed material from non-academic material—to reduce hits to a manageable number.
- Because it searches almost all of the databases and library online collections, Summon is highly interdisciplinary. Students from any program can use Summon as their first step in the research process, which can save you a lot of time and guesswork in choosing a database, especially if your research is cross-disciplinary.
- Summon has a simple citation formatting option: once you've sent items to your "saved" folder, you can view them in common citation styles including MLA and APA.
- If you've been asked to locate an article from a citation, you can usually locate it quickly by entering the title information into Summon.

FIGURE 7.3 Searching Summon by keyword on the University of British Columbia website.

- Summon provides an easy way to find full-text journal articles—it's usually quicker than working through traditional databases.

Weaknesses

- There is missing content in Summon—not all databases are included and print articles will not appear. For advanced and comprehensive projects, it is important to work with subject databases in order to ensure you do not miss valuable material.
- Summon can overwhelm you with results. Searches often provide thousands of responses, and even working with refine features can provide a vast amount of material, not all of it relevant. This is another reason why working with a database can be more valuable: you will be working with a smaller, more focused set of results that is going to be more closely related to your discipline.

- historical documents, including maps and public records
- collections of textual/graphic and archival material on special subjects, sometimes including original documents
- clipping files from newspapers and magazines
- bound volumes of journals
- collections of audio and film/video recordings
- current issues of journals that have an embargo on electronic versions (6–12 months after publication is common)

Alternative Information Sources

Although we have emphasized written research, many disciplines accept support for your thesis from visual or audio media, such as television, film, video, works of art, performances, surveys/questionnaires, interviews, and observations. Using these alternative sources of information requires the same attention to detail in note-taking as when using traditional materials, and most citation styles provide instructions for citing and referencing non-textual research information.

A Closer Look

Field Research: Interviewing

The purpose in field research, such as interviews, questionnaires, and personal observation, is to generate useful primary sources to augment secondary source material. The results of this research, whether field or interview notes or questionnaire results, can be interpreted and integrated along with your other findings.

If you have direct access to a noted authority in your area, interviewing can be an effective form of field research. For example, if your topic is "organic foods" and you want to objectively evaluate both sides of the issue, you might want to search out representatives of both the organic and the nonorganic food industries. Possible interview subjects could include spokespeople for organizations, growers of both kinds of food, or researchers.

The principal advantage of an interview, whether face-to-face, by telephone, or by email, is that you can ask questions directly relevant to your topic and subtopics. The university community—including, perhaps, one of your professors—is an ideal place to look for experts.

Tips for Effective Interviewing

- Determine the *purpose* of the interview; for example, is it to obtain information? What kind and level of information? How does the information differ from what is available through books or articles (more detailed, precise, current)? Is the interviewee a researcher in the field or an expert?

- Do you want the interviewee's informed opinion about something (for example, if the findings related to your topic are controversial—e.g., the benefits of chocolate, coffee, or red wine; links between TV viewing and violence)? An *informed* opinion implies that the person knows enough about the topic to understand the strengths and weaknesses of both sides.

- Choose your expert carefully; in addition to professors, there may be other experts both inside and outside your community. You may be able to get a list of experts through your library or your faculty/department office.

- Choose the interview medium (of course, the interviewee may prefer one medium over another):
  - *Telephone* interviews are quickest—for example, if you want to ask only one or two specific questions or to confirm information.
  - *Personal/face-to-face* interviews are flexible—for example, if you want your subject to expand on an answer. Sometimes letting an interviewee go slightly off topic can produce useful information or a colourful quotation, but make sure you *always* use quotations fairly and do not quote out of context.
  - *Email* interviews are convenient for the interviewee, who can take time to consider the question and respond at his or her convenience.

- Carefully explain to the subject the purpose of the interview; assure him/her of your interest in the topic and that the interviewee's comments are *integral to* your research.

- *Always ask* before recording an interview.

- The form of the interview will also help shape the interview itself, including the kinds of questions you ask:
  - In face-to-face interviews, remember that you should take notes even if you use a recording device; questions should be clear and direct.
  - Email interviews tend to be more formal than personal or phone interviews. Phrase the questions to encourage specific and detailed answers—avoid general, open-ended questions such as "What do you think about . . . ?", or those that could result in simple *yes* or *no* answers.

- In face-to-face interviews, consider giving the subject a list of questions in advance to enable him or her to think about them; however, it's usually acceptable to add follow-up questions during the actual interview.

- Structure your interview logically; for example, begin with more general questions before becoming more specific. Having a logical *order* of questions can also help create coherence in the responses.

- Don't ask unnecessary questions; make sure *each has a specific purpose* that is connected to your research question or a subtopic.

- Before leaving a personal interview or when you present your list of questions in an email interview, ask politely if you can contact the subject again, if necessary, for brief clarifications; don't forget to express your gratitude for the subject's time and expertise.

USING SOURCES IN THE COMPOSING STAGE

Summary and paraphrase are integral parts of the composing stage of a research essay. Scrupulous representation of the writer's ideas is the hallmark of good summarizing and paraphrasing.

Summary

Summary is the general term for the rephrasing of somebody else's ideas using your own words. Summarizing a book, article, or Internet source puts the main points before you when you come to write your essay. Summarizing also avoids the practice of *too much*

While a *summary* includes only the main point(s) of the source, using the same order as the original and putting it in your own words, a *paraphrase* includes all the original, changing the order of points, if possible, and putting them in your own words.

direct quotation. The précis (see chapter 4, p. 101), the abstract, and the annotated bibliography fulfill different summarizing functions.

Paraphrase

A **paraphrase** represents someone else's idea but uses your own phrasing and structure. It is usually about the same length as the original. You would normally paraphrase an important part of a text, perhaps a significant sentence or paragraph. Because a paraphrase doesn't omit anything of substance from the source, it is unlike a summary, which condenses the original, retaining only its essence.

The differences between a summary and a paraphrase are illustrated by the passage below, taken from the reading "The Teenage Brain: Self Control" by Casey and Caudle on page 229 of this chapter. In the summary, the main point accounts for the behaviour of adolescents: the evolving connections within the part of the brain responsible for self-control. In the paraphrase, the original passage is rephrased; as well, the order of the ideas and the sentence structure are changed.

> *Original*: Saying that one studies the adolescent brain is often met with comic skepticism and feigned relief that adolescents do indeed have a brain. There is no hole in the head or absence of parts to suggest a lesion-related impairment during this period. Moreover, the prefrontal cortex, a region important in self-control and rational decision making, is clearly present even from birth. What is changing during this period of development is the strength of connections within prefrontal circuitry as individuals learn to adapt to changing environmental demands (Liston et al., 2006). This development reflects a combination of evolutionarily shaped biological constraints and experiential history, which interact to shape the brain and behavior. (111 words)

> *Summary*: The adolescent brain has all its parts, including the region responsible for self-control. However, the connections in the prefrontal cortex are evolving in accordance with one's biology and experience. (33 words)

> *Paraphrase*: Biological dictates and past experiences combine to determine the brain and behavior of the adolescent. The connections that make up the wiring of the prefrontal cortex, the part of the brain responsible for logical decisions and the ability to regulate behavior, are changing as the adolescent adapts to new demands in the environment. When one states that one is studying the brain of 13–19-year-olds, the reaction is often one of skeptical amusement, but adolescents do indeed have brains without lesions or other biological impairments. It is the strength of the connections in the wiring of the prefrontal context that is developing and is responsible for the phenomenon of the adolescent brain. (111 words)

The Annotated Bibliography

An **annotated bibliography** is an expanded bibliography (*annotate* means "to note") that often accompanies large research projects, such as books. It is a critical survey,

→ For advice on when to use summary, paraphrase, or direct quotation, see page 217.

A **PARAPHRASE** uses your own words and structure to represent someone else's ideas. When you paraphrase, you include all ideas of the original.

An **ANNOTATED BIBLIOGRAPHY** is a bibliography that has been expanded to include brief summaries and appraisals of the sources in your essay.

A Closer Look

Other Types of Summaries—The Abstract

While a research proposal states your purpose for exploring a topic and, perhaps, what you hope to find out about it, an **abstract** is an overview of your essay; you write it *after* you have finished your essay, or, at least, after you have arrived at your conclusions. However, the abstract precedes the essay: it is placed after the title and author notation and before the Introduction, enabling readers to decide whether they wish to read the essay.

An abstract should be able to stand on its own, clearly but briefly representing the essay. Abstracts can include most or all of the following:

- background or overview of the field of study
- the specific problem and your purpose in investigating it
- methods or procedures
- results
- discussion

> An **ABSTRACT** is an overview of the text that follows.

It may end with a brief consideration of the significance or implications of the findings. For required length for an essay abstract, check with your instructor. For an example of an abstract, see page 229.

demonstrating the variety of approaches to the subject that other writers/researchers have taken. While an abstract concisely summarizes your own work for potential readers, an annotated bibliography concisely summarizes similar works in the field of study, telling your readers where each writer's piece of the puzzle fits into the whole.

Generally, each entry in an annotated bibliography provides a very brief summary of content, focusing primarily on thesis statement and major points or findings. If the entry refers to a book-length study, the main points may take the form of major section or chapter headings. Frequently, an annotated bibliography contains an appraisal of each study's usefulness, contribution to the field of study, or limitations. The 103-word example below is an entry from the annotated bibliography that accompanied the essay by Iain Lawrence (see p. 225), in which he concisely summarizes the source's main points and ends with a brief evaluation.

> Emery, McKay, Campbell, and Peters studied the attitudes of young hockey players to aggression and empathy in relation to their participation in either a non-bodychecking league or bodychecking league. Emery et al. discussed the differences between instrumental aggression and hostile aggression. They found that young bodychecking players showed little difference in their level of empathy when compared to their non-bodychecking counterparts; however, they did demonstrate a greater degree of aggression. The major limitation of the study was that the players themselves selected the league in which they would participate, meaning that no conclusion as to cause and effect can be drawn.

Source Citation and Plagiarism

Plagiarism is the unacknowledged borrowing of someone else's words or ideas. Intentional plagiarizing, such as using someone else's essay, buying an essay, or copying

> **PLAGIARISM** is the unacknowledged borrowing of someone else's words or ideas.

Examples of intentional plagiarism include

- copying another's work
- buying an essay
- using another student's essay or reusing your own essay from another class
- not following the guidelines set down by your institution about plagiarized material; such information is usually included in the university calendar or similar document

verbatim from a website, is considered by many the most serious academic crime, for which there are equally serious repercussions. The consequences for plagiarizing can range from a zero for that particular paper to failing the course or being expelled from your school.

It is often easy for an instructor to detect plagiarism through a shift in tone or word use. Many colleges and universities now subscribe to services such as Turnitin, which maintains an electronic copy of your essay and compares it to thousands of documents. If any matches are found, the results will be posted electronically for you and your instructor to see, along with the sources that match.

Unintentional plagiarizing often leads to the same repercussions, even if the reason for the plagiarism was careless note-taking, improper documentation, or a lack of knowledge about plagiarism itself. The questions and answers in table 7.2 are designed to prevent unintentional plagiarism. Examples of plagiarized content follow.

Audience is often a factor in whether a citation is given or not. General knowledge can vary according to audience. If you are writing for an audience with a scientific or medical background, for example, you may not need to cite the fact that the active ingredient in marijuana is tetrahydro-cannabinol; it is considered general knowledge within that audience. If you are writing a paper for historians or political scientists, you would not need to cite the fact that British Columbia became a Canadian province in 1871 because your readers could easily obtain this information. If the general knowledge or the easily obtainable standards do not apply, make the citation.

In the following examples, italicized words indicate sections of the original that are plagiarized.

Unintentional plagiarism could arise if you

- fail to cite a source in your essay, whether you quote directly, summarize, paraphrase, or simply use an idea
- fail to put quotation marks around the words you have quoted directly
- copy the structure of the source even if you change the words

Example 1

Original:

Anybody who will look at the thing candidly will see that the evolutionary explanation of morals is meaningless, and presupposes the existence of the very thing it ought to prove. It starts from a misconception of the biological doctrine. Biology has nothing to say as to what ought to survive and what ought not to survive; it merely speaks of what does survive.

—Stephen Leacock, "The Devil and the Deep Sea: A Discussion of Modern Morality"

Language of the source unchanged:

A person willing to see *the thing candidly* would realize that morals cannot be accounted for through evolution.

Sentence structure unchanged:

Biology does not distinguish between *what should and should not survive; it simply tells us "what does survive."*

TABLE 7.2 Seven Common Questions about Plagiarism

QUESTION	ANSWER
1. Do you need to cite information that you do not quote directly in your essay?	Yes. Specific content requires a citation, whether you use direct quotation, paraphrase, or summary to integrate it into your essay. Even general information may need a citation.
2. If you already knew a fact and you encounter it in a secondary source, does it need to be cited?	Probably. The issue isn't whether you know something but whether your reader would know it. If you are writing for an audience familiar with your topic, you may not need to cite "common knowledge," that is, knowledge that most readers would be expected to know. If you're uncertain about the common knowledge factor, make the citation.
3. What about specific information, such as a date, that is easy to look up, though it may not be common knowledge?	A fact that is easily obtained from a number of different sources (even if a typical reader wouldn't know it) may not need to be cited. Other factors could be involved (for example, would a typical reader know where to look?). Your instructor may be able to tell you how many sources constitute "easily obtainable" information; three common, accessible, and reliable sources is often the minimum.
4. If you use a source that you have already used earlier in the same paragraph, do you need to cite it a second time?	Yes, if another source, or your own point, has intervened. If all the content of the paragraph is from one source, you may not have to cite it until the end of the paragraph. However, always make it clear to the reader what is taken from a source.
5. Is it necessary to cite "popular" quotations, for example, the kind that appear in dictionaries of quotations? What about dictionary definitions?	Yes, these kinds of quotations should be cited unless the quotation has entered everyday use. For example, the first quotation below would not need a citation, though the second would—even though it's unlikely a reader would know either source:
	"When the going gets tough, the tough get going"; "Making your mark on the world is hard. If it were easy, everybody would do it." (Joan W. Donaldson is the author of the first quotation; Barack Obama is the author of the second.) Dictionary definitions should be cited.
6. Does a list of your sources on the final page of your essay mean that you don't have to cite the sources within the essay itself?	No. All major documentation methods require both in-text and final-page citations. (In some formats, the in-text citations consist only of numbers.)
7. What can you do to guarantee that the question of plagiarism never arises in your essay?	As suggested above, honesty alone is not enough, but it is a good start. Knowledge about what needs to be, and what may not need to be, cited is also essential and can be learned. Finally, being conscious of "grey areas" and checking with your instructor or another expert, such as a librarian, will make it unlikely that this serious issue will arise.

A good strategy for avoiding plagiarism (and consciously integrating the information) is to carefully study the passage you want to use; then, close the text and write the passage from memory completely in your own words. Finally, look at the passage again, ensuring that it is different in its structure as well as in its language—and that you have accurately restated its meaning.

Acceptable paraphrase:

An honest appraisal can tell a person that morals cannot be accounted for through evolution . . . . Biology tells us only "what does survive," not what should and should not survive (Leacock 57).

Example 2

Original:

This article highlights how self-control varies as a function of age, context, and the individual and delineates its neurobiological basis.
—Casey and Caudle reading, page 229

Language of the source unchanged:

This article outlines the neurobiological foundation of self-control and the way it changes *as a function of age, context, and the individual.*

Sentence structure unchanged:

The article demonstrates the variations of self-control due to situation, age, and the particular adolescent involved and outlines its neurobiological foundation.

Acceptable paraphrase:

The article outlines the neurological foundation of self-control and its variations according to factors like situation, age, and the particular adolescent involved.

EXERCISE 7.5

↻ Check answers to select questions

Decide whether the following paraphrases are acceptable or if they unintentionally plagiarize their originals. Rewrite them, if necessary.

1. *Original*: "The power of cultural standards of beauty emphasize slenderness as a key feature of feminine identity" (Haworth-Hoeppner 212).
   Paraphrase: The strength of our culture's standards of beauty stress thinness as a major aspect of feminine identity (Haworth-Hoeppner 212).
2. *Original*: "Restorative justice involves the victim, the offender, and the community in a search for solutions which promote repair, reconciliation, and reassurance" (Zher 5).
   Paraphrase: Restorative justice brings victim, offender, and community together in an attempt to find ways to fix damage, create harmony, and build confidence (Zher 5).
3. *Original*: "Changes in the atmospheric concentration of a number of air pollutants over the last century are hallmarks of the magnitude and extent of human impact on the environment" (Taylor et al., 1994, p. 689).
   Paraphrase: Variations in the atmospheric concentration of several contaminants during the last century highlight the extent of the impact of people on the environment (Taylor et al., 1994, p. 689).

4. *Original*: "The support of an outside role model, like a coach, helps improve an athlete's self-esteem as well as lower the chance of depression" (Stewart 17).
   Paraphrase: An athlete's self-esteem is improved and chance of depression is lowered if he or she can receive support from an adult role model like a coach (Stewart 17).
5. *Original*: "No matter how intense curiosity about public figures can be, there is an important and deep principle at stake, which is the right to some simple human measure of privacy" (Ostrow).
   Paraphrase: The basic right of public figures to a degree of privacy should be considered more important than the public's obsessive need to know every detail of their lives (Ostrow).

Methods of Integrating Sources

What method should you use to integrate information from a source with your own ideas?

- You can *summarize* the source.
- You can *paraphrase* the source.
- You can use a direct quotation.
- You can use *mixed format*—paraphrase and direct quotation combined.

Using a variety of methods is a good rule of thumb. However, general guidelines can help you make choices. With any method, remember that the source must be identified either in a signal phrase (see below) or in a parenthetical reference if you do not use a signal phrase (MLA and APA styles).

Summary

Summarize if you want to use a source's main ideas to provide background information, to set up a point of your own (to show similarity or difference, for example), or to explain findings relevant to your claim. You can summarize passages of just about any length—from a few words to several pages.

Paraphrase

A paraphrase restates the source's meaning using only your own words. Paraphrase when you want to cite a relatively small amount of material that is directly connected to your point. When you paraphrase, you include *all* of the original thought.

Direct Quotation

Use direct quotation when exact wording is important. You might want to preserve significant words in the cited passage or the unique way that the source expresses the idea. Avoid overly long direct quotations. If you choose to quote four or more consecutive lines, use the block format:

- Set the quotation in a separate paragraph indented one-half inch (1.25 cm) from the left margin.
- Double-space the text, but do not use quotation marks.
- Introduce the block quotation by a complete sentence followed by a colon.

See also Mixed Format below.

Use single quotation marks to indicate a word or passage in your source that is in quotation marks in the original. In this example, the single quotation marks around *elsewhere* inform the reader that quotation marks were used in the original:

> "In a number of narratives, the (usually female) character finds herself at a significant crossroad between home and a problematic 'elsewhere'" (Rubenstein 9).

Avoid unneeded direct quotations; use summary or paraphrase instead. Direct quotations are most effective when used *selectively* to preserve the original wording. You more clearly demonstrate your ability to understand and synthesize sources when you summarize and paraphrase.

Avoid a direct quotation if

- the idea in the passage is obvious, well-known, or could be easily accessed
- the material is essentially factual and does not involve a particular *interpretation* of the facts
- the passage can be readily paraphrased

The following are examples of direct quotations that are unnecessary or ineffective. The preferable alternatives are given after them.

> "About one-third of infants are breast-fed for three months or longer."

> *Paraphrase:* Approximately 33 per cent of infants receive breast-feeding for at least three months.

> "The greenhouse effect is the result of gases like carbon dioxide, nitrous oxide, and methane being trapped in Earth's atmosphere."

> *Paraphrase:* The accumulation of such gases as carbon dioxide, nitrous oxide, and methane in the atmosphere has led to the greenhouse effect.

The following are examples of direct quotations that are necessary or effective.

> Albert Einstein once said, "It always seems to me that man was not born to be a carnivore."

Quoting someone as well known as Einstein, even though he is speaking from personal opinion, would make direct quotation a good choice—though not an essential one.

In the following example, precise wording matters:

> "Neither capital punishment nor life imprisonment without possibility of release shall be imposed for offenses committed by persons below 18 years of age" (UN Convention on the Rights of the Child).

Mixed Format

Using a mixture of paraphrase and direct quotation demonstrates your familiarity with a source and your ability to integrate words and ideas smoothly into your essay; it also is efficient as you include only the most essential words and phrases from the source, as in this example:

> Although in his tribute to Pierre Elliott Trudeau in *The Globe and Mail* Mark Kingwell recalls the former prime minister as "the fusion of reason and passion, the virility and playfulness, the daunting arrogance and wit, the politician as rock star," behind this he finds "the good citizen."

Compare this paragraph with the original text below. The text crossed out shows what was not used.

> ~~It's hard to say anything about Trudeau now that has not been said a thousand times before:~~ the fusion of reason and passion, the virility and playfulness, the daunting arrogance and wit, the politician as rock star. ~~All true; all banal. But~~ underneath all that I find ~~a more resonant identity, one which is at once simpler and more profound:~~ the good citizen.

When you integrate a direct quotation using mixed format, you can remove the quotation marks and just look at the portion of the quoted text as words, phrases, or sentences that, like all sentences, must be written grammatically. Don't forget to put the quotation marks back in when you've integrated it grammatically, and also ensure that any changes you made to the original are indicated through brackets or ellipses (see Signal Phrases, Ellipses, and Brackets below).

When you use direct quotations, ensure that the quoted material is integrated grammatically, clearly, and gracefully. The examples below show poorly integrated quotations followed by corrected versions:

Ungrammatical: Charles E. Taylor discusses the efforts of scientists "are defining a new area of research termed artificial life" (172).

Grammatical: Charles E. Taylor discusses the efforts of scientists to "[define] a new area of research termed artificial life" (172).

Unclear: Art critic John Ruskin believes that the highest art arises from "sensations occurring to *them* only at particular times" (112).

Clear:

Art critic John Ruskin believes that highest art arises from "sensations occurring to *[artists]* only at particular times" (112).

or:

Art critic John Ruskin believes that *artists* produce the highest art from "sensations occurring to *them* only at particular times" (112).

Signal Phrases, Ellipses, and Brackets

Signal Phrases

The examples above under Mixed Format use signal phrases to introduce direct quotations. A signal phrase contains the source's name (e.g., Taylor or Ruskin) and a signal verb, such as *believes*, *discusses*, or *recalls*. A signal phrase shows the reader where the reference begins. It can also help guide the reader in places where you use two or more sources to explain a point. The following paragraph contains two citation formats: the first reference contains a signal phrase; the second one does not:

> *Richard Goldbloom states* that a surveillance video taken in Toronto showed that in more than 20 per cent of incidents where bullying was involved, peers actively became part of the bullying (2). Furthermore, recent statistics show not only the pervasiveness of the problem but that outsiders perceive bullying as a problem in schools today (Clifford 4).

The reader of this paragraph could easily separate the two sources, so a second signal phrase is unnecessary, though not incorrect.

Omitting Material: Ellipses

In direct quotations, you can use points of **ellipsis** (. . .) to indicate the omission of one or more words from a direct quotation. Three spaced dots (periods) show an ellipsis (omission). Four dots with a space at the beginning of the sequence (e.g., "childhood requires . . . .") indicate that the omitted text includes all the remaining words up to and including the period at the end of the sentence. The fourth dot is also used if you omit one or more complete sentences.

If a parenthetical citation follows an ellipsis, the fourth dot (i.e., the period) follows the citation:

> "Going green might cost a lot, but refusing to act now will cost us the Earth . . ." (*BBC News*, par. 5).

You can use points of ellipsis before or after the original punctuation to show exactly where you have dropped material, as in the following example, where the comma following *identity* is left in:

> "[U]nderneath all that I find a more resonant identity, . . . the good citizen."

When you omit significant amounts of material, such as entire paragraphs, or lines of verse, the points of ellipsis should occupy a line to themselves:

> . . . but were there one whose fires
>
> True genius kindles, and fair fame inspires;
>
> . . .
>
> View him with scornful, yet with jealous eyes,
>
> And hate for arts that caus'd himself to rise;
>
> Damn with faint praise, assent with civil leer,
>
> And without sneering, teach the rest to sneer; . . .
>
> —Alexander Pope, "Epistle to Dr. Arbuthnot," ll. 193–4, 199–202.

A signal phrase introduces a reference by naming the source (followed by the year in APA style) and including a verb.

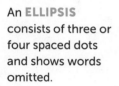

An **ELLIPSIS** consists of three or four spaced dots and shows words omitted.

An ellipsis before a direct quotation: Do not use an ellipsis at the beginning of a direct quotation, except, as in the example above, when part of a line of poetry has been omitted or if you break off a direct quotation and resume the same quotation later in the sentence or paragraph.

An ellipsis after a direct quotation: In general, do not use an ellipsis at the end of a direct quotation. However, if what follows the direct quotation in the original completes the thought, an ellipsis can be used in order to avoid a potentially incomplete statement. In the following sentence, an ellipsis would be optional:

> "[If] what follows the end of the direct quotation in the original completes the thought, an ellipsis can be used . . . ."

In the example, what follows *used* is treated as completing the thought.

Brackets

Square brackets (or just *brackets*) are used to show a change or addition to a direct quotation, such as

- a stylistic change (e.g., upper case to lower case)
- a grammatical change (e.g., the tense of a verb)
- a change for clarity's sake (e.g., adding a word to make the context clearer)

The following illustrates these kinds of changes (although you would probably paraphrase a passage that contained as many brackets and ellipses as this one):

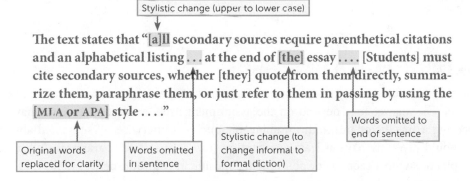

Stylistic change (upper to lower case)

The text states that "[a]ll secondary sources require parenthetical citations and an alphabetical listing . . . at the end of [the] essay . . . . [Students] must cite secondary sources, whether [they] quote from them directly, summarize them, paraphrase them, or just refer to them in passing by using the [MLA or APA] style . . . ."

Original words replaced for clarity

Words omitted in sentence

Stylistic change (to change informal to formal diction)

Words omitted to end of sentence

The original text:

All secondary sources require parenthetical citations and an alphabetical listing in the "Works Cited" section at the end of your essay (MLA) or the "References" section (APA). You must cite secondary sources, whether you quote from them directly, summarize them, paraphrase them, or just refer to them in passing by using the style preferred by your discipline.

Parentheses would be incorrect in the passages above as they are a form of punctuation (they enclose text that explains or expands on something, as these parentheses do); brackets indicate a change or addition to a direct quotation.

You may also use brackets to explain an unfamiliar term:

Emergency room nurse Judith McAllen said, "We triage [prioritize by severity of injury] patients if it's a non-emergency, and don't treat them on the basis of their arrival time."

(Brackets can also be used to indicate parentheses within parentheses [as in this sentence].)

Inserting *sic* (which means "thus") between brackets—[*sic*]—tells the reader that what immediately precedes [*sic*] occurs in the original exactly the way it appears in your quotation. One use of [*sic*] is to call attention to an error in the original:

As people often say, "vive le différence" [*sic*].

[*Sic*] here calls attention to the article error: *le* should be *la*. In APA style, italicize *sic* within brackets: [*sic*].

Punctuate a direct quotation exactly as it is punctuated in the original, but do not include any punctuation in the original that comes *after* the quoted material. Note the omission of the original comma after *recklessness*:

Original: "Any accounting of male–female differences must include the male's superior recklessness, a drive, not, I think, towards death . . . ."

Directly quoted: In his essay "The Disposable Rocket," John Updike states that "[a]ny accounting of male-female differences must include the male's superior recklessness."

OUTLINE FOR A RESEARCH ESSAY

How do you know when you have sufficient support for your points and can begin an outline? The answer may depend on the assignment itself, as your instructor may be expecting a specific or minimum number of sources. Otherwise, as suggested above, you should probably have at least one citation (direct quotation, paraphrase, idea, or example) to support each major point. Being specific in your outline will make it easier to write your first draft, where your main concern is integrating the sources with your own words.

Iain Lawrence's formal sentence outline is reproduced below (see his final draft, which follows on p. 225; see also his research proposal, p. 200). Because of the detail in his outline, Lawrence was able to closely follow the outline when he wrote his essay. In addition, he spent time organizing his points so that his structure could be clear. However, he made some changes when composing; for example, he combined the material in points I and II in his introductory paragraph, dropping a sub-point (II, B) in the interests of efficiency.

Other writers prefer less detailed outlines. Choose the kind of outline—topic, sentence, or graphic—you feel most comfortable with.

→ See chapter 2, Organization (p. 38), for more about the different kinds of outlines.

SAMPLE STUDENT OUTLINE

Outline for "The Impact of Sport on Childhood Aggression"

by Iain Lawrence

I. **Hypothesis: Participation in aggressive sport can mitigate inappropriate child-hood aggression.**

   A. Proponents of martial arts claim that participation encourages passive children to become more confident, while at the same time promotes respect for others and functions as a channel through which to direct inappropriate aggression for more hostile or violent children.

   B. Reasons why parents might have their children take part in organized sports are "enhanced self-esteem," "improved social interactions," and "development of leadership skills" (Emery, 2009, p. 207).

   C. Are such claims warranted, and do other "aggressive" sports, such as lacrosse, hockey, or perhaps even soccer, provide the same opportunity for a healthy out-let for aggression or do they simply encourage further inappropriate behaviour?

II. **There are two reasons why parents of aggressive children might have them participate in organized sport:**

   A. Sports may be thought to provide an outlet for unhealthy aggression.

   B. Aggressive behaviour may be modelled in such a way that the child learns environments in which aggression is appropriate.

III. **Key terms and their definitions**

   A. Three categories of aggressive behaviour within sport have been identified (Maxwell, 2004):

   1. Instrumental aggression: aggression used strategically within the rules of the game with no intent to cause physical harm to the opponent.

   2. Hostile aggression: aggressive acts engaged in the aim of injuring the opposing player.

   3. Reactive aggression: aggressive act resulting from an instinctive response to the act of another player. Reasoning plays little role in whether or not the act takes place.

   4. Maxwell argues that these terms are less useful than they appear because an athlete may have more than one motivation. Example: An athlete may be strategically aggressive in order to gain tactical advantage within the rules of play, but may take pleasure in causing injury at the same time.

   B. Definitions of aggressive sport can be arrived at through a summary of the literature:

   1. Aggressive sport has a high level of physical contact between participants.

   i. Examples would include tackling in rugby or football, bodychecking in ice-hockey, and punching and kicking in the martial arts.

   ii. Aggressive sport makes use of instrumental aggression, although differentiating between instrumental and hostile types may become blurred.

   2. Non-aggressive sport has little or no physical contact.

   i. Examples would include competitive cycling, running, swimming.

Continued

Lawrence's beginning point is a hypothesis, something that he believes might be true. However, his thesis, his final sub-point, is phrased as a question. Notice that the wording is identical to the wording of his thesis in his essay, page 225.

Lawrence does not provide the names of all authors of this study in his outline; the first author's name will enable him to locate the reference when he writes his draft.

Lawrence does not use this point in his introduction, probably in the interests of space and efficiency; however, he does consider this point in later paragraphs.

Notice the important role that definition plays in Lawrence's essay. Discussing the complexities of aggression and sport requires a grounding in clear terminology.

ii. Such sports may be high-energy and intensely competitive in spite of the absence of physical contact in order to gain an advantage.

IV. What aspects of emotional well-being are affected by aggressive behaviour?

A. No difference was found in levels of empathy between bodychecking and non-bodychecking leagues (Emery, 2009).

B. Negative outcome of contact sport (i.e., hockey) may be increased aggression (Emery, 2009).

1. A study of midget hockey league players in Calgary indicated that those in the bodychecking league had higher levels of aggression than those in a non-bodychecking league.

> In his essay, the writer focuses only on the result of the study and does not give details about the level of hockey or where the study of the children was carried out.

V. There appear to be beneficial emotional aspects of aggressive sports for aggressive children.

A. Benefits do not necessarily come from aggressive sports, but from sport in general.

1. Sports helps socialize children (Nucci).
   i. They learn how to compete, cooperate, and role-play.
   ii. They learn discipline regarding rules, regulations, and goals.

2. Both shy and aggressive children showed greater self-esteem when participating in sports (Findlay).

3. Aggressive children demonstrate greater anxiety, loneliness, and negative affect than "normal" children.
   i. They are less likely to have high physical ability and self-esteem.
   ii. There are links between these characteristics and "acting out" behaviour.
   iii. Sports are positively correlated with "higher positive affect and well-being and greater social skills" (p. 160). Decreased social anxiety has also been noted.

> In developing his outline, Lawrence has carefully considered the order of his points. After defining key terms, he briefly summarizes the literature on the pros and cons of sports and childhood aggression. He then turns to social learning theory to help explain some of the discrepancies in the findings. Finally, he notes some of the limitations in the research he has discussed. In his essay, he follows this same logical order, providing appropriate transitions to guide the reader from one point to the next.

VI. Social learning theory can be used to account for the mixed results of research.

A. The social learning theory of Albert Bandura can help explain the relationship between sports and aggression (Berk, p. 17).

1. The theory emphasizes modelling and observational learning.

2. It has been updated to reflect the recognition that children think about themselves and others. It is now referred to as the social-cognitive approach.

3. Nucci & Young-Shim stress the important role of coaches and parents in the use of strategies to reduce unsportsmanlike behaviour and increase moral reasoning:
   i. Coaches should use instruction with praise, modelling, and a point system.
   ii. There is evidence that athletes who have received coaching that demonstrates moral reasoning and promotes sportsmanship are better equipped than their non-athletic counterparts to effectively handle aggressive situations.
   iii. Further evidence suggests that under trained leadership, combative sports may be of benefit to athletes when faced with hostile situations.

> In this section, the writer uses critical thinking to discuss possible flaws in the studies he has used. This leads directly to his brief conclusion in which he provides an overview of and final comment on his topic.

VII. Discuss possible limitations in the current studies.

A. Most studies examine the attitudes of children who already are participating in a particular sport, whether an aggressive sport, a full-contact sport, or simply a high energy, non-contact sport.

B. Children self-select for their sports, meaning that a child scoring highly on an aggression test may naturally choose a full contact sport.

C. Randomized studies are required in order to gain a more accurate picture.

D. The effect of culture on the outcome of various studies is unclear, as suggested by Maxwell's study of Hong Kong Rugby Union participants.

VIII. Conclusion

A. Participation in sports, even aggressive sports, provides the opportunity for hostile children to receive proper instruction for dealing with misplaced aggression.

B. Sports in which positive modelling and reinforcement are present encourage sportsmanship and appropriate displays of aggression.

C. Some evidence suggests that combative sports better equip athletes to handle aggressive and hostile situations.

> The writer changed the order of sub-points in his essay, as the point about the need for randomized studies (C) follows more logically from A, B, and D.

Sample Student Essay

To conserve space, the student essay is not double spaced and the "References" section is not on a separate page; in addition, the essay does not follow essay format requirements for title pages or identification information (see appendix A, Essay Presentation, p. 388).

Sample Student Expository Essay—APA Style

The author of this essay uses reliable journal studies to explore and help answer his research question. Lawrence also wisely uses current sources. He combines the results of the research and his own critical thinking skills to explore a much-debated topic.

SAMPLE STUDENT RESEARCH ESSAY

The Impact of Sports on Childhood Aggression

by Iain Lawrence

[1]   Participation in sport has been recognized as an important source of childhood development: children involved in sports may learn to work with others to achieve a common goal, develop self-confidence, learn to abide by a set of rules, and acquire a sense of fair play. In some cases, parents of children with behavioural challenges, such as excessive shyness or aggression, look to aggressive sport as a means of helping their child integrate successfully into his or her peer group. Such solutions to social and emotional challenges like these have some support within both the scientific literature and the sporting community. Emery (2009), for example, identified three benefits realized by children taking part in organized sports: "enhanced self-esteem," "improved social interactions," and the "development of leadership skills" (p. 207). On the practical side, martial arts schools often claim that participation in their discipline will encourage passive children to become self-confident, while teaching aggressive children to become more respectful of others. These schools typically suggest that the martial arts function as a channel through which

> Lawrence begins with a generalization: the perception that sports aid in child development. His paragraph, however, provides detailed and specific support for the generalization. It successfully establishes the writer's knowledge and reliability.

Continued

to direct inappropriate aggression in more hostile or violent children. Are such claims warranted, and do other "aggressive" sports such as lacrosse, hockey, or perhaps even soccer, provide the same opportunity for healthy outlet for aggression, or do they simply encourage further inappropriate behaviour?

[2]   Within the field of psychology, two major categories of aggressive behaviour have been identified (Berk, 2008, pp. 386–387; Maxwell, 2004, p. 238), instrumental aggression and hostile aggression. In a sporting environment, instrumental aggression is characterized by behaviour that includes a high level of purposeful physical contact between opposing players. The participants use such aggression strategically with actions confined to those permitted under the rules of the game. In addition, players have no intention of causing physical harm to their opponents. Examples of this type of aggression include bodychecking in hockey and punching in boxing. The second type of aggressive behaviour, hostile aggression, is typified by acts engaged in with the intent of injuring an opposing player. Examples of this type of aggression include hitting an opposing player in the face with a stick in hockey or biting one's opponent in boxing. Maxwell (2004) includes a third type of aggression in his discussion: reactive aggression. As the name implies, this type of aggression involves instinctive acts in response to the action of another player. Reasoning plays little role in whether or not the athletes act aggressively. However, while these terms are useful for an introductory discussion on aggression, Maxwell argues that they have less value than initially thought since an athlete may have many different motivations for acting in a particular way (p. 238). For example, an athlete might be strategically aggressive in order to gain tactical advantage within the rules of play, but in addition, he or she may take pleasure in causing injury.

[3]   Two additional terms help provide a context for a discussion on childhood aggression and sport: aggressive sport and non-aggressive sport. An aggressive sport includes one with purposeful, physical contact between participants, such as tackling in rugby or football, bodychecking in ice hockey, or punching and kicking in the martial arts. An aggressive sport makes use of instrumental aggression, although as noted by Maxwell, determining when instrumental aggression spills over into hostile aggression may become difficult (p. 238). A high-energy, non-aggressive sport, on the other hand, has minimal or no purposeful contact between opposing players. In fact, any form of physical contact with the opposition may be prohibited under the rules of play. While a non-aggressive sport may seem "tame" at first glance, these sports remain highly competitive and can require a level of physical exertion equal to or higher than many aggressive sports. Examples of such high-energy activities include competitive cycling, running, and swimming.

[4]   Psychologists and other researchers have examined a possible link between emotional well-being and aggression in sports. In their study of minor hockey players, Emery, McKay, Campbell, and Peters (2009) described two major findings related to hockey where bodychecking is permitted and the child's emotional development. The first was that children in a league that permitted bodychecking showed similar levels of empathy as did their counterparts in a league that prohibited bodychecking. At the same time, Emery et al. noted players in the bodychecking league demonstrated increased aggression in comparison to those in the non-bodychecking league. They

---

Phrasing the thesis as a question is appropriate: through research, Lawrence will attempt to determine whether the perception of childhood sports is valid or not.

As he does in his outline (p. 223), Lawrence divides aggression into two categories, defines each, and gives examples. In paragraph 3, he gives two additional definitions. Definition is often a good starting point in expository essays (see p. 128).

Maxwell is an important source in this and the following paragraph. In APA style, publication year follows the author's name. After summarizing the source, Lawrence provides the page number. The absence of a citation in the last sentence shows that the example is Lawrence's.

suggested that increased aggression results from prolonged participation in the league with greater physical contact (p. 213).

[5]   Can it be said, then, that there are positive outcomes for children who participate in aggressive sports? Several researchers have highlighted a number of beneficial socio-emotional outcomes for aggressive children through participation in sports (Emery et al., 2009; Findlay & Coplan, 2008; Nucci & Young-Shim, 2005). However, these benefits come not from aggressive sports per se, but from sports in general. In terms of socialization, Nucci and Young-Shim (2005) point out that children enrolled in sports have the opportunity to learn how to compete, cooperate, and role-play. They also have the chance to develop an ethic of discipline as it relates to following regulations and pursuing goals. In addition, McHale et al. (2005) reported that both shy and aggressive children showed greater self-esteem after participating in sports (p. 130). These children share increased feelings of anxiety, loneliness, and negative affect more than their more confident and even-tempered peers (Findlay & Coplan, 2008, pp. 158–159). Such feelings also correlate with a greater likelihood of decreased physical ability and self-esteem, along with misbehaviour. By contrast, after participation in sports, they tend to experience "higher positive affect and well-being and greater social skills" (p. 160).

[6]   An important model for understanding the relationship between aggressive sport and the outworking of aggressive behaviour in children is the social learning theory developed by Albert Bandura in 1977. His theory emphasizes the importance of modelling by parents, teachers, and, in sport, coaches. The theory recognizes that children are likely to imitate the behaviour of their mentors (Berk, 2008, p. 17). Following Bandura's model, it is important that coaches and parents understand their contribution to the development of a child's social and emotional well-being. Specifically, Nucci and Young-Shim (2005) outline several strategies to reduce unsportsmanlike behaviour and increase moral reasoning. These include instruction and praise, modelling, and a points system, whereby children earn points for good behaviour. It follows that athletes who have received coaching that exemplifies moral reasoning and promotes sportsmanship are better equipped than non-athletic counterparts to effectively handle aggressive situations. Moreover, under trained leadership, combative sports may be of benefit to athletes when faced with hostile situations outside the sporting arena (pp. 128–129).

[7]   While research on aggression and sport seems to be divided on whether or not aggressive sports are beneficial for the development of children's social and emotional well-being, most of the studies themselves suffer from a number of limitations. The Emery (2009) study, for example, examined the attitudes of children who were already participating in one of two respective leagues. This was also true for other studies, whether focused on aggressive, full-contact sport, or simply high-energy, non-contact sport. With rare exception, children and their parents self-select the sports in which the children will participate. This means that a child scoring highly on an aggression test may naturally choose a full contact sport. In addition, the effects of culture on the outcome of various studies are unclear. Maxwell's (2009) study of Hong Kong Rugby Union athletes suggested that there is some correlation between culture and aggression as it relates to sport. Therefore, in order to gain a more accurate picture of the precise relationship between sport and aggression, randomized studies are required. In such studies, participants would be assigned to

| The question provides a transition between the last two sentences of paragraph 4, which mention increased aggression in children who play in a bodychecking league, and paragraph 5, which focuses on the benefits of children's participation in sports generally. |

| Sources can be combined in one citation with semicolons separating each source. |

| Unlike the previous citation, no signal phrase preceded the reference; therefore, author names, years and page numbers are included in the citation. |

| As this passage would be easy to summarize, Lawrence probably used direct quotation for emphasis, stressing the benefits of sports for shy and aggressive children. |

| In this paragraph, Lawrence turned to a classic theory of learning in order to examine the reasons why aggressive sports might benefit some but not all children. |

Continued

> Using critical thinking, Lawrence examines the limitations of two specific studies, implying that most studies on this topic have similar limitations. He concludes with a recommendation. In the final paragraph, Lawrence addresses parents, recalling the focus of his introduction on the parents of aggressive children.

aggressive sport and high-energy, non-aggressive sport groups based on research design criteria, rather than self-selection.

[8]   While opinion is divided on whether or not participation in aggressive sport contributes to or mitigates aggression, the act of participation provides the opportunity for hostile children to receive proper instruction for dealing with misplaced aggression. In accordance with the social learning theory, activities where positive modelling and reinforcement are present encourage sportsmanship and appropriate forms of aggression. What should concerned parents of aggressive children seek in sports programs if they wish to provide the best opportunity for social integration? At the present time, the most widely accepted answer appears to be a coach who is well-trained and is sensitive to both the needs of aggressive children and the potential of the sport to foster further aggression.

References

Berk, L. E. (2008). *Infants and children: Prenatal through middle childhood* (6th ed.). Boston, MA: Pearson.

Emery, C. A., McKay, C. D., Campbell, T. S., & Peters, A. N. (2009). Examining attitudes toward body checking, levels of emotional empathy, and levels of aggression in body checking and non-body checking youth hockey leagues. *Clinical Journal of Sport Medicine, 19*(3), 207–215. doi:10.1097/JSM.0b013e31819d658e

Findlay, L. C., & Coplan, R. J. (2008). Come out and play: Shyness in childhood and the benefits of organized sports participation. *Canadian Journal of Behavioural Science, 40*(3), 153–161. doi:10.1037/0008-400X.40.3.153

Maxwell, J. P., & Visek, A. J. (2009). Unsanctioned aggression in rugby union: Relationships among aggressiveness, anger, athletic identity, and professionalization. *Aggressive Behavior, 35*(3), 237–243. doi:10.1002/ab.20302

McHale, J. P., Vinden, P. G., Loren, B., Richer, D., Shaw, D., & Smith, B. (2005). Patterns of personal and social adjustment among sport-involved and noninvolved urban middle-school children. *Sociology of Sport Journal, 22*(2), 119–136.

Nucci, C., & Young-Shim, K. (2005). Improving socialization through sport: An analytic review of literature on aggression and sportsmanship. *Physical Educator, 62*(3), 123–129.

The Scholarly Essay

Scholarly essays, which usually appear in academic journals and can be accessed electronically through your school's databases, are longer and more complex than the kinds of essays you write for class. Many of the challenges they present, however, can be overcome by knowing where to look for information. Following the steps below will make the reading process easier:

1. Read the title and abstract to get an idea of the essay's purpose, topic, and results or findings. If the essay includes specific headings, they may also give useful information.

2. Read the introduction, especially the last paragraphs, where important information is placed.

3. Read the conclusion section (called "Discussion" in this essay), in which the findings are summarized and made relevant.

4. If you are trying to determine whether the essay is related to your research topic, scan the complete essay, looking for relevant concepts and key words. Use focused reading for important passages. Pay attention to tables, charts, and other visuals, which summarize important content.

From Theory to Practice: Sample Scholarly Essay

Many of the annotations on the essay below focus on advice for reading challenging essays. "The Teenage Brain: Self Control" represents a particular kind of scholarly essay, a literature review, or critical evaluation, in which the authors analyze previous studies on a topic to evaluate what researchers have discovered about it. As in most literature reviews, the authors discuss the results of previous studies throughout, organizing their essay by logical sections.

Like student writer Iain Lawrence (p. 225), Casey and Caudle draw attention to popular perceptions and use a combination of previous research and critical thinking to synthesize the findings and draw conclusions about their validity. Of course, Casey and Caudle cite many more studies than Lawrence, but the underlying processes are similar: both essays rely on analysis, synthesis, and critical thinking.

Before reading this essay, you can also review the questions discussed in chapter 1, Responding Critically and Analytically through Questions, page 8.

SAMPLE SCHOLARLY ESSAY

The Teenage Brain: Self Control

by B. J. Casey & Kristina Caudle

Abstract

Adolescence refers to the transition from childhood to adulthood that begins with the onset of puberty and ends with successful independence from the parent. A paradox for human adolescence is why, during a time when the individual is probably faster, stronger, of higher reasoning capacity, and more resistant to disease, there is such an increase in mortality relative to childhood. This is due not to disease but, rather, to preventable forms of death (accidental fatalities, suicide, and homicide) associated with adolescents putting themselves in harm's way, in part because of diminished self-control—the ability to suppress inappropriate emotions, desires, and actions. This article highlights how self-control varies as a function of age, context, and the individual and delineates its neurobiological basis.

Introduction

[1]   During adolescence, people are probably the quickest that they will ever be; their crushes will never be better, and their thrills will never quite be the same. That's the good news. The bad news is that during this time, relative to childhood, their chances of dying from putting themselves in harm's way will increase by 200% (Dahl, 2001). This

The abstract outlines the problem to be investigated and the focus of the article. Abstracts of scientific experiments often outline the stages of the experiment. However, this paper reports on the results of many experiments, not just the authors' own.

Although this definition of adolescence might seem unnecessary, the authors return to the idea that "successful independence" can be considered an adaptive mechanism that equips adolescents for adulthood. See paragraphs 3, 4, and 17.

The relationship between scholarly research and the media is an important one, but the authors point out that the results are usually simplified—and sometimes misrepresented—by the media seeking to make complex findings understandable to a general audience.

Academic authors often "justify" their study; in other words, they state directly or indirectly why it was necessary. In this sense, they argue for its importance.

Like most thesis statements, this one includes the topic and the authors' approach. However, rather than being placed at the end of the introduction, what follows expands on the three "overgeneralizations," clearly laying out the essay's structure as well as summarizing its content.

article focuses on the challenges of adolescence in the context of self-control— the ability to suppress inappropriate emotions, desires, and actions. We highlight the specific contexts in which adolescents' self-control is most likely to falter and its underlying neurobiological basis.

[2]   Over the past decade, there has been a marked increase in neurobiological research on the behavioral changes that occur during adolescence. Too often, in simplifying the findings for the media or for policymakers, this work is reduced to adolescents having no self-control and no prefrontal cortex, basically being "all gasoline, no brakes, and no steering wheel" (Bell & McBride, 2010, p. 565). Such simple claims can have positive and negative consequences for the treatment of adolescents, given that they can be used to justify both diminished responsibility for criminal acts (see Bonnie & Scott, 2013; this issue) and limited ability to make life choices (e.g., to terminate or continue a pregnancy). Reading popular science magazines that have made such claims led our group to undertake the studies of self-control described in this article. Here, we present our work in the context of three common "myths" or overgeneralizations about adolescence to clarify and temper some of these claims.

[3]   The first is that adolescent behavior is irrational or deviant. Such descriptions may be understandable in light of the peak incidence in criminal activity and many psychiatric disorders that arise during this developmental period. Yet this description pathologizes an important phase of normal development that allows individuals to learn how to function relatively independently in society. A second overgeneralization is that adolescents are incapable of making rational decisions because of their immature prefrontal cortex (Yurgelun-Todd, 2007), the so-called rational, vulcanized region of the brain (J. D. Cohen, 2005). Clearly, the prefrontal cortex is not the only part of the brain that changes during this developmental period, and the child's prefrontal cortex is even less mature than the adolescent's. Thus, this explanation does not sufficiently explain spikes in risky and emotive behavior during adolescence. We present evidence that underscores the importance of considering brain regions as part of a developing circuitry that is fine-tuned with experience during this time. Third is the century-old claim that all adolescents experience "sturm und drang"—that is, "storm and stress"—a claim originally proposed by G. Stanley Hall (Hall, 1904). Although adolescents show poor self-control as a group, we provide evidence for when self-control is most likely to break down during adolescence and for striking individual differences in this ability across the life span that may put some teens at greater risk than others. We address each of the preceding overgeneralizations in the context of a neurodevelopmental framework.

Overgeneralization 1: Adolescents are incapable of making optimal decisions

[4]   Adolescence, by definition, involves new demands on the individual as she or he moves from dependence on the family unit to relative independence. This developmental period is not specific to humans, as evidenced by the increases in novelty seeking, interactions with peers, and fighting with parents observed in other species (see Romeo, 2013; Spear, 2013; both in this issue). These behaviors are thought to have evolved to serve adaptive functions related to successful mating and obtainment of resources necessary for survival (Spear & Varlinskaya, 2010). A heightened sensitivity to socially relevant cues (e.g., peers, monetary gain) would seem to be an ideal mechanism for meeting some of

these developmental challenges. However, such a system may appear less than optimal when the pull by these socially relevant cues comes at the expense of long-term goals and the overall well-being of the adolescent.

[5]   To suggest that this period of development is one of no brakes or steering wheel (Bell & McBride, 2010) is to greatly oversimplify it. In a series of recent experiments in our laboratory (Somerville, Hare, & Casey, 2011), we measured self-control using a variant of a go/no-go paradigm that contained social cues (positive, negative, or neutral facial expressions). By using socially relevant and emotionally salient stimuli together with neutral stimuli, we could test how well adolescents regulated their impulses in both emotional and nonemotional contexts (Hare et al., 2008; Somerville et al., 2011).

[6]   Self-control—in this case, suppressing a compelling action—showed a different developmental pattern in the context of emotional information than in its absence, especially for males (Tottenham, Hare, & Casey, 2011). As illustrated in Figure 1 (also see Fig. 1 in Hare et al., 2008; National Research Council, 2011), when no emotional information is present, not only do many adolescents perform as well as adults, some perform even better. However, when decisions are required in the heat of the moment (i.e., in the presence of emotional cues; Fig. 2a), performance falters (Fig. 2b). Specifically, adolescents have difficulty suppressing a response to appetitive social cues relative to neutral ones. This diminished ability is not observed in children and adults, who show equal difficulty in suppressing responses regardless of the emotional content of the nontarget. Thus, the description of teens as "all gasoline, no brakes, and no steering wheel" more accurately

> Among the studies synthesized in this essay are those involving the lead author, B.J. Casey; the "References" section indicates six other studies in which she participated. A reader can infer that she is an expert in her field.

> Although this essay is written for knowledgeable readers, strategies for comprehension produce an efficient and readable paragraph—even for non-specialists. The authors carefully explain and clarify their statements, referring to visual material that both summarizes results and provides additional detail. The authors also use transitions to qualify (*However*), emphasize (*Specifically*), and summarize (*Thus*), helping the reader connect ideas. Repetition of the misleading phrase from paragraphs 2 and 5 also draws further attention to the inadequacies of the description.

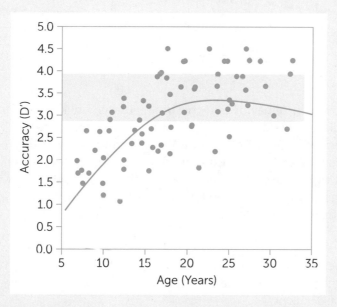

FIGURE 1

Performance on a standard go/no-go task as a function of age. D' was used as a measure of accuracy that includes both hits and false alarms. The data illustrate improvements in performance with age but also high variability, with some adolescents performing as well as or better than some adults (highlighted by the green box). Data are drawn from Hare et al. (2008) and National Research Council (2011).

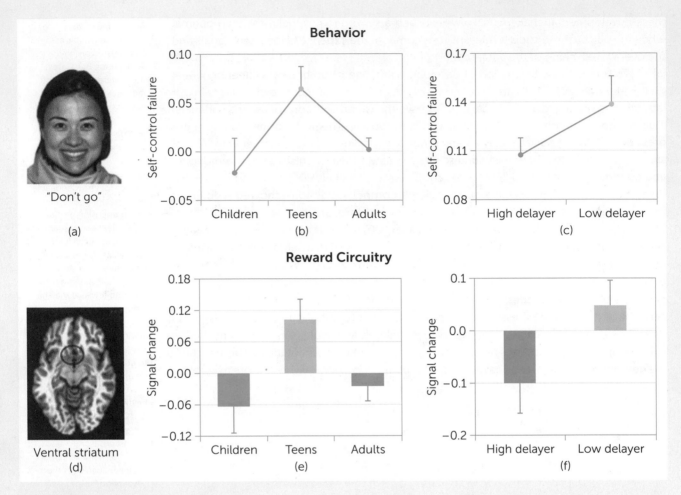

FIGURE 2

Developmental and individual differences in behavior and the brain. Teens, unlike children and adults, make more false alarms to positive social cues (a) than to neutral ones on a go/no-go task. This behavioral performance (b) is paralleled by enhanced activity in the ventral striatum (d), part of the reward circuit, in response to appetitive cues in teens relative to children and adults (e). Low delayers make more false alarms to positive social cues than do high delayers on a go/no-go task (c). This behavioral performance is paralleled by enhanced activity of the ventral striatum in low delayers relative to high delayers (f). Error bars represent ±1 *SE*. Data are drawn from Somerville, Hare, and Casey (2011) and Casey et al. (2011).

reflects their behavior in heated situations than in cool, less immediate, and less emotional ones. In these cool situations, the teen appears to be capable of acting rationally and making optimal decisions.

Overgeneralization 2: Adolescents have no prefrontal cortex

[7]   Saying that one studies the adolescent brain is often met with comic skepticism and feigned relief that adolescents do indeed have a brain. There is no hole in the head or absence of parts to suggest a lesion-related impairment during this period. Moreover, the prefrontal cortex, a region important in self-control and rational decision making, is

clearly present even from birth. What is changing during this period of development is the strength of connections within prefrontal circuitry as individuals learn to adapt to changing environmental demands (Liston et al., 2006). This development reflects a combination of evolutionarily shaped biological constraints and experiential history, which interact to shape the brain and behavior.

[8]   Evidence from human imaging and animal studies of regional neurochemical, structural, and functional brain changes over the course of development have led to a theoretical account of adolescence referred to as the imbalance model of brain development (Somerville & Casey, 2010). According to this view, reward-related subcortical regions and prefrontal control regions interact differently across development. Specifically, motivational and emotional subcortical connections develop earlier than do connections supporting prefrontal control. This developmental imbalance results in a relatively greater reliance on motivational subcortical regions than on prefrontal regions during adolescence (i.e., an imbalance in reliance on different systems), as compared with adulthood, when this circuitry is fully mature, and also as compared with childhood, when this circuitry is still developing. With age and experience, the connectivity between these regions is strengthened and provides a mechanism for top-down modulation of the subcortically driven emotional behavior that increases the capacity for self-control.

[9]   Recently, a number of human imaging studies have attempted to evaluate this model and test for unique patterns of brain activity in adolescents during stereotypical risky behavior in the context of incentives (Chein, Albert, O'Brien, Uckert, & Steinberg, 2011; J. R. Cohen et al., 2010; Geier, Terwilliger, Teslovich, Velanova, & Luna, 2010; Van Leijenhorst et al., 2010). This work has challenged the view that diminished self-control in adolescents is due to a less mature prefrontal cortex that leads to less successful exertion of regulatory control on behavior (Bell & McBride, 2010). In contrast, these studies have revealed a unique sensitivity to motivational cues during adolescence that appears to challenge the less mature cognitive control systems when called upon simultaneously in tasks that involve inhibiting attention or actions toward potential incentives. Accordingly, developmental differences in self-control arise because of maturational constraints of developing brain circuitry and the strengthening of the connectivity between these interacting brain systems with experience (Liston et al., 2006).

[10]   [a] To better understand changes in self-control during adolescence, we used functional brain imaging together with our previously described go/no-go task. [b] Specifically, we examined the neural correlates of self-control in the face of emotional and nonemotional cues. [c] We found that the ability to suppress a habitual response, regardless of emotional content, relied on the ventrolateral prefrontal cortex (Fig. 3). [d] Activity in this region showed a monotonic increase with age for correct trials that was correlated with behavioral performance. [e] In contrast, the ability to suppress a response to emotional cues revealed a different pattern of brain activity. [f] Specifically, diminished behavioral performance by adolescents in suppressing responses to positive emotional cues was paralleled by enhanced activity in the ventral striatum (Fig. 2d and 2e), a region critical for detecting and learning about novel and rewarding cues in the environment. [g] These findings suggest an exaggerated ventral-striatal representation of appetitive cues in adolescents that may serve to "hijack" a less fully mature prefrontal control response. [h]Thus, adolescents' decisions and actions are not due solely to a less mature prefrontal cortex but, rather, to a tension within neural circuitry involving the ventral striatum, implicated in reward processing, and the prefrontal cortex, implicated in control processing.

In paragraph 7, the topic sentence is placed in a non-traditional position. Such a structure is necessary as the authors address the nature of the "myth" in the first three sentences. More typically, the topic sentence is the first sentence of the paragraph, as in paragraph 8.

In paragraph 8, the authors explain how the *imbalance model* might account for the kind of patterns of behaviour characterizing adolescence. Thus, the model serves as a kind of hypothesis. In recent experiments, those mentioned in paragraph 9, researchers tested and refined this model. After further experimentation, researchers may be able to put forward a more sophisticated model that accounts more fully for adolescent behaviour.

Paragraph 10 explains the authors' study, which was designed to pinpoint the interactions between two parts of the brain. Sentences a and e make general statements; sentences b and f give detail, while sentences c and g summarize findings; sentence h conveys the study's significance, referring to the misconception that an undeveloped prefrontal cortex alone is responsible for risky behaviour. The paragraph's logical and predictable development makes the ideas easier to follow—even for a reader unfamiliar with the structure of the brain.

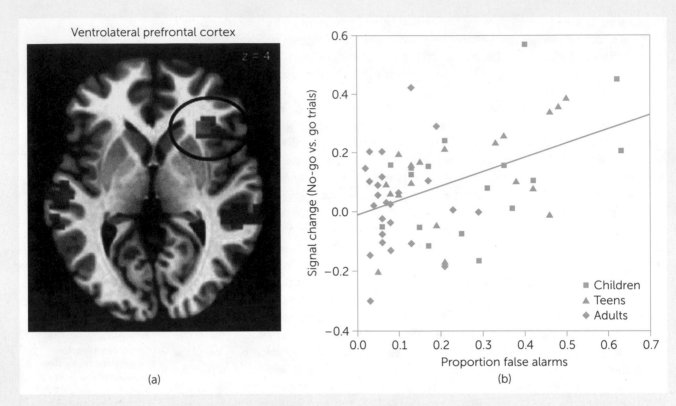

(a)   (b)

FIGURE 3

Correlation of ventral prefrontal activity with go/no-go task performance. Panel (a) illustrates localization of the ventral prefrontal cortical region that correlates with behavioral performance. Panel (b) illustrates the correlation between blood-oxygen-level-dependent (BOLD) signal in the ventral lateral prefrontal cortex and go/no-go task performance by age group. Adapted from "Frontostriatal Maturation Predicts Cognitive Control Failure to Appetitive Cues in Adolescents," by L. H. Somerville, T. Hare, and B. J. Casey, 2011, *Journal of Cognitive Neuroscience, 23.* Copyright 2011 by the Society for Neuroscience. Adapted with permission.

Overgeneralization 3: All adolescents experience similar degrees of storm and stress

[11]   Nearly everyone reading this article survived adolescence reasonably well. Clearly, we are not all doomed during adolescence, as was suggested by G. Stanley Hall's theory of adolescence (Hall, 1904). Rather, adolescence falls somewhere between the extreme views of Hall's storm-and-stress theory of adolescence and Margaret Mead's cultural–not-biological account of adolescence (Mead, 1928). Basically, our behavior is a reflection of environmental and genetic factors that impact our brain's ability to adapt to changing environmental demands. Some environmental demands are universally expected, and some are specific to an individual's experiences. How well we adapt to these changing environmental demands is a function of biological constraints and experiential history. Thus, even as adults, we may differ in our ability to face new challenges and to adequately regulate our behavior accordingly.

[12]   A hallmark of self-regulation is the ability to resist the temptation of an immediate reward in favor of a larger reward later, known as delay of gratification. A classic paradigm for assessing this ability was developed by Mischel (Mischel, Shoda, & Rodriguez, 1989)

> Scholarly writers rely on current studies directly relevant to their research along with well-established studies, such as Mischel's. Older still are Hall and Mead (see paragraph 11); though "classic" studies, decades of research have led to a reevaluation of their claims.

for use with young children. He examined whether children would choose a small reward (one marshmallow) sooner over a larger reward (two marshmallows) later. Children's behavior fell into two clusters: (a) they ate the treat almost immediately (low delayers), or (b) they waited for some amount of time in an attempt to gain two treats (high delayers). These two different patterns of behavior provide an example of individual differences in self-control that can be detected and measured in early childhood (Mischel et al., 1989). However, how did these individuals fare in their self-control ability later in life?

[13]   To address this question, we recently examined self-control in a 40-year follow-up of the original cohort of children Mischel tested on the delay-of-gratification task. Using both neutral ("cool") and emotional ("hot") cues in a go/no-go task, we examined the ability of these individuals, now in their mid-40s, to suppress habitual responses to emotional or neutral cues. Because marshmallows do not have quite the same appeal for adults as they do for children, we used social cues (e.g., happy faces relative to neutral and fearful faces) rather than marshmallows as nontargets in a go/no-go task.

[14]   The results indicated that even 40 years later, the same individuals who could not stop themselves from immediately eating the marshmallow and thus kept themselves from getting two marshmallows also had difficulty suppressing their responses when a positive social cue was present, even when they were instructed not to respond (Fig. 2c). However, they had no problem suppressing habitual responses to neutral cues (Casey et al., 2011). Thus, individuals who, as a group, had more difficulty delaying gratification at 4 years of age continued to show reduced self-control 40 years later. These findings highlight individual differences in self-control that are independent of age and can persist throughout the life span. However, a remaining question is whether the neural correlates underlying individual differences in self-control are similar to those observed in adolescents in our previously described study.

This represents an important finding as it contradicts overgeneralization 3, "All adolescents experience similar degrees of storm and stress." Casey and Caudle then use human imaging to determine whether the same physiological processes are at work as described in paragraph 10.

[15]   To address this question, high- and low-delaying individuals were imaged during performance of the "hot" go/no-go task (Casey et al., 2011). The findings showed that whereas prefrontal activity was associated with accurately withholding a response, activity in the ventral striatum mapped onto the behavioral finding of poorer performance when specifically suppressing a response to an appetitive social cue (Fig. 2f).

[16]   These findings underscore the importance of the stimulus qualities a person has to resist in an act of self-control. Sensitivity to characteristics of environmental cues (e.g., salience, reward value) can significantly influence an individual's ability to suppress inappropriate actions in favor of appropriate ones. This tension between regulation of behavior and sensitivity to positive environmental cues in many ways parallels observations from our adolescent study (Somerville et al., 2011). Perhaps unsurprisingly, children's ability to delay gratification at 4 years of age predicts parental ratings of these individuals' self-control during adolescence, too (Mischel, Shoda, & Peake, 1988). Both examples show how stimulus qualities such as rare, positive social cues can compromise an individual's self-control and suggest that both developmental and individual differences affect this ability. Thus, individuals who have diminished self-control may be especially vulnerable during adolescence, when a heightened sensitivity to emotional environmental cues can further hinder this ability.

Discussion

[17]   Our findings suggest that adolescents can show remarkable restraint in controlling habitual responses but tend to fail when attempting to control habitual responses to salient

In the Discussion section, the authors briefly summarize the latest findings from the three areas of their essay before again addressing the misperception of adolescents as "all gasoline, no brakes, and no steering wheel."

At the end of their essay, Casey and Caudle suggest an adaptive benefit in the developmental pattern of the adolescent brain: it helps the adolescent gain independence through the interaction with novel situations. Summarizing the results and suggesting real-world applications are two functions of conclusions of academic essays, especially in the sciences and social sciences. In addition, experimental studies may attempt to situate the current study relative to other studies; finally, they may include limitations of the current study and propose future research directions.

Like many social science essays, this essay's authors use APA citation style. This entry shows the correct format for eight or more authors; note the ellipses between the sixth and the last author. See page 258.

positive cues in the environment. Specifically, we showed that adolescents have impulse control that is comparable to or even better than that of some adults in neutral contexts (Fig. 1). However, in emotional contexts, adolescents' impulse-control ability is severely taxed relative to that of children and adults (Fig. 3). This behavioral pattern is paralleled by exaggerated responses in reward-related circuitry that presumably are difficult to regulate because of less top-down control from still-developing prefrontal connections in teenagers. This tension between motivational and control processes during adolescence can vary by individual, leading to enhanced or diminished self-control. To say that the adolescent is "all gasoline, no brakes, and no steering wheel" is to do a disservice to this essential phase of typical development. Indeed, if the objective of adolescence is to gain independence from the family unit, then providing opportunities for adolescents to engage in new responsibilities is essential. Without opportunities and experiences to help optimally shape the adolescent's brain and behavior, the objectives of this developmental phase will not easily be met.

References

Bell, C. C., & McBride, D. F. (2010). Affect regulation and prevention of risky behaviors. *Journal of the American Medical Association, 304*, 565–566.

Bonnie, R. J., & Scott, E. S. (2013). The teenage brain: Adolescent brain research and the law. *Current Directions in Psychological Science, 22(2)*, 158–161.

Casey, B. J., Somerville, L. H., Gotlib, I. H., Ayduk, O., Franklin, N. T., Askren, M. K., . . . & Shoda Y. (2011). Behavioral and neural correlates of delay of gratification 40 years later. *Proceedings of the National Academy of Sciences, USA, 108*, 14998–15003.

Chein, J., Albert, D., O'Brien, L., Uckert, K., & Steinberg, L. (2011). Peers increase adolescent risk taking by enhancing activity in the brain's reward circuitry. *Developmental Science, 14*, F1–F10. doi:10.1037/a0035696

Cohen, J. D. (2005). The vulcanization of the human brain: A neural perspective on interactions between cognition and emotion. *Journal of Economic Perspectives, 19*(4), 3–24. doi:10.1257/089533005775196750

Cohen, J. R., Asarnow, R. F., Sabb, F. W., Bilder, R. M., Bookheimer, S. Y., Knowlton, B. J., & Poldrack, R. A. (2010). A unique adolescent response to reward prediction errors. *Nature Neuroscience, 13*, 669–671. doi:10.1038/nn.2558

Dahl, R. E. (2001). Affect regulation, brain development, and behavioral/emotional health in adolescence. *CNS Spectrums, 6*, 60–72. Retrieved from http://www.cnsspectrums.com/

Geier, C. F., Terwilliger, R., Teslovich, T., Velanova, K., & Luna, B. (2010). Immaturities in reward processing and its influence on inhibitory control in adolescence. *Cerebral Cortex, 20*, 1613–1629. doi:10.1093/cercor/bhp225

Hall, G. S. (1904). *Adolescence: In psychology and its relation to physiology, anthropology, sex, crime, religion, and education* (Vols. I & II). Englewood Cliffs, NJ: Prentice-Hall.

Hare, T. A., Tottenham, N., Galván, A., Voss, H. U., Glover, G. H., & Casey, B. J. (2008). Biological substrates of emotional reactivity and regulation in adolescence during an emotional go-nogo task. *Biological Psychiatry, 63*, 927–934. doi:10.1016/j.biopsych.2008.03.015

Liston, C., Watts, R., Tottenham, N., Davidson, M. C., Niogi, S., Ulug, A. M., & Casey, B. J. (2006). Frontostriatal microstructure modulates efficient recruitment of cognitive control. *Cerebral Cortex, 16*, 553–560. Retrieved from http://cercor.oxfordjournals.org/

Mead, M. (1928). Coming of age in Samoa: A psychological study of primitive youth for Western civilisation. New York, NY: W. Morrow.

Mischel, W., Shoda, Y., & Peake, P. K. (1988). The nature of adolescent competencies predicted by preschool delay of gratification. *Journal of Personality and Social Psychology, 54,* 687–696. Retrieved from http://www.apa.org/pubs/journals/psp/

Mischel, W., Shoda, Y., & Rodriguez, M. I. (1989). Delay of gratification in children. *Science, 244,* 933–938. Retrieved from http://www.sciencemag.org/journals

National Research Council. (2011). *The science of adolescent risk-taking: Workshop report.* Washington, DC: National Academies Press.

Romeo, R. D. (2013). The teenage brain: The stress response and the adolescent brain. *Current Directions in Psychological Science, 22(2),* 140–145. doi:10.1177/0963721413475445

Somerville, L. H., & Casey, B. J. (2010). Developmental neurobiology of cognitive control and motivational systems. *Current Opinion in Neurobiology, 20,* 236–241. doi:10.1016/j.conb.2010.01.006

Somerville, L. H., Hare, T., & Casey, B. J. (2011). Frontostriatal maturation predicts cognitive control failure to appetitive cues in adolescents. *Journal of Cognitive Neuroscience, 23,* 2123–2134. doi:10.1162/jocn.2010.21572

Spear L. (2013). The teenage brain: Adolescents and alcohol. *Current Directions in Psychological Science, 22(2),* 152–157. doi:10.1177/0963721412472192

Spear, L. P., & Varlinskaya, E. I. (2010). Sensitivity to ethanol and other hedonic stimuli in an animal model of adolescence: Implications for prevention science? *Developmental Psychobiology, 52,* 236–243. doi:10.1002/dev.20457

Tottenham, N., Hare, T. A., & Casey, B. J. (2011). Behavioral assessment of emotion discrimination, emotion regulation, and cognitive control in childhood, adolescence, and adulthood. *Frontiers in Psychology, 2,* 39. doi:10.3389/fpsyg.2011.00039

Van Leijenhorst, L., Zanolie, K., Van Meel, C. S., Westenberg, P. M., Rombouts, S. A., & Crone, E. A. (2010). What motivates the adolescent? Brain regions mediating reward sensitivity across adolescence. *Cerebral Cortex, 20,* 61–69. doi:10.1093/cercor/bhp078

Yurgelun-Todd, D. (2007). Emotional and cognitive changes during adolescence. *Current Opinion in Neurobiology, 17,* 251–257. Retrieved from http://www.current-opinion.com/journals/current-opinion-in-neurobiology/

Source: *Current Directions in Psychological Science, 22*(2), 82–87.

CHAPTER SUMMARY

This chapter has focused on the many interrelated skills in which research plays a role. Although it covers many topics, it stresses three main areas: approaching research in orderly stages, finding reliable sources, and integrating them effectively. To begin, students need a firm understanding of what research entails. After coming up with a research question, students are encouraged to use their library's resources, especially peer-reviewed articles, to answer their question. Guidelines for successful searches are provided. In integrating sources, whether by summary, paraphrase, or direct quotation, writers should take great care they do not unintentionally plagiarize. Through detailed explanation and examples, students can learn to adopt strategies to avoid plagiarism and to integrate their research accurately.

8 Documentation Styles

Accurate and complete documentation is one feature that separates academic from non-academic writing. Student writers, too, need to be familiar with documentation methods when they write research essays. Correct and consistent documentation gives them credibility and enables others to check their sources. The purpose of this chapter is to introduce you to the three most commonly used documentation styles—MLA, APA, and CMS—providing information about and examples of the kinds of formats you are likely to encounter in your research. It is set up for easy access, beginning with in-text citations and concluding with bibliographical details, including those for electronic sources.

LEARNING OBJECTIVES

- to appreciate the reason for and value of citations as a part of the research process
- to learn efficiency in documentation in order to avoid unneeded citations
- to understand the differences between a citation, a reference, an in-text citation, and a bibliography
- to be aware of the major documentation styles, their uses, and the basic features of each
- to learn how to cite accurately whether referring to print sources, electronic sources, or non-textual sources

WHY DOCUMENT YOUR SOURCES?

Documentation is usually the final stage of research, but that doesn't mean you shouldn't prepare for it in advance. In fact, recording relevant bibliographic details of your sources in the early stages of research is essential, as it is time consuming to go back and retrieve these details later.

When you document, you are confirming that the information used in your essay comes from verifiable sources; thus, careful **citation** *gives you credibility as a researcher.* Other reasons for documenting include

- crediting the work of others
- avoiding plagiarism, a serious academic crime
- enabling interested readers and knowledgeable experts (such as your instructor) to trace or verify your sources
- finding the reference again if you need it for further research

A Closer Look

Using Citations Efficiently

Parenthetical **references** are intended to give the reader as *much* information as possible about the source while interfering as *little* as possible with the essay's content and readability. This is an especially important principle in the Modern Language Association (MLA); however, in both MLA and American Psychological Association (APA) documentation styles, you should not include unneeded citations.

You can avoid citing the same source repetitively in one paragraph *if it is clear you are referring to that one source throughout.* Thus, you can combine references from the same source in one citation. For example, let's say you used three pages from your source, Jackson; when you were finished drawing from that source, you could indicate your use of Jackson this way:

(Jackson 87–89)

This citation would tell the reader that you used that one source continuously for three of her pages—perhaps one idea from page 87, two facts from page 88, and a paraphrased passage from page 89.

Another strategy for direct and economical documentation is to use a signal phrase to indicate a forthcoming reference. After naming the source and following with the material from the source, for example, a direct quotation or paraphrase, provide the page number. The reader can then clearly see the beginning and end of the source material. Since you have named the author(s) in your own sentence, you do not repeat the name in the citation (see Signal Phrases in chapter 7 on p. 219).

A third strategy is combining in one citation sources that contain the same point. This method is useful when you are summarizing the findings of several studies in the same paragraph and want to avoid excessive citations:

(Drinkwater, 2010, p. 118; Hovey, 2009, p. 75).

Choosing Your Documentation Style

Handbooks are published for the major **documentation styles** and contain extensive guidelines. However, usage rules are updated every few years. University libraries provide a range of current **style manuals**. When using a manual, ensure that you have the most up-to-date edition; older editions and second-hand copies may not provide the latest rules.

Different areas of academia favour distinct styles. Below is a list of the styles used in common areas. However, your department or your instructor should be the final guide in your choice of documentation style.

- APA (American Psychological Association): business, education, psychology, many other social sciences and some sciences
- MLA (Modern Language Association): English literature, philosophy, religion, modern languages, some interdisciplinary subjects
- CSE (Council of Science Editors): biology and other sciences
- CMS (Chicago Manual of Style) notes and **bibliography** system/Turabian: history, some humanities
- In addition to the major styles, some subject areas, such as chemistry, engineering, mathematics, medicine, music, and sociology, have their own style specification.

Although there are many subtle differences among the various styles, the main elements of an **in-text citation** may include

- the name(s) of the author(s)
- the page number or a similar locator of the information cited
- the year of publication

Most styles require an abbreviated citation in the sentence where the referenced material appears. In parenthetical styles, the information is enclosed in parentheses.

Further details on each cited work are given in an alphabetized list at the end of the essay under a heading such as "References" or "Works Cited." The following references have been styled according to the rules of each handbook or manual:

- humanities
  Modern Language Association. MLA *Handbook for Writers of Research Papers*. 7th ed. New York: Modern Language Association, 2009. Print.

- social sciences
  American Psychological Association. (2010). *Publication manual of the American Psychological Association* (6th ed.). Washington, D.C.: Author.

Unlike the MLA and APA style guides, some other prominent documentation styles, such as the CMS notes and bibliography system, use numbered, detailed citations either at the bottom of the page or at the end of the essay (see pp. 264–266 for common examples).

THE MAJOR DOCUMENTATION STYLES: MLA AND APA

In the following MLA and APA sections, the basic standards for documenting sources are shown with examples to illustrate format.

MLA Documentation Style

In the humanities, the principal documentation style has been developed by the Modern Language Association of America. The MLA publishes two manuals: the MLA *Style Manual and Guide to Scholarly Publishing* for academics and the MLA *Handbook for Writers of Research Papers*, 7th edition (2009) for student researchers. The association also maintains a website (http://www.mla.org) that offers guidelines on Internet citations and updates.

MLA style is parenthetical, meaning that whenever you directly quote, paraphrase, or just use an author's idea, you give the author's last name and the location of the reference (usually a page or paragraph number) in parentheses. Then, you provide a more complete description of all the sources in the last part of your paper, titled "Works Cited" (see pp. 244–252).

MLA In-Text Citations

General Guidelines

- MLA in-text formats include the author(s) and page number(s): (Ashton 17). If the author is named in a signal phrase (e.g., "Ashton found that . . . ."), only the page number will be in parentheses: (17).
- Drop a redundant hundreds digit in the second page number (e.g., 212–47, *not* 212–247), but use both tens digits (e.g., 34–37).
- Leave one space between the author's last name and page number. Do not use commas to separate items unless you need to include both an author and a title in the citation or if you need to separate the author from the paragraph number in an electronic source.
- Readability and efficiency are key principles in MLA style: parenthetical references should not intrude in the text but should clearly indicate the cited sources.

Specific Examples

A citation including a direct quotation, paraphrase, or summary. Give the author's last name and page number in parentheses.

No signal phrase:

> During World Wars I and II, the Canadian government often employed masseuses because surgery and medical care were insufficient "to restore severely wounded men" (Cleather ix).

Signal phrase. Since a signal phrase names the author, the citation requires only the page number:

> Gillam and Wooden argue that Pixar studio films show "a kinder, gentler understanding of what it means to be a man" (3).

APA and MLA are both parenthetical styles, meaning that parentheses are used to enclose brief bibliographical information about the source.

Whenever you directly quote, paraphrase, or just use an author's idea, you give the author's last name and the location of the reference (usually a page or paragraph number) in parentheses.

MLA in-text formats include the author's last name(s) and page or paragraph number(s).

An indirect source is one that is cited in another source—not the original one. If you have to cite information from an indirect source, use the phrase *as qtd. in* ("qtd." is an abbreviation for *quoted*) followed by the place where you got the information.

Block quotation. Indent a quotation longer than four typed lines one inch (2.5 cm) from the left margin. Omit quotation marks, and use double spacing. The author's name and the page numbers appear in parentheses at the end of the quotation and *after* the final period:

> . . . and older children. (Gillam and Wooden 7–8)

A citation referring to an indirect source. If it is necessary to refer to a source found in another work, include the name of the original author in the sentence, along with the source of the information in parentheses. This is preceded by the abbreviation *qtd. in* and followed by the page numbers:

> Francis Bacon observed that language affects our thinking when he said "words react on the understanding" (qtd. in Lindemann 93).

In "Works Cited," list details for the indirect source.

Personal communication, including interviews and emails. This kind of communication needs the source's last name only, in parentheses:

> (McWhirter)

Multiple sources in one citation. You may cite more than one source in a single citation if the point you are making applies to both. Order sources alphabetically by last name and separate them by a semicolon:

> The practices of teaching composition in college have not radically changed in the last few decades (Bishop 65; Williams 6).

However, if the citation is lengthy, consider moving the entire citation to a note (see MLA Notes, p. 252).

If you cite two sources in the same sentence, placing the citation after each source may help with clarity:

> One study looked for correlations between GPA and listening to music (Cox and Stevens 757) while another study related academic performance to three types of music (Roy 6).

MLA In-Text Citations by Format

Kinds of Authors

Work by one author (book or article). Give the author's last name and page number:

> (Bloom 112)

Work by two authors. Give the last names of both authors with the word *and* between them, in addition to page number:

> (Higgins and Wilson-Baptist 44)

For four or more authors, you may give last name of first author followed by "et al."

Work by three authors or four or more authors. Include the last names of all authors with commas between them. To cite three authors, use the word *and* between the second and third names in the list in addition to the page numbers. For more than three authors, include all names as above or give only the last name of the first author with the abbreviation "et al." and page numbers:

(Higgins, Wilson-Baptist, and Krasny 102); (Terracciano et al. 96)

Two or more works by the same author. If you have used two or more works by the same author in one essay, give the author's last name, along with a shortened version of the work's title separated by a comma, and a page number:

"self-enforced discipline" (Foucault, *Power/Knowledge* 37)

Two authors with the same last name. Include each author's first initial along with page numbers:

(S. Taylor 225)

(D. Taylor 17)

Use first names if their initials are the same.

Group or organization as author (corporate author). If an author is not given, include the entire name of the organization in the sentence, if possible. For example, the organization commonly known as UNICEF would appear in the sentence as the United Nations Children's Fund (along with a page number in parentheses). However, it is also acceptable to shorten the organization's name within the citation:

> If no author is given, use the name of the group or organization in place of the author's name—in the sentence itself, if possible.

The United Nations Children's Fund reports that indigenous children are at exceptional risk of becoming refugees (204).

Some child protection advocates suggest that indigenous children are at exceptional risk of becoming refugees (UNICEF 204).

Work by an unknown author (including many dictionary and encyclopedia entries). Begin with the title, if it is short, followed by the page number. When the title is lengthy, a shorter version can be used. Distinguish articles from complete works by placing article titles in quotation marks:

("Plea to City Hall" 22)

MLA In-Text Citations: Electronic Sources

If your source is the entire website, use the author's name in the sentence without a citation. If you are citing a specific quotation or paraphrasing and the document uses paragraph numbers, use these (preceded by the abbreviation "par." for one paragraph, or "pars." for more than one, with a comma and space between the author's name and "par."). If sections are numbered, you may use these numbers (preceded by the abbreviation "sec."). If the document has no numbered pages, paragraphs, or section headings, the work must be cited without a page, paragraph, or section reference.

> For specific references from electronic documents without page numbers, use paragraph number(s) if visible, separated by a comma from author's name; the abbreviation for "paragraph(s)" is "par(s)." If sections are numbered, use these, preceded by a comma and the abbreviation "sec."

If you are referring to a website itself, rather than a specific part, include the author's name within the sentence and do not use any numbering.

Citation of entire website. Give the author's last name within the sentence:

> In his article, Dillon compares reading practices for print media to those for electronic media.

Citation from specific passage. The specific location is given in the parenthetical citation:

> One firmly entrenched belief is that reading screens will never replace reading books and other print media (Dillon, sec. 1).

Website by an unknown author. A site without an author's name follows the guidelines for a print document by an unknown author and uses the site title or an abbreviated form to direct readers to the source of any information:

> ("LHC Machine Outreach")

MLA In-Text Citations: Non-textual Sources

Film, video, audio, TV broadcasts, musical recordings, and other non-textual media. Give the name of the individual most relevant to your discussion in the text. In the case of a film, this could be the director, performer, screenwriter, or other contributor(s):

> Francis Ford Coppola's film *The Conversation* explores the psychology of surveillance.

If your focus is on the whole work, use only the title. In the "Works Cited" section, the entry would be alphabetized under *C* for Coppola, the film's producer.

MLA Entries in the "Works Cited" Section

The "Works Cited" section containing complete retrieval information appears at the end of your essay and on a new page that continues the numbers of your essay. The list is double-spaced with a one-inch (2.5 cm) margin. Omit words like "Press," "Inc.," and "Co." after the publisher name (but university presses should be abbreviated *UP*). Common abbreviations used in MLA style include

assn. (association)	
ch. (chapter)	pt. (part)
ed. (editor[s], edition)	rev. (revised)
fwd. (foreword)	rpt. (reprint)
introd. (introduction)	sec. (section)
P (Press)	trans. (translator)
par. (paragraph)	U (University)
pars. (paragraphs)	vol. (volume)

General Guidelines

- The title, "Works Cited," is centred an inch (2.5 cm) from the top of the page without underlining or bolding.

- The list is alphabetized by author's last name; each entry begins flush with the margin with subsequent lines indented half an inch (1.25 cm). Do not number entries.
- The standard MLA citation begins with the author's last name, followed by a complete first name (unless the author has published only initials). Italicize book titles and titles of other complete works, such as plays, films, and artistic performances—along with journal titles and websites; place quotation marks around titles of articles, essays, book chapters, short stories, poems, web pages, and TV episodes.
- The first letter of every major word in the title is capitalized, even if the source did not do so.
- The medium of publication or a similar descriptor is included, usually as the last element, unless the date of access is required in an electronic source.

Specific Examples

Sample book entry. List book (or pamphlet/brochure) data in this sequence: author; title (italicized); place of publication; shortened version of the publisher's name (remove articles *A* or *The* and abbreviations); year of publication; publication medium:

> Thompson, Neville. *Canada and the End of the Imperial Dream*. Don Mills: Oxford UP, 2013. Print.

Sample journal entry. List journal article data in this sequence: author; title of article (in quotation marks); title of journal (italicized); volume number; issue number; year of publication; inclusive pages; publication medium:

> Valkenburg, Patti M., and Peter Jochen. "Who Visits Online Dating Sites? Exploring Some Characteristics of Online Daters." *CyberPsychology and Behavior* 10.6 (2007): 849–52. Print.

Kinds of Authors

Work by one author (book). See above, "Sample book entry."

Work by two or three authors. Only the first author's complete name is inverted, with a comma before *and*:

> Saul, Nick, and Andrea Curtis. *The Stop: How the Fight for Good Food Transformed a Community and Inspired a Movement*. Toronto: Random House, 2013. Print.

Work by more than three authors. MLA style provides two possibilities: (1) the complete names of all authors, reversing the name of the first author only and including a comma between authors' names; or (2) the complete name of just the first author plus the abbreviation "et al." ("and others"):

> Festial, Lawrence, Harold Inch, Susan Gomez, and Komiko Smith. *When Economics Fails*. Minneapolis: U of Minnesota P, 1956. Print.

Or:

> Festial, Lawrence, et al. *When Economics Fails*. Minneapolis: U of Minnesota P, 1956. Print.

The order for most "Works Cited" entries is author's last name and first name; title of work; publication details, which vary depending on whether the work is a book, a journal article, or an electronic document; and medium of publication.

In a work by two or three authors, all authors are listed with only the first author's name inverted. Use a comma between first author's first name and the word *and*. With more than three authors, you may name all authors or only the first and use abbreviation "et al." to indicate there are at least three more authors.

Two or more works by the same author. Works by the same author are arranged chronologically from earliest to most recent. The author's name appears in the first listing only, with three em dashes (long dashes) substituted for it in the additional citations:

> Foucault, Michel. *Discipline and Punish: The Birth of the Prison*. Trans. Alan Sheridan. New York: Random, 1977. Print.
>
> — — —. *The History of Sexuality*. Trans. Robert Hurley. 3 vols. New York: Random, 1978. Print.

Different works by two authors with the same last name. The alphabetical order of the first names determines the sequence:

> Taylor, Dylan. "The Cognitive Neuroscience of Insight." *Psychological Inquiry* 18.4 (2009): 111–18. Print.
>
> Taylor, Sara. "Creativity Unbound: New Theoretical Approaches." *Creative Being* 2.1 (2009): 14–23. Print.

One work with two authors. If two works have the same first authors, the order is determined by the last name of the second author:

> Srivastava, Sarita, and Margot Francis. "The Problem of 'Authentic Experience.'" *Critical Sociology* 32.2–3 (2006): 275–307. Print
>
> Srivastava, Sarita, and Mary-Jo Nadeau. "From the Inside: Anti-Racism in Social Movements." *New Socialist* 42 (2003): n. pag. 18 May 2006. Web. 8 Dec. 2009.

Group or organization as author (corporate author). Use the full group name in place of an author's name (if the organization name begins with an article such as *The*, omit it):

> Education International. *Guide to Universities & Colleges in Canada*. Victoria: EI Education International, 2014 ed. Print.

When a work has a group, rather than an individual, author, the group name takes the place of the author's name.

Work with unknown author, publisher, or publication location (non-electronic). If the work does not provide an author's name, list it alphabetically by title. For missing publication details, use the following abbreviations: Before the colon, "N.p." means "no place," and after the colon it means "no publisher"; "N.d." means "no date." Use square brackets to identify any information that isn't from the source; if information may be unreliable, add a question mark.

No author name (unsigned encyclopedia entry):

> "Interveners." *Canadian Encyclopedia*. 2014 ed. Print.

No publisher. In this example, the publisher is unknown; place of publication is tentatively identified as Ontario:

> Webb, Noah. *The Great Haileybury Forest Fire*. [Ontario?]: n.p. 1971. Print.

No publishing place or date:

> Case, Michael. *Opus Dei*. N.p.: Slipshod P, n.d. Print.

Source Type

Work by author with an editor or translator. Begin with the author's name unless you refer primarily to the work of the editor (for example, his or her introduction or notes); the original publication date can be included after the title. Follow the same format for a translated work. "Ed." is used for one or more editors.

Referring primarily to the text. The first date indicates the year that the book was originally published:

> Hawthorne, Nathaniel. *The Scarlet Letter*. 1850. Ed. John Stephen Martin. Peterborough: Broadview, 1995. Print.

Referring primarily to editor's work:

> Martin, John Stephen, ed. *The Scarlet Letter*. By Nathaniel Hawthorne. 1850. Peterborough: Broadview, 1995. Print.

Translated work. The abbreviation "Trans." precedes the translator's name after the work's title:

> Calvino, Italo. *Why Read the Classics?* Trans. Martin McLaughlin. New York: Pantheon, 1999. Print.

Chapter or other type of selection, such as an essay, in edited volume. Begin with the author's name and the chapter (or essay) title. Follow with the book title and the book editors' names, preceded by "Ed." and not inverted. Conclude with the publication information, complete page range, and publication medium:

> Sanders, Douglas E. "Some Current Issues Affecting Indian Government." *Pathways to Self-Determination: Canadian Indians and the Indian State*. Ed. Leroy Little Bear, Menno Boldt, and J. Anthony Long. Toronto: U of Toronto P, 1984. 113–21. Print.

If you use more than one work from the same collection, you can economize by creating one entry for the work as a whole and abbreviated entries for specific works.

Main entry:

> Little Bear, Leroy, Menno Boldt, and J. Anthony Long, eds. *Pathways to Self-Determination: Canadian Indians and the Indian State*. Toronto: U of Toronto P, 1984. Print.

Specific entry using Sanders, above; other essays in the work would follow the same format:

> Sanders, Douglas E. "Some Current Issues Affecting Indian Government." Little Bear, Boldt, and Long. 113–21.

> In an edited volume, including an anthology, begin with the author's name and the work title. Follow with the book title and the editor name, preceded by "Ed." and not inverted. If you use more than one selection from the volume, you can create one entry for the work as a whole and abbreviated entries for specific works.

Introduction, preface, foreword, or afterword. Begin with the name of the author of the section, followed by the section name (not in quotation marks). The title of the complete work comes next, then the work's author preceded by *By*:

> Scholes, Robert. Foreword. *The Fantastic: A Structural Approach to a Literary Genre*. By Tzvetan Todorov. Trans. Richard Howard. Ithaca, NY: Cornell UP, 1975. v–xi. Print.

Volume in multivolume work. State the volume number if you use just the one volume:

> Bosworth, A. B., ed. *A Historical Commentary on Arrian's History of Alexander*. Vol. 1. London: Oxford UP, 1980. Print.

If you use more than one volume, give the number of volumes in the whole work instead of specific volume numbers:

> Bosworth, A. B., ed. *A Historical Commentary on Arrian's History of Alexander*. 2 vols. London: Oxford UP, 1980. Print.

In your essay, the parenthetical reference would include the author's name and volume number followed by a colon; after a space, include page numbers:

> (Bosworth 1: 212)

Second or subsequent edition of a work. Include the edition number after the title (or editor, translator, etc.):

> Suzuki, David, Aaron Griffiths, and Rebecca Lewontin. *An Introduction to Genetic Analysis*. 4th ed. New York: Freeman, 1989. Print.

Book published before 1900. The publisher's name can be omitted; between the place of publication and the year, insert only a comma:

> Baring Gould, S. *Old Country Life*. 5th ed. London, 1895. Print.

Article in a journal. Whether the numbering of the journal continues with each succeeding issue in a volume (continuous pagination) or begins at *1* in every issue, you should include both volume and issue number:

> Machado, Mariana V., and Helena Cortez-Pinto. "The Dark Side of Sports: Using Steroids May Harm Your Liver." *Liver International* 13.1 (2011): 280-81. Print.

If the journal does not use both volume and issue in its numbering, follow the journal's numbering system.

Article in a magazine. Cite the complete date (day, month, year) if the magazine is issued every week or every two weeks; if issued monthly or every two months, include the month and year:

> Knapp, Lonny. "Licensing Music to the Film and Television Industries." *Canadian Musician* Sept./Oct. 2007: 49–56. Print.

After the journal name, always include the volume and issue number in your citation, and follow with the year (in parentheses), colon, page range, and medium.

→ For an article in a journal accessed electronically, see page 250.

If the article breaks off and continues later in the work, cite the first page number followed by a plus sign—not the page range (e.g., "12+" indicates the article begins on page 12 and continues somewhere after page 12).

Article in a newspaper. Cite the author if given; if no author, begin with the title. Give the day, month, and year; give the page number, preceded by the section number or letter if the newspaper contains more than one section:

> "Lawyer Seeks Mistrial for Client Accused of Illegal Midwifery." *National Post* 20 April 2013: A8. Print.

If the article breaks off and continues later in the work, cite the first page number followed by a plus sign—not the page range. A letter to the editor follows the same format and includes *Letter* after the title.

Book/movie review. Follow the reviewer's name by the title of review; if there is no title, continue with *Rev. of* and the book/movie title followed by *by* and the author's or director's name. Conclude with publication information:

> Mihm, Stephen. Rev. of *Swindled: The Dark History of Food Fraud, from Poisoned Candy to Counterfeit Coffee*, by Bee Wilson. *Business History Review* 83.2 (2006): 379–81. Print.

Government document. If the author is unknown, begin with the government name followed by the agency (e.g., ministry, department, crown corporation) and document name:

> British Columbia. Office of the Auditor General. *Salmon Forever: An Assessment of the Provincial Role in Sustaining Wild Salmon*. Victoria: Office of the Auditor General of British Columbia, 2009. Print.

Indirect source. Cite the work where you found the citation rather than the original text:

> Lindemann, Erika. *A Rhetoric for Writing Teachers*. 4th ed. New York: Oxford University Press, 2001. Print.

See above, "A citation referring to an indirect source" under MLA In-Text Citations, for the in-text format.

Personal communication, including interview. Include a description of the communication. *TS* in this example stands for "typescript":

> Carr, Emily. Letter to Lawren Harris. 12 December 1940. TS.

MLA Web Publication Citations

Where some relevant information is unavailable (such as page or paragraph numbers), cite what you can to enable the reader to access the source. Note that a URL, enclosed in angled brackets, is given only if the specific page of the website would be otherwise hard to locate. (If you need to divide the URL between two lines, break it after single or double slashes.) The date of access, however, is an essential part of web citations.

When you type In a URL, most word processing programs automatically flag it as a hyperlink. This means that the URLs are underlined and usually show up in blue. However, before printing your essay, make sure all URLs show up as plain text and not as hyperlinks.

The first date in a web entry is the date of the site itself or most recent update; the second is the date you last accessed the site. The medium of publication precedes the access date.

Sample electronic citation. Give the website title after work's title, followed by the site's publisher or sponsor; if unavailable, use "N.p." The first date is that of the website creation or its latest update. The date that follows the publication medium (Web) is the date of your latest access:

Czekaj, Laura. "Promises Fulfilled: Looking at the Legacy of Thousands of Black Slaves Who Fled to Canada in the 1800s." *InnovationCanada.ca*. Canada Foundation for Innovation, 7 Feb. 2009. Web. 19 Apr. 2010.

Group, organization (e.g., corporate or government) **website**. If there is no author, list the entry by the organization's name. In this example, the URL is included because the page might be hard to locate otherwise:

Environment Canada. "10 Things You Should Know About Climate Change." 12 Aug. 2012. Web. 10 May 2014. <http://www.ec.gc.ca/cc/default.asp?lang=En&n=2F049262-1>.

Article in online-only journal. Online-only journals may not include page numbers, in which case use the abbreviation "n. pag." (no pagination) after the website date:

Rye, B. J., Pamela Elmslie, and Amanda Chalmers. "Meeting a Transsexual Person: Experience within a Classroom Setting." *Canadian On-Line Journal of Queer Studies in Education* 3.1 (2007): n. pag. Web. 21 Oct. 2010.

Internet article based on a print source and retrieved from a database. In addition to the information required for the print version of a journal article, the database name and date of access are included:

Barton, Sylvia S. "Discovering the Literature on Aboriginal Diabetes in Canada: A Focus on Holistic Methodologies." *Canadian Journal of Nursing Research* 40.4 (2008): 26–54. *Ingenta*. Web. 11 May 2010.

In addition to the information included in the print version, journal articles retrieved from a database require the database name and date of access, which follows the medium of publication.

Work found online that originally appeared in print. Include details of the print source and follow with the website title, publication medium, and date of access:

Douglass, Frederick. "My Escape from Slavery." *The Century Illustrated Magazine* Nov. 1881: 125–31. *Electronic Text Center, University of Virginia Library*. Web. 14 Jan. 2011.

Letter or email. If the letter is published, cite it as you would a work in an edited volume, adding the date of the letter. If it is a personal letter or email, include a description, such as *Message to the author*, and date:

Barrett, Anthony. "Re: *Lives of the Caesars*." Message to the author. 15 Aug. 2014. Email.

If the message is a typed letter, use *TS* (typescript) as publication medium.

Message posted to online forum, discussion group, or blog post. Follow the guidelines for "Sample electronic citation," above. If no title is given, the entry should include a generic label after the author's name. In this example, the author did not include a first name, so this information cannot be given:

> Koolvedge. Online posting. *Adbusters.org*. Adbusters Media Foundation, 8 Aug. 2009. Web. 30 Aug. 2010. <https://www.adbusters.org/blogs/dispatches/massacre-peru.html#comments>.

MLA Citations for Non-textual Sources

Your citation should begin with the name of the person(s) most relevant to your discussion, along with an abbreviated description of their role. For example, if your paper is about actors, you can cite their contribution in a film either with or instead of the name of the director.

Lecture or other oral presentation. Begin with the speaker's name, presentation title, meeting and/or sponsor (if applicable), location detail, and date. Conclude with the equivalent of publication medium (e.g., *Lecture*, *Reading*):

> Armstrong, Nancy. "Darwin's Paradox." Department of English. David Strong Building, University of Victoria, Victoria. 2 April 2014. Lecture.

Film or video. Begin with the work's title unless you are referring mainly to one person's contribution (for example, a performer or writer). Follow with the names of the most relevant individuals and conclude with the distributor's name and year of release.

Citing the film:

> *Apocalypse Now*. Dir. Francis Ford Coppola. United Artists, 1979. Film.

Citing a specific individual (the abbreviation "perf." stands for *performer*):

> Brando, Marlon, perf. *Apocalypse Now*. Dir. Francis Ford Coppola. United Artists, 1979. Film.

Video-posting website. This format closely follows that of an electronic citation (see p. 250) with addition of "media type text" after title. If the author is not given, begin with the poster's username:

> BrokenRhythms. "Grim Promo." Online video clip, *YouTube*. YouTube, 9 Aug. 2013. Web. 1 Sept. 2013.

Performance (e.g., play, concert). Begin with the title of the performance and follow with relevant information, usually names of the writer, director, and main performers. Conclude with the company name, theatre, city, date of performance, and the word *Performance*:

> *Macbeth*. By William Shakespeare. Dir. Des McAnuff. Perf. Colm Feore and Yanna McIntosh. Stratford Shakespeare Festival Company. Festival Theatre, Stratford, ON. 1 June 2013. Performance.

If you are citing one individual's contribution, begin with that person's name (see "Film or video," above).

Episode of a television or radio series. Use the following order: title of episode (in quotation marks), title of program (italicized), network, call letters of local station, and city, if relevant. Conclude with broadcast date and medium of reception:

"Man of Science, Man of Faith." *Lost*. Dir. Jack Bender. CTV. CFTO, Toronto, 21 Sept. 2005. Television.

Information relevant to the episode (e.g., the writer or director) follows the episode title; information relevant to the series follows the series title. If you are citing one individual's contribution, begin with that person's name (see "Film or video," above).

Music. Use the following order: performer (or other most relevant individual), recording title, label, year of issue, and medium (e.g., CD, LP):

Morrison, Van. *Too Long in Exile*. Polydor, 1993. CD.

If citing a specific song, place its name in quotation marks after the performer's name; use a period before and after the song's name.

Work of visual art. Use the following order: artist, title (italicized), date of composition (or "n.d." if this is unavailable), medium of composition, name of institution that contains the work, and city:

Escher, M. C. *Drawing Hands*. 1948. Lithograph. Cornelius Collection, National Gallery of Art, Washington.

Interview. Begin with the name of the interview subject and follow with the interviewer's name preceded by *Interview by*. Conclude with publication details:

Murakami, Haruki. Interview by Maik Grossekathöfer. *Spiegel Online International* 20 Feb. 2008. Web. 8 Dec. 2012.

If you are the interviewer, give the name of the interview subject followed by the interview medium and date:

McWhirter, George. Email Interview. 2 June 2013.

MLA Notes

MLA permits either footnotes (at the bottom of the page) or endnotes (at the end of the document) for information you feel is valuable but which does not fit well within the text. You may use notes to expand on a point, to cite multiple sources, to suggest additional reading, or to cite related points of interest. Each note is indicated by a superscript (raised) number directly to the right of the word most related to the note, or at the end of a phrase; they are numbered consecutively through your paper. Format the notes to match the rest of the document by double-spacing and indenting each note.

APA Documentation Style

In the social sciences, the principal documentation style has been developed by the American Psychological Association (APA). It is sometimes used in the sciences as well. The APA publishes a manual (*Publication Manual of the American Psychological*

Association, 6th ed.) and maintains a website (http://www.apastyle.org) with updates, FAQs, and specific information on Internet citations.

APA style is parenthetical, meaning that whenever you directly quote or paraphrase an author in your essay, or use an author's idea, you give the author's last name and the year of the work in parentheses; you usually include page numbers as well. Then, you provide a more complete description of all the sources in the last section of your essay, titled "References."

APA In-Text Citations

General Guidelines

- APA in-text formats include the authors and year. If the author is named in a signal phrase (e.g., "Ashton found that . . ."), the year follows the author's name and precedes the verb: "Ashton (2008) found that . . . ." Otherwise, the publication year follows the author's name in the end parentheses: (Ashton, 2008).
- A specific reference, such as a direct quotation or paraphrase, requires a page number. Use the abbreviation "p." for "page" and "pp." for "pages."
- Use commas to separate items in the citation.

APA in-text style includes the author's last name, year of publication, and, usually, page number(s).

Specific Examples

Citation including a direct quotation. Give the last names of the authors, a comma, year of publication, a comma, and page number(s) all in parentheses.

No signal phrase. In this example, the author, Cleather, is not named in a signal phrase, so the parenthetical citation includes the author's name:

> During World Wars I and II, the Canadian government often employed masseuses because surgery and medical care were insufficient "to restore severely wounded men" (Cleather, 1995, p. ix).

Signal phrase. After the author is named in the signal phrase, follow with the year in parentheses. Place the page number at the end of the reference. In this example, the authors, Gillam and Wooden, are named in the signal phrase, so the parenthetical citation consists only of the page number. Note that the year follows the authors' names:

> Gillam and Wooden (2008) argue that Pixar studio films show "a kinder, gentler understanding of what it means to be a man" (p. 3).

When you name the source in a signal phrase, the publication year (in parentheses) follows the author's name.

Block quotation. A quotation of 40 words or more is placed on a new line and indented one half-inch (1.25 cm) from the left margin. Quotation marks are omitted, and the quotation is double-spaced. The author's name, publication year, and page number appear in parentheses at the end of the quotation *after* the final period:

> . . . and older children. (Gillam & Wooden, 2008, pp. 81–82)

Citation including a specific reference (such as a paraphrase). Give the name of the authors, year of publication, and page numbers:

> Most of the profits from BC's aquaculture industry go to Norwegians, who control 92 percent of the industry (Macdonald, 2009, pp. 148–149).

You do not include the page number(s) in a citation that refers to the work as a whole rather than to a specific page(s).

Citation for a non-specific reference. A non-specific reference applies to the essay as a whole rather than to a specific page in the work. Give the author's last name and publication year:

> Conservation biologists agree that protecting habitats is the most effective way to conserve biological diversity (Primack, 2000).

An indirect source is cited in another source. If you have to cite information from an indirect source, use the phrase *as cited in* followed by the place where you got the information.

Citation referring to an indirect source. If it is necessary to refer to a source found in another work, include the original author in the sentence. In parentheses, use the phrase *as cited in*, followed by the name of the source of the information and publication year:

> Francis Bacon (as cited in Lindemann, 2001) observed that language affects our thinking when he said that "words react on the understanding" (p. 93).

In the "References" section, list the details for the indirect source.

Personal communication, including interviews. Give the author's name, including initials, the phrase *personal communication,* and a date:

> (J. Derrida, personal communication, September 20, 2000)

Personal communications are not listed in the "References" section.

You may include more than one source in a single citation. Order them alphabetically and separate them by semicolons.

Multiple sources in one citation. You may cite more than one source in a single citation if the point you are making applies to both. Order sources alphabetically by last name and separate them by semicolons:

> The practices of teaching composition in college have not radically changed in the last few decades (Bishop, 2005; Williams, 2007).

APA In-Text Citations by Format

Kinds of Authors

Work by one author (book or article). Give the author's last name, comma, year of publication, comma, and page numbers (if required):

> (Bloom, 2002, p. xviii)

Note that a book with both an author and an editor is usually cited by author.

When you refer to a work with more than one author, use an ampersand (&) to separate the last author's name from the preceding name.

Work by two authors. Give the last names of both authors with an ampersand (&) between them, comma, date, comma, and page numbers (if required):

> (Higgins & Wilson-Baptist, 1999, p. 44)

When naming the authors in the text of your essay, as in a signal phrase, use the word *and* instead of an ampersand:

> Higgins and Wilson-Baptist (1999) argue that "a tourist exists outside of experience. A traveller, though, submerges herself in the new" (p. 44).

Works by three, four, or five authors. List the last names of all authors for the first citation. For later citations, give the last name of the first author followed by the abbreviation "et al." with the publication year. If the authors are mentioned more than once in a paragraph, the publication year is not included after the first reference:

> (Higgins, Wilson-Baptist, & Krasny, 2001); later citations in the same paragraph: (Higgins et al.)

Work by six or more authors. Give the last name of the first author followed by the abbreviation "et al.", comma, and publication year:

> (Terracciano et al., 2005)

Two or more works by the same author in the same year. Add alphabetical letters in lower case (a, b, c) to distinguish works chronologically in that year. In this example, the *a* after the year indicates that this is the first of at least two works by the same author in 1980 that you have used:

> . . . self-enforced discipline (Foucault, 1980a, p. 37)

Two authors with the same last name. Include the authors' initials separated from the last names by commas:

> (Sinkinson, S., & Sinkinson, B., 2001, pp. 225–237)

Group or organization as author (corporate author). If the group title is long, or is well known by an acronym or abbreviation of the name (for example, the United Nations Children's Fund is commonly known as UNICEF), for the first citation include the entire title where the author's name would appear; also give the acronym in square brackets, comma, and publication year. Use the abbreviation with the publication year throughout the rest of the paper. If the group name is not well-known, use the full name with the publication year each time:

> (American Educational Research Association [AERA], 2001), later citations: (AERA, 2001)

Work by an unknown author (including many dictionary and encyclopedia articles). Put the first few words of the article/chapter title in quotation marks followed by a comma and the year of publication:

> ("Plea to City Hall," 2003)

Author designated as "Anonymous." Cite in the same way as a named author:

> (Anonymous, 1887, p. 12)

Republished book. Give both original and current publication dates:

> (Lacan, 1966/1977)

For three to five authors, list the last names of all authors in parentheses for the first citation, and the name of the first author and abbreviation "et al." in later citations. For six or more authors, name the first author followed by "et al."

If no author is given, use the name of group or organization in place of the author's name.

If you cannot locate page or paragraph numbers in an electronic document, include the section heading in quotation marks and count by paragraphs from the heading to the appropriate paragraph(s).

APA In-Text Citations: Electronic Sources

If no page numbers are given, cite by the paragraph number preceded by the abbreviation "para." If neither page nor paragraph numbers are given but the document includes section headings, cite the heading title in quotation marks, count the paragraphs, and include paragraph number(s) in which the material occurs:

(Kao & Choi, 2010, "Economic Variables," para. 5)

Sample in-text Internet citation. Include the author's last name, comma, year site was mounted or updated, comma, title (if applicable), comma, and page or paragraph number:

(Gregoire, 2000, "Bones and Teeth," para. 5)

Internet site with an unknown author. Give the title (abbreviated if needed) in quotation marks, a comma, the year site was created or updated, a comma, and a page or paragraph reference:

("Muchinfo's Poll," 2002, para. 16)

Internet site without a date. Use the abbreviation "n.d." if no date is available:

(Hannak, n.d., para. 2)

APA In-Text Citations: Non-textual Sources

Film, video, audio, TV broadcasts, and musical recordings. Give the most senior production person's name, comma, and year of public release or broadcast:

(Coppola, 1979)

Installation, event, performance, or work of art. Give the name of the artist, comma, and date of showing or creation:

(Byrdmore, 2006)

APA Entries in the References List

In APA style, the "References" section containing complete retrieval information appears at the end of your essay and begins on a new page that continues the page numbering of your essay. The references list is double-spaced with a one-inch (1.25 cm) margin. Omit words like "Publishers," "Inc.," and "Co." after publishers' names, but write out complete names of associations, corporations, and university presses. Some of the most common abbreviations include

ed. (edition)	para. (paragraph)
Ed. (Editor)	Pt. (Part)
Eds. (Editors)	Rev. ed. (Revised edition)
No. (Number)	Trans. (Translator[s])
p. (page)	Vol. (Volume)
pp. (pages)	Vols. (Volumes)

General Guidelines

- The title is centred an inch (2.5 cm) from the top of the page.
- The list is alphabetized by author's last name; each entry begins flush left with the margin; subsequent lines are indented one inch (2.5 cm) from margin. Items are not numbered.
- The standard APA reference begins with the author's last name followed by initials, not given names. Titles of full-length works are italicized.
- Capitalize only the following elements of book and article titles: first letter of the first word, first letter after a colon, first letter of all proper nouns, and acronyms like NFB or CBC, regardless of how the original is capitalized. Capitalize the names of journals exactly as they appear in the published work.

Specific Examples

Sample book entry. List book and report data in the following order: author, publication date, title, place of publication, publisher:

> Thompson, N. (2013). *Canada and the end of the imperial dream*. Don Mills, ON: Oxford University Press.

Sample journal entry. List journal article data in the following order: author, date of publication, title of article, title of journal, volume number, issue number (if required), page range, and DOI or URL:

> Valkenburg, P. M., & Jochen, P. (2007). Who visits online dating sites? Exploring some characteristics of online daters. *CyberPsychology and Behavior, 10*, 849–852. doi:10.1089/cpb.2007.9941

A digital object identifier (DOI) is included in many journal articles whether in print or electronic format; it is not followed by a period. A DOI enables readers to locate documents throughout the Internet.

> The order for most final-page citations is the author's last name and initial(s); publication date; title of work; and publication details, which vary depending on whether the work is a book, a journal article, or an electronic document.

Kinds of Authors

Work by one author. See above, "Sample book entry."

Work by two authors. Use an ampersand (&) to separate the authors' names, and invert the names of both authors with commas between the last name and initial and a period at the end:

> Saul, N., & Curtis, A. (2103). *The Stop: How the fight for good food transformed a community and inspired a movement*. Toronto, ON: Random House.

> With two to seven authors, invert all authors' names and use an ampersand (&) between the last and second-last name.

Work by three to seven authors. List all the authors:

> Festial, L., Ian, H., & Gomez, S. (1956). *When economics fails*. Minneapolis, MN: University of Minnesota Press.

With eight or more authors, list the first six authors and the last author, with three ellipsis points between the sixth and the final author.

Work by eight or more authors. List the first six authors and the last author, with three ellipsis points between the sixth and the final author:

Terracciano, A., Abdel-Khalek, A. M., Ádám, N., Adamovová, L., Ahn, C.-K., Ahn, H. N., . . . McCrae, R. R. (2005). National character does not reflect mean personality trait levels in 49 cultures. *Science, 310*, 96–100. doi:10.1126/science.1117199

Two or more works by the same author. Works by the same author are listed chronologically, earliest to latest:

Arrange works by same author chronologically from earliest to latest.

Foucault, M. (1977). *Discipline and punish: The birth of the prison*. A. Sheridan (Trans.). New York, NY: Random House.

Foucault, M. (1980). *The history of sexuality* (Vol. 1). R. Hurley (Trans.). New York, NY: Random House.

Works with the same publication year are listed alphabetically by first major word of the title; lowercase letters follow the year within the parentheses. Below, the *h* in *history* precedes the *P* in *Power*:

Foucault, M. (1980a). *The history of sexuality* (Vol. 1). R. Hurley (Trans.). New York, NY: Random House.

Foucault, M. (1980b). *Power/knowledge: Selected interviews and other writings 1972–1977*. C. Gordon (Ed.). Brighton, England: Harvester Press.

Different works by two authors with the same last name. Alphabetical order of the first names determines the sequence:

Taylor, D. (2009). The cognitive neuroscience of insight. *Psychological Inquiry, 18*(4), 111–118.

Taylor, S. (2009). Creativity unbound: New theoretical approaches. *Creative Being, 2*(1), 14–23.

One work with two authors. If two works have the same first authors, the order is determined by the last name of the second author:

Jason, L. A., & Klich, M. M. (1982). Use of feedback in reducing television watching. *Psychological Reports, 51*, 812–814.

Jason, L. A., & Rooney-Rebeck, P. (1984). Reducing excessive television viewing. *Child & Family Behavior Therapy, 6*, 61–69.

When a work has a group author, rather than an individual author, use the group name in place of the author's name.

Group or organization as author (corporate author). Use the full group name in place of the author's name (if the organization name begins with an article such as *The*, omit it):

Education International. (2014). *Guide to universities & colleges in Canada*. Victoria, BC: EI Education International.

Work by an unknown author (non-electronic source), such as an entry in a reference book. List it alphabetically by the first major word in the title:

> Interveners. (2014). In *Canadian Encyclopedia* (Vol. 11, pp. 344–348). Ottawa. ON: Smith Press.

When an author is listed as "Anonymous," alphabetize by the letter *A*.

Work with no date. Replace the date with "n.d.":

> Gaucher, D. (n.d.).

Source Type

Work with an editor. Begin with the name of the editor(s) followed by "Ed." (one editor) or "Eds." (more than one editor) in parentheses:

> Corcoran, B., Hayhoe, M., & Pradl, G. M. (Eds.). (1994). *Knowledge in the making: Challenging the text in the classroom*. Portsmouth, NH: Boynton/Cook.

Chapter or other type of selection, such as an essay, in edited volume. Begin with the author name, year, and chapter or essay title. Follow with *In* and the name(s) of the book editor(s), not inverted, and the abbreviation Ed. or Eds. The citation concludes with the book title, page range in parentheses, and publication information:

> Sanders, D. E. (1984). Some current issues affecting Indian government. In L. Little Bear, M. Boldt, & J. A. Long (Eds.), *Pathways to self-determination: Canadian Indians and the Indian state* (pp. 113–121). Toronto, ON: University of Toronto Press.

The usual order for an essay or other selection in an edited book is author name, year, essay title, book editor's name preceded by *In*, the abbreviation "Ed.," the book title and page range, and other publication details.

Translated work. The translator's name is placed in parentheses after the work's title, followed by "Trans."

> Lacan, J. (1977). *Écrits: A selection* (A. Sheridan, Trans.). New York, NY: W. W. Norton. (Original work published 1966)

Volume in multivolume work. Include the volume number after the title:

> Bosworth, A. B. (Ed.). (1995). *A historical commentary on Arrian's history of Alexander* (Vol. 1). London, England: Oxford University Press.

If referring to more than one volume, give the specific volumes or range (e.g., Vols. 1–3).

Second or subsequent edition of a work. Include the edition number after the title:

> Suzuki, D. T., Griffiths, A. J., & Lewontin, R. C. (1989). *An introduction to genetic analysis* (4th ed.). New York, NY: W. H. Freeman.

Article in a journal with continuous pagination. If the numbering in each issue continues from the previous issue, include the volume but not the issue number. Page numbers in journals are not preceded by "p." or "pp.":

> Garner, R. (2003). Political ideologies and the moral status of animals. *Journal of Political Ideologies, 8*, 233–246.

Whether you include the issue number depends on whether each journal issue is numbered separately (include the issue number) or numbering continues from the previous issue (do not include the issue number).

If the article is assigned a DOI, it should be included after the page range (see APA Internet Entries in the "References" Section, below).

Article in a journal that is paginated by issue. If every issue begins with page number *1*, include both the volume (italicized) and issue number (in parentheses and not italicized):

→ For an article in a journal accessed electronically, see pages 261–262.

> Machado, M. V., & Cortez-Pinto, H. (2011). The dark side of sports: Using steroids may harm your liver. *Liver International, 13*(1), 280–281.

Article in a magazine. Cite the complete date beginning with the year; follow with a comma and month or month and day. Include the volume and issue number if available:

> Knapp, L. (2007, September/October). Licensing music to the film and television industries. *Canadian Musician, 29*(5), 49–56.

Article in a newspaper. List the author if it is given; if no author is given, begin with the title. For page numbers, use the abbreviation "p." or "pp." If the article breaks off and continues later in the work, give all page numbers, separated by commas, or the page range:

> Lawyer seeks mistrial for client accused of illegal midwifery. (2013, April 20). *National Post*, p. A8.

A letter to the editor or an editorial follows the same format and includes specific information in square brackets after the title (e.g., [*Letter to the editor*]).

Book/movie review. Follow the article format but in brackets include the book title and the reviewer's name, preceded by *Review of* and the medium (e.g., "Review of the DVD . . ."):

> Mihm, S. (2009). Swindled: The dark history of food fraud, from poisoned candy to counterfeit coffee [Review of the book *Swindled: The dark history of food fraud, from poisoned candy to counterfeit coffee*, by B. Wilson]. *Business History Review, 83*(2), 379–381.

Government document. If the author is unknown, begin with the name of the government followed by the agency (e.g., ministry, department, Crown corporation) and the document name. In this example, because the publisher is the same as the author (i.e., Office of the Auditor General of British Columbia), *Author* replaces the publisher's name:

If the author is unknown, begin with the name of the government followed by the agency (e.g., ministry, department, Crown corporation) and the document name. Report numbers can be included in parentheses right after the work's title.

> British Columbia. Office of the Auditor General. (2005). *Salmon forever: An assessment of the provincial role in sustaining wild salmon*. Victoria, BC: Author.

For government reports, along with similar documents, like issue briefs and working papers, the report number can be placed in parentheses after the work's title: (e.g., "Research Report No. 09.171").

Indirect source. List the work the citation comes from, not the original text:

> Lindemann, E. (2001). *A rhetoric for writing teachers*. (4th ed.). New York, NY: Oxford University Press.

Personal communication. Because they cannot be verified by the reader, personal communications (including emails, phone calls, interviews, and conversations) are not included in the list of references.

APA Internet Entries in the "References" Section

Online sources should include the elements of print sources in the same order with exact location information added as needed. If available, include the DOI, which is found with other publication information, such as the journal title and volume number, on the first page of the article. The DOI is a number–alphabet sequence that begins with *10*. It forms the last element in your citation sequence and, like a URL, is *not* followed by a period.

Cite the URL of the home page of the journal or book publisher if the DOI is unavailable or if your instructor tells you to do so. If the document would be hard to locate from the home page, provide the exact URL or as much as is needed for retrieval. More information on electronic reference formats recommended by the APA is available at http://blog.apastyle.org/apastyle/electronic-references/.

Sample electronic reference. Citation formats follow those of print sources with the website title replacing the journal title:

> Czekaj, L. (2009, February 7). Promises fulfilled: Looking at the legacy of thousands of black slaves who fled to Canada in the 1800s. *InnovationCanada.ca*. Retrieved from http://www.innovationcanada.ca/en/

Note the absence of a period after the URL. If it is necessary to break the URL from one line to the next, break *before punctuation*, such as the period before *innovationcanada* above; don't use a hyphen to break a URL unless it is part of the URL. Remember to remove the hyperlink from the URL before printing your essay.

Group or organization (e.g., corporate or government) **website**. If no author is given, list it by the organization's name. In this example, the complete URL is given because it might be hard to locate the document from the organization's home page:

> Environment Canada. (2009, August 12). 10 things you should know about climate change. Retrieved from http://www.ec.gc.ca/cc/default.asp?lang=En&n=2F049262-1

Article in online-only journal. In this example, the home page of the journal has been used for retrieval information:

> Rye, B. J., Elmslie, P., & Chalmers, A. (2007). Meeting a transsexual person: Experience within a classroom setting. *Canadian On-Line Journal of Queer Studies in Education, 3*(1). Retrieved from http://jps.library.utoronto.ca/index.php/jqstudies/index

---

Personal communications (including emails, phone calls, interviews, and conversations) are not included in the list of references.

Include the DOI (digital object identifier) for journal articles if available; otherwise, cite the URL of the home page of the journal or book publisher. The date of access is not usually required.

> If there is a DOI, or if there is no DOI and you include the journal home page, the database name can be omitted.

Article from a database (with a DOI). The database name is not usually required. In this example, the first part of the article is in quotation marks, indicating that a direct quotation is part of the title:

> Martel, M. (2009). "They smell bad, have diseases, and are lazy": RCMP officers reporting on hippies in the late sixties. *Canadian Historical Review, 90,* 215–245. doi:10.3138/chr.90.2.215

Article from a database (no DOI). The home page of the journal is used; the database name is not usually required:

> Barton, S. S. (2008). Discovering the literature on Aboriginal diabetes in Canada: A focus on holistic methodologies. *Canadian Journal of Nursing Research, 40*(4), 26–54. Retrieved from http://cjnr.mcgill.ca/

No author or date. Place "n.d." in parentheses:

> Hegemony. (n.d.). In *Merriam-Webster online dictionary*. Retrieved from http://www.merriam-webster.com/dictionary/hegemony

Electronic-only book. In this example, the hyphen after the first *mod* is part of the URL:

> Radford, B. (n.d.). *Soil to social*. Retrieved from http://on-line-books.ora.com/mod-bin/books.mod/javaref/javanut/index.htm

Electronic version of print book. Do not include publication details of the print version but include the reader version, if applicable, in brackets, and the DOI or URL:

> Douglass, F. (1881). My escape from slavery [MS Reader version]. Retrieved from http://etext.lib.virginia.edu/ebooks/

Message posted to online forum, discussion group, or blog post. Give the format of the message, such as *Web log message* or *Video file*, in brackets:

> Koolvedge. (2009, August 8). Reply to massacre in Peru [Web log message]. Retrieved from https://www.adbusters.org/blogs/dispatches/massacre-peru.html#comments

APA Citations for Non-textual Sources

Lecture or other oral presentation. Include the name of the lecturer, date (year, month day), lecture (topic) title, followed by *Lecture presented at* and location details, such as sponsoring agency or school department and/or building name, name of school, and location of school:

> Armstrong, M. (2009, April 2). *Darwin's paradox*. Lecture presented at David Strong Building, University of Victoria, Victoria, BC.

Film, video. Use the following order: producer, director, year, and film title, followed by *Motion Picture* in square brackets. Conclude with the country of origin and the studio:

> Coppola, F. F. (Producer & Director). (1979). *Apocalypse now* [Motion picture]. USA: Zoetrope Studios.

Video-posting website. Begin with the name of poster, if available, and follow with the screen name in brackets; if the poster name is unavailable, just use the screen name, as below. Conclude with retrieval information:

> BrokenRhythms. (2013, Aug. 9). *Grim promo*. [Video file]. Retrieved from http://youtube.com/dAe5b7vUXgU

Episode from a television series. Use the following order: writer, director, year, and episode title, followed by *Television series episode* in brackets. Conclude with the city and broadcasting company:

> Lindelof, D. (Writer), & Bender, J. (Director). (2005). Man of science, man of faith [Television series episode]. In J. J. Abrams (Executive producer), *Lost*. New York, NY: American Broadcasting.

Music. Use the following order: writer, copyright year, and song title, followed by the recording artist in brackets (if different from writer). Conclude with the album title preceded by *On*, the medium of recording in brackets, the city, and the label:

> Morrison, V. (1993). Gloria. On *Too long in exile* [CD]. London, England. Polydor.

If the recording date is different from the copyright year, provide this information in parentheses.

CMS Documentation (Notes) Style

The *Chicago Manual of Style* (CMS) numbered notes and bibliography system is used primarily in history and other humanities disciplines. This CMS style may also include at the end of the essay a list of sources in alphabetical order by last name. Sometimes the bibliography is omitted, when the notes provide all the details; however, you should include it unless told otherwise.

If you take history courses, you may be asked to document your essays using the CMS notes style (or a variant, Turabian style). You may also encounter this documentation style in your research. For this reason, the rudiments of CMS notes style are discussed below. You can consult a reliable online source, such as a library website, for information about hard-to-find formats. The *Chicago Manual of Style* website offers updates and sample formats at http://www.chicagomanualofstyle.org/home.html.

Guidelines are found in the 16th edition of *The Chicago Manual of Style* (2010), published by the University of Chicago Press, and *Chicago Manual of Style Online*. The CMS style uses footnotes (at the bottom of each page) or endnotes (at the end of the paper) to direct readers to the sources of the information cited. Most word-processing programs will format these notes for you (under References). A superscript number (in a smaller point size raised above the level of the rest of the sentence) immediately follows the final punctuation of the reference (e.g., appears after the last word and quotation mark of a direct quotation). This number refers to a note at the bottom of the page or the end of the document.

General Guidelines

- Each note is single-spaced with the first line indented five spaces and successive lines flush left.
- Full bibliographical details are given for first references: author's name (first names followed by surname); work's title; place of publication, publisher, date (in parentheses); and page number(s). Successive references are condensed. Unlike in-text numbers, the corresponding footnote/endnote numbers are the same point size as the rest of your text.
- Block quotations should be used for important passages of at least 100 words. Indent them five spaces from the left margin and omit quotation marks.
- The final section, usually titled "Bibliography," alphabetically lists by last name all works used in the essay. Not all works cited in notes are included in the bibliography—for example, personal communications, brief dictionary/encyclopedia entries, and newspaper articles may be omitted.
- Bibliography entries are single-spaced. Leave a blank line between each entry.

Sample Notes and Bibliographic Entries

Book—one author:

In-text reference:

Pringle believed "there is real need of authentic information" about social usage in Canada as distinct from the U.S. or Britain.[1]

Note for first reference:

1. Gertrude Pringle, *Etiquette in Canada: The Blue Book of Canadian Social Usage* (Toronto: McClelland & Stewart, 1932), vi.

Note for subsequent reference to same work:

3. Pringle, 28.

If more than one work by Pringle had been used, the title of the work (or a short form of it) would follow the author's last name with a comma to separate it from the page number.

Note for successive reference to same author:

4. Ibid., 16.

"Ibid." means "in the same place." If the page number is the same as in the preceding note, only "Ibid." is used; do not use "Ibid." unless the reference that *immediately* precedes is from the same source.

Bibliography:

Pringle, Gertrude. *Etiquette in Canada: The Blue Book of Canadian Social Usage.* Toronto: McClelland & Stewart, 1932.

Book—two or three authors:

Note:

> 2. Jung Chang and Jon Halliday, *Mao: The Unknown Story* (London, Vintage Books, 2005), 53.

Bibliography:

Chang, Jung, and Jon Halliday. *Mao: The Unknown Story.* London: Vintage Books, 2005.

Book—more than three authors. In the note give the name of the first author followed by *and others* or "et al." All authors are named in the bibliography entry. See "Journal article" below for examples.

Journal article:

Note:

> 5. Todd G. Morrison et al., "Canadian University Students' Perceptions of the Practices That Constitute 'Normal' Sexuality for Men and Women," *The Canadian Journal of Human Sexuality* 17, no. 4 (2008): 163.

Bibliography:

Morrison, Todd. G., Travis A. Ryan, Lisa Fox, Daragh T. McDermott, and Melanie A. Morrison. "Canadian University Students' Perceptions of the Practices That Constitute 'Normal' Sexuality for Men and Women." *The Canadian Journal of Human Sexuality* 17, no. 4 (2008): 161–71.

If the journal is **paginated by issue** (i.e., each issue begins with page 1), the issue number is included after the volume number; see example above. The season or month should be included if the issue number is not given: e.g., 165 (Spring 2010).

If the article is **accessed from a database**, follow the format above, but also include the DOI (if available) or URL, preceded by a comma (note) or period (bibliography entry). Include the date of access if your instructor requires it. (Examples below include access dates.)

Note:

> 6. Peter John Loewen, "Affinity, Antipathy and Political Participation: How Our Concern for Others Makes Us Vote," *Canadian Journal of Political Science* 43 (2010): 666, accessed October 2, 2013, doi:10.10170500084239100065X.

Bibliography:

Loewen, Peter John. "Affinity, Antipathy and Political Participation: How Our Concern for Others Makes Us Vote." *Canadian Journal of Political Science* 43 (2010): 661-87. Accessed October 2, 2013. doi:10.10170500084239100065X.

Magazine article:

Note:

> 7. Katelyn Friel, "Seven Tips for a Winning Website," *Dance Magazine*, August 2009, 12.

Bibliography:

> Friel, Katelyn. "Seven Tips for a Winning Website." *Dance Magazine*, August 2009.

Newspaper articles follow a similar format, but section (sec.) number or name replaces page number(s) as the last element. If the author is unknown, begin with the newspaper's name and follow with the article title. Newspaper articles are not included in the bibliography unless your instructor requires it.

Selection in an edited work:

Note:

> 8. David Henry Feldman, "Creativity: Dreams, Insights, and Transformations," in *The Nature of Creativity: Contemporary Psychological Perspectives*, ed. Robert J. Sternberg (New York: Cambridge University Press, 1988), 275.

Bibliography:

> Feldman, David Henry. "Creativity: Dreams, Insights, and Transformations." In *The Nature of Creativity: Contemporary Psychological Perspectives*, edited by Robert J. Sternberg, 271–97. New York: Cambridge University Press, 1988.

If you are referring to the collection as a whole, the name(s) of the editor(s) would replace the article author's name at the beginning of the citation and would be followed by "ed(s)." Use a comma for a note and a period for a bibliographic entry.

Electronic reference:

Note:

> 9. The Internet Encyclopedia of Philosophy, "Deductive and Inductive Arguments," accessed October 7, 2013, http://www.iep.utm.edu/d/ded-ind.htm.

Bibliography:

> The Internet Encyclopedia of Philosophy. "Deductive and Inductive Arguments." Accessed October 7, 2013. http://www.iep.utm.edu/d/ded-ind.htm.

If the author is known, both the note and bibliography entries begin with his or her name. In the bibliography, the item should be alphabetized by the first major word in the title (*Internet*). The access date is added before the website URL with a comma before the URL. Encyclopedia articles and dictionary entries are not usually included in the bibliography; however, your instructor may require them.

The following exercises ask you to apply information from chapters 7 and 8. They test your ability to use summary, paraphrase, direct quotation, mixed format, block format, signal phrases, ellipses, brackets, and MLA and APA in-text citations.

1. Following the instructions given in this text, complete parts a, b, and c, creating sentences that show your understanding of how to use sources. The excerpts are from the website article "Comets May Have Led to Birth and Death of Dinosaur Era," by Hillary Mayell. It was published in *National Geographic News* on 16 May 2002. The information for part a is taken from numbered paragraphs 1 and 2 of the source; part b is taken from paragraph 4; part c is taken from paragraph 3.

   a. Paraphrase the following in one or two sentences. Do not use a signal phrase or any direct quotations. Use MLA style for the parenthetical citation.

   > Comets slamming into the Earth may be responsible for both the birth and the death of the dinosaur era, an international group of researchers report. There is a considerable amount of evidence that a bolide [a comet or asteroid] collision with Earth triggered the end of the dinosaur era 65 million years ago.

   b. Paraphrase the following sentence, but include one direct quotation that is no more than eight words (choose the most appropriate words for the quotation). Use a signal phrase to set up the paraphrase (i.e., the source's name and a signal verb).

   > "We have been able to show for the first time that the transition between Triassic life-forms to Jurassic life-forms occurred in a geological blink of an eye," said Paul Olsen, a geologist at the Lamont-Doherty Earth Observatory of Columbia University.

   c. Using brackets, grammatically integrate the direct quotation into the complete sentence. Do not use a signal phrase.

   > The cause of the end of the dinosaur age might have been "a giant ball of ice, rock, and gases smashed into the supercontinent Pangaea."

2. a. Integrate the passage below as if you planned to use it in your essay, following the instructions. Use a signal phrase and APA style, which includes source's name, year, and signal verb, followed by a direct quotation of the passage. In sentence three, omit (i) "oral contraceptives, transoceanic phone calls" and (ii) "just to mention a few," indicating to the reader that material is omitted. Format the quotation in the most appropriate way—i.e., either as part of the text or in block format. The author is David Suzuki; the name of the article is "Saving the Earth"; publication date is June 14, 1999; the quotation is from page 43 of *Maclean's*.

   > In this century, our species has undergone explosive change. Not only are we adding a quarter of a million people to our numbers every day, we have vastly amplified our technological muscle power. When I was born, there were no computers, televisions, jet planes, oral contraceptives, transoceanic phone calls, satellites, transistors or xerography, just to mention a few. Children today look at typewriters, vinyl records and black-and-white televisions as ancient curiosities.

b. Paraphrase the passage below, which is from page 45 of the same Suzuki essay as in part a, and cite it using APA style. Include one direct quotation no longer than three words as part of your paraphrase. Do not use a signal phrase.

> In biological terms, the globe is experiencing an eco-holocaust, as more than 50,000 species vanish annually, and air, water and soil are poisoned with civilization's effluents. The great challenge to the millennium is recognizing the reality of impending ecological collapse, and the urgent need to get on with taking the steps to avoid it.

c. Summarize the above passage in one sentence of no more than 20 words (there are 54 words in the original); begin with a signal phrase and use APA style. Do not use any direct quotations.

3. The following passage appeared as a block quotation in an essay on video-game addiction. Reduce the word count of the quotation by one-third (i.e., reduce it to approximately 100 words from the current 155). Your answer should include (a) at least two ellipses indicating material omitted; and (b) at least one use of square brackets, indicating a grammatical or stylistic change, or added words.

> *Example*: The game offers an experience many other activities cannot offer. . . . [with] stimulating auditory and visual components.

> The game offers an experience many other activities cannot offer. There are stimulating auditory and visual components, as well as "raids" that keep the players coming back. The players always want to be on top. I can understand why they would want to stay home from work or school to play. To "keep up with the Joneses," you have to raid four days a week, but the company that oversees *World of Warcraft* recently cut it down to two or three because players were burning out. The rewards totally help too. It is set up so you get better rewards depending on the difficulty of the content. I would say a good number of *WoW* players are enslaved by it; it just adds purpose to their lives. A lot of people get depressed when they have to stop playing. I quit cold turkey a few years ago, but since I moved, I started playing again. (Castigliano)

4. **Collaborative activity.** Decide which of the following direct quotations should be paraphrased and which should be left as direct quotations; then, write a paraphrase for each that should be paraphrased. To justify your choices, you could refer to the criteria in chapter 7, page 217. (For the purposes of this exercise, you can omit the citation; the author is provided to help you decide or help in a paraphrase if one is required.)

Example:

> "A person would need to gain an additional 75 to 100 pounds in order to equal the health risks associated with smoking one pack of cigarettes a day." (John Polito)
> • is easily paraphrased
> • is factual information

Paraphrase:

According to John Polito, by consuming only one pack of cigarettes daily, you are doing as much damage to your body as you would by gaining 75 to 100 pounds.

a. "In Canada, over 26 percent of children and youth (1.6 million in all) are considered overweight or obese." (Childhood Obesity Foundation)

b. "Everything great that we know has come from neurotics. Never will the world be aware of how much it owes to them, nor above all what they have suffered in order to bestow their gifts on it." (French novelist Marcel Proust)

c. "The hippocampus is a component of the brain's limbic system that is crucial for learning, memory, and the integration of sensory experiences with emotions and motivations." (Council on Alcohol & Drug Abuse)

d. "Research shows that children raised by same-sex parents are just as healthy as those raised by heterosexual parents because stable family relationships are more important in the long run than parental sexual orientation." (Alyssa Judd)

e. "Our media and entertainment industry remains vibrant and ripe with opportunity; you just have to look in the right places. Television has never been better; the audiences have never been bigger, programming has never been more diverse, or distribution more available. And, as a result, our industry has never had greater potential for growth." (John Foote, Research Manager, Department of Canadian Heritage)

f. "The increase in carbon dioxide–related air pollution is posing a serious health risk threat to residents of inner-city communities, especially children." (Gale Jurasek)

g. "Although there are signs of mild cognitive impairment in chronic cannabis users, there is little evidence that such impairments are irreversible or that they are accompanied by drug-induced neuropathology." (Leslie L. Iversen)

h. "In 2006, 11 million cosmetic plastic surgeries were performed in the United States, where any doctor, no matter what the specialty, may perform these procedures." (Martin Anderson).

i. "It is a well-known fact that dramatic musical scores and operas written by Richard Wagner, with their intense, romantic and mythic qualities, heavily influenced the Nazi party and its idealism." (Leopold von Konigslow)

j. "Congress shall make no law respecting an establishment of religion, or prohibiting the free exercise thereof; or abridging the freedom of speech, or of the press; or the right of the people peaceably to assemble, and to petition the Government for a redress of grievances." (US Constitution: First Amendment)

CHAPTER SUMMARY

This chapter has focused on the important "final" stage of the research project: documentation. Although it provides general information, answering questions like, What are citations? and What is the value of documentation?, its main function is to enable you to correctly document your sources both in the text of your essay and at the end of your essay where full details of each source are arranged in alphabetical order by author name. The chapter provides brief descriptions of MLA, APA, and CMS formats with examples for each.

PART III
Handbook

Many students have come to associate grammar and punctuation with fussy, fault-finding teachers who are stuck in a bygone era of sentence-parsing and rote learning. It is true that much of the informal writing you do outside of class will not depend on your knowing the difference between a preposition and a pronoun or where to place commas in a non-restrictive clause. Moreover, if having many online friends is important, it is best to refrain from correcting a person's grammar too often!

But if your purpose is to communicate complex ideas, as it usually is when you analyze a text or research a topic, *how* you communicate these ideas in writing will be vital. Correctness is important when you write to an educated audience, such as your instructor or your peers. Correct grammar and precise punctuation demonstrate your reliability as a writer as much as a well-structured essay with unified, coherent, and well-developed paragraphs do, as mentioned in the model of the essay discussed in Chapter 3. Even if your reader is unfamiliar with grammar or punctuation rules, he or she could become confused if, for example, you omit commas, as in the following Internet meme: I like cooking my family and my pets.

However, writing well is not just a matter of being correct and following rules: the first goal of the careful writer is clarity. Thus, in chapter 9 you will learn strategies to help make your writing clear and direct. Effective writers also try to create interest and emphasis to engage their readers and guide them to important points. Chapter 9, then, discusses many useful techniques applicable to most of your writing, as clear, interesting writing is always valued.

Chapter 10 introduces the basic concepts of the parts of speech, the sentence, and phrases and clauses. In chapter 11, you will learn how to use commas and other punctuation, along with apostrophes. Chapter 12 focuses on typical "trouble spots" for writers: agreement, pronouns, modifiers, and parallelism. The simplified but comprehensive approach in part III will enable you to approach your future writing with greater confidence.

9 Achieving Clarity and Depth in Your Writing

This chapter focuses on writing style, the *way* you convey your ideas to a reader so they are understandable. It is divided into sections that match the goals of good writing: writing that is concise, direct, precise, and specific. It offers examples and guidelines for producing clear, straightforward prose, and includes a list of the most commonly confused word pairs. Good writing means not only efficient communication but also interesting, sophisticated prose; examples and guidelines to help with this goal are given. The chapter includes two annotated samples, applying many of the features discussed in the chapter: a revised passage from a student essay and an excerpt of professional prose demonstrating successful rhetorical strategies.

LEARNING OBJECTIVES

- to appreciate what writing style is and why it is important to learn the characteristics of an effective writing style

- to learn strategies for concise writing including eliminating unneeded words or phrases or replacing them by shorter alternatives

- to learn strategies for direct writing, such as using active sentence constructions; to learn how passive constructions are formed and when it is acceptable to use them in your writing

- to learn the features of formal writing and informal writing in order to write for different audiences

- to be able to identify words that are often confused and learn hints to avoid misusing them
- to learn strategies for providing depth and emphasis in your writing, such as sentence length and variety

EFFECTIVE STYLE: CLARITY

What is style? If you have written a research essay, you will know that the word *style* is applied to documentation formats, such as the rules for citing sources using MLA or APA guidelines. Style is also a term applied to individual writers—say, a descriptive writing style versus an economical style. Although every writer has a unique style, when you are writing factually with a specific purpose for a specific audience, you need to put *clarity* above your distinctive writing style. More than a half-century ago, Wendell Johnson stressed the importance of clarity:

> For writing to be effective . . . it may or may not be grammatically correct, but it must be both clear and valid. It can be clear without having validity, but if it is unclear its validity cannot well be determined. . . . We ask of the writer, "What do you mean?" before we ask, "How do you know?" Until we reach agreement as to precisely what he is writing about, we cannot possibly reach agreement as to whether, or in what degree, his statements are true.

> —Wendell Johnson, "You Can't Write Writing"

Clarity depends on various factors. If you were writing for a general audience on a specialized topic and used words that were unfamiliar to most readers, you would not be writing clearly, though a specialist might understand you.

The "art" of writing clearly is really not an art or talent at all: it is the result of hard work and attention to detail. Few writers—experienced or inexperienced—write clearly without making several revisions. Much of the revising process, in fact, consists of making the language reflect the thought behind it.

One of the differences between experienced and inexperienced writers is that the former expect to spend much of their time revising their prose; they ask not just, "Is this clear?" but also, "Can this be put *more clearly*?" Student writers should ask themselves the second question, too. If the answer is "maybe," try paraphrasing it (rephrasing it). Can you do this easily? Does your paraphrase express the point more clearly? When you paraphrase something you've written, you often find that the second version is closer to your intended meaning.

What, then, is clear writing? Writing is clear when it is grammatical, concise, direct, precise, and specific. When you revise, you can ask yourself not just, "Is the writing clear?" but also the following questions:

- *Is it grammatical?* Chapters 10, 11, and 12 provide most of the information you need to write understandable, grammatically correct sentences.

When you are writing for an audience, it is not enough that *you* understand your ideas. *Your readers* need to understand what is being written. Revise your work with this thought in mind.

Chapter 10 introduces you to the parts of speech and the sentence.

Chapter 11 teaches you uses of the comma, semicolon, colon, and apostrophe.

Chapter 12 explains subject–verb and pronoun-antecedent agreement, pronoun use, modifier problems, and parallelism.

> **CIRCUMLOCUTION**, meaning "speak around," refers to using more words than necessary to express an idea, or not coming to the point.

- *Is it concise?* Do you use as many words as you need and no more than you have to? Have you used basic words and simple constructions that reflect what you want to say?
- *Is it direct?* Have you used straightforward language and avoided **circumlocutions**? Is the structure of your sentences as simple as possible given the complexity of the point you are trying to express?
- *Is it precise?* Does it say exactly what you want it to say? When you are writing for a reader, *almost* or *close enough* is *not* enough. Would another word or phrase more accurately reflect your thought?
- *Is it specific?* Is it as detailed as it needs to be? Is it concrete—not vague or abstract?

Writers who carefully work to make their writing more grammatical, concise, direct, precise, and specific will likely produce an essay that is clear. However, experienced writers aim also for forceful writing. To this end, they may introduce freshness, variety, and emphasis in their writing.

EXERCISE 9.1

The following paragraphs are from student essays. The first is from an argumentative essay; the second is from a literary analysis. Try to find examples that illustrate stylistic problems summarized above. How could the writer be more concise, direct, precise, and specific? Do stylistic problems impair understanding? Where?

1. There is an idea in society today that suggests that all embryonic stem cells are the result of destroyed embryos. This comes from the fact that this branch of science is still in its developing stages, and the overall public is largely unaware of the real situation when it comes to stem cells. There is an idea circulating that suggests that innocent human embryos would be killed to cure someone who doesn't take care of his or her physical being. However, the fact is that there are other resources for embryos, such as leftover or discarded embryos from in-vitro fertilization. What is more recent is the idea that one could turn typical adult cells that are produced throughout the body into powerful stem cells . . . .

2. In the second work discussed in this paper, "Borders," by Aboriginal writer Thomas King, a young boy travels with his mother to the border where they run into multiple problems relating to identity. The lack of communication between characters, namely, the mother of the narrator and the border guards, is very evident in the entirety of the story and creates a symbolic connection to real-life issues that pertain to aboriginal peoples in North America today. These issues have to do with acceptance and, arguably, the ability to impose your standards on people whose standards are very different from those you possess.

Cutting for Concision

To achieve concision, cut what is inessential. How do you determine what is unnecessary? The simple test is whether you can omit words without changing the meaning.

Many common stylistic patterns that student writers adopt, especially in their early drafts, are described below under specific categories. Your instructor may indicate

A Closer Look

Revising for Style

Why should so much effort be devoted to concise and direct writing? For one thing, such writing is easy to follow and keeps the reader's interest. Unnecessary repetition and other kinds of clutter may cause a point to lose its sharpness. Furthermore, just as concise and direct writing makes you seem reliable, wordy, indirect writing may give the impression that you lack confidence in what you're saying, that you are just trying to impress the reader, or that you are trying to use more words to reach a word count. Finally, when you use more words than you have to or express yourself in a roundabout way, you greatly increase the odds of making grammatical and mechanical errors.

Where directness and concision are discussed, it is not just a question of *more versus less*. Thus, it would be absurd to generalize that less is *always* best. However, wordy structures are usually weak as they shift the emphasis from strong words to weaker ones, for example, from an active subject or strong verb—substantial words—onto a passive subject or a weak verb. Of course, occasionally, you may want to use a longer structure if it conveys a better rhythm or stresses a particular meaning. Reflecting on stylistic choices during revision gives you more control over the ideas you want to communicate,

just as other features of the writing process do, as discussed in earlier chapters.

Consider the two sentences below and why you might choose to use one or the other if you wanted to advise someone about a choice of university to attend or job to apply for. The two sentences say much the same thing, but their stress is subtly different:

> It is important that you make the right decision as your future will depend on it!

> Decide carefully, for your future is at stake!

Clearly, the second sentence is more concise, but is it the better sentence? Perhaps it is—if you wanted to stress the decision-making process more than the decision. The first sentence is longer and begins weakly with the expletive structure "It is . . . ." It also contains a weak verb, *make*. But the sentence might be preferable if you wanted to stress the decision itself. Its tone is also gentler: it is insistent but not threatening. When you revise for style, consider your purpose and audience, just as you do when planning your essay, drafting your introduction, and focusing on other stages.

---

problems with concision by putting parentheses around unneeded words or by writing *wordy* or *cut* in the margin.

Student writers may also unconsciously shift the stress away from where it should lie—the main nouns and verbs. The strategies that follow can guide you as you revise your essay. (See Revising for Concision, Directness, and Diction: A Sample Student Draft on p. 294 for an example of revisions that one student made as she moved from rough to final draft.)

Doubles: The Noah's Ark Syndrome

Editors sometimes offer this formula: one + one = one-half. In other words, if you use two words when one is enough, you are halving the impact of that one word. When you do choose to use two of the same parts of speech, ensure that the two words don't convey the same thing:

> The administrative officer came up with an ~~original,~~ innovative suggestion for cost-cutting. (Anything innovative is bound to be original.)

> The event will be held at ~~various~~ different venues.

Ensure that one of the words doesn't incorporate the meaning of the other, as does *different* with *various* in the second example. This also applies to phrases containing words that are unnecessary because the meaning of the phrase can be understood without them. Be especially wary of verb–adverb combinations; ensure that the adverb is necessary:

The airport was ~~intentionally~~ designed for larger aircraft. (Can a design be unintentional?)

She ~~successfully~~ accomplished what she had set out to do. (The word *accomplished* implies success.)

Needless nouns steal the thunder from other parts of speech, including other nouns and verbs. In the following example, we are not really talking about a world, but about politics:

The world of politics demands that you kowtow to the ineptitude of others.

In this sentence, the phrase *the fields of* is redundant because *ecology* and *biodiversity* are fields of study:

The efforts of conservationists in *the fields of* ecology and biodiversity are leading to renewed efforts to save old-growth forests.

Below, the phrase containing *author* and *name* is redundant because these nouns are implied in the context:

An author by the name of Seth Grahame-Smith wrote a bestseller lampooning Jane Austen's *Pride and Prejudice.*

Redundant Verb–Adverb Pairings

Here are some common verb–adverb pairings and other combinations that usually are redundant:

(clearly) articulate	estimate/approximate	ponder (thoughtfully)
climb (up)	(roughly)	praise (in favour of)
combine/join	(eventually) evolve	progress (forward/
(together)	(over time)	onwards)
(harshly) condemn	examine (closely)	protest (against)
(carefully) consider	(anxiously) fear	(successfully) prove
descend (down)	fill (completely)	refer/return/revert
dominate (over)	finish (entirely)	(back) to
drawl (lazily)	(strictly) forbid	rely/depend (heavily) on,
dwindle (down)	gather/assemble	(symbolically) represent
emphasize/stress	(together)	sob (uncontrollably)
(strongly)	gaze (steadily)	(completely) surround
(better/further) enhance	hurry (quickly)	unite (as one)
(totally) eradicate/	(suddenly) interrupt plan	vanish (without a trace)
devastate	(ahead)	

Repetitive Adjective–Noun Pairings

Be wary, too, of such repetitive adjective–noun pairings as the following:

advance warning	knowledgeable specialist	powerful blast
brief encapsulation	mutual agreement	sharp needle
dead carcass	new beginning	terrible tragedy
exact same	past memory	timeless classic
future plan	positive benefits	total abstinence

When using transitions of addition, be careful to avoid redundancy:

In addition, *another* factor that *also* has degraded agriculture today is farmers' reliance on fertilizers and pesticides.

→ For examples of transitions of addition, see chapter 3, page 62.

Phony Phrases and Clumsy Clauses

Phrases you can do without. Many prepositional phrases are more economical as one-word modifiers. Look for redundant prepositional phrases after verbs and nouns:

Unnecessary: For now, the patient's kidneys are functioning *at a normal level*.

The prepositional phrase *at a normal level* can be replaced by the adverb *normally*:

Better: For now, the patient's kidneys are functioning *normally*.

Here the phony phrase is introduced by the preposition *for*:

Unnecessary: The bill was legislated in 1995 *for a brief period of time*.

Better: The bill was *briefly* legislated in 1995.

Non-specific nouns may be connected to phony phrases beginning with *on*, *to*, or other prepositions. Watch for prepositional phrases that include non-specific nouns like *basis, degree, extent, level, manner,* and *scale*:

on/at the international level

on a larger scale

on a regular basis

to a great/considerable degree/extent

Such phrases can usually be replaced by appropriate adverbs:

Unnecessary: Jindra checks her answering machine *on a regular basis*.

Better: Jindra checks her answering machine *regularly*.

Clauses you can do without. Relative clauses are adjectival and may sometimes be replaced by a corresponding adjective preceding the noun or omitted entirely. In this example, *that is high in protein* is a relative (adjectival) clause modifying *diet*:

Unnecessary: Most body-builders follow a strict diet *that is high in protein*.

Better: Most body-builders follow a strict, *high-protein* diet.

EXERCISE 9.2

Replace or omit any wordy phrases or clauses in the following sentences.

1. The writer's bias calls into question much of the evidence that has been used.
2. Gender stereotypes sometimes challenge the success of women in the international arena.
3. The process of hiring today often involves the administration of a personality test to determine the suitability of a candidate.
4. The poet's theme is that nature is something that is to be feared.
5. Brain imaging has shown that musicians have a larger auditory cortex than those who do not play a musical instrument.

Weedy Words

English contains many unimportant words whose function is to join more important words or parts of the sentence. But when these words pop up throughout a sentence, they can distract a reader. Small words, such as prepositions and articles, can often be omitted. In the examples below, parentheses indicate words that can be omitted:

He was (the) last out (of) the door.

(The) taking (of) life can never be condoned.

Look at the following passage and consider what can be deleted—big words and small—without changing the meaning of the sentence. Also consider unneeded phrases and clauses:

The city of Toronto has one of the most ethnically diverse of cultures in all of North America. The city has a population of 2.7 million people and is also the home of a wide variety of sports teams that play in professional leagues.

The word *that* can be used as a pronoun (demonstrative and relative), an adjective, and a subordinating conjunction. It can often be omitted if the subject of the second clause introduced by *that* is different from the subject of the preceding clause. By methodically checking your first draft for unnecessary *that*s, you can improve sentence flow. Look back at the first paragraph in Exercise 9.1. How many *that*s can you take out of the paragraph?

Taking *that* out of the sentence below does not affect the structure of the sentence—even though it makes the sentence more readable. In both cases, *that* introduces a dependent clause; the independent clause in the sentence is *I thought*:

I thought (that) Silas was going to go to the same school (that) his brother went to.

Now unravel the meaning of the following statement:

It's certain that that *that* that that person used is ungrammatical.

Prepositions are usually short words, like *to*, *at*, or *in*, that introduce phrases and are followed by a noun or pronoun. Using lengthy prepositions can distract the reader by calling attention to the joiner instead of the more important noun. The list below contains mostly prepositions but also some awkward conjunctions and adverbs:

amidst	in accordance with	notwithstanding the
amongst (use *among*)	in comparison to	oftentimes
analogous to	in conjunction with	pertaining to
as a result of	in connection with	so as to
as to	in reference to	subsequent to
at this point in time	in regard to	thusly
cognizant of	in terms of	whether or not
consequent to	in the final analysis	whilst (use *while*)
despite the fact that	in view of the	within (when you mean *in*)
due to the fact that	inasmuch as	with regard to
fact that	irregardless (use *regardless*)	with respect to

Rabbit Words

An *intensive* is an example of a "rabbit word," one that reproduces quickly and may over-run the landscape of your prose. An intensive adds emphasis to the word or expression it modifies but has little meaning on its own. However, due to overuse, it often does not emphasize at all. In all levels of formal writing, intensives should be rooted out whenever they do not truly add emphasis, such as in the simple sentence below:

She is ~~certainly~~ a(n) ~~very~~ impressive speaker.

Words like *certainly* and *very* are overused. Many intensives are adverbs modifying verbs or adjectives. In some instances, you can simply use a stronger verb in place of a weak verb and an intensive, or a stronger adjective in place of the intensive plus a weak adjective; or, you can just eliminate the intensive, as in

It was a ~~very~~ unique idea.

Unnecessary: He was very grateful for his warm reception.

Better:

He was gratified by his warm reception.

or:

He appreciated his warm reception.

The words and phrases in the two lists below can be used in your writing if you truly want to stress or qualify a point. Most often, though, they can be omitted.

Overused Intensives

absolutely	definitely	incredibly	particularly
actually	effectively	indeed	significantly
assuredly	extremely	inevitably	surely
certainly	fact	interestingly	totally
clearly	fundamentally	markedly	utterly
completely	highly	naturally	very
considerably	in	of course	

If you need to use words like *definitely* or *extremely*, note the spelling. They are two of the most commonly misspelled words.

Overused Qualifiers

apparently	hopefully	perhaps	somewhat
arguably	in effect	quite	sort of
basically	in general	rather	virtually
essentially	kind of	relatively	
generally	overall	seemingly	

Examples:

Overall. In most cases, the word *overall* can be omitted. For example, in the sentence below, it can be added as a modifier almost anywhere—yet, wherever it is, it contributes nothing to the sentence's meaning:

> *Overall* in the poem "Easter 1916," Yeats uses imagery to convey a theme of sadness.

> In the poem "Easter 1916," Yeats uses imagery *overall* to convey a theme of sadness.

> In the poem "Easter 1916," Yeats uses imagery to convey an *overall* theme of sadness.

Arguably. Using this adverb is too often a way of saying something and not saying it at the same time:

> Maurya's fate at the end of the play "Riders to the Sea" is arguably worse than that of her husband and sons.

If her fate is worse than her sons, say it; if the point is "arguable," argue it!

EXERCISE 9.3

Go to one of your school's databases and find some corporate annual reports. See if you can find any examples of unnecessary words or redundant constructions. Choose two or three examples and rewrite them in more concise prose.

Writing Directly

Writing should get straight to the point, but indirect writing stresses the less important parts of the sentence. Passive constructions are indirect because they place the active subject at the end of the sentence or clause, although they may be preferable when you do not want to stress the subject or if it is unknown.

Passive Constructions: The Lazy Subject

Effective, direct English is geared toward the *active*, not the *passive*, voice. In a passive construction, the subject of the sentence is *not* doing the action. Ordinarily, the subject *is* acting, as in the following:

> *Ezra placed* the book on the table.

Changing the sentence so that the object becomes the (non-active) subject requires changing the word order and adding words:

The book was placed on the table by Ezra.

Note the differences between these two sentences. In the second sentence, the direct object, *book*, has become the subject and the original subject, *Ezra*, is now at the end of the sentence, the object of the preposition *by*. The verb form has changed too. The sentence now has a subject that is acted on rather than acting itself. The passive subject sentence requires more words to provide the same information.

The passive voice uses a form of the verb *to be* followed by a past participle. If the actor is named, it will be the object of a prepositional phrase that begins with *by*. Don't confuse the identifying verb forms of the passive with a construction in which a form of the verb *to be* is used along with the past participle as a predicate adjective. For example, in the following sentence, the subjects are clearly the actors; you can't add the preposition *by* after *determined* or *pleased*. This sentence, then, uses an active construction:

Dana was determined to succeed at any cost; I am pleased to see him succeed.

In the following sentence, there are three indicators of a passive construction:

The door was opened by a tall, sinister man.

- The subject (*door*) is not doing the action expressed by the verb *open*.
- The preposition *by* precedes the actor (*man*).
- The simple past of *to be* combines with the past participle of the main verb to form the passive voice of the verb.

To change a passive to an active construction:

1. Move the subject so that it follows the verb as the direct object.

   was opened *the door* by a tall, sinister man

2. Move the object of the preposition *by*, the actor, to the beginning of the clause to replace the passive subject.

   a tall, sinister man was opened the door by

3. Get rid of the identifying passive forms of the verb and the preposition *by*.

   A tall, sinister man ~~was~~ opened the door ~~by~~.

Below is a slightly more complicated example. In its active form, the sentence contains fewer words and the thought is expressed more directly:

Passive: The special commission was informed of its mandate by a superior court judge last Monday.

Active: A superior court judge informed the special commission of its mandate last Monday.

A Closer Look

Academic Writing and the Passive

There are cases in academic writing, especially in the sciences, in which the passive may be used to stress the object of the study or the method of research, as below, where the method, *comparison*, is the subject:

> Through case studies, a comparison of two common methods for treating depression will be made [*by the writer*].

In the following examples from academic writing, the passive is preferred either because the actor doesn't matter or because the writer wants to stress the receiver of the action:

> The emergence of second-hand smoke (SHS) [as a cancer hazard] has been offered as a viable explanation for the increased enactment of local smoking restrictions (Asbridge, 2003, p. 13).

> In 1891 the science of embryology was shaken by the work of the cosmopolitan German biologist and vitalist philosopher Hans Driesch (Bowring, 2004, p. 401).

As a general rule, *don't use the passive voice if the active will serve*. However, the passive is acceptable or is even the better choice when

- the subject isn't known, or is so well known it doesn't need stating. In the following example, it is unnecessary to mention that *the voters* elected the prime minister:

> Pierre Trudeau was first elected prime minister in 1968.

- passivity is implied, or the context makes it seem natural to stress the receiver of the action. In this sentence, the massages are more important than the person giving them:

> When a cyclist completes a hard workout, massages are usually performed on the affected muscles.

EXERCISE 9.4

↻ Check answers to select questions

The following sentences use passive constructions. Determine which are appropriately in passive voice and which inappropriately. Change unnecessary uses of the passive voice to form active constructions. In some sentences, the actor or "active" subject is not part of the sentence, so you may have to add it to the sentence (see the example below). Be prepared to justify your decisions to leave some sentences as passive constructions.

Example:

> *Passive*: The suspect's behaviour had been watched for more than one month.

> The suspect's behaviour had been watched (by the police) for more than one month.

> *Active*: The police had watched the suspect's behaviour for more than one month.

> *Decision*: Leave as passive because *suspect's behaviour* is more important to the meaning than *the police*.

1. I was given two choices by my landlord: pay up or get out.
2. It was reported that more than 1,000 people were left homeless by recent flooding.
3. Theo's protest was heard by the fairness committee.
4. At Wednesday's committee meeting, the problem of parking in the downtown core was discussed.
5. Beethoven's Third Symphony, the *Eroica*, originally was dedicated to Napoleon, but the dedication was erased after Napoleon proclaimed himself emperor.
6. Education needs to be seen by the government as the number one priority.
7. Many acts of self-deception were committed by Bertha, the protagonist of "Bliss."
8. The belief in a powerful and infallible Creator is commonly held today.
9. Poverty in First Nations communities must be addressed by the federal, provincial, and First Nations' governments.
10. There are two ways of looking at rights-based ethics that were put forward by Immanuel Kant.

Black Hole Constructions

In addition to the passive, other indirect constructions can weaken a sentence. You can consider them the black holes of writing: they swallow up the substance of the sentence.

- *It was . . .*

  It was Mary Shelley who wrote *Frankenstein* in 1816.

  As simple as this sentence is, it begins weakly by displacing the logical subject, *Mary Shelley*, and substituting the unnecessary *It was*. The sentence is stronger and more direct when the most important noun is made the subject:

  Mary Shelley wrote *Frankenstein* in 1816.

- *There is/are . . .*

  There are many reasons that exist for attempting to avoid weak sentence openings.

  Like *It is*, *There is* begins the sentence weakly.

  Many reasons exist for avoiding weak sentence openings.

  For many reasons, avoid weak sentence openings.

  Occasionally, you may want to use *It was*, *there is*, or a similar construction for rhetorical effect. In such a case, emphasis, rather than directness, may determine your choice.

- *One of. . .*

  Poor: The path you have chosen is one of danger and uncertainty.

  Better: The path you have chosen is dangerous and uncertain.

  You have chosen a dangerous, uncertain path.

- *The reason . . . is because*, which is both illogical and redundant:

  Incorrect: The reason Jessica is lucky is because she has a horseshoe on her door.

  Correct: Jessica is lucky because she has a horseshoe on her door.

Weak Verb + Noun

Writers often fall into the habit of using a weak verb and a corresponding noun rather than a verb that directly expresses the meaning. Often the noun that follows the verb can be changed into a strong verb; at other times, a one-word verb can sum up the verb phrase. In these examples, a weak verb phrase supplants the more direct alternative:

Weak constructions:

1. I had a meeting with my staff, and I am now asking you to provide a list of all your clients.
2. Inexperienced writers have a tendency to be wordy.
3. She made changes to the document, making clear what was ambiguous.

Stronger constructions:

1. I met with my staff and now ask you to list all your clients.
2. Inexperienced writers tend to be wordy.
3. She changed the document, clarifying ambiguities.

Do not needlessly use the present progressive tense where the simple present will suffice:

Although both authors *are discussing* [*discuss*] multiculturalism, only Iyer *is understanding of* [*understands*] the uniqueness of Canada's version.

Global warming *affects* shifting major weather patterns. Its *effects* are being widely felt throughout the globe.

→ See Tense Encounters with Verbs on the inside cover.

In the weak phrase *has an effect on*, where *has* is the verb and *effect* is the noun, remember that the corresponding verb form is *affect*.

→ See page 281 for tips on the unnecessary use of forms of the verb *to be*.

EXERCISE 9.5

↻ Check answers to select questions

Make the following sentences more concise and direct by revising the weak verb + noun structure.

1. Historians agree that Canada made a significant contribution to the war effort in France and Belgium.
2. To determine whether video games are addictive, researchers have had many interviews with gamers and designers.
3. It is important for schools to take into consideration the ways that the school environment has an effect on behaviour.
4. Several devices in the story bring to prominence the theme of revenge.
5. The first-person point of view in Raymond Carver's "Feathers" provides the reader with a connection to the simple, working-class narrator.

TABLE 9.1 Nominals

NOMINAL	VERB	SENTENCE WITH NOMINAL	SENTENCE WITHOUT NOMINAL
conclusion	conclude	We have reached the conclusion that the defendant is guilty.	We have concluded that the defendant is guilty.
classification	classify	We will now proceed with the classification of Vertebrata.	We will now classify Vertebrata.
intention installation	intend install	Our intention is to complete the installation of the new system this month.	We intend to finish installing the new system this month.

Numbing Nouns

Nouns that pile up in a sentence can create a numbing effect. This is especially true with *nominals*, nouns formed from verbs. There is nothing wrong with using a polysyllabic noun formed from a verb—unless a more concise and direct alternative exists. Table 9.1 shows how nominals can be turned back into verbs.

Euphemisms

A **euphemism** is an indirect expression considered less harsh or offensive than the term it replaces. Many ancient cultures used euphemisms to avoid naming their enemies directly. They believed that naming gave power to those they feared, so they invented ways around saying their names; the word *euphemism* comes from the Greek word that means "to use words for good omen." We sometimes do the same today out of consideration and kindness to those who may be suffering, as a way of speaking about taboo subjects and objects, or as a form of satire or irony. For example, the euphemisms for *die* are numerous, with *pass away* or *pass on* being the most common.

Although euphemisms can be used to protect us from the unpleasant, they can be used also to falsely reassure. For example, *urban renewal* avoids the implications of *slum clearance*, *revenue enhancement* has a more positive ring than *tax increase*, and *collateral losses* attempts to sidestep the fact that civilians can be killed during military action.

We also sometimes use euphemisms to try to give more dignity and a sense of importance to special objects, actions, or vocations: *pre-owned automobile* for *used car* and *job action* for *strike*. The following classified ad uses some verbose and euphemistic language:

> We are seeking an individual who possesses demonstrated skills and abilities, a sound knowledge base coupled with the experience to provide service to mentally challenged teenagers with "unique" and significant challenging behaviours.

The requirements of the position could have been written in half the words:

> Applicants need proven skills, knowledge, and experience to serve mentally challenged teenagers with challenging behaviours.

> A **EUPHEMISM** is an indirect expression considered less harsh or offensive than the term it replaces.

A special category of "acceptable euphemisms" are those that we, as a society, agree should be substituted for expressions that have acquired inappropriate connotations. For example, to refer to someone in a wheelchair as a *cripple* inappropriately stresses the disability and its limitations. More sensitively and more accurately, this person is *physically disabled* or *physically challenged*.

EXERCISE 9.6

Collaborative Exercise: Indirect Writing

The Plain English Campaign gives Golden Bull awards for the "worst written nonsense." Identify examples of indirect writing in the 2012 "winner" below, a rejection of an application to open a pharmacy. Discuss what the author is attempting to say. Identify wordy joiners; intensives, or qualifiers; nominals; or other examples of wordiness. Rewrite the passage in no more than 25 words (half the original length):

> The Committee concluded, having regard to the totality of the factors considered above, that choice could not be given significant weight and that there was not currently a gap on the spectrum of adequacy sufficient to conclude that the provision of pharmaceutical services is not currently secured to the standard of adequacy.

EXERCISE 9.7

Collaborative Exercise: Euphemism Maker

In groups, think of 10 euphemisms, either ones you've heard of or made-up ones. Then, read them to the rest of the class, who will guess what they are meant to describe.

Prepackaged Goods: Clichés

A **CLICHÉ** is an overworked and unoriginal expression.

Clichés are overworked and unoriginal expressions. Inexperienced writers may reach for them in a vain attempt to "spice up" their writing. Clichés may be *dead metaphors*: expressions drained of their novelty through overuse. Although they may appear in some informal writing, they are poor substitutes for informative, imaginative words.

EXERCISE 9.8

In this short passage adapted from a travel feature, find evidence of tired and predictable writing, citing particular words and phrases that could be made more effective or accurate. Although newspaper features use informal writing, it should be descriptive and concrete. How could you make this passage more interesting?

> We're up and about at the crack of dawn, and from outside our cabin we can see the peak of a small mountain looming in the distance. Our ship glides effortlessly over the fathomless blue sea, and soon the mountain's craggy features come into view.

"It's breakfast, honey," my wife, Jen, sings from inside the cabin, and soon our impeccably dressed waiter knocks softly on our door. As we sit down to partake of the delectable repast, I feel as though I could pinch myself. Yes, here we are, aboard a luxurious liner, about to drop anchor off the coast of one of the world's most fabled isles.

The following sentences can be revised for greater concision and directness. Make whatever changes you believe are necessary and be prepared to justify these changes.

1. Tanya has been invited to provide us with a summary of the significant main points of her findings.
2. The unexpected eruption of the volcano changed the Western Samoan island into a fiery, blazing inferno.
3. At first the wallpaper is completely detested by the narrator, but she later comes to believe that it is the path leading her to the freedom that she so much desires.
4. Individuals who are bullied are not responsible in any way for their victimization, yet there seems to be a reason as to why they are chosen to be victims.
5. It was in 1964 that the Beatles first made their inaugural tour of the North American continent.
6. The disappearance of even one single species at the lower end of the food chain can have dire adverse effects in many instances on the survival of various other species.
7. Although Copernicus's radical idea that the earth made revolutions around the sun was once considered an extreme heresy and was ridiculed mercilessly by his peers, the idea eventually gained gradual acceptance.
8. The fact is that for a great many years now antibiotics have been utilized on a regular basis by many people as a cure for each and every symptom that they develop over the course of their entire lifetimes.
9. Perhaps in the heat of emotion the act of capital punishment would seem to be a feasible idea, but when you come to think of it rationally, this act would accomplish virtually next to nothing at all.
10. In protest of their salary freeze, all of the teachers who teach at the high school in Oak Bay have made the unanimous decision not to undertake any tasks of a supervisory nature until the school board has conducted a fair and impartial salary review.
11. Vehicles that have the four-way drive feature option are an extremely practical and pragmatic form of transportation for the majority of the Canadian population in this day and age.
12. There are many people in our society today who have serious drug addictions that take complete and utter control over their lives.
13. From the beginning of its conception, Canada has been a country concerned with promoting an active multicultural society, although the reality of unity within the country is still a large, unanswered question in the minds of most of the people of Canada.

EXERCISE 9.9

↻ Check answers to select questions

14. A French scientist by the name of Louis Pasteur was the first individual to make the discovery that microbes were harmful menaces to the well-being and healthy functioning of the human body.

15. The reason yoga allows us to live a healthy lifestyle is due to the fact that it provides a strong basis for the efficient functioning of the body's endocrine system.

Fast Track

Ten Categories of Wordy Writing

Exercise

Revise the sentences in column 3 to make them more concise and direct. (More than one problem may exist in some examples.)

CATEGORY	DESCRIPTION	EXAMPLE
doubles	Using two words that mean almost the same thing	Some of today's new technological innovations have unwelcome disadvantages.
phony phrase & clumsy clause	Unnecessary or wordy phrase/clause that follows a noun or verb	The concept of bullying that is engrained within the school system is not a new one.
weedy word	Unimportant word that distracts from more important ones	The labelling of additives in accordance with regulations is oftentimes ignored on the packaging of consumer products.
rabbit word	Word used to intensify or qualify that in fact adds little to the sentence	The essay was very effective overall but was lacking somewhat in solid evidence.
passive construction	The grammatical subject is not performing the action of the verb	Tigers are used by the poet to symbolize pride.
black hole construction	Construction that begins a sentence weakly or draws attention to less important words	There have been a large number of studies that show natural supplements are just as effective as prescription drugs.
weak verb + noun construction	A weak verb followed by a word, often a noun, that could replace the verb	Athletes have the unique ability to have an effect on their young admirers.
numbing noun	Multi-syllable noun formed from a verb that can clog a sentence.	The investigation of antibiotics and a consideration of their effects must be a priority.
euphemism	Expression considered less harsh or offensive than what it replaces.	The division lost two souls due to friendly fire at the height of the altercation.
cliché	Overworked and unoriginal expression	*Life of Pi* is a heartwarming story of a plucky boy who never says die.

Rewrite the following passage, aiming for concise, direct writing.

EXERCISE 9.10

> It is clear that teenagers have learned behaviour deemed to be aggressive by watching violent acts on TV or due to being exposed to violence within video games. There have been hundreds of studies that have attempted to explain or clarify the relationship between aggression and a person's exposure to violence. In one of these studies, the adolescents who participated were divided into two groups. One of these groups was assigned to play a racing game that was non-violent, and the other group was assigned to play a violent first-person shooter game. After the allotted time, the subjects were the recipients of brain scans. The overall result was found to be an increase in activity in the part of the brain that is involved in aggression in those adolescents who played the shooter game.

Working toward Precision: Wise Word Choices

Informal Writing

For most university writing assignments, you will need to use formal writing. Because you may be used to writing informally when using the Internet or when texting, you may puzzle over the ways that **informal writing** differs from formal writing. In informal writing

- language may be close to speech or chatty with **colloquialisms**, **idioms**, or even slang
- contractions are acceptable (e.g., *don't, can't, shouldn't, it's*)
- the first person (*I, me*) and second person (*you*) voice may be used
- sentence fragments may be used occasionally for dramatic effect
- short paragraphs are the rule rather than the exception
- citations for research sources are not given

In your essays, you should avoid contractions, unless your instructor tells you otherwise. Unless you are quoting someone, you should always avoid slang, colloquialisms, and jargon. For example, you would not use any of the following in a formal essay: *mindset, price tag, quick fix, downside, upfront, stressed (out), okay, do drugs, give the green light, put (someone) down, fall for, obsess (about something), pan out, put on hold, put a positive spin (on something), opt for, tune out, no way, the way to go, go overboard, way more (of something), a lot.*

In addition, avoid merely quantitative words and phrases, such as *great, incredible, beautiful, terrible,* and the like; they are non-specific. Of course, you also should refrain from using words and expressions that might suggest to some readers a gender, sexual, racial, cultural, or other bias.

INFORMAL WRITING is writing intended for general readers; its language, style, and format distinguish it from formal writing.

COLLOQUIALISMS are words and expressions acceptable in conversation but not in formal writing.

An **IDIOM** is a phrase whose meaning is understood only within the context of the phrase itself. For example, "his bark is worse than his bite" cannot be understood by the meanings of the individual words but only by its customary usage.

Avoid using informal verbs such as *saw, has seen,* etc., when you mean *resulted in* or *occurred*:

> The policy implemented two years ago *has seen* a 40 per cent drop in crime.

Revised: The policy implemented two years ago *has resulted in* a 40 per cent drop in crime.

Precision and Word Meaning

Your word choices involve much more than thinking about the level of formality. Effective writers choose their words and phrases carefully to mean exactly what they intend.

Rather than making extreme blunders, more often a writer chooses an imprecise word. These "near misses" can confuse the reader. You should not let the search for the exact word prevent you from fully expressing your ideas in a first draft. But when revising, you should look up the meaning of each word you're in doubt about—even if you're only a little unsure about its meaning.

You can use a thesaurus to look for words similar in meaning to avoid repeating a word too often. But a thesaurus should always be used along with a reliable dictionary. Most thesauruses, such as the ones included with word-processing programs, simply list words similar in meaning; they do not provide connotations for the words. A word's connotation includes its possible meanings in its given context, and since contexts can vary, so can the meanings of the same word.

Some dictionaries help with precision not only by defining the main entry but also by providing distinctions among similar words. In addition to illustrating the way a word is used by providing examples, many mid-sized dictionaries distinguish the main entry from other words with similar meanings. For example, the *Gage Canadian Dictionary*, which lists more than six meanings for the adjective *effective*, also defines two words similar to *effective* in meaning but different in connotation:

> *Syn. adj.* 1. Effective, effectual, efficient = producing an effect. Effective, usually describing things, emphasizes producing a wanted or expected effect: *several new drugs are effective in treating serious diseases*. Effectual, describing people or things, emphasizes having produced or having the power to produce the exact effect or result intended: *his efforts are more energetic than effectual*. Efficient, often describing people, emphasizes being able to produce the effect wanted or intended without wasting energy, time, etc.: *A skilled surgeon is highly efficient*.

Similarly, the *Student's Oxford Canadian Dictionary*, which lists seven meanings for the adjective *nice*, offers the following examples of words that may be more appropriate or more forceful than *nice* in certain contexts:

we had a **delightful/splendid/enjoyable** time

a **satisfying/delicious/exquisite** meal

a **fashionable/stylish/elegant/chic** outfit

this is a **cozy/comfortable/attractive** room

she is **kind/friendly/likeable/amiable**

our adviser is **compassionate/understanding/sympathetic**

a **thoughtful/considerate/caring** gesture

For more about determining a word's meaning from its context, see chapter 1, Using Context or Similarities to Determine Word Meanings, page 12.

Finally, do not write ironically or sarcastically unless you are certain that your reader shares your attitude:

> It is well known that college students under stress need to exercise their livers on the occasional Friday night.

Remember that the hallmark of academic writing is an objective voice, one without bias.

Precision and Logic

Choosing your words carefully will help make your writing precise. But sometimes, imprecision may result from illogical thinking or from writing down an idea quickly. To determine if something you've written really makes sense, you need to look carefully at the relationship among the parts of the sentence, especially at the *relationship between the subject and predicate*. **Faulty predication** exists if a verb (**predicate**) cannot be logically connected to its subject. In general, avoid the phrases *is when* and *is where* after a subject in sentences that *define* something. For example, in the following sentence *faulty predication*, a thing, is illogically referred to as a time or a place:

> *Incorrect:* Faulty predication is when/where a verb cannot be logically connected to its subject.

> *Correct:*

> Faulty predication *occurs where* [i.e., in a sentence] a verb is not logically connected to its subject.

> Faulty predication *is* an illogical juxtaposing of a subject and a verb.

Consider this comment on the setting of Joseph Conrad's *Heart of Darkness*:

> The Congo represents an inward journey for the character Marlow.

The Congo is a country and a river. How can a country or a river represent a journey? Of course, a *trip* through a country or on a river could represent an inner journey.

In another kind of faulty predication, an inanimate object is falsely linked to a human action:

> Some opponents claim that PE *programs are unwilling* to accommodate the needs of all students.

The programs aren't "unwilling," since this implies a will, though teachers or administrators may be "unwilling":

> Some opponents claim that the *administrators* of PE programs *are unwilling* to accommodate the needs of all students.

> **FAULTY PREDICATION** occurs where a verb (predicate) isn't logically connected to the subject.
>
> The **PREDICATE** consists of a verb and any verb modifiers or objects.

When checking for faulty predication, identify the subject and verb; then, ensure that the subject can perform the action that the verb describes.

Be careful that a linking verb (e.g., *be* and its various forms, such as *is*, *are*, *were*) does not illogically connect a subject to a predicate noun or adjective (See "3. Linking Verbs" under Verbs in Chapter 10, p. 312):

The *twenty-first century* may well *be a step* in a new direction for the human race as we gradually come to embrace alternative energy sources.

A time period cannot logically *be* a step, so the sentence should be revised:

In the twenty-first century, the human race may gradually embrace alternative energy sources, taking a step in a new direction.

EXERCISE 9.11

Identify the subject and verb in the sentences below, revising to avoid faulty predication and/or other illogical statements.

1. The science of physiognomy believed that a person's facial features could reveal one's character and moral disposition.
2. Previous research studying motorists using hand-held devices while on the road claimed that 20 per cent of all accidents were directly related to these devices.
3. The use of social networking sites can be used to talk to someone who is hard to contact through other means.
4. The theme of the poem is the fact that she hates her father for leaving her when she was only eight years old.
5. The crucial line in Margaret Avison's poem claims that everyone will eventually encounter his or her life's whirlpool.

Verbs with Vitality

→ See page 284 to learn more about using strong verbs in your sentences.

Verbs are the action words in a sentence. Look at the verbs in your sentences. Could you replace them with stronger, more descriptive verbs? Could you replace verbs like *be* and *have*, which convey a state or condition, with verbs of action? Common verbs, such as *do*, *make*, *go*, and *get*, are not specific. Could you replace them with more precise or emphatic verbs?

EXERCISE 9.12

↻ Check answers to select questions

Read the following paragraph and underline places where you would revise verbs to make them more expressive and descriptive.

By the 1800s, inventions were beginning to put people out of work. One of the first inventions that resulted in rebellion was in the craft guild. In 1801, Joseph Jacquard became known as the inventor of the Jacquard loom. This loom was capable of being programmed by pre-punched cards, which made it possible to create clothing design patterns. This invention led to the creation of the Luddites, who were a group made up from the craft guild. These people were against any type of manufacturing technology and went about burning down several factories that were using this new technology. The Luddites were around only for a couple of years, but the name Luddite is still used to describe people who are resistant to new technologies. The Jacquard loom was, in effect, an invention that replaced people. It could do great designs quickly and without making any errors. The replacement of people by machines was beginning.

The most common verb in English, *to be*, takes many different forms as an irregular verb: *am, is, are, was, were, will be*, etc. and appears frequently as a helping verb. Your writing will be more concise if you omit the forms *being* or *to be* whenever they are unnecessary.

The results of the study can be interpreted as ~~being~~ credible.

Hypnosis has been proven ~~to be~~ an effective therapy for some people.

Decide whether the form of the verb *to be* is needed in the sentences below and revise accordingly.

1. She dreamed of a carriage being pulled by two fine horses.
2. In 313 BCE, Constantine I declared Christianity to be the official religion of Rome.
3. One source on the website is about the research today being done on twins.
4. Being able to perceive life from varying angles is one of the key elements to being a good writer.
5. Helga Dittmar considers the mass media to be the most "potent and pervasive influence" on young women today, being the strongest contributor to negative body image.

EXERCISE 9.13

↻ Check answers to select questions

Suggest how the following passage could be improved by using more specific language and by omitting unnecessary words and phrases.

The time period between 1985 and 1989 was a difficult one for graffiti artists in New York City. This was a time when graffiti barely stayed alive because of the harsh laws and efforts of the Metropolitan Transit Authority, which is known as the MTA. This period was called the period of the "Die Hards" because of the small number of die-hard artists who were able to keep graffiti from dying out completely. As a result of the measures of the MTA against graffiti art and artists, there was a lack of paint available for use and the level of enforcement was extremely high. The only important thing that was happening during these years was the use of markers for tagging. These tags were usually small, of poor artistic quality, and were finished quickly by the artists. These tags can be seen today at some bus stops and in some washrooms throughout the city.

EXERCISE 9.14

Revising for Concision, Directness, and Diction: A Sample Student Draft

Using the editing form on page 414, peer editor Dawn-Lee Ricard suggested changes to her classmate Adrienne Poirier's essay on aggression. She also commented in the text and margins of the draft itself, providing helpful suggestions for direct and concise prose. Most of the introduction and the first body paragraph with editing by Ricard and Poirier herself appear below.

First Draft

It has long been debated whether aggression and violence are inherent or learned; to this day , there are ~~still many~~ varying opinions. ~~In~~ the beginning of the [*At*] 1900s, it was widely accepted that the way humans behaved ~~had everything to do with~~ their ~~biological makeup~~ (Macionis, Jansson, & Benoit, 2008, p. 169). Sigmund [*depended on*] [*biology*] Freud, creator of ~~the psychoanalysis~~ theory, believed ~~that~~ each person had an [*psychoanalytic*] aggressive drive ~~within them~~. ~~He called this drive~~ "the death instinct," ~~and held~~ [, *which he called* , *believing*] that it was impossible to rid ~~completely~~ yourself of it (p. 166). However, ~~more~~ recent studies ~~have begun to~~ show that aggressive and violent behaviour have less to do with natural instinct and more to do with how people learn to deal with situations that may lead to such behaviour. Research states that ~~the majority of~~ [*most*] violent behaviour is ~~in fact~~ learned ~~behaviour~~ (Elliott, 1994, p. 3). Studies have shown that when someone participates in aggressive acts, that person becomes more aggressive, backing up the opinion that aggression and violence are learned . . . .

Early childhood is ~~a very~~ important stage for demonstrating non-aggressive [*an*] behaviour, as children can begin to show aggressive behaviour as early as two and a half years ~~of age~~ (Murray-Close & Ostrov, 2009, p. 830). Once a [*old*]

Margin comments:

2nd person is not used in formal academic work

Check agreement? "behaviour" is singular

"Researchers state" or "studies demonstrate"

Supporting the view?

Modelling? Adrienne, do you mean that parents need to model this kind of behaviour?

child has established an aggressive personality~,~ it can be ~~very~~ difficult to

restore positive behaviour in them. Farrington (as cited by Pepler & Rubin,

> Consider "constructive"

1991) observed that aggression in childhood could worsen and turn into

"delinquency and hostility" in ~~the teenage years~~ *adolescence* and remain throughout the

child's life (p. xiii). ~~What~~ parents often ~~don't~~ realize ~~is~~ they ~~are teaching~~ *teach*

> No contractions in formal writing

their children aggressive behaviour when trying to do the ~~exact~~ opposite.

For example, r Reprimanding ~~a child's aggression~~ *a child for aggressive behaviour* by shouting, grabbing, or threats is almost

worse than not reprimanding the child at all (Fraser, 1996, p. 349). Witnessing

> This citation can be deleted

this ~~kind of behaviour~~ *type of reprimand* causes the child to revert ~~back to it~~ as soon as he or

she is upset (Fraser, 1996, p. 349). Even worse is ~~the direct witnessing of~~ *directly experiencing* physical

or emotional abuse (Elliott, 1994, p. 3). Such negative reinforcement does

not have to come from a parent but can ~~be as simple as~~ *occur when simply* watching a violent TV

program.

Final Draft

In her final draft, Poirier used most of Ricard's suggestions for concision, directness, and diction, rewording some passages herself.

> It has long been debated whether aggression and violence are inherent or learned; to this day, there are varying opinions. At the beginning of the 1900s, it was widely accepted that the way humans behaved depended on their biology (Macionis, Jansson, & Benoit, 2008, p. 169). Sigmund Freud, creator of psychoanalytic theory, believed each person had an aggressive drive, which he called "the death instinct," holding that it was impossible to rid oneself of it (p. 166). However, recent studies show that aggressive and violent behaviour has less to do with natural instinct and more to do with how people learn to deal with situations that may lead to such behaviour. Researchers believe that most violent behaviour is learned behaviour (Elliott, 1994, p. 3). Studies have shown that when someone participates in aggressive acts, that person becomes more aggressive, which supports the idea that aggression and violence are learned . . . .

Early childhood is an important stage for demonstrating non-aggressive behaviour to children, as they can begin to show aggressive behaviour as early as two and a half years old (Murray-Close & Ostrov, 2009, p. 830). Once a child has established an aggressive personality, it can be difficult to restore constructive behaviour in them. Farrington (as cited by Pepler & Rubin, 1991) observed that aggression in childhood could worsen and turn into "delinquency and hostility" in adolescence and remain throughout the child's life (p. xiii). Parents often do not realize that they teach their children aggressive behaviour when trying to do the opposite. For example, reprimanding a child for aggressive behaviour by shouting, grabbing, or threats is almost worse than not reprimanding the child at all. Witnessing this type of reprimand causes the child to revert to it as soon as he or she is upset (Fraser, 1996, p. 349). Even worse is directly experiencing physical or emotional abuse (Elliott, 1994, p. 3). Such negative reinforcement does not have to come from a parent but can occur when simply watching a violent TV program.

PROVIDING DEPTH: VARIETY AND EMPHASIS

When you revise an early draft to improve clarity, you will likely find opportunities to make your prose more interesting. Variety and emphasis in your writing will make what is competent also *compelling*. Variety and emphasis are worthwhile goals in all forms of essays: literary, argumentative, and expository.

Sentence Variety

Length

You can vary sentence length for rhetorical effect. Just as short paragraphs suggest underdeveloped points, short, choppy sentences could suggest a lack of content. On the other hand, several long sentences in a row could confuse a reader. Consider revision if you find you have written several short or long sentences in a row.

To connect short sentences you can use appropriate conjunctions. Simple sentences can be joined by one of the seven coordinating conjunctions. If the idea in one sentence is less important than the idea in the sentence before or after it, use the subordinating conjunction or relative pronoun that best expresses the relationship between the sentences. You can also join independent clauses with a semicolon or a colon:

Stephenie Meyer wrote the *Twilight* saga. E.L. James wrote *Fifty Shades of Grey*.

Stephenie Meyer wrote the *Twilight* saga, *and* E.L. James wrote *Fifty Shades of Grey*. (coordinating conjunction used as joiner—see p. 315)

E.L. James's heroine begins a provocative relationship with millionaire Christian Grey, *although* she initially believes he will not be interested in her. (subordinating conjunction used as joiner—see p. 315)

Grey has a scarily controlling personality: *he* is both physically and emotionally abusive to Anastasia. (colon used as joiner—see p. 315)

Coordinating conjunctions—*and, or, but, so, for, nor,* and *yet*—join equally important ideas, whereas subordinating conjunctions—such as *whereas*—introduce less important information.

You can also join independent clauses with a conjunctive adverb or transitional phrase, ensuring that a semicolon precedes the connecting word or phrase. You may be able to grammatically connect phrases or clauses through a parallel relationship, such as apposition. The second phrase or clause could also modify the preceding word, phrase, or clause—for example, a relative (adjectival) clause could give information about a preceding noun clause:

Fifty Shades of Grey was soundly criticized for its poor writing. It quickly became an international best seller.

Fifty Shades of Grey was soundly criticized for its poor writing; *however,* it quickly became an international best seller. (conjunctive adverb joiner—see p. 313)

Fifty Shades of Grey became an international best seller. It has sold 60 million copies.

Fifty Shades of Grey, an international best seller, has sold 60 million copies. (appositive)

Fifty Shades of Grey has sold 60 million copies, *which makes it an international best seller.* (relative clause—see p. 328)

You waste space when you begin a new sentence or paragraph by repeating part of the previous one. Although repetition can be used to build coherence, it should not create redundancy:

Redundant: In 1970, Gordon O. Gallup created the mirror test. ~~This test was~~ designed to determine whether ~~or not~~ animals are self-aware.

Revised: In 1970, Gordon O. Gallup created the mirror test, designed to determine whether animals are self-aware.

See chapter 11 to review punctuation rules.

An *appositive* consists of a noun or noun phrase that is parallel to a preceding noun and names it or restates its meaning (see page 310).

EXERCISE 9.15

The following paragraph consists of too many short sentences. Using the strategies mentioned above, revise the paragraph to make it more effective.

[1] During the earth's long history, there have been various periods of glaciation. [2] This fact is well known. [3] There is also evidence of one great glacial event. [4] It is possible that the earth was once completely covered by ice and snow. [5] Skeptics argue this is impossible. [6] They say that the earth could never have become this cold. [7] The idea of the tropics being frozen over is unlikely, they believe.

To learn about sentences that have two or more clauses, see Sentence Types in chapter 10 (p. 327).

When checking your work for overly long sentences, consider breaking up sentences with more than two independent clauses or one independent clause and more than two dependent clauses. See if the relationships between the clauses are clear. If they are not, divide the sentences where clauses are joined by conjunctions, by transitional words and phrases, or by relative pronouns.

A **PREPOSITIONAL PHRASE** begins with a preposition and acts as an adjective or adverb.

A **PARTICIPIAL PHRASE** is a type of verbal phrase that acts as an adjective, usually at the beginning of the sentence/clause.

The following sentence is a little hard to read because of the number of dependent clauses, numbered below:

> Thirty years ago, China's population growth became a serious social problem [1] since the nation's capacity to produce resources, like food and water, would be exceeded [2]if the population kept growing at a rapid pace, [3]which would put China's stable economy in jeopardy.

One solution is to put a period after the independent clause and choose the most important idea among the dependent clauses for the independent clause in a separate sentence. In the revision below, the most important idea is that China's economy would be endangered:

> Thirty years ago, China's population growth became a serious social problem. If the population kept growing at a rapid pace, China's stable economy would be jeopardized since the nation's capacity to produce resources, like food and water, would be exceeded.

EXERCISE 9.16

↻ Check answers to select questions

The following paragraph consists of sentences that are too long. Using the strategies mentioned above, revise the paragraph to make it more effective.

[1] Finding a definition for "the homeless" is difficult, but the most common definition, which is used both in the media and in current research, defines the homeless as those who lack visible shelter or use public shelters. [2] Literature about homelessness is sparse, and it was not until the 1980s that the incidence of homelessness began to be reported in the media, but homelessness has existed for centuries, and literature on the subject dates back to the feudal period in Europe.

An **INFINITIVE PHRASE** consists of *to* followed by the bare verb; as a sentence opener, it can act as an adjective or adverb.

An **ABSOLUTE PHRASE** consists of a noun/pronoun and a partial verb form, modifying the entire sentence.

Structural Variety

You can experiment with phrasal openings to sentences. Consider beginning the occasional sentence with a prepositional phrase, a verbal phrase, or an absolute phrase instead of the subject of the sentence.

Prepositional phrases begin with a preposition followed by a noun or pronoun (see p. 324); they are adjectival or adverbial and modify the closest noun (adjectival) or verb (adverbial). A **participial phrase**, which ends in *-ing*, *-ed*, or *-en*, is a verbal phrase acting as an adjective. An **infinitive phrase**, which is preceded by *to*, can act adjectivally or adverbially as a sentence opener. An **absolute phrase**, consisting of a noun/pronoun and a partial verb form, modifies the entire sentence.

In this short excerpt from an essay about the death of a moth, Virginia Woolf uses a prepositional phrase opening, an absolute phrase that introduces an independent clause, and two verbal phrase openings:

After a time, <u>tired by his dancing</u> apparently, he settled on the window ledge in the sun, and **the queer spectacle being at an end**, I forgot about him. Then, <u>looking up</u>, my eye was caught by him. He was trying to resume his dancing, but seemed either so stiff or so awkward that he could only flutter to the bottom of the window-pane; and when he tried to fly across it, he failed.

Note the types of modifiers:

After a time: prepositional phrase

<u>tired by his dancing</u>, <u>looking up</u>: verbal phrases

the queer spectacle being at an end: absolute phrase

Creating Emphasis

Writers may create emphasis by presenting main points or details in a particular order. Two kinds of sentences vary in the order in which they present the main idea: *periodic* and *cumulative* sentences.

A **periodic sentence** begins with a modifier—word, phrase, or clause—before the independent clause. A **cumulative sentence** works the other way: it begins with an independent clause, followed by a modifying or parallel word, phrase, or clause. While a periodic sentence delays the main idea, creating anticipation, a cumulative sentence develops the main idea by drawing it out. Many sentences are slightly or moderately periodic or cumulative, depending on whether the writer has begun or ended with modifiers. However, a writer can employ either periodic or cumulative sentences to create a specific effect. Independent clauses are shown by italics in the examples below:

Periodic:

Unlike novelists and playwrights, who lurk behind the scenes while distracting our attention with the puppet show of imaginary characters—and unlike the scholars and journalists, who quote the opinions of others and take cover behind the hedges of neutrality—*the essayist has nowhere to hide* (Scott Russell Sanders, "The Singular First Person").

Cumulative:

The root of all evil is that we all want this spiritual gratification, this flow, this apparent heightening of life, this knowledge, this valley of many-colored grass, even grass and light prismatically decomposed, giving ecstasy (D.H. Lawrence, *Studies in Classic American Literature*).

A writer can delay the main idea, generating tension by beginning with a prepositional phrase:

Behind the deconstructionists' dazzling cloud of language lie certain more or less indisputable facts (John Gardner, *The Art of Fiction*).

Other ways to achieve emphasis include parallel structures and repetition—techniques that also help in paragraph coherence—and rhythms that call the reader's

> When you use a participial phrase at the beginning of a sentence, make sure that you include the word it is intended to modify so that it does not dangle. (See Dangling Modifiers, p. 379.)

> A **PERIODIC SENTENCE** begins with modifiers, building toward the main idea.
>
> A **CUMULATIVE SENTENCE** begins with the main idea and is followed by modifiers that expand on this idea.

attention to important ideas. The end of a sentence in itself provides emphasis, since a reader naturally slows down when approaching the last part of a sentence and pauses slightly between sentences.

Sample Essay for Rhetorical Analysis

Several stylistic choices have been discussed above, which you can use in your own writing. When you write a rhetorical analysis, you can read an essay to ask why the writer made the choices that he or she did, whether they were effective, and what they contribute to the essay. In the excerpt below, from Michael Ignatieff's book *Fire and Ashes*, the author reflects on his learning experience as a former leader of the Liberal Party of Canada. A skilled and sophisticated writer, Ignatieff employs many of the strategies discussed in this chapter, while making his prose concise and direct. He also uses some of the strategies for coherence discussed in chapter 3. The marginal annotations could be used as the basis for a rhetorical analysis.

→ For some differences between a critical and a rhetorical analysis, see chapter 4, page 106.

SAMPLE PROFESSIONAL ESSAY

Excerpt from *Fire and Ashes*

by Michael Ignatieff

Sophisticated writers often vary paragraph structure, including placement of the topic sentence. In this paragraph, Ignatieff begins with an epigrammatic opening, attracting the reader's attention, before introducing the topic of the paragraph in the second sentence.

Epigram: a concise, witty saying.

[1]   What you learn from your mistakes is that politics is a game with words, but it isn't Scrabble. No one who enters the political arena for the first time is ever prepared for its adversarial quality. Every word you utter becomes an opportunity for your opponents to counter-attack. Inevitably you will take it personally, and that is your first mistake. You have to learn what the lifers, wise with years of experience, have long since understood: it's never personal; it's strictly business. . . .

[2]   You can try complaining about the bad faith of an opponent to the press, but they aren't referees. They've come to watch the fight, and they want a good one. As one of them said to me, "Our job is to watch the battle and then come down on the field and shoot the wounded." Once you've been shot at, you handle all your interactions with the media with utmost care. You become strategic. You become as careful as your appearance, every hair in place, tie well knotted, suit immaculate, armoured for the day of battle. In entering politics, you have to surrender spontaneity and one of life's pleasures—saying the first thing that comes into your head. If you are to survive, you have to fit a filter between your brain and your mouth. When words are weapons and can be turned against you, freely expressing yourself is a luxury you can't afford. Your language, like your personality, becomes guarded. You can still have fun. Indeed you must have fun, since everyone likes a happy warrior, but every happy warrior is a watchful one.

Ignatieff uses an analogy (comparison) in the first four sentences to expand on the adversarial nature of politics. He ends the paragraph by returning to the analogy, referring to "happy warriors" who must be "watchful"; thus, he makes an effective word choice, which helps provide a transition to the topic of the next paragraph, the need for caution when speaking to the press.

After a short simple sentence, Ignatieff uses a cumulative sentence, beginning with the main idea and following with a list, which adds detail. Although it is more associated with literary writing, Ignatieff uses alliteration in two of the last three sentences, repeating the *w* sound at the beginning of words in close proximity.

[3]   Obviously, a straight answer to a straight question is a good idea, and when citizens put a question to you, such candour becomes an obligation. They elect you, after all. The rules are different with the press. In the strange kabuki play of a press conference or interview, candour is a temptation best avoided. Be candid if you can, be strategic if you must. All truth is good, the African proverb goes, but not all truth is good to say. You never try to lie, but you don't have to answer the question you're asked, only the question you want to answer.

> This paragraph, like others, is notable for its use of parallel structure, like the highlighted passage. Note the use of the coordinating conjunction *but* to join equal grammatical units, independent clauses.

[4]   As you submit to the compromises demanded by public life, your public self begins to alter the person inside. Within a year of entering politics, I had the disoriented feeling of having been taken over by a doppelganger, a strange new persona I could barely recognize when I looked at myself in a mirror. I wore Harry Rosen suits—and Harry himself had chalked the trousers—and my ties were carefully matched to my shirts. I had never been so well-dressed in my life and had never felt so hollow. Looking back now, I would say that some sense of hollowness, some sense of a divide between the face you present to the world and the face you reserve for the mirror, is a sign of sound mental health. It's when you no longer notice that the public self has taken over the private self that trouble starts. When you forget that you have a private realm that you want to keep separate from the public gaze, you'll soon surrender your whole life to politics. You become your smile, the fixed rictus of geniality that politics demands of you. When that happens, you've lost yourself.

> Ignatieff begins and ends the paragraph by using the second person (you, your), which is appropriate because he is generalizing about the public versus the private selves. In between, he uses his own experiences to support the claim in the topic sentence. The "I" voice also helps convey the self-reflective tone of the passage.

Source: *Fire and Ashes: Success and Failure in Politics.* Random House, 2013.

> The use of the word *rictus* is another example of careful diction. A rictus is a fixed, gaping smile. Why might this be an apt choice to convey Ignatieff's meaning?

> Ignatieff uses devices of emphasis in the second half of this paragraph. His use of "It is . . . when," Instead of a more concise choice, creates emphasis through rhythm. In the last three sentences, he uses decreasing sentence length to build towards the final, shortest sentence, drawing attention to the epigrammatic, "When that happens, you've lost yourself."

Write a rhetorical analysis of "Why Politicians Should Be More Like Professors," by David D. Perlmutter, page 151, focusing on the kinds of strategies discussed in this chapter as well as in chapter 3, Essay and Paragraph Structure, page 60.

EXERCISE 9.17

Common Words That Confuse

English has many word pairs that are confusing either because the two words look similar (e.g., *affect* and *effect*) or because they have similar, but not identical, uses (e.g., *amount* and *number*)—or both. In most cases, the dictionary is the best resource for unravelling difficulties that pertain solely to meaning, but usage can be more complicated. The words below are the "Top 15" that continue to give student writers the most trouble. Hints and examples are provided to help you distinguish them.

For a guide to spelling, there is no better resource than the dictionary; if you have the slightest doubt about the spelling of a word, consult a dictionary—don't rely on a spell-checker.

- **affect**, **effect**. **Affect** is a verb meaning "to influence or have an effect on." **Effect**, a noun, means "a result." As a verb, effect is less often used; it means "to bring about" or "to cause"—not "to have an effect on."

  Hint: Try substituting *influence* in the sentence; if it fits your intended meaning, *affect* is the word you want.

  The news of Sidney Crosby's return to hockey greatly affected his fans. The effect was also felt in Pittsburgh where a dramatic increase in attendance was effected.

- **allot**, **a lot**. **Allot**, a verb, means "to portion out"; **a lot** can be an adverb (*I sleep a lot*) or a noun (*I need a lot of sleep*) meaning "a great deal." *A lot* is too informal for most academic writing; you should use the more formal *a great deal*, *many*, *much*, or similar substitutes. The one-word spelling, *alot*, is incorrect.

  My parents allotted me $500 spending money for the term, which was not a lot considering my shopping habit. (informal)

- **allusion**, **illusion**. A literary **allusion** is a historical, religious, mythic, literary, or other kind of outside reference used thematically or to reveal character. An **illusion** is something apparently seen that is not real or is something that gives a false impression.

  Hint: Since the most common mistake is misspelling *allusion* as *illusion* in literary essays, you could remember that *allusion*, meaning an outside reference, *al*ways begins with *al*.

  The title of Nathanael West's novel *The Day of the Locust* is an allusion to the Book of Exodus in the Bible.

  Optical illusions often use graphics to fool our senses.

- **amount**, **number**. Use **amount** to refer to things that can't be counted; **number** refers to countable objects.

  Hint: Think of using numbers when you count.

  The number of errors in this essay reveals the amount of care you took in writing it.

- **bias**, **biased**. **Bias** is a noun that refers to a "tendency to judge unfairly"; **biased** is an adjective that means "having or showing a preferential attitude." A person can have a bias (a thing); be a biased person (adjective modifying *person*); or can be biased (predicate adjective after a linking verb). A person cannot *be bias*. Also, a person is biased or has a bias *against* (not *to*, *toward*, or *for*) something or someone.

  His bias against the Rastafarian lifestyle caused him to overlook some of its ideals.

- **cite, sight, site**. **To cite**, a verb, is "to refer to an outside source." (The complete naming of the source itself is a citation.) **Sight** (noun or verb) refers to seeing, one of the five senses. **Site**, when used as a noun, is a location or place (usually of some importance). The most common error in essays is the use of *site* when *cite* is meant.

  Hint: Remember that *cite* is a verb referring to "the act of giving a citation"; *site* is "where something is situated or sits."

  She said the ruins were excavated in 1926, citing as proof the historic plaque that commemorated the site.

- **e.g., i.e. E.g.** is an abbreviation for the Latin ***exempli gratia***, meaning "for the sake of example"; **i.e.** is an abbreviation for the Latin ***id est***, meaning "that is." Use "e.g." before one or more examples; use "i.e." if you want to elaborate on or clarify a preceding statement. In both cases, use a period after each letter and a comma after the abbreviation. Because they are abbreviations, they should be avoided in formal writing.

  Hint: The first letter in *example* tells you that examples should follow "e.g.".

  J.K. Rowling defied the common formula for success in the children's book market by writing long novels, e.g., *Harry Potter and the Goblet of Fire*, *Harry Potter and the Order of the Phoenix*. Some of Rowling's novels have episodic plots that contain many well-developed characters; i.e., they tend to be long.

- **its, it's**. **Its** is a possessive adjective meaning "belonging to it." Remember that a pronoun possessive form (except some indefinite pronouns) does not include an apostrophe. **It's** is the contraction for *it is*, the apostrophe indicating that the second letter *i* is left out.

  Hint: Try substituting *it is* if you're having problems identifying the correct form; if it fits, then use *it's*; if it doesn't, use *its*. (*Its* is usually followed by a noun.)

  It's foolish to judge a book by its cover.

- **led, lead**. **Led** and **lead** are forms of the irregular verb **to lead** (long ē); the present tense is also **lead**. However, the past tense and the past participle are **led** (short ě). Writers may become confused by the noun *lead*, the metal, which looks like *to lead*, but is pronounced like *led*. Therefore, when they come to write the past tense *led*, they may wrongly substitute the noun *lead*, rather than the verb.

  Hint: Don't be led astray by thinking there is an *a* in *led*.

  Although she led in the polls by a 2:1 margin three months ago, today she leads by only a slight margin.

- **loose, lose**. **Loose** is the adjective meaning "not tight"; **lose** is a verb meaning "not to be able to find," or "to be defeated."

Hint: When you lose something, it is lost. *Lost* is spelled with one *o*.

If you don't tighten that loose button, you're going to lose it.

- **than**, **then**. **Than** is a conjunction used in comparisons (*He's happier than he knows*). **Then** is an adverb with temporal connotations meaning "consequently," "at that time," "after that," etc.

  Hint: If you're comparing one thing to *another*, use "th*an*." *Then* "tells when."

  Warren said he was better at darts than Mark, and then he challenged him to a game to prove it.

- **their**, **there**, **they're**. **Their** is a possessive adjective meaning "belonging to them"; **there** is an adverb meaning "in that place"; **they're** is the contraction of *they are*, the apostrophe indicating that the letter *a* is left out.

  Hint: If you're uncertain about *they're*, substitute *they are*; *there* (meaning "in that place") is spelled the same as *here* ("in this place") with the letter *t* added.

  There is no excuse for the rowdy behaviour in there; they're supposed to be in their rooms.

- **to**, **too**. **To** is a preposition indicating "direction toward"; **too** is an adverb meaning "also."

  Hint: *To* will usually be followed by a noun or pronoun as part of a prepositional phrase; substitute *also* for *too*.

  The next time you go to the store, may I come along, too?

- **usage**, **use**. Many writers overuse **usage**, which refers to "a customary or habitual pattern or practice." It applies to conventions of groups of people, such as "language usage of the English." Usage shouldn't be used simply to characterize a repeated action.

  Incorrect: The usage of fax machines and email has allowed businesses to increase their efficiency.

  Example: I have no use for people who are always correcting my usage of *whom*.

- **you're**, **your**. **You're** is the contraction of *you are*; **your** is a possessive adjective that means "belonging to you."

  Hint: Try substituting *you are*. If it fits, then *you're* is the correct form.

  You're going to be sorry if you don't take your turn and do the dishes tonight.

Here is a list of 50 additional words that often give students trouble. Although students may confuse them, more often they use the term in the first column when that in the second column is intended.

Don't Say . . .	**When You Mean**
adolescents	adolescence (the *time* one is an adolescent)
around	about (in reference to numbers)
associated to	associated with
attribute to	contribute to
based off of/around	based on
in comparison to	compared to
compliment	complement
conscience	conscious
continuous	continual (meaning *often*)
could of/would of	could have/would have
council	counsel
demise	death
different than	different from
downfall	disadvantage
downside	disadvantage
farther	further (*farther* applies to physical distance)
first off	first
imply	infer
insure	ensure
issues	problems
lifestyle	life
like (a preposition)	as (a conjunction)
locality/location	place
majority of	most
man	human/humanity
manpower	resources
mindset	belief
misfortunate	unfortunate
multiple	many
none the less	nonetheless
obsess about	to be obsessed about
obtain	attain
passed	past
popular	common
principal	principle
references	refers to (*references* is a plural noun)
reoccur	recur
seize	cease
so	very
thanks to	due to
that	who/whom (to refer to people)
thru	through
till	until

to transition	to change
uninterested	disinterested
upon	on
weather	whether
were	where
which	who/whom (to refer to people)
within	in

As you progress through your course, you may find other groupings of words that you have problems with. Add them, along with definitions and correct usage, to the list above.

EXERCISE 9.18

Choose 10 of the words from the list above that you know give you trouble. Find the definitions of these words and then write sentences using the words correctly.

CHAPTER SUMMARY

This chapter has focused on clear, effective writing that is concise, direct, precise, and specific. You are encouraged to identify areas in your writing that may be unclear in your early drafts. Identifying and revising wordy or imprecise writing will also strengthen your prose as the stress will fall on the important words in the sentence. Effective prose, however, consists of more than just avoiding stylistic awkwardness: it provides freshness, variety, and emphasis. When writing factually, whether informing or arguing, you need to put clarity above a distinctive writing style.

Sentence Essentials

10

As a writer, you are responsible for ensuring that readers can understand your message, so you need to become familiar with grammatical rules if you are to write effectively; as well, just as dressing for the occasion improves your standing in the group you are interacting with, the proper use of language creates a positive image, adding to your credibility as an academic writer. In this chapter, you will be introduced to the basic concepts of grammar that you can build on in chapters 11 and 12 to help you succeed as a grammatical writer. After beginning with the smallest word units in the sentence, the parts of speech, we look at what a simple sentence is, how to recognize phrases and clauses, and how to join clauses to form more complex sentence types.

LEARNING OBJECTIVES

- to recognize and be able to identify the seven major parts of speech and their functions in the sentence
- to understand the two definitions of a sentence: a completed thought; a group of words with a subject and predicate that needs nothing else to complete it
- to recognize two types of sentence fragments and to be able to fix them
- to learn how to identify two types of clauses and to join them to create different sentence types, such as compound and complex sentences

- to identify run-on sentences as two independent clauses with no punctuation to separate the thoughts and to fix them in your writing
- to identify comma splices as two independent clauses joined only by a comma and to fix them in your writing

GRAMMATICAL GROUNDWORK

Guidelines for usage determine what words are suitable for a typical reader or listener. The typical reader of academic prose is different from the typical reader of a popular book, an office memo, a blog, or an email. Therefore, the level of usage is different.

Learning grammar is a way to improve your writing and further your understanding of English syntax. Like clear writing, correct grammar helps create a channel of clear communication between you, the writer, and the reader. In university, learning the rules of formal usage and correct grammar is vital. However, not all the writing you do at university is formal. For example, you might correspond with classmates using a tablet or cellphone, in which case you will probably write more informally, using colloquialisms or other "casual," everyday language.

Informal writing may also apply to certain kinds of business, technical, or journalistic writing. Some writing samples in this book, like "Embrace the Mediocrity Principle" in chapter 1, page 19, are designed for a wider reading public than are academic studies and employ more informal language and looser sentence structure. For more information on the differences between formal and informal writing, see chapter 9, page 289.

EXERCISE 10.1

Find one example each of formal and informal prose from a magazine, newspaper, or book. Consider how the formal example could be changed into informal prose, taking into account such factors as vocabulary, sentence length and variety, tone of voice, and audience. Rewrite it as informal prose, keeping it about the same length. Then, rewrite the informal example as formal prose, considering the same factors and keeping it about the same length.

INTRODUCING . . . THE PARTS OF SPEECH

A **SENTENCE** is a group of words that includes a subject and predicate and expresses a complete thought.

PARTS OF SPEECH are categories that words belong to depending on their functions in the sentence.

Before considering the **sentence**, the basic unit of written communication in English, you need to be able to identify what makes up a sentence. A sentence can be divided into words, which have specific functions within the sentence as the parts of speech. Phrases and clauses are larger units than individual words. Being able to identify the forms and functions of the parts of speech will help you understand these larger units, too. The seven major **parts of speech** are

- nouns
- pronouns
- adjectives
- verbs
- adverbs
- prepositions
- conjunctions

Interjections, such as *oh!* and *hey*, usually express surprise or other emotion, and are not grammatically related to the rest of the sentence.

The Parts of Speech at Work

When you are hired by an organization, given a job title, and a detailed job description, the job title is what you will be called, but the full job description explains your responsibilities, duties, or functions within the organization. The parts of speech, too, have specific, assigned roles within their organizational structure, the sentence.

Each part of speech is described below, with examples of its uses. The chart introducing each section gives definitions to help you identify that part of speech; it also lists its major functions in the sentence. Being aware of the functions of the parts of speech within the sentence (their job descriptions) will help you apply the rules of grammar.

Nouns and Pronouns

Nouns are important words in a sentence because they name people, places, things, and ideas. Nouns and their replacements, pronouns, appear in the chart below.

TABLE 10.1 Nouns and Their Functions

IDENTIFICATION	FUNCTIONS
Noun: name of a person, a place, a thing, or an idea. • *Proper* nouns refer to names and begin with a capital letter. • *Common* nouns refer to class or a general group and are not capitalized. • *Concrete* nouns refer to physical objects and things experienced through the senses. • *Abstract* nouns refer to concepts, ideas, and abstractions. • *Count* nouns name things that can be counted. • *Non-count* nouns refer to things that can't be counted. • *Collective* nouns refer to groups comprising individual members.	1. **Subject**: performs the action of the verb (the doer of the action); is sometimes called the *simple subject* to distinguish it from the *complete subject*, which includes the simple subject plus its modifiers 2. **Object** (also called the *direct object*): receives the action of the verb 3. **Object of a preposition** (also called the *indirect object*): is usually preceded by a preposition (such as *between, in, with*) 4. **Subjective complement** (also called the *predicate noun*): follows a linking verb (often a form of *to be* such as *is, are, was, were*) and can be linked to the subject 5. **Appositive**: is grammatically parallel to the previous noun or noun phrase
Pronoun ("in place of the noun"): usually takes the place of a noun in a sentence. See Pronouns on page 310.	Since pronouns generally replace nouns, they share the functions of nouns listed above.

1. *Subject.* The subject noun usually performs the action (but see chapter 9, p. 280, for examples of the passive construction, where the subject does not perform the action). In the following examples, the subject is in boldface; the action word, the verb, is italicized:

   Dan *stood* at the front of the line-up.

   She *awoke* before dawn.

   The **rain** in Spain *falls* mainly on the plain.

   The subject usually comes before the verb but sometimes follows it, as, for example, with some questions:

   Was the final **exam** difficult?

2. *Object (of the verb)* is also called the *direct object*. It is the receiver of the action of the verb. Here, the object is in boldface; the verb is italicized:

   James *beat* **Dan** into the movie theatre.

   Erin *let* **him** into the house.

   They *chopped* the **logs** for firewood.

3. *Object of the preposition* (also called *indirect object*). The noun or pronoun is usually preceded by a preposition. Here, the object is in boldface; its preposition is italicized:

   She awoke *before* **dawn**.

   The rain *in* **Spain** falls mainly *on* the **plain**.

   I never heard *of* **it** before.

4. *Subjective complement (completion).* The noun or pronoun that "completes" the subject after a linking verb. Here, the subjective completion is in boldface; the linking verb is italicized; the subject is underlined:

   <u>Rayna</u> *was* the first **person** to get a job after graduation.

5. *Appositive.* A noun, noun phrase, or pronoun that is grammatically parallel to a preceding noun or pronoun and that rephrases or (re)names the preceding noun. Here, the appositive is in boldface; the preceding noun is italicized:

   Madeline's *cats*, **Evie and Nanny**, have very different personalities.

   The subject of the sentence is *cats*; the names of the cats are in apposition to the subject (the names are not part of the simple subject).

Pronouns

1. **Personal pronouns** refer to people and things; in the possessive case, they can function as adjectives, as does *her* in the second example below. Here, the pronouns are in boldface:

   He ran all the way to the sea.

   She sat down because **her** feet were blistered.

A **PERSONAL PRONOUN** refers to people and things.

2. **Relative pronouns** (*that, which, who*) introduce dependent clauses that *relate* the clause to the rest of the sentence; these clauses act as adjectives. Here, the relative pronouns are in boldface:

   The book, **which** I lost on the bus, was about Greek history. The student **who** found it returned it to me.

3. **Interrogative pronouns** (*how, what, when, where, which, who, why*) introduce questions. Here, the interrogative pronouns are in boldface:

   Where is the book I lost on the bus? **How** can I thank you enough for returning it?

4. **Demonstrative pronouns** (*that, these, this, those*) point to nouns; they can function as adjectives when they precede nouns. Here, the demonstrative pronouns are in boldface, and the nouns they refer to are italicized:

   This is the *day* of reckoning.

   This *day* will be long remembered.

5. **Indefinite pronouns** (such as *any, everything, some*) refer to unspecified individuals or groups; they do not require an antecedent and may form their possessives in the same way as nouns. Here, the indefinite pronouns are in boldface:

   It is **anyone's** guess when the boat will arrive, but **everyone** should wait on the dock.

6. **Reflexive pronouns** have the form of personal pronouns with the *-self* suffix; they refer *back* to the subject as the receiver of an action. Here, the subject is italicized and the reflexive pronoun is in boldface:

   Ben congratulated **himself** on his successful election.

7. **Intensive pronouns** also have the form of personal pronouns with the *-self* suffix; they serve to reinforce their antecedents. Here, the subject is italicized and the intensive pronoun is in boldface:

   The *teacher* **herself** was often late for class.

8. **Reciprocal pronouns** refer to the separate parts of a plural antecedent. Here, the reciprocal pronoun is in boldface and the antecedent is italicized:

   People need to accept and tolerate **one another**.

Verbs

Verbs convey an action, a state, or a condition. There are three different kinds of verbs, each having different functions.

The various tenses of English verbs are printed on the inside cover.

1. *Main verbs* express action, condition, or a state of being. Some kinds of action are not necessarily visible—*imagine, suggest,* and *think* are examples of action verbs in which the "action" is interior or mental.

   Nicole **helps** her father at the store every Saturday.

A **RELATIVE PRONOUN** introduces a dependent clause that *relates* the clause to the rest of the sentence.

An **INTERROGATIVE PRONOUN** introduces a question.

A **DEMONSTRATIVE PRONOUN** points to specific things.

An **INDEFINITE PRONOUN** refers to unspecified individuals or groups.

A **REFLEXIVE PRONOUN** refers back to the subject as the receiver of an action.

An **INTENSIVE PRONOUN** serves to reinforce its antecedent.

A **RECIPROCAL PRONOUN** refers to the separate parts of a plural antecedent.

The predicate consists of one or more words and contains the main verb.

TABLE 10.2 Verbs and Their Functions

IDENTIFICATION	FUNCTIONS
Verb: conveys an action, a state, or a condition, or precedes another (main) verb. The different kinds of verbs have different functions.	1. **Main verb** may be *transitive* (takes a direct object) or *intransitive* (does not take a direct object) and usually conveys an action (not necessarily physical) in the predicate. 2. **Helping** or **auxiliary verb** precedes main verb to form a complex tense (indications of the time, continuance, or completeness of the action) or to express a *mood* such as obligation, necessity, probability, or possibility; or *voice*, (whether the relation of verb to subject is active or passive). 3. **Linking verb** is followed by a *predicate noun* or *adjective* that refers back to the subject.

A **MODAL** is a verb form placed before a main verb to express necessity and similar conditions.

2. *Helping verbs* (also called **auxiliary verbs**) combine with main verbs. The two most common helping verbs are *to be* (*am, are, is, was, were, will be*, etc.) and *to have* (*have, has, had*, etc.) Forms of *to be* are used in the *progressive* tenses; forms of *to have* are used in the *perfect* tenses (see inside cover).

    She has helped her father at the store for two years.

    Modals are verb forms placed before the main verb to express necessity, obligation, possibility, probability, and similar conditions: *can, could, will, would, shall, should, may, might, must*, and *ought to* are modals (see inside cover).

    She would help on Sunday, too, if not for her other weekend job.

Although verbs often convey an action, some verbs do not express what a subject is doing, but rather express a condition or state of being. The most common of these verbs are forms of *to be*: *is, are, was, were, has been, have been, will be*, and so on. Because you will use these verbs often, you need to become familiar with them and recognize them as a particular kind of verb.

3. *Linking verbs* like *to be* are used to connect a subject and the word following the verb (a predicate noun or adjective). The linking verbs are in boldface:

    I am upset. (*upset* is an adjective)

    These are my colleagues. (*colleagues* is a noun)

    The words that follow the linking verb name or describe the subject. Similar verbs that may be linking verbs according to their context include *act, appear, become, feel, grow, look, prove, remain, stay, seem, smell, sound*, and *taste*.

Modifiers: Adjectives and Adverbs

Adjectives and adverbs modify, or give more information about, the major parts of speech—nouns and verbs. *Articles*, such as *a, an*, and *the*, and determiners, such as *her* and *this*, may precede nouns and can be considered to function adjectivally.

TABLE 10.3 Adjectives and Adverbs and Their Functions

IDENTIFICATION	FUNCTIONS
Adjective: a word that modifies and precedes a noun or follows a linking verb; it answers the question *Which?*, *What kind?*, or *How many?*	1. **Adjectival modifier** describes or particularizes a noun and precedes it. 2. **Subjective complement** (also called the *predicate adjective*) follows a linking verb (see Nouns and Pronouns above on page 309) and modifies the subject.
Adverb: a word that modifies a verb, adjective, adverb, or even an entire sentence; it often ends in *-ly* and answers the question *When?*, *Where?*, *Why?*, *How?*, *To what degree?*, or *How much?*	1. **Adverbial modifier** describes or particularizes a verb; may also modify an adjective or another adverb; a *sentence adverb* may modify the entire sentence. 2. **Conjunctive adverb** may be used to connect two independent clauses.

Adjectives modify nouns and usually precede them. Here, the adjective is in boldface and the modified noun is underlined:

They attended the **delightful** <u>party</u>.

Adjectives can also follow linking verbs, where they *modify the subject* as *predicate adjectives*. Here, the predicate adjective is in bold, the linking verb is italicized, and the subject is underlined.

The <u>party</u> *was* **delightful**.

Adverbs modify verbs, adjectives, and adverbs.

1. Here, the boldface adverb modifies the italicized verb:

   Jake *turned* **suddenly**.

2. Here, the boldface adverb modifies the italicized adjective:

   That looks like a **very** *contented* cow.

3. In this example, the boldface adverb modifies another adverb (italicized):

   They lived **quite** *happily* together.

Some adverbs can also act as conjunctions to connect two independent clauses. Here, the **conjunctive adverb** is in boldface:

Richard was hired by the publicity firm on Monday; **however**, he was fired on Tuesday.

Note the semicolon separating the clauses and the comma after *however*.

Joiners: Prepositions and Conjunctions

Prepositions and conjunctions are classed together here as they connect different parts of a sentence.

TABLE 10.4 Prepositions and Conjunctions and Their Functions

IDENTIFICATION	FUNCTIONS
Preposition: ("to put before"): a small word or short phrase that often refers to place or time.	1. Preposition joins the following noun or pronoun to the rest of the sentence.
Conjunction: a word or phrase that connects words, phrases, and clauses of equal or unequal weight or importance. For a list of common subordinating conjunctions, see page 321.	1. **Coordinating conjunction** joins *equal* units, including independent clauses; there are seven coordinating conjunctions. (See p. 315.)
	2. **Subordinating conjunction** introduces a dependent clause. (See p. 321.)
	3. **Correlative conjunction** joins *parallel* units; they join in pairs.

Prepositions join nouns and pronouns to the rest of the sentence, thus adding detail to the subject or predicate. Prepositions introduce prepositional phrases, which function as *adjectives* or *adverbs*, depending on what part of speech they modify. In the following examples, the preposition is in boldface, the object of the preposition is italicized, and the prepositional phrase is underlined:

You will find the letters **in** the *attic*. She worked **during** the summer *vacation*.

They laughed **at** *him*.

Commonly used prepositions. Listed below are 50 commonly used prepositions. Prepositions can also be more than one word (see list below) but can often be recognized as such by the fact that a noun or pronoun follows and that the phrase that the preposition begins acts as an adjective or adverb.

about	despite	outside (of)
above	down	over
across	during	regarding
after	except	since
against	for	than
along	from	through
among	in	throughout
around	inside	to
as	into	toward(s)
at	like	under
before	near	until
behind	next (to)	up
below	of	upon
beside(s)	off	with
between	on	within
beyond	onto	without
by	opposite	

Conjunctions have two main joining functions: they can join equal or unequal units.

1. *Coordinating conjunctions* join *equal* units—words to words, phrases to phrases, clauses to clauses. An important use of coordinating conjunctions is to join *independent clauses* in compound sentences. Here, the coordinating conjunction is in boldface. Note the comma before the conjunction:

   Tanya objected to their new roommate, **but** Mercedes liked her.

   Coordinating conjunctions are often referred to as the **FANBOYS** (*for, and, nor, but, or, yet, so*).

2. *Subordinating conjunctions* join *unequal* units—a *dependent* clause, which it begins and is part of, to an *independent* clause. Here, the subordinating conjunction is in boldface. Note the comma in the second sentence:

   He plans to exercise his option **once** the season is over.

   Once the season is over, he plans to exercise his option.

3. *Correlative conjunctions* occur in pairs and require parallel structure. Here, the correlative conjunctions are in boldface:

   Either you will support me, **or** you will not be able to borrow my car.

   Both Ali **and** his father work at the community centre on Saturdays.

> The seven coordinating conjunctions are *for, and, nor, but, or, yet, so*. The coordinating conjunctions spell out the acronym **FANBOYS**.

EXERCISE 10.2

↻ Check answers to select questions

In the following numbered sentences, which make up a complete paragraph, identify the parts of speech indicated in parentheses:

1. Once we left the main road and turned down a narrow side street, we were in nothing more than an extended slum. (2 nouns, 2 adjectives, 1 verb, 1 conjunction, 1 pronoun)
2. The car came to a stop in front of a house that was far better than any of the others around it. (2 nouns, 1 verb, 1 preposition, 1 pronoun)
3. Set back a little from the street, it was a well-kept bungalow. (2 nouns, 1 verb, 1 adjective, 1 preposition)
4. The cemented front garden had a garish marble fountain in the middle, with an arrangement of plastic flamingos and penguins around it. (3 nouns, 1 verb, 2 adjectives, 1 pronoun, 2 prepositions, 1 conjunction)
5. The windows had heavy bars across them, and even the front door had an extra door of iron bars in front of it. (2 nouns, 1 verb, 2 adjectives, 1 preposition, 1 conjunction)
6. My grandmother did not get out; instead she had the driver toot his horn imperiously. (2 nouns, 2 verbs, 1 adverb)
7. A woman stepped out of the front door, and when she saw the car, she immediately nodded and smiled and went back inside. (3 nouns, 3 verbs, 1 pronoun, 1 adjective, 1 adverb, 1 preposition, 2 conjunctions)

   —Selvadurai, Shyam. "The Demoness Kali." *Short Fiction & Critical Contexts*. Ed. Eric Henderson and Geoff Hancock. Don Mills: Oxford UP (2010). 384. Print.

INTRODUCING . . . THE SENTENCE

The sentence is the basic unit of written communication. As a result, you need to know how to identify incomplete sentences in early drafts so you can make them complete in formal writing. First, you need to first familiarize yourself with the sentence itself.

What Is a Sentence?

Most complete sentences express a completed thought or idea.

Which of these word groups is a sentence?

Rules of grammar.

Grammar rules!

If we accept *rules* in the second example as a colloquialism (an informal word or expression), then the second word group would form a sentence with *rules* as the verb. The first, however, is not a sentence because nothing is happening and no comment *about* the rules of grammar is being made. Some groups of words can be recognized as sentences because a word or words suggest something is happening or something is being observed about the subject: it expresses a completed thought.

The word *rules* in the second sentence tells us something the writer is observing about *grammar*. The first word also is necessary to make the sentence complete; it indicates *what* "rules." Grammatically, you can say that complete sentences need two things:

1. A *subject* that answers the reader's question "What or who is this about?"
2. A *predicate* that tells us something the subject is doing or what is being observed about it.

A question that can help determine the subject of a sentence is, Who or what is doing the action in the sentence? Consider a very simple sentence:

Dogs bark.

The answer to the question "Who or what is doing the action in the sentence?" is *dogs*. So, *dogs*, a noun, is the subject.

To determine the predicate of a sentence, you can ask the question, What does the subject do? The answer is *bark*. A predicate will always include a *verb*. The line in this sentence divides the subject from the predicate:

Dogs | bark.

Adding words or phrases to a subject makes this sentence more informative. The line between subject and predicate will remain; the difference will be that a reader will know more about the dogs. Similarly, we could add words or phrases to the predicate so we would know more about their barking:

Dirty, dangerous dogs | bark balefully behind the barn.

The longer sentence illustrates how you can make statements more interesting by adding words or phrases, *modifiers*, to the subject and to the predicate. The subject has

> A sentence is a word or group of words that expresses a complete thought. It can be defined grammatically as a group of words that contains at least one subject and one predicate and needs nothing else to complete its thought.

been particularized; we know the dogs are *dirty* and *dangerous*. Similarly, the reader has been told *how* the dogs barked (*balefully*) and *where* they barked (*behind the barn*). The subject with its adjectival modifiers is called the **complete subject**; the main noun or pronoun alone is sometimes called the **simple subject** to distinguish it from the complete subject.

Another way you can give more information in a sentence is to add more subjects and predicates. This changes the sentence type: while simple sentences convey one completed thought, compound or complex sentences can convey more than one completed thought, or subject–predicate unit.

When you look to see whether the word group has a subject, make sure you don't mistake a noun or pronoun in a prepositional phrase for a subject. In this sentence, there are two nouns in the complete subject: *end* and *troubles*. The first noun is the true subject; *travels* is preceded by the preposition *of*. It is the *end* that is in sight, not *our travels*.

> The *end* of our travels | *is* in sight.

The Invisible-Subject Sentence

The need for a subject and a predicate in every complete sentence suggests that the minimum English sentence must contain at least two words. There is one exception: an **imperative sentence**, which is a command, may consist only of a predicate (verb). The subject, which is always implied, is the pronoun *you*, although it is invisible.

For example, in the imperative sentence, "Listen!" the subject *you* is understood to be the subject: "[You] listen!" In the command, "Go to the store!" *you* is understood to be the subject: "[You] go to the store."

> The **COMPLETE SUBJECT** includes the noun/pronoun subject and any modifiers.
>
> The **SIMPLE SUBJECT** includes only the noun/pronoun subject.

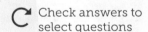

See page 327 for different sentence types.

> An **IMPERATIVE SENTENCE** issues a command, demand, or wish.

Which of the following are complete sentences? Draw a line between the subject and the predicate. Mark with an *S* those that contain only a subject and with a *P* those that contain only a predicate. Indicate an *N* if there is neither subject nor predicate.

1. The cat on the window ledge.
2. Wanted to bury his treasure where it would never be found.
3. A door in the wall.
4. Dropped the ball with only ten yards to go.
5. A sweet-smelling fragrance.
6. Opportunity knocks.
7. Is willing to give a presentation.
8. The high levels of stress of today's students.
9. Can schizophrenia be cured?
10. Hundreds of geese in the field.
11. Send in the clowns!
12. An enemy of the people.
13. Pay attention to the number of times that you end a sentence with a preposition.
14. All dressed up with no place to go.
15. This term will be my most successful one ever.

EXERCISE 10.3

↻ Check answers to select questions

Two Types of Sentence Fragments

The first step to ensure that all your sentences are complete is to check that there is a noun or pronoun subject to connect with a verb in the predicate. However, a dependent clause fragment has a subject and a predicate yet is still not a complete sentence (see page 321 to find out why).

Fragment 1—Fragment Lacks Subject, Predicate, or Both

In sentence 10 of Exercise 10.3, *Hundreds of geese in a field*, something essential is missing. What about geese in a field? What did they look like? Who saw them? Are they doing anything? To answer any of these questions is to complete a thought—and the sentence. For example:

Hundreds of geese in the field | *were resting before the next stage of their long journey.*

Mr. Elford | *imagined* hundreds of geese in the field.

In the first example, a predicate has been supplied. In the second example, a subject, Mr. Elford, and a verb, *imagined*, have been introduced, and the words *hundreds of geese in the field* have become part of the predicate, the direct object of the verb *imagined*.

The following sentence is also incomplete because it consists only of a subject. In this case, the noun *instructor* is followed by a word group that expands on the subject. The subject is not doing anything:

An instructor who never gives an A.

Who never gives an A tells us what kind of instructor he or she is but goes no further. To turn this into a complete sentence, you would need to complete the thought by adding a predicate:

An instructor who never gives an A | *marks too hard!*

An instructor who never gives an A | *sets very high standards.*

Come up with two other ways to complete this fragment.

EXERCISE 10.4

C Check answers to select questions

Complete the following fragments, all of which lack a predicate.

1. The cellphone that I lost yesterday.
2. The brilliant idea that came to me in the middle of the night.
3. A leader who is capable of motivating others.
4. The kind of doughnut that doesn't have a hole in the middle.
5. The baseball bat that was put in the museum.

EXERCISE 10.5

C Check answers to select questions

Add a subject and/or predicate to the remaining fragments in Exercise 10.3 to create grammatically complete sentences.

One example of a fragment lacking *both* a subject and predicate consists of a phrase that adds onto the previous sentence. Writers can mistake them for complete sentences because in speech a pause is usual between them and the preceding sentence; you may mistakenly associate a pause or drawn breath with a new sentence. The easiest way to fix these kinds of fragments is to make them part of the previous sentence or to supply missing essentials, such as a subject and predicate.

Add-on fragments may begin with transitional words and phrases: *such as, like, for example, including, also, as well as, except (for), besides, especially,* and similar words. They may also begin with prepositions like *on, in,* and *to.* In the examples below, the fragments are underlined:

Fragment: Exaggerated images of fitness are everywhere. <u>Especially in teen-oriented magazines</u>.

Correction: Exaggerated images of fitness are everywhere, *especially* in teen-oriented magazines.

Fragment: Sewage contains more than 200 toxic chemicals that are flushed down sinks or toilets. <u>Not to mention the runoff from roads</u>.

Correction: Sewage contains more than 200 toxic chemicals that are flushed down sinks or toilets, *not to mention* the runoff from roads.

When you begin a sentence with a word like *in, to,* or *at* (i.e., a preposition), ensure that the sentence expresses a completed thought and includes both a subject and a predicate.

Fragment: On a mountaintop in the remotest region of the Yukon.

Who or what is there and what is taking place? Although there are three nouns in the word group, none is acting as a subject. Similarly, nothing is happening or being observed.

Corrections:

A confused goat | stood on a mountaintop in the remotest region of the Yukon.

On a mountaintop in the remotest region of the Yukon, *the climbers | unfurled a flag.*

Another kind of fragment that often lacks a subject and predicate occurs when an incomplete verb form ending in *-ing* or *-ed/en*, or a base verb form, is mistaken for a complete verb. To avoid sentence fragments, always ensure you write a *complete* verb form.

Here are some examples of incomplete verb forms:

being, listening, studying, thinking (present participle form of verb)

given, taken, thought, written (past participle form of verb)

to be, to begin, to look, to tell (infinitive form of verb)

You can check if a verb form is incomplete or complete by adding a subject. An incomplete verb form can't be joined to a subject. By adding a helping verb, however, you can make the verb form complete:

Incomplete: She listening, they given . . .

Complete: She *was listening*, they *are given* . . .

A common sentence error is mistaking the *-ing* part of a verb form for a complete verb form. The following are examples of fragments with incomplete verb forms:

Holiday crowds | *milling* around shopping malls.

What are the crowds doing? If you said "they *are* milling," you have changed the fragment into a complete sentence by adding the helping verb *are*:

Holiday crowds | *are milling* around shopping malls.

Fragment: As a new doctor | fascinated by innovative surgery procedures.

Correction: As a new doctor, he | *was fascinated* by innovative surgery procedures.

A Closer Look

Fixing *-ing* Fragments

You can recognize an *-ing* form of the verb as incomplete because it is missing the helping verb that would make it complete. One way to fix an *-ing* fragment, then, is to complete it by adding a helping verb and a noun or pronoun.

Fragment: Looking ahead to chapter 8 of the textbook.

Correction: The students were looking ahead to chapter 8 of the textbook.

It's important to be able to identify these kinds of incomplete verb forms in your sentences and not treat them as if they were complete forms. However, they have useful roles to play in your writing—not as verbs but as nouns, adjectives, and even adverbs. *Eating* is the subject of this sentence:

Incomplete verb form as noun: *Eating* sensibly | is the best way to lose weight.

Incomplete verb form as adjective: My *growling* stomach | told me it was time to eat.

Growling is an adjective modifying *stomach*, the noun subject. Note that there is another incomplete verb form in this sentence, *to eat*, which is also acting as an adjective, modifying *time*.

There is more than one way to fix the following fragment error:

Fragment: City Hall instigating a new policy despite tough economic times.

Corrections:

City Hall | *was instigating* a new policy despite tough economic times.

Instigating a new policy | is inadvisable in tough economic times.

In the first correction, a complete verb form has been made from the incomplete form. In the second one, *instigating* has become the noun subject of the sentence.

Complete the following fragments, all of which lack a subject and a predicate.

1.　Ensuring that you write in complete sentences.
2.　He promised to call on her tomorrow. To see if she was still all right.
3.　For example, the famous TV show American Idol.
4.　Learning about people from different ethnic groups.
5.　On the side of the room facing the door.

Fragment 2—Dependent Clause Fragment

A dependent clause fragment is the most common type of fragment and, at first glance, looks a lot like a grammatical sentence.

Independent clauses are equivalent to simple sentences: they have a subject and a predicate and need nothing else to complete them. *Dependent* clauses also contain a subject and a predicate, but they express incomplete thoughts because the information they contain is *dependent on* information in the independent clause. That is one way you can tell a dependent from an independent clause. (Recall that a sentence expresses a *complete* thought.)

Another way that dependent clauses can be identified is by the word they begin with—a subordinating conjunction or a relative pronoun. Here are some of the most common subordinating conjunctions and relative pronouns to help you identify dependent clauses:

after	ever since	though	whether
although	if	unless	which
as	if only	until	whichever
as if	in case	what	while
as long as	in order that	whatever	who
as soon as	once	when	whoever
as though	rather than	whenever	whom
because	since	where	whose
before	so that	whereas	why
even though	that	wherever	

Dependent clause fragments sound incomplete and leave us wondering about the missing part. Consider this fragment:

Because his car wouldn't start this morning.

What happened because his car wouldn't start? When you answer the question in an independent clause, you will have a complete sentence. You can also test a sentence for completeness by asking whether the word group is true or false. *Because his car wouldn't start this morning* can be neither true nor false due to missing information.

→ For more information about subordinating conjunctions as joiners, see page 315.

A dependent clause could precede or follow the independent clause. The placement of the dependent clause often determines whether you use a comma to separate it from the main idea. See page 315.

→ See pages 311 and 328 for information about relative pronouns.

Because his car wouldn't start this morning, *he was late for his first day of work.*

The subordinating conjunction that introduces the dependent clause indicates the relationship of that clause to the independent clause, such as one of cause–effect (*as, because*), time (*before, since, when, while*), or contrast (*although, though, whereas*).

Without the subordinating conjunction, you will have a simple sentence expressing one idea. However, it may not be the idea you intended to convey:

His car wouldn't start this morning.

This is a complete sentence, but it does not explain the consequences of his car not starting.

Like subordinating conjunctions, relative pronouns introduce clauses that sound incomplete by themselves. Dependent clauses introduced by relative pronouns usually follow the word or phrase that they modify (*images* in the sentence below):

Fragment: The media bombards us with images of underweight women. Which give an unrealistic representation of the female body.

Corrected: The media bombards us with images of underweight women, which give an unrealistic representation of the female body.

Fast Track

Finding Fragments

Does the word group contain a subject (tells who or what), and is there an action performed by the subject?	If NO . . . ⟶	it's a fragment
Does the word group consist of only nouns/pronouns preceded by prepositions?	If YES . . . ⟶	it's a fragment
Is the only identifiable verb form in the word group an infinitive (e.g., *to be, to know, to learn*)?	If YES . . . ⟶	it's a fragment
Does the only identifiable verb form in the word group end in *-ing, -ed,* or *-en* and is not preceded by a helping verb (e.g., *is, were, has been*)?	If YES . . . ⟶	it's a fragment
Does the word group begin with a subordinating conjunction (one of the words on p. 321), and express a incomplete thought?	If YES . . . ⟶	it's a fragment

Most of the following are sentence fragments. If applicable, identify the kind of fragment (lacks a subject and/or predicate or is a dependent clause fragment) and make them into complete sentences with a subject and a predicate.

1. Being that she was insured as the principal driver.
2. Huge tears rolled down his cheeks.
3. I won't vote tomorrow. Unless I hear something that makes me change my mind.
4. Whenever they called her into work.
5. Stress can make us victims of illnesses. Including mild to life-threatening ones.
6. Introducing our next prime minister.
7. A row of stately elms interspersed with sprightly cedars.
8. He must be guilty. Since he's already confessed.
9. Which leads to another popular argument for lowering the drinking age.
10. Because spiritual values are more enduring than material ones.
11. Golf courses always include obstacles. These being water hazards and sand traps.
12. The opposition to vaccinations is a manifestation of fear. That the side effects will be more harmful than the disease itself.
13. More than half of depressed adolescents are given antidepressants. Which raises the question of whether they are the best long-term solution.
14. This is the information age. When ideas are literally at your fingertips.

EXERCISE 10.7

C Check answers to select questions

Each of the following passages contains four sentence fragments. Underline them. Then, correct them by joining them to complete sentences or by adding information.

1. Although it is known that the people who inhabited the island were of Polynesian descent. In 1994, DNA was extracted from 12 skeletons found on the island, and it was proven to be from people of Polynesian descent. Furthermore, it was suggested that these Polynesians came from Southeast Asia. From the fact that the crops grown by the indigenous people were native to Southeast Asia. For example, bananas, sugar-cane, taro, and sweet potato. For more than 30,000 years prior to human settlement of the island, the area was a subtropical forest of trees and woody bushes. Towering over a ground layer of shrubs, herbs, and grasses.

2. International concern has grown in recent years over the proliferation of weapons of mass destruction, but weapons used to exterminate enemy forces are nothing new. In World War I, artillery was used. In addition to gas, machine guns, grenades, and bombs. The 1940s brought more powerful weaponry. As well as the first nuclear weapon. A weapon capable of killing hundreds of thousands of people. After World War II, the Cold War began, as Russia and the US became involved in an arms race. Building hundreds of nuclear weapons more potent than those used in World War II.

EXERCISE 10.8

C Check answers to select questions

→ To find out more about conjunctions, see page 315.

A **PHRASE** is a group of two or more grammatically linked words which, lacking a subject and/or predicate, can be thought of as functioning as a single part of speech.

ADVERBIALLY means acting as an adverb.

ADJECTIVALLY means acting as an adjective.

INTRODUCING . . . PHRASES AND CLAUSES

Phrases and clauses are grammatical units within the sentence. Prepositions introduce phrases that as a unit join nouns and pronouns to the rest of the sentence.

Phrases

Phrases function as nouns, verbs, adjectives, and adverbs. When they act as these parts of speech, it is important to remember that they do so as a unit, though each word *within* the unit may be made up of a different part of speech and have a function distinct from that of the unit itself.

> Phrases | function <u>as a unit</u> <u>within the sentence</u>.

As a unit and *within the sentence* are functioning as adverbs, modifying the verb *function*. (Recall that adverbs modify verbs.) The first phrase answers the question *how* while the second answers the question *where* of the verb. But though each phrase is acting adverbially, the individual words within the unit have distinct functions, none of which is adverbial.

> as = preposition
>
> within = preposition
>
> a = indefinite article
>
> the = definite article
>
> unit = noun (object of preposition *as*)
>
> sentence = noun (object of preposition *within*)

Prepositional Phrases

Prepositional phrase units act as either adverbs or adjectives. As you've seen above, a group of words that includes more than one part of speech can, as a unit, modify a verb. It is then said to be functioning **adverbially** (as an adverb) within the sentence.

> She drove me <u>into town</u> so I could do my laundry.

The prepositional phrase *into town* begins with the preposition *into* and is followed by the noun *town*, the object of the preposition. But if you look at the phrase as a unit, you can see that *into town* is functioning as an adverb modifying the verb *drove* by explaining where the action took place: "Drove where? Into town."

Similarly, a group of words can modify a noun or pronoun, in which case it is functioning **adjectivally** (as an adjective). Consider the prepositional phrases (indicated by underlining) in these sentences:

> An obsession <u>with *Star Wars*</u> | led to her career <u>as an astronomer</u>.

"With *Star Wars*" is a prepositional phrase that gives us more information about (i.e., modifies) the noun *obsession*. It is functioning as an adjective.

> with = preposition
>
> *Star Wars* = proper noun (object of preposition *with*)

The second phrase, *as an astronomer*, modifies the noun *career*, functioning as an adjective.

> as = preposition
>
> astronomer = noun (object of preposition as)

Adjectival phrases usually *follow* the noun or pronoun they modify. This order is different from that of one-word adjectives, which usually *precede* the noun they modify.

Prepositional phrases do not contain the actual subject of a sentence. In the following sentence, *at the beginning of class* does not contain the actual subject even though it begins the sentence:

> <u>At the beginning of class</u>, students in Japan bow to their teacher.

The subject here is *students*; *at the beginning of class* is a prepositional phrase telling *when* they bow. Since it answers *when* of the verb *bow*, you know it is acting adverbially in the sentence.

Noun and Verb Phrases

In this example, the indefinite pronoun *some* combined with its modifier, *of the injured*, makes up a **noun phrase**. The entire phrase *some of the injured passengers* functions as the subject in this sentence because it tells us who had to be hospitalized:

> *Some of the injured passengers* | had to be hospitalized.

Phrases, then, can function as noun subjects or objects.

Finally, consider the following sentence, in which a **verb phrase** acts as a unit in the sentence, conveying the action of the subject *we*:

> We *will be looking* carefully for the person with a red flag on her backpack.

Verb phrases are very common since you will often need to use helping verbs with main verbs to create different tenses beyond the one-word simple tenses (verb phrases are italicized):

Simple present: I think, you say, she takes

Simple past: I thought, you said, she took

Present progressive: I *am thinking*, you *are saying*, she *is taking*

Past perfect: I *had thought*, you *had said*, she *had taken*

In addition to forms of *to be* and *to have*, verb phrases occur when modals, a special kind of helping verb, combine with main verbs to convey ability (*can, could*), possibility (*may, might*) necessity (*must, have*), and other meanings.

For more information about tenses and modals, see the inside cover.

> Do not assume that a noun near the beginning of a sentence is the subject. If a preposition precedes it, it could be the object of the preposition, and the subject will be found later in the sentence.

> A **NOUN PHRASE** is a group of words acting as a noun.
>
> A **VERB PHRASE** is a group of words acting as a verb.

First, identify each underlined word group as adverbial, adjectival, noun phrase, or verb phrase. Then, identify the subject of the sentence.

1. Yesterday, <u>the price of food</u> was the main item <u>in the news</u>.
2. <u>Some of my favourite</u> <u>books</u> <u>have gone</u> out of print.
3. The room <u>with the two computers</u> <u>has been locked</u> <u>from the inside</u>.

EXERCISE 10.9

↻ Check answers to select questions

4. A search <u>of the abandoned house</u> <u>turned up</u> several cartons <u>of stolen goods</u>.
5. The best player <u>on our paintball team</u> broke his arm and <u>will be lost</u> <u>for the season</u>.

Clauses

A word group larger than a phrase that can be broken down into two grammatical units, a subject and a predicate, is called a **clause**. In the following sentence, the subjects are in bold, the verbs are italicized, and the conjunction (joiner) is underlined. Clauses can be combined to create compound or complex sentences:

> **Frances** never *answers* questions in class <u>unless</u> **the teacher** *calls* on her.

First clause: Frances never answers questions in class

Second clause: unless the teacher calls on her

The sentence above illustrates two kinds of clauses:

1. an **independent clause**, which can stand alone as a sentence (*first clause*)
2. a **dependent clause**, which cannot stand alone as a sentence (*second clause*)

It is especially important to be able to distinguish an independent clause from a dependent clause in order to avoid sentence fragments. As discussed under Fragment 2—Dependent Clause Fragment (p. 321), a dependent clause contains an idea subordinate to (dependent on) the idea of the main clause.

A **CLAUSE** is a group of words containing both a subject and a predicate.

An **INDEPENDENT CLAUSE** is a group of words with a subject and a predicate that can stand alone as a sentence.

A **DEPENDENT CLAUSE** is a group of words with a subject and predicate that cannot stand alone as a sentence.

EXERCISE 10.10

↻ Check answers to select questions

Identify all independent and dependent clauses in the following sentences by underlining independent clauses and placing parentheses around any dependent clauses. For help, you can refer to the list of subordinating conjunctions below, page 327; these kinds of conjunctions introduce dependent clauses. Remember that pronouns, such as *I* or *it*, can act as subjects.

1. While drug testing has become more common, athletes are still taking drugs.
2. Although I think winter is here, the temperature is not cold enough for snow.
3. I became hooked on reality shows when I began watching them with my roommate.
4. In most parts of North America, Daylight Saving Time begins in March.
5. The battle against cancer will continue until a cure is found.
6. While it is important that students volunteer, mandatory volunteerism introduced at many schools does not instill a sense of civic duty.
7. The folk music of the '60s and '70s often encouraged peace; however, the message was not always received.
8. Studying grammar does not guarantee good grades, but it certainly helps.
9. Despite her good intentions, the governor general has not been able to satisfy many Canadian politicians.
10. Plastic water bottles have become the focus of public scorn, though more pressing moral concerns need attention.

Using Conjunctions to Join Clauses

An independent clause by itself is equivalent to a *simple sentence*. However, clauses are used as building blocks to construct other types of sentences. The function of a coordinating conjunction is to connect *equal* units, such as two independent clauses. The function of a subordinating conjunction is to connect *unequal* units, such as an independent clause and a dependent clause. Different rules for punctuation apply to independent and dependent clauses connected this way.

Sentence Types

Compound. Sentences formed by two or more independent clauses joined by a coordinating conjunction are called **compound sentences**. We can see these kinds of conjunctions (italicized) operating as joiners in the following examples:

The woodwinds warbled, *and* the strings sang sweetly.

Our profits in the first quarter showed a 10 per cent increase, *but* in the second quarter, they dropped again.

I discovered there was a great deal written on my topic, *so* I knew I would have to narrow my search.

Complex sentences. A sentence formed by one independent clause joined by a subordinating conjunction to a dependent clause is called a **complex sentence**. In a complex sentence, two or more subordinating conjunctions may connect two or more dependent clauses to an independent clause. We can see these kinds of conjunctions operating as joiners in the following examples:

1. Plagiarism is a problem at many universities *where* much research these days is conducted through the Internet.

2. *Although* much work has gone into developing artificial organs, the results have been disappointing.

In sentence 1, *where* is the subordinating conjunction that begins a dependent clause and joins it to the preceding independent clause. In sentence 2, the dependent clause comes first, but the subordinating conjunction *although* nevertheless joins the dependent to the independent clause.

You need to carefully distinguish clauses in order to punctuate them correctly. For example, in the sentence below, a second dependent clause (italicized) intervenes between the subordinating conjunction *that* and the rest of the dependent clause:

The students felt it was unfair that, *because the instructor was late*, they weren't given enough time for the test.

A **COMPOUND SENTENCE** consists of two or more independent clauses joined by a coordinating conjunction.

A **COMPLEX SENTENCE** consists of one independent clause joined by a subordinating conjunction to a dependent clause.

Common subordinating conjunctions and relative pronouns:

after	so that
although	that
as	though
as if	unless
as long as	until
as soon as	what
as though	whatever
because	when
before	whenever
even	where
though	whereas
ever since	wherever
if	whether
if only	which
in case	whichever
in order	while
that	who
once	whoever
rather	whom
than	whose
since	why

A Closer Look

Compound Predicates and Sentence Type

A sentence can have two subjects or two verbs and still be a simple sentence (but not two subjects *and* two verbs). Coordinating conjunctions join equal units, so as well as joining two independent clauses, they can join two nouns that are the subject of one verb or two verbs governed by one subject. Such compound—subject and predicate—constructions can occur in simple sentences. However, a compound *sentence* contains two independent clauses, *each* with its own subject and verb.

Here is an example of a simple sentence with a compound predicate (one subject, two verbs):

Jason *awoke* before dawn *and listened* happily to the sounds of the new day.

Note that there is no comma before the conjunction *and* because the two verbs it connects are parts of the same clause. The sentence below contains two subjects and two verbs:

Jason awoke before dawn, *and he listened* happily to the sounds of the new day.

Don't use a coordinating conjunction to begin a sentence. Words like *and*, *but*, and *or* should occur *within* a sentence where they join two equal units, such as two independent clauses:

Incorrect: The Korean Wave has become a worldwide phenomenon with the success of Psy's "Gangnam Style." And it shows no sign of abating.

Corrected: The Korean Wave has become a worldwide phenomenon with the success of Psy's "Gangnam Style," *and* it shows no sign of abating.

A Closer Look

Dependent Relative Clauses

One kind of dependent clause begins with a relative pronoun. Such adjectival clauses "relate" back to the noun they follow, specifying it or giving additional information about it. Relative pronouns include *who*, *whom*, *which*,

→ For more on relative pronouns, see page 311. For more on omitting relative pronouns, see Weedy Words in chapter 9.

A **RELATIVE PRONOUN** introduces an adjectival clause that "relates" back to the noun it follows.

A **RELATIVE CLAUSE** is a type of dependent clause that acts as an adjective by modifying the noun that precedes it.

and *that*. The **relative clause** is underlined and the **relative pronoun** italicized:

Environmentalist David Suzuki wrote the essay *that we read last week*.

The guest speaker was introduced by the college's vice-president, *who was clearly unprepared*.

In the last sentence, *who* is a relative pronoun introducing a dependent (relative) clause that modifies *vice-president*.

Relative pronouns introducing dependent clauses can sometimes be omitted. For example, in the sentence below, *whom* can be omitted, yet it is understood to introduce the dependent (relative) clause *[whom] she admires most*, which modifies *actresses*:

One of the actresses she admires most is Kate Beckinsale.

Compound-complex sentence. The last sentence type, a **compound-complex sentence**, combines a compound sentence (independent clause + coordinating conjunction + independent clause) with a complex sentence. It will contain two independent clauses along with one or more dependent clauses. For example:

> The woodwinds warbled, the brass bellowed, *and* the strings sang sweetly, *though* the timpani thundered, almost drowning out the other instruments.

A **COMPOUND–COMPLEX SENTENCE** is formed by two or more independent clauses and at least one independent clause.

Examples of the four sentence types appear below.

a. Identify the type of sentence.
b. For compound, complex, and compound-complex sentences, underline independent clauses, circle conjunctions, and put parentheses around dependent clauses.

1. Salmon oil is a supplement that lowers cholesterol.
2. She ran the race in record time but collapsed at the finish line.
3. Snowboarding began in the early '70s, and it has grown in popularity ever since.
4. Expository writing explains or informs the reader about something.
5. The committee began its search in September and has not yet found a suitable candidate.
6. His library privileges have been suspended, and his transcripts have been sealed until he pays his fines.
7. Music is essential in schools because it gives students a chance to excel in a non-academic subject.
8. She is convinced that she will get an A in the course.
9. After Orri learned Greek cooking, we ate psomi with every meal, but since he switched to Indian cuisine, we seldom have it anymore.
10. The first non-Inuit to reach the North Pole was James Peary, though his claim has often been disputed.

EXERCISE 10.11

↻ Check answers to select questions

To demonstrate your familiarity with the different kinds of clauses and joiners, construct compound, complex, and compound-complex sentences from the independent clauses (simple sentences) below. After you have joined the clauses in the most logical way, identify the sentence type: compound, complex, or compound-complex. Ensure that you have at least one example of each type of sentence. Small changes can be made so that it is easier to make up complex sentences, and sentence order may be changed.

1. They intended to eat at Benny's Bistro.
   They saw a long line-up outside Benny's.
   They went to Kenny's Kitchen instead.
2. There may be nearly 2 million kinds of plants in the world.
   There are likely at least as many different kinds of animals.
   No one can know how many species have evolved, flourished, and become extinct.

EXERCISE 10.12

↻ Check answers to select questions

3. Timothy Findley's story "Stones" takes place in Toronto.
   Norman Levine's "Something Happened Here" takes place in northern France.
   Both stories describe the tragic assault by Canadian troops on Dieppe during the Second World War.
4. We may suspect that earth is not unique as a life-bearing planet.
   We do not as yet have any compelling evidence that life exists anywhere else.
   We must restrict our discussion of the pervasiveness of life to our own planet.
5. Drug-testing procedures for Olympic athletes are becoming more and more elaborate.
   Athletes often feel they have to boost their performance.
   They want to compete at the same level as their competition.

Errors of Combining

A RUN-ON
SENTENCE consists
of two independent
clauses run together
without anything
between them.

A COMMA SPLICE
consists of two
independent clauses
with only a comma
between them.

A fragment in formal writing suggests the writer does not fully understand what a sentence is. But sometimes writers run one sentence into another, suggesting they don't know where to end the sentence. The two major errors in ending a sentence are the **run-on sentence** (sometimes called "the fused sentence") and the **comma splice**, or the comma fault.

The Run-On Sentence

A writer of a run-on sentence joins two independent clauses without stopping. Doing this is like running a stop sign without changing speed. The writer charges through the end of the first complete thought and into the second one without separating the statements. This writer does not place a period at the end of the first sentence and so does not capitalize the first letter of the word that should begin the second sentence.

A sentence may contain one, two, or more subject–predicate units, and these units (independent clauses) must be either separated by a period or joined correctly so the reader can distinguish one main idea from another.

Incorrect:

The cruise to Alaska was full Yumi decided to fly to Jamaica instead.

The Dene peoples live in Northern Canada they speak different languages.

Once you determine where the first clause ends and the second one begins, make them into two simple sentences or use a comma and the appropriate coordinating conjunction to join them.

Corrected:

The cruise to Alaska was full. Yumi decided to fly to Jamaica instead.

The cruise to Alaska was full, *so* Yumi decided to fly to Jamaica instead.

The Dene peoples live in Northern Canada. They speak different languages.

The Dene peoples live in Northern Canada, *and* they speak different languages.

The run-on sentences below contain two complete thoughts, or two main ideas. Lines indicate the division between subject and predicate; double lines show where the first sentence ends and the second begins, and where a period or a comma and coordinating conjunction should be placed.

Incorrect:

Few Koreans | have animals in their homes | | pets | are not a large part of Korean culture.

Toxic chemicals and pollutants | do not disappear | | they | accumulate in our natural resources.

Corrected:

Few Koreans have animals in their home. Pets are not a large part of Korean culture.

Few Koreans have animals in their homes, *for* pets are not a large part of Korean culture.

Toxic chemicals and pollutants do not disappear. They accumulate in our natural resources.

Toxic chemicals and pollutants do not disappear, *but* they accumulate in our natural resources.

A run-on sentence isn't just a long sentence: it's a major grammatical error in which two subject–predicate units (two "sentences") are not properly separated.

The Comma Splice

An error more common than the run-on sentence is the comma splice—the joining of two complete sentences by only a comma. This error is like slowing down at a stop sign without coming to a full stop, then charging through. The comma has many uses *within* the sentence, but, by itself, a comma cannot be used to connect two sentences.

The simplest way to avoid a comma splice is to think about where one complete thought (independent clause) ends and the next begins and to place a period there or use a comma and a coordinating conjunction. A comma splice sometimes occurs when two clauses are very closely related or the second clause seems a continuation of the first one. In formal writing, it's important to be able to separate two independent clauses.

Incorrect:

Fights in hockey are more than pointless, they are often dangerous.

Legalizing marijuana is not just the better choice, it is the right choice.

Although the second clauses in these sentences are closely related in meaning to the preceding clauses, they are not part of those clauses and must be separated from them by something stronger than just a comma:

Corrected:

Fights in hockey are more than pointless. They are often dangerous.

As you will see in later sections (pp. 345 and 348), a "stop" form of punctuation, such as a semicolon or colon, may be a good choice in these cases.

Fights in hockey are more than pointless; they are often dangerous.

Legalizing marijuana is not just the better choice. It is the right choice.

Legalizing marijuana is not just the better choice; it is the right choice.

Remember that a pronoun generally replaces a noun that precedes it in a sentence. Like a noun, a pronoun can act as the subject of a clause. In the following sentence, a pronoun is the subject of the second clause. A line indicates the division between subject and predicate; a double line shows where the first sentence ends and the second begins, and where a period or the comma and coordinating conjunction should be placed:

Incorrect:

Working in a busy office environment | was completely new to her, | | she | had always worked at home.

Corrected:

Working in a busy office environment was completely new to her. She had always worked at home.

Working in a busy office environment was completely new to her, *for* she had always worked at home.

Remember that if you wish to use a comma to connect two independent clauses, you must also use one of the seven coordinating conjunctions. You cannot use a comma before words like *however*, *therefore*, or *thus* to join two independent clauses. When you use these words between independent clauses, choose one of two options: (1) Put a period after the first independent clause and begin the next sentence with the "joiner," such as *however*; or (2) precede the joiner by a semicolon, so that it will now introduce the second independent clause.

> A comma splice isn't just a problem in comma usage; it's a major grammatical error in which a comma by itself is used to separate two complete thoughts.

> → For more information about using words other than coordinating conjunctions to join two main ideas, see page 296.

For more information about using words other than coordinating conjunctions to join two main ideas, see page 296.

Fast Track

Errors of Combining

Does one independent clause follow another one with no punctuation in between?	If YES . . . ⟶	you may have written a run-on sentence
Have you separated one independent clause from another with only a comma?	If YES . . . ⟶	you may have written a comma splice
Have you joined two independent clauses with a comma followed by a joining word that is not a coordinating conjunction?	If YES . . . ⟶	you may have written a comma splice

Fix the sentences below by using a period to make two separate sentences (or if you already know the rules for using other forms of punctuation to join independent clauses, you can use them). Also, identify whether the sentence is a run-on or a comma splice.

1. I took two buses to get downtown it was a long way.
2. Our neighbour's dog howled all last night, it was just impossible to get a night's sleep.
3. I was frightened during my first driving lesson the instructor yelled at me.
4. It's easy to punctuate sentences, just put a comma whenever you pause.
5. Janne ate as quickly as he could then he went upstairs to finish his homework.
6. The incidence of breast cancer has increased, it takes the lives of many women today.
7. Homelessness has existed for centuries, literature on the subject dates back to the feudal period in Europe.
8. Mozart composed his first minuet at the age of five he wrote his first symphony before he turned nine.
9. Humans are imitators, conforming is something they are good at.
10. Asthma is a common problem among Canadians, exposure to second-hand smoke in public places can intensify this condition.

EXERCISE 10.13

↻ Check answers to select questions

Determine what is wrong in the following sentences; it could be a fragment, a run-on sentence, or a comma splice. Then, make the correction.

1. While books are still the main source for acquiring knowledge.
2. The opening ceremonies were delayed. On account of rain.
3. Understanding the theory of relativity and its impact on our daily lives.
4. The concept that "bigger is better" is part of our culture, it is promoted by both advertisers and the media these days.
5. Martin Luther King led protests during the civil rights movement, his enthusiasm and his will to end discrimination made him a leader.
6. Although TV can corrupt the minds of innocent children if it is not monitored closely.
7. It seems that the North American mass media prescribes two roles for women, they can be sex objects or passive housewives.
8. Martial arts are attracting more people than ever before. Especially those who want to gain self-control and self-awareness.
9. We can no longer turn our backs to what is happening in the north it is time to take action.
10. Racism in Canada exceeded just social and personal racism, it was institutional racism.
11. A story of an Indo-Canadian woman who rejected her arranged marriage.
12. Carpal tunnel syndrome has many causes, the most common is repetitive wrist movements.
13. The tobacco in cigarettes is not the only problem, they contain many dangerous chemicals as well.
14. In the final book of the series, Harry visits his parents' grave and sees two inscriptions on their graves the inscriptions refer to passages from the Bible.
15. Many factors contribute to poverty. Including geographic factors, disease, and lack of education or health care.

EXERCISE 10.14

↻ Check answers to select questions

EXERCISE 10.15

Identify the sentence errors in the following paragraph; they may include fragments, run-on sentences, and comma splices. Then, correct them.

In recent decades, our society has become obsessed with body image through fitness and weight loss this infatuation can be seen in the popularity of fad diets. Such as the Atkins diet and its many variants. Fitness routines popular today include yoga and Pilates, there has also been a marked increase in the number of women having plastic surgery. In general, the obsession with body image is a greater concern for females than for males. Since many women are socialized to equate self-worth with physical appearance. One of the causes of this socialization is the popular media. Which often portrays unrealistic standards of the ideal body type.

CHAPTER SUMMARY

This chapter is designed to give you the foundations for grammatical writing by focusing on the key concepts of the parts of speech, phrases and clauses, and sentences. Learning to identify the seven major parts of speech is important, but learning their functions within the sentence will help you apply the grammatical and punctuation rules given in chapters 9 and 11. As larger units, phrases and clauses also have vital functions within sentences. Finally, understanding what a sentence is and the different sentence types will enable you to write in complete sentences and join simple sentences to form more complex structures.

Punctuation and Apostrophes

The most common errors in student writing—indeed, probably all writing—are punctuation ones. Some are critical and may interfere with your ability to communicate your meaning; others could be considered minor. However, all could affect your credibility as a writer. The correct use of punctuation guides your reader through the sentence, clarifying the relationships among its parts. This chapter presents the major rules for punctuation without using intimidating terminology or complex explanations. Many examples are provided, along with exercises through which your skills can develop.

LEARNING OBJECTIVES

- to learn how to use commas in a series, with independent clauses, with non-essential information, and with dates, addresses, and the like

- to learn how to use semicolons to join independent clauses and to punctuate a series

- to learn how to use colons to set up a list or a quotation or complete an idea

- to learn how and when you should use dashes and parentheses

- to learn how to use apostrophes to express possession and similar relationships between two nouns and to form contractions

COMMAS: DO THEY REALLY MATTER?

Does the precise placement of commas *really* matter? The short answer is *yes*, because readers look for commas in specific places to help them read. When a comma is missing or out of place, the sentence could take on a different meaning from the intended one, or the reader could become confused and have to reread the sentence.

Missing commas in the short sentences below could confuse a reader:

1. The day after a deadly tornado ravaged much of the countryside.

2. Although dating services may ask you for a photo appearance is less important than personality.

Applying one of the comma rules discussed below means placing commas after *after* in sentence 1 and after *photo* in sentence 2.

Myths about comma use abound, such as the "one breath rule," which states that wherever you naturally stop to pause, you should insert a comma. However, commas are there to assist the silent reader. If you are coaching yourself to read a speech aloud, you may want to place commas where you plan to pause for breath, but in formal writing, the "one breath rule" is simply too vague to be of use; it can even lead you astray.

The word *comma* comes from the Greek word *komma*, meaning "cut" or "segment." In general, commas separate (segment) the smaller or less important units in a sentence. Working with coordinating conjunctions, however, they also separate large units, independent clauses. In a sentence, commas separate

1. items in a series
2. independent clauses
3. parenthetical (non-essential) information
4. some adjectives; parts of dates, addresses, titles; and the like (conventional uses)

Rule Category 1: Items in a Series

Use a comma after each item in a list or series. This rule category applies to three or more grammatically parallel items whether single words—such as nouns, verbs, or adjectives—phrases, or clauses.

A series of three nouns:

It doesn't matter whether the items in the series are words, phrases, or clauses.

A series of three predicates:

A typical pattern for email addicts is to check their email, work for a few minutes, and recheck their email.

A series of three clauses:

Come to the Broadmead Art Tour tomorrow: view artworks in a variety of media, add to your collection, and meet with talented artists on their doorstep.

A Closer Look

Use of a Comma before *and* in a Series

The comma before the last item in a series of three or more items, referred to as the *serial comma*, is often omitted in informal writing:

> *Informal*: My three favourite months are April, June and September.

However, sometimes using the serial comma makes a sentence easier to follow. It should *not* be omitted if the last element or the one that precedes it is a compound, as in the following example where *toast and jam* comprises two elements but refers to a single thing:

> She ordered orange juice, an omelette with cheese, and toast and jam.

The serial comma is also helpful where the second-last or last item is significantly longer than the other items:

> The two-year specialization includes 10 half-courses, two full courses that involve internships in health-care facilities, and a research paper.

A series or list is *three* or more of something. When you refer to *two* of something with a joiner in between like *and*, you do *not* usually use a comma unless *and* is joining two independent clauses. The grammatical name for a group of words made up of two of something (such as two nouns or two verbs) is a **compound**.

> A **COMPOUND** is a word group made up of two of something.

Rule Category 2: Independent Clauses

The rule for independent clauses applies to three related situations:

a. two independent clauses joined by a coordinating conjunction
b. an introductory word, phrase, or clause followed by an independent clause
c. an independent clause followed by a concluding word or phrase

2a. Compound Sentence

Use a comma before the coordinating conjunction in a compound sentence (two joined independent clauses).

> The course was supposed to be offered in the fall, *but* it was cancelled.

> Dyana was the best dancer on the cruise ship, *and* she won an award to prove it.

Remember that the comma goes *before*, not after, the coordinating conjunction.

Short independent clauses. The comma between independent clauses may be omitted if the second clause is very short or if the clauses are so closely related that they could be considered compounds (i.e., the ideas are hard to separate). In this example, the comma may be omitted between *dress* and *and* because the clauses are short:

> "She wore the dress and I stayed home," sang Danny Kaye in the movie *White Christmas*.

> **COMBINING RULES**
> In the following example, independent clause rules 2a and 2b are illustrated:
>
> In America, [2b] 20 per cent of homeless children repeat a grade in school, [2a] *and* another 16 per cent of these children are enrolled in special education classes.

A **SENTENCE ADVERB** is an adverb that modifies the independent clause that follows it.

2b. Introductory Word, Phrase, or Clause

Use a comma after an introductory word, phrase, or clause followed by an independent clause.

In the following example, the introduction is one word, a **sentence adverb**, an adverb that modifies the independent clause that follows it:

Unfortunately, we have run out of mineral water.

When a sentence begins with a dependent clause that is followed by an independent clause, a comma follows the dependent clause (italicized here):

While the drinking age is 19 in most provinces, it is only 18 in Alberta.

When she first encountered the Canadian educational system, she was surprised by the many differences between the North American and Japanese systems.

Compare with rule 2c, below.

2c. Concluding Word or Phrase

In general, use a comma after an independent clause that is followed by a concluding word or phrase.

W.J. Prince wrote to his client Larry Drucker, asking direction in the case.

Concluding dependent clause. If you begin with an independent clause and conclude with a dependent clause, you do *not* generally use a comma (but see A Closer Look, below).

A Closer Look

Essential and Non-essential Dependent Clauses

Consider these examples:

1. He seldom visits the zoo, though he lives only one block away.
2. He often visits the zoo when he is in town.

In sentence 1, the dependent clause gives additional information; it is not essential to the main idea of the sentence, which is that the man seldom visits the zoo. But in sentence 2, the dependent clause, *when he is in town*, completes the thought, giving us essential information.

You will be right more often than not if you use the simplified rule that depends on the order of the independent and dependent clauses (see above). However, dependent clauses that begin with *although, even though, though,* or *whereas* often suggest a contrast with the independent clause and do not "complete" its meaning. In these cases, the dependent clause containing additional information should be preceded by a comma.

The sleek Siamese cat lay on the sofa *where* it was sunny. (essential, completes the thought in the independent clause)

The sleek Siamese cat lay on the sofa, *whereas* the old Labrador retriever curled up by the fire. (additional information)

Rule Category 3: Parenthetical Information

When you place something in parentheses, you signal that it is less important than what is outside the parentheses. Similarly, commas separate less important from more important information in the sentence. The three rules in this category will help you decide whether the information is non-essential (additional) or essential; then, you can punctuate accordingly.

3a. Non-restrictive (Non-essential) Phrase or Clause

Use commas before and after a non-restrictive phrase or clause. A non-restrictive clause often begins with one of the relative pronouns *which*, *who/whom*, or *that*. It follows a noun, which it modifies.

Although the information in **non-restrictive clauses** may be important, it *can* be left out without changing the essence of the sentence:

> *Non-restrictive:* Many students, *who have the burden of tuition fees*, have a hard time making ends meet.

The main idea is *Many students have a hard time making ends meet.* The relative clause helps explain why but is not essential to the meaning of the sentence.

By contrast, a **restrictive clause** is *essential* to the meaning of the sentence. If you left it out, the sentence would mean something different or would be ungrammatical. If the information in the clause is essential, omit the commas. This example is a more specific statement about *only* those students who take out loans, so no commas are used:

> *Restrictive:* Many students *who take out loans* have a heavy debt burden on graduation.

3b. Appositive

Use commas to set off an **appositive**, a noun or noun phrase that is grammatically parallel to a preceding noun or phrase. It *names, rephrases, specifies, or explains* the first noun or noun phrase. In these examples, the appositives are underlined, and an arrow points to the noun that each identifies or explains:

Her first work, <u>a short story collection</u>, was given outstanding reviews.

Seal hunting, <u>a traditional means of livelihood among the Inuit</u>, has been criticized by some environmentalists.

Use commas only for a true appositive. Sometimes the second noun completes the first noun, giving essential information. In such cases, you do not set off the second noun with commas. If in doubt, take the second noun or noun phrase out of the sentence and see if the sentence is complete without it and makes grammatical sense.

A **NON-RESTRICTIVE CLAUSE** is a type of adjectival clause that gives non-essential information.

A **RESTRICTIVE CLAUSE** is a type of adjectival clause that gives essential information.

An **APPOSITIVE** is a noun or noun phrase that is grammatically parallel to a preceding noun or phrase and gives non-essential information.

Use *who* to refer to people in restrictive and non-restrictive clauses. Use *which* to refer to non-humans in non-restrictive clauses, and *that* to refer to non-humans in restrictive clauses:

> The actor who [not *that*] appeared in the movie *Outbreak* also appeared in *Sweet Home Alabama*.

COMBINING RULES
In the following sentence, the appositive rule 3b and independent clause rule 2a are illustrated:

His first purchase, [3b] the painting of the Northern Ontario Landscape by Tom Thompson, [3b] is now worth thousands of dollars, [2a] but he says he will never sell it.

Can you explain why commas are placed around *king of the beasts* in the following sentence but not before *Aesop*, the name of the Greek writer? Which is the true appositive? Hint: try taking *king of the beasts* and *Aesop* out of the sentence to test for essential versus non-essential (additional) information:

The lion, king of the beasts, is the subject of many fables by the Ancient Greek writer Aesop.

You can also use the appositive rule for a word or phrase that can be considered a subset of a larger set—like a phrase beginning with *such as* or *including*.

The celebration of certain holidays, such as Christmas and Halloween, has been banned by several local school boards.

3c. Adverb or Adverbial Phrase

Use commas to set off an adverb or adverbial phrase that interrupts the flow of the sentence. Such a word or phrase often emphasizes or qualifies a thought, or presents a contrast.

Use commas to set off the name of a person being directly addressed. The following sentence has two interrupters, *Frank* and *beyond a doubt*:

I must say, Frank, that your performance on the aptitude test demonstrates, beyond a doubt, that you would make an excellent engineer.

There are times, especially in informal or semi-formal writing, when two commas around a small word that interrupts the sentence may produce clutter. Except in the most formal writing, commas around adverbial interruptions can be omitted if they directly follow a coordinating conjunction, such as *but*, to avoid three commas in close proximity.

Commas can be omitted: Leslie worried about her driver's test, but in fact she passed easily.

Not incorrect, but cluttered: Leslie worried about her driver's test, but, in fact, she passed easily.

Rule Category 4: Conventional and "Comma Sense" Uses

Stylistic convention more than grammar requires you to use commas between coordinate adjectives before a noun; in dates, addresses, and titles; and before and after direct quotations.

Commas between adjectives. Adjectives modify nouns and usually precede them. When two or more adjectives are *coordinate*, or equal and interchangeable, separate them with a comma. When the adjectives are *non-coordinate*, or unequal and not interchangeable, do not use a comma.

Coordinate adjectives: big, friendly dog; tall, white tower; proud, condescending man

Non-coordinate adjectives: white bull terrier; welcome second opinion; incredible lucky break

You can determine if adjectives are coordinate by mentally placing the word *and* between the adjectives, as in *big (and) friendly dog*. If this makes sense, then the adjectives are coordinate and commas are required. Applying this test to *white (and) bull terrier* produces a meaningless phrase, as it contains non-coordinate adjectives; therefore, commas are not used.

Quotation in a sentence. Use a comma before and after a direct quotation if a source is named:

> The sign says, "trespassers will be prosecuted."

> "I am not a crook," said Richard Nixon.

If the word *that* precedes the quotation, do not use a comma:

> The sign says that "trespassers will be prosecuted."

In other cases, let the grammar of the sentence determine whether a comma should be used:

> *Comma incorrect:* The computer is often accused of, "promoting superficial and uncritical thinking."

> *Comma correct:* According to the writer, "the computer promotes superficial and uncritical thinking."

Address. Commas separate names and locations in an address:

> The Prime Minister of Canada, 24 Sussex Drive, Ottawa, Ontario, Canada

Convention also dictates that you place a comma *after* the name of the province or state if the sentence continues:

> I lived in Calgary, Alberta, until I moved back to Cambridge, Ontario.

Date:

> October 7, 1951

A comma is not used if you begin with the day and follow with the month and year, nor is it used with the month and year alone:

> 7 October 1951; October 1951

Degrees, titles, and similar designations:

> Sabrina Yao, M.D., Ph.D., F.R.C.P.S.

Numbers. Under the metric system, there is a space rather than a comma between every three digits in a number of more than four digits (the space is optional with four-digit numbers). You will often see the non-metric format where a comma separates every three digits starting from the right:

> *Metric:* In 2011, the population of Nunavut was 31 906, according to Statistics Canada.

> *Non-metric:* The US Defense Department listed 2,356 casualties earlier in the year.

Quotation marks. The convention in North America is to place commas and periods *inside* quotation marks:

The new topic, "Where Ecological Ends Meet," has been posted.

Other marks of punctuation, such as colons and semicolons, are placed *outside* quotation marks:

A new study on bullying suggests a problem with the policy of "zero tolerance": it may increase the suicide rate of bullies.

If a citation follows a direct quotation, however, the period or comma is put *after the citation*:

Accounting for psychology's minimal role in climate change research, Gifford (2008) says, "we must lay the blame in part on ourselves" (p. 457), but he goes on to explain how this role can be expanded.

In some cases, you will have to apply "comma sense." If a sentence sounds confusing when you read it over, it may be necessary to insert a comma. The comma in the following sentence ensures the sense intended:

He told the student to come now, and again the following week.

EXERCISE 11.1

↻ Check answers to select questions

Add commas to the following sentences if required, and name the rule category that applies. There is one comma rule to apply in each sentence.

1. After her inaugural speech several members of the House rose to congratulate her.
2. The optional package includes bucket seats dual speakers and air-conditioning.
3. We have collected more than $20,000 and there is a week remaining in our campaign.
4. Metaphors similes and personification all are examples of figurative language.
5. Although many are called few are chosen.
6. The magnificent country estate is hidden behind a long elegant row of silver birches.
7. "We can't achieve peace in our time if we assume war is inevitable" he said.
8. As well as the Irish many Africans were forced to leave their families behind during times of famine.
9. Because of the humidity levels it feels hotter than the actual temperature.
10. Joe Clark the former prime minister has a famous wife.
11. Even though most people are aware of global warming and climate change fewer are aware of the term *carbon footprint*.
12. James Earl Jones who is the voice of Darth Vader in *Star Wars* is a well-known actor.
13. *The Globe and Mail* is a popular paper across Canada whereas the *Toronto Star* was created for the Toronto and area market.
14. Trust is important in any relationship and it always takes time to develop.
15. People have immigrated to Canada from countries in Asia Europe the Middle East and Central and South America.
16. Caffeine a stimulant is unregulated and completely legal.
17. Since climate change is a global problem it requires global solutions.

18. Diesel-powered cars have long been on the North American market yet they have never been widely accepted by the typical motorist.
19. The aggression effect of a video game depends on the type of game the way it is played and the person playing it.
20. Now a widely accepted theory evolution was discounted when Charles Darwin published *On the Origin of Species* in 1859.

Fast Track

Using Comma Rules

Have you written *three* or more items in a series?	If YES . . . ⟶	use commas to separate them
Have you referred to *two* items joined by a coordinating conjunction?	If YES . . . ⟶	do *not* use a comma
Have you written a compound sentence (i.e., two independent clauses joined by a coordinating conjunction)?	If YES . . . ⟶	use a comma before the coordinating conjunction
Have you begun a sentence with a word, phrase, or dependent clause where an independent clause follows?	If YES . . . ⟶	use a comma before the independent clause
Have you ended a sentence with a word or phrase where an independent clause precedes it?	If YES . . . ⟶	use a comma before the concluding word or phrase
Have you ended a sentence with a dependent clause where an independent clause precedes it?	If YES . . . ⟶	do *not* use a comma (but see p. 338 for exceptions)
Have you written a dependent clause that begins with *who*, *which*, or *that*?	If YES . . . ⟶	use two commas if the clause gives additional information and can be omitted without changing sentence meaning
Have you written a word group (appositive) that names or explains the preceding noun?	If YES . . . ⟶	use two commas that enclose the word group
Have you used a word or phrase that interrupts sentence flow (for example, for emphasis)?	If YES . . . ⟶	use two commas that enclose the interrupter
Have you used two coordinate (interchangeable) adjectives before a noun?	If YES . . . ⟶	use a comma between them
Have you used direct quotations, addresses, dates, numbers, or titles in your sentence?	If YES . . . ⟶	use commas as required by convention (see Conventional and "Comma Sense" Uses, p. 340)

EXERCISE 11.2

↻ Check answers to select questions

Add commas to the following sentences if and where required. There is more than one comma rule to apply in most sentences.

1. I had planned to go to Calgary but my bus was delayed for more than four hours so I decided to go back home.
2. Juliet studied medicine at Western University in London Ontario before becoming a doctor near Prince Albert Saskatchewan.
3. Like Jane Austen's character Emma the heroine of *Clueless* Cher is less superficial than she first appears.
4. Nick and Nicole were married on April 20 1995 but they separated two years later.
5. Jessica Julep the mayor of Nowhere Nova Scotia provided inspirational leadership.
6. The simple sentence as we've seen is easily mastered by students but compound sentences necessitate an understanding of various forms of punctuation.
7. The waste of our resources including the most precious resource water is the major environmental problem that Canada is facing today.
8. British general Sir Frederick Morgan established an American-British headquarters which was known as COSSAC.
9. The book with the fine red binding on the highest shelf is the particular one I want.
10. Agnes Campbell Macphail the first woman elected to Canadian Parliament served for 19 years beginning her career in 1921.
11. The first steam-powered motorcycle known as the "bone-shaker" led to the bikes we use today.
12. Following successful completion of the English test another skills test is taken which is in a written format.
13. He combed through directories of professional associations business and trade associations and unions looking for possible contributors to his campaign.
14. Oliver Wendell Holmes an American was known as a master essayist but Canadian Barry Callaghan is also internationally respected as an essayist.
15. After visiting her ancestral homeland China and meeting her sisters from her mother's first marriage Amy Tan wrote the novel *The Joy Luck Club.*
16. The soldier with the red coat in the picture fought on the side of our enemies the Americans.
17. In 1885 the Canadian government introduced a racist bill the Chinese "head tax" which forced every Chinese person entering the country to pay a $50 fee.
18. Currently ranked fourth behind heart disease stroke and respiratory infections AIDS is set to become No. 3 say researchers in a new report.
19. Leslie Hornby known as "Twiggy" became a supermodel overnight and was identified by her skinny 90-pound body.
20. Jeff Deffenbacher Ph.D. a specialist in anger management thinks that some people have a low tolerance for everyday annoyances.

EXERCISE 11.3

↻ Check answers to select questions

Add commas in the paragraphs below, following the rule categories as discussed above and avoiding comma splices. A few commas have been included to help with comprehension, but they may be incorrect.

1. If you asked people to name the most gruelling and challenging race in the world most of them would probably say that it was an auto race such as the Indianapolis 500, few

people would name the Tour de France which is a bicycle race. Thousands of cyclists however vie for an elite position in this annual event. Even with the modern advances in bicycle technology cyclists still find the course very challenging, it offers a variety of climbs including slight inclines hills and steep grades. The Tour de France has a history that dates back about one hundred years, in the years to come the race will continue to challenge inspire and glorify new riders.

2. Autism is a much misunderstood problem, often children with autism are viewed as a "handful" and "hyperactive." Very little is known of its causes and characteristics can vary making a diagnosis difficult. In children it is even harder because normal children can exhibit some of the characteristics associated with autism. Although autism can cause many behavioural difficulties autistic children can still live near-normal lives if they are surrounded by understanding caregivers. Working with autistic children can change a person and make one realize the need for better understanding and education. Treating autism can be difficult because often there is no feedback from the patient. Over the years there have been many ideas of how to treat autism but not all were correct and have at times made treatment problematic.

OTHER FORMS OF PUNCTUATION

The colon and semicolon are stronger, more emphatic marks of punctuation than the comparatively mild-mannered comma. The careful use of semicolons, colons, dashes, and parentheses gives your writing polish and precision.

Semicolon

As discussed, one of the major functions of commas is to separate independent clauses in a compound sentence. Two rules for semicolon use also involve independent clauses; the third rule is to separate items in a series that contains commas.

1. Joined Independent Clauses

You may use a semicolon rather than a comma and a coordinating conjunction to join independent clauses to show a close connection between the ideas. Consider the following examples:

a. Strong economies usually have strong school systems, *and* investment in education is inevitably an investment in a country's economic future.

b. Strong economies usually have strong school systems; weak economies generally have weak school systems.

In sentence a, the second clause is logically related to the preceding one; however, they have different subjects and are not so closely related that a semicolon would be called for. In sentence b, however, both clauses are concerned primarily with the relationship between economic strength and school systems. That focus in each clause justifies the use of a semicolon. A semicolon is often used if you want to stress a contrast between two independent clauses as in the example below:

Organically grown food is generally high in nutrients; processed food is not.

Note that the semicolon could be replaced by a comma and the coordinating conjunction *but*—they could *not* be replaced by a comma alone.

Here are other examples where a semicolon is a good choice to stress the close relationship between independent clauses:

> Gymnastics is not just any sport; it's one of the most challenging and physically taxing of all sports.

> Some children may have lost a parent because of illness or divorce; others may have been cared for by grandparents or other relatives.

Do *not* use a semicolon to separate an independent clause from a *dependent* clause.

2. Independent Clauses Joined with a Conjunctive Adverb

A semicolon precedes a conjunctive adverb/transitional phrase when it joins independent clauses. Note the comma *after* the conjunctive adverb in each example:

> My roommate lacks charm, friendliness, and humour; *still*, he is an excellent cook.

> A recent study has found a surprising correlation between a rare form of sleeping disorder and those with telephone numbers that include the number six; *however*, the conclusion is being challenged by several researchers.

Here are some of the most common conjunctive adverbs and transitional phrases:

accordingly	further(more)	later	otherwise
afterward	hence	likewise	similarly
also	however	meanwhile	still
as a result	if not	moreover	subsequently
besides	in addition	namely	that is
certainly	in fact	nevertheless	then
consequently	in the	next	therefore
on the contrary	meantime	nonetheless	thus
finally	indeed	on the other	undoubtedly
for example	instead	hand	

Be careful not to confuse conjunctive adverbs/transitional phrases with another large group of joiners, subordinating conjunctions, which join dependent to independent clauses (see p. 315).

→ The rules for separating independent and dependent clauses are given on page 338; they may involve commas but not semicolons.

Although and *whereas* are sometimes mistaken for conjunctive adverbs, but they are subordinating conjunctions that introduce dependent clauses; they cannot be used to join two independent clauses and are not preceded by semicolons.

A Closer Look

Using Adverbs to Join Independent Clauses

A common error is to miss the distinction between adverbs like *however* and *therefore* acting as ordinary adverbs (e.g., interrupters) and these same words acting as conjunctive adverbs (joiners). The following sentence pair illustrates this distinction. In sentence 1, commas are required because the adverb occurs in the middle of the clause as an interruption between the subject *he* and most of its predicate. In sentence 2, a semicolon is required before the conjunctive adverb because *however* is joining two independent clauses:

1. Dr. Suzuki will not be in his office this week; he will, *however*, be making his rounds at the hospital.
2. Dr. Suzuki will not be in his office this week; *however*, he will be making his rounds at the hospital.

In the following sentences, the word that changes its function from interrupter to joiner is *therefore*:

3. The CEO has been called away for an emergency briefing; her secretary, *therefore*, will have to cancel her appointments.

4. The CEO has been called away for an emergency briefing; *therefore*, her secretary will have to cancel her appointments.

Notice that the only apparent difference between these sentences is word order: in sentence 3, *therefore* is the third word of the clause, whereas in sentence 4, it begins the second clause. If you look closely, though, you can see that changing the position of a word like *however* or *therefore* can change its function. In sentence 4, an independent clause precedes and follows *therefore*, necessitating the semicolon before and the comma after.

The following sentences are punctuated correctly. The italicized word or phrase is either an ordinary adverb acting as an interrupter or a conjunctive adverb (joiner). Rewrite the sentence by moving this word/phrase to another place in the second clause in which its function will be different. Punctuate accordingly.

EXERCISE 11.4

↻ Check answers to select questions

Example:

The weather this summer was very wet; *however,* it did not make up for the drought we have experienced.

The weather this summer was very wet. It did not, *however,* make up for the drought we have experienced.

or:

The weather this summer was very wet; it did not, *however,* make up for the drought we have experienced.

1. One of my roommates rode her bicycle to school most of the time; she was more physically fit, *as a result*, than my other roommate, who didn't even own a bicycle.
2. SPCA officers work for but are not paid by the government. It is donations, *in fact*, that provide their salary.
3. If homelessness continues to increase, it will be costly for taxpayers; *moreover*, homelessness affects downtown businesses.
4. Many professional golfers use the same caddy for years; *for example*, Steve Williams caddied for Tiger Woods for 12 years.
5. Scientists tend to strongly support stem-cell research. Most evangelical Christians, *however*, just as strongly oppose it.

3. Items in a Series

Serial semicolons can be used to separate items in a series if one or more of the elements contain commas. Without semicolons, these sentences would be confusing:

> Her company included Alex Duffy, president; Marie Tremble, vice-president; John van der Wart, secretary; and Chris Denfield, treasurer.

> Bus number 1614 makes scheduled stops in Kamloops, BC; Valemount, BC; Jasper, AB; and Drayton Valley, AB, before arriving in Edmonton.

You may also use semicolons to separate items in a list where each item is a long phrase or clause, especially if there is internal punctuation. Using semicolons to separate the items makes this sentence easier to read:

> The role of the vice-president will be to enhance the school's external relations; strengthen its relationship with alumni, donors, and business and community leaders; implement a fundraising program; and increase the school's involvement in the community.

Colon

While a semicolon brings the reader to a brief stop, the colon leads the reader on. The colon has three main uses:

1. to set up a quotation
2. to set up a list or series
3. to set up an answer to, completion of, or expansion on what is asked or implied in the preceding independent clause

1. Before a Quotation

When you use direct quotations in your essays, you can set them up formally with a colon:

> The *Oxford English Dictionary* defines the word *rhetoric* this way: "The art of using language so as to persuade or influence others."

> Health Canada has made the following recommendation for dentists: "Non-mercury filling materials should be considered for restoring the primary teeth of children where the mechanical properties of the material are safe."

Direct quotations can also be set up less formally. In such cases, a comma, or perhaps no punctuation at all, may be required. To determine which is needed, look at the sentence as if it contained no quotation marks and see if one of the rules for using commas applies:

> According to the American Academy of Dermatology, "a tan is the skin's response to an injury, and every time you tan, you accumulate damage to the skin."

> The most general definition of evolution is "any non-miraculous process by which new forms of life are produced" (Bowler 2).

You should use semicolons to join independent clauses in one of the two ways discussed above or to separate items in a series where, otherwise, confusion might result.

In the first sentence, a comma rule dictates the use of a comma before the quotation; in the second sentence, there is no rule that would necessitate a comma before the quotation. A comma after *is* is incorrect.

2. Before a List or Series

The most formal way to set up a list or series is to write an independent clause and follow with a colon and the list of items:

> In 1998, the CBC outlined three challenges for the future: to attract more viewers to Canadian programming, to increase the availability of "under-represented" categories, and to direct its resources toward this kind of programming.

Avoid the temptation to insert a colon if the thought is incomplete before the colon. You do *not* use a colon after *including* or *such as*, or right after a linking verb like *is* or *are*, though these words are often used to set up a list or series.

> *Incorrect colon:* Caffeine withdrawal can have many negative effects, such as: severe headaches, drowsiness, irritability, and poor concentration. (**A comma is also incorrect after** *such as*.)

> *Unnecessary colon:* One of the questions the committee will attempt to answer is: Does our current public health system work?

3. After an Independent Clause

When an independent clause is followed by a word, phrase, or clause that answers or completes it, end the independent clause with a colon:

> There is only one quality you omitted from the list of my many wonderful characteristics: my modesty. (**states** *what* **quality**)

> David's driving test was a memorable experience: he backed over a curb, sailed through two stop signs, and forgot to signal a left turn. (**states** *why* **the test was memorable**)

> The New Testament of the Holy Bible gives the ultimate rule for Christians: to treat others the way you want them to treat you. (**states** *what* **rule**)

If what follows the colon is at least the equivalent of an independent clause, you may begin it with a capital letter. It is acceptable to begin with a small letter, however, as in the examples above.

Dashes and Parentheses

Imagining this scenario might help you decide whether to use parentheses or dashes in a sentence: you are in a crowded room where everyone is talking. Somebody takes you aside and begins speaking in an unnaturally loud voice about the latest rumour. You look around. People are listening, which is the speaker's intent. A couple of minutes later, somebody else approaches and very discreetly begins whispering the same information in your ear.

In your reading, you may sometimes see a colon used unnecessarily to set up a list or a quotation (especially before a block quotation). In such cases, the writer has made a stylistic choice. However, bear in mind that unnecessary colons, like unnecessary commas, can impede more than assist understanding.

Remember that unless you are using semicolons to separate items in a series, both what *precedes* and what *follows* a semicolon should be an independent clause.

What *precedes* a colon should be an independent clause.

Don't use one hyphen (-) if you want to set off a word or phrase. Hyphens are a mark of spelling— not of punctuation.

Using dashes is like giving information that is meant to be overheard, to be stressed. But information in parentheses is more like an aside. It conveys additional information which is not important enough to be included in the main part of the sentence.

Dashes, then, set something off and can convey a break in thought. You can use dashes sparingly to emphasize a word or phrase; two dashes (one dash if the material comes at the end of a sentence) draw the reader's attention to what is between the dashes.

You can type two hyphens to indicate a dash (--); if you don't leave a space after the second hyphen, your computer may automatically convert the hyphens to an em dash like this: —.

Use parentheses sparingly to include a word or phrase, even occasionally a sentence, that isn't important enough to be included as part of the main text; where dashes emphasize, parentheses de-emphasize:

"Crayolas plus imagination (the ability to create images) make for happiness if you are a child" (Fulghum 10).

Fast Track

Rules for Semicolons, Colons, Dashes, and Parentheses

Have you written two independent clauses that are closely related in meaning or that strongly contrast?	If YES . . . →	use a semicolon between clauses
Have you used a word/phrase like *however* to join two independent clauses?	If YES . . . →	use a semicolon before the joiner and a comma after it
Have you written a list or series in which one or more items contain commas or are very long?	If YES . . . →	use semicolons between main items
Have you used a direct quotation?	If YES . . . →	you may use a colon before the direct quotation if the statement before the quotation is an independent clause
Have you written a list or series?	If YES . . . →	you may use a colon before the series if the statement before the series is an independent clause
Does a word, phrase, or clause answer or complete a preceding independent clause?	If YES . . . →	use a colon between the independent clause and the word, phrase, or clause that follows
Do you want to stress or set off a word, phrase, or clause from the rest of the sentence?	If YES . . . →	you may use dashes for emphasis
Do you want to include less important information in your sentence?	If YES . . . →	you may use parentheses to show that this information is less important

You may also use parentheses to refer to a source in a research essay. This parenthetical use is illustrated in the example above to refer to the source of the quotation about Crayolas.

Punctuating parenthetical insertions depends on whether the statement in parentheses is (1) a complete sentence in itself or (2) part of the larger sentence. If the parentheses enclose a complete sentence, the period should be placed *inside* the second parenthesis, as the period ends only what is between parentheses. The following sentence illustrates this rule:

> (The period in this sentence goes inside the second parenthesis.)

If parentheses do not enclose a complete sentence, punctuate the sentence just as you would if the parenthetical insertion were not there. The sentence below shows a comma that has nothing to do with the parenthetical insertion but that is required to separate independent clauses; note that this comma follows the closing parenthesis. Notice also that *both* begins with a lower case letter:

> Cassandra wanted to be an actor (both her parents were actors), but she always trembled violently as soon as she stepped on a stage.

→ For information about parenthetical documentation methods, see chapter 7.

EXERCISE 11.5

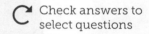

Replace commas in the sentences below with the most appropriate form of punctuation (semicolon, colon, dashes, parentheses). In some cases, the commas are correct and should not be replaced.

↻ Check answers to select questions

1. Every essay needs three parts, an introduction, a body, and a conclusion.
2. The following is not a rule for comma use, put a comma wherever you pause.
3. It is probable, though not certain, that she will be promoted to the rank of corporal next year.
4. It was the best of times, it was the worst of times.
5. The *Online Dictionary* defines animal cruelty this way, "treatment or standards of care that cause unwarranted or unnecessary suffering or harm to animals."
6. In my health sciences class, we studied the four main food groups, dairy products, meats, carbohydrates, and fruits and vegetables.
7. The tuition increase has affected many lower income families, therefore, there is an even greater demand for student loans.
8. Whenever I order designer clothing for my boutique, I shop in Toronto, Canada, Buffalo, New York, and London, England.
9. Each kind of stem cell has potential advantages and disadvantages, however, the least successful today are those harvested from human embryos.
10. First advice to those about to write a novel is the same as Punch's to those about to wed, don't (Victor Jones).
11. His plans for the new development included the following, an apartment complex, single-family residences, a 60-store mall, and a multi-use recreation centre.
12. In a compound sentence, use a comma to join independent clauses where there is a coordinating conjunction, use a semicolon where two such clauses are not joined by a coordinating conjunction.

13. The tour includes visits to the following museums, the Prado in Madrid, Spain, the Louvre in Paris, France, and the Rijksmuseum in Amsterdam, the Netherlands.

14. Oil, electricity, and solar power are popular sources for heating homes in Ontario, however, the most popular is natural gas.

15. School cafeterias often offer unhealthy options, such as hot dogs, which have virtually no nutritional value, hamburgers, which have a high fat content, and poutine, known as "heart attack in a bowl."

16. The zero emissions of a battery-electric vehicle come with a drawback, the emissions are only as clean as the means used to generate the power.

17. This year's conference on the environment is intended to focus concern on three main areas, global warming, pollution, and the destruction of natural habitat.

18. The art of writing the news lead is to answer as many of the following five questions as possible, *Who?*, *What?*, *Where?*, *When?*, and *How?*

19. A lack of essential nutrients can result in deficiencies, for example, a vegetarian may have iron deficiency.

20. Freewriting can be a useful means of overcoming blocks, it can help you write when you're not in the mood, it can generate ideas, even if you are the kind of writer who has a hard time coming up with main points, and it can energize your writing.

EXERCISE 11.6

↻ Check answers to select questions

Below is Edward Lear's nonsense poem "The New Vestments." Write it in paragraph form, making sense out of nonsense by punctuating it for correctness and effectiveness. Most of the original end-of-line punctuation has been taken out, and some internal punctuation also has been omitted; some of the nineteenth-century spellings have been changed.

There lived an old man in the kingdom of Tess
Who invented a purely original dress
And when it was perfectly made and complete
He opened the door and walked into the street
By way of a hat he'd a loaf of Brown Bread
In the middle of which he inserted his head
His Shirt was made up of no end of dead Mice
The warmth of whose skins was quite fluffy and nice
His Drawers were of Rabbit-skins so were his shoes
His Stockings were skins but it is not known whose
His Waistcoat and Trousers were made of Pork Chops
His Buttons were Jujubes and Chocolate Drops
His Coat was all Pancakes with Jam for a border
And a girdle of Biscuits to keep it in order
And he wore over all as a screen from bad weather
A Cloak of green Cabbage leaves stitched all together.
He had walked a short way when he heard a great noise
Of all sorts of Beasticles Birdlings and Boys
And from every long street and dark lane in the town
Beasts Birdles and Boys in a tumult rushed down

Two Cows and a half ate his Cabbage-leaf Cloak
Four Apes seized his Girdle which vanished like smoke
Three Kids ate up half of his Pancaky Coat
And the tails were devoured by an ancient He Goat
An army of Dogs in a twinkling tore up his
Pork Waistcoat and Trousers to give to their Puppies
And while they were growling and mumbling the Chops
Ten boys prigged the Jujubes and Chocolate Drops
He tried to run back to his house but in vain
Four Scores of fat Pigs came again and again
They rushed out of stables and hovels and doors
They tore off his stockings his shoes and his drawers
And now from the housetops with screechings descend
Striped spotted white black and gray Cats without end
They jumped on his shoulders and knocked off his hat
When Crows Ducks and Hens made a mincemeat of that
They speedily flew at his sleeves in trice
And utterly tore up his Shirt of dead Mice
They swallowed the last of his Shirt with a squall
Whereon he ran home with no clothes on at all
And he said to himself as he bolted the door
"I will not wear a similar dress any more
"Any more any more any more never more!"

Correct or add commas in the following passages. Among your changes and additions, include at least one semicolon and one colon. Some commas have been included to help with reading; however, they may not be correct.

EXERCISE 11.7

↻ Check answers to select questions

1. Cocaine an alkaloid obtained from coco leaves is a stimulant to the nervous system, unfortunately it is one of the most addictive drugs and it is possible to overdose and die on first use. Among the 3 million users today 500,000 are highly addicted. Cocaine users describe the high as a euphoric feeling, they feel energetic and mentally alert, however this feeling wears off in as little as 20 minutes. Users responses to the drug vary but may include the following, hyperactivity elevated blood pressure and heart rate and increased sexual interest. Large amounts of cocaine such as more than 100 milligrams can cause bizarre erratic and violent behaviours.

2. Labour shortages during the late nineteenth century in Canada became an impediment to progress and something had to be done to fix this problem. For white politicians and business owners the solution seemed obvious, exploit cheap labour. Chinese immigrants provided exactly what was needed to boost the labour scene, they were male unskilled and cheap. Between 1881 and 1885 approximately 17,000 Chinese immigrants arrived in Canada, Chinese men were employed in masses, their jobs included those in mining forestry canning and above all railroad construction. Sir Matthew Begbie the Chief Justice of BC said "Chinese labourers do well what white women cannot do and what white men will not do."

THE APOSTROPHE

Technically, the apostrophe isn't a mark of punctuation; it is a mark used within a word that has two main uses:

1. to indicate the possessive case of a noun or indefinite pronoun
2. to show where one or more letters have been omitted, as in a contraction

1. Apostrophe for Possessive Case

The possessive case in nouns and pronouns indicates ownership and similar relationships between two nouns, such as association, authorship, duration, description, and source of origin. The possessive is a short form indicating that the second noun belongs to or is associated with the first noun. When a noun has an apostrophe to show the possessive, it is functioning adjectivally and can be replaced by the corresponding possessive pronoun. Most *pronouns*, however, do not show the possessive through an apostrophe.

> the hard drive of the computer = the computer's hard drive (*its* hard drive)
>
> the landlady's apartment (ownership: *her* apartment)
>
> the tenants' rights (association: *their* rights)
>
> Dvorak's *New World Symphony* (authorship: *his* symphony)

Singular noun. The usual rule for a *singular* noun, including proper nouns (nouns that begin with a capital letter) ending in *s*, *ss*, or the *s* sound, is to add "'s" to make it possessive.

> the attorney's portfolio; Mr. Price's car; the week's lesson

Indefinite pronoun. Like nouns, but unlike other kinds of pronouns, many indefinite pronouns add an apostrophe + *s* to show the possessive:

> In times of stress, it is not in *one's* best interest to act quickly or reflexively. (the best interest *of one*)

Plural noun. To make a plural noun possessive, add an apostrophe after the *s*:

> the islands' inhabitants; the Hansons' children; the Gibbses' marriage certificate; two weeks' lessons; the readers' perceptions

Make sure you carefully distinguish between singular and plural when applying the rules for possessives:

> company (singular) + 's ⟶ the company's profits (one company)
>
> companies (plural) + ' ⟶ the companies' profits (more than one company)
>
> society (singular) + 's ⟶ our society's attitude toward war (one society)
>
> societies (plural) + ' ⟶ past societies' attitudes toward war (many societies)

A few plural nouns do not end in *s*: *children, women, men, people*. Because they have irregular endings, they are treated as singular nouns for the possessive:

the popular children's book; the women's group

Proper noun ending in s. Because it may look and sound awkward to add an apostrophe + *s* to a proper noun ending in *s*, some authorities would write *Tracy Jarvis' book*, meaning "*the book of Tracy Jarvis*." Others would follow the rule for singular nouns by adding an apostrophe + *s*: *Tracy Jarvis's book*. Whichever rule you follow, be consistent in applying it.

Joint ownership. In joint ownership, where two nouns share or are equal parties in something, only the last noun should show the possessive. In the following sentences, Salem and Sheena shared duties as hosts at one party, but the general manager and the district manager are paid separate wages:

I attended Salem and Sheena's party.

Morana raised the general manager's and the district manager's wages.

In the example below, the two educators do *not* share the same belief or theory:

Incorrect: Piaget and Montessori's beliefs about how children learn were similar in many ways.

Correct: Piaget's and Montessori's beliefs . . . .

2. Apostrophe to Show Contraction

The second main use of the apostrophe is to show missing letters within a word. Contractions are not generally used in formal writing. You should check with your instructor to see if they are acceptable in your assignment.

People often confuse the contraction *it's* (*it is*) with the possessive form of the pronoun *its* (as in *I gave the dog its bone*). The contraction *who's* (*who is*) is sometimes confused with *whose*, the possessive form of *who* (*the man whose house I'm renting*).

> An apostrophe is not used with a simple plural unless it is needed for clarity with numbers, letters, or symbols. Example: Adrian got two A's and three B's on his transcript.

Decide which nouns in the following sentences require the possessive; then add apostrophes and make any other necessary changes.

1. In South Africa, the current crime rate is using up much of the countrys GDP.
2. Parents and teachers often complain about television's influence in today's society.
3. The schools biggest draw for new students was the brand new recreation complex.
4. Ones education should not depend on the financial resources of ones parents.
5. The mayor's biggest asset is her commitment to the citys future growth.
6. The course I took required two hours homework a day.
7. Apples, oranges, mangoes, and tomatoes are the stores specials today.
8. Work songs and street vendors cries are examples of traditional African-American music styles.
9. Our societys fascination with celebrities lives is a product of the medias daily obsession.

EXERCISE 11.8

↻ Check answers to select questions

10. The topic of the term paper is a comparison between George Grant's and John Ralston Saul's theories of Canadian identity. [The last names are Grant and Saul.]
11. The young man stated his churchs mission is to spread Jesus message to people throughout the world.
12. Climate change is caused by harmful chemicals that trap the suns energy in the earths atmosphere.
13. Nowadays, rap is used to express a persons experiences, feelings, and opinions.
14. The desire of Pip in Charles Dickens Great Expectations to find his place in the world illustrates the works main theme.
15. The introductory paragraph should capture the readers interest while developing the writers credibility.

EXERCISE 11.9

Punctuate the following passage for correctness and effectiveness, using commas and other forms of punctuation as appropriate. Minimal punctuation has been provided in places to aid in understanding; however, some punctuation may be incorrect. Correct all errors in apostrophe use. The passage concerns the response to an investigative article entitled "Spin Doctors," posted on the Canadian news and information website Canoe.

Reader reaction was swift and impassioned. The sites traffic which averages 65 to 70 million views each month experienced an additional 50,000 page views within the first 10 days of the posting. The investigation drew more than 400 letters to the editor hundred's of emails to the message boards and more than 16,000 responses to an online poll.

The intensity of the response surprised veteran investigative journalist Wayne MacPhail the articles author. Although the sheer volume of letters was unexpected it proved to him that there was an audience for online journalism in Canada. MacPhail has experimented with hypertext reporting since the late 1980s but outside of "Spin Doctors" he believes that by and large newspapers have done a "woeful job" of building an audience for Web-based investigative reporting . . . .

Unlike it's media rivals Canoe has never made journalism it's only or even its most important focus. A headline announcing the top story of the day appears underneath the Canoe banner but there are so many other things to do, shopping email contests Web utilities and lifestyle tips all compete with the news.

The CNEWS section isnt necessarily the first place people are expected to go on the network though it is usually at the top of the highlighted sections. It is also part of the site that changes the most during daylight hours. In other words when CNEWS changes the entire home page changes. A "This Just In" feature was recently added but theres no set schedule for posting stories. Despite this expansion of the news section Canoes promotional material drives home the message that the site is about much more than current events. One recent ad reads, "shop chat email read, in that order."

—adapted from Tara Stevens, "Paddling into Cyberspace."

CHAPTER SUMMARY

Building on the grammatical foundations of chapter 10, this chapter has given you straightforward rules for using punctuation, beginning with the often misused comma. Three major rule categories for comma use are given: series, independent clauses, and non-essential elements; guidelines follow for adjectives, quotations, and numbers, such as dates. Three rules are given for both semicolon and colon use; dashes and parentheses are also covered. You can practise these rules by doing the many exercises, including paragraph correction, drawn from student writing. Guidelines for apostrophes enable you to identify situations where apostrophes are needed and to focus on correct usage.

12 Agreement, Pronouns, Modifiers, and Parallelism

Although punctuation errors are common in student writing, other errors can affect your credibility. In this chapter, we discuss grammatical errors often overlooked in early drafts, beginning with agreement errors. Although most native English speakers do not have to think too much about subject–verb agreement, we look at specific instances that can present problems for all writers. Several problems related to pronouns are then identified and solutions provided: pronoun–antecedent agreement, pronoun reference, pronoun consistency, and pronoun case. Modifier errors are discussed next; often the product of first drafts, they can give a sentence an unintended meaning. The chapter concludes by identifying instances in which parallel structures are required. Mastering the basic grammatical concepts discussed in this chapter will make you both a more successful and a more confident writer.

LEARNING OBJECTIVES

- to understand the principles of subject–verb and pronoun–antecedent agreement and learn the rules that apply to them

- to recognize the importance of gender-neutral writing and learn strategies for dealing with pronouns that reference gender

- to understand the principle of pronoun reference and to ensure that your pronouns clearly refer back to the nouns they replace

- to understand the principle of pronoun case and the forms that personal, relative, and interrogative pronouns should take depending on their function in a sentence

- to identify misplaced and dangling modifier errors and how to fix them

- to understand the importance of parallelism in your writing and how to ensure parallelism in lists, compounds, and comparisons

AGREEMENT

A verb must agree in number with its subject; that is, they must be both singular or both plural. Similarly, a pronoun must agree in number, person, and gender with its antecedent. These forms of agreement underscore the close connection between a subject and the verb it governs, along with that between a noun and the pronoun that replaces it.

Agreement errors and other errors common to non-native English speakers are discussed in Appendix C.

Subject–Verb Agreement

You may not have to stop and think about whether a verb agrees in number with its subject, especially if English is your first language. However, determining whether a subject is singular or plural is not always straightforward. In the specific instances explained below, the rules help you apply the important principle of subject–verb agreement.

Finding the Subject

Usually, the subject of a sentence or clause is the noun/pronoun that performs the action of the verb. In most cases, the subject precedes the verb and can be found near the beginning of the sentence (the subject is italicized below):

Kevin and Nigel are happy that they passed the exam.

Sometimes the subject is harder to spot for one of the following reasons:

1. The sentence begins with *Here is/are, There is/are, There has/have been*, etc. The subject follows the verb, rather than precedes it; you have to look ahead in the sentence to the first noun/pronoun to determine whether the subject is singular or plural.

   There *are* many *reasons* for supporting the legalizing of marijuana.

   Here *is* one *person* who supports raising the drinking age.

2. The sentence is phrased as a question. You may need to look ahead to determine the number of the subject:

   What *is* the main *reason* for legalizing marijuana?

   Where *are* all of the *people* who are in favour of raising the drinking age?

3. The subject is delayed. Because the sentence begins with a prepositional phrase, the noun in the phrase may *seem* to form the subject, but the true subject is found later

in the sentence. You can rearrange this kind of sentence to confirm that you have, in fact, used a delayed subject construction:

With the dependence on caffeine *come withdrawal symptoms.*

Sentence rearranged with subject first: *Withdrawal symptoms come* with the dependence on caffeine.

Among Graham's favourites *was the recent album* by Green Day.

Sentence rearranged: *The recent album by Green Day was* among Graham's favourites.

In the examples in 3, one of the nouns *dependence* or *caffeine* in the first sentence, and *favourites* in the second sentence, could be mistaken for the subjects of *come* and *was*, respectively; however, these nouns are preceded by prepositions. A noun or pronoun that directly follows a preposition cannot act as a subject; it is the object of the preposition.

→ To understand more about prepositional phrase openings, see chapter 10, page 314.

4. The subject is governed by a linking verb that has a plural complement. Don't be distracted by what follows the verb; the subject alone determines plurality of the verb:

The *topic* for discussion tomorrow *is* the pros and cons of indoor tanning.

5. The subject is followed by one or more prepositional phrases that contain nouns and/or pronouns that are *not* the subject. If there are two or more nouns before the verb, backtrack carefully to find the noun or pronoun that governs the verb. In the examples below, the prepositional phrases are crossed out so that the subject and verb (italicized) stand out:

A long *list* of items, ~~including vegetables, fruits, meats, and several kinds of bread,~~ *was* handed to Tao.

The *roots* ~~of his dissatisfaction with the course~~ *go* very deep.

Mistaking the Subject

Writers sometimes forget that the common word *of* is a preposition and that the following noun or pronoun is the object of the preposition, not the subject.

Do not mistake a prepositional phrase or a dependent clause for a subject. The sentences below can be fixed by omitting the preposition and beginning the sentence with the noun subject. In the incorrect sentence below, *by choosing* has been mistaken for the subject:

Incorrect: By choosing to take a few correspondence courses may afford a student athlete greater flexibility in meeting academic requirements.

Correct: Choosing to take a few correspondence courses may afford a student athlete greater flexibility.

In the example below, *although Edna thinks of her children at the last moment before her death*, a dependent clause, has been mistaken for the subject (dependent clauses contain their own subjects):

Incorrect: Although Edna thinks of her children at the last moment before her death does not change the fact she is still willing to leave them.

Correct: Although Edna thinks of her children at the last moment before her death, she is still willing to leave them.

Edna thinks of her children at the last moment before her death, though this does not change the fact she is willing to leave them.

Rules for Subject–Verb Agreement

1. **Compound subject joined by *and*.** Two subjects joined by the conjunction *and* require a plural verb form:

   Thanh *and* his friend *are* visiting Ottawa.

   Occasionally, a compound subject expresses a single idea. In both examples below, the compound subject can be treated as a singular subject, since the elements are so closely connected that they can't be separated without changing the meaning:

   Rhythm and blues was always popular with younger audiences.

   To compare and contrast the roles of setting in the novels *is* sure to be a question on the exam.

→ See also
Precision and
Logic in chapter 9
for information
about faulty
predication (p. 291),
in which subject and
predicate are not
logically aligned.

2. **Compound subject joined by *or*.** When the compound subjects are linked by the conjunction *or,* or with the correlative (or paired) conjunctions *either . . . or* or *neither . . . nor,* the verb form is determined by *the noun or pronoun nearest the verb*:

   The chairs *or the table is* going to auction.

   Neither famine nor *floods are* going to force the people to leave their homes.

   If you changed the order of the nouns making up the compound subject in the above sentences, you would need also to change the number of the verb.

   Or and *nor* suggest a choice between one thing or the other, while *and* clearly suggests two or more of something, requiring the plural verb.

3. **Compound subject joined by prepositional phrase.** A prepositional phrase can also be used to join two nouns in a compound subject. *Along with, as well as, combined with, in addition to,* and *together with* are examples of such phrases, which stress the first noun/pronoun more than the second one. Logically, then, the verb is *singular* if the first element of the compound is *singular*:

   The *instructor, as well as* her students, *is* going to be attending the symposium on the environment.

   If the writer of the sentence above wanted to stress equality, the sentence should read: "The instructor *and* her students *are . . . ."*

   Prepositional phrase joiners do not have the strength of the conjunction *and.* When you use one of these joiners, you stress the *first* element more than the second one. The rule for agreement is therefore logical: it depends on the number of the *first* noun/pronoun.

4. **Collective noun as subject.** A collective noun refers to a group. It is singular in form but may be either singular or plural in meaning, depending on the context. Examples of collective nouns include *audience, band, class, committee, congregation, family, gang, group, jury, staff,* and *team.*

   Whenever the context suggests the members of the group are to be thought of as *one unit,* all doing the same thing or acting together, the verb form is *singular*; when the members are considered as *individuals,* the corresponding verb form is *plural*:

   Singular (jury acts as unit): The jury *is* out to consider the evidence before it.

   Plural (class will ask questions individually): After the lecture, the class *are* going to ask questions of the guest speaker.

Most often, collective nouns are considered singular, so, if in doubt, choose the singular form. If a plural verb with a collective noun sounds odd, you can rephrase the subject so that the collective noun functions adjectivally before a clearly plural noun:

After the lecture, *class members are* going to ask questions of the guest speaker.

5. **Singular subject followed by plural noun.** With the following phrases, the verb form is singular, even though the noun or pronoun that follows is usually plural: *each of, either/neither of, every one of, one of,* and *which one of.* The verb form following *the only one of* also is singular:

One of our 115 students *has* written an A+ essay.

Alec is *the only one of* those attending who *has* difficulty speaking before a large group.

> When you use a compound subject, look at the word(s) doing the joining to determine whether the subject is singular or plural.

6. **Indefinite pronoun.** An indefinite pronoun refers to a nonspecific individual or object. Most indefinite pronouns are considered singular and take a singular form in agreement. *Anybody, anyone, anything, each, either, everybody, everyone, everything, neither, nobody, no one, nothing, one, someone,* and *somebody* are singular indefinite pronouns.

7. **Portions and fractions.** With phrases expressing a portion or a fraction followed by *of,* such as *all, a lot, a number, any, a variety, (one-)half, more, most, much, none, part, plenty, some,* and *the majority/minority,* the form of the verb depends on whether the noun or pronoun following *of* is singular or plural:

Half of the *pie is* gone.

One-third of the *employees are* out on strike.

> Some authorities believe that when context clearly warrants the use of plural agreement with the antecedents *everyone* and *everybody*, as in the second sentence below, you may use the plural pronoun:
>
> When the pepper was spilled, *everyone* rubbed *his or her* nose.
>
> When the pepper was spilled, *everyone* rubbed *their* noses.

8. **Collective quantity.** Subjects expressing collective distance, time, money, weight, or mass are singular:

Twelve miles is not a great distance to an experienced hiker.

When the subject is *the number of,* the verb is singular (in contrast with rule 7):

The number of people attending the courses *has dropped* in the last two years.

9. **Singular noun ending in s.** Some nouns end in *s,* but because they usually refer to a singular concept or subject, they require the singular form of the verb. Examples include *athletics, billiards, darts, economics, gymnastics, politics, physics, mathematics, measles, mumps, news,* and *statistics.*

Statistics is an inexact science.

No *news is* good news.

Depending on their context, many of these nouns can be considered plural and should then take a plural verb form. For example, *statistics* could refer to a set of facts, rather than to one subject:

The *statistics* on global warming *are* alerting politicians to the need for worldwide action.

10. **Titles or names**. Whether the titles of artistic works or the names of companies are singular or plural in form will not affect the verb. A singular verb will be needed to agree with the subject:

    Montreal Stories is a collection of Mavis Gallant's fiction; McClelland & Stewart *is* the publisher.

11. **Gerunds**. Gerunds (noun verbals) can act as subjects; you can recognize them by their *-ing* ending. They are singular, so they will be followed by a singular verb form, though what follows them may be plural:

    Understanding quantum physics *is* essential for today's theoretical physicist.

12. **Plural indefinite pronouns**. Logically, the following are plural and require the plural form of the verb: *both, few, many, parts of, several*:

    A well-educated *few seem* to care about correct grammar and punctuation these days, but *both are* essential parts of the writing process.

Pronoun–Antecedent Agreement

Most problems in pronoun–antecedent agreement apply to **personal pronouns**, such as *she, he, they*, and *them*, as well as the possessive pronoun forms, such as *its* and *their*. The **antecedent** of a pronoun is the noun it replaces, and a pronoun must agree with its antecedent noun in number. If you have difficulty finding the antecedent, see if it, or an equivalent form, can be substituted for the pronoun in the sentence, as in the example below:

The dieter should realize that diets will only work when he or she [*the dieter*] restricts his or her [*the dieter's*] caloric intake.

Most of the rules for subject–verb agreement also apply to pronoun–antecedent agreement. For example, a compound antecedent requires the plural form of the pronoun and of an adjective formed from a pronoun (possessive pronoun):

Connie *and* Steve *have* invited me to *their* cottage.

If the compound subject includes the words *each* or *every*, the singular form should be used:

Each book and magazine in the library *has its* own entry.

When two antecedents are joined by *or* or *nor*, the pronoun agrees with the closest antecedent (see rule 2 of subject–verb agreement on p. 361):

Neither the prime minister *nor his advisors were* certain how to implement *their* proposal.

As with subject–verb agreement, a collective noun antecedent requires the singular pronoun form if it is thought of in the collective sense, as a unit; if the context suggests

Most errors in subject–verb agreement are due to one of these three situations: (1) use of a compound subject; (2) use of an indefinite pronoun as the subject; (3) intervening words between the subject and the verb.

A **PERSONAL PRONOUN** refers to people and things.

The **ANTECEDENT** is the noun that the pronoun replaces in the sentence.

that individuals are being referred to, the pronoun takes a plural form (see rule 4 of subject–verb agreement on p. 361):

> Our hockey team will play *its* final game against *its* archrivals. **(The team will be playing as a unit.)**

> The team will be receiving *their* new jerseys Friday. **(Individual team members each will be given a jersey.)**

With a pronoun referring to a portion or fraction, agreement depends on whether the noun following *of* is singular or plural (see rule 7 of subject–verb agreement on p. 362):

> Studies show that *a* large *number of college and university students are* cheating on *their* exams and essays; however, a much larger number are not.

If the pronoun has an indefinite pronoun antecedent such as *one*, *anybody*, or *someone*, the singular form applies, as it does with subject–verb agreement (see rule 6 of subject–verb agreement on p. 362):

> *One* should be careful about pronoun agreement, or *one's* teacher will certainly point out the error to *one*.

Although grammatically correct, the sentence above could be improved by using a personal pronoun to replace the indefinite pronoun *one*. However, you must be careful to use a *singular* pronoun to replace an indefinite pronoun like *one* as the writer of this sentence has failed to do:

> *Incorrect:* *One* should be careful about pronoun agreement, or *their* teacher will certainly point out the error to *them*.

In the sentence below, a singular pronoun replaces the singular antecedent *one*—; however, the sentence is faulty because the possessive adjective *his* and the personal pronoun *him* refer to only one gender:

> *Also incorrect:* *One* should be careful about pronoun agreement, or *his* teacher will certainly point out the error to *him*.

In the next section, we discuss problems that can arise when you want to replace an indefinite pronoun or a generic singular noun by a singular pronoun.

Problematic Pronouns: Inclusive Language

In recent years, the efforts of some writers to avoid gender bias have driven them to a gender-neutral, but grammatically incorrect, use of *they*, *them*, or *their* with the singular indefinite pronoun. The inclusion of both correct pronouns in the form *him or her* or *his or her* is awkward compared to the inclusive *him*, but is preferable to an incorrect *their* and better than a form that may appear sexist. In the sentence below, the writer has used both singular forms to replace the antecedent *student*:

> *Correct:* A student must footnote *his or her* references, or the teacher will expect *him or her* to correct the oversight.

The problem of pronoun–antecedent agreement is especially common among student writers when the antecedent noun is either an indefinite pronoun or a singular noun referring to a person whose gender is unspecified—a generic noun such as *reader, writer, student, teacher, individual, character,* or *person*. Here are three options to consider when you have used an indefinite pronoun or a generic singular noun and want to follow with a pronoun.

Option 1. Replace the plural pronoun with both singular personal pronouns (or possessive adjectives). This option is nearly always acceptable in academic writing, but can be seen as awkward and repetitive in journalistic and workplace writing.

> *Ungrammatical:* Anybody not willing to put in long hours for little pay should give up *their* idea of becoming a writer.

> *Faulty (not gender-neutral):* Anybody not willing to put in long hours for little pay should give up *his* idea of becoming a writer.

> *Correct*: Anybody not willing to put in long hours for little pay should give up *his or her* idea of becoming a writer.

Option 2. Change the singular antecedent into the equivalent plural form and use the plural pronoun.

> *Those* not willing to put in long hours should give up *their* ideas of becoming writers.

Option 3. Where possible, revise the sentence to omit the pronoun.

> *Informal:* If you are not willing to put in long hours for little pay, you should give up the idea of becoming a writer.

In the short paragraph below, fix pronoun–antecedent agreement errors, using at least one of each of the three inclusive language options discussed above.

> If a child begins to perform poorly at school nowadays, they will likely be sent to a school counsellor to deal with the situation. Everyone assumes that attention deficit disorder is the culprit, and they just as automatically assume that drugs are the answer. On the other hand, perhaps the child is just not interested in a particular subject, or they do not understand the material. Parents, in turn, treat the child as if he is the problem instead of listening to him to find out how he can be helped.

EXERCISE 12.1

C↻ Check answers to select questions

Choose the correct form of the verb and/or pronoun in the sentences and make any other necessary changes in agreement. Rewrite the sentence if that will produce a better result.

1. Everybody who supported the motion raised (his/her/their) hand.
2. Neither the film's director nor its producers (was/were) on hand to receive (his/her/their) prestigious award.
3. The instructor as well as the students (thinks/think) the room is too small.

EXERCISE 12.2

C↻ Check answers to select questions

4. It is unfortunate when a person no longer cares what others think about (him/her/them).
5. One should never expect to succeed unless (one/they) (is/are) willing to persist—even against the odds.
6. It is the tried and true that (provides/provide) the ultimate refuge in mediocrity.
7. Everyone who works during the year (is/are) obliged to file (his/her/their) income tax return.
8. Her set of baby teeth (was/were) complete when she was only 18 months old.
9. He was one of those few candidates who (was/were) able to win re-election.
10. None of the company's products (requires/require) testing on animals.
11. Lining the side of the highway (is/are) a lot of billboards advertising fast food restaurants.
12. Every specimen of the horned grebe (has/have) a distinctive tuft on each side of (its/their) head.
13. Media and information technology training (provides/provide) students today with important communication skills.
14. Neither team members nor their coach (expects/expect) the season to last another game.
15. The maximum number of people allowed on this elevator (is/are) 30.

EXERCISE 12.3

C Check answers to select questions

Most of the following sentences contain one or more subject–verb agreement and/or pronoun antecedent agreement errors. Correct the sentences as needed.

1. Every person in the community should have the right to attend a university and create new opportunities for themselves.
2. Especially unique to adolescent depression are physical symptoms, such as headaches.
3. Use of the leaves of the coca plant for its stimulant effects dates back thousands of years.
4. Over the past week, there has been some unexplained occurrences on the girls' floor of the residence.
5. Everyone who has purchased tickets is eligible for the grand prize, but they must be residents of Canada to claim their prize.
6. A coalition of neighbourhood organizations, students, and unions are currently forming to oppose the university's proposed plan.
7. Participation and public education is necessary in a true democracy.
8. When a person contracts jaundice, their skin as well as the white part of their eyes turn yellow.
9. Another round of intense labour negotiations have not produced a settlement, so each union member has been told to do his duty on the strike line.
10. Before rendering its unanimous verdict, the jury was polled individually.
11. Almost nothing shapes a person's true character as much as their home.
12. The nature and role of human resources in organizations have undergone tremendous change in the last two decades.

13. In P.K. Page's poem, it is apparent that the landlady's prying nature and lonely life has made her forget her place.
14. Stereotyping and the use of degrading language in the book serves to reinforce its theme.
15. His overriding concern with rules and regulations, together with his excessive neatness and demand for order, suggests a mild obsessive-compulsive complex.
16. In Japanese culture, a person's reputation along with their social standing depend on the concept of "saving face."
17. The encouragement of curiosity, questioning, and discussion is vital to the success of today's school environment.
18. The give and take in any relationship is the most important factor in sustaining it.
19. Medieval universities established a system of education and academic credentials that continue to function in today's universities.
20. Although the Canadian Forces is still one of the best-trained military in the world, the training standards and morale of the forces is declining, according to some people.

In addition to agreement problems, there are other potential pronoun pitfalls: errors in *pronoun reference*, *pronoun case*, and *pronoun consistency*.

PRONOUN REFERENCE

For a moment, consider life without pronouns.

A Lost Loonie Leads to a Lesson Learned

Alex and Alex's lawyer, Alan, left in Alex's limousine for Loonies Unlimited to buy Alex's landlady, Alice, a litre of light lemonade. Alice told Alex and Alan to also buy a litre of light lemonade for Alice's long-time lodger, Alison. When Alex and Alan alighted at Loonies Unlimited, Alex and Alan were alarmed that Alex had left Alex's loonie in Alex's loft. So Alphonse, of Loonies Unlimited, allowed Alex and Alan only one litre of lemonade, along with a length of limp licorice, and Alphonse loudly lamented Alex's and Alan's laxness.

Newsflash: The pronoun has just been invented! Rewrite the "Lost Loonie" paragraph, replacing as many nouns as possible with pronouns, ensuring that it is clear what noun (antecedent) the pronoun is referring to. If in doubt about the clarity of antecedents, refer to the section that follows.

EXERCISE 12.4

C Check answers to select questions

The noun that the pronoun replaces in the sentence is called the antecedent—literally, the one that "goes before" the pronoun. *Each pronoun you use in your writing should refer clearly to its antecedent*. You can test for pronoun reference errors in your writing by seeing whether you can replace a pronoun by its specific noun antecedent:

Pronoun replaced by specific noun:

As reality shows become more popular, they [*reality shows*] have become more and more bizarre.

Unclear which noun acts as antecedent:

Reality shows have become more popular while their participants have become more and more bizarre; consequently, they [*reality shows? participants?*] can no longer be believed.

There are three categories of pronoun reference errors, which can be repaired in different ways.

1. **No reference (missing antecedent)**. This error occurs where the pronoun has no apparent noun antecedent. Consider this sentence:

   Following the prime minister's speech, *he* took several questions from reporters.

   The personal pronoun *he* apparently replaces *prime minister's*, which is a possessive adjective. Pronouns replace nouns, not adjectives.

   In the following sentence, the noun antecedent is implied but not actually stated; grammatically, the reference, *Canada*, is missing:

   One thing that Canadians are especially proud of is *its* national health-care system.

   Where there is no antecedent, one must be provided or the pronoun changed into an appropriate noun:

   After the *prime minister* spoke, *he* took several questions from reporters.

   or:

   After speaking, the prime minister took several questions from reporters.

   One thing that Canadians are especially proud of is their national health-care system.

   Don't begin a sentence with a preposition, such as *at, by, for, in, on,* or *with,* and then use a pronoun whose antecedent is the object of the preposition. The sentence should be revised to include an antecedent/subject of the clause. The examples below illustrate this problem (and its solutions), which sometimes occurs in a rough draft when a writer is trying to get ideas down quickly:

   Incorrect: With the new Formula One scoring system, *it* keeps fans excited throughout the season.

   Correct: The new Formula One scoring system keeps fans excited throughout the season.

A tendency in speaking, and sometimes in informal writing, is the use of the impersonal third-person pronoun *it* or *they* to refer vaguely to some unmentioned authority. In formal writing, you should avoid this habit:

They say there's nothing like a nice car to make you popular.

or:

With the new Formula One scoring system, fans remain excited throughout the season.

2. **Ambiguous reference**. This error occurs when the pronoun seems to refer to two or more nouns, either of which could be the antecedent:

When *Peter* gave *Paul his* driver's licence, *he* was very surprised to see that it had expired.

Who was surprised in this sentence? The pronoun *he* could refer to either Peter or Paul.

Other examples:

The problem for readers aspiring to look like the models in women's magazines is that their photos have been airbrushed. (*Their* **has two possible grammatical antecedents:** *readers* **and** *models*.)

While it is sometimes possible to correct ambiguous reference by repeating the noun intended to act as the antecedent, the result is not always pleasing:

When *Peter* gave *Paul* his driver's licence, *Peter* was surprised to see that it had expired.

Rewriting may be the better solution:

On giving his driver's licence to Paul, Peter was surprised to see that it had expired.

The problem for readers aspiring to look like the models in women's magazines is that the models' photographs have been airbrushed.

3. **Broad reference (vague reference)**. This error occurs when the pronoun (often *that*, *this*, or *which*) refers to a group of words, an idea, or a concept, rather than one specific noun:

Children these days are too prone to lazy habits, such as watching television. *This* shows we have become too permissive.

This replaces too much—in effect, the whole preceding sentence. By contrast, the meaning of the sentence below is unambiguous, even though the pronoun *which* doesn't replace a specific noun here, but rather the fact that she *received top marks*:

She received top marks for her final dive, *which* gave her the gold medal in that competition.

In the following sentence, the pronoun *this* appears to refer to an idea, rather than a noun antecedent; as a result, the precise meaning of the second independent clause is unclear:

Many older drivers are retested if they have had medical problems, but *this* needs to go further.

Broad reference often requires that a sentence be rewritten. Sometimes, the easiest way is to provide a noun and change the demonstrative pronoun into a

---

While there is perhaps a "broad" allowance for broad reference error, depending on the level of formality required, *it* is a personal pronoun, and, like all personal pronouns, should always have a clear noun referent.

Poor: We try not to mention specific businesses by name in our article; however, it can't be avoided in some situations.

Better: We try not to mention specific businesses by name in our article; however, we can't avoid names in all situations.

demonstrative adjective. (Demonstrative adjectives have the same form as demonstrative pronouns—*that*, *these*, *this*, *those*—but, as adjectives, they precede nouns as modifiers, rather than take their place.)

Children these days are too prone to lazy habits, such as watching television. *This tendency* shows that we have become too permissive.

Many older drivers are retested if they have had medical problems, but *this retesting* needs to go further.

You could also omit *this* in the second sentence.

EXERCISE 12.5

Broad pronoun reference errors are particularly distracting when they occur repeatedly as a writer tries to develop a point. After reading the following paragraph, revise it to fix the errors in broad pronoun reference:

Genetically modified foods have been engineered to flourish in harsh environments. This will help alleviate the need for usable farmland as it will enable farming to occur on lands once considered unsuitable for growing crops. This will be a major benefit to many nations in Africa, Asia, and South America where there is a shortage of food and available land.

EXERCISE 12.6

↻ Check answers to select questions

Identify the kind of pronoun reference errors in the following sentences; then, correct the errors by making necessary revisions. In the first five sentences, the pronoun that needs to be changed is italicized.

1. *It* says in my textbook that pronouns should always have a clear referent.
2. Whenever a staff meeting is called, *they* are required to attend.
3. Racism is a disease that will continue to plague society until *it* is non-existent.
4. Sixty per cent of our pesticides are used on cotton, and *this* is our major groundwater pollutant.
5. During Roosevelt's Pearl Harbor speech, *he* identified the US as a peaceful and tolerant nation.
6. I know it said *No Parking*, but I went ahead and parked there anyway. They gave me a $20 fine.
7. Her second novel was far different from her first. It was set in the remote Hebrides.
8. Previous Afghan successes were significant victories; for example, they last waged war against the powerful Soviet Union.
9. In Andrew Nikiforuk's essay, he discusses the harmful consequences of Alberta's Tar Sands.
10. During the dinosaur age, they lived in a rapidly changing environment.
11. It is the right of everybody to have access to knowledge, and this means access to the education of choice.
12. In chapter 21 of my textbook, it analyzes the success of the Liberal Party in Canada.

13. Supervisors may discourage workers from reporting injuries since they receive annual bonuses for low injury rates.
14. Children often hide their compulsive behaviours from friends and family because of feelings of shame, causing them to remain undiagnosed.
15. To experienced "gamers," the quality of the video card is crucial; this is because the latest games require a high standard of video card.
16. The Catholic kings of Spain rallied the country to fight their enemies, the Moors. This became known as the "Reconquista."
17. Huck Finn was the physically abused son of Pap, who harasses Judge Thatcher when he is drunk. This creates sympathy in the reader, which makes him more likeable.
18. By teaching today's youth safe and healthy approaches to sexuality, it will elevate their self-esteem.
19. Part of the appeal of driving an SUV is that they are big and look impressive beside the "merely mortal" car.
20. Japanese smokers consume more than twice the number of cigarettes as American smokers do, and it continues to increase steadily.

PRONOUN CASE

Some personal, relative, and interrogative pronouns change their form to reflect their function in the sentence. The grammatical term for this form is *case*. You need to be aware of those situations and look at the pronoun's function in order to use the correct form.

Personal Pronoun

A personal pronoun refers to a person. The *first person* refers to the one *doing* the speaking or writing; *second person* refers to the one *spoken to*; *third person* refers to the one *spoken about*. Most nouns can be replaced by third-person pronouns.

Table 12.1 can help you distinguish between one group of pronouns and another. It's important to be able to distinguish between them because the role that a personal pronoun plays in a sentence will determine whether you use the pronoun form from the first group (subjective) or from the second one (objective). Notice that the second-person pronoun *you* doesn't change its form.

TABLE 12.1 Personal Pronouns

	SUBJECTIVE SINGULAR	SUBJECTIVE PLURAL	OBJECTIVE SINGULAR	OBJECTIVE PLURAL
First person	I	we	me	us
Second person	you	you	you	you
Third person	he, she, it	they	him, her, it	them

In the table, consider the pronoun forms under Subjective Singular and Subjective Plural:

He was swimming in the pool.

He is subject of the sentence, the third-person singular masculine form of the pronoun.

He is the correct form because it is the subject of the clause/sentence, so it is said to be in the **subjective case**. The following sentence illustrates what happens when the pronoun plays a grammatical role other than subject:

I was swimming in the pool with *her*.

The subject *I* is first-person singular, but the other pronoun in the sentence is acting as the object of the preposition *with*. When it acts as the object of a verb or of a preposition, it is in the **objective case**.

If you are in doubt about the correct form of a personal pronoun, determine the grammatical role it plays in the sentence, and then use the corresponding case form:

She spoke so softly to the teacher that it was difficult for *him* to understand *her*.

She is the *subject* of the verb *spoke*; *him* is the *object* of the preposition *for*; *her* is the *object* of the infinitive *to understand*.

Notice the different pronouns in these two sentences:

Anna, the King, and *I* are going out for Chinese food tonight. (***I* is part of the subject.**)

Anna arrived late for her dinner with the King and *me*. (***Me* is part of a prepositional phrase; it is the object of the preposition *with*.**)

To decide which form to use:

1. Determine the grammatical relationship involved: Is the pronoun the subject of a clause/sentence, or the object of a verb, a preposition, or an infinitive? Then,
2. Choose the appropriate form (subjective or objective). Until the forms become familiar, you can refer to the pronoun chart above.

Although the principle of pronoun case with personal pronouns is quite straightforward, it can be tricky to apply in compounds:

Tina and (*I/me*) plan to attend Mavis's wedding on May 15.

Strategy: Isolate the pronoun from the noun to determine the correct form:

~~Tina and~~ I plan to attend Mavis's wedding on May 15.

Mavis's wedding will be a joyous occasion for ~~Tina and~~ me.

We ~~students~~ believe firmly that our rights should be given back to us.

Our rights should be given back to us ~~students~~.

A noun/pronoun acting as a grammatical subject or as a subjective complement is in the **SUBJECTIVE CASE**.

A noun/pronoun acting as a grammatical object of a verb or of a preposition is in the **OBJECTIVE CASE**.

TABLE 12.2 Possessive Personal Pronouns with Complements

	ADJECTIVAL SINGULAR	ADJECTIVAL PLURAL	SUBJECTIVE COMPLEMENTS SINGULAR	SUBJECTIVE COMPLEMENTS PLURAL
First person	my	our	mine	Ours
Second person	your	your	yours	Yours
Third person	his, her, its	their	his, hers, its	Theirs

Possessive pronoun. A pronoun also changes its form in the possessive (adjectival) form (e.g., "my *uncle's* pet alligator"; "*his* pet alligator").

> The book doesn't belong to Anthony but to Kristy; it is *hers*.

Hers is the noun form of the possessive pronoun replacing the antecedent *Kristy*. The adjectival form is seen in the following sentence:

> The book doesn't belong to Anthony but to Kristy; it is *her* book.

Table 12.2 completes Table 12.1 by including the possessive forms of pronouns.

Relative Pronoun

A relative pronoun *relates* the dependent clause it introduces to the noun that it follows (see p. 311). A relative clause, then, functions adjectively, modifying the preceding noun. Of the major relative pronouns (*that, which, whichever, who, whoever*), only *who* and *whoever* change their form (to *whom* and *whomever*) depending on whether they are being used as the subject of the clause or as the object of either the verb or a preposition in the clause.

To determine the case of a relative pronoun, look at the role the relative pronoun plays within the clause; in other words, the answer to whether you use *who* or *whom* will be found in the clause that the relative pronoun introduces.

If either of the pronouns is the subject of the clause or is the subjective completion, use the subjective form: *who* or *whoever*. If the pronoun is acting as an object of the verb or of a preposition in the clause, use the objective form: *whom* or *whomever*. Consider these two sentences; italics indicate the dependent (relative) clause:

1. The old man shouted at *whoever happened to be within listening distance.*
2. The old man should be free to shout at *whomever he chooses.*

In sentence 1, *whoever* is the subject of the clause it introduces (*whoever happened to be within listening distance*). In sentence 2, *he* is subject of the clause, and the relative pronoun is in the objective case. If the relative clause has a subject, the relative pronoun will *not* be the subject of the clause. In sentence 2, *he* does the choosing and is the subject of the verb; *whomever* is the object of the preposition *at*.

Acting as an adjective, a **POSSESSIVE PRONOUN** indicates ownership or a similar relationship with the noun that follows.

Never use an apostrophe when you use a form like *hers* ("belongs to her") or *theirs* ("belongs to them.")

One test for case is to substitute the third-person form of the personal pronoun for the relative pronoun in the relative clause:

whoever [relative pronoun] happened to be within listening distance

would become

he/she [personal pronoun] happened to be within listening distance

This is a grammatical sentence, so *whoever* is correct in sentence 1.

If you apply this test to sentence 2, the relative clause would read, *he chooses he*, which sounds, and is, incorrect. The grammatical clause would read *he chooses him*; therefore, *whomever* is the correct relative pronoun.

Interrogative Pronoun

The **interrogative pronouns** (*what, which, whichever, who, whoever*) are always asking questions. Of these interrogatives, it is again *who* and *whoever* that change, depending on their function in the sentence:

> An **INTERROGATIVE PRONOUN** introduces a question.

With whom did you go out on Saturday night? **(object of the preposition)**

Who says you should never reveal your feelings? **(subject of the verb)**

Whom would you recommend for the new opening? **(object of the verb)**

If a pronoun is part of a prepositional phrase, it normally follows the preposition. However, it's possible to structure the sentence so the pronoun precedes the preposition (e.g., *Whom is the note for?*). If you end a sentence with a preposition, you can rearrange the sentence so the preposition comes before the pronoun. It is then clearer to see that the *objective case* should be used for the pronoun:

Whom did Professor LeGuin direct the question *to*?

The more formal usage makes it easier to determine case:

Rearranged sentence: *To whom* did Professor LeGuin direct the question?

It is now clear that *whom* is the object of the preposition *to*.

EXERCISE 12.7

↻ Check answers to select questions

Choose the correct form of the pronoun.

1. Management often forgets about the needs of (we/us) wage-earners.
2. (Who/whom) should run for office this election?
3. You recommend (who/whom) for the position?
4. The person (who/whom) finishes first will be rewarded.
5. Margaret Laurence was a novelist (who/whom) entertained her readers with well-developed plots and realistic characters.
6. People (who/whom) use memory aids tend to be better spellers.
7. The instructor explained the different cases of pronouns to Gail and (I/me).
8. The last person (who/whom) she wanted to see at the track meet was her former coach.

9. The young narrator's goal is to bring back a present for his friend's sister (who/whom) he admires from afar.

10. I wanted to ask her (who/whom) the note should be addressed to.

11. Chris's rival, Mike, lasted longer in the ring than (he/him).

12. I proposed that Geordie and (I/me) would stack chairs after the meeting.

13. We were allowed to invite (whoever/whomever) we wanted to the party.

14. The newly renovated house is a very pleasant place for my brother and (I/me) to live.

15. "Only certain areas will be affected," said Marc Bierkens, (who/whom), along with two other researchers, conducted the study.

16. Prejudices decrease when children observe non-prejudiced behaviour by peers (who/whom) children associate with during their preteen years.

17. During his career, Jackie Robinson was subjected to racial hatred from many people (who/whom) he came in contact with.

18. "[I]n these fits I leave them, while I visit / young Ferdinand, (who/whom) they suppose is drowned." —Shakespeare

19. Christy so drastically changes his personality that his own father can barely believe it is (he/him).

20. Choose the grammatical poem:
    a. Roses are red, / Butterflies are free; You must choose / Between him and me.
    b. Roses are red, / Birds can fly; You must choose / Between he and I.

Pronoun Consistency

A pronoun must agree in number, gender, and person with its antecedent. In many instances, you will refer to different persons in the same sentence, and it's acceptable to do so, as long as the change isn't arbitrary. On the other hand, if you want simply to replace a preceding noun with a pronoun, the pronoun should be the same *person* as its antecedent. Remember that nouns are usually treated as third person and are replaced by third-person pronouns.

Incorrect: During final exams, if *students* must go to the washroom, raise *your* hand so *you* can be escorted there. (*Students* is third person; *your* and *you* are second person.)

Correct:

During final exams, if *students* need to go to the washroom, *they* should raise their hands . . . .

or, informally:

During final exams, if *you* need to go to the washroom, raise *your* hand . . . .

Another example:

Incorrect: Educators today should teach *students* learning skills, such as how to manage *your* money.

Correct: Educators today should teach *students* learning skills, such as how to manage *their* money.

EXERCISE 12.8

↻ Check answers to
select questions

The following paragraph contains errors in pronoun consistency, along with some awkward use of third-person pronouns. When you rewrite the paragraph, strive for correctness and effectiveness. First decide which person you want to refer to consistently. First- and second-person pronouns, such as *I/me* and *you*, are considered more informal than third-person pronouns, such as *he/she* and *him/her*.

> You can definitely learn a lot from educational TV; we can learn things that we cannot learn from written texts. If one is a major in commerce, for example, and if he or she watches the business news, he or she can understand the commerce textbook better by applying what he or she learns from the news. Similarly, I think that watching sports programs can provide people with excitement. Watching sports can also give us a better understanding of the game. On the other hand, if one chooses to watch comedy all the time, people are not going to gain any real benefits. I feel comedies are generally meaningless.

SENTENCE CONSTRUCTION ERRORS

Writing in complete sentences and using the appropriate conjunctions to join clauses will help you form grammatical sentences. However, there are other potential problems in constructing sentences. Major sentence construction errors are discussed below under three categories:

- misplaced modifiers
- dangling modifiers
- faulty parallelism

Sentence construction errors result from forgetting two basic principles in English grammar:

- Modifiers need a word to modify in the sentence and should be placed as close as possible to this word.
- Coordinate (equal) elements in a sentence must be grammatically parallel and complete.

Misplaced modifiers and dangling modifiers are examples of errors that can result when the first principle is not adhered to. Faulty parallelism and faulty comparisons result when the second principle is not followed.

Misplaced Modifiers

The main function of adjectives is to modify nouns, while the main function of adverbs is to modify verbs. Prepositional phrases can also function as adjectives or adverbs. Misplaced modifiers, then, can be either adjectives or adjectival phrases, or adverbs or adverbial phrases. They are misplaced when mistakenly placed next to a part of speech they are not intended to modify.

The meaning of a sentence in English heavily depends on word order, or *syntax*; it is partly through syntax that writers communicate their meaning and that the reader understands the message.

Modifiers should have a word to modify in the sentence, and they should be placed as close as possible to this word; coordinate (equal) elements in a sentence must be grammatically parallel and complete.

Adjectival Modifiers

The usual position for a one-word adjective is immediately before the noun it is intended to modify, but adjectival phrases and clauses usually *follow* the noun they modify. Most misplaced adjectival modifiers are phrases or clauses. Consider the following examples of misplaced modifiers:

Incorrect: They headed for a child in the front row *with a long overcoat.*

It is the child, not the front row, wearing the long overcoat. The adjectival phrase should follow the noun *child*:

They headed for a child with a long overcoat in the front row.

The furnace thermostat is located upstairs, *which displays the temperature settings.*

In this sentence, the adjectival (relative) clause, "which displays the temperature settings," is placed next to the adverb *upstairs* instead of closest to the noun *thermostat*.

The furnace thermostat, which displays the temperature settings, is located upstairs.

Adverbial Modifiers

Misplaced adverbs and adverbial phrases are more common than misplaced adjectives and adjectival phrases because adverbs can often be moved in a sentence without affecting meaning. However, moving them does sometimes affect meaning, and it is safest to place them right before or after the word or phrase they are supposed to modify.

The meaning of the following sentence could be misconstrued:

Students should buy this book because it will give them all the information they need to know about writing *in a convenient form.*

Presumably, the writer did not want to highlight convenience in writing, but that the book *will give them . . . information . . . in a convenient form.*

Correct: Students should buy this book because it will give them, *in a convenient form*, all the information they will need to know about writing.

Fixing Misplaced Modifiers

When the misplaced modifier *in a convenient form* in the previous example is placed closer to the verb it should modify, *give*, the problem is fixed. The solution to misplaced modifiers, whether an entire clause, a phrase, or a single word, is simple: move them.

The following misplaced modifier makes the sentence awkward or misleading:

Incorrect: The instructor marked the essay I wrote *unfairly.*

Correct:

The instructor *unfairly marked* the essay I wrote.

or:

I thought the instructor *marked my essay unfairly.*

When you are writing quickly, trying to get your ideas down, misplaced modifiers can occur anywhere in a sentence; however, they often occur at the end, almost as an afterthought. That is the place to begin checking:

Incorrect: Cars today produce large amounts of toxic chemicals that can damage human cells *if inhaled*.

Correct: Cars today produce large amounts of toxic chemicals that, *if inhaled*, can damage human cells.

A Closer Look

One-Word Modifiers

You need to be careful in placing one-word modifiers in the sentence, especially with limiting adverbs like *almost, barely, even, just, only, merely, nearly,* and the like.

Does one little word out of place *really* affect the meaning of the sentence? Consider how the meaning of the following statement changes, depending on where the "little" word *only* is put:

Jared didn't do his homework yesterday.

Seven Answers to the Question, "Is Jared a Lazy Student or a Conscientious One?"

1. *Only Jared* didn't do his homework yesterday.

Everyone but Jared did his or her homework; *only* is an adjective modifying *Jared*.

2. Jared *only didn't do* his homework.

The meaning of this sentence is ambiguous. It could mean the same as sentence 1 or that Jared did other things—but not his homework. It could also mean that the fact Jared didn't do his homework wasn't important.

3. Jared didn't *only do* his homework yesterday.

Now *only* is an adverb modifying the verb *do* and suggests that Jared did do his homework and other things as well.

4. Jared didn't do *only his homework* yesterday.

Placing *only* before *his homework* means that Jared definitely did his homework and other things as well. It might also mean that Jared was involved in doing someone else's homework in addition to his own.

5. Jared didn't do his *only homework* yesterday.

Placing *only* between *his* and *homework* implies that Jared might under other circumstances have had much more homework, but yesterday had only a lesser amount, which he nevertheless did not do.

6. Jared didn't do his homework *only yesterday*.

Jared normally does his homework but only yesterday did not.

7. Jared didn't do his homework *yesterday only*.

Perhaps Jared is not such a lazy student after all: the only day he didn't do his homework was yesterday!

Dangling Modifiers

Dangling modifiers grammatically modify nouns they are not intended to modify, often producing an unintended meaning. Consider the following sentence from a résumé, which never mentions the applicant at all:

> When not working or attending classes, my hobbies are gardening, doing macramé, and bungee-jumping.

As dangling modifiers are often *-ing* participle (adjectival) phrases, they are sometimes called **dangling participles**. Grammatically, they modify the closest noun. These adjectival phrases, then, are dangling because the intended noun or noun phrase is not in the sentence. That's why it doesn't help to move the modifier.

There are two ways to correct dangling modifiers:

1. provide the noun or noun phrase in the independent clause to give the modifier something to modify
2. turn the dangling phrase into a dependent clause with a subject:

> When not working or attending classes, I enjoy several hobbies, including gardening, doing macramé, and bungee-jumping. **(1)**

> When I am not working or attending classes, my hobbies include gardening, doing macramé, and bungee-jumping. **(2)**

While misplaced modifiers frequently appear at the end of a sentence, dangling modifiers usually are found at the beginning—somewhat less often at the end—of a sentence, and even occasionally in the middle. Unlike misplaced modifiers, a modifier dangles if the essential information *is not in the sentence*. The examples below will show you how to identify dangling modifiers by asking appropriate questions.

In this example, poetic description is undercut by the statement that the clouds are arriving in Calgary, when more likely the writer is describing his or her arrival:

> When arriving in Calgary, the clouds had scattered, and the sky was aglow with bands of pink and red.

In the next example, the book seems to have written itself:

> Though a well-known writer, his latest book failed to make the best-seller's list.

The question to ask in the first example is, "Who is arriving in Calgary?" In the second, we must ask, "Who is the well-known writer?" Since the answers are not in the sentences, the modifiers must be dangling. In both cases, (1) the missing information needs to be provided in the independent clause, or (2) the dangling phrase needs to be turned into a dependent clause that can modify the independent clause that follows:

Corrected:

> When arriving in Calgary, I saw that the clouds had scattered, and the sky was aglow with bands of pink and red. **(1—information has been provided in the independent clause)**

A **DANGLING PARTICIPLE** is an adjective or adjectival phrase that has no noun to modify in the sentence.

Dangling modifiers usually occur at the beginning of a sentence. However, they can also occur later in the sentence if information is missing.

When I arrived in Calgary, the clouds had scattered, and the sky was aglow with bands of pink and red. **(2—dangling phrase has been changed to a dependent clause)**

Corrected:

Though a well-known writer, he failed to make the bestseller's list with his latest book. **(1)**

Though he was a well-known writer, his latest book failed to make the bestseller's list. **(2)**

EXERCISE 12.9

↻ Check answers to select questions

The intended meanings of the following sentences are obscured or distorted due to modifier problems. Working in groups, identify the particular problem (misplaced or dangling modifier) and determine the grammatical (incorrect or ambiguous) meanings of the sentences. Then, fix the sentences using one of the methods above. The sentences are either headlines or leads to actual news stories.

1. Elderly Alberta woman fends off purse snatcher with walker.
2. Jellyfish injures swimmers from beyond the grave.
3. Deriving inspiration from the novel *Uncle Tom's Cabin*, Walker's characters embody the racial tropes that reinforce stereotypical representations of African-Americans.
4. A mother and her daughter were recently reunited after 18 years in a checkout line.
5. The oilsands giant was recently found guilty of failing to take appropriate steps to prevent the deaths of more than 1,600 birds in a St. Albert courtroom.
6. Explorer who first reached North Pole indisputably dies at 80.
7. Scientists have been trying to determine why people need sleep for more than 100 years.
8. Cougar attacks five-year-old boy, expected to survive.
9. Officer fired for waitress photo on cop car with rifle.
10. The googly-eyed Puss-in-Boots looks nothing like the cat fans used to love in the new movie.

EXERCISE 12.10

↻ Check answers to select questions

Correct the following sentences, each of which contains a modifier error. In some instances, it will be necessary to reword the sentence for clarity and correctness.

1. In our city, shady characters lurk on quiet corners that offer a variety of drugs.
2. Over the years, several world-class cyclists have had spectacular careers, such as Eddie Merckx and Greg LeMond.
3. Built in mere minutes, you will have a fully interactive website for your business or for your personal use.
4. Being a member of the Sikh community, my paper will be given a strong personal focus.

5. Germany has built an extensive network of highways through its countryside, known as the Autobahn.
6. Benefits will only result from a smoke-free environment.
7. People's rights to privacy should be forfeited when caught in criminal behaviour.
8. Trying to find a job today, employers are stressing verbal and written communication skills more than ever before.
9. Walking through the streets of Srinigar, devastation and fear are immediately evident.
10. This species of snake will eat frogs, mice, and small pieces of meat in captivity.
11. Tylenol and Aspirin effectively reduce pain when experiencing a fever.
12. As a beginner, my instructor taught me about the respect one karate student must show to another.
13. Moving to Nebraska at the age of 10, Jim Burden's narrative reveals the reflections of one his age.
14. Speaking from experience, tans that dye the top layer of the skin last for about one week.
15. Opening the door unexpectedly, his eyes fell upon two of his employees sleeping in front of their computers.
16. Being an Elizabethan playwright, I am certain that Shakespeare would have been a major influence on Marlowe.
17. Darwin's theory of evolution may be contested on the grounds that species may cease to appear abruptly.
18. As a serious snowboarder, it is exciting to observe the growth of this sport.
19. Based primarily on the work of Karl Marx, socialists see the creation of profit as a complex process.
20. Another example of imagery of light and dark in *Heart of Darkness* occurs when Marlow encounters an African dying in a clearing with a white scarf.

The Parallelism Principle

Balanced constructions give a sentence grace and strength, while unbalanced constructions make a sentence weak and unstable. A sentence must be constructed so that words and phrases parallel in the logic of the sentence are parallel (i.e., balanced) in the grammatical structure of the sentence. Checking for **parallelism** is checking to ensure that the elements in a sentence that have the *same grammatical function* are expressed in parallel structures.

When studying paragraph coherence (chapter 3), you looked at using repetition and balanced structures. Learning the fundamentals of parallelism in this section will help ensure that your writing is both grammatically correct and easy to read. Apply the principle of parallelism carefully to ensure grammatical correctness, and work to ensure that the grammatically parallel structures you use lend clarity and smoothness to your writing.

Experienced writers have mastered the principles of parallel structures and use them routinely in their writing; balanced structures are rhetorically effective. Consider, for example, the following excerpt from Francis Bacon's essay "Of Youth and Age" (1601),

> **PARALLELISM**
> is using the same structure for elements that have the same grammatical structure.

which is made up almost entirely of parallel words, phrases, and clauses. Without parallel elements, shown by italics, this paragraph would be very hard to follow:

> Young men, in the conduct and manage of actions, *embrace* more than they can hold; *stir* more than they can quiet; *fly* to the end, without consideration of the means and degrees; *pursue* some few principles, which they have chanced upon absurdly; *care not* to innovate, which draws unknown inconveniences; *use* extreme remedies at first; and, that which doubleth all errors, *will not acknowledge or retract* them; like an unready horse, that will neither *stop* nor *turn*. Men of age *object too much, consult too long, adventure too little, repent too soon*, and seldom *drive* business home to the full period, but *content* themselves with a mediocrity of success.

Read the following sentences. Although their meanings are clear, they don't *sound* balanced. In fact, they're not balanced because the important words in the compound or list aren't all the same part of speech: each sentence contains an error in parallel structure. The words you need to pay attention to are italicized:

> Ian would rather *snack* on some chips than *eating* a regular dinner.

> The basic human needs are *food, clothes, shelter*, and *having a good job*.

> After her 10-kilometre run, she felt *weak, tired*, and *she badly needed water*.

> Our cat enjoys *watching* TV, *looking* out the window, and *to sleep* at the foot of our bed.

> Neither a *borrower* be, nor *lend* to others.

Identifying and Fixing Parallelism Problems

Use a two-stage approach to identify and fix parallel structures in your writing:

1. Identify structures where there should be parallelism: *lists, compounds, correlative conjunctions*, and *comparisons*.
2. When you have identified which part(s) are not grammatically parallel, make them so by using two of the same parts of speech or sentence structures.

In the following sentence, *food, clothes,* and *shelter* are nouns, but *having a good job* is a gerund (non-finite verb form):

> The basic human needs are *food, clothes, shelter*, and *having a good job*.

> *Fixed:* The basic human needs are *food, clothes, shelter*, and ~~having~~ *a good job*.

In the following sentence, the list is composed of two adjectives and an entire independent clause. Using three independent clauses would make the list parallel—but not concise:

> After her 10-kilometre run, she felt *weak, tired*, and *she badly needed water*.

> *Fixed:* After her 10-kilometre run, she felt *weak, tired*, and *thirsty*.

When checking for parallel structure, consider first the structurally essential words like nouns and verbs (not their modifiers). But if adjectives or adverbs appear in a list *by themselves* without words to modify, ensure they are in parallel form. Look at any larger grammatical units, such as prepositional phrases, which also should appear in parallel relationships with other prepositional phrases. Similarly, dependent clauses should be parallel with dependent clauses, and independent clauses with independent clauses.

The examples below apply the two-step method to lists, as well as compounds, correlative conjunctions, and comparisons.

Parallelism in a List or Series

A list or series comprises three or more items. If you use an expanded thesis statement that lists your essay's main points, you need to ensure that all the items are grammatically parallel:

> *Incorrect:* Research into cloning should be encouraged as it could lead to cures for diseases, successful organ transplants, and put an end to infertility problems.

> *Correct:* Research into cloning should be legalized as it could lead to | *cures* for diseases, | successful organ *transplants*, | and *solutions* to infertility problems.

The line before the first item shows where you should begin to look for parallelism. Notice that to avoid repeating the word *cures*, a word with a similar meaning has replaced it.

Note: Length is not necessarily a factor in parallelism: for example, a simple noun would normally be considered parallel with a noun phrase (but not with a prepositional phrase) because both have the same grammatical function.

The following sentence contains two nouns preceded by adjectives and a noun followed by an adjectival (prepositional) phrase. The important words here are the nouns:

> Discipline in single-sex schools has been shown to directly affect | regular *attendance*, good *grades*, and *standards* for dress and behaviour.

You also need to be careful that items in a list are *logically*, as well as grammatically, parallel. The following list contains five nouns/noun phrases, but not all of the items are logically parallel. Which item does not belong in the list? Why?

> Common injuries in the meat-packing industry include chemical burns, broken bones, lacerations, amputations, and even death.

Parallelism in Compounds

You need to apply the principle of parallel structure to compounds. A coordinating conjunction, such as *and*, *or*, or *but*, can signal a compound, as can a prepositional phrase joiner such as *as well as*; in a comparison, *than* or *as* may join the two elements being compared.

After identifying a compound, look at the important word or phrase in the first element of the compound and ensure that the second element that follows the joiner uses the parallel grammatical structure:

> *Incorrect:* It is actually cheaper | *to convert* a used vehicle into an electric vehicle than | *buying* a new gas-powered model.

A Closer Look

Correlative Conjunctions

A specific kind of compound involves correlative conjunctions. These are joiners that work in pairs (*both . . . and, either . . . or, neither . . . nor, not . . . but, not only . . . but also*). Logically, the part of speech that follows the first half of the compound should also follow the second half. It might be helpful to draw a line after each conjunction:

> *Incorrect*: A college diploma today is an investment *not only* | in students' financial resources *but also* | their time.

What follows *not only* is a prepositional phrase that begins with *in*; therefore, a prepositional phrase, not just a noun (*time*), must follow the second member of the pair:

> A college diploma today is an investment *not only* | *in* students' financial resources *but also* | *in* their time.

> *Correct*: It is actually cheaper | *to convert* a used vehicle into an electric vehicle than | *to buy* a new gas-powered model.

Some compounds that cause trouble are those with helping verbs. In these cases, it may be helpful to draw a line where the first element begins and another where the second begins (after the conjunction). Then, see if both parts line up with the main verb that follows; you can draw a line there too. The main verb in the sentence below is *worked*:

> *Incorrect:* The prohibition of marijuana and the laws in place for it | *do not* and | *have never* | worked.

> *Test:* The prohibition of marijuana and the laws in place for it | *do not* . . . worked and *have never* worked.

> *Correct:* The prohibition of marijuana and the laws in place for it *do not work* and *have never worked*.

Faulty Comparisons

Than is the word for comparisons, not the adverb related to time, *then*. Other words and phrases can also signal comparisons: *as, compared to, different (from), like, similar (to)*, etc.

Under Parallelism in Compounds, above, we looked at comparisons as compound structures requiring parallelism. However, sometimes faulty comparisons have less to do with grammar than with logic.

Because comparisons are always made between one thing and another thing, both these elements must be fully expressed for the comparison to be complete. Often either the comparison is left incomplete or the terms being compared are incompatible; that is, they cannot be compared because there is no basis for comparison.

Writers need to ask if the two parts of a comparison are grammatically parallel, if both parts of the comparison are fully expressed, and if the two objects of the comparison can logically be compared. In this sentence, the reader is left to assume whom males are being compared to:

Incomplete: An unfortunate stereotype is that males are more scientific and less intuitive.

Complete: An unfortunate stereotype is that males are more scientific and less intuitive *than females*.

Incompatible: I have found that students are less judgmental in university compared to high school.

You can ask what precisely is being compared to what and if the comparison is logical; in this case, the writer is comparing a perceived trait of students at university to high school itself. People must be compared to people:

Compatible: I have found that people are less judgmental in university than they are in high school.

The two sides of the comparison are now complete and compatible.

In the word groups that follow, there are three or four main points related to a topic. Build parallel structures in thesis statements for each topic. Make whatever changes are necessary to achieve parallelism and use whatever order of points seems natural.

Topic 1: The advantages of yoga:
- to relax and reduce stress
- to exercise
- also can meet people in yoga classes

Topic 2: Living with roommates:
- they can create a lot of mess
- invade your personal space
- you can talk to them about your problems

Topic 3: The benefits of coffee:
- coffee helps you wake up
- its rich, satisfying flavour
- it improves your concentration

Topic 4: School uniforms are beneficial:
- promote school identity and school pride
- they save parents money and hassle
- to make it easier for school authorities to enforce discipline

Topic 5: The legalization of marijuana:
- it is less addictive than some other illegal drugs
- the Canadian government has already made it legal under certain circumstances
- governments could increase their revenue by selling it
- making it legal would reduce crime since people wouldn't have to obtain it illegally

EXERCISE 12.11

↻ Check answers to select questions

EXERCISE 12.12

↻ Check answers to select questions

The sentences below contain parallelism errors. Identify each kind of error (series, compound, correlative conjunction, or comparison) and fix the errors.

1. A good journalist is inquisitive, persistent, and must be a good listener.
2. Music can directly affect your thoughts, emotions, and how you feel.
3. In this essay, I will be looking and writing about the role of women in the military.
4. There are three main qualities that a leader must possess: a leader must be enthusiastic, organized, and have creativity.
5. Television can affect children in a variety of negative ways since children often lack judgment, are naturally curious, and easily influenced.
6. She was not only the best teacher I have ever had, but also I was impressed by her wardrobe.
7. Aman never has and never will be good at golf.
8. There are many reasons why people choose to or enjoy watching television.
9. We can help combat global warming by using renewable energy sources, researching carbon sequestration, starting carbon taxes, and all the little things we can do as individuals.
10. Being imprisoned for a long time can result in a dependency on the institutional environment, a lack of meaningful relationships, and there can be a loss of personal identity.
11. When Jim has the choice of either jumping or to stay on the doomed ship, he chooses to jump.
12. Physical education teaches children not only to work well together but also patience and discipline.
13. Smoking should be banned because it raises health-care costs, physically harms both smokers and non-smokers, and because cigarette production damages the environment.
14. Allowing prostitution in controlled environments will reduce the risk of violence, decrease drug abuse, and even combats disease through regular testing.
15. What made Beethoven's music different from other composers was his expressive style.

CHAPTER SUMMARY

Studying the topics covered in this chapter will enhance your ability to write grammatically. Applying the rules for agreement will prevent illogical errors in which a subject and its verb or a pronoun and the noun it replaces do not match up. Pronoun errors are often caused by misunderstanding the different categories of pronouns and their functions; the sections on pronouns clarify pronoun functions within sentences or clauses. Finally, modifier and parallelism errors can make a sentence more difficult to read or even mean something different from what the writer intended.

Appendix A

PROOFREADING: PERFECTION IS POSSIBLE

In publishing, *editing* refers to the revising of a work before it is formatted, whether for a book, a newspaper, a magazine or journal, or another medium. *Proofreading* refers to the final check of the formatted material—done either on screen or in the form of paper "proofs" printed from the formatter's electronic files.

While someone who edits and suggests revisions to a document is mainly concerned with improving it, the proofreader is looking for errors. The proofreader is the document's last line of defence before it falls under the public eye. Ironically, poor proofreading may be the first thing noticed in the published document.

In spite of its importance, proofreading is usually one of the neglected stages for student writers working under deadline to submit an essay. However, errors may strike your instructor as carelessness, a sign of a lack of effort or respect for the reader.

Proofreading is best performed as a mechanical process. By taking a systematic approach to the essay at this stage, you can be more confident that the work of many hours, days, or even weeks will be more readable to the person marking it.

Proofreading Methods

Reading forward is the method of reading the paper aloud or to yourself but more slowly and carefully than you would usually do, paying attention both to the words and to the punctuation. Because it can be hard to concentrate solely on the words apart from the meaning, it's best to read through the essay at least once for meaning and then at least once again for spelling and other errors.

Reading backward is the method by which you start at the end and read to the beginning word by word or sentence by sentence. This technique forces your attention on the writing; it works well for catching spelling errors. However, it is time-consuming, and you may miss some punctuation and other "between the words" errors, as well as words that are dependent on their context.

Reading syllabically, you read from the beginning, breaking every word into syllables. This is faster than reading backward, works well for catching internal misspellings, and is quite effective for catching missing and extra words and for correcting word endings (which may be overlooked when you read forward). However, it is a slower method than reading forward word by word, requires some discipline to master, and can be hard on the eyes if done for a long time.

> When you proofread your work, it is a good idea to read aloud since you may more easily catch errors you've missed as a writer.

Guidelines for Proofreading

- Probably the main reason for essays with careless errors is that not enough time was allotted for proofing. The half hour not set aside for proofreading can undo the work of several hours.
- Let at least a few hours pass before you look at the essay for the final time.
- Having someone else go over the essay can be helpful but is no substitute for your own systematic proofing. Instructors are not likely to be sympathetic to the cry of baffled frustration, "But my roommate read it over!"
- Use a spell-checker but don't rely on it. A spell-checker will not see any difference between *there house is over their two* and *their house is over there too*.
- Experiment with the different proofreading methods discussed above and use the ones you feel most comfortable with and that work best for you. When you start proofreading using one particular method, though, you should use it until you finish reading.

Common Errors

Categories of typical errors to watch for and correct in your writing:

- Areas where consistency is required—for example, spelling, capitalization, abbreviations, hyphenation, numbers, and punctuation
- Proper nouns , acronyms, etc. Are names of authors and titles spelled correctly?
- Middles and endings of words, for spelling and for agreement
- Small words, such as articles and prepositions (*a, an, and, as, at, if, in, it, of, or, the, to,* etc.)
- Words that have different spellings but the same pronunciation (homophones)— e.g., *to/too, its/it's, their/there/they're, role/roll, cite/site, led/lead, manor/manner*
- Font style (italic, bold, Roman: applied correctly and consistently? Applied to *all* necessary words?). Have you used italics for complete works, such as books and films, and used quotation marks for works within larger works, such as essays, articles, short stories, and poems?
- End punctuation (periods and question marks)
- Appropriate use of quotation marks. Are both opening and closing quotation marks present? Are periods and commas inside; colons and semicolons outside? Similar checks can be made for parentheses.
- All citations, both in-text and on the final page of the essay. Check both for accuracy (author, title, journal name, date, and page numbers) and for consistency. Are all citations documented according to the style of your discipline— including capitalization, punctuation, and other conventions?

Essay Presentation

Your audience and purpose are relevant to how you present your essay; for example, a scientific or engineering report probably would look quite different from an essay for English class—for one thing, it might have headings, whereas the English essay would probably not. A research essay, too, must conform to the documentation style of your discipline; on the other hand, presenting your essay may mostly be a matter of following directions for title, typeface, margins, spacing, indentation, page numbering, and identifying information.

Although document design can vary, you can be sure of one thing: if your instructor asks you to format your essay a certain way, he or she will look to see that you followed these instructions. Therefore, if you are unsure about essay presentation, ask for help.

Unless you are told otherwise, you can refer to the following (based on MLA guidelines):

- Essays should be typed. Use good-quality white paper. Many instructors will let you print on both sides of the page, but you should check.

- Leave 2.5-centimetre (1-inch) margins on all sides. The first page should include identification information positioned flush left (i.e., starting at the left margin). List information in the following order: your name and student ID, if applicable; instructor's name (use the title that your instructor prefers—e.g., Professor Robert Mills, Dr. M. Sonik, Ms. J. Boswell, etc.); course number and section, if applicable; submission date. Leave a double space, then insert the essay's title, centred.

- Double-space the text of your essay; this makes it much easier for the instructor to correct errors and add comments. *Also double-space* any "Notes," the "Works Cited" page, and block quotations.

- Indent each paragraph 1.25 centimetres (one-half inch)—do *not* use additional spaces to separate paragraphs, and leave a single space after each period before beginning the next sentence.

- Number pages using Arabic numerals in the upper right-hand corner preceded by your last name; place about 1.25 centimetres (one-half inch) from the top and flush right. If you need to include prefatory pages (such as a Contents page or a formal outline), use lower-case Roman numerals (i, ii, iii) for those pages.

- Title pages are often optional. If used, position the essay's title down one-third of the page with your name about half-way down; near the bottom of the page include the course number, instructor's name, and submission date. All items should be centred. Begin your essay on the second page (numbered 1) under the centred title.

- No illustrations or colours, other than black and white, should be on any pages unless you use graphics directly relevant to your essay—for example, charts or diagrams for a scientific study. Use a paper clip to attach the pages (some instructors ask for stapled pages)—especially, don't dog-ear them. Don't use folders, clear or coloured, unless asked for. (If you do use a folder, the left-hand margin should be slightly wider than the other margins to enhance readability.)

- Prefer common fonts, such as Times New Roman, Arial, or Garamond (not Courier New or cursive ones). Use 10- to 12-point type size. *Do not* justify lines to the margins in academic papers or reports (i.e., set the paragraphing for flush left and use a *ragged* right line at the margin). Finally, ensure that the text of your essay is easy to read. An essay printed in draft mode or from a cartridge that is almost out of ink will not be easy to read.

Appendix B

THE IN-CLASS ESSAY OR EXAMINATION ESSAY

You will likely have to do in-class writing, at least occasionally, during your academic career. Timed activities, for many, can be stressful, as you need to demonstrate both your knowledge of a subject and your writing skills. You may be able to use a text, notes, or a dictionary; or it may just be you, your pen, and some paper (or a computer).

Although in-class writing—especially exams—might be considered a necessary evil for many, it serves several practical purposes, demonstrating your ability to think, read, and write under pressure. Although these kinds of essays often test recall, they also test other important qualities, such as organization and time management, adaptability, and, sometimes, creativity and imagination.

Recall

In-class or examination essays require you to remember information from lectures, textbooks, and discussions; however, other factors may also be crucial. Being familiar with the *terminology* of your discipline is vital, meaning that you need to be able to communicate effectively in the language of the discipline. For example, if you are writing an English literature exam, you will need to be able to understand and refer to terms such as *metaphor* or *analogy* that are used to analyze prose, poetry, and drama.

You also need to be aware of *basic principles*, *procedures*, and *methods* stressed throughout the year.

- If you are asked to write one or more essays, you will need to know the basics of essay format and structure.
- If you are asked to write a summary of a text, you will need to know how to summarize.
- If you are asked to write a critical analysis of an essay, you will need to know how to think critically.

Nobody can remember everything that was taught, so you should allow enough time for a leisurely review of your notes, highlighted sections of course texts, and instructor comments on term essays and tests. The goal is to distinguish the essential from the less-than-essential and to focus on what you *need* to know. Although it's important to have a grasp of basic facts and details, essays often test the *application* of facts. For example, in English literature, applying key terms like *irony*, *point of view*, or *dramatic structure* may be more important than defining them.

Organization and Time Management

Once you have decided how you will divide up the exam and how much time to spend on the various parts, stick to your plan. It is common to spend too much time on the first question. If you find yourself doing this, jot one or two points in the margin to follow up on, time permitting, and move on to the next question.

Do you begin with the longest question, the shortest one, the hardest or the easiest one, the one worth the most marks or those worth fewer marks? It is probably safest to begin with a question you feel comfortable with. Writing a confident answer can make you feel at ease when responding to the other questions.

Obviously, you should read the general exam instructions carefully before beginning. Underline key words or phrases to reinforce their importance and to keep them in mind as you write. The same applies to each question. This is especially important when the question makes a distinction of some kind: "answer *three* of the following five questions"; "respond to *either* question one *or* question two." Also pay attention to the verb used to introduce or frame the question; *discuss*, *compare and contrast*, and *explain* give three different instructions. Dictionaries, if allowed, are useful for interpreting questions and helping you find the right word, not to mention spelling.

Finally, plan for at least five minutes per question to look over the exam after you have finished writing to ensure that nothing has been omitted and that the marker will be able to follow you. Final checks and careful proofreading are important—as are small additions, such as transitions to connect ideas. Instructors prefer to read a thoughtfully revised and carefully proofed essay to one that is meticulous looking but unclear. Neatness is important, but completeness and accuracy are more so.

Adaptability

Once you have done the necessary planning and are focusing on the individual question(s), you need to

1. distinguish what is important from what is less important
2. focus on strong, well-chosen points and supporting details, adapting the question, if necessary

In the question for the Sample Student In-Class Essay below, the writer has underlined the important parts of the question and has already begun to shape her answer by attempting to rephrase or elaborate on the question. At this stage, she is looking for clues, hints, and suggestions for writing.

Before she can proceed from topic to thesis statement, she has to decide on her approach. One of the common weaknesses of in-class essays is the tendency to generalize, to be too broad. Therefore, first limiting the topic and finding a distinct area to make your own will result in a more manageable essay.

When you limit or refine a general topic, you want to achieve focus and intensity. Ask yourself the following questions to help limit the topic:

- What do you know about the topic?
- Have you or has anyone you know had experience with it?
- How can you relate the topic to your own knowledge base or skills?

The main reason for asking such questions is not to enable you to write using the first-person (*I*, *me*, etc.) but to consider *how you can use your experience as an asset.* Finding where you are knowledgeable is the key to refining the topic in order to use your demonstrable strengths.

Every essay benefits from examples and illustrations that give solid support for your points. Examples turn the general and abstract into the concrete and specific. Details are essential. Consider using a pre-writing technique, such as questioning or brainstorming, to generate detail.

The student who wrote the in-class essay was given 60 minutes for her response, enough time to develop an approach to her topic and a thesis statement, and to prepare a scratch outline. Although the assignment did not test factual recall, it did test typical writing skills, such as organization, topic development, and the ability to write clearly and grammatically.

SAMPLE IN-CLASS STUDENT ESSAY

by Kristen Carlton

Exam question: Paperbacks continue to be the largest sector of the book publishing industry, but ebooks are now outselling hardcovers. From your knowledge, experiences, or observations, compare reading text on screen (books, if possible) to reading books in paper form.

Kristen's Response

[1]   Reading is a pastime that many people enjoy. It provides a release from ordinary life and can be a way to relax, laugh, reflect, and gain knowledge. Since the dawn of the computer age, however, reading has begun to take on a different form as ordinary bound and printed books are beginning to be replaced by online texts and electronic books, or ebooks. Some students are even being asked to purchase online rather than printed textbooks. While paperbacks are still maintaining strong sales, hardcovers are dwindling away. It comes as no surprise that hardcovers are decreasing in popularity as paperbacks were usually preferred due to being smaller, lighter, and less expensive than the hardcover equivalents. Ebooks take the idea of size and weight to a whole different level.

Side annotations:

I can refer to this as a fact as it's mentioned in the question. From this fact, certain inferences can be drawn about current reading habits and trends—for example, paperbacks and ebooks are more convenient than hardcovers.

I can speak from personal experience or use experience of friends, etc.

Compare means looking at similarities and differences; in this case, I believe there are more differences than similarities.

The student begins with a general observation on the uses of reading, making the transition to her topic in the third sentence.

Although the beginning of this sentence repeats some information from the previous sentence, the writer uses reader preferences for paperbacks over hardbacks to provide a transition into her next point: ebooks provide even more convenience than paperbacks. Logical connections between ideas enables Carlton to develop her introduction.

While some consumers may prefer traditional forms of reading, ebooks are making their way into the marketplace with astounding vigour as more consumers realize their benefits.

[2]   Ebooks provide a new format with which to enjoy literature. With electronic readers like Kindle and Kobo, and Smartphones and tablets that come equipped with ebook applications, the world of reading has never been as efficient and accessible to consumers. Readers can purchase ebooks online, usually at reduced prices compared to hardcovers, from wherever they have Internet access. This form of shopping for books involves no crowds, lines, or waits. With the press of a button and a credit card or PayPal number, a book can be in your hands—or, at least, downloaded to your e-reader—in seconds. Another bonus of ebooks is that they are easy to take anywhere. One electronic reader can hold hundreds of books, all accessible within moments, giving you a choice of reading matter that is dependent on mood as well as necessity. Ebooks are lightweight, easy to hold, and compact. They also provide privacy if you are reading an ebook you don't want everyone to see. Ebooks have become popular because they are easy to use and easy to access.

[3]   While ebooks have several advantages, there are many people who prefer the traditional reading experience with a book in paper form. Some people don't appreciate staring at screens; they prefer holding the book in their hands and flipping the pages themselves. Ebooks are not for those who do not get along with technology or, obviously, those who don't have access to the Internet. Clearly, ebooks are not for everyone.

[4]   The experience of reading has been revolutionized by ebooks, but like all great changes, there always will be opposition. Ebooks provide efficient and compact access, while traditional books in paper form provide the familiar experience that many grew up with and grew accustomed to. It doesn't matter whether you are a tech-savvy ereader or a traditional page flipper, there are many reading experiences to choose from. Reading, no matter what form it takes, appears to have a permanent place in society.

Note the precise phrasing of the simple thesis: Carlton begins with a dependent clause acknowledging the preferences of traditional readers. She places the main idea, the advantages of ebooks, in an independent clause.

The writer's longest paragraph focuses on her main point, the advantages of ebooks. The paragraph is well developed with three subpoints. Can you identify them? She also shows credibility by demonstrating knowledge (gained through her own experiences or through observing or talking to others); by demonstrating reliability—for example, by writing clearly and organizing her points logically; and by demonstrating fairness—for example, she doesn't make extreme claims for ebooks. As in the next paragraph, she includes a topic sentence and a brief paragraph wrap.

The writer's conclusion focuses on summary. She ends her essay by making a general comment about the popularity of reading itself. Although she could, perhaps, have used more strategies to attract the reader's interest, her attention to essay and paragraph structure, along with her reasonable points, creates an effective essay.

Appendix C

A CHECKLIST FOR EAL WRITERS

The following are some English idiomatic expressions and rules for usage, organized alphabetically by the parts of speech. Although they are not a major part of speech, articles can be confusing for EAL writers, so they have been allotted a separate section, beginning on page 396.

For more complete information, many useful references, including OUP's general ESL dictionaries, can be consulted.

Adjectives

One-word adjectives usually precede the words they modify, except predicate adjectives that follow linking verbs (see p. 313). However, relative (adjectival) clauses follow the nouns they modify and present special challenges for writers (see p. 396).

The following adjectives often give students trouble:

Ago: When you want to refer to a time in the past and relate this time to today, you can use the adjective *ago*; it follows the noun. To refer to a *specific* point in the past, you can give the date (month, day, year) preceded by *on*. See "Times and dates," below.

> The first truly successful cloning of an animal occurred more than *ten years ago*. The first truly successful cloning of an animal occurred *on July 5, 1996*.

Few* versus *a few: Both can precede nouns that can be counted, but *few* means "not many," and *a few* means "some." So, *few* usually refers to fewer of something than *a few*! (Since *a few* has more letters than *few*, you can associate it with more of something than *few*.)

> *Few* Canadians know how to play cricket. However, *a few* people on my listserv said they would be interested in learning how to play it.

Much* versus *many: Use *much* before nouns that cannot be counted and *many* before countable nouns. Similarly, use *amount* before uncountable nouns and *number* before countable nouns (see p. 302); use *less* before uncountable nouns and *fewer* before countable nouns (see p. 402).

> The Canadian television channel *MuchMusic* features *many* different kinds of music.

Adjectives as Participles

When a participle ending in *–ed* or *–en* precedes a noun and acts as an adjective, don't drop the ending it requires as a past participle:

Although Patrick lived a *fast-paced* [not fast-pace] life, he had the *old-fashioned* [not old-fashion] habit of stopping and reading a newspaper every day before work.

Adjectives and Present Participles versus Past Participles

When participles are used to modify nouns, it can be confusing knowing whether to use the present (*–ing*) form or the past (*–ed* or *–en*) form, especially after a linking verb like *was*. In verbs related to feeling or emotion, the present particle is used when the subject *causes* the feeling; the past participle is used when the subject *experiences* the feeling.

Dennis felt *embarrassed* to receive a C on his essay; the mark was *depressing*.

Dennis experiences embarrassment; the mark causes him to feel depressed.

The surprise ending of the football game was *exciting*; the few fans left in the stadium were *excited*.

Comparatives and Superlatives

Use the comparative of adjectives and adverbs when you want to compare one person or thing to another person or thing. Usually, the suffix *–er* is added if the quality being compared is one syllable, while the word *more* precedes a word of two or more syllables:

In BC, summers are usually *drier* than they are in Ontario.

According to *the most recent* statistics, it is *more dangerous* to drive a car than to take an airplane.

Use the superlative of adjectives and adverbs when you want to compare more than two of something. The definite article is usually not used with comparisons, but it is used with superlatives (see Articles, below).

In my opinion, BC is a *better* province than Alberta [there are two]; in my friend's opinion, Alberta is *the best* of the western provinces [there are four].

Plural Nouns as Adjectival Phrases Concerning Distance, Money, and Time

When these kinds of plural nouns appear in hyphenated phrases before other nouns, they drop the final *s*, as in the following examples:

a *10-kilometre* run (*not* a 10-kilometres run), a *30-day* refund policy (*not* a 30-days refund policy), a *70-year-old* man (*not* a 70-years-old man).

Relative (Adjectival) Clauses

A relative clause modifies the noun it follows (known as the *antecedent*). These clauses begin with a relative pronoun (usually *who*, *that*, or *which*, but sometimes *whom*, *whose*, *when*, *in which*, or *where*). Make sure you include the introductory relative pronoun at the beginning of the clause. Below, the complete relative clause is underlined, the relative pronoun is bolded, and the antecedent is italicized:

> In China, there is a *high school* **that** was painted green because green is considered a relaxing colour. The *students* **who** attended the school reported better study habits.

When you use a phrase like *in which* to introduce a clause, do not repeat the preposition at the end of the clause:

> Happiness for some people is measured by their success in the society in which they live ~~in~~.

Agreement in Relative Clauses

The relative pronoun that introduces the relative clause refers back to the noun antecedent, as mentioned above. The antecedent determines whether the verb in the relative clause is singular or plural. The relative pronoun is bolded in the sentence below, the verb is underlined, and the antecedent is italicized:

> The Hyundai hybrid car has a small *engine* **that** consumes less fuel than ordinary cars.

Adverbs

Adverbs with Adjectives

Adverbs can modify adjectives and other adverbs, along with verbs. Ensure you always use the correct adverbial form. In the sentence below, *environmental* is the adjectival form; *environmentally* is the adverbial one:

> The average Canadian household has become more environmental*ly* conscious than in the past.

Although many adverbs end in *–ly*, some do not; furthermore, some adjectives end in *–ly* and modify nouns: a *friendly* neighbour, some *fatherly* advice, a *cowardly* act. These adjectives cannot be made into adverbs.

Comparative and Superlative of Adverbs

See Comparatives and Superlatives, under Adjectives, above.

Articles—*A*, *An*, and *The*

Indefinite articles precede some singular nouns, and definite articles precede some singular and plural nouns. Context often determines whether an article precedes a noun or whether it is omitted; idiom also can determine usage. However, general guidelines can be used to determine whether to include the article or not.

The Indefinite Article

General rule: Use the indefinite article *a* or *an* if you want to identify a general or non-specific noun. Use *an* rather than *a* if the noun begins with a vowel that is not pronounced or with a silent *h*.

> When I was bird watching, I looked for *a* Rufus hummingbird. (no specific bird is referred to)

> When *the* hummingbird saw me, it darted into the trees. (a specific bird is referred to)

The indefinite article is *not* used before most uncountable concrete nouns, nor do these nouns form plurals. It is easier to remember these nouns if you divide them into categories:

Kinds of liquids: beer, blood, coffee, milk, oil, soup, water, wine, etc.

Kinds of food: bread, cheese, corn, flour, food, fruit, lettuce, meat, pasta, popcorn, rice, sugar, etc.

Names of languages: Arabic, Mandarin, Dutch, French, Japanese, Vietnamese, etc.

Names of areas of study: biology, economics, geography, mathematics, etc.

Names of gases: hydrogen, methane, ozone, oxygen, etc.; air, fire, smoke, and steam also belong here

Sports and games: baseball, bowling, football, hockey, jogging, surfing, tennis, etc. But, baseballs and footballs (the objects, not the sports) are countable.

Others: chalk, clothing, equipment, feedback, furniture, health, help, homework, housework, laughter, luggage, mail, money, research, scenery, soap, software, weather, wood, work, etc.

However, if preceded by a word like *piece* or *item*, such nouns may be countable: *a piece* (or *pieces*) *of chalk*; *an item* (or *items*) *of furniture*; *a glass of water*. As well, many nouns can be used adjectivally before countable nouns: *a cheese stick*; *a hockey game* . . .

Some of the nouns above can be used in a countable sense if they can be divided into different types:

> Red *wine* in moderation can be beneficial to one's health.

> Different *wines* are classified by their place of origin.

Note: Although *mail* is an uncountable noun, *email* can be used as a countable noun; thus, you can talk about receiving *an* email. As a noun, email can also be pluralized:

> Flora was shocked to see that she had received more than 100 *emails* over the weekend; as a result, she vowed to get rid of her *email* by the end of the week.

See also Uncountable and Countable Nouns under Nouns.

The Definite Article

General rule: Nouns that refer to a specific person, place, or object are usually preceded by the definite article, *the*:

> Please give me *the* pen on *the* table.

A specific pen (distinct from other pens) on a specific table is requested.

> Please give me *a* pen on *the* table.

This request implies that there is more than one pen on the specific table.

> Please give me *a* pen.

Any pen from anywhere will do.

> Young children, especially in *the* 3–5 age group, are always asking questions.

Other age groups exist, making the reference specific.

Using definite articles before nouns:

(a) **First versus second reference:** Use *a* when something is first mentioned, *the* when the same noun is mentioned again (it can now be identified). Several examples are shown in the brief story below:

> Mike, who was 18 and lived in Canada, had *a strange experience* as he was walking on *a beach*: he found *a brown bottle* that had washed ashore. When he cleaned it up, he saw that *the bottle* had *a note* inside. With much effort he was able to dislodge *the note*, which was from *a person* in another country. *The person* had written simply "Hi, I'm Mike. I'm 18, and I live in Australia."

(b) **Nouns that refer to a species or class of objects:** Use the definite article before this group; an example is *the definite article* in this sentence. Here is another example:

> In her English class, Izumi studied *the argumentative essay* before *the research essay*.

(c) **Unique nouns:** If the noun has a unique identity, precede it by the definite article.

> *Examples*:
>
> *specific eras or time periods*: *the* Industrial Revolution, *the* Age of Reason, in *the* twentieth century, etc.
>
> *the* Sun, *the* Moon, *the* North Star (unique celestial objects)
>
> *Newspapers, museums, theatres, and hotels*: *The* Vancouver Sun (newspaper), *the* Royal Ontario Museum, *the* Imax theatre, *The* Banff Springs Hotel

(d) **Superlatives** could also be considered unique, in a category by themselves; the definite article precedes superlatives (see also Comparatives and Superlatives). The sentence below includes three superlatives.

I have found that *the best courses* at university are usually *the most challenging ones*, and they are taught by *the best professors*.

Compare with:

I have found that *courses* at university are usually *challenging*, and they are taught by good *professors*.

(e) **Ordinals:** *the first*, *the second*, etc. (versus cardinal numbers: one, two, etc.)

Maria was *the first* to cross the finishing line; Linden was *the second*. They finished *one* and *two*, respectively.

Omitting definite articles before nouns. When using nouns that fall into the following groups, omit the definite article. However, there are exceptions to the guidelines.

(a) Omit before most *plural nouns*:

If animals have no consciousness, it is meaningless to discuss whether eating meat is immoral.

Animals is a plural noun; *meat* is an uncountable noun.

(b) Omit before *proper nouns*, though there are many exceptions to this general rule. For example, the article is used before some geographical names:

Bodies of water: Hudson Bay, Lake Ontario, but *the* Pacific Ocean, *the* Fraser River

Countries and continents: Canada, China, Japan, Asia, Africa, North America; but *the* United States, *the* Philippines, *the* Arctic. Omit before Nunavut and all the *provinces and American states*; but *the Province of Quebec*, *the Province of Ontario*, etc., *the* Northwest Territories, *the* District of Columbia (in the US). Omit before Hawaii, but *the Hawaiian Islands*.

National, social, and cultural groups: Canadians, Americans; but *the* English, *the* Japanese, *the* middle class, *the* Inuit peoples

Lonnie is a member of *the* Chipewyan First Nations and lives near Prince Albert in northern Saskatchewan.

(c) Omit before *abstract nouns* unless a prepositional phrase follows the noun; abstract nouns are usually uncountable and also cannot be pluralized:

It is said that while truth is relative, reality is what we perceive through our senses.

Truth and *reality* are abstractions.

The reality of the situation, unfortunately, is that *justice* does not always prevail.

A prepositional phrase follows *reality* but not the abstract noun *justice*.

Other abstract nouns include *advice, anger, curiosity, employment, enjoyment, evidence, freedom, fun, health, information, intelligence, knowledge, love, music, peace, pollution, research, respect, wealth, weather,* etc.

(d) Common nouns that often result in errors in article use include *government, nature, society, Internet,* and *media*:

Government: if you are referring to a *specific* government, use the definite article; otherwise, do not use *the*:

> *The government* [meaning, for example, the government of Ontario] has no right to raise student tuition fees.

Nature: If you are referring to the natural world, the noun *nature* is *not* preceded by *the*. If the sense is of a quality, essence, or habit, *the* may be required. The noun *environment*, which has a similar meaning to *nature*, is usually preceded by an article.

> The wonders of *nature* surround us every day. It has been *the nature* of previous generations [their habit] to take *nature* [the natural world] for granted.

> Evidence of damage to *the environment* is all around us.

Society: It is *not* preceded by *the* if the reference is a general one. Note that *society* is usually singular and requires the singular verb form. If the reference is specific, *the* may be required (for example, if it is followed by a phrase that particularizes society):

> *Society does* not look kindly on those who fail to respect *its* rules.

> I find *the society* of like-minded people unfulfilling.

> When used as a noun, *Internet* is preceded by *the* as is *media* when it refers to *the news media* as a form of mass communication, such as television, radio, newspapers, and magazines; it usually takes a singular verb form when used this way.

> With the rise of *the Internet, the media has* become even a more powerful influence on *society*.

For article use with gerunds, see Gerunds, under Nouns, below.

Nouns

The following nouns often give students trouble:

Human: This noun can be used in the singular or the plural, but possessive forms should be avoided. Instead, consider using *humanity*, an adjectival form, or *our*.

> It is a *human* [*not* a human's] need to aim for perfection.

> *Humanity's* [*not* Humans'] need for perfection is unending.

> *or*:

> *Our* need for perfection is unending.

Humanity: Humanity refers to humans collectively. Don't use *man* or *mankind* to refer broadly to human beings: many consider these words sexist as, by implication, they exclude women. *Humanity* is not preceded by the definite article (or possessive adjective) unless it refers to an inner quality (see "Nature," above).

> One quality that *humanity* shares with other organisms is the need to solve problems. She demonstrated *her humanity* [an inner quality] by forgiving her enemies.

Opinion, express an opinion: Don't write, "In my point of view," "As for myself," or "As far as I am concerned. . . ." The most direct way of stating your opinion is simply to write, "In my opinion . . ." or, "I believe that . . .", and follow with a clause that states your opinion. However, it is often more objective just to express your opinion without announcing that it is your opinion.

If you want to express someone else's opinion, you can write: "According to the point of view of people who smoke . . ."; "according to smokers . . .", etc., or simply, "Scientists believe that. . . ."

Every + Noun

Every one of, like *each one of, either one of*, etc., will be followed by a plural noun but a *singular* verb form. But when one of these words is followed directly by a noun, that noun will be *singular*, not plural (and the verb will be singular, too):

> Almost *every* drafting *course* in schools *involves* computers.

> Almost *every kind* of species *has its* own social group.

> Many high school students in China are not allowed to use calculators, so they have to do *every* mathematical *step* in their heads.

Using *every one of* would result in a plural noun in the *of* phrase: *Every one of the* drafting *courses*; They have to do *every one of the* mathematical *steps* in their heads.

Gerunds

Gerunds are incomplete verb forms that act as nouns in a sentence (they end in *–ing*). They are *always singular* and *are usually not preceded by articles*.

> *Learning* many new skills *is* enjoyable if you have the time for *it*.

> *Eating* fast foods *has* quickly *become* a part of our stressful lives today.

The subject *eating*, a gerund, is singular. Below, the subject, *fast foods* is plural, so the verb is plural.

> *Fast foods have* quickly *become* a part of our stressful lives today.

Kind(s) of/Type(s) of + Noun

What follows *kind of* and *type of* will be a singular noun; what follows *kinds of* and *types of* will be a plural countable noun (uncountable nouns could be used with either) since more than one kind/type will be referred to. Often, a demonstrative adjective will precede *kind/type*: *this* or *that* (both are singular) can precede *kind/type*; *these* or *those* (plural) can precede *kinds/types*.

What *type of car was* Natalie driving?

Many *kinds of cars are* on the market today.

That *type of incident* occurs every day.

Uncountable and Countable Nouns

For a list of common uncountable nouns, see The Indefinite Article, above. The following uncountable nouns are responsible for many writing errors and may require your particular attention:

Clothing: As an uncountable noun, it will never be preceded by the indefinite article and will never form a plural. *Clothes*, however, is a countable noun. *Cloth* is a material that is sometimes used in the manufacture of clothing; it does not mean the same thing as *clothing*.

People have used *clothing* to cover their body for thousands of years; however, we often choose our *clothes* today for their fashion rather than their practicality.

At lululemon, you can buy *various kinds of clothing*; at a store that sells sewing supplies, you can buy *different kinds of cloths*.

Information: This and similar nouns, such as *knowledge*, *evidence*, and *advice*, are uncountable abstract nouns: they are not preceded by *a* or *an* and are never plural.

Importance: You can never say *an importance* or *importances*. You can say *the importance* if a prepositional phrase beginning with *of* follows. As with a few other noun–adjective pairs, the noun ends in *–ance* or *–ence* and the adjective ends in *–ant* or *–ent* (*important*).

I am going to discuss *the importance of getting a good job* in today's society.

The most *important* thing about a job is that it will make you *confident* and *independent*.

Research: A non-count noun, it is singular. However, *researcher*, a person who *does* or *conducts* research, is a countable noun. As a verb, *research* is usually followed by a direct object (not by *about*).

The Journal of Wildlife Management has been covering *research* in the field for more than 30 years. I *am researching* the topic of wildlife management by looking for articles from this journal.

As an adjective, *research* can be followed by a plural noun: *research projects, research studies*.

Some nouns can be either countable or uncountable depending on context.

> In their youth, most people have at least 100,000 *hairs* on their head.

If you're determined, you could count the number of hairs!

> Shaving your *hair* today is more often a matter of personal choice than of hygiene.

The sense here is of hair as a mass, therefore uncountable.

For examples of countable and uncountable nouns with articles, see Articles, above.

Prepositions

Despite; **in spite** *of*: Both act as prepositions, so a *noun*—not a clause—needs to follow each.

> *In spite of* her best efforts to create interest in the performance, only a few people attended it.

You can also say, "*Despite* her best efforts. . . ."

Times and dates, referring to: The preposition used for time expressions will vary according to context: e.g., "I will be there *for* Christmas." (I will arrive sometime *on* or *before* Christmas); "I will be there *during* Christmas" (I will be there for the entire time).

For specific times:

> He will arrive *at* 9 a.m. *on* Tuesday; *on* December 24

For less specific times:

> He will arrive *in* the morning (*in* the evening, but *at* night); *in* December; *in* 2014

See Verbs and Prepositions.

Verbs

The following verbs sometimes give students trouble:

Conclude: There are a few ways to express a conclusion. In most cases, a clause should follow the verb:

> One can *conclude that* commercialism destroys culture; *one can come to the conclusion [or draw the conclusion] that commercialism destroys culture.*

You can also write "In conclusion . . . ," or "To conclude," + clause.

To announce the conclusion of your essay, don't write, "As a conclusion . . ." Instead, write, "In conclusion . . . ."

Remember: When you are remembering something now (for example, when you're writing about an incident in the past), *remember* is put in the present tense, though the action described will be in the past tense.

> I *remember* when I was little how I *thought* my parents *knew* everything.

Verbs as Modal Auxiliaries

Modals can be considered a special category of helping verb that make the meaning of a main verb more precise. They are usually followed by the bare infinitive, which does not include *to*. Some common uses of modals are listed below.

Can expresses capability:

> Clothing *can* really say a lot about a person.

> Compare the following sentences and note their different meanings:

> In the summer, Nina *swims* every day.

The simple present tense is used to show a repeated action.

> In the summer, Nina *can swim* every day.

The modal *can* is used with the bare infinitive to show ability or capability; *is able to* can be substituted for *can*.

Could expresses capability in the past tense:

> When she lived near a lake, Nina *could* swim every day.

Should expresses necessity or obligation. Compare the following sentences and note their different meanings:

> *Incorrect statement (i.e., not factually true)*:

> There *are* gun laws in all states in the US that prevent people from killing each other.

> *Correct but weak*:

> There *have to be* gun laws in all states in the US.

> *Correct and effective*:

> There *should be* (or *must be*) gun laws in all states in the US.

May and *might* express possibility. *May* often conveys a stronger possibility than *might*:

> Since she has the prerequisites, Bianca *may* enroll in the second-year course.

> Although she worked late, she *might* decide to go to the party.

May also expresses permission:

> Students *may* bring beverages into the study area but not food items.

Will expresses probability:

> Since she has the prerequisites, Bianca *will* enroll in the second-year anthropology course.

Would expresses a repeated action in the past:

> When she lived near a lake, Nina *would* swim every day. (Compare with "Could," above.)

Similar Verbs and Nouns

Because nouns are sometimes formed from verbs and often look like them, they can be confused. Use a dictionary to ensure you have used a verb where one is required and a noun where one is required. Here are four sets of commonly confused words:

Belief, believe: *belief* is a noun; *believe* is a verb. *Believe* is often followed by *in* or *that*, depending on whether a word/phrase (*in*) or a clause (*that*) follows:

> She firmly *believed in* his innocence.

> She firmly *believed that* he was innocent; this was her true *belief.*

Breath, breathe: *breath* is a noun; *breathe* (pronounced with a long ē) is a verb. You can *take* or *draw a breath*, meaning "breathe in." Somewhat idiomatically, to *take a deep breath* can mean to prepare yourself for a difficult task (whether or not a deep breath is actually taken).

> The guest speaker, Madeleine, *took a deep breath* before she entered the crowded room. After she began speaking, she *breathed* normally again.

Effect, affect: see page 302.

Life, live: *life* is a noun; *live* (pronounced with a short ĭ) is a verb; *live* (long ī) is an adjective meaning "alive." Like many English nouns, *life*, the noun, can precede another noun and act as an adjective.

> While someone born today in Canada can expect to *live* about 81 years, in Botswana the quality of *life* is much lower, and the average lifespan is about 51 years.

Verbs and Prepositions

The following alphabetical list includes verbs that have become confusing, usually because of idiomatic prepositional use.

Access: This verb means to get information from (e.g., the Internet); *to have access to* means to be able to obtain information from, or to be able to use something or go somewhere to get it.

> She *accesses* her bank account every day.

> Thanks to the Internet she *has access to* her bank account every day.

> Although she has no stove or refrigerator in her room, she *has access to* a shared kitchen at the end of the hallway.

Agree/disagree with: You agree or disagree *with* someone or with a person's views or opinions on something. There are other prepositions that can follow both these verbs, but in most essays where you argue a thesis, you will use *with* following *agree* and *disagree*.

> I agree *with* space exploration in general, but I disagree *with* those who want us to spend billions of dollars per year on something with no practical benefit for humanity.

> Hassan and I agreed *on* the issue of space exploration.

Agreed followed by *to* means "to consent" (to).

> I agreed *to* give a speech on the merits of space exploration to my philosophy class.

Apply *for* a loan, a scholarship, a position, a job; **to apply *to*** (a place or situation) a school, etc.; **to be accepted *to*** is usually followed by an object (a place or position):

> Joshua *applied to* several Ontario colleges before he *applied for* a student loan.

> After he was *accepted to* the business program at Conestoga College, Joshua learned that loans don't *apply to* scholarship students.

Attend (a university, class, concert, wedding, etc.; this means "to be present at"); **to study *at*** (a university). To *attend to* means to "apply oneself to something."

> The school counsellor told Braden he would have to *attend to* academic matters, which included *attending* tutorials.

> Before he decided *to study at* Red Deer College he had been considering the business program at the University of Alberta.

See "Graduate from."

Avoid versus to prevent: To *avoid* indicates a passive activity. When you *avoid* something, you stay away from it; the verb is usually followed by a direct object (the thing that is avoided). When you *prevent* something, you take an action so that it does not occur; *prevent* can be followed by a direct object or by a direct object + *from* and a gerund phrase (a gerund is a noun ending in *–ing*):

> Inoculations are designed to *prevent the flu*.

> You should *avoid people* when you are sick as this will *prevent others from catching* your virus.

Call/draw attention *to*: To *call/draw attention to* is followed by a noun and means to "point something out." A noun or possessive adjective often precedes *attention*, as in the following sentence:

> The *Intergovernmental Panel on Climate Change* (IPCC) was founded in 1988 in order to *draw* world *attention to* the link between climate change and human activity.

To *pay attention to* means to "take note of or to look at closely."

All Canadians should *pay attention to* the next *IPCC* report in 2014.

To *get attention*, meaning to "attract notice," is not usually followed by a preposition:

After failing to *get* the teacher's *attention* any other way, Harmon shouted "fire!"

See "Pay"; "Point out."

Care: To *care about* means to "be concerned about" (see "Concern"):

She cares *about* good grades.

To *care for* or *take care of* means to look after:

Thomas *took care of* his sister when his mother was working.

Commit: A person can *commit a* crime, *a* murder, *an* error, but a person *commits suicide* (no article). Another meaning of the verb *commit* is "to dedicate to" or "resolve to do something"; it is *often* followed by the reflexive pronoun and the preposition *to*.

After *committing a* serious crime, he thought briefly about *committing suicide*, but decided instead to *commit himself to* a life of helping others.

Compare and contrast: When you compare, you focus on similarities; when you contrast, you focus on differences. *Compare* is usually followed by *to* or *with*:

In our class assignment, we were asked to *compare* the Canadian system of government *with* the system in another country.

Note that what follows *compare* (or *contrast*) is the direct object; *with* or *to* then follows, and the indirect object follows *with* or *to*.

If you use the verb phrase *make a comparison*, the preposition you use is *between*:

He made a comparison *between* one political system *and* another.

Compared to/with: In this construction, the grammatical subject is what is being compared:

Compared to the small town that I grew up in, Victoria seems like a big city.

Victoria is the subject as it is being compared to the small town.

The author *compares and contrasts* two different time periods by analyzing the standards of dress in each one.

The writer will look at similarities and differences.

The transitional phrase is *by contrast*.

Compete for (something); compete *against* (someone):

They *competed for* the honour of being named captain of the team.

Siblings often *compete for* attention from their parents.

Mohammed *competed against* his friend to see who could get the higher mark.

Concern: The meaning you want determines the preposition to use:

- *To be concerned about* means "to be troubled or worried about" *something*
- *To be concerned for* means "to be worried about" *someone* (or, occasionally, *something*)
- *To concern oneself about* means "to take an active interest in" something or someone.

When it is not followed by a preposition, *concern* means "applies to" or "is relevant to":

She *was concerned about* the implications of the new driving regulations; specifically, she *was concerned for* her daughter, who would soon be getting her licence.

The matter I have to discuss, Yuto, *concerns* your future with this organization.

Consider, discuss, mention: When you consider something, you think carefully about it, usually in order to take some kind of action. *Consider*, like *discuss* and *mention*, is followed by a direct object—not by *about*. Unlike *discuss*, however, *consider* and *mention* may be followed by a clause beginning with *that*.

Before Yoshi decided to get married, he *considered the matter* by talking it over with his married friend Eizad. Then he *discussed it with* Sanjeet.

Before Yoshi *discussed* his marriage plans with his fiancée, he *mentioned* to Eizad and Sanjeet *that* he was considering marriage.

See "Think."

Depend, rely, count: These verbs can mean "have confidence in someone or something" and are followed by *on* + a noun that states who or what is depended/relied on. They may then be followed by *for* + another noun that expands on the first noun:

Shaun *depends on* email *for* most of his business.

Maheen *relies on* her friend Amy *for* fashion advice.

Discriminate *between*: This means "to tell differences between"; two nouns must follow.

Discriminate *against*: This means to treat the individual(s) or group(s) unfairly; one or more nouns could follow.

It is good to be able to *discriminate between* a true friend and somebody who only wants you to do something for him or her.

We often unconsciously *discriminate against* groups like the homeless by not seeing them when we walk downtown, even when they are a few feet away.

Discrimination is the noun that means "the practice of discriminating."

Discuss: See "Consider."

Encourage/discourage: You encourage someone *to* do something, but you discourage someone *from* doing something. You can also *offer encouragement to* someone (which means to actively encourage him/her), but you cannot offer discouragement.

Raising tuition may *discourage* students *from* enrolling in other courses.

The president of the students' union is *encouraging* all students *to* protest the tuition increase.

Note that an infinitive follows *to*, but a gerund follows *from*.

Annie *offered encouragement to* John, who was worried about the tuition increase.

Graduate *from* university, etc.; **to be a graduate *of*** (this is the noun; the second *a* is a short vowel); to have/get/obtain/pursue *an* education:

After Kasey *graduated from* college, she went to graduate school and became a *graduate of* UBC.

Hire (someone; *employers* hire); **to be hired by** (someone, a company, etc.; *employees* are hired):

After applying for several positions during the summer, Teh *was hired by* another company.

See "Apply for."

Know *something*: This means to have information or expertise *about* something; **to know *someone*:** the person's name should follow the verb as the direct object.

When I got *to know Teh*, I learned about computers, and I now *know* everything *about* them; Shelley *knows* that she has a test tomorrow.

Lack: As a verb, it is followed by a direct object; as a noun, it is usually preceded by an article or other determiner (e.g., *its*, *that*, *this*, *your*) and followed by *of*:

The first thing she noticed about the bedroom was *its lack of* privacy. The kitchen also *lacked* dishes and other utensils.

Lead to: This means the same as *result in* (see below). In both cases, a result or consequence follows the preposition.

The cloning of animals, according to many people, is certain *to lead to* (or, result in) the eventual cloning of humans.

Look at/around/for/into/over:

look at (examine): In my essay, I will *look at* solutions to the problem of homeless people.

around: Dazed by the accident, he slowly sat up and *looked around*.

for (search): Simon *looked for* his lost notes on his messy desk.

into (investigate): After being laid off for the second time this year, Natalie began to *look into* self-employment.

over (scan): She *looked over* her notes from the previous class.

Mention: See "Consider."

Participate *in*: You participate *in* something—activities, sports, etc.:

Dong Hun often *participates in* classroom discussions.

Pay (*for*): *Pay* means to give (usually money) what is due for goods, services, or work, etc. *For* + a noun may follow if you want to indicate what was purchased:

She *paid* less than $80 *for* all her textbooks since she bought them used.

Point out: This verb means to "call attention to" (something). It is generally followed by a noun/pronoun or a clause beginning with *that*. One of the meanings of *to point* is to indicate, to single out, using a finger; it is followed by *to*.

Ruji *pointed out* her sister among the bystanders.

Ruji *pointed out that* her sister was always late for a meeting.

Ruji *pointed to* her sister, who was standing in a crowd.

Refer: *Refer* is followed by *to* when the meaning is "to make a reference or to make mention of something." If a clause beginning with *that* follows, a noun such as *fact*, *idea*, etc. should intervene between the verb *refer* and the clause.

In his letter of recommendation, he *referred to* the many occasions in which Duy had demonstrated his sense of humanity and compassion.

Specifically, he *referred to the fact that* Duy had often volunteered for work in local hospices.

Result in/result from: When you use the verb *result*, you must be careful about the preposition you use after it. To result *in* means that what follows the verb will be a *result* or consequence; to result *from* means that what follows the verb will be a *cause*.

Most murders in the US *result from* the use of guns.

Guns are a cause.

Being convicted of the crime of murder *usually results in* long prison terms.

Prison terms are the consequence.

Stress and **emphasize:** They mean the same thing and are usually followed by direct objects (not prepositions). But if you want to use the verb phrase *put stress/emphasis on*, note the preposition that is required. A *that* clause may also follow these verbs.

The writer *emphasized* the main point of her argument by providing examples.

The writer *put emphasis on* the main point of her argument by providing examples.

The instructor *stressed that* all students should arrive on time for class.

Avoid informal expressions like *stress out*, meaning to experience feelings of stress.

Think is a verb with many uses. To think *about* means to "reflect on," and to think *over* means to "consider"; note the word order of *it* in the sentence below. Use *think* + a clause beginning with *that* if you want to refer to a belief or an opinion.

William originally *thought that he would take a commerce class* in the second term, but when he thought *about it* (or *thought it over*), he decided to enroll right away.

Verbs and Their Subjects (subject–verb agreement)

Always ensure that you use the singular form of any verb that has a singular subject. But if the subject is plural (indicating more than one of something or someone), the verb should be plural.

Remember that the third-person *singular* form of a *verb* usually ends in *s*. This can be confusing because it is the *plural* form of most *nouns* that ends in *s*.

See Every + Noun, under Nouns, above. *Each, either,* and *neither* are singular and require a singular verb form. For agreement rules, see chapter 12.

See Gerunds, under Nouns, above, for agreement with gerund subjects.

Also see Agreement in Relative Clauses above.

Verb Tenses

See the inside cover for a summary of verb tenses.

Appendix D

PEER EDIT FORMS

Peer Edit Form: Formal Outline

The essay outline provides the structure on which the essay itself will be built. Therefore, as an editor, you should pay special attention to the relation among the parts (introduction, body paragraphs, conclusion), to the order of points (least important to most important? Most to least? Some other logical order?), as well as to the strength and effectiveness of each main point. Is each one adequately developed? Is the claim supported/ question answered/hypothesis proved?

Instructions

Use the check boxes below to record the fact that you have considered and evaluated the criteria. Use the space following to add suggestions, comments, questions, and advice.

Introduction

- ☐ Does it attract your interest?
- ☐ Does it announce the topic?
- ☐ Does it contain a two-part direct thesis statement announcing the topic and showing the reader what the writer contends about the topic?
- ☐ Is the claim one of fact, value, or policy?
- ☐ Is the thesis statement interesting, specific, and manageable?
    - ☐ Interesting?
    - ☐ Specific?
    - ☐ Manageable?
    - ☐ Clear?
- ☐ Does the essay appear expository? Argumentative? What shows you this?

Body Paragraphs

- ☐ Does each paragraph contain at least one main idea that can be easily identified as such? If not, which paragraphs don't do this?
- ☐ Does each paragraph contain at least two sub-points that help develop the main point? If not, which paragraphs don't?
    - ☐ Formal *topic* outline used?
    - ☐ Formal *sentence* outline used?
    - ☐ Other kind of outline?

☐ Has the writer been able to provide support for his/her argument? If not, suggest ways that he/she could use kinds of evidence to do this (e.g., examples, facts/statistics, personal experience, outside sources, etc.).

☐ Do the paragraphs appear to be organized using any of the rhetorical patterns discussed in chapter 5 (e.g., definition, cause–effect, problem–solution, compare and contrast?) If not, can you suggest methods for any of the paragraphs?

☐ Are the main points ordered in a logical and persuasive way? If not, what could you suggest as an alternative arrangement?

☐ Are there at least two levels represented in the outline (main points and sub-points)? Are the elements of coordination and subordination applied correctly? Is parallel structure applied to main points and the levels of sub-points?

Conclusion

☐ Does it successfully summarize or restate the argument without sounding repetitious?

☐ Does it go beyond the introduction by enlarging on the implications of the thesis, by urging a change in thought or call to action, or by making an ethical or emotional appeal?

Final comments or suggestions?

Writer's Name: _____

Editor's Name: _____

Peer Edit Form: Research Essay First Draft

Your first draft is the stage at which you make the transition from large-scale structural concerns to those focusing on integrating your research with your own ideas to create a synthesis—in your final draft, you will work further on these areas, along with the attempt to achieve conciseness, clear expression, grammatically sound prose, etc.

Instructions

Use the check boxes below to record the fact that you have considered and evaluated the criteria. Use the space following to add suggestions, comments, questions, and advice. In addition, underline places in the essay where you would like to draw the writer's attention to possible grammatical problems, such as fragments, comma splices, apostrophes, lack of parallelism, misplaced or dangling modifiers, pronoun agreement and/or consistency; stylistic problems, such as passive constructions or other instances where the writing could be made more concise, direct, or forceful; and spelling errors, along with errors in mechanics and presentation.

Introduction

- ☐ Is the introduction successful?
  - ☐ Interesting?
  - ☐ Announces subject and contains thesis statement with a claim of fact, a hypothesis to be tested, or a question to be answered?
  - ☐ Suggests the main way the argument will be organized?
- ☐ Does the writer establish him- or herself as credible and trustworthy? How?

Body Paragraphs

- ☐ Does the essay seem complete, and does the order of the paragraphs appear logical?
- ☐ Look at paragraphs individually. Are any too short? Too long?
- ☐ Is each paragraph unified (relates to one main idea)? If not, which ones aren't?
- ☐ Is each paragraph coherent? If not, which ones aren't?
- ☐ Do paragraphs contain topic sentences?
- ☐ Is the order of the sentences natural?
- ☐ Are there appropriate transitions between sentences, enabling you to see the relationship between consecutive sentences?
- ☐ Does the writer successfully use repetition, rephrasing, synonyms, or other devices to achieve coherence?
- ☐ Does each paragraph seem developed adequately?
- ☐ Has the writer used secondary sources effectively? Note any exceptions.
- ☐ Do all the sources seem reliable?
- ☐ Does the writer use a sufficient number of sources? Is there an over-reliance on one source? Which one?
- ☐ Does the writer show familiarity with the sources used?
- ☐ Do the secondary sources appear to be relevant to the points discussed?

☐ Is each reference integrated smoothly into the essay?
  ☐ Stylistically?
  ☐ Grammatically?
☐ Has the context been made sufficiently clear in each instance?
☐ Are brackets and ellipses used correctly?
☐ Are any other kinds of evidence produced in addition to secondary sources (for example, analogies, personal experience, illustrations, examples, or field research—e.g., interviews)?
☐ Does the essay appear to be fundamentally focused on exposition (explaining) rather than argumentation (persuasion)?

Conclusion

☐ Does the conclusion function as a satisfying ending? Does it summarize and/or generalize?

Other Criteria

☐ Has the writer presented him- or herself credibly?
  ☐ Conveyed knowledge?
  ☐ Seems trustworthy and reliable?
  ☐ Appears to be fair?
☐ Is the writer's voice impartial and objective?
☐ Has the writer used any elements of style to assist in the argument (e.g., imagery, analogies—figurative language, distinctive voice or tone, particular choice of words, sentence variety, etc.)? Can you suggest any additional stylistic features that might help?
☐ Are there any places in the draft where the language seemed unclear or an incorrect word was used?

Final comments or suggestions?

Writer's Name: _____

Editor's Name: _____

Peer Edit Form: Argumentative Essay First Draft

Your first draft is the stage at which you make the transition from large-scale structural concerns to those focusing on your developing argument—in your final draft, you will work further on these areas, along with clear expression, grammatically sound prose, etc., responding to editorial suggestions as well as your clearer conception of your argument as a result of having written the draft.

Instructions

Use the check boxes below to record the fact that you have considered and evaluated the criteria. Use the space following to add suggestions, comments, questions, and advice. In addition, underline places in the essay where you would like to draw the writer's attention to possible grammatical problems, such as fragments, comma splices, apostrophes, lack of parallelism, misplaced or dangling modifiers, pronoun agreement and/or consistency; stylistic problems, such as passive constructions or other instances where the writing could be made more concise, direct, or forceful; and spelling errors, along with errors in mechanics and presentation.

Introduction

- ☐ Does the introduction function successfully?
    - ☐ Interesting?
    - ☐ Announces subject and contains thesis statement; is the claim arguable? Is the claim one of value or policy?
    - ☐ Suggests the main way the argument will be organized (e.g., definition, cause–effect, time order, division, compare and contrast, question–answer, etc.)?
- ☐ Does the writer establish him- or herself as credible and trustworthy? How?
- ☐ Is the argumentative purpose clear?

Body Paragraphs

- ☐ Does the argument seem complete, and does the order of the paragraphs appear logical?
- ☐ Look at paragraphs individually. Are any too short? Too long?
- ☐ Is each paragraph unified (relates to one main idea)? If not, which ones aren't?
- ☐ Is each paragraph coherent? If not, which ones aren't?
- ☐ Do paragraphs contain topic sentences?
- ☐ Is the order of the sentences natural?
- ☐ Are there appropriate transitions between sentences, enabling you to see the relationship between consecutive sentences?
- ☐ Does the writer successfully use repetition, rephrasing, synonyms, or other devices to achieve coherence?
- ☐ Does each paragraph seem developed adequately? If not, which ones aren't?
- ☐ What kinds of evidence are produced? Are they used effectively?
    - ☐ Examples, illustrations?
    - ☐ Personal experience?

- ☐ Analogies?
- ☐ Precedents?
- ☐ Outside authorities/secondary sources?
- ☐ Other?
- ☐ Are there points where the argument seems strained, weak, incomplete, and/or illogical? Are there any fallacies (e.g., cause–effect fallacies, fallacies of irrelevance, emotional/ethical fallacies)?

Conclusion

- ☐ Does the conclusion function as a satisfying ending? Does it summarize and/or generalize?

Other Criteria

- ☐ Has the arguer presented him- or herself credibly?
  - ☐ Conveyed knowledge?
  - ☐ Seems trustworthy and reliable?
  - ☐ Appears to be fair?
- ☐ Is the opposing view acknowledged?
- ☐ Is the writer's voice impartial and objective?
- ☐ Are there any examples of slanted language?
- ☐ Is the opposing view successfully refuted (as in the point-by-point method)?
- ☐ Has the writer used any elements of style to assist in the argument (e.g., imagery, analogies—figurative language, distinctive voice or tone, particular choice of words, sentence variety, etc.)? Can you suggest any additional stylistic features that might help?
- ☐ Are there any places in the draft where the language seems unclear or an incorrect word is used?
- ☐ If the writer used sources, are they integrated smoothly and grammatically? Are all direct quotations, summaries, paraphrases, and ideas acknowledged?

Final comments or suggestions?

Writer's Name: _____

Editor's Name: _____

Peer Edit Form: Literary Essay First Draft

Your first draft is the stage at which you make the transition from large-scale structural concerns to those focusing on your developing analysis—in your final draft, you will work further on these areas, along with clear expression, grammatically sound prose, etc., responding to editorial suggestions as well as your clearer conception of your analysis as a result of having written the draft.

Instructions

Use the check boxes below to record the fact that you have considered and evaluated the criteria. Use the space following to add suggestions, comments, questions, and advice. In addition, underline places in the essay where you would like to draw the writer's attention to possible grammatical problems, such as fragments, comma splices, apostrophes, lack of parallelism, misplaced or dangling modifiers, pronoun agreement and/or consistency; stylistic problems, such as passive constructions or other instances where the writing could be made more concise, direct, or forceful; and spelling errors, along with errors in mechanics and presentation.

Introduction

- ☐ Is the introduction successful?
  - ☐ Interesting?
  - ☐ Announces subject and contains thesis statement with a claim of interpretation? Suggests the writer's purpose: Review? Text-centred analysis? Context-centred analysis?
  - ☐ States the work(s) being discussed and the organizational method, if appropriate (e.g., compare and contrast)?
  - ☐ Suggests most important focus (character, point of view, setting, mood, tone, analysis of technique)?
  - ☐ Gives appropriate background, if needed?
- ☐ Does the writer establish him- or herself as credible and trustworthy? How?

Body Paragraphs

- ☐ Does the reading/analysis seem complete, and does the order of the paragraphs appear logical?
- ☐ Look at paragraphs individually. Are any too short? Too long?
- ☐ Is each paragraph unified (relates to one main idea)? If not, which ones aren't?
- ☐ Is each paragraph coherent? If not, which ones aren't?
- ☐ Do paragraphs contain topic sentences?
- ☐ Is the order of the sentences natural?
- ☐ Are there appropriate transitions between sentences, enabling you to see the relationship between consecutive sentences?
- ☐ Does the writer successfully use repetition, rephrasing, synonyms, or other devices to achieve coherence?
- ☐ Does each paragraph seem developed adequately?

- [ ] What kinds of evidence are produced?
  - [ ] Examples from the text(s)?
    - [ ] Representative and relevant?
    - [ ] Are there a sufficient number?
  - [ ] Textual references cited appropriately (according to the conventions for citing poetry, fiction, and drama)?
  - [ ] Has the context been made sufficiently clear in each instance?
  - [ ] Are brackets and ellipses used correctly?
- [ ] If secondary sources have been used, are they integrated smoothly and grammatically? Are all direct quotations, summaries, paraphrases, and ideas acknowledged?
  - [ ] Secondary sources used effectively (to introduce or provide general information; support, explain, or expand; disagree or qualify)?
  - [ ] Other kinds of evidence used?
- [ ] Are there points where the reading seems strained, weak, incomplete, and/or illogical?

Conclusion

- [ ] Does the conclusion function as a satisfying ending? Does it summarize and/or generalize?

Other Criteria

- [ ] Has the writer presented him- or herself credibly?
  - [ ] Conveyed knowledge?
  - [ ] Seems trustworthy and reliable?
  - [ ] Appears to be fair?
- [ ] Has the writer used any elements of style to assist in the argument (e.g., imagery, analogies—figurative language, distinctive voice or tone, particular choice of words, sentence variety, etc.). Can you suggest any additional stylistic features that might help?
- [ ] Are there any places in the draft where the language seemed unclear or where an incorrect word was used?

Final comments or suggestions?

Writer's Name: _____

Editor's Name: _____

Appendix E

ANSWERS TO EXERCISES

Note that your responses may vary from those given here.

Chapter 1

Exercise 1.6 (p. 16)

1. b. The instructor announced class cancellation yesterday.
2. b. Todd is sarcastically voicing his displeasure (c is a possible inference).
3. c. The school has been designed for students with behavioural problems.
4. a. Meghan will likely face many challenges at the university,
5. d. No inference is possible.

Chapter 2

Exercise 2.6 (p. 30)

1. high school history teachers: neutral?
   phys-ed teachers: positive
   high school students: mixed
2. NHL hockey fans: mixed?
   referees' union: positive
   NHL team owners: negative
3. pet owners: mixed?
   city council: positive
   pet breeders: negative
4. a citizen's rights group: negative
   RCMP officers: positive
   dentists: neutral
5. students who own laptops: positive
   students who do not own laptops: negative? neutral?
   instructors who have taught for 20 years or more: negative

Exercise 2.7 (p. 34)

2. Borderline personality disorder is a controversial condition.
   It is a topic (it is not complete enough to serve as a thesis).
   Possible subject: personality disorders

4. More hybrid cars are on the market than ever before.

It is a topic.

Possible subjects: cars; alternative energy sources; consumerism

6. "Managed trade" involves government intervention, such as the imposition of tariffs.

It is a topic (it simply says what managed trade is).

Possible subjects: economic theories; international commerce

8. Studying the classical languages in school is unnecessary today.

It is a thesis.

Topic: classical languages

Possible subjects: university subjects; languages; Greek and Roman history

10. Enrolling in a dance class can help people with disabilities.

It is a thesis.

Topics: teaching/learning dance; coping with disabilities

Possible subjects: dance; disabilities

Chapter 3

Exercise 3.1 (p. 58)

2. A (extended value)
4. E (fact)
6. A (value)
8. E (fact)
10. E (fact)
12. A (value)
14. (interpretation)

Exercise 3.2 (p. 59)

In these answers, the original claim is identified below.

2. value
4. fact (could be used as a value claim)
6. policy
8. value
10. policy
12. policy
14. policy

Exercise 3.3 (p. 61)

2. c. Cellphones dominate the lives of many Canadians today.

Exercise 3.4 (p. 63)

2. In addition, exercise is a solution to the ever-growing problem of obesity.

Exercise 3.5 (p. 68)

I. Coherence through Word Choice

2. The *amount* of competition and training that goes into golf requires a high level of physical fitness.

4. The narrow *structure* (*shape*) of glacial fjords protects them from the effects of high waves and storm damage.

6. Sports today have become more competitive, and parents may *enroll* their children in competitive sports at too young an age.

8. Adopting a vegetarian lifestyle would no doubt have a major *impact in* ending world hunger.

10. To *ensure* that teenagers do not drive drunk, the drinking age should be raised to 19, when teens are mature enough to deal *responsibly* with alcohol.

IV. Coherence through Transitions

2. Massive energy consumption is having a negative impact on the planet. *For example*, in the summer of 2006, western Europe experienced some of the hottest weather on record. <u>*Moreover*</u>, this temperature increase is not an isolated occurrence. *In fact*, almost every credible scientist today believes that the earth is experiencing climate change due to the emissions of greenhouse gases from cars and coal-burning power plants. Ninety per cent of the energy used in the US comes from fossil fuels such as oil, coal, and natural gas (Borowitz 43), *but* problems arise from other sources, too. *For example*, nuclear power plants leave radioactive by-products, making storage difficult. *Unfortunately*, dams are not much better, as nearby populations must be relocated, and the surrounding habitat is destroyed.

V. Coherence through use of Repetition, Parallel Structures, and Transitions

2. The topic sentence is the first sentence.
   But, *Instead* (transitions of contrast or qualification)
   As a result (transition of cause and effect)
   in effect (transition of emphasis or summary)
   Since this paragraph ends by defining "the trivialization effect," it is logical to expect that the following paragraph will expand on this definition in some way, perhaps by discussing one or more effects that trivializing the news has on its audience.

Exercise 3.7 (p. 77)

2. Although email began as a modern communications miracle, it has become the greatest nuisance ever invented. (4 abrupt)

4. There are many issues surrounding end-of-life treatment of terminally ill individuals. (2 general)

6. The movement of people away from the Catholic Church today is mostly due to its teachings on issues like abortion, women's equality, and homosexuality. (4 abrupt)

8. In all American literature, no character ever gave more thought to moral decisions than Huckleberry Finn does. (4 exaggerated)

14. Western society today increasingly accepts different lifestyles and personal choices, giving many marginalized individuals greater freedom to live as they choose. (2 or 3)

Exercise 3.8 (p. 80)

C. 2. Simple. *Expanded:* As consumers, we must keep ourselves informed about the activities of the industries we support in order to be knowledgeable consumers, which will ultimately make us better citizens of today's world.

4. Simple. *Expanded:* Education is viewed as a benefit to individuals, but too much education can have negative results by narrowing one's vision and separating one from others who are less educated.

Exercise 3.10 (p. 82)

2. a. logical
   b. effective; develops logically
   c. "Anabolic steroid abuse plays a large role in bodybuilding, often resulting in adverse health effects." Simple
   d. credible: reveals knowledge of bodybuilding and IFBB
   e. cost–benefit, focusing on costs

Exercise 3.12 (p. 91)

The classification and example rhetorical patterns are used. The final sentence (thesis statement) suggests that the essay itself will be organized according to the cost–benefit method (arguing the benefits of vegetarianism).

Chapter 5

Exercise 5.4 (p. 124)

2. Not specific; phrases like *a major problem* and *make sense* lack precision
4. Not interesting; it's an obvious claim. A more controversial, but arguable, claim might be that the costs of using email outweigh its well-known benefits.
6. Not interesting; a general audience would likely not be interested in this specific benefit of no-fault insurance (though an audience of auto insurers probably would be).
8. Not arguable; it would make a better thesis statement for a personal essay in which the writer could make full use of personal experience and, perhaps, narration.
10. Not manageable; writers need to show that policy claims are viable and can realistically be instituted.

Exercise 5.5 (p. 126)

2. Inductive reasoning is flawed as the means for gathering the evidence was faulty; hence, a conclusion could not be drawn.

Exercise 5.10 (p. 140)

Tina rebutted, "But nobody actually drives 30 on those streets!" (bandwagon)
Steve replied, "But we could get stuck behind a little old lady, and everybody knows how slowly they drive." (false authority)

"Besides, we can speed on the main street; there are never any cops on that street, so we won't get a ticket." (hasty generalization)

Tina said, "No, let's take the side streets: we always go that way." (tradition)

"And there have been two accidents recently on the main street, so the side streets are safer." (hasty generalization)

Exercise 5.11 (p. 141)

2. The legalization of marijuana would destroy society as we know it today (desk-thumping)

    sentences 2–6 (certain consequences or slippery slope)

    "sink to a despicable level" (slanted language)

Chapter 7

Exercise 7.5 (p. 216)

2. *words changed, but sentence structure same: better paraphrase:* In an attempt to find ways to fix damage, create harmony, and build confidence, restorative justice brings together community, victim, and victimizer (Zher 5).

4. *sentence structure changed, but words identical: better paraphrase:* To reduce the odds of depression and increase feelings of self-worth in athletes, a supportive coach or other role model is beneficial (Stewart 17).

Chapter 8

Exercise 8.1 (p. 267)

1. b. Paul Olsen said it has now been proven that the shift from Triassic to Jurassic forms of life "occurred in a geological blink of an eye" (Mayell, par. 4).

2. b. Our most urgent challenge today is recognizing the need to act to prevent the destruction of our environment. Biologically speaking, the world is "experiencing an eco-holocaust," as the world is becoming polluted with society's wastes, and more than 50,000 life forms disappear each year (Suzuki, 1999, p. 45).

4. The following are suggested answers. There may be purposes for which other kinds of integration are better suited.

    b. no paraphrase: memorably phrased; authoritative source

    d. factual information; can be paraphrased:

    Over the long term, the sexual orientation of a family's parents is not as important as harmonious relationships among family members, and same-sex parents produce children who are as well-adjusted as those of heterosexual parents, according to research.

    f. factual information; can be paraphrased:

    The health of people in inner cities, particularly those under 13 years old, is threatened by excessive carbon dioxide in the air.

    h. statistical information; can be paraphrased:

Doctors in the US do not need special qualifications to perform aesthetic plastic surgery; approximately 11 million such surgeries by specialists and non-specialists were recorded in 2006.

j. no paraphrase: wording of important legal document

Chapter 9

Exercise 9.4 (p. 282)

2. Acceptable passive. (The grammatical subject does not need to be specified.)
4. Acceptable passive if the matter was discussed by members of the committee. (The grammatical subject does not need to be specified.)
6. Change to active: The government needs to see education as the number one priority. (Making "government" the active subject gives more force to the statement.)
8. Change to active: Many people today believe in a powerful and infallible Creator. (It is important to know *who* believes this.)
10. Change to active: Immanuel Kant proposed two ways of looking at rights-based ethics. (The sentence is wordy and indirect without an active subject.)

Exercise 9.5 (p. 284)

Your sentences might be different from the examples below.

2. To determine video game addiction, researchers interviewed many gamers and designers.
4. Several devices in the story stress the revenge theme.

Exercise 9.9 (p. 287)

Your sentences might be different from the examples below.

2. The volcano's eruption changed the Western Samoan island into an inferno.
4. Victims of bullying are not responsible for their victimization, but there may be a reason why they become victims.

    Or:

    Although victims of bullying are not responsible for their victimization, there may be a reason for it.
6. The disappearance of even one species near the bottom of the food chain often adversely affects other species' survival.
8. For many years, people regularly have used antibiotics to cure a variety of diseases in their lives. (Indirect writing increases the likelihood of errors in usage—indeed, errors of all kinds: symptoms may be "relieved" but not "cured.")
10. To protest their salary freeze, all Oak Bay high school teachers have decided not to undertake supervisory tasks until the school board conducts an impartial salary review.
12. Many people have drug addictions that control their lives.
14. French scientist Louis Pasteur was the first to discover that microbes were menaces to the human body.

Exercise 9.12 (p. 292)

By the 1800s, inventions <u>were beginning</u> (had begun?) to put people out of work. One of the first inventions that <u>resulted in</u> (triggered? provoked?) rebellion <u>was</u> (affected those?) in the craft guild. In 1801, Joseph Jacquard <u>became known as the inventor of</u> (invented?) the Jacquard loom. This loom <u>was capable of being</u> (could be/was?) programmed by pre-punched cards, which made it possible to create clothing design patterns. This invention <u>led to the creation of</u> (gave rise/birth to? spawned?) the Luddites, a group made from the craft guild. These people <u>were against</u> (opposed?) any type of manufacturing technology and <u>went about burning down</u> (set fire to?) several factories that <u>were using</u> (used?) this new technology. The Luddites <u>were around only</u> (existed?) for a couple of years, but the name Luddite is still used to describe people who <u>are resistant to</u> (resist?) new technologies. The Jacquard loom, in effect, replaced people. It could <u>do great designs</u> (create complex patterns?) quickly and <u>without making any errors</u> (flawlessly?). The replacement of people by machines <u>was beginning</u> (had begun?).

Exercise 9.13 (p. 293)

2. In 313 BCE, Constantine I declared Christianity the official religion of Rome.
4. Perceiving life from varying angles is a key element of a good writer.

   Or:

   Perceiving life from varying angles is a sign of a good writer.

Exercise 9.16 (p. 298)

Revision suggestions:
Defining "the homeless" is difficult. However, both the media and current research commonly refer to the homeless as those who lack visible shelter or who use public shelters. Literature about homelessness is sparse, as the media did not report on the incidence of homelessness until the 1980s. Nevertheless, it has existed for centuries with literature on the subject dating from the feudal period in Europe.

Chapter 10

Exercise 10.2 (p. 315)

The answers often include more examples of the parts of speech than required in the instructions. Phrases and clauses can also act as different parts of speech, but they have not been included in the answers.

1. **nouns**: road, street, slum; **adjectives**: main, narrow, side, extended; **verbs**: left, turned, were; **conjunctions**: once, and, than; **pronoun**: we
2. **nouns**: car, stop, house, others; **verbs**: came, was; **prepositions**: to, of; **pronouns**: that, it
3. **nouns**: street, bungalow; **verb**: was; **adjective**: well-kept; **preposition**: from
4. **nouns**: garden, fountain, middle, arrangement, flamingos, penguins; **verb**: had; **adjectives**: cemented, front, garish, marble, plastic; **pronoun**: it; **prepositions**: in, with, of, around; **conjunction**: and

5. **nouns**: windows, bars, door, bars; **verb**: had; **adjectives**: heavy, front, extra, iron; **prepositions**: across, of; **conjunction**: and
6. **nouns**: grandmother, driver, horn; **verbs**: get, had, toot; **adverbs**: not, out, imperiously
7. **nouns**: woman, door, car; **verbs**: stepped, saw, nodded, smiled, went; **pronoun**: she; **adjective**: front; **adverb**: out, immediately, back, inside; **pronoun**: she; **preposition**: of; **conjunctions**: and, when, and

Exercise 10.3 (p. 317)

2. Wanted to bury his treasure where it would never be found. (P)
4. Dropped the ball with only ten yards to go. (P)
6. Opportunity | knocks. (complete sentence)
8. The high levels of stress of today's students. (S)
10. Hundreds of geese in the field. (S)
12. An enemy of the people. (S)
14. All dressed up with no place to go. (N)

Exercise 10.4 (p. 318)

2. The brilliant idea that came to me in the middle of the night seemed ordinary by the light of day.
4. I have a strange craving for the kind of doughnut that doesn't have a hole in the middle.

Exercise 10.5 (p. 318)

2. The imaginative child wanted to bury his treasure where it would never be found.
4. The wide receiver dropped the ball with only ten yards to go.
8. The high levels of stress of today's students can lead to illnesses.
10. Hundreds of geese in the field create a big mess!
12. An enemy of the people should never be alone in a dark alley.
14. It is sad to be all dressed up with no place to go.

Exercise 10.7 (p. 323)

2. Huge tears rolled down his cheeks.
4. Whenever they called her into work, *she was about to leave town for a holiday.* (dependent clause fragment)
6. *The party president is* introducing our next prime minister. (*–ing*)
8. He must be guilty *since* he's already confessed. (dependent clause)
10. Because spiritual values are more enduring than material ones, *most of my memories of Christmas are of joyous occasions, not of expensive gifts.* (dependent clause)
12. The opposition to vaccinations is a manifestation of fear that the side effects will be more harmful than the disease itself. (lacks predicate in original)
14. This is the information age when ideas are literally at your fingertips. (dependent clause)

Exercise 10.8 (p. 323)

2. International concern has grown in recent years over the proliferation of weapons of mass destruction, but weapons used to exterminate enemy forces are nothing new. In World War I, artillery was used. <u>In addition to gas, machine guns, grenades, and bombs</u>. The 1940s brought more powerful weaponry. <u>As well as the first nuclear weapon</u>. <u>A weapon capable of killing hundreds of thousands of people</u>. After World War II, the Cold War began, as Russia and the US became involved in an arms race. <u>Building hundreds of nuclear weapons more potent than those used in World War II</u>.

Corrected:

International concern has grown in recent years over the proliferation of weapons of mass destruction, but weapons used to exterminate enemy forces are nothing new. In World War I, artillery was used, in addition to gas, machine guns, grenades, and bombs. The 1940s brought more powerful weaponry, as well as the first nuclear weapon, a weapon capable of killing hundreds of thousands of people. After World War II, the Cold War began, as Russia and the US became involved in an arms race, building hundreds of nuclear weapons more potent than those used in World War II.

Exercise 10.9 (p. 325)

2.   **S**
<u>Some of my favourite books</u> <u>have gone</u> out of print.
       noun   **verb**

4.   **S**
A search <u>of the abandoned house</u> <u>turned up</u> several cartons <u>of stolen goods</u>.
  noun   **adjectival**   **verb**   **adjectival**

Exercise 10.10 (p. 326)

2. (Although I think winter is here), <u>the temperature is not cold enough for snow</u>.
4. In most parts of North America, <u>Daylight Saving Time begins in March</u>. (*In most parts of North America* is a phrase modifying the verb in the independent clause.)
6. (While it is important that students volunteer), <u>mandatory volunteerism introduced at many schools does not instill a sense of civic duty</u>.
8. <u>Studying grammar does not guarantee good grades</u>, but it <u>certainly helps</u>.
10. <u>Plastic water bottles have become the focus of public scorn</u>, (though more pressing moral concerns need attention).

Exercise 10.11 (p. 329)

2. <u>She ran the race in record time</u> (but) <u>collapsed at the finish line</u>. (simple—*but* is joining *ran* and *collapsed*, two verbs. You can see that it is not joining two independent clauses as *collapsed* has no separate subject from *ran*.)
4. <u>Expository writing explains</u> (or) <u>informs the reader about something</u>. (simple)

6. His library privileges have been suspended, (and) his transcripts have been sealed (until) he pays his fines). (complex)
8. She is convinced (that) she will get an A in the course). (complex)
10. The first non-Inuit to reach the North Pole was James Peary, (though) his claim has often been disputed). (complex)

Exercise 10.12 (p. 329)

2. Although there may be nearly 2 million kinds of plants in the world, and there are likely at least as many different kinds of animals, no one can know how many species have evolved, flourished, and become extinct. (compound–complex)
4. We may suspect that Earth is not unique as a life-bearing planet, but since we do not as yet have any compelling evidence that life exists anywhere else, we must restrict our discussion of the pervasiveness of life to our own planet. (compound–complex)

Exercise 10.13 (p. 333)

2. Our neighbour's dog howled all last night. It was just impossible to get a night's sleep. (comma splice)
4. It's easy to punctuate sentences: just put a comma whenever you pause. (comma splice)
6. The incidence of breast cancer has increased. It takes the lives of many women today. (comma splice)
8. Mozart composed his first minuet at the age of five. He wrote his first symphony before he turned nine. (run-on sentence)
10. Asthma is a common problem among Canadians. Exposure to second-hand smoke in public places can intensify this condition. (comma splice)

Exercise 10.14 (p. 333)

2. The opening ceremonies were delayed on account of rain. (fragment)
4. The concept that "bigger is better" is part of our culture. It is promoted by both advertisers and the media these days. (comma splice)
6. Although TV can corrupt the minds of innocent children if it is not monitored closely, many programs are suitable for children (fragment).
8. Martial arts are attracting more people than ever before, especially those who want to gain self-control and self-awareness. (fragment)
10. Racism in Canada exceeded just social and personal racism: it was institutional racism. (comma splice)
12. Carpal tunnel syndrome has many causes. The most common is repetitive wrist movements. (comma splice)
14. In the final book of the series, Harry visits his parents' grave and sees two inscriptions on their graves; the inscriptions refer to passages from the Bible. (run-on sentence)

Chapter 11

Exercise 11.1 (p. 342)

2. The optional package includes bucket seats, dual speakers, and air-conditioning. (items in a series)
4. Metaphors, similes, and personification all are examples of figurative language. (series)
6. The magnificent country estate is hidden behind a long, elegant row of silver birches. (miscellaneous: coordinate adjectives)
8. As well as the Irish, many Africans were forced to leave their families behind during times of famine.
10. Joe Clark, the former prime minister, has a famous wife.
12. James Earl Jones, who is the voice of Darth Vader in *Star Wars*, is a well-known actor.
14. Trust is important in any relationship, and it always takes time to develop.
16. Caffeine, a stimulant, is unregulated and completely legal.
18. Diesel-powered cars have long been on the North American market, yet they have never been widely accepted by the typical motorists.
20. Now a widely accepted theory, evolution was discounted when Charles Darwin published *On the Origin of Species* in 1859.

Exercise 11.2 (p. 344)

2. Juliet studied medicine at Western University in London, Ontario, before becoming a doctor near Prince Albert, Saskatchewan.
4. Nick and Nicole were married on April 20, 1995, but they separated two years later.
6. The simple sentence, as we've seen, is easily mastered by students, but compound sentences necessitate an understanding of various forms of punctuation.
8. British general Sir Frederick Morgan established an American-British headquarters, which was known as COSSAC.
10. Agnes Campbell Macphail, the first woman elected to Canadian Parliament, served for 19 years, beginning her career in 1921.
12. Following successful completion of the English test, another skills test is taken, which is in a written format.
14. Oliver Wendell Holmes, an American, was known as a master essayist, but Canadian Barry Callaghan is also internationally respected as an essayist.
16. The soldier with the red coat in the picture fought on the side of our enemies, the Americans.
18. Currently ranked fourth behind heart disease, stroke, and respiratory infections, AIDS is set to become No. 3, say researchers in a new report.
20. Jeff Deffenbacher, Ph.D., a specialist in anger management, thinks that some people have a low tolerance for everyday annoyances.

Exercise 11.3 (p. 344)

2. Autism is a much misunderstood problem. **O**ften children with autism are viewed as a "handful" and "hyperactive." Very little is known of its causes, and characteristics

can vary, making a diagnosis difficult. In children, it is even harder because normal children can exhibit some of the characteristics associated with autism. Although autism can cause many behavioural difficulties, autistic children can still live near-normal lives if they are surrounded by understanding caregivers. Working with autistic children can change a person and make one realize the need for better understanding and education. Treating autism can be difficult because often there is no feedback from the patient. Over the years, there have been many ideas of how to treat autism, but not all were correct and have, at times, made treatment problematic.

Exercise 11.4 (p. 347)

2. SPCA officers work for but are not paid by the government; in fact, it is donations that provide their salary.
4. Many professional golfers use the same caddy for years; Steve Williams, for example, caddied for Tiger Woods for 12 years.

Exercise 11.5 (p. 351)

2. The following is not a rule for comma use: put a comma wherever you pause.
4. It was the best of times; it was the worst of times.
6. In my health sciences class, we studied the four main food groups: dairy products, meats, carbohydrates, and fruits and vegetables.
8. Whenever I order designer clothing for my boutique, I shop in Toronto, Canada; Buffalo, New York; and London, England.
10. First advice to those about to write a novel is the same as Punch's to those about to wed: don't (Victor Jones).
12. In a compound sentence, use a comma to join independent clauses where there is a coordinating conjunction; use a semi-colon where two such clauses are not joined by a coordinating conjunction.
14. Oil, electricity, and solar power are popular sources for heating homes in Ontario; however, the most popular is natural gas.
16. The zero emissions of a battery-electric vehicle come with a drawback: the emissions are only as clean as the means used to generate the power.
18. The art of writing the news lead is to answer as many of the following five questions as possible: Who?, What?, Where?, When?, and How?
20. Freewriting can be a useful means of overcoming blocks; it can help you write when you're not in the mood; it can generate ideas, even if you are the kind of writer who has a hard time coming up with main points; and it can energize your writing.

Exercise 11.6 (p. 352)

The first 15 lines are shown below. Of course, there are punctuation options for these and the rest of the poem.

There lived an old man in the kingdom of Tess, who invented a purely original dress, and when it was perfectly made and complete, he opened the door and walked into the street. By way of a hat, he'd a loaf of brown bread, in the middle of which he inserted his head. His shirt was made up of no end of dead mice, the warmth of whose skins was quite fluffy and nice. His drawers were of rabbit-skins (but it is not known whose). His waistcoat and trousers were made of pork chops; his buttons were jujubes and chocolate drops. His coat was all pancakes with jam for a border and a girdle of biscuits to keep it in order. And he wore over all, as a screen from bad weather, a cloak of green cabbage leaves stitched all together.

Exercise 11.7 (p. 353)

2. Labour shortages during the late nineteenth century in Canada became an impediment to progress, and something had to be done to fix this problem. For white politicians and business owners, the solution seemed obvious: exploit cheap labour. Chinese immigrants provided exactly what was needed to boost the labour scene: they were male, unskilled, and cheap. Between 1881 and 1885, approximately 17,000 Chinese immigrants arrived in Canada. Chinese men were employed in masses; their jobs included those in mining, forestry, canning, and, above all, railroad construction. Sir Matthew Begbie, the Chief Justice of BC, said, "Chinese labourers do well what white women cannot do and what white men will not do."

Exercise 11.8 (p. 355)

2. Parents and teachers often complain about **television's** influence in **today's** society.
4. **One's** education should not depend on the financial resources of **one's** parents.
6. The course I took required two **hours'** homework a day.
8. Work songs and street **vendors'** cries are examples of traditional African-American music styles.
10. The topic of the term paper is a comparison between George **Grant's** and John Ralston **Saul's** theories of Canadian identity.
12. Climate change is caused by harmful chemicals that trap the **sun's** energy in the **earth's** atmosphere.
14. The desire of Pip in Charles **Dickens's** *Great Expectations* to find his place in the world illustrates the **work's** main theme.

Chapter 12

Exercise 12.1 (p. 365)

If a child begins to perform poorly at school nowadays, **he or she** will likely be sent to a school counsellor to deal with the situation. ~~Everyone~~ **Parents (People) assume** ~~assumes~~ that attention deficit disorder is the culprit, and they just as automatically assume that drugs are the answer. On the other hand, perhaps the child is just not interested in a particular subject or ~~they do~~ **does** not understand the material. Parents, in turn, treat the child as if he **or she** is the problem instead of listening ~~to him~~ to find out how he **or she** can be helped.

Exercise 12.2 (p. 365)

2. Neither the film's director nor its producers were on hand to receive their prestigious award.
4. It is unfortunate when a person no longer cares what others think about him or her.
6. It is the tried and true that provides the ultimate refuge in mediocrity.
8. Her set of baby teeth was complete when she was only 18 months old.
10. None of the company's products require testing on animals.
12. Every specimen of the horned grebe has a distinctive tuft on each side of its head.
14. Neither team members nor their coach expects the season to last another game.

Exercise 12.3 (p. 366)

Alternatives are given in some cases, and other alternatives may be possible.

2. Especially unique to adolescent depression are physical symptoms, such as headaches. (correct)
4. Over the past week, there have been some unexplained occurrences on the girls' floor of the residence.
6. A coalition of neighbourhood organizations, students, and unions is currently forming to oppose the university's proposed plan.
8. When a person contracts jaundice, his or her skin as well as the white part of his or her eyes turns yellow.

Alternatives:

When people contract jaundice, their skin as well as the white part of their eyes turns yellow.

When a person contracts jaundice, the skin as well as the white part of the eyes turns yellow.

10. Before rendering its unanimous verdict, the jury was polled individually. (correct)
12. The nature and role of human resources in organizations have undergone tremendous change in the last two decades. (correct)
14. Stereotyping and the use of degrading language in the book serve to reinforce its theme.
16. In Japanese culture, a person's reputation along with his or her social standing depends on the concept of "saving face."
18. The give and take in any relationship is the most important factor in sustaining it. (correct)
20. Although the Canadian Forces is still one of the best-trained military in the world, the training standards and morale of the forces are declining, according to some people.

Exercise 12.4 (p. 367)

Alex and his lawyer, Alan, left in Alex's limousine for Loonies Unlimited to buy Alex's landlady, Alice, a litre of light lemonade. She told them to also buy a litre of light lemonade for her long-time lodger, Alison. When they alighted at Loonies Unlimited, they were alarmed that Alex had left his loonie in his loft. So Alphonse, of Loonies Unlimited, allowed them only one litre of lemonade, along with a length of limp licorice, and he loudly lamented their laxness.

Exercise 12.6 (p. 370)

2. Whenever a staff meeting is called, employees are required to attend. (no reference)
4. Sixty per cent of our pesticides, our major ground water pollutant, are used on cotton. (ambiguous reference)
6. I know the sign indicated *No Parking*, but I went ahead and parked there anyway. An officer gave me a $20 fine. (no reference in both sentences)
8. Previous Afghan successes were significant victories; for example, the country last waged war against the powerful Soviet Union. (no reference)
10. During the dinosaur age, dinosaurs lived in a rapidly changing environment. (no reference)
12. In chapter 21 of my textbook, the author analyzes the success of the Liberal Party in Canada. (no reference)
14. Children often hide their compulsive behaviours from friends and family because of feelings of shame, causing these behaviours to remain undiagnosed. (ambiguous reference)
16. The Catholic kings of Spain rallied the country to fight their enemies, the Moors. This movement became known as the "Reconquista." (broad reference)
18. Teaching today's youth safe and healthy approaches to sexuality will elevate their self-esteem. (no reference)
20. Japanese smokers consume more than twice the number of cigarettes as American smokers do, and this trend continues to increase steadily. (broad reference)

Exercise 12.7 (p. 374)

2. Who should run for office this election?
4. The person who finishes first will be rewarded.
6. People who use memory aids tend to be better spellers.
8. The last person whom she wanted to see at the track meet was her former coach.
10. I wanted to ask her whom the note should be addressed to.
12. I proposed that Geordie and I would stack chairs after the meeting.
14. The newly renovated house is a very pleasant place for my brother and me to live.
16. Prejudices decrease when children observe non-prejudiced behaviour by peers whom children associate with during their preteen years.
18. "[I]n these fits I leave them, while I visit / young Ferdinand, who they suppose is drowned." —Shakespeare
20. a. Roses are red, / Butterflies are free; You must choose / Between him and me.

Exercise 12.8 (p. 376)

Informal: You can definitely learn a lot from educational TV; you can learn things that cannot be learned from written texts. If you are a major in commerce, for example, and if you watch the business news, you can understand the commerce textbook better by applying what you learn from the news. Similarly, watching sports programs can be exciting and can also give you a better understanding of the game. On the other hand, if you choose to watch comedy all the time, you are not going to gain any real benefits. In general, I think that comedies are meaningless.

Formal:
Educational TV has many benefits and can teach people things they cannot learn from written texts. If a person is a major in commerce, for example, and watches the business news, he or she can understand the commerce textbook better by applying what is learned from the news. Similarly, watching sports programs can provide people with excitement and also give them a better understanding of the game. On the other hand, if people choose to watch comedy all the time, they will not gain any real benefits as comedies, generally, are meaningless.

Exercise 12.9 (p. 380)

2. Jellyfish from beyond the grave injures swimmers.
4. After 18 years, a mother and her daughter were recently reunited in a checkout line.
6. Explorer who indisputably first reached North Pole dies at 80.
8. Cougar attacks five-year-old boy, who is expected to survive.
10. The googly-eyed Puss-in-Boots in the new movie looks nothing like the cat fans used to love.

Exercise 12.10 (p. 380)

2. Over the years, several world-class cyclists, such as Eddie Merckx and Greg LeMond, have had spectacular careers.
4. As I am a member of the Sikh community, my paper will be given a strong personal focus.
6. Benefits will result only from a smoke-free environment.
8. When they look for employees today, employers are stressing verbal and written communication skills more than ever before.
10. In captivity, this species of snake will eat frogs, mice, and small pieces of meat.
12. When I was a beginner, my instructor taught me about the respect one karate student must show to another.
14. Speaking from experience, I can say that tans dyeing the top layer of the skin last for about one week.
16. I am certain that Shakespeare, being an Elizabethan playwright, would have been a major influence on Marlowe.
18. As a serious snowboarder, I find it exciting to observe the growth of this sport.
20. Another example of imagery of light and dark in *Heart of Darkness* occurs when Marlow encounters an African with a white scarf dying in a clearing.

Exercise 12.11 (p. 385)

Topic 2: One disadvantage of having roommates is that they can create a lot of mess and invade your personal space, but having a roommate gives you someone to talk to about your problems.

Topic 4: School uniforms are beneficial as they promote school identity and school pride, save parents money and hassle, and make it easier for school authorities to enforce discipline.

Exercise 12.12 (p. 386)

2. Music can directly affect your thoughts, emotions, and feelings. (series)
4. There are three main qualities that a leader must possess: a leader must be enthusiastic, organized, and creative. (series)
6. She not only was the best teacher I have ever had but also had an impressive wardrobe. (correlative conjunctions)
8. There are many reasons why people choose to watch or enjoy watching television. (compounds)
10. Being imprisoned for a long time can result in a dependency on the institutional environment, a lack of meaningful relationships, and a loss of personal identity. (series)
12. Physical education teaches children not only to work well together but also to have patience and discipline. (correlative conjunctions)
14. Allowing prostitution in controlled environments will reduce the risk of violence, decrease drug abuse, and even combat disease through regular testing. (series)

Glossary

absolute phrase A group of words that consists of a noun/pronoun and a partial verb form, modifying the entire sentence.

abstract A condensed summary used in many scholarly essays; it is placed before the study begins, is written by the study's author, and includes its purpose, methods, and results.

adjectivally Acting as an adjective in a sentence.

adjectival modifier A word or phrase that describes or particularizes a noun and usually precedes it.

adjective A word that modifies and precedes a noun or follows a linking verb; it answers the question *Which?*, *What kind?*, or *How many?*

adverbially Acting as an adverb in a sentence.

adverbial modifier A word or phrase that describes or particularizes a verb; may also modify an adjective or another adverb; a **sentence adverb** may modify the entire sentence.

adverb A word that modifies a verb, an adjective, an adverb, or even an entire sentence; it often ends in *–ly* and answers the question *When?*, *Where?*, *Why?*, *How?*, *To what degree?*, or *How much?*

alliteration Identical sounds at the beginning of closely placed words.

allusion A historical, religious, mythic, literary, or other kind of outside reference used thematically or to reveal another aspect of the work.

analogy A logical comparison between two objects in order to help the reader understand the first object. *See also* **metaphor**.

analysis The act of taking something apart or breaking it down in order to look at it closely.

analytical Refers to the activity of breaking something down to see how it is put together and the relationship between the parts.

anapest A foot of poetic metre consisting of two unstressed syllables and one stressed syllable.

anaphora The repetition of words or phrases at the beginning of lines or clauses.

annotated bibliography An expanded bibliography that includes not only the information of standard bibliographies but also brief summaries of related works and, sometimes, appraisals of each work.

antecedent The noun that the pronoun replaces in the sentence.

apostrophe In poetry, an address to an absent or dead person or to a non-human object.

appositive A word or phrase that is grammatically parallel to the previous noun or noun phrase and gives non-essential information.

argument A rhetorical mode concerned with persuading a reader to adopt a specific point of view or course of action.

aside In drama, a brief speech intended for the audience, not for other onstage characters.

assonance The repetition of vowel sounds in the middle of closely placed words.

audience Readers with common knowledge, interests, attitudes, reading habits, and/or expectations.

audience orientation The attitudes and emotional/ethical positions that define a typical reader; it could be positive (agreeing with your position), neutral (having no opinion), negative (disagreeing with your position), or mixed (including those who agree and those who disagree).

bibliography A list at the end of the essay of all the sources used in the essay. The title of this list varies by citation style.

blank verse Poetry written in unrhymed iambic pentameter.

block method A method of comparing and contrasting in which a writer considers all points related to one subject of comparison before moving on to the second subject.

Boolean operators Small words used to combine, include, or exclude specific search terms.

cacophony   Words that sound harsh or disagreeable.

caesura   A pause in the middle of a line of poetry.

case study   A carefully selected example that is closely analyzed to support a claim.

catastrophe   The resolution or denouement in a tragedy; it usually results in the tragic hero's death.

cause–effect   A rhetorical pattern in which a writer considers the reasons for or consequences of something.

chiasmus   In the second of two parallel phrases, the inversion of the order followed in the first.

chronology   A rhetorical pattern in which a writer traces a topic's development over time.

circular conclusion   An ending to an essay that recalls and reinforces the thesis. *See also* **spiral conclusion**.

circumlocution   Using more words than necessary to express an idea, or not coming to the point.

citation   A brief acknowledgement of the source of your information, whether paraphrased, summarized, or quoted directly.

citation style   *See* **documentation style**.

claim   A statement that a writer will attempt to prove in an essay.

claim of extended value   A claim that asserts the need for an action; an interpretive claim that analyzes a text or trend or argues for an outcome.

claim of fact   An assertion supported by empirical methods such as measurement and observation.

claim of interpretation   A claim that analyzes a text or trend or argues for an outcome.

claim of value   An assertion of a value or moral quality.

classification   A rhetorical pattern in which a writer organizes items into manageable groups.

clause   A group of words containing both a subject and a predicate.

cliché   An overworked and unoriginal expression.

climax order   A sequencing of points in an argument from least important to most important.

coherent   Describes writing that is easy for the reader to follow.

colloquialism   A word or an expression acceptable in conversation but not in formal writing.

comma splice   Two independent clauses with only a comma between them.

comparison and contrast   A rhetorical pattern in which a writer considers similarities and/or differences between two objects.

complete subject   A group of words that includes the noun/pronoun subject and its modifiers.

complex sentence   A sentence formed by one independent clause joined by a subordinating conjunction to one or more dependent clauses.

composing   Getting down your ideas in paragraph form. *Also called* **first draft**.

compound   A word group made up of two of something.

compound sentence   A sentence formed by two or more independent clauses joined by a coordinating conjunction.

compound–complex sentence   A sentence formed by two or more independent clauses and at least one dependent clause.

confessional poetry   An autobiographical form of poetry in which the poet expresses intense emotion.

conflict   In fiction, obstacles a character must overcome to achieve a goal.

conjunction   A word or phrase that connects words, phrases, and clauses of equal or unequal weight or importance.

conjunctive adverb   An adverb that may be used to connect two independent clauses.

connotation   A word's associations or implications; connotations may depend on context. *Compare* **denotation**.

contextual symbol   A symbol that derives meaning from the context in which the author uses it.

coordinating conjunction   A word that joins *equal* units, including independent clauses; there are seven coordinating conjunctions (the FANBOYS).

correlative conjunctions   A word that joins a pair of parallel units in a sentence.

cost–benefit analysis   A rhetorical pattern in which a writer weighs the advantages and disadvantages of something.

couplet A poetic unit containing two lines.

credibility A writer's knowledge, reliability, and fairness, which help back up a claim.

critical Describes the activity of weighing or evaluating something, such as the validity of a statement.

critical analysis A type of analysis that demonstrates an ability to analyze such elements as the writer's purpose, audience, use of reason, and argumentative strategies.

critical thinking A series of logical mental processes that lead to a conclusion.

cumulative sentence A sentence that begins with the main idea and is followed by modifiers that expand on this idea.

dactyl A foot of poetic metre consisting of one stressed syllable and two unstressed syllables.

dangling participle An adjective or adjectival phrase that has no noun to modify in the sentence.

deductive reasoning A method of reasoning that arrives at a conclusion based on a general statement (major premise) applied to a specific statement (minor premise).

definition A rhetorical pattern in which a writer tells the reader what he or she will be talking about.

delayed claim A claim that is not announced until the evidence has been provided.

demonstrative pronoun A pronoun that points to a specific thing.

denotation The basic, or dictionary, meaning of a word. *Compare* **connotation**.

denouement The outcome or resolution of the play's conflicts.

dependent clause A group of words with a subject and predicate that cannot stand alone as a sentence.

description A rhetorical mode in which concrete, sensual information is used.

diction A writer's choice of words.

digital object identifier (DOI) A number–alphabet sequence that begins with the number 10 and is often found on documents obtained electronically through databases. In APA documentation style, it is the last element in the citation.

direct object *See* **object**.

division A rhetorical pattern in which a writer breaks a topic down into parts.

documentation (citation) style A system used in academic disciplines and by publishers to identify source formats. Disciplines often favour one system over another and publish their guidelines in style manuals or handbooks.

dramatic poetry A poem that has drama-like qualities, such as a speaker who addresses an imaginary listener.

dramatic irony A literary device in which the reader or audience possesses an awareness about the character or situation that the character does not have.

dramatic monologue *See* **monologue**.

ellipsis Three or four spaced dots indicating that words have been omitted.

emphasis Drawing the reader's attention to specific parts of a text through word choice, repetition, rhythm, or other techniques to stress their importance.

empirical Denoting a scientific method based on observation and measurement.

end-stopped Denoting a line of poetry that ends with a logical and syntactic stop.

enjambment The continuation of a thought from one line of poetry to the next.

essay plan A form the thesis can take in which the author outlines the parts of the essay, often using the first-person voice.

ethos Aristotle's term for ethics or morality as the basis of an argument.

euphemism An indirect expression considered less harsh or offensive than the term it replaces.

euphony Words that have a pleasing or melodic sound.

evidence Studies, examples, and so on, that help support a claim.

example A specific instance that helps a reader understand or relate to a point.

expanded thesis statement A thesis statement that includes your main points in the order in which they will appear in your essay. *See also* **essay plan**, **simple thesis statement**.

exposition A rhetorical mode concerned with informing or explaining, as distinct from arguing or persuading.

extended value claim *See* **claim of extended value**.

factual claim *See* **claim of fact**.

fairness A writer's objectivity, shown through the proper use of reason and emotion.

faulty predication A grammatical error that occurs where a verb (or predicate) isn't logically connected to the subject.

final draft *See* **revising**.

find or search A database function that scans through many journal articles looking for keywords.

first draft *See* **composing**.

fixed forms of poetry Styles of poetry that rely on conventions, such as structural or metric ones.

focused reading A close and detailed (i.e., word-by-word) reading of a specific, relevant passage.

formal outline An outline that shows the relationships between the different levels of points.

formalist Denoting a text-centred approach to a poem that explores the connections between the formal elements of the work and its meaning.

genres Divisions within literature such as poetry, drama, the novel, the short story, and nonfiction prose.

hamartia *See* **tragic flaw**.

hard evidence Authoritative evidence that includes facts, statistics, and expert opinions.

helping verb A verb form that precedes the main verb to form a complex tense or to express a grammatical mood or voice. *Also called* **auxiliary verb**.

hubris Pride that leads to a protagonist's downfall in classical tragedy.

hyperbole Extreme exaggeration used as a literary device.

hypothesis A prediction or probable result. Experiments are often set up to test a hypothesis.

iamb A foot of poetic metre consisting of one unstressed and one stressed syllable.

iambic pentameter Lines of poetry consisting of five iambs.

idiom A phrase whose meaning is understood only within the context of the phrase itself.

illustration A detailed example that helps make your essay readable and understandable.

imperative sentence A sentence that issues a command, demand, or wish.

indefinite pronoun A pronoun that refers to unspecified individuals or groups of people or things.

independent clause A group of words with a subject and a predicate that can stand alone as a sentence equivalent.

indirect object *See* **object of the preposition**.

inductive reasoning Reasoning that leads to a conclusion based on specific occurrences that are observed and recorded. Errors in inductive reasoning can develop (1) where there is not enough evidence to make a generalization, or (2) where the means for gathering the evidence are faulty or biased. *Also called* **scientific reasoning**.

inference A conclusion based on the evidence presented (i.e., the reader is not directly told what to conclude from the evidence).

infinitive phrase A group of words that consists of *to* followed by the bare verb.

informal writing Writing intended for general readers where the language, style, and format vary from formal writing.

intensive pronoun A pronoun that reinforces its antecedent.

internal rhyme In poetry, a rhyme occurring in the middle of a line.

interrogative pronoun A word that introduces a question.

in-text citation (or **reference**) An acknowledgement of a source that occurs in the text of an essay, usually immediately after the information from that source.

inverted climax An essay plan in which the points in an argument are presented from most important to least important.

irony A literary device in which two levels of meaning are present: the apparent (literal or surface) meaning and another intended (non-literal or deeper) meaning.

jargon Words and expressions used within a designated group or in a particular discipline that its members would understand but that people outside the group would not necessarily understand. Jargon is a kind of specialized diction.

juxtaposition Words or images placed beside others, usually to show contrast.

knowledge Familiarity with a topic that is shown through strong, well-supported points.

linking verb   A verb that is followed by a predicate noun or adjective that refers back to the subject.

literary canon   The set of literary works considered to meet high artistic standards and thus most worthy of study.

literary present   In a literary analysis, the use of the present tense to describe action and character.

literature review   A condensed survey of articles on one topic that appears in the introduction of many scholarly essays and informs the reader about previous research.

loaded language   *See* **slanted language**.

logos   Aristotle's term for reason or logic as the basis of an argument.

lyric   A category of poetry that expresses strong emotions in a relatively brief form.

magic realism   A kind of fiction that combines the objectively real and the surprise of the unreal or unexpected.

main verb   A word or phrase that conveys an action or a state of being in the predicate.

major premise   A general statement that is the first part of a syllogism, which can be used to show how deductive reasoning works.

manageable claim   A claim that can be adequately addressed within the given length of an essay, using the support available to the writer.

metafiction   A kind of fiction that defines its own boundaries of the real by focusing on the story itself as the testing ground of the "real."

metaphor   An indirect comparison between two things not usually considered similar.

metonymy   The substitution of an object or idea for a related one.

minor premise   A specific statement that is the second part of a syllogism, which can be used to show how deductive reasoning works.

modal   A verb form placed before a main verb to express necessity and similar conditions.

monologue   In drama, a continuous speech by one character.

mood   The emotions associated with a particular literary work or part of a work.

narration   A rhetorical mode in which incidents are related and character may be revealed.

narrative point of view   The perspective or angle of vision from which the narrative is told.

narrative poetry   A long poem that tells a story.

naturalism   An outgrowth of realistic writing that stresses humanity's helplessness before external forces, such as those of one's society or natural environment, or before internal ones, such as heredity.

near rhyme   Words with identical vowel or consonant sounds on the last stressed syllable.

non-restrictive clause   A type of adjectival clause that gives non-essential information, usually beginning with *who*, *which*, or *that*.

noun phrase   A group of words acting as a noun.

novel   A fictional narrative of more than 40,000 words involving one or more characters undergoing significant experiences over a span of time.

novella   A fictional narrative of 15,000–40,000 words; a short novel.

object   The part of the sentence, often a noun or pronoun, that receives the action of the verb. *Also called* **direct object**.

object of the preposition   The part of the sentence, often a noun or pronun, that is preceded by a preposition. *Also called* **indirect object**.

objective case   The form of a noun or pronoun when it is acting as the grammatical object of a verb or of a preposition.

octave   A stanza of poetry containing eight lines.

onomatopoeia   Words that sound like their meanings.

open forms of poetry   Styles of poetry, such as free verse, that do not conform to set conventions of stanza, rhyme, or metre.

organization   The process of determining the order of points; outlining.

paragraph wrap   An ending to a paragraph that reinforces its main idea.

parallelism   In poetry, repetition or "echoing." In grammar, using the same structure for elements that share a grammatical function.

paraphrase   Using your own words and structure to represent someone else's ideas. When you paraphrase, you include all of the original.

parody   Poking fun at a literary work or revealing its weaknesses.

participial phrase   A type of verbal phrase that acts as an adjective, usually at the beginning of the sentence/clause.

parts of speech   Categories that words belong to depending on their functions in the sentence.

pathos   Aristotle's term for emotion as the basis of an argument.

pentameter   A line of poetry containing five feet.

periodic sentence   A sentence that begins with modifiers, building toward the main idea.

personal pronoun   A word that replaces a noun referring to one or more people or things.

phrase   A group of two or more grammatically linked words that, lacking a subject and/or predicate, can be thought of as functioning as a single part of speech.

plagiarism   The unacknowledged borrowing of someone else's words, ideas, or sentence structure.

point-by-point method   A method of comparing and contrasting in which a writer considers one point of comparison as it applies to each subject before moving on to the next point.

possessive pronoun   A pronoun that acts as an adjective to indicate ownership or a similar relationship with the noun that follows.

postmodernism   In literature, a tendency to reject such assumptions as the authority of the author, univocal (one-voice) perspectives, unifying narratives, and other "absolutes"; it stresses plurality, possibility, and "play."

precedent   An example of how a particular situation was dealt with in the past that may be used in an argument to convince a reader that a similar situation exists today and would benefit from a similar action.

premise   A statement, assumed to be true, that leads to a conclusion.

prepositional phrase   A group of words that begins with a preposition and acts as an adjective or adverb.

preposition   A small word or short phrase that often refers to place or time.

pre-writing   Thinking about, coming up with, and narrowing a topic through an associative technique, such as freewriting or brainstorming.

primary sources   Original material. *Compare* **secondary sources**.

problem–solution   A rhetorical pattern in which a writer analyzes a problem, solutions to a problem, or both.

process analysis   A rhetorical pattern in which a writer gives the step-by-step stages of a process.

quatrain   A stanza of poetry containing four lines.

question claim   A claim (thesis) in the form of a question.

reader-based prose   Writing that is focused on the reader by making clear communication a priority and acknowledging the role of the reader in the communication process.

rebuttal   The process of raising an opponent's points in an argument in order to reveal their weaknesses, thereby strengthening one's own argument.

reciprocal pronoun   A pronoun that refers to the separate parts of a plural antecedent.

reflexive pronoun   A pronoun that refers back to the subject as the receiver of the action.

relative clause   A type of dependent clause that acts as an adjective by modifying the noun that precedes it.

relative pronoun   A word that introduces a dependent clause and that relates the clause to the rest of the sentence.

reliability   A writer's trustworthiness, shown through well-structured, clear, and grammatical writing.

research   The stage in writing a research paper in which you locate background information and supporting evidence, such as academic studies, to help support a thesis.

restrictive clause   A type of adjectival clause that gives essential information.

revising   The stage in writing in which you reconsider an essay's structure as well as work towards readability and correctness. *Also called* **final draft**.

rhetoric   Applied to argument, the structure and strategies of argumentation used to persuade the members of a specific audience.

rhetorical modes of discourse   Argument, exposition, narration, and description.

rhetorical patterns   Methods of breaking down information and presenting it to the reader.

rhyme   Words with identical vowel and/or consonant sounds in the last stressed syllable.

run-on sentence   Two independent clauses run together without punctuation between them.

satire   Humour and an ironic tone used to poke fun at an individual, a group, or society.

scanning   A reading strategy in which you look for key words or sections of a text.

scansion   The reading of a line of poetry to determine the pattern of stressed and unstressed syllables.

scientific reasoning   *See* **inductive reasoning**.

secondary sources   Studies or other sources that comment on or analyze primary sources. *Compare* **primary sources**.

selective reading   A reading strategy designed to meet a specific objective, such as scanning for main points or reading for details.

sentence   A group of words that includes a subject and predicate and expresses a complete thought.

sentence adverb   An adverb that modifies the independent clause that follows it. *See also* **adverbial modifier**.

sentence outline   A kind of outline that shows more detail than a topic outline and uses complete sentences in parallel format.

sestet   A stanza of poetry containing six lines.

setting   In fiction, the place and time of the work.

short story   A fictional narrative of fewer than 15,000 words that focuses on situation rather than character development.

simile   A comparison using *like* or *as* or a similar word/phrase.

simple subject   A word or phrase that includes only the noun/pronoun subject without modifiers.

simple thesis statement   A statement that announces the topic and main point. *See also* **expanded thesis statement**.

situational irony   A literary device in which a situation appears to point to a particular outcome but results in the reverse of the expected one.

slanted language   Statements used in an argument that are extreme or that convey a bias. *Also called* **loaded language**.

soft evidence   Examples, illustrations, case studies, precedents, and so on, that help make an essay readable and understandable.

soliloquy   A continuous speech by one character alone on the stage.

sonnet   A poem of 14 lines that follows specific conventions. The Italian, or Petrarchan, form has an eight-line octave and a six-line sestet; the English, or Shakespearean, form has three quatrains of four lines each and a couplet of two lines.

specific claim   A precisely worded claim about a specific topic and the writer's approach to it.

spiral conclusion   An ending to an essay that recalls the thesis but also leads beyond it, applying it or suggesting further research. *See also* **circular conclusion**.

stanza   A unit of two or more lines of poetry that often share metre, rhyme scheme, etc.

style manual (or handbook)   A set of guidelines for following a discipline-specific documentation system.

subject   A broad area of study that contains many potential topics. In grammar, the part of the sentence that performs the action of the verb.

subjective case   The form of a noun or pronoun when it is acting as the grammatical subject or the subjective complement.

subjective complement (or completion)   The part of a sentence that follows a linking verb and that adds information about the subject.

subordinating conjunction   A word that introduces a dependent clause.

summary   A brief overview of a source text in which the main points are included and less important information is left out.

support   Validation of the claim made by presenting evidence and showing credibility.

syllogism   The three-part structure illustrating deductive reasoning: the major premise (general statement), the minor premise (specific statement), and the conclusion.

symbol   An image that accumulates meaning according to its context and traditional associations.

syntax   The order of words in a sentence.

synthesis   In a research essay, the process of putting together findings of different sources.

tetrameter   A line of poetry containing four feet.

thesis   A formal statement that includes both your topic and your approach to, or a comment on, the topic. A more developed thesis would include your main points. *See also* **simple thesis statement** and **expanded thesis statement**.

tone   The writer's attitude toward the subject matter or audience; it can be determined by the writer's language and style.

topic   An area of study that is narrower and more focused than a subject.

topic outline   A kind of outline that shows paragraph topics and their development, usually through just a word or phrase.

topic sentence   The sentence that contains the paragraph's main idea.

traditional (or Western) canon   The set of literary works by European and North American authors meeting high artistic standards and once considered most worthy of study.

tragic flaw   A character trait that leads to a protagonist's downfall in a classical tragedy. *Also called* **hamartia**.

tragic irony   A literary device in which the reader/audience is aware of a situation that the hero is oblivious to and which will lead to disaster.

trimeter   A line of poetry containing three feet.

trochee   A foot of poetic metre consisting of one stressed and one unstressed syllable.

understatement   A literary device that draws attention to something by minimizing it.

unity of action   The idea that the action of a play should be limited to one set of incidents with a beginning, middle, and end.

unity of place   The idea that the action of a play should be limited to one place.

unity of time   The idea that the action of a play should be limited to one day.

value claim   *See* **claim of value**.

verb   A word that conveys an action, a state, or a condition, or that precedes another (main) verb.

verb phrase   A group of words acting as a verb.

verbal irony   A literary device in which the literal and intended meaning conflict; verbal irony resembles sarcasm but is usually more indirect and subtle.

warrant   A statement that tests the logical connection between a claim and its support.

wit   The humour of high comedy that appeals to the intellect, having such targets as social pretensions and character inconsistencies.

working bibliography   A list of books, articles, and other texts you plan to look at.

writer-based prose   Writing focused on the writer and the expression of his or her feelings or thoughts.

Index

Credits